Robert Clifton Weaver

# Robert Clifton Weaver

* AND THE *

# American City

*The Life and Times of an Urban Reformer*

WENDELL E. PRITCHETT

*The University of Chicago Press* Chicago and London

The University of Chicago Press, Chicago 60637
The University of Chicago Press, Ltd., London

Paperback edition 2014
Printed in the United States of America

23 22 21 20 19 18 17 16 15 14 2 3 4 5 6

ISBN-13: 978-0-226-68448-2 (cloth)
ISBN-13: 978-0-226-21401-6 (paper)
ISBN-13: 978-0-226-68450-5 (e-book)
10.7208/chicago/9780226684505.001.0001

Library of Congress Cataloging-in-Publication Data

Pritchett, Wendell E.
Robert Clifton Weaver : a biography / Wendell E. Pritchett.
p. cm.
Includes bibliographical references and index.
ISBN-13: 978-0-226-68448-2 (cloth : alk. paper)
ISBN-10: 0-226-68448-2 (cloth : alk. paper)
1. Weaver, Robert Clifton, 1907– 2. Cabinet officers—United States—Biography. 3. African Americans—Biography. 4. United States Dept. of Housing and Urban Development—Officials and employees—Biography. 5. Urban policy—United States—History—20th century. 6. African Americans—Government policy—History—20th century. 7. Cabinet officers—New York (State)—Biography. 8. African American college presidents—Biography. 9. Bernard M. Baruch College—Biography. I. Title.
E748.W425P75 2008
352.2'93092—dc22
[B]

2008000927

♾ This paper meets the requirements of ANSI/NISO Z39.48-1992 (Permanence of Paper).

FOR ANNE

# Contents

# Acknowledgments

This book has been many years in the making, and I have incurred many debts during the process. When I began research, I was a member of the history department at Baruch College, the former home, for a short while, of Robert Weaver. I was lucky, in my first permanent academic position, to have wonderful colleagues there who helped me grow as a teacher and scholar. In particular, I am grateful to my friends Carol Berkin and Myrna Chase for their continuing support.

I have been even more fortunate in my academic life since moving to the University of Pennsylvania, where I have found an intellectually rigorous and supportive community. Two people, more than any others, were responsible for giving me this opportunity: Dean Mike Fitts and Sally Gordon. Throughout my years at Penn, they have been stalwart supporters and terrific friends. Thanks to Mike for enabling me to take a year's sabbatical to get the manuscript in shape and for providing the financial and moral support necessary to bring this book to completion. Words cannot express my gratitude to Sally for all that she has done to help me. I have also been fortunate to work with an amazing staff who have helped me throughout the research process. I want to give special thanks to my research librarians, Ron Day and Merle Slyhoff, for all of their assistance in accessing documents and books for this project. The years of work on this book have also been enlivened by my interaction with the wonderful students of the University of Pennsylvania Law School. They have blessed me with their passion for learning and some of the best research assistance a person could ask for.

Along the way, I have also been aided by some terrific archivists. I want to thank in particular the staffs at the Schomburg Center for Research in Black Culture, the John Fitzgerald Kennedy Library, and the Lyndon Baines

Johnson Library for their assistance and for their support of the historical profession. Several libraries also provided financial assistance to enable me to conduct research. This project was supported by a Theodore Sorenson grant from the Kennedy Library, two travel grants from the Johnson Library, and a travel grant from the Franklin Delano Roosevelt Foundation.

I am grateful to my many friends and colleagues in the history profession who were willing to share with me their time and knowledge. Thanks to my dissertation advisor and constant advocate Walter Licht, as well as Robert Fishman, Josh Freeman, Howard Gillette, Walter Hill, Michael Katz, and Rhonda Williams, all of whom took time out of their busy schedules to read an earlier (and longer!) draft of the manuscript and provide detailed comments. This book is much better because of their involvement. Thanks also to Mark Rose and an anonymous reader for the University of Chicago Press for their helpful comments. I have been privileged to have had the opportunity to share many of the ideas in this book with some of the best scholars in the field. I am grateful to, among others, Regina Austin, Martha Biondi, Steve Conn, Risa Goluboff, Arnold Hirsch, Gideon Parchomovsky, Wendy Plotkin, Len Rubinowitz, Phyllis Santacroce, Rich Schragger, Robert Self, Tom Sugrue, and Clarence Taylor, for their friendship and insights.

The University of Chicago Press published my first book, and I was fortunate to have Robert Devens as my editor. I am even more blessed to have the opportunity to work with him for a second time. Thanks to Robert for his enthusiasm and commitment to history.

Nothing I have done could have been possible without the support of my parents, Wendell and Carolyn Pritchett. Racial pioneers themselves, they have provided me with constant intellectual and emotional support and have been role models in more ways than they know. I am grateful to them for all the sacrifices they have made for me and the rest of our family. Thanks also to my in-laws, Mary and Jerry Kringel, who have been unwavering in their encouragement of me and this project.

This book is dedicated to my wife, Anne Kringel. For over fifteen years, Anne has been my partner, my best friend, my toughest critic, and my heartiest fan. She has provided me with love, affection, two wonderful children, and a life full of happiness. I can only hope to someday be worthy of all that she has given me. The other two women in my life, Ellie and Clara, budding scholars both, are my constant inspiration. Ellie's precision of thought and Clara's warmth of spirit are my daily models. I hope this book meets their exacting standards.

# Introduction

Over one hundred years ago, in one of the era's most accurate prognostications, the scholar W. E. B. DuBois predicted that the central question of the twentieth century would be that of "the color line." Since that period, American race relations have occupied a dominant position in the nation's public debates. As the century progressed and millions of African Americans left the South, that line was drawn in, and around, American cities. Bringing with them their labor, culture, and aspirations, these migrants dramatically transformed the face of cities at exactly the same time that the country was changing from a rural society into an urban one. American cities and the race relations that influenced them were two of the most important themes of the twentieth century, and Robert Clifton Weaver was at the center of both.

For almost half of the century Robert Weaver shaped the development of American racial and urban policy. A member of a privileged group of upper-middle-class African Americans that DuBois dubbed the "Talented Tenth," Weaver was the first of the small number of black "New Dealers" hired by President Franklin Delano Roosevelt in his effort to bring the country out of the Great Depression. For more than a decade, Weaver was a crucial participant in the rise of the federal government as a major influence in American society. After World War II, Weaver was a founder of a new approach to race relations known as racial liberalism, and he held a series of high-level positions in public and private agencies that were working to promote racial cooperation in American cities. Although he was less well known than other advocates for civil rights such as Rev. Martin Luther King Jr. and A. Philip Randolph, Weaver was a leading figure in the movement, particularly through his role in the National Association for the Advancement of Colored People (NAACP). By the early 1960s, Weaver was widely considered one of the nation's foremost authorities on urban issues, and President Kennedy appointed him administrator of the Housing and Home Finance Agency (HHFA). When Congress created the Department of Housing and Urban Development (HUD), President Johnson named Weaver its first secretary, making him the first black to hold a cabinet position. Weaver also served as president of Baruch College in 1969 and 1970 and as a professor at the City University of New York for several years thereafter.

American cities at the turn of the last century were chaotic, dangerous, and dirty places, and many people feared that their growth would result in the country's moral decline. The most important goal of the Progressive movement that emerged during this era was to tame the city and bring order to the lives of its residents. Throughout the first half of the century, politicians, business leaders, and activists labored to incorporate the millions of migrants and immigrants who flocked to the city into urban society, to rebuild the neighborhoods in which these newcomers lived, and to improve the provision of government services by professionalizing its organization. Through the work of public officials like New York master builder Robert Moses and Senator Robert Wagner and urban reformers such as attorney Charles Abrams and planner Catherine Bauer, a new type of city emerged. Public housing, urban renewal, mass transportation, civil service reform, mass public education, and urban planning were among the many initiatives these men and women created or nurtured. Though they debated specific policies, all of these reformers shared a belief that government had an important part to play in transforming cities into safe, healthy environments that enabled their residents to flourish. The initiatives they promoted, although they failed to bring about the complete transformation of the city, left an indelible imprint.

Urban reformers played a major role in the rise of a new political philosophy that came to be known as New Deal liberalism. Rejecting the old laissez-faire approach—which held that economic and social inequalities were the result of free-market competition—these reformers created strong public institutions to deal with domestic problems. As America transformed from a society of small businessmen to one of large corporations and its institutions grew from voluntary groups to national professional organizations, these policymakers sought to harness the public sector to protect the interests of Americans struggling to deal with the changes. During the 1930s, Franklin Roosevelt put the weight of the federal government behind these efforts, creating new bureaucracies to organize the economy in the public interest. The New Deal increased the regulation of labor, business, housing, health, education, and other sectors and resulted in a profound restructuring of the relationship between individual Americans and their government.

During the postwar years, presidents from Harry F. Truman through Lyndon B. Johnson (even, to a limited extent, Dwight D. Eisenhower) all committed to two basic principles: that government should play an important role in protecting Americans against the vagaries of the marketplace and that professionally managed institutions using rational, scientific methods were the means to accomplish societal change. They were joined by liberals across the country—Senator Hubert Humphrey, Philadelphia mayor Joseph Clark, labor leader Walter Reuther, economist John Kenneth Galbraith, among many others—in refining and promoting this ideology. Although they disagreed about specific approaches, these policymakers created a new understanding of domestic policy, one that remains dominant in the twenty-first century.

Few of the men and women who re-created America during the first half of the last century paid attention to the needs or desires of the millions of African Americans who were also struggling to become full members of society. Since the Reconstruction Era following the Civil War, most white Americans had chosen to ignore the discrimination, violence, and subjugation that were the daily lot of their darker compatriots. However, throughout the twentieth century, African Americans were increasingly vocal in their demands for equal rights under the law and an equal opportunity to exploit their abilities. The founding of the NAACP in 1909 was just one of many statements by blacks that they would no longer accept second-class status. From the beginning of the century through the 1960s and thereafter, activists demanded legal, political, economic, and social reforms to allow blacks and other minorities to fully participate in American life.

The movement's leaders, senior statesmen like NAACP head Walter White, educator Mary McLeod Bethune, and labor leader A. Philip Randolph, along with second-generation leaders, including United Nations mediator Ralph Bunche, attorneys Thurgood Marshall and William Hastie, White's NAACP successor Roy Wilkins, and foundation leader Edwin Embree, all fought to transform a culture that considered blacks inferior to other Americans. Over time, these men and women expanded the definition of liberalism to include the protection of minority rights, and they harnessed the support of government to achieve their goals. The racially integrated civilization they sought to create has yet to become a reality, but, through their efforts, the civil rights movement changed the way Americans think about race relations and brought about dramatic improvements in the legal, economic, and social status of African Americans.

It is these ideas, people, and policies that Robert Weaver engaged throughout his long life. Weaver's career, which spanned the creation, expansion, and contraction of New Deal liberalism, provides an excellent window through which to examine the struggles over the future of the city and the racial tensions that these battles engaged. He was instrumental in the implementation of almost every major urban initiative, including public housing, urban renewal, affirmative action, rent control, and fair housing, and he served as advisor to governments and advocacy organizations on these issues. As a federal official during the New Deal and World War II, Weaver helped shape the country's urban policy and worked to secure opportunities for African Americans through government programs. As the first HUD secretary, Weaver was a leader of the federal response to the urban racial conflicts of the 1960s, an effort that left an indelible imprint on American cities.

In the field of civil rights, Weaver was a leader of the NAACP's endeavor to promote racial integration, and he played a crucial role in the organization's legal victory against restrictive covenants in the Supreme Court case *Shelley v. Kraemer.* The framework of racial liberalism, most famously explicated by Gunnar Myrdal's polemic *An American Dilemma,* claimed that racial prejudice was the result of ignorance and could be overcome by education. Through his leadership of several organizations, including the American Council on Race Relations, the NAACP (where he served as vice chair and chair during the 1950s and early 1960s), the National Committee against Discrimination in Housing, and the Whitney Foundation, Weaver was a major contributor to the rise of racial liberalism as the dominant approach to racial progress. This framework served as the foundation of the Supreme Court's pathbreaking decision in *Brown v. Board of Education* as well as the organizing principle behind the civil rights acts of the 1960s, and it continues to profoundly influence American race relations today.

A prolific writer, Weaver wrote four books and dozens of articles for scholarly and popular journals, and he published two important studies on black America: *Negro Labor: A National Problem* (1946) and *The Negro Ghetto* (1948). Through these works, Weaver contributed greatly to the expanding sociology of black America, and his writings influenced a generation of scholars. Weaver pioneered many of the modern approaches to racial cooperation, and he was instrumental in the creation of the government and private institutions that regulate American race relations.

Because of his high-profile role in American race relations, Weaver was often a controversial figure. For example, as a government official working on black employment during World War II, he was criticized by African Americans as an apologist for discrimination at the same time he was damned by whites who wanted to continue business as usual. When appointed HUD secretary in 1966, Weaver achieved the highest position ever attained by an African American. His success came just as the problems of American cities in general, and of their African American residents in particular, emerged as national concerns. During his term as secretary, Weaver was a lightning rod for critics of federal urban and racial policies from across the political spectrum. Lauded in their early years, by the 1960s public housing and urban renewal were blamed for intensifying racial segregation and poverty in cities. Because he participated in the implementation of these initiatives, Weaver was implicated in the failure of government to deal with the ghettoization of urban areas.

Like many other African Americans in his cohort, Weaver chose to work within existing institutions; he believed that advances in race relations were made through the accumulation of small victories within the political system. He never wavered from this philosophy throughout his long career. Weaver eschewed grassroots and popular movements that sought more radical change and instead focused on reform of existing institutions. During the post–World War II years, the careful, quiet work of Weaver and his peers, combined with the more vocal protest of others, such as Martin Luther King and A. Philip Randolph, resulted in numerous achievements and significant progress for blacks in American politics, economy, and social life. However, in the changing political climate of the 1960s, many activists rejected this "accommodationist" stance. To Weaver's critics, black and white, the growing racial violence, combined with the decline of American cities, testified to the failure of this approach. As a result, like the liberals with whom he toiled, Weaver's influence declined as his power within the government reached its apex. At the same time, the causes that he championed, racial integration and an activist government, also came under attack during these years. Weaver's story is, therefore, an important one in the broader history of civil rights, illuminating the potential and limitations of American liberalism.

As a member of a very small black professional class, Weaver attained power never before achieved by a member of his race. His attempts to balance advocacy for African Americans with his faith in a meritocratic, democratic society are emblematic of the conundrum of DuBois's Talented

Tenth. Like every other policymaker, Weaver was influenced by the social milieu in which he lived, that of a small number of upper-middle-class professionals. For decades, this group worked to break down barriers for themselves, believing that, over the long run, such changes would benefit all African Americans. This strategy brought significant improvements, but often at a cost. For example, Weaver and other civil rights leaders pushed successfully to open housing opportunities to middle-class blacks in urban renewal projects, but these same developments uprooted poor blacks, diminished the supply of affordable housing, and intensified racial segregation. Prisoners to economic and social trends they could not control, and frustrated by the continued intransigence of many white officials, Weaver and his cohort made only piecemeal progress toward racial integration in the postwar years.

Throughout his life, Weaver struggled to reconcile his obligations to his race with his personal aspirations. His close friends were among the most accomplished blacks in the nation—federal judge William Hastie, Nobel Prize winner Ralph Bunche, medical expert Charles Drew—but he was considered aloof and reticent by those who did not know him well. His family's careful oversight of his childhood years prepared him for a life of professional success, but Weaver struggled to gain the acclaim of the "average person." Weaver owned summerhouses on Chesapeake Bay and in Connecticut, and his world was much more similar to that of the wealthy whites with whom he interacted than with that of the struggling African Americans he so often represented. The tensions between the ideal of the "black leader" and the reality of the complex and contested goals of the nation's colored population were constantly revealed during Weaver's long and tumultuous career.

Weaver's life is a story of the ambiguities of race in America. He was a man who had received all of the training and experience required to excel in a meritocratic society, but his career was shaped by his color. His goal was to make his race irrelevant: instead, white and black Americans looked to him to mediate between the races, a position that became increasingly untenable as the years went on. During Weaver's career, which witnessed significant progress in race relations, African Americans continued to be "hyphenated citizens," neither completely assimilated into nor separate from mainstream American culture. Weaver himself embodied this dilemma. Throughout his career, Weaver, moderate by temperament, light-skinned, and married for half a century to a woman who had "passed" as white during her youth, was viewed with suspicion by both the white power structure to which he pledged his allegiance and the African Americans whose lives he devoted his career to improving.

At the beginning of the twenty-first century, despite his significant accomplishments, Weaver is an obscure figure, forgotten by white and black Americans. But his story is an important one in American history and a crucial one for understanding the momentous changes in cities and race relations that the country experienced during the past century. The nation still has a long way to go to fully complete the job of ending poverty and despair in its urban (as well as rural) areas, and just as far to go to achieve Dr. King's dream of a society where everyone is judged by the content of their character and not the color of their skin. By putting Weaver back into this story, this book seeks to grapple with several of the crucial questions of recent American history, questions that remain unanswered and continue to vex the country today.

* 1 *

# Preparing the Talented Tenth

## *The Weaver Family and the Black Elite*

In the summer of 1867, Robert Tanner Freeman took the train from his hometown of Washington, DC, to Boston, Massachusetts. The son of a former slave and future grandfather of Robert Clifton Weaver, Freeman had graduated from high school and taken a job as an assistant to a white dentist named Noble in Washington. After a short period, Freeman, with Noble's support, decided to apply to dental school, but he was rejected on the basis of his race. However, in 1867, when Harvard University opened its dental school, Freeman decided to present himself to the dean, Nathan Keep. After meeting with Freeman, Keep reported to his faculty that he had "decided that Harvard University should consider right and justice above expediency," and he accepted Freeman in the school's first class of six. Two years later, Freeman graduated, becoming the first professionally trained black dentist in the country. Two other African Americans, Edwin Howard (School of Medicine) and George Ruffin (School of Law), joined Freeman as the first blacks ever to receive degrees from Harvard.[1]

Freeman moved back to Washington and opened a practice, but he died less than a decade later. By then, however, he had established himself as a member of the black elite in the nation's foremost African American community, Washington, DC. From the mid-1800s through the 1900s, Weaver's family were prominent members of that city's small but influential black professional class. When he was born in 1907, Weaver entered a world of both prejudice and privilege. Unlike the overwhelming majority of African Americans (and other Americans) at the time, Weaver grew up in a community that expected him to master the arts and letters, to excel at school, to attend an elite college, and to enter the professional world. It also expected him to be both a "credit to" and an advocate for his race. In this cultured, racially segregated world, Weaver interacted with other youth who would take their place among the group that W. E. B. DuBois named the "Talented Tenth." Weaver's family and friends—refined, educated, aloof from the masses, and determined to advance by means of the methodical acquisition of economic and political power within the existing system—would profoundly influence him, shaping the personality traits that would carry him to academic and professional success throughout his career.

WEAVER'S GRANDFATHER ROBERT Tanner Freeman was born a member of the Washington, DC, free black community, but his great-grandfather Walter Freeman was born a slave in North Carolina. Trained as a carpenter, Walter hired himself out to the builders of the city of Raleigh. Like many other skilled blacks, Walter was permitted to keep part of his pay. Over several years, Walter accumulated enough to purchase his freedom. In 1842, for the sum of $1,800, Walter purchased the freedom of his wife and six children. Soon thereafter, they moved to Washington, DC, where Robert was born.[2]

Robert became a man during a short-lived golden age for blacks in Washington. The years immediately following the Civil War saw the city emerge as a true national capital, one in which African Americans played an extremely important role. The Union's war effort resulted in a dramatic expansion of federal power and of government agencies to administer the new system. During the 1860s, the number of people working for the federal government grew significantly. The arrival of tens of thousands of new residents ignited an economic boom that reshaped the city's geography and social structure.[3]

After the war, with the Republican Party firmly in power, Washington presented an opportunity for experimentation in racial integration. In 1866, Congress approved unrestricted male suffrage for the District. The arrival of the first African American members of Congress, including Senator Blanche K. Bruce of Mississippi, gave blacks their first real political influence, which they used to secure economic resources for their community. The founding of Howard University in 1867 is one of the many examples of profound change that Reconstruction represented for the nation's capital. Although the creation of a society without racial discrimination would not be achieved during this short-lived period, Washington continued to be a city of aspiration for African Americans for decades to come because of the economic and political power blacks were able to achieve there during Reconstruction.

Freeman entered his profession at a time of promise for African Americans, particularly black professionals. Soon after returning from Boston, he wed another member of DC's black elite, Rachel Turner. Rachel's story, while it is more difficult to document than Robert's, is equally illuminating of the complicated state of American race relations. According to Weaver family history, Rachel's mother, whose name has been lost to history, was the daughter of a wealthy white Philadelphia Quaker family. While in her teens, this girl became pregnant as the result of an illicit liaison with a white employee of the family. Because this relationship would have been an embarrassment to the family, the girl was sent to Arizona under the pretense of health problems, accompanied by her "mulatto" nurse, whose last name was Turner. When they returned several months later, the family declared that baby Rachel was the offspring of the nurse. For several years, Rachel Turner lived with both her biological and social mother. After her biological mother was married, Rachel and her nurse moved to Washington. Supported financially by her biological mother's family, Rachel was educated by tutors and trained in the social mores of the upper class. In addition, her skin color gave her entrée to the world of the black elite, many of whose members, as products of liaisons between slaves and slave owners, were of similarly light complexion.[4]

Weaver remembered his grandmother as "a warm, affectionate, talented woman" and "a person with a great ability to give love." She was a major presence during his childhood and thereafter. According to Weaver, along with his mother, Rachel was responsible "for helping to instill within" him the "values of drive and push and fastidiousness in choosing associates and friends." In the early 1870s, she married Freeman, but Rachel and Robert had only one child before he died: Florence, Weaver's mother. A few years later, Rachel married Albert J. Farley, another member of the District's black elite. When he died in 1935, the Republican Party stalwart had served as the clerk of the District of Columbia Supreme Court for forty-five years. They had one daughter, Louise, who later married musician Harry T. Burleigh.[5]

During his short professional career, Freeman was an active member of black society and a vocal proponent of civil rights. In 1873, he joined twenty-four other city leaders, including Charles R. Douglass (son of Frederick Douglass), in a petition to Congress. The "Memorial of Colored Citizens," printed by the Forty-second Congress, demanded that Congress "obliterate" distinctions between the races under the law and bar "any discrimination in respect of citizens by reason of race, creed, color or previous condition." The group was particularly upset about continuing discrimination in public transit and hotels and restaurants, and they demanded open and equal access to these facilities.[6]

As Robert's participation in the petition to Congress reveals, the Freemans were part of a small but vibrant black elite in Washington, a city many called the "Capital of the Colored Aristocracy." During the late 1800s and early 1900s, the so-called black 400, a group of DC families, were nationally renowned for their wealth, education, political influence, and social standing. Among the leaders of this group were a small number of black politicians who won elective office during Reconstruction: Blanche K. Bruce, senator from Mississippi; P. B. S. Pinchback, former lieutenant governor of Louisiana; Congressman John R. Lynch; and several wealthy black businessmen and professionals, including James Wormley, John and George Cook, and Judge Robert Terrell and his wife, Mary Church Terrell.[7]

Even more than in other cities, DC's black elite guarded their membership closely. Family status and ancestral history were the most important requirements for inclusion in the group. A majority of the group came from families that had been free before the Civil War and from those who were the offspring of liaisons between slaves and white owners. Although not all of the elite were light-skinned, most were, and most had achieved educational credentials unavailable to most black, and white, Americans. The Freemans had joined this group before the Civil War, as Walter Freeman's success as a businessman gave the family the ability to live in relative comfort. Robert Freeman's achievement as one of the first black Harvard graduates was further evidence of their status. But the Freemans did not possess the wealth of the Bruces, Wormleys, or Cooks, and neither before nor after Robert's death did they entertain in the manner of these families. They did, however, maintain close social ties with many wealthy blacks, particularly the Bruces, an affiliation which enabled family members to secure coveted positions in the DC government.

In 1893, Charles Douglass, in response to his family's exclusion from a white resort, purchased a forty-acre tract of land on the Chesapeake Bay near the Naval Academy in Annapolis and created the resort community of Highland Beach. Over the years, the community would grow to approximately seventy houses and would include many of DC's black elite. The Freemans, and later the Weavers, purchased land in the development and were frequent visitors to this exclusive retreat. The Weavers' property would remain in the family until Robert Clifton Weaver sold it in the 1950s.[8]

DC's black leadership was deeply involved in promoting the interests of all African Americans, and they fought against discrimination in employment and services. These men and women created dozens of charitable organizations, including orphanages, health and welfare centers, and recreational centers for the expanding black working class. At the same time, the black elite generally remained aloof from the daily life of most black residents. Hoping that their refinement, wealth, and training would exempt them from racial discrimination, they separated themselves physically and socially. "There is more discrimination among the colored people than there is among the white against the colored," one journalist wrote in 1896. Nothing to "the colored aristocrats of Washington . . . was more absurd than the idea that all blacks were social equals." Though there were many factions within the black elite, they socialized almost exclusively among themselves and frequently complained about the lack of manners and morals of most of the city's African Americans. They rejected the "over-dressing, over-acting and over-prancing" that they argued characterized poor and middle-class blacks and chose to engage in the refined pursuits of the salon and dining room.[9]

DC's black elite also formed religious institutions that reflected their beliefs in a traditional, reserved form of Christianity. According to one historian, elite blacks in DC "wanted a religion that would speak to earthly as well as spiritual issues, and hoped to move beyond the old-time slave religion." After Robert died, Rachel Freeman Farley was one of a small group of African Americans, which included several members of the Wormley family and other wealthy blacks, who left the Nineteenth Street Baptist Church to form their own congregation. The church they left was described by one historian as "a hightone church that bore little resemblance to low-class Baptist congregations," but Rachel and the others departed out of concern that it was being populated by the wrong kind of members, and they formed the Berean Baptist Church. In 1877, the congregation constructed a new church at Eighteenth and M streets NW. There, they presided over a ministry that was puritanical in character and where fastidiousness and reserve were expected of all members and their children.[10]

In the late 1800s, the social pages of DC's African American newspapers were filled with notices of parties and other events led by the city's black elite such as the Bruces and Terrells. Although the Freeman and Farley family names did not make many appearances on the social calendar of the Washington *Bee* or the *Colored American* (the leading journals of the period), the members of this small group knew them well. The family's place in the black power structure was well established by the time Weaver's parents came of age.

ALTHOUGH FLORENCE FREEMAN Farley and her sister, Louise, were raised in comfort, they came of age in a time of increasing backlash against Republican efforts to reconstruct American society. Viewed as the model for racial progressivism in the 1860s and 1870s, by the 1880s Washington had joined the rest of the nation in imposing limitations on black aspirations, and discrimination in jobs, housing, and social life increased dramatically. Soon after establishing a foothold in local government and business, the black middle class saw itself increasingly marginalized as Reconstruction ebbed. The tentative efforts at social interaction also abruptly ended during this period. The changes particularly disturbed the black elite, who had believed that they would ultimately be assimilated into white society. This was not to be, but the group continued to maintain its status relative to other members of the race.[11]

Exclusion increased, but black Washington continued to be the most prosperous such community in the country. Although the Republican Party lost political influence, its continued power in the city enabled black professionals to maintain many patronage positions. African Americans secured jobs in the federal government, particularly in the local offices controlled by the executive branch, and out of 23,144 federal jobs in 1891, blacks held nearly 2,400. This proportion was much smaller than the percentage of blacks in the city, but it was still significant. The black middle class, combined with the large number of working-class blacks who held stable employment, supported an expanding black business sector, much of which gravitated toward the area surrounding Howard University.[12]

Weaver's mother, Florence, grew up in this changing climate. As was expected by the determined community of educators in which she lived, Florence was among a very small number of black women who pursued her education through high school, obtaining a diploma from the prestigious M Street High School in Georgetown. Weaver later told interviewers that she was "very cultured and well-versed in Latin" and that she read Tennyson and Longfellow to him as a child. After graduating, Florence was engaged to Mortimer Grover Weaver, a DC native described by his family as "a fair-skinned mulatto who could have passed for white but chose not to." Weaver, who talked frequently about his mother, said much less about his father. He remembered Mortimer as "a puritan who didn't smoke, drink or gamble; a man very devoted to his family and actually quite compassionate, although he talked very little." Mortimer also graduated from M Street High School. Introduced by Florence's half sister, the two were married as the new century began.[13]

Through family connections, Mortimer obtained a position as a clerk in the Post Office, among the highest government positions available to blacks at the time. By 1908, the number of blacks in federal service had declined to 1,450, and the overwhelming majority of them were clerks, messengers, or laborers. The postal service was by far the largest employer of blacks, with seventy-nine black clerks and fifty-five black mail carriers among almost nine hundred workers. In 1925, Mortimer's salary was $2,200. Not a princely sum, but one that placed the family firmly in the middle class.[14]

In 1905, their first child, Mortimer Jr., was born. Robert Clifton followed in 1907. Most of Washington's black elite lived in the Northwest section of the city that surrounded Howard University. However, even in the midst of the tightening grip of Jim Crow, blacks lived in many parts of the capital. Mortimer and Florence chose to locate their family in Brookland, a bucolic neighborhood in the far section of the Northeast quadrant near Catholic University. Originally owned by Colonel Jehiel Brooks, who had served under President Andrew Jackson, the estate was subdivided in the 1880s by Benjamin Leighton, a white lawyer who was also the dean of Howard Law School. Although the subdivision was intended for middle-class whites, Leighton also sold to a small number of black families (fifteen according to the 1900 census). The first black to build in the area was W. H. A. Wormley, a longtime family friend of the Weavers.[15]

The Weavers moved to a house at 3519 North Fourteenth Street soon after they were married. They would remain there until their deaths. The decision to move to Brookland represented an effort to create some distance for the family from the social milieu of the black elite. Weaver's parents wanted their children to grow up in a world they controlled, where the focus would be on family and achievement and not on material possessions or social pretensions. Although they interacted with other members of the black elite, the Weavers remained generally separate from that world. Their son would adopt the same approach to black society. Robert would have many lifelong friends among the city's leading black families, but he also generally refrained from participation in African American (or white) parties and clubs.

From early in their youth, Mortimer and Robert had distinct personalities. Mortimer was serious and studious, while baby Robert was gregarious and playful. The boys and their friends spent hours wandering the countryside, which would soon fill up with homes and businesses. Weaver remembered his childhood as generally happy, even though the family's race influenced their relations with other residents. "We had some neighbors who were very friendly, we had other neighbors who didn't speak," he recollected. The boys' mother carefully supervised their interactions with white neighbors to protect them from racial prejudice. "My mother had the rule that we would play in our own yard, and if the other kids were to play, they played in our yard, we didn't play in theirs. . . . We didn't go to their houses to eat, and we didn't feed them at our house." Florence watched over the boys carefully, seeing to their educational and social needs. "The way to offset color prejudice is to be awfully good at whatever you do," she told both of them. Weaver later commented that his parents professed "no militancy, no call to arms . . . merely an affirmation of their right to enjoy the integrity and self-respect that are the birthright of every American." As a result, Weaver felt a strong obligation to succeed. "If you did not do well, you felt that you had let your parents down—and they let you know it," he later recalled.[16]

While his quiet father worked six days a week and spent his leisure hours on investments and projects around the house, Florence was the dominant person in the boys' lives. Weaver later told a reporter that she had several rules that puzzled him, one that "they had to wear shoes in summer when all the other kids were going barefoot," even though they lived in a rural area. Asked by Robert the reason for the rule, his mother told him that "the Weavers always hold their heads high." Although she "tongue-lashed" them once in a while, in general she established her authority "less through fear than through a subtle approach which shamed them and implied that their behavior fell below the standard of conduct expected of them." Throughout his life, Weaver frequently referenced his mother's demanding standards as a crucial part of his maturation.[17]

Florence and Mortimer raised their children in a period of instability for African Americans. Relations between the races were quiet in Brookland, but, as Jim Crow intensified, racial violence in the city increased. The 1919 riots were among the worst of the dozens of such conflagrations that occurred around the nation in that year. They started on 19 July when a group of white soldiers went on a rampage through a black area in the city's Southeast section. The pretext for the attacks was a number of assaults upon white women that local newspapers alleged were perpetrated by black men. In reality, the conflict resulted from increasing competition between whites and blacks for jobs and housing. The violence continued for several days, spreading across the city, with blacks arming themselves and defending their homes. Only the entrance of the cavalry and marines quelled the attacks. Weaver, who was twelve when the riots occurred, remained safely ensconced in his rural neighborhood, but the attacks disturbed all of the city's black community.[18]

Although Weaver's early childhood was relatively free from racial prejudice, his earliest memories of discrimination arose from the fact that he and his brother had to commute six miles every day to go to school. Like most institutions in Brookland, the elementary school was closed to blacks, and Robert and Mortimer took the streetcar, past one public and one parochial school, to Lucretia Mott Grade School. None of the Weavers complained about this situation. Their mother told them that "there is nothing inherently inferior in black blood" and argued that the education they were receiving was just as good as that of their white neighbors. Weaver later told an interviewer that "the realization of this peculiar racial arrangement was gradual and without any particular emotional upset."[19]

After grade school, Weaver would have an even longer commute, to the nation's most prestigious black secondary school, Paul Laurence Dunbar High School. By the time Robert arrived, the same year that Mortimer graduated (at the age of sixteen, heading for Williams College, in Williamstown, Massachusetts), Dunbar was widely known among African Americans in Washington as the crown jewel of the segregated system. During the late 1800s and early 1900s, Dunbar and its predecessor, M Street High School, produced an astounding percentage of the nation's black leaders, including Benjamin O. Davis, the first black general, civil rights lawyer Charles Hamilton Houston, and educator Nannie Helen Burroughs. Among the future elite whom Weaver joined during his years there were Charles Drew, the doctor who would make blood plasma a widespread product, William Hastie, the first black federal judge, and Montague Cobb, future dean of Howard Medical School. From its establishment in 1870 as the first high school for blacks in the country, through the end of legal segregation in the 1950s, Dunbar held its place as a leader in black education. It sent more students to ivy-league and other elite colleges than almost any public school (black or white) in the nation. During the 1920s alone, according to William Hastie, the school sent twenty students to Amherst College. The training Weaver received, as well as the contacts he made there, would shape his character and career.[20]

Dunbar was one of the few areas in DC where "separate" was at least approximately equal. In 1864, Congress directed that education funds be allotted to black and white schools on the basis of the number of children. Although black schools were generally physically inferior and older during the years that followed, pay for black teachers was equal to that of whites, and blacks maintained significant control over the operation of their schools. The superintendents of the black schools were African Americans, and each of them (including Weaver family friend Roscoe Conkling Bruce, who was the son of Senator Blanche K. Bruce and who led the schools in the early 1900s) worked to maintain a strong educational program.[21]

Washington schools also benefited from discrimination by the nation's colleges. During the early 1900s, a small number of blacks (many educated in DC) obtained advanced degrees. Even though they frequently graduated from the nation's elite universities, they were unable to secure teaching positions in white colleges. Excluded from other opportunities, and drawn by the fact that Washington schools paid relatively well, a significant number of black PhDs joined their faculties, among them historian Carter G. Woodson, founder of Black History Month. These teachers adopted rigorous curricula and placed high demands on the students. Weaver later wrote that he remembered "at least half a dozen outstanding teachers who not only exposed me to the subject matter and instilled an appreciation for high standards of achievement, but also inspired me as human beings."[22]

The school that Robert and Mortimer attended was new when they arrived, having opened in 1917. The construction of Dunbar, located at First and N streets NW, was the result of two decades of lobbying to replace M Street School, which was overcrowded when it opened in 1891. Dunbar itself was at capacity soon after it opened, and its facilities were not as luxurious as those of nearby all-white Central High School, but it had a gymnasium, a large auditorium, and a significant library. In 1921, the school had 1,556 students, 520 men and 1,036 women.[23]

Dunbar also had strict admissions standards and was known as a school for the children of black professionals. Although many working-class students also attended, the image of the school as an elite institution remained well into the twentieth century. The large number of middle-class students distinguished the school from other black schools at the time. Dr. Kenneth Clarke, the psychologist whose studies played a major role in the battle against school segregation, described Dunbar as a "white school in a segregated system. . . . excellence at Dunbar represented the few—the percentage of Washington's black community that was middle-class and upwardly mobile." Even within the school, class distinctions often prevailed, and the poorer and darker-skinned children frequently complained that they did not receive the same amount of attention as their light-skinned peers.[24]

The curriculum of the school focused on preparing students for college, requiring that they master Latin, the sciences, and English literature. The American history that they learned gave particular attention to the achievements of African Americans and incorporated their stories into the larger narrative of America, because Dunbar teachers "committed themselves to uplifting the race through their students." The culture of the school was based on the expectation that the students would prove themselves worthy of participation in the broader American society and, through their efforts, would open doors for less-fortunate blacks. One former graduate from Weaver's years remembered that there "were constant reminders of what it meant to be black in America" and of their obligations to their race. By its own standards, Dunbar was a dramatic success during these years. In 1975, a study of Dunbar students concluded that the school had produced 2,500 teachers, 1,000 doctors, 1,500 nurses, 400 lawyers, and 8,000 federal government professionals.[25]

The demands of his teachers, Weaver later recalled, prepared him well for the challenges of the future. "Perhaps the finest tribute I can pay to Dunbar . . . is the fact that, when I graduated, I went to Harvard College where many of my classmates had been trained in some of the best preparatory schools in the nation. I found myself on the whole about as well able to survive in college as they were." He praised several teachers, including one who taught him a "love for literature," another who taught him "the structure and proper usage of language," and a third, a math teacher, who gave Weaver confidence by asking him to step in and teach the class during his absence. His course load included two years of Latin, two of French, algebra, geometry, and two English courses a year. With the exception of his math courses (where he infrequently scored a 90) and French (where he received an 85 once), Weaver consistently received grades of 95 in all of his courses.[26]

Weaver fondly remembered his years at Dunbar, where he was among the most active members of his class. He served as the captain of the Cadet Drill Team, which won an award during his senior year in a competition attended by President and Mrs. Calvin Coolidge. Weaver also served as business manager of the school newspaper and was a member of the honor society. But Weaver's strongest memories involved his participation in speech and debate competitions. During his senior year, he won the prestigious city-wide Oratorical Competition, a success that was reported in the *Washington Star.* Weaver later told Ralph Bunche that the contest opened his eyes to the struggles that his race presented. During his speech, Weaver noticed that a white judge had stopped listening. "I realized what a terrible barrier race prejudice was. . . . I soon decided that it would demand just a little more effort and a little more subtlety for me, as a Negro, to get ahead than was required of a white person," he wrote.[27]

During his summers, Weaver first worked for an electrical business and then started his own, hiring himself out to families to wire their houses; he made a good deal of money, much of which he saved for college. Watched over by the careful eye of his mother, he did not spend much time socializing but focused on study. On Sundays, the family went to church at Berean Baptist. The congregation there was composed of socially conservative professionals who expected much from Weaver and his peers. There is little in Weaver's background that would predict his nascent liberal philosophy. Most of his family and friends were rock-ribbed Republicans. One source for alternative political views, however, was Weaver's pastor, David Rivers, whom Weaver remembered as a thoughtful, probing man who introduced him to the *New York Times* and national politics.[28]

By the time Weaver graduated from Dunbar in 1925, he had developed into an intelligent, mature, and sometimes-rambunctious young man. He excelled at many activities, though he never thought himself the equal of his brother, Mortimer, when it came to intellectual pursuits. At the same time, Weaver was secure in his place as a young member of the black elite, a society where summer beach vacations, classical music lessons, and high educational expectations were the norm. He was, in all ways except one, identical to the young men he would join in Cambridge that fall.

AT GRADUATION, WEAVER'S grade average placed him sixth in a class of 266 and second out of 68 among the boys, a more important score, as almost all of the elite colleges were for men only. The school principal, Walter Smith, told the Harvard Admissions Office that Weaver was "a young man of excellent ability and character," who was "thoroughly dependable and capable." His grades and recommendations enabled Weaver to gain admission to Harvard without the necessity of an entrance examination, and he secured a scholarship which paid most of his tuition for the first year. As evidence of the strong historical connections between Harvard and Dunbar, the Admissions Office told Weaver that he would be allowed to enroll without taking the entrance exam, provided that he was in "the highest seventh of boys" in the graduating class. So confident was Weaver of his admission that he did not apply to any other schools.[29]

Weaver talked about his years at Harvard with the attitude of one who had expected to attend the nation's most prestigious institution and had not been particularly impressed by the place. Most Americans could not have aspired to such a goal, but Weaver's family history, background, and training were all such that Harvard University was a natural step after graduation from Dunbar. By the time that Weaver arrived at Harvard in the fall of 1925, the college had a fifty-five-year history of admitting African American students. Weaver's family had known many black Harvard graduates, including Richard Greener, who was the first black to receive a degree from the college and who later served as principal of Dunbar High School. Throughout the late 1800s and early 1900s, Harvard admitted a very small number of blacks, in the early years selecting one or two per class and increasing that number to three to five by the 1920s. In 1923 there were forty-two black men, seventeen undergraduates and twenty-five graduate students, at Harvard. Guided by the tradition of abolitionism and controlled by Republicans, the university claimed that it did not discriminate on the basis of race. However, few Harvard leaders believed that their black students were truly equal, and the philosophy of equality did not apply to "social relations." Although there were exceptions, African Americans at Harvard generally created their own social circle. Most lived off-campus in Cambridge and took their meals separately.[30]

For most of this period, racial separation at Harvard was informal, but in the years immediately before Weaver's arrival, segregation became more rigid. The most significant example of this changing atmosphere was President Lawrence Lowell's 1923 announcement that the freshman halls be restricted to whites. Soon after taking office, Lowell had created the college system to provide students with a more intimate community within the larger university. His secondary goal was to reduce elitism by creating residences in which all Harvard students, the extremely wealthy and the less well-to-do, would live together. He made no provision for black students, however, and for several years they were denied admission to the dorms on the grounds that there was not enough space.[31]

By 1921, however, the administration was receiving complaints, from black and white alumni, about racial discrimination in housing. In 1922, Roscoe Conkling Bruce, a 1902 graduate, wrote the Registrar's Office to reserve a place for his son, a good friend of Weaver's who was then a student at the Exeter School. President Lowell replied that he had decided to bar blacks from the freshman dormitories, though not from other residential halls. Blacks, Lowell stated, were entitled to admission to all academic facilities but not to social ones. "It seems to me that for the colored man to claim that he is entitled to have the white man compelled to live with him is a very unfortunate innovation which, far from doing him any good, would increase a prejudice that, as you and I will thoroughly agree, is most unfortunate, and probably growing," Lowell wrote Bruce. He argued that allowing blacks to live in the dorms would result in many white students, particularly those from the South, deciding to attend other universities and would hurt Harvard's standing.[32]

Black and many white alumni strongly opposed the decision and organized a petition that was signed by 142 alums, including Herbert Croly, Oswald Garrison Villard, and Walter Lippmann. Harvard students, they argued, were not opposed to living next to African Americans. Of the seventeen black college students, ten lived in dorms, and there was no record of any white opposition to these students, they stated. Later that year, both the *Harvard Graduate's Alumni Magazine* and the *Harvard Alumni Bulletin* issued editorials opposing the restriction. The policy, the *Bulletin* wrote, was "disloyalty to a principle for which the University has hitherto taken an open and unshaken stand." It reported that, of the sixty letters it received on the issue, two-thirds of them opposed the policy of exclusion. None of this, however, convinced Lowell of his error.[33]

Years later, Weaver told an interviewer that Lowell's decision "was one which affected me rather personally," adding that "it was general knowledge among Negroes that they were not welcome in the freshman dormitories." As a result, Weaver did not apply to be admitted to the dorms. Instead, he found housing with his brother, Mortimer, who had graduated, at the top of his class, from Williams College and was pursuing a master's degree in literature at Harvard.[34]

Throughout his career, Weaver frequently referred to his training as an electrician as evidence that he was not solely an intellectual. According to Weaver, Mortimer was the "brain" in the family, and not wanting to compete with his adored brother, he focused on practical pursuits. Weaver chose to enroll in the School of Engineering, hoping to secure a degree in electrical engineering. But he struggled with several aspects of the program, particularly German (in which he received an E). By his own account, Weaver enjoyed the freedom of being so far from his mother too much during his freshman year. He participated heartily in Boston's black society events and was described by one friend as "the brother who made most of the noise" and a "lady's man around Boston." By the end of the year, Weaver was on academic probation, and he lost his scholarship aid. The academic difficulties weighed on him physically, and his files record several absences from class for medical reasons.[35]

In the spring of 1926, Weaver decided to transfer out of the School of Engineering to the liberal arts college. He later remarked that the engineering curriculum was like that of a graduate school, and tongue-in-cheek, he claimed that he had been having too good a time to do the work. Engineering "interfered with my courting and also it called for much more energy than I wanted to extend in intellectual pursuits at that time. So I shifted over to economics." The transfer was approved during the summer, and Weaver began his sophomore year with a new major. Weaver never lost his interest in engineering, and he would be a lifelong tinkerer. During summers in college, he worked as an electrician at Howard University, doing "inside work," which, he remembered, made him the envy of his peers who toiled in the hot summer sun.[36]

He also said goodbye to Mortimer, who took a job in Greensboro, North Carolina, as assistant professor of English at North Carolina Agricultural and Technical College, a school for blacks. Robert felt Mortimer's loss but found support with a group of African American students who would become some of the most illustrious members of the American civil rights movement. Weaver's sophomore-year roommate at 419 Broadway in Cambridge was Louis L. Redding, a law student who would become a leading civil rights activist and one of the lawyers in the school desegregation cases during the 1950s. Their next-door neighbors were William Hastie, Ralph Bunche, and John P. Davis. Hastie, a Dunbar graduate, had been a family friend for years. He was attending Harvard Law School after graduating with honors from Amherst College. Hastie, who would achieve a number of firsts, including becoming the first black governor of the Virgin Islands and the first black federal judge, was well known at the Law School as one of the student body's leading intellects. His roommate, Ralph Bunche, was a westerner who had graduated from the University of California at Los Angeles and won a scholarship to pursue a doctorate in political science. He would remain a lifelong friend who amassed many accomplishments, including the Nobel Peace Prize for his work in the Middle East. Davis, another family friend and Dunbar graduate, would help Weaver move into the world of New Deal politics. Together, the five young men formed a formidable association that would last their lifetimes. Through poker, dinner, socializing, and studying, they provided each other with the support that Lowell's college system was supposed to have provided.[37]

After his freshman struggles, Weaver's academic performance improved dramatically. During his junior year, he made the dean's list, and he stayed on the honor roll through his senior year. Weaver was also an active participant in the university's oral competitions. During his junior year, he won the Pasteur Medal for the best speech on "contemporary French politics." His topic was "Resolved, That the United States Adopt Foreign Minister Briand's Treaty Outlawing War between France and the United States." Later that spring, Weaver won the Boylston Speaking Prize for a speech entitled "Abraham Lincoln." These prestigious awards brought him notice in Cambridge as well as at home, where both announcements were reported in the *Washington Post*. He was also a member of the Liberal Club, an organization whose members were a distinct political minority at Republican Harvard, a place that chose Herbert Hoover over alum Franklin Delano Roosevelt in a 1932 straw poll. At the club's meetings, Weaver had his first significant exposure to the debates over the appropriate role of government in society. There is, however, little evidence that Weaver was experiencing a political awakening. His work at Harvard focused on the traditional college subjects and extracurricular activities, managed by a faculty that was among the nation's most conservative.[38]

As he had been at Dunbar, Weaver was a leader of the university's debating club. He was a member of the traveling debating team and was elected secretary of the Debating Council during his senior year. The debating competitions were among the most prestigious and widely attended functions in the university, and Weaver participated in several competitions, including debates with Williams College and Brown University. He did not, however, travel with the team to its competitions at Duke or Emory universities and others in the South, because his race disqualified him. Although such exclusion was to be expected at the height of Jim Crow, Weaver experienced what he described as his only example of discrimination at Harvard when he was removed from the team that was set to visit Princeton. As Weaver later recalled, "One of the eager beavers, who was the coach, sent a telegram saying that I was a Negro and would there be a problem. They got sort of a wishy-washy reply. And the great liberal, Mr. Abbott Lawrence Lowell, came up with sophistry that since we were not the hosts but the guests, we would have to abide by their rules and I was not permitted to go, though the team felt very strongly to the contrary."

Nevertheless, he remembered his years at Harvard as academically productive, and he stated that he "certainly did not encounter any discrimination as far as anything academically was concerned or any other extra-curricular activities in which I engaged."[39]

Although he increased his focus on academics, Weaver maintained an active social life in Boston, in DC, and elsewhere. He frequently visited his cousin Alston Burleigh, a musician in New York City, who was the son of Harry T. Burleigh and Weaver's aunt Louise. Harry Burleigh was among the most famous black musicians of the early twentieth century. A native of Erie, Pennsylvania, Burleigh won a singing scholarship to study at the National Conservatory of Music. There, he developed a lifelong friendship with the famous Russian composer Antonin Dvorak, who encouraged him to use the music of Negro spirituals in his compositions. Between 1900 and 1930, Burleigh wrote several hundred songs and performed them for numerous luminaries, including the king of England and President Teddy Roosevelt. Burleigh's success enabled him to create a very comfortable life for his family in Harlem. Weaver was a frequent guest at their house, and while there he participated in the salons, jazz, and parties of the Harlem Renaissance. According to Weaver, both the Burleighs "introduced me to the theater, concert life, and other cultural aspects of New York City." Alston also initiated Weaver into the Omega Phi Psi fraternity, an institution that played a major supportive role for black professionals throughout their lives.[40]

Burleigh was not the only entrée Weaver had into the city's black society. In 1928, Weaver participated in what many blacks at the time called the "wedding of the century," the marriage of Yolande DuBois, only child of W. E. B. DuBois, and poet Countee Cullen, son of one of the nation's most famous black ministers. In 1928 the two were married in front of 1,500 people at Salem Methodist Church in Harlem. Weaver was one of ten groomsmen (there were fifteen bridesmaids), joining several of the leading lights of the Harlem Renaissance, including Arna Bontemps and Langston Hughes. Weaver and Cullen had met at Harvard, where Cullen was studying literature, but they had long-standing family connections. In his report on the wedding for *Crisis,* the journal of the National Association for the Advancement of Colored People, DuBois described the wedding party as evidence of "a new race; a new thought." Almost all of the nation's black elite attended the festivities. Throughout his early career, Weaver kept up a sporadic correspondence with DuBois and sought his advice on a variety of matters. As the old lion of the civil rights movement became increasingly controversial among blacks and whites during the 1930s, Weaver's interaction with DuBois decreased.[41]

Although his social life was full, Weaver's family life was not as stable. In May 1929, his beloved brother, Mortimer, died suddenly of an unexplained illness. After Harvard, Mortimer had moved to North Carolina to teach and then to Howard University, where he was an assistant professor of English. Long after Mortimer's death, Weaver remained in awe of his brother, who had achieved more distinctions than almost anyone in his cohort. Weaver described him as "a brilliant mind" who "would have been a great man." At Williams College, Mortimer was Phi Beta Kappa and received a $100 graduation prize for winning the "the greatest number of prizes" during his years in college. Mortimer was particularly adept at public speaking and won several regional college competitions in this area. In his short time at Howard, Mortimer revitalized the debate team, arranging, with his brother's aid, a competition with Harvard.[42]

Mortimer's death, Weaver later remembered, was "the greatest loss I had ever known until that time," and with the clarity of hindsight Weaver said that it had changed his life. He told an interviewer in the 1960s, "I always felt I had a smart brother, so I didn't have to do much. But now . . . everything depended on me." According to Weaver, he and Mortimer had been planning to go to law school and open a firm together. But after Mortimer's death, Weaver said "to hell with law school" and started taking academic life more seriously. According to one journalist, Weaver "turned over two new leaves. He suddenly felt obligated to be all that his parents expected of him *and* Mortimer." Over the years, several of his friends remarked that Weaver's "'terrible drive' to get ahead" would often cause him to "push [himself] too far." Mortimer's death immediately aroused these ambitions. When he graduated later that year, Weaver was admitted to the Cum Laude Society.[43]

IT SAYS A great deal about the value the black elite placed on education that Weaver felt that opening a law practice would disappoint his parents. Like many other African Americans, Weaver's family believed that the attainment of a doctorate was the pinnacle of all professional aspirations. The fact that Weaver could become the first black to secure a doctorate in economics from Harvard, following in the footsteps of W. E. B. DuBois, the first black to receive a Harvard doctorate, made the goal even more worthwhile. Though his degree would remain a distinction that Weaver pointed to proudly, its actual pursuit was surprisingly painless and uneventful.

After graduation Weaver moved immediately into the graduate economics program. Although many other people were profoundly influenced by the training and proselytization of their economics professors, Weaver left Harvard showing few effects of this indoctrination. If anything, despite the efforts of his professors, Weaver departed Cambridge with a stronger belief in the necessity of government reform to support the needs of the poor and excluded. Armed with the credential, Weaver used very little of his education in his professional life.

Weaver joined a department that, while still considered among the best in the country (it was Harvard, after all), was led by academics at the end of their careers and working in a field whose central tenets were rapidly changing. By 1920, argued J. S. Davis, an economist who left for Stanford in 1921, the department "had lost much of its earlier quality." Edward Mason, who joined the department just before Weaver came to Harvard and was later dean of the college, called the 1920s a "dead period" in the department's history. By 1929, when the country entered a period of unprecedented economic turmoil, the scholars who dominated the economics department had done their best work decades before, when classical economic theory was dominant. Few of them participated in the rethinking of the basic principles that John Maynard Keynes would launch when he published his 1936 tome *The General Theory of Employment, Interest, and Money*.[44]

Few of Weaver's professors engaged in applied economics—that is, used their tools to study pressing problems in industry and agriculture. Most of them focused on economic history and theory. Even those involved in analyzing current phenomena agreed with their colleagues that the economic system was controlled by the "natural laws" of supply and demand and that government intervention was almost always wrong. They were particularly opposed to the dramatic increase in federal involvement in the economy that began under Herbert Hoover and accelerated when Franklin Roosevelt took office in 1933. According to one historian of the department, "the ideas embodied in the New Deal were anathema, because they represented an overt interference by government in the otherwise efficient workings of markets."[45]

Large among the leading lights of the profession with whom Weaver studied was Frank Taussig, who had joined the department in 1883 after serving as personal secretary to Harvard president Charles Eliot. During his long tenure, Taussig molded not only the department but the economics profession as a whole. He held steadfastly to the principles of neoclassical economics, arguing that worker protections such as the minimum wage and unemployment insurance were unnecessary. Thomas Nixon Carver, one of Weaver's advisors, shared a belief in natural laws of economics as well as of other parts of society. A teacher of sociology who was supportive of a wide range of empirical studies, Carver was described by colleagues as a "devout Social Darwinist." President Lowell, no liberal, characterized Carver as seeing "things clearly but through a very small keyhole." Weaver's main thesis advisor, William Ripley, described by a colleague as "sort of an intellectual Colonel Sanders of Kentucky Fried Chicken," focused on applied economics, particularly the railroad industry. He also, according to one historian, "for many years championed the biological superiority of Anglo-Saxons as the reason for the United States' and England's economic success." Such views dominated the department during Weaver's tenure.[46]

One would expect the period Weaver was in school to be a tumultuous one for the economists who taught him, but even though it tested all of their economic theories, the depression that began in 1929 did nothing to alter these men's core beliefs. In 1934, these men, along with other members of the department, would publish a full-scale attack on the New Deal entitled "The Economics of the Recovery Program," which called the president's efforts to regulate the economy doomed to fail and claimed that Roosevelt's monetary policy would create an "orgy of inflation." When a group of young instructors (professors not on the tenure track) wrote in praise of the New Deal, they were systematically pushed out of the department. Just a few years later, many of the department's conservative faculty would also be gone, replaced by a diverse group of brilliant young economists that included Joseph Schumpeter, Alvin Hansen, and John Kenneth Galbraith. Along with others, these men would play a major role in rethinking the structure of economic systems, but when Weaver was taking classes, the department's renaissance had yet to arrive.[47]

Despite the fact that he disagreed with much that he was being taught, Weaver did very well in his coursework, earning As in almost every class. Through years of training by family and teachers, Weaver had mastered the skill of ascertaining what his professors wanted and regurgitating it back to them lucidly. He wrote nothing at the time about his experiences and little about Harvard later, but Weaver remembered most of the classes as dull and the teachers as extremely conservative.

His scholarly success, however, did not enable him to overcome the racial barriers between him and the faculty. Given their economic and social views, it is not surprising that Weaver never developed a lifelong mentor-student relationship with any of his professors at Harvard, and none of them played an important role in Weaver's career. At the same time, when he needed academic recommendations, Weaver's professors were without exception warm in their praise, albeit cognizant of the limitations his race would impose. Professor Arthur Cole called Weaver's examination "the best in the entire group" and stated that Weaver was "a pleasant, well-appearing fellow so agreeable, in fact, that one forgets at once that he has some negro blood in him." William Crum, who taught Weaver statistics, wrote that "he has a good personality and abundant energy" and was "well qualified for a teaching position where he is socially fitted." Frank Taussig, who Weaver later said "didn't think black men had aptitude for economics," was also positive about Weaver's performance. Taussig wrote that he was "a good thinker and has independence and some originality," with "every promise of making an excellent teacher." Only Professor Frederick Packard held any confidence that Weaver might break the academic color barrier. He wrote that Weaver was "universally admired by students and associates." At the end of his recommendation, Packard added a note to the career placement staff that stated, "It would be a pity to allow racial prejudice to handicap him, but his splendid appearance and the fact that he is clean and fine in every respect should prevent that." At least in the short term, Packard would be proven wrong.[48]

Two years after entering the program, in the spring of 1931, Weaver easily passed his general examination, and all that remained was the completion of his dissertation. Like many of his classmates, Weaver chose at this point to find a teaching position with the expectation that he would return to Harvard on a fellowship to write his thesis. Packard hoped that Weaver's light skin and refinement might enable him to secure a position no other blacks had attained, but this hope was misplaced. Though he was widely respected by his professors and peers, Weaver had few of the employment options available to other Harvard graduate students. The hiring of the first African American to a tenure-track position at a prestigious white college (Dunbar grad Allison Davis, who was appointed to the University of Chicago faculty in 1942) was a decade away. Since the turn of the century, all of the department's own hires had been its own students, but even though he was among the best students in his class, it does not appear that the faculty ever considered keeping Weaver in Cambridge. In later years, the Harvard economics department would add several assistant professors (most of whom were *not* Harvard graduates), but Weaver's job opportunities were limited to black colleges. He had hoped to secure a position at Howard University, but they had no openings at the time. Instead, as his brother, Mortimer, had done a few years earlier, Weaver moved to Greensboro, North Carolina, to take a position at North Carolina Agricultural and Technical College. His career as a professor would not last long.[49]

North Carolina Agricultural and Technical College, the most important secondary school for blacks in the state, was founded in 1891, a year after Congress passed the Morrill Act to subsidize the expansion of colleges in the nation. The law required any state applying for funds to provide facilities for qualified blacks, and like other southern states, North Carolina decided to do this on a segregated basis. Located in Greensboro, the school had a traditional curriculum that focused on farming and vocational skills, with a limited number of classes in liberal arts. Weaver was the whole economics and sociology department. His salary was $2,450, less than he would have made at Harvard but a significant sum for the time.[50]

Although it was not his first choice, North Carolina Agricultural and Technical College had many advantages for Weaver. It was easily accessible to Washington, DC, so Weaver could maintain his social ties there. Also, the school had a capable and credentialed faculty that included Dr. Percy Julian, one of the nation's leading chemists. During his first year, Weaver was responsible for teaching introductory courses in economic theory, agricultural economics, and sociology. He later recollected that, unlike his brother, he was not a good teacher, and he did not feel that being a college professor was the best job for him. However, school administrators were impressed with his performance: In 1932 Dean Warmoth Gibbs wrote that Weaver "has made a fine impression on both the students and faculty of this institution. . . . He shows that he has a fine grasp of the subject matter in his field . . . makes friends easily, and cooperates well inp a faculty group."[51]

In the spring of 1932, Weaver applied for, and received, a fellowship to return to Harvard to complete his doctorate. Before he arrived, he seemed to be leaning toward a study of African Americans. Weaver wrote W. E. B. DuBois that his future work would "concern Negroes," and the topic he gave his thesis committee was "Industrial Education and Industrial Opportunities for the Negro." Though Weaver would devote much of his career to studying the labor problems of African Americans, when he returned to Harvard he chose a different dissertation topic. Weaver's thesis, "The High Wage Theory of Prosperity," was an examination of the theoretical debates over the role of consumption and saving in the business economy. The paper provided a detailed analysis of the major theories on the relationship between labor and capital, focusing in particular on the arguments made by several economists that improving wages was crucial to maintaining a healthy economic system. Walking the line between his professors, who were deeply skeptical about arguments for higher wages (since they involved alterations of natural economic laws), and his own predilections in favor of such interventions, Weaver concluded that, although improved wages produced many benefits, they were not the solution to economic instability. He told friends that he wrote the thesis "in about six months time" and that it "was rather bad." It would be his one and only foray into economic theory.[52]

In June 1933, when Harvard University bestowed upon him a doctorate of philosophy in economics, Weaver became the first African American to achieve such a distinction from Harvard and only the second black person to receive a doctoral degree in economics (the first was Sadie T. M. Alexander, a Philadelphia lawyer who received her degree from the University of Pennsylvania in 1921). None of his family or friends had any doubt that Weaver was going to make a major mark in society. But the question remained, what kind of mark would he make? Certainly he could expect a successful teaching career, but it would likely be (at least until he was able to secure a position at Howard) at an underfunded institution. During the 1920s, economists had become more fully engaged in the business world, but Weaver's color prevented him from exploiting such opportunities. Fully trained in the techniques of data collection and analysis, Weaver was certainly qualified to move in many directions, and given his personal connections in the nation's capital, the rapidly expanding national government seemed to be an obvious choice. But, despite his degree, there was little evidence that the federal government was ready to open itself to aspiring African American professionals. That would soon change, however, and Weaver would be responsible for breaking down the barriers.

* 2 *

# Fighting for a Better Deal

On 30 June 1933, John P. Davis and Robert C. Weaver took their places at the hearing table of the National Recovery Administration (NRA). Meeting in a temporary building constructed behind the White House, the board of the NRA sat to hear testimony on a proposed "Code of Fair Competition" for the textile industry, an industry particularly hard hit by the deepening depression. Davis, the executive secretary of the Negro Industrial League, told NRA leaders that he was accompanied by the organization's director of research, Robert Weaver. In fact, the two young men were the only staff of the organization, which had no office, no funding, and had been created just days before.[1]

"The Negro Industrial League," Davis began, "is a national organization which concerns itself with the bettering of the labor and economic conditions of Negroes as workers and consumers." Even though the proposed code said nothing about race, Davis asserted, the operators of the textile plants that crafted it had designed the code to deny minimum wage and work protections to their black workers. These provisions, Davis argued, were contrary to the intent of the act which created the NRA. If the government was to achieve its goal of putting people back to work and increasing buying power, then the black worker "must be dealt with on a parity with his white fellow workers," Davis asserted.[2]

Decades later, it is difficult to understand why a couple of young men, both with advanced degrees from Harvard, would attract such a great deal of attention just by testifying at what amounted to an administrative hearing. But, in a country where Jim Crow segregation ruled throughout the South and racial discrimination was a matter of course across the country, the sight of two African Americans before the national government was a major event. The *New York Times*, *Washington Star*, and *Washington Tri-*

*bune* all described their efforts. "You'd have thought Jesus Christ had come back," Weaver later recalled. "All of a sudden people knew who we were. We had no idea we would get this sort of recognition." Weaver's and Davis's appearance would set the two men on a course that would take both, albeit in dramatically different directions, to positions of leadership in the civil rights movement. For Weaver, the hearing would be the beginning of a long and illustrious career in government service. It would also mark the first in a series of decisions Weaver would make regarding the path toward racial justice. Though they started their efforts together, Weaver and Davis would soon part ways—Davis choosing to agitate from outside the system, and Weaver choosing a career within government institutions, prodding and pulling them toward reform.[3]

BY THE SUMMER of 1933, when the two men came to the nation's capital, the Depression had reached severe proportions. Because of the seemingly unending spiral of unemployment and declining production, the average worker, who had earned $25 a week in 1929, took home, if he was lucky to have a job, only $16.73 in 1933. Unemployment was particularly high in the Northeast and Midwest, reaching 50 percent in Chicago, Detroit, and Cleveland and a staggering 90 percent in Gary, Indiana (home to the largest steel plant in the world). The farm economy, where more than 80 percent of blacks toiled, had never really reaped the benefits of economic growth during the 1920s, but the Depression years were even harder. Agricultural prices declined 61 percent between 1929 and 1933 and foreclosures took one-third of all homesteads. As a result, hundreds of thousands of Americans took to the roads looking for any kind of work or assistance. In 1932, over two-thirds of black cotton farmers made no profit at all.[4]

During the 1920s, the increasing number of blacks seeking work in industrializing urban America fared relatively better than their rural brothers and sisters, but in the modern economy blacks faced deeply entrenched patterns of discrimination. By far, most occupations for blacks were in the menial services: black men were unable to move past custodial positions, while black women who sought paid work overwhelmingly found it in the homes of others as domestics. When the Depression deepened, they were lucky to hold on to these occupations, as many of them were replaced by whites who banded behind the slogan "No Jobs for Niggers until Every White Man Has a Job." Others saw their jobs disappear as employers were no longer able to afford them. By 1932 black unemployment in American cities was at more than 50 percent.[5]

Into this devastation came Franklin Delano Roosevelt. A member of one of the nation's most elite families, Roosevelt had enjoyed every advantage—private tutors, private schools, Harvard College, Columbia Law School. Elected governor of the nation's most populous state in 1928, Roosevelt was immediately an early front-runner for the Democratic nomination to run against Republican Herbert Hoover. During the campaign, Roosevelt promised a "New Deal" for the American people, but the specifics of this program were less than clear. Although Roosevelt beat Hoover by almost 18 percentage points, the election was more a rejection of Hoover than a recognition of the Democrat's strengths.[6]

When he took office, few people were sure what the president would do, but he quickly responded with a flurry of proposals. The first one hundred days of FDR's presidency were unlike any previous period in the history of the federal government. Between his inauguration in March 1933 and Congress's summer recess, the president succeeded in passing fifteen major bills that sought to bring economic recovery to the nation. Several of these laws dramatically and permanently changed the relationship between the federal government and the American people.

The New Deal also significantly altered the path of American race relations, though these changes were slow and hard fought. While they were wary of the new president, many African Americans also felt that 1933 marked a significant moment in the struggle for equality. That spring, the National Association for the Advancement of Colored People (NAACP), the nation's most influential civil rights group, announced the convening of a conference of young leaders in Amenia, New York. NAACP officials sought to evoke positive memories of the 1916 Amenia conference, which was a formative moment in the group's history. Among the twenty-two men and eleven women invited were Weaver's friends Louis Redding, Ralph Bunche, and William Hastie. Other members of the Talented Tenth chosen were attorney Charles Hamilton Houston and sociologist E. Franklin Frazier.[7]

NAACP leaders hoped that the interaction of these young men and women with their older counterparts would produce new approaches to the civil rights cause, but they were also concerned with continuing the group's influence in a period of crisis. The Depression placed the NAACP under extreme pressure to bring about relief to the millions of impoverished African Americans. Many young blacks were increasingly critical of the group's leaders, who, they argued, were isolated and removed from the needs of the black masses. The organization's almost-exclusive focus on legal rights, critics claimed, blinded it to the fact that most blacks were too poor to enjoy the liberties (such as dining out or traveling in first class) these groups sought to secure. By selecting thirty-three young people to meet and chart the course of black America, NAACP leaders sought to mute this criticism and bestow influence on young people who would be "responsible" race leaders.[8]

Weaver, who at twenty-six was younger than Hastie, Bunche, and most of the attendees, was not invited to the Amenia conference. Though he was known to DuBois and other black leaders, Weaver had yet to make any contributions to the cause of black progress. But within a year of Roosevelt's election, Weaver would be one of the most influential members of this new generation. Working with a small number of African American professionals within the federal government, in cooperation and less frequently conflict with an array of black advocacy groups, and with increasing assistance from white liberals who understood the importance of governmental intervention in the areas of civil rights, Weaver would become a crucial participant in the debates over American domestic policy during the New Deal years.

ALTHOUGH TODAY PEOPLE understand the New Deal to refer to a specific philosophy about the role of government in American society and to a series of coherent programs, Roosevelt and his aides were far from consistent in their approaches to the economic crisis. No agency better captured the spirit of New Deal experimentation than the National Recovery Administration (NRA). The goal of the NRA was to bring economic growth through the rationalization of the country's chaotic industrial system. By serving as a mediating body responsible for creating codes of conduct for the nation's major industrial sectors, the NRA, proponents argued, would lessen destructive competition between companies and increase buying power among workers. From the moment of its inception until the Supreme Court declared the program unconstitutional a little less than two years later, the NRA was vilified by many who believed that it was a step toward socialism and government control of the economy. Many people in the administration viewed the NRA's authority to enforce the codes it negotiated as legally problematic, and from the beginning NRA director

Hugh Johnson had to resort to public campaigns to pressure businesses to comply.[9]

The overwhelming majority (more than three-quarters) of blacks toiled in agriculture and domestic service, and these two fields were specifically exempted from the provisions of the NRA. However, the law still had the ability to influence the lives of at least two million black workers. Like many of the new programs, the NRA offered both great potential benefits and serious threats to the interests of African Americans. Blacks had generally been excluded from participating in the industrial economy, and sympathetic federal regulation, many hoped, could result in increased pressure on businesses to provide equal opportunities at decent wages. However, the administration's opposition to any measures that angered the segregationist wing of the Democratic Party prevented the law from being used in this manner. In the end, discrimination within the NRA would spur a dramatic increase in activism among African Americans, bring about the creation of new organizations to fight for equal rights, and cause an important shift in the strategies of existing institutions toward economic concerns. Weaver would play a crucial role in this process.[10]

Immediately after the NRA was created in June 1933, it began organizing hearings to set production standards in many industries. Just as quickly, it became clear to at least some black activists that the codes would be damaging to the interests of black workers. The first hearings, held just eleven days after Roosevelt signed the act creating the NRA, focused on textiles, an industry that had been subject to a great deal of turmoil for more than a decade. Although most of the northern textile factories employed eastern European immigrants, blacks toiled in large numbers (generally in the lowest-paid positions) in southern companies. At the hearings, industry leaders and union representatives presented their views on the appropriate production schedules and wage rates, but no representative spoke for black workers (who were not unionized).[11]

One of the most important decisions that had already been agreed to was that the codes would allow different wage rates according to the region of the country. Factories in the South, where, owners argued, the cost of living was lower and workers were less efficient, would be allowed to pay their workers a minimum wage substantially lower than northern factories. In addition, and even more importantly for most black workers, the proposed code would exempt manufacturers from paying "cleaners and outside employees" the proscribed minimum wage of $12.00 per week and from limiting those employees to the maximum workweek of forty hours set by the code. The majority of black workers fell in these categories. While the proposed codes made no racial distinctions, the impact of this decision would fall predominantly on African Americans.[12]

One of the members of the audience for the first hearing was Weaver's Harvard and Dunbar friend John P. Davis. By this time Davis had finished his law degree and was back in Washington, DC. Like his Harvard classmates, Davis had taken a keen interest in the New Deal and had discussed the administration's proposals frequently with his professors, including Felix Frankfurter, who had provided advice to the administration. Unlike his classmates, however, Davis was not able to partake in the employment service that Frankfurter ran between Harvard and the federal government. Davis came to the NRA hearings as a private citizen, not as a New Dealer. However, he quickly saw an opportunity to inject himself into the debates. Noticing that no black organizations had signed up to give testimony, Davis created an organization, the Negro Industrial League, on the spot and asked to be listed to represent black workers at the hearings.[13]

Histories of the two men provide different memories of how they began their collaboration. Davis stated that he had created the Negro Industrial League on his own and then asked Weaver to join him, but Weaver argued that he and Davis created the organization together. Sitting around his parents' house waiting to go back to his teaching position in North Carolina, Weaver hoped that he might have a chance to join the Roosevelt administration. As it was for lawyers, the New Deal was a boon for social scientists of all kinds, particularly economists. Hundreds of them converged on Washington in 1933 to participate in the great experiment. For men like Berkeley economics graduate John Kenneth Galbraith, who started an illustrious economics career in the Department of Agriculture, the government expansion was a godsend. Weaver, who had written his dissertation on the role of wages in economic growth, was a natural choice to investigate the impact of the codes on blacks. However, just as Weaver's color prevented him from exploiting the teaching opportunities available to his Harvard classmates, racial discrimination obstructed access to these new government jobs. His applications to several agencies were rejected without consideration.[14]

Weaver was fortunate to have as a friend the flamboyant John Davis, who set in motion the process that would end with Weaver's entrance into the federal government. Forming their group, Davis took the title of executive secretary; and Weaver, director of research. The two-man organization spent the next two days and nights preparing their testimony, pulling together statistics on the cost of living in southern textile areas. Weaver later recalled that he had written most of the presentation, and, three decades later, he was somewhat dismissive of Davis's role: "John, a little short guy, sort of pompous, he liked to speak, well he read it," he told an interviewer. Davis's testimony brought a positive response from the committee members. NRA head Hugh Johnson called the presentation a "comprehensive and forceful brief," and Secretary of Labor Frances Perkins also praised Davis. In an attempt to co-opt the group, textile company lobbyist George Sloan offered to pay Davis and Weaver for a "supplementary brief" providing further detail for their claims. The two unemployed men agreed to do so, but they did not temper their criticism of the proposed rules.[15]

Caught off guard by the young upstarts, established civil rights groups jumped to participate in the formulation of the NRA codes. At the NAACP annual convention, held just days after Davis's presentation, the board adopted a resolution demanding that a black person be appointed to the NRA's Labor Advisory Board and that blacks be appointed to other boards and governmental positions involved in implementing the program. The National Urban League, which had been the dominant advocacy group for black economic interests, announced the creation of Emergency Advisory Councils in its local branches to help blacks to participate in relief programs.[16]

In order to maintain their position as representatives of black workers, Davis and Weaver realized that they had to turn the Negro Industrial League into an actual organization. They secured an office on Florida Avenue and began to search for financial support. They first asked George Hayes, the semiretired founder of the National Urban League, who they hoped would provide liaison with wealthy liberals and progressive organizations, to join them. To avoid complaints that they were competing with established groups, Davis and Weaver told prospective supporters that they would serve as a representative for other civil rights organizations, providing them with information about the changes in government policy in Washington, DC, where neither the NAACP nor the National Urban League had an office.[17]

Davis and Weaver then contacted NAACP director Walter White for support. White had only recently ascended to the organization's top position, following James Weldon Johnson's retirement, and he was in the midst of a battle with W. E. B. DuBois for control. Since the early 1920s, White had cut a dashing figure as a crusader for equal rights. Born in Atlanta to a middle-class family, White attended Atlanta University and expected to start a career in business. However, the entrenchment of the Jim Crow system within the city led him to join the civil rights cause. One of the founders of the city's NAACP branch in 1910, White would devote his life to the agency. So light-skinned that he frequently passed as white, the activist became famous for his investigations of lynchings during the 1920s. Posing as a journalist sympathetic to the murderers, he was able to get detailed, damning information about attitudes throughout the South and the lack of government protection for African Americans. Because of his still-tenuous position, White was wary of any efforts that weakened the image of the NAACP as the leading civil rights organization, and he was reluctant to commit to support Davis and Weaver. But he realized that they had taken the spotlight on an extremely important issue to African Americans, and so he did not reject them out of hand.[18]

To generate support for the group, Davis issued a press release that was published in several black papers. The Negro Industrial League, he argued, was small but had "affiliates in thirty states," which was an extreme exaggeration. The purpose of the group was to "protect the interests of Negroes" in the debates over the NRA codes and to show employers "the wisdom of improving the Negro market in America by increasing the number of jobs available to Negroes," Davis claimed.[19]

In the weeks after their first presentation, Davis and Weaver made several more appearances at code hearings. In late July, Weaver testified at the hearing on the lumber and timber products industry, where the committee envisioned a similar differential between southern workers and those in other parts of the country. Under the proposed code, the southern industry (which employed over 90,000 blacks) would pay workers 22½ cents an hour, and employees would have a maximum workweek of forty-eight hours, while in the rest of the country workers would receive 40 cents an hour and be limited to forty hours a week. In what the *Pittsburgh Courier* described as a "masterful brief," Weaver argued that this violated the intent of the act. Attacking arguments made by southern employers that their workers were "contented," Weaver stated that "the only reason why the Negro has not rebelled against low wages paid him has been because intimidation and fear, coupled with enforced ignorance and economic destitution, have conspired to vitiate his bargaining power." As a result of Weaver's and Davis's complaints, the committee agreed to a minimum wage of 23 cents an hour and a forty-hour week. The differential was still discriminatory, but Davis and Weaver estimated that the change resulted in an added weekly income of $125,000 to black lumber workers as well as spreading work to 15,000 additional laborers. This was a material contribution to black welfare that exceeded almost any made by the established civil rights groups.[20]

The men appeared at several additional hearings during the summer, protesting differential wage rates in the iron and steel industry and the shipbuilding industry, arguing for higher wages for coal miners, and protesting labor unions that maintained closed shops that denied benefits to black workers. They also conducted studies of other sectors of the economy, including the construction industry, and put together a brief that examined the plight of black domestics. In all of their statements, the men worked to counter the widely accepted view that southern black workers were less efficient. This claim, Weaver argued, could not be supported by the evidence. Furthermore, if the goal of the NRA, as the president stated, was to increase the buying power of Americans, the regional wage differential ran counter to this mandate.[21]

In the debates over the lumber code, this argument garnered some sympathy. But that battle was one of the men's few concrete successes. While they were able to raise attention about discrimination against black workers, they won only small victories in changing NRA policies. For example, after agreeing to review their criticisms of the proposed textile code, the committee approved it without change. President Roosevelt, announcing finalization of the first code, stated that he had directed the NRA to adopt minimum wages and maximum hours for those exempted by the end of the year, but that deadline passed without any action. In general, NRA officials expressed concern to Davis and Weaver and then ignored their arguments.[22]

Regardless of the group's weaknesses, the black press treated Davis and Weaver as heroes. Columnist Kelly Miller argued that the men were making "a valiant fight for Negro workers," and writers in other papers concurred. Even though the organization declined to support them financially, the National Urban League's journal, *Opportunity*, praised their efforts, stating that Davis and Weaver had "waged a brilliant battle for justice to Negro workers." By the end of the summer, because of their consistent advocacy for black workers, the two men could not be ignored by leaders of the race.[23]

While Weaver and Davis were toiling away in the heat of summer in the nation's capital, forty of the race's current and future leaders were meeting at J. E. Spingarn's Hudson River valley estate, Troutbeck, near Amenia, New York. For three days, the participants debated the future of black activism in the United States, and the events in Washington were a primary topic in their discussions. Several of the young attendees, particularly Weaver's friends Ralph Bunche and William Hastie, along with sociologist E. Franklin Frazier and economist Abram Harris, argued that the NAACP should shift its focus away from civil rights and toward economic concerns. Black workers, they argued, needed to secure economic power through labor organizations that would enable them to work toward interracial class cooperation. They also agreed that, given the increasing power of the state, blacks needed to secure representation within government to protect their interests. Not surprisingly, the established members were reluctant to support a major reenvisioning of their organization, and they chastised the younger members for disregarding the importance of racial uplift. The conference produced little agreement on the future course of black activism, but it highlighted Davis's and Weaver's work as well as the institutional tensions it created.[24]

In the aftermath of the conference, Davis wrote potential supporters arguing that the NRA and other laws had given "vast power" to the president to administer a federal relief program. These changes, Davis continued, "made necessary a different set of tactics for Negro organizations engaged in advancing the welfare of the American Negro." He called for "a powerful Negro lobby" to be established in Washington, and he recommended that black organizations "pool" their resources to create one. The new coalition, which he named the Joint Committee on Negro Affairs (JCNR), would be responsible for appearing at NRA hearings, keeping in contact with administration officials, and studying economic and labor trends. It would also monitor the activities of other New Deal agencies. To establish an office with clerical help and hire staff to conduct research, Davis asked member organizations to contribute $200 each. In the fall, after almost two months of lobbying from Davis and Weaver, several groups agreed to support the organization, including the African Methodist Episcopalian Church, the National Negro Business League, and the National Baptist Convention.[25]

Crucial to the survival of the coalition was the support of the NAACP. Even before the Amenia conference, White's assistant Roy Wilkins gave Davis and Weaver his ringing endorsement. "They seemed to be the only Negroes in Washington who had any intelligent idea of what was going on down there," he told White. "These youngsters succeeded in getting the confidence and respect of official Washington." While Wilkins and White were somewhat skeptical of Davis, whose activities, Wilkins told Hastie, "heretofore have not been such as to create confidence in his straightforwardness," Wilkins believed that others, including Hastie and Charles Hamilton Houston, who were both at Howard Law School, could provide oversight for Davis and Weaver and protect the NAACP's interests, and he recommended that the NAACP make a contribution. By the end of August, White had agreed, and he called on other organizations to join in supporting the young men.[26]

September provided a lull in the NRA hearings so that the administration could organize its staff and publish the codes that had been agreed to, and this afforded Davis and Weaver the time to lobby other organizations for financial support. Both had worked the whole summer without salary. But they struggled to get the members to make good on their pledges. Even the NAACP delayed its contribution, sending only a $100 advance. Davis had proposed a six-month budget of $2,600, which most of the board viewed as extremely conservative, but they were not able to raise close to that amount. "I am pretty goddamn sick of all these people trying to hamstring us and then not producing a dime," Davis complained to Weaver. Recognizing that whatever money they received could pay only one salary, in early September Weaver returned to Greensboro to resume his teaching position at North Carolina Agricultural and Technical College. He joked that he was the chairman of the economics department (a department of one). Despite the accolades, it appeared that Davis's and Weaver's days as federal lobbyists were numbered. They were, in a sense. But the young men's summer sojourn piqued the interest of a leading white liberal, Edwin Embree. Their interaction would bring Weaver into the New Deal and push Davis in a more radical direction.[27]

While Weaver and Davis continued to serve as a clearinghouse for information on the New Deal, they awaited word from the Julius Rosenwald Fund regarding a request they hoped would support their efforts. Created in 1917 by Sears, Roebuck, and Company founder Julius Rosenwald, the organization had been from its inception dedicated to promoting "the welfare of Negroes." By the early 1930s it supported a wide variety of racial-uplift causes, providing hundreds of fellowships to talented black youths to help them achieve advanced degrees. The fund was responsible for the construction of 5,000 schools for blacks in the South, supported improvements in health care facilities, and enabled numerous black colleges to improve their facilities. It also provided crucial assistance to civil rights groups, including the NAACP.[28] In late October, Edwin Embree, president of the fund, rejected their application, stating the fund was "unwilling at the present time to make any further appropriations to the established Negro agencies."

Because he was "much impressed" by the "heroic work" that the men had done, Embree offered Davis and Weaver each an "emergency fellowship" of $600 to cover their expenses for a three-month period.[29]

Raised in Berea, Kentucky, Embree had long contact with progressive, but paternalist, attitudes on race relations. His grandfather was a well-known abolitionist, and several members of his family had been active in promoting racial cooperation in the northern parts of the South. After attending Berea College, Embree received a degree in philosophy from Yale. There he made contacts in the world of philanthropy that led him to the Rockefeller Foundation and later to the presidency of the Rosenwald Fund. From 1928 to the fund's closure twenty years later, Embree was a leader of the white philanthropic effort to promote the economic and social development of African Americans. Embree's contact with Weaver would have a profound influence on the young economist's career, more than that of any other individual.[30]

Embree's rationale for denying a larger grant to the JCNR obscured another agenda that he maintained regarding the role of black activists in the federal recovery effort. He supported the goals of Davis and Weaver, but he believed that the fund's money would be put to better use by supporting other approaches to equal treatment. Embree envisioned a "generalissimo of Negro welfare" who would "look after the Negro's interests in all phases of the recovery." It was unlikely, Embree argued, that a black person could undertake such as task. "A black administrator would labor under the disability of prejudice against his abilities and would be constantly under assault by southern segregationists." "Only a white," he told federal officials, "could carry the kind of influence that is necessary for results."[31]

His leadership of the Rosenwald Fund placed Embree close to the New Deal's leaders and gave him great influence over administration racial policy. Embree believed that the New Deal, by moving the locus of power from local governments and the states to the federal government, presented an opportunity to weaken the barriers to the educational and economic advancement of blacks. Weaver concurred, later recalling that he and his peers felt that "the precedents were in the Reconstruction period, and that you had to look to the federal government. This was the only way you were going to get meaningful activity because, of course, by this time all the states in the South had completely disenfranchised blacks." But, unlike Weaver and his friends, Embree had real influence within the administration. During the summer of 1933, he pressured government officials to take race into account in the shaping of their programs, and he argued that blacks should have representation, by whites, in the administration so that their interests would be protected.[32]

Weaver and other black leaders concurred with Embree that the New Deal represented an opportunity for significant change and that blacks needed representation, but they differed over how that representation should be provided. Though they disagreed about tactics, both the established leaders and the youth who met at Amenia agreed that African Americans were best suited to represent the interests of the black masses within the government. They envisioned professionally trained administrators—people like Bunche, Hastie, and Weaver—with advanced degrees in economics, political science, and law, who would protect the interests of African Americans in the federal government.[33]

This argument was, of course, self-interested. The young professionals promoting this approach were the only blacks suited to play this role. At the same time, their plan represented a significant shift in the approach of blacks to power within the federal government, which had previously focused on achieving influence through politics. Since the turn of the century, a small number of black Republicans had been able to secure patronage positions—often as clerks and other low-level positions—through involvement in party activities. These positions were mostly ceremonial, and they provided no real influence over government policy. The failure of black Republicans to secure any influential voice for black Americans was in part responsible for the shift of young blacks to the Democratic Party. "All of us were completely disgusted with and critical of the so-called Republican Negro leaders," Weaver later recalled. They had "not done anything for the mass of black people" and were, in Weaver's view, an impediment to positive change.[34]

Embree shared Weaver's disdain for the traditional black government official, but he had a different vision for black representation. "This is not a question simply of a political job for which Negroes are naturally hungry," he stated. "No thoughtful person," he told black columnist Kelly Miller, "can believe that any Negro, however capable, can accomplish as much as a white man." The person should, preferably, be a southerner familiar with the situation of blacks. Throughout the spring and summer of 1933, Embree lobbied FDR and his friends in the administration to support his plan. To assuage the president's concern about creating a government position for a specific race, Embree promised that his fund would pay the salary of the so-called Negro Advisor.[35]

Embree already had a person in mind when he developed his idea of a

Negro Advisor: a staff member named Clark Foreman. Natives of Atlanta, Foreman's family were leaders of the "New South" movement. The *Atlanta Constitution,* published by Foreman's grandfather Henry Grady, and then his uncle Clark Howell, supported economic development and law and order in the region. Although they held paternalistic views toward blacks, by southern standards both men were considered progressive, since they opposed lynching and promoted black institutions. Foreman received a bachelor's degree from the University of Georgia and then continued his liberal arts studies at Harvard and the London School of Economics. At twenty-two, Foreman joined southern liberal (and future New Deal official) Will Alexander at the newly formed Commission on Interracial Cooperation (CIC). An attempt to improve southern race relations by introducing southern elites to the problems of African Americans, the CIC exposed Foreman to the realities of poverty and discrimination in the South and introduced him to the race's leaders.[36]

After two years of activism, Foreman left the CIC, frustrated by the lack of progress the group had made in convincing southern whites of the problems facing their black neighbors. "We were treating the symptoms on the assumption that eventually the disease would be cured," he later recalled. Foreman moved to New York City to pursue a doctorate in philosophy, but with the support of Alexander, he continued his contacts with southern progressives. In 1928, Foreman joined the Rosenwald Fund and worked on the institution's southern programs in education. After receiving his doctorate in 1932, Foreman spent almost a year, at the Rosenwald Fund's expense, studying rural life in eastern Europe, particularly the Soviet Union. Embree called Foreman back to the states in July 1933 with the express purpose of making him the "generalissimo." Originally, Embree hoped to place Foreman within the Department of Labor, but Secretary of Labor Frances Perkins rejected the idea. Interior Secretary Harold Ickes, a native of Chicago (where the Rosenwald Fund was headquartered) and former president of that city's NAACP chapter, was more amenable to the proposal, and he agreed to take on Foreman as the "Special Advisor on the Economic Status of Negroes."[37]

Black leaders were livid when Foreman's appointment was announced in August. While making "no objection to Mr. Foreman personally," Roy Wilkins stated, "the age of paternalism in the relations of the races is past so far as the Negroes are concerned, and they bitterly resent having a white man officially designated by the government to advise on their welfare. Only a Negro can know true conditions of Negro people and voice their hopes." Furthermore, there were "a number of colored men" who were as qualified as Foreman and of "far richer experience who could fill this post to the satisfaction of the administration and colored people." Foreman's appointment, Wilkins concluded, would "be regarded as most unfortunate by colored citizens of every section and station in life." W. E. B. DuBois seconded Wilkins's position, arguing that "it is an outrage that we again, through the efforts of some of our best friends, should be compelled to have our wants and aspirations interpreted by one who does not know them."[38]

Ickes, however, agreed with Embree that a white person would be better equipped to tackle the job. He defended Foreman as well qualified for the task and argued that any "fair minded individual" would acknowledge that solving the problems of African Americans required the "efforts of both races." When even Foreman suggested that the job should go to a black person, Ickes replied that if Foreman did not want the job, he would give it to another white person, because a white person would provide "better service than a Negro in his position." Stung by the questions about his qualifications, Foreman convinced Ickes and Embree to allow him to hire a black person as an assistant. To get Foreman to accept the job, Embree agreed to pay the assistant's salary, and Embree already had a person in mind: Robert Weaver.[39]

When they founded the Negro Industrial League, Davis and Weaver agreed that neither would accept any offers of government jobs that were made during their lobbying activities. They did not want their efforts to be viewed as self-promotion. But by September, Weaver, who had no desire to continue in North Carolina, was strongly interested in securing a job in the federal government. Frustrated by the lack of support for their efforts from black groups, Davis tried to get Weaver appointed to the Department of Commerce's Colored Advisory Council (a public relations effort concocted by Secretary Daniel Roper that had no authority), but those efforts failed to bear fruit.[40]

Weaver's luck would soon change. At the end of October, Foreman invited Weaver to Washington for a meeting and offered him the job of assistant advisor on the economic status of Negroes at a salary of $3,200. Weaver immediately accepted the job, requesting and receiving a leave of absence from North Carolina Agricultural and Technical College. While others would profess reservations to Weaver about the position, he appeared to have no doubts about his decision. "I had no desire to be in North Carolina," he later told an interviewer. "I wanted to be in Washington where the action was." In a formal letter that was more for public relations than for his friend, he told Davis, "I believe that such a position will offer me an opportunity to influence the operation of the recovery program as it affects Negroes," and he assured Davis that he would be "guided by the same principles" in the new job as he had been in his work with the JCNR. The decision was the first of many Weaver would make in which he chose a path within the system rather than one that sought more radical change.[41]

Davis, like most other black leaders, was still steaming about Foreman's appointment, and he called Weaver's selection "no more than a makeshift palliative which fails to remove the original and the basic ill." He sent Weaver two letters, one public and one personal. The public letter thanked Weaver for his services to the JCNR and urged him to "not become either the creature of a system or the burden bearer of an administration's errors in regard to race." He included a jab at the Rosenwald Fund, regretting that "white Americans have adopted the subtle policy of robbing us of our independence by subsidies, subventions and material aid—all of which we need." However, he wished Weaver "every success in your new position."[42]

Davis frequently told people that he had been offered several positions in the administration but that he had rejected them. Because of Davis's Republican connections and personality, it is unlikely that Foreman considered him for the position of his assistant. Weaver, the soft-spoken technocrat, was an obvious choice for Foreman and Embree: a talented, hardworking but less risky choice for a sensitive position. Davis's private correspondence with Weaver reveals several emotions: concern of an older brother for a young man about to enter a hornet's nest, a touch of envy that Weaver would be close to power, and a desire for continued friendship. Davis stated that the "disagreement over the appointment is not personal and that any criticism which we make will be on the high plane of policy," and he hoped that "outside of office hours, both of us may see a great deal of each other."[43]

On 9 November, Foreman formally announced the appointment in a press release that described Weaver as an honors graduate of Dunbar and Harvard. Most black leaders responded positively to Weaver's appointment. Roscoe Conkling Bruce wrote Foreman to congratulate him on his choice. Weaver, Bruce argued, had "exceptional native gifts and personality. . . . A man of such stock, such education, such training will never fail you or the Administration you so ably represent," he told Foreman. The editors of the *Pittsburgh Courier* called Weaver's appointment "far more beneficial to the Negro masses than any previously made." Most black papers, however, remained neutral on the announcement, reporting it but making no comment.[44]

Other black leaders expressed reservations about Weaver's position. George Hayes argued that Weaver would have more influence outside the government. NAACP official George Streator wrote to declare his hope that Weaver would "not become just another one of these insincere and bumptious race leaders." Streator compared Weaver's job to "working in a Church school while compiling the facts to show the total hypocrisy of 'Christian Education.'" While Streator understood Weaver's reasons for taking the job, he was opposed to "these Foundations forever dictating the thinking of Negroes through the control of his education, his 'uplift' and now federal patronage." Streator believed that Embree and Foreman "visualize the future very clearly—some sort of DICTATORSHIP. Their place in the cabinet will be 'in charge of Negroes, though surrounded by his best brains.'" Streator concluded his letter by stating, "We may differ and yet be friends." Weaver came to this difficult job under fire: with many of his friends expecting him to fail. Given the tense atmosphere that characterized his hiring, Weaver had a great deal of work to do to win over the critics.[45]

SOON AFTER HIS appointment, Weaver moved into a house near Howard University, returning home to a city that was rapidly changing. The New Deal brought an influx of young intellectuals to the tradition-bound city, forever changing its culture. At the same time, the expansion of the government created thousands of professional and blue-collar jobs and spurred an economic boom in the nation's capital. Housing and commercial services expanded dramatically, and a significant share of the benefits went to the city's black population. The city's transformation affected all of the institutions of black Washington, and nowhere was this change more evident than at the nation's foremost institution of higher learning for African Americans, Howard University. In the early 1930s, civil rights agitation increased dramatically at the university, much of it led by Weaver's friends Bunche and Hastie, both of whom had recently joined the faculty.

Activism at Howard was only one aspect of increasing protest throughout the black community. At the same time that Weaver and Davis were organizing their attack on discrimination in federal relief programs, activists in DC were fighting for work opportunities in local businesses. Spurred by the August firing of three black workers at the white-owned Hamburger Grill, a restaurant in the heart of the black commercial area, Weaver's friend

John Aubrey Davis led others in a protest of the dismissals. After a day of picketing, the owner agreed to rehire the workers. Energized by the victory, the activists formed a group they named the New Negro Alliance (NNA). The goal of the NNA, Davis stated, was to promote grassroots organizing against discrimination and in support of black economic interests.[46]

Like other civil rights efforts of the period, this one marked a changing philosophy among young blacks. Davis stated that he and other young leaders felt an "irritation" with "the complete lack of militancy" in other local groups, particularly the NAACP, which he claimed was run by "stuffed shirts." In the following years, the NNA was a leader of a national trend, the "Don't Buy Where You Can't Work" movement; they demanded jobs for blacks at businesses dependent on their patronage. Though organized by local youth, the NNA drew the support of many black professionals, including Hastie and other Howard professors.[47]

Though he supported the campaigns to get more jobs for blacks, Weaver was not an active member of the NNA. He chose to focus his efforts on the insider work of governmental reform. Soon after his appointment, Weaver was joined at the Interior Department by William Hastie. Hastie, in addition to civil rights work with the NAACP and other organizations, had been teaching law at Howard and practicing with William Hamilton Houston and his son Charles Hamilton Houston. The Interior Department's head lawyer, Nathan Margold, was a former NAACP counsel who had first been impressed by Hastie when Margold was an instructor at Harvard. On Margold's recommendation, Interior Secretary Harold Ickes hired Hastie to serve as Margold's assistant.[48]

Weaver and Hastie immediately made their presence felt at the Interior Department, breaking the two-decades-old Jim Crow system in the lunchroom. The department had two cafeterias—one for professional staff and one for "service" employees (laborers, messengers, elevator operators, and the like, the majority of whom were black). Black employees were expected to lunch with the service staff, but Weaver and Hastie refused to do this because "it was just a subterfuge for a segregated lunchroom." Instead, they went to lunch with their colleagues, where a startled cashier asked them if they worked at the department. After proving their identity, the two men took their seats with little fanfare, but half an hour later a group of white women entered the secretary's office to protest. According to Weaver, when the women asked what Ickes was going to do about "Negroes eating in the lunchroom," Ickes replied, "Not a damn thing, ladies." The integration of many other federal lunchrooms quickly followed.[49]

Two weeks after taking office, Weaver sent Foreman a long memo with advice about the priorities of their office. Weaver viewed their role as investigating the operation of the various relief programs to make sure that they benefited African Americans. Resources for the construction of public facilities, particularly hospitals, schools, and housing, he argued, should be allocated fairly to benefit black communities. He recommended that Ickes issue an order declaring racial discrimination a breach of any contract which the department entered. To promote equal treatment, Weaver argued that their office "should be allowed to review all projects before they take final form." He called for investigation into the use of funds in conservation programs, particularly those already under way in southern construction projects, where, Weaver argued, more than 30,000 blacks were laboring "often at low wages, and invariably under inhuman labor conditions." In addition to efforts to promote blue-collar workers, Weaver recommended that their office work to increase opportunities for black professionals in the federal government.[50]

Weaver spent much of his first year on the road, reviewing projects and meeting with black leaders to make them aware of his office. He spent two weeks touring the Deep South and investigating claims of discrimination in all the federal government's relief programs. During this trip, he focused in particular on public works programs funding the construction of elementary and secondary schools.[51]

When in DC, Weaver devoted a great deal of time to working with the various agencies to promote equal treatment for blacks. He and Foreman secured the appointment of advisors in other departments, and by early 1934 Weaver was joined by six other black professionals in similar positions. With the support of Ickes, Foreman convinced the president to allow him to set up an Interdepartmental Committee on Negro Affairs, which Foreman chaired. At the group's first meeting, black appointees, including Eugene Kinkle Jones, head of the National Urban League who was appointed to the Commerce Department, Harry Hunt, of the Farm Credit Administration, and Forrester Washington, of the Federal Emergency Relief Administration, met with white representatives from other federal departments to discuss the specific problems of blacks in labor, agriculture, and government service. Throughout the spring and summer, with Foreman and Weaver providing guiding hands, the group of about twenty met to discuss reports from their members and share information on specific complaints about discrimination. However, after less than a year, the group stopped meeting. While successful in gathering information about the problems facing blacks, the group was unable to convince the major departments actually undertaking the relief program to change their operations.[52]

Throughout his first year, Weaver developed a close relationship with Foreman and Embree (who kept close tabs on his experiment) and had many opportunities to work with Ickes. Weaver called Foreman an "emancipated southerner," and he described Ickes as "quite gruff" but "a very decent human being and a good administrator." At the same time, Weaver continued to keep in close contact with John P. Davis and other civil rights leaders, providing them with inside information about policy decisions that affected African Americans.

When the NRA code hearings resumed in late 1933, John P. Davis continued to voice his opposition to regional differentials in wage rates, and Weaver and Foreman worked within the government to get NRA and Labor officials to look more carefully at the impact of their decisions. Davis argued that the regional differentials were bad policy and that they were inconsistently applied. The code for the fertilizer industry, for example, classified the state of Delaware (where thousands of black workers toiled in these factories) as southern, while other codes, those for industries with few black workers, classified the state as northern. In industries with a small number of blacks, regional differentials were much smaller than in those sectors that employed many blacks. The common denominator for all decisions on classification of industries and regions was the race of the workers.[53]

None of these arguments swayed NRA administrators. In fact, during the winter of 1933–1934, the situation of black workers continued to deteriorate as southern manufacturers started to use the code as an excuse to displace African Americans. One widely publicized example of discrimination occurred at the Maid-Well Garment Company in Forest City, Arkansas. There, the company had continued to pay its workers a wage of $6.16 per week even though the code required $12.00. When a worker lodged a complaint with the NRA, the company shut down the plant, arguing that it would lose money if it was forced to abide by the code, and putting 194 black women out of work. The black workers, the managers argued, were too inefficient to justify the NRA wage rate. The NRA's own research staff concluded that this action was not unusual and reported that "there is a great deal of displacement going on and a large amount of plain cheating on wages." Their report, however, was shelved.[54]

The elimination of black workers was a significant problem that had begun before the NRA codes were enacted, but the continued loss of jobs was used by southern manufacturers as evidence to support their arguments that black workers should be paid a lower wage than their white counterparts. "Progressive" white newspapers joined with businessmen who contended that such differentials would assist blacks by protecting them from displacement. Virginia attorney Charles Kaufman argued that "differentials in wages and working hours have kept the colored people in many jobs which would have otherwise been filled by whites."[55]

When the Southland Corporation in Alabama took a similar action, laying off three hundred black workers, the plight of the employees caused some black leaders to support the wage differential. The Tuskegee College secretary G. Lake Imes appeared before the NRA board to ask that the plant be granted an exception allowing it to pay its workers a lower wage if it reopened, at least until the plant could "bring up the efficiency of the workers" to the point that they "earned" the higher wages. Imes's argument was supported by columnist Kelly Miller and several other black leaders. Southland owner Herbert Mayer argued that his request for substandard wages was based on his concern for the workers "as people, as human beings and as individuals." He could not, however, operate the factories "as a charitable institution."[56]

The closure of the plants divided blacks between those who argued that priority should be given to employment now, at any wage rate, and those who claimed that the precedent set by a wage differential would be disastrous. Weaver, Davis, and other black leaders vocally opposed "racial differentials," arguing that "there is more involved in this question." These differential wage scales, Weaver claimed, would affect "the whole industrial position of colored Americans." The difference would "increase the ill-will and friction between white and colored workers" and make labor organization more difficult. It would also destroy the gains that blacks had made in northern industries. Finally, and most seriously, the differential would "brand black workers as a less efficient and submarginal group." This stigma would take years to overcome.[57]

NAACP head Walter White argued that it was in the South's interest to protect the wages of black workers. Since blacks were such a large part of the population, the South's economic recovery, he charged, was dependent on the consumption power of these residents. However, while civil rights activists received some support from southern whites, most of the latter favored the idea of a differential. Even though it was against their economic interests, Roy Wilkins concluded, "the truth of the matter is that the southerners want a lower wage scale because they do not wish Negroes to have wages equal to whites." Unlike most battles, civil rights leaders were able to prevent the NRA from sanctioning racial differentials, which the administration never approved, at least explicitly.[58]

The continuing discrimination by employers and the neglect of NRA officials led many civil rights leaders to lose interest in Davis's still fledgling organization. YWCA official Frances Williams, one of the Negro Industrial League's earliest supporters, wrote Davis in May 1934 that his efforts had resulted in no "material advantages to Negroes" and had failed to increase blacks' awareness of the problem. Davis, who granted that not enough had changed, of course disagreed. However, during the year, Davis saw the financial support of several member institutions decrease. Edwin Embree, who had now achieved his goal of getting federal agencies to include racial advisors, declined to continue Davis's fellowship grant, arguing that the time had come for black organizations to "raise the relatively small amount of money to carry on this work." Black groups were unable, or unwilling, to do this. Davis reported monthly on the financial crisis facing the organization, but he received little support. By the end of the year the board was forced to consider allowing the NAACP to take over the group.[59]

Davis saw his organization waning at the same time that Weaver's personal prospects were growing. When Foreman hired Weaver, he said that he wanted "to work himself out of a job," and Weaver hoped that when Foreman left he would be promoted. Many others, however, were surprised when Foreman announced at an October dinner of the JCNR supporters that Weaver would be taking over as advisor to Harold Ickes for Negro Affairs. Unlike Foreman's, Weaver's $6,000 yearly salary would be paid by the government, and Weaver would be a full member of the secretary's staff. Although Roosevelt was not particularly supportive of the work Weaver was doing, Ickes had decided it was useful, and he succeeded in getting the position in his budget. The black press celebrated the decision. The *Chicago Defender* called Weaver's "rise in governmental circles almost phenomenal," and he received letters of congratulation from across the country. The appointment received little attention outside the black press, and Ickes's and Embree's fear that the appointment of a black person would be attacked by southerners did not occur. In less than a year, Weaver went from an outsider unable to break into the federal government to an official of some influence, with a secretary and small staff. His ability to push for fair treatment within the rules of the system disarmed opponents and placed Weaver on the path to power.[60]

* 3 *

# A Liberal Experiment

## *Race and Housing in the New Deal*

Before and after his promotion, Weaver spent the majority of his time working on the administration's public housing experiment. Federal housing programs were a crucial part of New Deal urban policy, and these initiatives significantly changed the relationship between the federal government and the cities. Weaver's involvement in the construction effort would begin a career of engagement with housing and urban development and prepare him for the leadership roles he would take in the 1950s and 1960s. Because he was present at the formative moment of these important policies, Weaver would gain unsurpassed knowledge about urban policy and make contacts in the field that sustained him throughout his career. In addition, although his part would later be forgotten, Weaver played a crucial role in the development of antidiscrimination policies that over time became models for other government programs.

That Franklin Roosevelt would have such an impact on cities is ironic considering his disdain for these areas. The president was raised in the idyllic setting of the Hudson Valley, and he never enjoyed his trips to New York City, a metropolis that, at the turn of the century, overwhelmed most visitors. Rexford Tugwell, one of the president's most important advisors, called him "a child of the country," who believed that cities were a "necessary nuisance." During the 1932 presidential campaign, FDR talked frequently about his desire to move people out of the cities and into the countryside. Early in his administration he urged a redistribution of the population to deal with what he called the "overbalance of population in our industrial centers."[1]

Whether Roosevelt liked it or not, cities were where his political support lay. During the first three decades of the century, American cities grew dramatically. By 1920, a majority of Americans lived in urban areas. The

Roaring Twenties brought dramatic advances to cities. Flush with investment for housing, factories, and entertainment, American cities flourished as they had at no previous time. The increasing tax revenues created by this growth enabled city governments to expand and provide improved services. However, when the Depression hit, local officials faced a dire financial situation. Fiscal turmoil, caused in part by a property market that had collapsed, combined with unemployment, created in the nation's cities a deepening spiral—increasing relief needs at the same time that tax revenues plummeted. Cities facing bankruptcy called on the federal government for loans to pay off existing debts and to pay for public services, and they organized the United States Conference of Mayors to lobby for jobs programs. The fiscally conservative president, who hated the political machines that ran most big cities, was reluctant to provide direct support to city governments.[2]

However, it was clear to Roosevelt's advisors, most of whom had deep financial and political ties to the nation's largest cities, that the president had no choice but to intervene. To provide relief, Roosevelt created the Public Works Administration (PWA), which provided desperately needed funds for employment efforts across the nation. Between 1933 and 1939, the program spent $4.8 billion on housing, bridges, highways, public buildings, water projects, airports, and other types of construction. The initiative was managed by Harold Ickes, who, through his careful oversight of federal funds, slowly gained the respect of fiscal conservatives and the ire of mayors and progressives who wanted to produce jobs and public works quickly. The program was the largest federal intervention into the economy ever undertaken, and it forever changed the relationship of the federal government to cities. From then on, the idea that federal tax dollars could support local efforts was no longer an aberrant one.[3]

One of the major aspects of the PWA program was the public housing initiative. Promoted for more than a decade by activists in the nation's largest cities, many viewed public housing as the answer to the long-standing problems of the slum. Reviled by real estate interests as "socialistic," public housing was controversial from the beginning. If conservatives grudgingly accepted the need for government-funded work programs, they violently opposed the idea of publicly owned housing, which, in their view, was antithetical to the bedrock American principle of private ownership. Despite the constant opposition to the initiative, the federal government provided the first concrete example that affordable housing could be produced on a large scale. Between 1934 and 1937, the PWA would construct, or finance the construction of, 25,000 units of housing in fifty-eight developments across the country.[4]

Weaver announced his interest in the housing program almost immediately after his hiring. Because the program was new, he believed, it would be easier to shape it to promote the principles of equal opportunity. In addition, since contractors, their employees, and the unions that represented them were so desperate for work, they might, Weaver thought, be more amenable to federal requirements to share the benefits with African Americans. He later referred to the PWA as the "guinea pig" of antidiscrimination efforts in the federal government. Their office, Weaver told Foreman, should "insist upon the inclusion of qualified Negroes and the granting of equal opportunities to Negro artisans and laborers," and soon thereafter he asked Ickes if he could serve as a consultant to the housing program. The always-prickly secretary replied, "Young man, what do you know about housing?" When Weaver stated, "very little," Ickes told him, "You'll do fine. None of those sons of bitches know anything about it either."[5]

Weaver immediately began to insinuate himself into the program. His most important contribution was the creation of an aggressive effort to secure jobs for blacks at PWA construction projects. Long before "affirmative action" became an issue of national debate, Weaver and his colleagues at the Interior Department promoted the principle. The construction industry was well suited to their initiative, because there were thousands of blacks who had been employed in this field before the Depression. Particularly in the South, a large number of blacks worked as bricklayers, plasterers, and stone masons and in other construction trades. In some southern cities, blacks were a majority of the workers in the trades.[6]

To exploit this labor pool, in September 1933, Ickes issued an order that prohibited discrimination on account of color or religion in all PWA programs. However, his staff immediately faced the problem of defining discrimination. Often employers would hire one black person for a project on which hundreds worked. In other instances, they would hire black workers and soon thereafter fire them. Frequently, employers argued that they were willing to hire African Americans, but their agreements with unions required them to use only union members, and the unions did not admit blacks.[7]

To deal with this problem, Weaver secured the support of the Department of Labor, which told labor unions that they would get support for their participation on PWA projects only if they allowed blacks to get work permits or join the union. Then, since the PWA was actually a party to all housing construction contracts, Weaver and his friend, attorney William Hastie, included in each agreement a clause requiring that a specific percentage of employees on each project—based on the percentage of blacks who held that occupation according to the 1930 census—be African Americans. If contractors failed to meet this requirement, it would be considered prima facie evidence of discrimination, and they would be in breach of the agreement. This scheme shifted to the contractors the burden of proof that they were abiding by their obligations.[8]

Weaver later remembered it as "my idea and Bill's law." In later years, as demands for equal opportunity in employment increased, affirmative-action programs would be hotly debated and their legal status questioned. Many would call affirmative action "reverse discrimination" which denied opportunities to whites in favor of predetermined requirements that mandated the hiring of a set number of minorities. But in the pre–civil rights era, when the "separate but equal" framework expounded by the Supreme Court in the case *Plessy v. Ferguson* dominated the law, the PWA "quota" program was on strong legal ground. *Plessy* envisioned the treatment of Americans according to racial categories. As a result, the designation of certain percentages of jobs as "black" jobs was not constitutionally suspect. There is no evidence that the Interior Department asked for a legal opinion on the program from the Justice Department, and the constitutionality of the program was never questioned.[9]

Over the next three years, Weaver and his staff reviewed each housing proposal to determine the appropriate percentage of African American hires. They also reviewed the weekly payrolls of every housing project managed by the PWA to determine if the contractors were meeting their obligations. Members of his team described Weaver as a demanding but fair boss who was a stickler for details. Weaver worked to ensure that black architects and other professionals participated in the construction program. Hilyard Robinson, the black architect who designed and oversaw the construction of the Langston Houses in Washington, DC, was one of several professionals who benefited from Weaver's efforts, as was Paul Williams, a Los Angeles architect who would later become architect to movie stars such as Lena Horne. So successful was Weaver in this effort that Oscar Stonorov, one of the nation's leading architects in the field of multifamily housing, complained to his associates that Weaver was preventing whites from getting a decent share of the contracts.[10]

Throughout 1935 and 1936, Weaver traveled the country reviewing housing projects and mediating work disputes. In Indianapolis, he negotiated with a carpenters union that barred black members. In Miami, he aided black mechanics struggling to secure work on the Liberty Square project. And in Atlanta, he worked to get black painters a fair share of work on the PWA construction projects there. In general, he used moral suasion with contractors, and the Interior Department never actually declared a project in breach of its agreement. However, after a year and a half implementing the program, Weaver wrote that he was "convinced that it is a workable solution to a difficult problem. In this instance, the Federal Government has done more than make a gesture in the direction of effectively preventing discriminations against colored workers."[11]

According to one analyst, his efforts "resulted in unprecedented wages for many black laborers and led to the admission of hundreds of Negroes into previously lily-white Southern construction unions." But not everyone was pleased with the initiative. Weaver's friend John Davis was one of a few blacks to criticize the initiative. "Without doubting the good intentions of the sponsors of this ingenious scheme," Davis complained that the percentages employed by the department were too low and the number of projects too small to have much effect on unemployment. Furthermore, and somewhat presciently given the complicated future history of affirmative-action programs, Davis argued that the scheme could be used by employers to break labor unions and weaken efforts at racial cooperation by pitting white job seekers against blacks. However, most civil rights leaders considered Weaver's efforts one of the most positive outcomes of the New Deal. James Hubert, director of the New York Urban League, called the program "one of the most advanced steps taken by the Labor Department in recent years." Even Howard University historian Rayford Logan, a vociferous critic of the New Deal, acknowledged that the housing program had brought benefits to blacks. After the PWA housing program was dismantled, Weaver and Hastie's initiative disappeared for several decades, only to be resuscitated in the 1960s.[12]

ALTHOUGH THE PWA was a federal agency, the public housing program relied on local initiative to plan and build the projects. Public housing represented one of the first federal-local partnerships, a framework that would be the model for almost every urban program in the decades to follow. The effort was among the first examples of an expanding federal urban policy, the area that Weaver would oversee three decades later. The first housing project of this initiative was built in the capital of the

South: Atlanta. The story of that city's housing program, which produced two projects, the Techwood Homes and the University Homes, illuminates both the successes and limitations of Weaver's efforts to secure equal treatment for blacks.

The redevelopment of the Techwood area, a deteriorated district between Georgia Technical College and downtown, was first proposed by Atlanta developer Charles Forrest Palmer, who wanted to increase the value of his holdings in the area and connect the educational institution with the business district. The Techwood flats were a collection of cheap, wood-frame houses built in the 1880s that had quickly deteriorated. By 1930, the area had one of the city's highest crime rates. Palmer organized a powerful coalition of business and political leaders, including Mayor James Key and Clark Howell Sr., publisher of the *Atlanta Constitution* (and Clark Foreman's grandfather), to support the project.[13]

At the same time he promoted his own project, Palmer supported a proposal by Dr. John Hope, the president of Atlanta University, for a development that would occupy the space that separated the campuses of Hope's institution and Spellman College and Morris Brown College. These three institutions, which played a central role in the rise of the black middle class, bordered on an area called Beaver Slide, a district of extreme poverty and inhuman living conditions. Fewer than half of the apartments in the district had electricity or indoor plumbing and almost none had heat. The University Homes that would replace them, Hope argued, would provide modern accommodations for black Atlantans and enable all three colleges to flourish.[14]

The coalition of white and black leaders, who told President Roosevelt that new housing was needed to avert an "insurrection" in the city, increased the attraction of the proposal to the PWA, which approved both projects in 1934. The 604-unit Techwood Homes and the 675-unit University Homes were among the first completed by the agency. Housing reformers, business leaders, and architectural critics all celebrated both projects, praising the two-story town houses at University and the three-story, European-style apartments at Techwood. The University Homes project organized a series of buildings around a central courtyard, and the larger Techwood buildings were surrounded by green spaces. They both had centrally located community facilities, including health and educational facilities. Both projects used modern construction techniques and included modern utilities and appliances. In 1936, Franklin Roosevelt celebrated the opening of Techwood with a nationally broadcast speech in which he declared "people who never before could get a decent roof over their heads will live here in reasonable comfort amid healthful, worth-while surroundings."[15]

Weaver was involved in the developments from the beginning, promoting the University Homes project within the administration and working to see that blacks received a share of work at both construction sites. Ickes strongly supported the efforts to promote equal opportunity, telling the administrator of the housing program "that it is our purpose, so far as possible, to avoid race discrimination in our housing projects." The contract for both the projects required that "there shall be no discrimination due to race, creed, or color" and declared that variations of more than 10 percent from the required ratio of black workers would be considered "prima facie evidence of discrimination."[16]

Despite Weaver's creativity in promoting fair treatment, the affirmative-action program did have limitations. Because some on the PWA staff were concerned about the enforceability of the clause, they agreed that the contract would require that at least 12 percent of all skilled workers be African American. According to the 1930 census, however, 24 percent of skilled construction workers in Atlanta were black. And, as John Davis would later complain, the "minimum" requirement was also the maximum that the contractor did: 12.7 percent of the skilled workers on the sites were black. The projects did, however, bring needed employment to a significant number of black Atlantans. Ninety percent of the unskilled workers on the projects were African American. Weaver and his staff determined that, overall, blacks received 36 percent of the wages for both the projects, a total of more than $360,000 during a period of desperately high unemployment.[17]

Weaver was equally concerned that the program provide benefits to black professionals, and he got Ickes to support the hiring of a black manager for the University Homes. That manager, Alonzo Moron, was a graduate of Brown University who had served as commissioner of public welfare for the Virgin Islands. Moron worked with Weaver to develop a training program in public housing management at Atlanta University to increase the pool of eligible black applicants at subsequent projects, and they were able to place several graduates in other developments.[18]

In subsequent projects, contracts required that the percentage of black workers more closely parallel the actual percentage of blacks in the trade, and these provisions were enforced by PWA staff. In 1935, Ickes told NAACP officials that "we believe that these contracts will point the way to doing away with discrimination against Negro labor, and the results so far warrant this belief." In 1938, Weaver reported that blacks had received

$3 million (out of a total of $19 million) in wages from PWA housing projects. A later review of the program declared that it had been moderately successful. According to the study, approximately two-thirds of the projects met the requirements in employing black workers. The total number of people benefited was relatively small (approximately 3,000), and the program's effect on long-term gains in union membership was negligible, but it provided good-paying jobs during the three years that the PWA was in the construction business.[19]

The Atlanta projects, although both were modern, did not receive the same amenities. The Techwood Homes had wading pools for children and tennis courts for adults, while the University Homes did not. Techwood was constructed of the most modern materials, while designers described University Homes as a "modified modern design" of brick and cinderblock. One historian of the projects has argued that decisions such as this one were made in recognition of the fact that black residents had less income to devote to rent, and the rental prices at University Homes were lower than those at Techwood. But neither project was built for the poor. The residents of the Techwood Homes were office workers and public employees. The occupants of the University Homes included workers at the three educational institutions, skilled workers, and porters. Very few of the residents whose housing was demolished for the projects secured units in the new buildings.[20]

The fact that the Techwood Homes were for whites and the University Homes were for blacks was unremarkable to all the participants in the project, and this highlights the most problematic aspect of the PWA housing program. Of course, in Depression-era Atlanta, the leading city of the South, segregation was considered unavoidable. When John Hope proposed the University Homes, he specifically stated that they were to house blacks. The "separate but equal" approach was practical for a variety of reasons. First of all, an assault on Jim Crow in housing would have undoubtedly resulted in severe opposition to the projects and the likely rejection of the proposal. Second, although the project would only begin to meet the severe shortage of decent housing in the city, black Atlantans desperately needed housing.[21]

That all of the projects the PWA built or funded in the Deep South were segregated is, given the political climate, understandable. When Weaver initially argued that the housing program should receive special focus, he did not contest the fact that the projects would be divided by race. Instead, Weaver focused on the allocation of units. "Usually it will be desirable to place the white and colored projects together so that the Negro section forms a part of a larger program," he argued to Clark Foreman. Recognizing that this might not be the case, Weaver concluded, "In any event, the accommodations should be equal."[22]

More troubling was the fact that a large number of the projects in other parts of the country were also segregated, even in cities where racial integration was common. The "Great Migration" that began during World War I brought several million African Americans to northern cities in search of economic opportunity and social freedom. Though blacks found jobs, they continued to face unbending discrimination. One of the worst aspects of northern racial exclusion was that blacks were forced to accept the most decrepit shelter. Public housing provided an opportunity to solve the housing crisis of blacks. However, in general, the program achieved that goal by entrenching residential segregation of the races.

In the North, Weaver originally argued that "our policy should be the complete integration of Negroes into housing projects." The PWA, however, had a mixed record at best on that radical idea. While successful in providing desperately needed decent housing to African Americans—a third of the 21,000 units that the PWA produced were rented to blacks—the majority of these were in segregated developments. Of the forty-seven projects in the continental United States, seventeen were for African Americans, twenty-three for whites only, and six were designated for "mixed occupancy" (the term used at the time). In northern cities like Chicago, Detroit, Philadelphia, and New York City, the PWA allowed housing authorities to construct segregated communities where they had not existed before.[23]

In New York City, the newly established housing authority planned two projects. One, in the Williamsburg section of Brooklyn, would provide 1,622 apartments to white New Yorkers. The other would be located in the heart of the nation's largest black urban community, Harlem. Its 574 apartments would be for African Americans. Walter White protested this system, arguing that racially mixed projects had been produced elsewhere. "Surely, if this can be done in South Carolina it can be done in New York City," he told housing officials, but they ignored his pleas.[24]

Weaver later justified the decision to allow segregation by arguing that federal policy "attempted to avoid the problems of residential segregation in the North by concentrating on slum cities and giving preference in tenant selection to the racial groups previously in the site and the surrounding neighborhood." He meant that the program did not itself create segregation but merely reflected the racial makeup of the prior neighborhoods—but that assertion elided important questions. For example, during the planning for the Techwood Homes, Weaver himself noted that the Techwood site, which was designated for whites, was home to many African Americans. He was concerned that the plan implied "that federal funds are to be used to encourage the segregations of Negroes in certain areas of Atlanta." He told Foreman that "such displacement is, I believe, contrary to the best housing theory." Unfortunately, the use of public housing to separate the races was widespread.[25]

The PWA projects that had racially mixed tenant bodies were exceptional, and segregation was the norm in almost all federal programs. In FDR's pet projects, the Tennessee Valley Authority (TVA) and the Homestead program, federal officials fought against any attempts to weaken the Jim Crow system. The idea of the Homestead program was to build sustainable subsistence farming communities. The act allocated $25 million to create communities where families would maintain one-to five-acre plots of land while living in modern housing built by the government. Early in its administration, officials of the Homestead Subsistence Bureau declared that its Arthurdale, West Virginia, colony would be open to whites only, and the TVA announced that it would maintain the same policy at its model town of Norris, Tennessee.[26]

Walter White and other civil rights leaders protested these decisions. "We feel that it would be a backward step and a very grave mistake for the government to establish or countenance any segregated colony. Negroes and whites have been living together in the South for three hundred years and we can see no logical reason why taxpayers' money should be used to foster separation," White claimed. Instead of yielding to prejudice, officials had "the opportunity to do a great service to America" by refusing to approve any project that did not contemplate integration. While Weaver was also concerned about the program, he did not push his case as strongly as White did. Immediately after his appointment in 1933, Weaver told Foreman that "the notion of such communities is not popular" and argued that, "in the North, care should be taken to see that qualified Negroes are admitted to the projects," but he did not press the matter, and few homestead projects admitted blacks.[27]

The dispute over homestead communities arose at a time when black leaders were engaged in an aggressive and very personal debate over the merits of segregation, spurred by W. E. B. DuBois. In January 1934, DuBois initiated a yearlong discussion within the pages of *Crisis*, the NAACP's journal (which DuBois edited), on the matter of segregation. "The thinking colored people of the United States must stop being stampeded by the word segregation," he argued. Segregation was the norm in American society, DuBois claimed. Few people objected to blacks or other racial and religious groups living or worshiping separately. The problem was not segregation but the discrimination that often came with it. "Voluntary segregation" with the end of securing adequate resources for black advancement was a goal that blacks should pursue, DuBois argued. While integration should remain a long-run objective, it would be wrong for blacks to "wait for the millennium" to occur when they could be uniting to secure power today.[28]

In making his case for voluntary segregation, DuBois specifically cited the example of the Homestead program. Since blacks were not going to secure entrance to white homestead communities, he argued, "it would be nothing less than idiotic for colored people themselves to refuse to accept or neglect to ask for subsistence homestead colonies of their own." Other NAACP officials, including board chair Joel Spingarn, Walter White, and founder Francis Grimke, strongly objected to DuBois's statements. Segregation is an evil, Spingarn argued, that the NAACP should consistently oppose. Segregation, White asserted, means "spiritual atrophy for the group segregated." William Hastie also attacked DuBois, claiming that segregation could exist without discrimination in theory but "any Negro who uses this theoretical possibility as a justification for segregation is either dumb or mentally dishonest." The conflict ended in August with DuBois's resignation from the organization.[29]

Weaver, who later argued that DuBois had "always supported" him, continued to be "doubtful of the desirability of separate projects for Negroes," but Foreman supported the idea. Under the Homestead Act, Foreman argued, blacks could build their "own self-sufficient communities." With PWA backing, blacks could create full-fledged "industrial centers" that would be completely controlled by them. He cited DuBois's arguments in support of his conclusions.[30]

As a result, Weaver found himself in the same position regarding homestead communities that he had experienced in the PWA housing program: arguing for integration while accepting the necessity to provide resources to blacks for projects he philosophically opposed. Because no blacks had been placed in any homestead communities, black leaders pressured Secretary Ickes to intervene. He convinced Homestead officials to give blacks priority in future developments. But when they agreed that a homestead community in New York would be integrated (15 percent black and 85 percent white), several black leaders protested that the decision would lead to the continued underrepresentation of blacks in the program.[31]

Weaver's early New Deal years were a whirlwind of activity. As one of a small number of African American professionals in the federal government, Weaver had numerous responsibilities. In addition to participating in the Interior Department's programs, Weaver investigated claims of discrimination in the federal government, including one that described in detail discrimination at the TVA. Weaver's report concluded that the TVA had systematically excluded blacks from job opportunities and after pressure had allowed blacks to occupy only the most menial, lowest-paid positions. Unlike his work at the PWA, however, Weaver's efforts regarding the TVA failed to significantly modify its practices.[32]

Weaver served as both a critic of and spokesman for the New Deal, and he provided outreach to black communities across the country. He also made dozens of speeches to black groups on the progress of the federal government's programs. And there was a lot of work to do. Although Weaver's bosses were sensitive to claims of racial discrimination, most New Deal officials, like the officials in the National Recovery Administration (NRA), were not. The Agricultural Adjustment Administration was among the most discriminatory agencies. Henry Wallace, secretary of the Department of Agriculture, would later support the cause of civil rights, but in 1934 he urged Weaver and other officials meeting to discuss the needs of blacks to "go slow" and avoid "making trouble for other groups." Weaver had little influence over federal farm programs, which directed aid to white farmers while denying it to blacks.[33]

Weaver's efforts during the rise of the New Deal earned him praise and criticism. Arthur Logan, conducting a yearlong study of the New Deal for the Alpha Phi Alpha fraternity, argued that Weaver had been the most successful of the "Negro Advisors." Although he was the "most inconspicuous," Logan argued, Weaver had also been the "most conscientious in the discharge of his duties." Weaver's "high sense of honor," while it had not brought all that blacks might have wished, had accomplished "more for the Negroes of America . . . than has been accomplished by any of the other Negro New Dealers," Logan concluded.[34]

But other black leaders criticized the impotence of black government officials and made veiled attacks on Weaver himself. The editors of the *Chicago Defender* wrote in 1935 that the total improvement in the situation of blacks could be summed up in one word: "NOTHING." The writers blamed black advisors for the failure of federal programs to serve blacks. "The sum total of their influence," the editorial stated, "has exemplified itself in their ability merely to hold a job." The editors called the advisors "spineless." Despite his brother's praise for Weaver, Rayford Logan also criticized black advisors, arguing that they were "not sufficiently militant." Rather, they were "the type of Negro that the white people wanted—one who knew what to say and what not to say; one who gladly accepted what the white officials gave Negroes and never made any further inquiry or complaint." The report did not single out Weaver for criticism, but Logan's biographer has concluded that Weaver was the target of the attack.[35]

When the Supreme Court declared the National Recovery Act unconstitutional on 27 May, 1935, few people shed a tear for the program. By that time, most Americans considered it a failure. The Depression continued, unemployment had not improved at all and was worse in some regions, and many businesses had figured out how to avoid NRA regulations. The demise of the NRA signified to many the end of the most radical phase of the New Deal. Black Americans, who had been systematically excluded from participating in that aspect of the recovery program, were not sad when the agency was dismantled.[36]

However, although the NRA failed to achieve either its goal of putting the economy back on track or responding to the hopes of civil rights leaders, there were several other bright spots in the first years of the New Deal. Weaver's first three years as a New Dealer were ones of rapid change for the federal government and for African Americans. Though opponents battled every aspect of the president's program, many initiatives suffered from haphazard organization, and, most importantly to the average American, the economic crisis continued, these early efforts created a new framework for government policy that would reshape the economic system. At the same time, FDR's support of equality for African Americans, though extremely timid and limited, still represented a quantum leap forward in the political system for blacks. For Weaver, the early years of the New Deal were formative moments: a period when he would develop the political and economic philosophies that carried him through three decades of civil rights activism and government service.

* 4 *

# Creating a New Order

## *Black Politics in the New Deal Era*

Lino Rivera, a sixteen-year-old resident of the Harlem neighborhood in New York, stole a knife from a store on 19 March 1935. Store employees confronted him, took him to the basement, and beat him. While Rivera was in their custody, rumors quickly spread down 125th Street, the area's largest business district, that the boy had been killed. In a short time, several thousand black Harlemites congregated. Incited by speakers who gave speeches claiming that the boy had been "mercilessly beaten" and was "near death," many began to break store windows and loot the shops. The New York City police soon arrived, and a full-scale conflict ensued. When the rioting subsided, fifty-seven residents and seven police officers were injured, and seventy-five people were under arrest. The riot was just one of the expressions of frustration at the continuing discrimination and brutality that was African Americans' daily experience.[1]

Though a small number of New York blacks turned their anger into violence, most African Americans continued to focus on incremental change through the political system. And, while discrimination continued to shape the lives of black Americans, the federal government gave them some reason for cheer. A short time after the Harlem riot, Weaver made the case for the Roosevelt administration in the National Urban League journal *Opportunity.* In "The New Deal and the Negro: A Look at the Facts," Weaver reminded readers of the economic hardships facing African Americans when FDR took office, and he described the numerous benefits that the New Deal had already provided. Acknowledging that racial discrimination in the implementation of several programs continued to be a serious problem, he nonetheless called the federal government's efforts "a godsend to the unemployed." After describing the gains made by blacks in the Public Works Administration (PWA) housing program and in the allocation of funds for schools in the South, Weaver concluded that the New Deal represented "a departure which can do much to reach the Negro citizens" and had succeeded in many areas. Blacks should both continue to fight discrimination and "admit that we have gained" from the program. Weaver wrote these words at a time when the influence of blacks, within both the federal government and the Democratic Party, was on the rise. While still small in number, black officials established a foothold during the 1930s that was the beginning of the incorporation of African Americans into government service.[2]

During the late 1930s, Weaver and John Davis would pursue dramatically different paths in pursuit of racial equality. While Davis moved closer to the Communist Party and became a leader of grassroots leftist politics, Weaver positioned himself within the Democratic Party, cultivated the liberal wing of the party's leadership, and helped create opportunities for African American professionals in the federal bureaucracy. By the war years, the "Black Cabinet"—a collection of black government professionals—would achieve mythic status and be ascribed powers by both its supporters and its detractors that far exceeded its actual influence, but the activities of the group reveal a level of influence previously unavailable to blacks. Weaver was the undisputed leader of this coalition.

Weaver remained a leader in the continually controversial but expanding field of public housing. First in the Interior Department and then in the newly created U.S. Housing Authority (USHA), Weaver struggled to protect the interests of blacks in the initiative. As the federal government's support for publicly owned shelter was institutionalized, Weaver worked to see that the program provided employment for black construction and professional workers and to ensure that black families received a substantial share of the housing produced, while at the same time promoting racial integration. Weaver's efforts were successful in the area of employment and also in the creation of a small number of experimental ventures in integration. However, opposition to these efforts, as well as to public housing in general, remained strong, so powerful, in fact, that Weaver's promotion of integration would imperil the program and ultimately cost him his job. The 1935 Harlem riot presaged the increasing racial conflict of the postwar years. Weaver was one of a very small group of people responding to the problems created by the ghettoization of African Americans. The struggles among civil rights activists, government officials, and local political leaders would have a profound impact on the nation's racial landscape.

NOT ALL BLACK activists were as sanguine as Weaver about the New Deal. In May 1935, just a week before the Supreme Court struck down the National Recovery Act, John Davis and Ralph Bunche convened a conference at Howard University titled "The Position of the Negro in Our National Economic Crisis." More than 250 people, including Weaver, attended the event, which examined the economic situation of African Americans, analyzed the problems of New Deal programs, and debated the most productive approaches to ensure economic advancement for blacks. While several government officials defended their programs, the majority of the presentations attacked the New Deal, frequently in vitriolic tones. Bunche was among the most strident critics, arguing that "after two years of frantic trial and error, the New Deal, and most of its elaborate machinery, remains suspended in mid-air, bewildered and innocuous." With regard to the impact of the program on blacks, Bunche claimed that "New Deal planning only serves to crystallize those abuses and oppressions which the exploited Negro citizenry of America have long suffered."[3]

After the conference, a small group of attendees met at Ralph Bunche's house. There, they agreed to convene a national meeting of labor and civil rights organizations geared at developing ways to improve the economic status of black Americans, and they selected Davis as the organizer of the group, which he named the National Negro Congress (NNC). Though Weaver was good friends with many of the participants, he did not take part in the meeting at Bunche's house, a fact that, twenty-six years later, he would trumpet in his congressional confirmation hearings.[4]

In Davis's call to potential attendees of the congress, he stated that "there has been a wholesale denial of the constitutional rights of the Negro. Hardly anywhere in America does there exist for Negroes an effective weapon to compel respect and justice from the government under which they live." The NNC, he claimed, would not replace existing organizations but would "accomplish unity of action of already existing organizations on issues which are the property and concern of every Negro in the nation." The NNC would bring together the nation's black leaders and their supporters to fight for racial justice. With financial support from many national organizations, the meeting occurred in Chicago in February 1936. According to organizers, there were between 4,000 and 8,000 attendees. They heard from Davis, union leader A. Philip Randolph, Communist Party leader Max Yergan, and an envoy from the emperor of Ethiopia, Haile Selassie. At the end of the conference, the participants agreed to a wide variety of resolutions covering everything from America's policy in the Caribbean and Africa to the needs of black women and farmers, and they endorsed a program of industrial unionism for black workers. Black newspapers across the country called the meeting a major success, and it pushed Davis higher in the ranks of national black leaders.[5]

NNC organizers, who viewed both the Republican and Democratic parties with suspicion, hoped that their group could lead the way to nonpartisan organization of blacks and working-class whites. However, the majority of African Americans, just four years ago staunchly in the Republican fold, were won over by FDR and his activist wife. The 1936 election represented a sea change in American politics, and African Americans were among the most vigorous participants. In 1932, the majority of blacks voted for Hoover, but just four years later they went overwhelmingly for FDR. In Harlem, Roosevelt received 81 percent of the vote; in Philadelphia, 69 percent; and in Detroit, 65 percent. This was the beginning of an affiliation between blacks and the Democratic Party that would last into the next century.[6]

African Americans supported the president despite the constant criticisms of the New Deal in mainstream black journals like *Crisis* and *Opportunity*. Black voters acknowledged the limitations of the federal program but also realized that the New Deal brought them many benefits. After living through decades of violence and discrimination, few blacks expected radical changes in the nation's race relations and, therefore, were not disenchanted by the limited reach of the New Deal. Rather, they appreciated what the president had done. Programs like Weaver's housing effort resulted in real jobs that paid for food and other necessities. Even if federal relief payments were less than those received by whites, they were more than any other president had provided. "I know me and my children would have starved this winter if it was not for the President," a black woman in Memphis wrote. Blacks were particularly appreciative of the Works Progress Administration, which required fair treatment for minorities and employed tens of thousands of them across the country.[7]

More importantly, blacks felt an affinity for FDR, who, more than any other president, made efforts to personally connect with African Americans. Even though he generally followed his aides' counsel of passivity with regard to civil rights issues, Roosevelt's public attitudes toward black Americans seemed different from those of his predecessors. As one historian argued, "blacks not only voted for Roosevelt, they idolized him as well." FDR's portrait hung in the living rooms of thousands of black Americans, and thousands more wrote the president thanking him for his concern.[8]

The president's campaign assiduously avoided discussions of racial integration, but he did other things that drew the support of black Americans. At the 1936 Democratic Convention, Arthur Mitchell, congressman from Illinois (the only black member of Congress), spoke to the audience, the first black ever to do so. The small number of black delegates at the convention were also the first of their race to participate fully in the proceedings, raising the ire of many southern segregationists. In a speech at Howard University that was widely reported by the black press, Roosevelt claimed that there would be "no forgotten men and no forgotten races." Even that vague statement was remarkable to many African Americans.[9]

The Democrats also creatively used black officials like Weaver to draw support from black voters. During the 1936 campaign, Weaver worked diligently for the president, helping to organize a political action committee called Independent Voters for Roosevelt that sought to "appeal to colored voters who have not been active in politics" and to draw Republicans into the Democratic orbit. Weaver and other black officials aided campaign staff in reaching out to black voters in northern cities, and he made dozens of speeches to black groups during the campaign. After FDR's reelection, Weaver's friend Paul Williams told him that Democrats "should see that you are well rewarded for your valued service."[10]

Though he won by a landslide, the period after the president's reelection was marked by the stagnation of the New Deal, and few of FDR's proposals were adopted. Administration efforts to further expand the federal government's role in the lives of urban residents, initiatives that were not a priority with the anti-city president, also foundered. In the area of civil rights, activists would lose more battles than they would win. But the period was also one of consolidation for black professionals, as they entrenched themselves in government service and secured a grudging acknowledgment by white officials that the racial concerns they voiced were not going away. During these years, Weaver established himself as the leader of the small group of blacks in government, creating relationships and acquiring knowledge that he would use throughout his career.

FDR's effort to secure the black vote in the 1936 campaign revealed the increasing importance of black professionals in the New Deal. During the late 1930s and early 1940s, this group, which journalists dubbed the "Black Cabinet," would garner increasing attention from African Americans, who looked to these bureaucrats to secure equality in the government, and from critics, who feared that Weaver and his cohort were looking to overthrow the traditions of Jim Crow.[11]

The informal group began to coalesce in 1935 as Weaver, Hastie, Mary McLeod Bethune, and several others began to meet sporadically to share ideas and provide each other with material and moral support. Weaver played a crucial role in the group's development during his eleven-year stint in the federal government. Over the years, many referred to him as the "chief recruiter," the person responsible for increasing the number of blacks in government service. Among the people Weaver recruited was Frank Horne. Born and raised in Brooklyn to an elite black family (he was the uncle of singer and movie star Lena Horne), Horne graduated from City College and received a doctor of optometry degree from Northern Illinois College. He had worked for several years as a teacher and administrator at black colleges in the South when Weaver recruited him to join Bethune at the National Youth Administration (NYA). Like many black academics, Horne was somewhat reluctant to enter the federal government, which he viewed with much trepidation since it had not treated blacks well in the past. But Weaver told Horne that the opportunities for blacks were increasing. Other early Weaver recruits were Booker McGraw and William Trent, both of whom would have important civil rights roles in the postwar years (among his many positions, Trent would become the head of the United Negro College Fund). By the early 1940s, almost all of the black professionals in the group worked for, or were recruited by, Weaver.[12]

While Weaver provided the organization, the group's public persona was embodied in its eldest and most widely known member, Mary McLeod Bethune. The daughter of sharecroppers, Bethune graduated from Scotia Seminary in South Carolina and attended Moody Bible College in Chicago. She then moved to Florida and founded a black primary school which grew until it became Bethune-Cookman College. Bethune was a founding member of the National Council of Negro Women, one of the leading black advocacy groups. Because of her consistent lobbying on behalf of black youth, Bethune became increasingly close to Eleanor Roosevelt. They first met in 1927, and by the time FDR took office, Bethune was considered the First Lady's closest black confidant. Bethune used this connection to secure access to the president. In 1936, Aubrey Williams, then head of the NYA, asked her to run the newly created Office of Minority Affairs in the NYA.[13]

Throughout the 1930s and thereafter, Bethune was a constant presence in campaigns for civil rights. She was a board member of the NAACP and many other national organizations, but she was equally active in grassroots organizing efforts like the "Don't Buy Where You Can't Work" campaign. An imposing personality who inspired awe among both the black masses and the black elite, she was referred to as "Ma Bethune." Weaver later said that Bethune was "a catalyst and a symbol, dramatizing the knowledge and learning of younger Negroes who were working as race advisors in the various New Deal Agencies."[14]

Bethune called the first formal meeting of black New Dealers in 1936. Their goal was to work together to bring about fair treatment for blacks across federal agencies. Although the group struggled to make significant progress, they did celebrate many small victories. One such achievement was FDR's decision to appoint Hastie a federal judge in 1937. When the president selected the thirty-two-year-old lawyer to serve as district judge for the Virgin Islands, he made Weaver's good friend the first African American to attain such a status. By 1938, members were meeting regularly at Bethune's home or office and referring to themselves as the Federal Council on Negro Affairs, with Bethune as chair and Weaver as vice chair. Bethune led the business meetings, but members also met informally, frequently at Weaver's house, where they played poker, drank, and discussed issues. Bethune, who was the only woman to play an important role in the council, did not participate in these activities. In general, the members of the group aided each other by sharing information and providing constructive criticism of each other's plans and programs.[15]

Although Bethune was the group's titular head, Weaver provided much of the leadership and organizational effort. Weaver later told an interviewer that "Mrs. Bethune, as time went on, was the spokesman, I was the secretariat. I got the guys together and prepared the policy memorandums." Bethune, because of her political contacts, was the most appropriate person to represent the group at White House and other meetings. The membership of the group varied greatly over time, and some members were more active than others. The core participants were professionals with advanced degrees, but black political appointees like *Pittsburgh Courier* publisher Robert Vann (who served for a brief time in the Justice Department) were also members, although they were not active in the group.[16]

During the late 1930s, the group created a coordinated program to fight discrimination in New Deal programs. One target Weaver and others consistently attacked was the Civilian Conservation Corps (CCC). Established early in the New Deal to put young men to work (with the additional benefit of keeping them off the streets and out of trouble), throughout its nine-year history the agency served about 2.5 million of them, establishing camps across the country in which young men could live, train, and work. The CCC legislation included a prohibition on racial discrimination in the operation of the program, but from the beginning, the CCC director, Robert Fechner, a white South Carolinian, made it clear that he did not take this mandate seriously. Fechner set a limit of 10 percent for black youth in the program, arguing that this corresponded to the percentage of blacks in the population, but the number of blacks in the program never approached this percentage. The CCC created only a few black camps and then justified its inability to enroll blacks on the grounds that there were no vacancies. CCC officials offered a myriad of other excuses, arguing that blacks were still needed in the fields and that communities would oppose the creation of camps if blacks were allowed to participate.[17]

After several years of lobbying by Weaver and others, the CCC increased the number of black youth participating in the program, creating segregated camps for them not only in the South but in the North. Accepting that there was little he could do to combat segregation of the CCC camps, Weaver focused his attention on the employment of "educational advisors" at the camps. If blacks were to be segregated, he argued, at least these camps should provide employment opportunities for black professionals to train and teach the residents. With the support of Secretary Ickes, Weaver fought with CCC officials and J. W. Studebaker, commissioner of education, to get them to hire more black professionals. Progress was slow, but by 1937, almost all the camps for blacks had at least one black advisor.[18]

Weaver also took other approaches to secure work for black professionals. He convinced Ickes to authorize a major study of black professional and skilled workers. The project was similar to many conducted by the Works Progress Administration to study aspects of American life and to—more importantly—prop up the nation's academic sector, which had been hurt badly by cutbacks at the country's colleges and universities. Weaver served as administrator, and the project was supervised by several leading black academics, including Ira D. Reid of Atlanta University and Charles Spurgeon Johnson of Fisk University. Over the three years of its operation, the office spent over $500,000 and employed 1,800 people in thirty-two states to conduct surveys and collect information such as work histories of thousands of black workers. Through this program, Weaver provided desperately needed work for the black professionals who conducted the surveys and further cemented his position as a leading scholar of black America.[19]

The report, written by Weaver, Ira Reid, Preston Valien, and Charles S. Johnson, found "a marked decrease in the number of Negro skilled workers" during the preceding decade. More than one-fourth of black skilled workers had left their fields between 1925 and 1936. Moreover, unemployment among black skilled workers had more than doubled since 1930, from 8.4 to 17.7 percent. The authors blamed this increase on the lack of apprentice and vocational opportunities for blacks, noting that a major reason (in addition to discrimination) that many blacks had been pushed out of their fields was their lack of understanding of modern techniques. This was particularly true in the construction trades, as employees were required to have knowledge of the mechanics of large buildings. The report recommended federal legislation to require that an equitable share of education funds be devoted to training black Americans.[20]

The report was one of many publications produced by Weaver in the late 1930s. Throughout these years, Weaver wrote numerous articles for black periodicals such as *Crisis* and *Opportunity* and for scholarly publications like the *Journal of Education* and *Social Forces* that sought to explain New Deal programs to the general public and academics. As spokesman for the Roosevelt administration, Weaver acknowledged the limitations of the New Deal but forcefully made the case that federal initiatives had aided blacks by providing jobs, building schools and housing, and creating a more productive approach toward the issue of blacks in American society.[21]

By the early 1940s, the Black Cabinet would be a topic of frequent conversation among African Americans, who were fascinated by the journalistic reports (frequently exaggerated) of their exploits. At the same time, Weaver and his colleagues would be subject to increasing scrutiny by southern congressmen who believed they represented a conspiracy to undermine the Jim Crow system. Both groups overestimated the officials' actual impact on federal policy; nevertheless, the Black Cabinet did provide a forum for professionals to promote equal treatment from within the dramatically expanding bureaucracy.

ALTHOUGH WEAVER'S POSITION enabled him to avoid many of the daily inequities facing working-class blacks, he was not himself immune to discrimination. In July 1935, while returning from Baltimore, Weaver was pulled over by a Maryland police officer who told him he had been speeding. When Weaver protested that he had been driving within the speed limit, the officer arrested him. Unable to post the $26.70 bond, Weaver had to spend several hours in jail while his party went on to Washington to get the money. He believed that the highway patrolman had targeted him because of his race and that he pressed charges just to show Weaver that he had no power. In a letter to the commissioner of motor vehicles, with copies to the state's senators, Weaver stated that the officer "lacked courtesy, veracity and common politeness, as well as good judgment."[22]

Though only Weaver's feelings and pocketbook were hurt by the incident, the potential for a violent encounter with the police or white thugs was a constant worry that influenced the daily lives of all blacks in the nation's capital. Persistent discrimination limited the economic and social opportunities of most African Americans, and they generally stayed within their own communities, creating a vibrant culture of theater, music, and other arts. However, caught up in the whirlwind of the New Deal, Weaver had little time for a social life. He traveled frequently, and when he was in Washington, he began work early in the morning and often did not finish until late at night. At work, he had few close friends. Though he developed a strong relationship with the African American secretary he hired, Corienne Robinson, he did not socialize with the department's white professionals.

Much of Weaver's social life revolved around his close friends, William Hastie, Ralph Bunche, Charles Hamilton Houston, and others affiliated with Howard University, and his family. Still influenced by his parents' training, Weaver did not participate much in DC's black society, and he, Hastie, and Bunche all disdained most of the social circuit. Although they sometimes went out to dinner or a movie or a show, they preferred to meet in their respective homes to drink and play cards. Though Weaver was reserved in public, he was very warm and loving to his close friends, particularly his friends from his Harvard days. To his younger peers, he took on the role of big brother, chiding, for example, Bill Dean (who was following him in the Harvard economics department) to finish his dissertation: "If you keep on at the rate you are going now you will be writing it for the next 50 years. However, that is enough of Dorothy Dix advice from me."[23]

Given how little time he spent socializing or dating, many of Weaver's friends were surprised when they were informed, after the fact, that Weaver had married Ella Haith in July 1935. Ella's father had died when she was a young child. Her mother, a schoolteacher, had raised the family by herself in Wilmington, North Carolina. After graduating from high school at fifteen, Ella moved to Washington to attend Howard University. As a freshman, she took an English class with Mortimer Weaver. The two began dating, but upon the recommendation of her Howard counselors, Ella transferred to Carnegie Technical College (later Carnegie-Mellon University) to study drama. Attending the white university, the light-skinned Ella died her hair red and passed as a white student. After graduating, Ella went to the University of Michigan and received a master's degree in speech therapy. While she was in Michigan, Mortimer died. Ella later told reporters that she and Robert Weaver began corresponding while she was in Michigan. She returned to the East Coast in January 1935 to take a job with the Baltimore Board of Education. Just six months later, she and Weaver were married in a small private ceremony attended almost exclusively by family. Even Ella's mother, whom Ella frequently described as her best friend, received only two weeks' notice of the impending nuptials.[24]

Like Weaver, Ella was reserved and proper, and she did not enjoy socializing in large groups. When they agreed to marry, Weaver told her that he felt it important that they acknowledge that they were African Americans and live in that world. However, Ella did not emphasize her racial heritage, and she later told reporters that she did not disabuse people of their belief that she was white.[25]

Marrying Ella without telling people was typical of Weaver, who shared his feelings with very few people. By the time of his marriage, Weaver was twenty-eight years old and well established. He had no doubt received much lobbying from his mother and grandmother about the need to "settle down." Ella was a beautiful and accomplished woman from the "right kind of people." The couple did not know each other well when they joined hands in marriage, but this was not unusual for people of their social circle. Weaver and Ella would remain together until her death in 1991. During their marriage of fifty-six years, she would be a stalwart supporter who achieved significant accomplishments of her own. Friends and acquaintances called Ella a sophisticated person who, although warm, was reserved and demanded the respect of her peers.[26]

The newlyweds settled into Weaver's house near the Howard campus, and within a year Ella had obtained a position at the school as an assistant professor in the speech department. The couple frequently attended faculty and social events there and provided intellectual and moral support to the student body. After his marriage, Weaver's social life closed even further. His dominant occupations were work and home. In his limited correspondence with friends he wrote, "I am getting some good cooking done these days," and he never forgot to close his messages with "Ella sends her regards." But the couple did not participate in the party circuit. In 1937, writing to his friend Hastie in the Virgin Islands about goings-on in Washington, Weaver stated, "Socially I assume there is much of a startling nature. However, I am not familiar with what is going on in that field."[27]

During the summers, the couple frequently joined Weaver's family at Highland Beach in Maryland. There, they enjoyed the company of a small number of close friends. The Weavers' friend Mary Washington described the place as one that, "if you didn't have friends there, you wouldn't know about it," because it was accessed by a dirt road with no signs. On the road were "a lot of ruts, but once go beyond that, there were these gateposts that led into Highland Beach and there was this wonderful community of single houses." There were about seventy residences altogether, and there was also a small hotel and a pavilion on the beach where young people would congregate. The Weaver's house was all the way down the beach at the end. According to Washington, it was "a lovely house, two-story, frame house with a large screened porch that went from the front of the house around to the side. None of the houses were elaborate, no heat, they had hot and cold running water and inside baths. It was a delightful place to spend time away from everyone." Weaver, who would build several small boats over his lifetime, fondly looked back at his time spent there. In 1942, the family added another person when the couple adopted a baby they named Robert Weaver Jr. It is unclear where the baby came from, but it is likely that he was the offspring of an unmarried relative. Robert Jr. was the only child they would ever have.[28]

Although he was devoted to Ella, a large part of Weaver's life was his work. As Weaver organized black federal workers in support of equal treatment within the New Deal, he continued to play a major role in the implementation of the public housing program. By 1936, Weaver had established himself as one of a small number of housing experts in the nation. His job within the Interior Department put him in close contact with the group of reformers, based primarily in New York City, who called themselves "housers" and lobbied for increased government involvement in the clearance of slums and construction of decent, affordable housing. Their movement, its roots in the Progressive Era, had both scholarly and activist wings. Developed by social scientists and "settlement house" officials, its underlying tenet was that the way to improve the lives of working-class Americans was through urban planning. With the help of professionals who carefully designed communities for the immigrant and rural poor, these disadvantaged segments of the population would be acclimated into modern urban society, ending the social ills that troubled them. The production of decent housing, these advocates believed, was crucial to the broader goal of social improvement.[29]

The contacts Weaver made in this period—with Charles Abrams, Catherine Bauer, Leon Keyserling, and others—deeply shaped his political philosophy. An avid reader, Weaver consumed all of the materials on urban planning and housing that he could, and he soon became an expert himself on these matters. Though they would not always agree, he would count Abrams and Bauer as lifelong friends and collaborators. Weaver shared with these progressives a strong belief in the power of government intervention to improve people's lives through economic and social planning. Even though the planning framework would come under attack in the 1960s, Weaver never wavered from the philosophical approach he adopted during these years.

During FDR's second term, as the always-contentious subject of the New Deal garnered increasing attention from supporters and opponents, events conspired to turn Weaver's career fully toward the public housing program. With the 1937 creation of the USHA, Weaver's term at the Interior Department would end, setting Weaver on a path that would end three decades later with his leadership of the Department of Housing and Urban Development (HUD). The battles over the funding and racial composition of public housing in the 1930s were precursors of the struggles that Weaver would engage in during the postwar years and that he would vainly attempt to resolve during his years at HUD's helm. Throughout these years, Weaver would balance demands for full equality within public housing with a desire to produce decent shelter for the millions who needed it. The choices that Weaver and the other participants in the public housing program made during these formative years would influence the program's successes and limitations for years to come.

During the first years of the PWA housing program, although local officials and housing reformers celebrated the federal government's support for modern housing, they constantly complained about the program's administrator, Harold Ickes. Ickes, they claimed, prevented the program from achieving its full potential through his obsession with costs and his dictatorial oversight of every aspect of the projects. Charles Abrams called Ickes "ironhanded and puritanical," and local officials claimed that their views were completely ignored. Even though he had overseen the construction of more than 21,000 units of housing, progressives disliked Ickes so much that the *Nation* called the program a "public scandal."[30]

Housing reformers wanted a program that would be operated at the local level, where they would have greater control of the initiative (as they would soon learn, reformers were wrong in this belief). They were aided by Robert Wagner, senator from New York, who introduced legislation to fund local housing initiatives in three successive congresses. The specifics of the legislation varied, but each envisioned a federal agency that provided grants and loans to local housing authorities, which would build, own, and manage these units. FDR's landslide reelection carried into office several liberal legislators who also backed an expanded housing effort. After strenuous opposition, Congress approved the proposal. The Housing Act of 1937 created the USHA and authorized it to issue bonds to fund very low interest loans to local authorities for construction of public housing.[31]

To run the agency, the president chose his friend and New York ally Nathan Straus. Son of the founder of Macy's department store, the thirty-eight-year-old Straus had attended the University of Heidelberg in Germany and received a degree from Princeton University. After working in Macy's administration, Straus was elected to the New York State Assembly in 1921. He served three terms before retiring and was widely rumored to be Roosevelt's choice for lieutenant governor in 1928 before FDR settled on Herbert Lehman. Straus had been involved in housing issues as a legislator and worked with housing reformers to create several programs in New York State, and he was the developer of the Hillside Homes, a major affordable housing project built in Queens during the early 1930s.[32]

Most observers expected Straus to hire the existing PWA housing staff, and Straus did offer jobs to many of these officials, but he also populated the new agency with many of his own people, appointing Wagner aide Leon Keyserling as general counsel and Catherine Bauer as director of research and information. Recognizing the severe housing shortage for blacks, civil rights leaders strongly supported the Housing Act, and even before the law passed, they organized to protect the interests of blacks in the new agency. Black leaders from across the country, including NAACP head Walter White, Chicago housing official Robert Taylor, and Los Angeles architect Paul Williams, agreed that Weaver should be appointed to a high-level position at the USHA.[33]

White, who publicly stated that his group had "a strict rule against asking for positions for individuals since that would put us under obligations," lobbied aggressively behind the scenes for Weaver's appointment, calling Straus, Harold Ickes, and others. Ickes told White that Weaver would do an excellent job at the USHA, but the secretary, who was in no mood to lose one of his staff, refused to intervene in the matter. After some mediation between the two bureaucrats by White, however, Ickes agreed to release Weaver. Straus's announcement of the appointment was delayed over a month by Weaver's hospitalization for an appendectomy. Accepting the appointment to the post of special assistant to the administrator on race relations, Weaver issued a public statement declaring that "past experience of government in housing has shown the need for planning for Negro participation from the beginning. It is my hope that I will be instrumental in stimulating such planning."[34]

Weaver's 1933 appointment as deputy to the administrator on race relations, Clark Foreman, brought a mixed response from African American leaders, but by 1938, because of the increasing influence of blacks within the federal government as well as Weaver's personal success in the Interior Department, there were no reservations about his transfer. His selection, stated Campbell Johnson of the Washington, DC, YMCA, "was the logical result of the excellent work which you have done." It was "surprising," Johnson noted, because "somehow we are not much used to seeing the thing that should happen actually come about in the manner of public appointments." "The race will have reason to be proud of a young man of your ability in the Housing Authority," Forrester Washington wrote from Atlanta University. C. L. Alexander of the Harlem YMCA, commenting on Weaver's past performance, told Weaver that "the many benefits which Negroes have secured . . . through your influence with the department with which you serve, are a tribute to you." T. Arnold Hill of the National Urban League told Straus he "could not have made a better choice."[35]

Like his friends in the field, Weaver held high hopes for the public housing initiative. Soon after his appointment, he wrote, "the whole theory behind public housing is that the individual is affected greatly by his environment. Not only does the person develop more fully if he is given better surroundings, but society benefits because a better citizen is produced." Like many others, Weaver believed that public housing could change the lives of the poor. But Weaver worried that he would need all the power he could muster to do his job. While housing reformers celebrated the transfer of control of the housing program from the federal government to local entities, Weaver and other black leaders feared this change. After all, what had local governments done for African Americans in the past? In the South, blacks were disenfranchised and therefore unable to wield influence over the allocation of resources. In the North, the Promised Land for thousands of blacks since World War I, African Americans remained a distinct minority—blacks represented just 5 percent of the population in New York City, for example. The power of the federal government to overcome local prejudices and protect against discrimination was what had attracted Weaver and his peers to the nation's capital in the first place.[36]

Protection of blacks in the new program would require new approaches. Early in his tenure, Weaver told the readers of *Crisis* magazine that "Negroes as individuals and groups must become increasingly articulate in regard to low-rent housing." Weaver was particularly concerned about the viability of his affirmative-action program for black workers. Since the USHA decided which projects received funding, it would still wield a great deal of power over the public housing program, and with Weaver's prodding the agency told local housing authorities that racial discrimination would be prohibited. But the USHA did not directly enter into agreements with contractors—that was done by local housing authorities—and it therefore could not hold them in violation if they failed to abide by the pledges to hire minorities. As a result of their shaky legal position, Weaver and his staff were forced to be creative in promoting equal treatment. "We bluffed a little bit," he told an interviewer several decades later, recalling their efforts to use their federal status to get contractors to comply. "I had to do the identification for my staff. It looked like an FBI agent. They sealed with 'Government' and stamped it." Contractors were fooled by the badges. "Nobody ever read it and we got along very famously," Weaver recalled.[37]

Although they did not have the power they once had, Weaver and his staff traveled the country to actively promote their affirmative-action program. They continued to calculate the percentages of black workers in each city and recommend contractual clauses that provided for fair participation in the building program. With the help of Walter White, who brought reports of discrimination to Weaver's attention, they mediated disputes in dozens of cities, lobbying against a proposed Jacksonville, Florida, law that would have limited participation in the program to union members (the unions that barred blacks), attacking the Houston Housing Authority for placing obstacles in the way of black job seekers, and working to protect the gains made by blacks in the Atlanta housing program. As a result of their efforts, black workers participated in USHA-funded projects at significant levels. According to one study, the percentage of black skilled workers in public housing projects was larger than the percentage of blacks in the construction industry. In 1940 Weaver reported that, on USHA projects, black workers represented 11.6 percent of all workers, 4.1 percent of skilled workers, and 26.3 percent of unskilled workers.[38]

Success was much harder to achieve regarding the issue of the projects' tenantry. The small number of integrated PWA projects were a noble experiment that a few housing authorities continued under the new program, but with Weaver and his staff weakened by the USHA's decentralized system, many local housing authorities sought to use housing development to create segregation where it had not previously existed. In Detroit, at the behest of merchants, the local housing authority decided that a project planned for a racially diverse area that was to have housed blacks would now serve whites exclusively. When asked where the African Americans uprooted by the project would go, housing officials stated, "they will just have to find another place to live." In Los Angeles, officials planned two racially based projects. In one, two-thirds of the units were allocated to Latinos, and blacks received the remainder. The second project, in the Watts area, would be exclusively for blacks. The Atlanta Housing Authority, to save money, planned one large development, the Clark Howell Homes. To protect the Jim Crow system, however, they decided to erect a wall between the black and white sections. When Weaver and others objected, they altered the plan, replacing the wall with a boulevard.[39]

The desperate need for decent housing for blacks in American cities shaped the response of many leaders in these debates and strongly influenced Weaver's participation in the program. In the Atlanta dispute, Weaver did not contest the segregated aspects of the program. He did, however, push for an increase in the number of units that would be allocated to blacks in recognition of the fact that a large percentage of the area's population was African American. "The division should not be 50/50," he told Al Moron, his local contact. "That is the point which we can fight on."[40]

In New York City, the desire to produce housing also overwhelmed concerns about racial separation, a decision that had far-reaching implications for what would quickly become the nation's largest public housing program. Despite pledges that the program would be color-blind, the staff of the New York City Housing Authority planned a segregated system from the beginning. Blacks, housing officials argued, were served by the Harlem Houses. At the Williamsburg Houses, the second project completed, there was 1 black family out of 1,630. At Brooklyn's massive Red Hook project, home to 2,545 families, there were 2. In defending the segregated system, housing authority chair Alfred Rheinstein argued that "blacks and whites just don't mix." Settlement official and board member Mary Simkovitch, who was expected by some to be more circumspect in her comments, stated that attempts to promote integration in the projects would imperil the whole system. "You may say it is up to the white population to receive the colored people in equal numbers everywhere because that is justice," she told protestors. "But you know very well we haven't arrived at that condition of social justice." If the authority tried to integrate the Red Hook Houses, she argued, "the thing would not go."[41]

Weaver later argued that most blacks were not concerned about segregation; they were more worried about jobs and decent housing. "If you went too far out on the segregation issue, you were apt to lose your followership," he told an interviewer. As a result, he concluded, "we didn't get much done" on that issue. While not objecting directly to racially segregated projects, Weaver fought against efforts to entrench segregation. The USHA rules required that projects not change the existing racial makeup of a neighborhood. Therefore, he argued, plans must protect against the removal of African Americans from integrated areas. The regulations stated that, in areas "which are either inhabited now by members of more than one race or, in the case of vacant sites, are contiguous to neighborhoods which are inhabited by different races, local authorities should plan projects open to the members of these different groups." A few local authorities followed these guidelines, but the USHA in the end had little influence over the racial policies of public housing developers.[42]

Racial segregation in the present concerned Weaver, but he also worried about the impact of decisions on future neighborhood change. Segregated housing, he claimed, set "a dangerous precedent by encouraging families of other races to believe that they have a prior claim, by virtue of race, to sole occupancy of a given neighborhood." Weaver argued that it was in the long-term interests of housing authorities to establish flexible racial policies now. When a development is designated for whites only, he asserted, "the existence of such a label will create resistance to the introduction of Negro families at a later date, regardless of whether this innovation is due to the failure of white families to be attracted to the neighborhood or because of the political pressure exerted by the minority group." For this reason, he concluded, housing authorities should support integration from the beginning. Weaver would return to this argument frequently over the next two decades, but by the time he had the power to influence these decisions, his predictions had come true: public housing was overwhelmingly African American.[43]

The desire of housing officials to avoid the problem of race relations proved a constant obstacle to Weaver in his job, but his efforts were not without some success. In Newark, New Jersey, pressure from Weaver and local activists succeeded in convincing the housing authority to open all projects to white and black residents. Across the country, a significant number, though not a majority, of public housing authorities experimented with integration. In 1940 White praised Straus and Weaver for their efforts: "They have courageously and wisely tackled the problem and have stood firmly against the extension of segregation even when it has perhaps been politically dangerous for them to take such a position."[44]

Weaver concluded in 1940 that the housing program had made many positive contributions. "The Negro," he claimed, was "more nearly integrated into the program than is usually his experience, and he has received benefits on the basis of his need and eligibility." That year, he found that 145 of a total of 468 USHA-approved projects were designated for black occupancy, and another 50 were racially integrated. Weaver also pointed to the 22 (out of 300) public housing authorities where blacks served on the boards of directors, and he cited statistics showing that black workers had received 11.6 percent of the total amount of money allocated for public housing projects as of September of that year. He further noted that public housing had provided professional opportunities to many blacks in the planning and management of the developments. While he could not forecast the future, Weaver asserted that positive first steps had been taken and argued that the program had "an opportunity to perfect a rational approach to racial relations."[45]

A full-scale evaluation of the USHA program has yet to be written, but most historians have given the agency a mixed review. Although over 130,000 units of affordable housing were built under the program, many of the projects were problematic from the beginning. In New York, for example, the cost restrictions resulted in enormous developments, such as Red Hook and Queensbridge, that architectural critics have called "unnecessarily barrackslike and monotonous" and inhumane. To save money, projects were built without amenities or even basic things like closet doors. At the Red Hook development, the elevators stopped on only every other floor. These projects were immediately recognized as housing for the poor, marginalizing the projects from the start and creating long-term perception problems. Housing reformers criticized Ickes for his ironfisted management, but most historians agree that the PWA projects were far better designed. In the long run, however, the decisions about the projects' racial makeup would be even more important than those about architecture.[46]

Liberals celebrated the passage of the 1937 Housing Act, but in retrospect it marked the end of the New Deal era and the last significant piece of domestic legislation. A variety of factors, including FDR's aborted efforts to reconstruct the Supreme Court and the federal bureaucracy and public discontent over continued high unemployment, contributed to the reinvigoration of conservatives in Congress, who fought any further expansion of the president's program. In contrast to the liberals' landslide victory in 1936, the 1938 congressional elections added new members to the conservative coalition of southern Democrats and northern Republicans set on rolling back the growth of the federal government.[47]

Public housing was high on the list of targets for congressional conservatives. From the passage of the act, they fought to obstruct the program and to limit the resources devoted to it. They were aided by the business lobby, particularly the realtors, who organized a national campaign against the program, calling it "undiluted socialism." Although the main reason for opposition to the USHA was philosophical, personal animosity in Congress toward Administrator Straus also played a role in the declining support for public housing. Harold Ickes called him "the most unpopular man in the administration," and several of FDR's advisors told the president that Straus had to go if the program was to be saved. FDR received constant complaints from local housing agencies about "bureaucratic red tape" that prevented them from operating. Straus found himself under attack from all sides, castigated by housing reformers for moving too slowly to produce housing and vilified by conservatives for undermining American values.[48]

In the spring of 1940, Weaver provided fodder for opponents in their assault on the public housing program. In a 28 April speech to the third convention of the NNC, Weaver praised the efforts of his agency to promote racial integration. "What effect the Government's housing program will have on the problem of residential segregation only time will tell," Weaver told the audience. However, he continued, public housing had already shown that "Negro occupancy need not result in depreciation of property, that the Negro is a responsible tenant in a decent home." In addition, the program had shown that "the two races can live harmoniously together in the same project, that the Negro can be a good neighbor as well as a good tenant."[49]

The expansive tone of Weaver's remarks was, no doubt, partially affected by the audience. The third convention of the NNC marked the organization's most prominent moment. In a year in which most political observers felt that the black vote would be influential in the election, the convention gained added importance. That the group would, because of concerns about Communist influence, precipitously decline soon thereafter was not obvious when Weaver made his speech. Rather, he made these remarks to a large group of African Americans and their supporters who were dissatisfied with the New Deal and critical of its black spokesmen. Weaver sought to impress the group with a dramatic statement about the successes and potential of the Democratic administration, but his statement would soon come back to haunt him.

Soon thereafter, opponents used Weaver's remarks, specifically those praising integration within projects, to attack the public housing program. Early that year, Senator Robert Wagner introduced a bill to allow the USHA to borrow additional funds. The proposal experienced strong opposition from conservatives in Congress, and throughout May and June, congressional opponents used Weaver's remarks as another argument against the program. "Unfortunately, one of the officials of the U.S.H.A. talked too much," a congressional supporter of the program told Walter White. Other members of Congress told White that they did not think Weaver's statement had a significant impact on the fate of the program, but the bill never did reach the floor of the House for a vote before Congress recessed in June. It is impossible to say how much impact Weaver's remarks had on the program's travails, but they did not help.[50]

Less than a month after the failure of the public housing funding bill, Weaver resigned his position, taking a job in the growing national defense program. Although he never stated his reasons for the move, it is clear from Weaver's correspondence with White that Weaver felt that the conflict had weakened his position within the agency. Despite the fact that he was forced out of the agency, Weaver continued to view his participation in the effort positively. Two years later he argued that public housing had been a model for new approaches to racial equality. "Fundamentally, participation by Negroes in any public program approaches adequacy as it is planned with and by Negroes rather than for them by others more or less acquainted with Negroes' needs and specific problems." No program had gone as far in meeting this goal as public housing, he asserted.[51]

The demise of the USHA did not mean the end of government-owned housing. The initiative was extremely resilient, which is unsurprising given the fact that millions of Americans continued to live in squalid conditions. But opposition to the agency illuminated the limitations of New Deal liberalism. As the war in Europe heated up and conservative opposition to domestic programs increased, FDR's attention turned increasingly to foreign affairs. The war had negative implications for the government's racial policy, as increasing focus on defense programs undermined efforts toward racial equality. During the 1940s, as several million African Americans flocked to cities, race relations and urban policy would become increasingly intertwined, but policymakers responded to these dilemmas in an ad hoc manner. The emergence of new approaches to racial and urban problems would have to wait until after World War II had ended.

At the same time that Weaver was toiling to promote racial equality within the government, his friend John P. Davis was following a radically different path. After the first NNC convention, many people believed that the group offered blacks a new opportunity for real economic power. During the late 1930s, its focus on local organizing, in contrast to the NAACP's cultivation of elite support, marked an important change in civil rights activism. From 1936 through the early 1940s, the NNC spurred the organization of branches in many cities, and the group played an important role in the movement of black workers into labor unions. To manage their expanding effort, Davis relied increasingly on Communist activists as organizers, and by 1940 a substantial number of the group's members were affiliated with the Communist Party. This resulted in a backlash against the group, the resignation of several board members, and Davis's marginalization in the civil rights movement.[52]

Even though Weaver was pushed out of the public housing program, his role as racial mediator would continue. During the war years, Weaver's professional, methodical approach to racial progress would lead him to positions of influence in new areas of the federal government. In these positions, he would continue to serve as a lightning rod in the struggle for racial equality.

* 5 *

# World War II and Black Labor

One evening in late October 1940, Weaver got a call at his home from the White House asking for his help. In the midst of a heated campaign against Republican nominee Wendell Wilkie, President Roosevelt's campaign had made a major blunder that threatened to lose him the black vote. The incident involved Roosevelt's chief aide, Stephen Early. Attending an October campaign affair at Madison Square Garden, Early got into an altercation with a black police officer working the event. The officer, who was on alert against an assassination attempt on the president, refused to allow Early, who had no identification, to go through the gate. In frustration, Early kneed the policeman in the groin. At first, Early bragged about his actions, but within days several civil rights leaders and journalists publicly criticized him. Early backtracked and apologized, but Republicans made the incident a major event, taking out advertisements in black papers across the country. Administration officials pleaded with black leaders to help them control the damage resulting from the incident.[1]

Fearing a backlash, presidential advisor Jonathan Daniels called Weaver, who was in the midst of a poker game in his basement with Bill Hastie, Ralph Bunche, and a few others. Not knowing that most of the "Black Cabinet" were there in the basement, Daniels asked Weaver to get his friends together to write a speech for the president to deliver to a black audience in Baltimore. Weaver told his friends, "We've got 'em now—what do we want?" He informed Daniels that a speech would not be enough to stem the criticism and that the president needed to take more dramatic action. After some discussion, the group recommended that Roosevelt promote Colonel Benjamin O. Davis Sr. to brigadier general, which would make him the first African American to achieve that rank. They also advised him to appoint a black advisor to Selective Service and the secretary of war, an important position given the growing war threat. The president agreed and announced Davis's promotion two days later. He also asked Hastie to serve as advisor to Henry Stimson, secretary of war, an offer that Hastie accepted after some deliberation.

The promotions, and the Black Cabinet's role in them, were widely reported in the black press, greatly elevating Weaver's profile. Although the media exaggerated his influence in the matter, Weaver welcomed the acclaim, particularly since, just six months before, he had resigned from his position at the U.S. Housing Authority. Whether he left of his own accord or was pushed out by his superiors, Weaver departed the U.S. Housing Authority at a propitious time. By 1940, domestic concerns were quickly being eclipsed by worries about the war in Europe. Weaver's candor may have cost him one job, but he quickly moved into one that had the potential to reach far beyond anything he had previously done to impact the lives of African Americans. World War II presented a major opportunity to African Americans in their struggle for civil rights, and Weaver was at the center of this battle. Throughout the war, Weaver and his friends would fight racial discrimination in the military and in the war mobilization effort. They would experience many victories, but the wall of segregation would be hard to pull down. For his efforts, Weaver received as much criticism, from all sides, as acclaim. Four years later, frustrated by the slow process of change, he would leave government service.[2]

Although President Roosevelt foresaw early in the European conflict that the United States would have to play an important role in preventing the spread of fascism, the American public remained resolutely opposed to intervention. Congress, fearing the wrath of its constituents, passed two neutrality acts to prevent American involvement and generally gave the president little flexibility in aiding the Allies. Most Americans did not oppose, however, the economic benefits that the conflict brought to the country. By 1940, spurred by FDR's efforts to build up the nation's defense capabilities, along with the funds released by his Lend-Lease Act and other agreements with the Allies, American factories were back in operation, and unemployment started to drop. The strongest growth was in the aircraft industry, which was ignited by a $300 million appropriation that Roosevelt pushed through Congress to increase the nation's capacity.[3]

White workers celebrated the nation's improving economic prospects in 1940, but blacks saw few gains. Discrimination in the more than 250,000 war-related jobs was the norm across the country. More than 50 percent of employers polled by the U.S. Employment Service stated that they would not employ blacks under any circumstances. "We have not had a Negro worker in twenty-five years, and do not plan to start now," an official of Kansas City's Standard Steel Corporation stated. The rapidly expanding aircraft industry, for example, was completely closed to blacks. Out of 107,000 workers in the industry in 1940, 240 were African American, and almost all of them were in janitorial services. The Glenn Martin Company of Baltimore employed over 10,000 workers but never hired a black person.[4]

Civil rights leaders vigorously opposed this exclusion. On the July 1940 cover of *Crisis* was a picture of an airplane factory with the caption "For Whites Only." Inside, the leaders of the National Association for the Advancement of Colored People (NAACP) asked readers to organize to protest this discrimination. "Warplanes, Negro Americans may not build them, repair them, or fly them, but they must help pay for them," the editors complained. Black newspapers across the country blasted discrimination in the military buildup. "Why die for democracy for some foreign country when we don't even have it here?" the *Chicago Defender* asked, and a writer to the *Cleveland Call and Post* wondered if the government was "trying to make a traitor of him" by denying him the chance to work.[5]

To say that World War II changed the nation is to state the obvious. The impact of the war was felt in every community across the country, and its repercussions shaped the United States for decades to come. The war further accentuated the already-significant urbanization trends in the nation, bringing millions of Americans to the cities, where war jobs were located. These changes were particularly powerful for African Americans. Black migration from the South to northern and western cities increased dramatically during the war. These trends would have significant long-term implications, but in the short term they forced policymakers to deal with issues of employment, housing, and the racial tensions that arose out of competition in both these areas.

As one of the nation's leading black policymakers, Weaver played a central role in the slow growth of black employment prospects during World War II. Weaver continued to toil within the government to promote equal opportunity for blacks. Working together, and sometimes in conflict, with other activists, Weaver saw significant gains for African Americans in their efforts to enter industrial society. At the same time, discrimination in both employment and housing continued to limit the opportunities of blacks and other minorities. As it did during the New Deal, Weaver's position as an insider placed him in the middle, caught between intransigent government officials, who complained that he was asking for too much when the focus of the nation should be completely on national security, and civil rights activists, who claimed that he was an apologist for a racist government. The tensions raised by World War II not only would have broad implications for the future of American race relations but would also be emblematic of the fundamental contradictions of Weaver's career.

BETWEEN THE START of the European conflict and the end of the war, the president and his staff would create an alphabet soup of agencies to manage the war economy. In 1939, FDR created his first, the War Resources Board (WRB), a collection of government officials given the responsibility of coordinating the country's defense activities. This organization failed the difficult task of managing the government's already-significant production program, and in the spring of 1940, soon after the Nazi blitzkrieg over France, Roosevelt created two new entities, the Office of Emergency Management (OEM), a White House agency charged with coordinating government defense efforts, and the National Defense Advisory Committee (NDAC), a group of business leaders and government officials tasked with overseeing war production. While the OEM had some success, the NDAC, whose purview was vague and its powers limited, did little to bring together the competing business, labor, and governmental interests that controlled the war economy.[6]

Although several titans of business served on the NDAC board, William Knudsen, chairman of General Motors, was viewed by all as the leader of the group. His second-in-command, appointed to represent labor interests, was Sidney Hillman. Born in Lithuania to a family with a long tradition in rabbinical studies, Hillman immigrated to the United States in 1907. Having gained significant political experience in Russia through his activities in the socialist Bund society, Hillman took a job as a garment cutter in Chicago, quickly rose in the ranks of the labor movement, and helped to found the Amalgamated Clothing Workers of America. During the 1930s, as leader of his union, Hillman was a crucial participant in the formation of the Congress of Industrial Organizations (CIO).[7]

An early supporter of FDR, during the New Deal Hillman was widely known as the most powerful labor advocate in the administration. Hillman's increasing power, however, placed him at odds with his labor comrades, because, like Weaver, he frequently had to make compromises to secure benefits for his constituency. Hillman's activities during the war, which frequently involved subordinating the goals of workers in the name of production, would greatly strain his relationships with the labor movement.[8]

While Roosevelt organized the government for war, civil rights leaders continued to press for equal treatment in war industries and in the military. In the spring of 1940, several activists formed a coalition called the Committee on Participation of Negroes in the National Defense Program, led by Howard University professor Rayford Logan, to pressure the government to deny contracts to employers that discriminated and to secure a "fair share" of positions for blacks in the armed forces. One of their first requests was to ask Hillman to appoint a "Negro consultant" to his office in the NDAC.[9]

During the spring and early summer, while he was still working at the U.S. Housing Authority, Weaver participated in the meetings of Logan's committee and conducted research for them on discrimination in war industries. The record does not show who promoted Weaver as Hillman's consultant, but he was the obvious choice. As leader of the black professionals in the government, Weaver brought instant credibility to the office and muted complaints that the agency did not take discrimination seriously. Weaver's stature was such that civil rights lawyer Thurgood Marshall told him that he was "the only man to handle the job." Hillman also received pressure from Eleanor Roosevelt to protect the interests of black workers, and it is possible that she recommended Weaver to Hillman. On 9 July, Hillman announced that he had hired Weaver "to assist him in integrating colored persons into the training and industrial phases of the defense program."[10]

Though Hillman was committed, in principle, to opportunities for blacks, Weaver's appointment was also political: an early effort to secure the votes of African Americans in the upcoming elections. Soon after Weaver's appointment, Hillman issued a press release stating that "workers should not be discriminated against because of age, sex, race or color." The release argued that the policy was "similar to protective measures developed by Dr. Robert C. Weaver," for the Public Works Administration. It further noted that the U.S. Office of Education had also issued a policy prohibiting discrimination. The *Pittsburgh Courier* reported that these provisions were due to Weaver's advocacy. For several years, however, they would be empty statements with little practical impact.[11]

Weaver later described Hillman as "the smartest man I ever worked under, and the hardest man to get to do anything on this [the race] problem, being a minority himself." According to his biographer, Hillman's approach to the matter was to "equivocate and placate." He "deliberately avoided any vigorous effort to enforce the government's nondiscrimination policy." Lacking much support in his new job, Weaver spent much of his time lobbying companies in search of small victories, for example, the hiring of 150 black carpenters in St. Louis and 300 bricklayers in Indiana. The limitations of Weaver's agency were due to its lack of legal influence. The committee was powerless to order employers or labor unions to do anything, and unsurprisingly, its statements of support for equal treatment had little impact.[12]

Stymied by employers and labor unions, Weaver worked to prepare blacks for jobs he hoped would be opened up to them later. To meet the increasing need for skilled workers in new fields such as aircraft production, Congress created the National Defense Training Program. However, in December 1940, out of 115,000 trainees in the pipeline, only 1,900 were black. Black participation in the vocational system, particularly in the South but also in the North, had always been restricted by local officials who wanted to reserve these benefits for white males. They were supported by federal officials, who generally started their careers in the local offices. Training opportunities for blacks were also limited in the South by the rudimentary provisions for vocational training at black high schools and colleges. As in all parts of the segregated system, separate was not equal in the education of skilled workers.[13]

A supplementary appropriation for vocational education passed by Congress in 1940 specifically banned discrimination on the basis of sex, race, or color. But, as they had in the past, education officials argued that it was pointless to train blacks for jobs that they could not secure even if qualified, continuing the vicious cycle of exclusion. In some northern cities, protest opened vocational training programs, but in many places schools devised tests that excluded blacks. Throughout his first year, Weaver constantly peppered federal education officials with requests for information on the status of black applicants and provided them with contacts at companies that were willing to hire blacks for jobs if they received training. New occupations, which were not yet racially restricted, he argued, provided the potential for progress. Weaver's efforts were successful in creating opportunities for a small number of individuals but achieved no structural reforms. According to Weaver, the agency "for two years resisted any and all changes in racial policy which would modify the states' traditional approaches to vocational education."[14]

In addition to lobbying for policy reform, Weaver spent a great deal of time talking to African Americans about the defense program and urging them to participate. Although discrimination was a reality, he argued, that did not absolve blacks of the responsibility to fight to enroll in training. "We know there are psychological resistances to all change. Often they are exaggerated. But we must face their existence and reckon with them," he told readers of the National Urban League journal *Opportunity.* When shortages in labor occurred, there would be expanded job opportunities for minority racial groups, and employers would "change their minds about using colored labor," he argued.[15]

Although Weaver's forecast eventually came true for many blacks as the war intensified, in 1940 discrimination was the norm in both war industries and the military. The exclusion of blacks from almost all aspects of military service was enforced with an iron hand by the predominantly southern military leadership. Under pressure from Roosevelt, the services agreed to admit blacks, but only in segregated units.[16]

Civil rights leaders were pleased with the president's statements on the importance of blacks to the defense effort, but they opposed the expansion of Jim Crow. At the urging of Eleanor Roosevelt, FDR agreed to meet with a small group of civil rights leaders, including Walter White and T. Arnold Hill of the National Urban League to discuss the issue. They presented to the president a memo prepared by Charles Houston, William Hastie, and Weaver that called for the integration of blacks into all aspects of the defense program, including officer training, the use of black medical professionals, and the appointment of blacks to advisory positions throughout the military. But Secretary of the Navy Frank Knox and Assistant Secretary of the Army Robert Patterson objected. Knox argued that blacks could not serve in the navy, because the races could not operate together in the close quarters of a ship. Patterson, who was later described as a man who believed that "anyone who disagrees with him is not only wrong, but wrong from bad motives—probably treasonable," argued that an integrated program would cause great problems for the army's activities in the South.[17]

The president listened attentively to the requests of civil rights leaders but, fearing a mutiny from his military leaders, issued a declaration that the government's policy was "not to intermingle colored and white personnel in the same regimental organizations." Although the October appointments of Hastie and Davis to the president's war team enabled Roosevelt to survive the election without further complaints, civil rights leaders were livid, and these palliatives would not be sufficient to end the objections of African Americans.[18]

After his reelection, FDR continued to face pressure from civil rights leaders to open up the military and the defense industries, but he had other worries on his plate. Large among his concerns was the failure of the existing governmental system to manage the expanding war economy. The increasing number of military contracts led to supply shortages and profiteering by companies that held monopolies in their industries. To improve the efficiency of war production, in January 1941 FDR created a new organization, the Office of Production Management (OPM). He appointed Hillman and Knudsen cochairs and charged them with mediating disputes among business leaders, military officials, and union leaders that were impeding war production. Though their titles had changed, little else was different about the new agency, and it continued to struggle to meet its mandate.[19]

In his many radio addresses before the United States declared war, FDR frequently stated that all Americans should benefit from the improving economy. "There will be no divisions of party or section or race or nationality or religion," as there was "not one among us who does not have a stake in the outcome of the effort," he argued in March 1941. But FDR's staff did little to implement the president's flowery promises. If Hillman was afraid of pushing too hard on nondiscrimination, his colleague William Knudsen was adamantly opposed to any action at all in that area. Knudsen frequently argued that it was not the government's job to interfere in an employer's decision on whom to hire. His company, General Motors, received hundreds of millions of dollars to construct facilities to build tanks, artillery, ammunition, and other products for the military from 1940 on. However, despite the promises of the administration, from the beginning of his tenure, Weaver received numerous complaints that many of the company's divisions refused to hire blacks. Several plants told black prospects that they would not even accept their applications. In January, Walter White, who had personally investigated many claims against the company, told Knudsen that discrimination at General Motors was "more wide-spread now than it has ever been before." He asked the chair to "use your great influence" to change General Motors policy, but Knudsen blandly replied that he had "severed active relationship" (which was not true) with the company when he accepted his government position.[20]

Discrimination in the rapidly expanding aircraft industry remained particularly strong. Just weeks after the president's promise of equal treatment, J. H. Kindleberger, the North American Aviation official who was spearheading the construction of a massive new plant in Kansas City, announced even before the plant opened that, in staffing the operation, "Negroes will be considered only as janitors and in other similar capacities." The company, a subsidiary of General Motors, had received $133 million from the federal government in construction contracts to build planes in several facilities that would, when completed, employ several thousand workers. But these opportunities would be closed to blacks. Kindleberger told reporters that "under no circumstances would Negroes be employed as aircraft workers or mechanics . . . regardless of their training."[21]

This bold rejection of equal opportunity was met with swift condemnation by civil rights leaders. "Such an edict could very easily bear Berlin as its place of origin with the substitute of the name of Adolf Hitler for that of J. H. Kindleberger," Walter White argued. "We respectfully submit that if the stake of Negro Americans is in the maintenance of a system in which they are to be denied employment and restricted in opportunity, then the effort is not one which can command their full loyalty and unstinted support." Knudsen, who remained chair of General Motors, told civil rights leaders that the OPM "had no authority to force plants to employ Negro workers." Weaver told Wilkins that his office was "formulating plans for a discussion" with Kindleberger and would "exert every effort to secure equitable employment opportunities" at the plant, but these efforts did not produce any immediate results.[22]

NAACP leaders continued to use political connections and lobbying to reform government and business policies, but the bald denial of jobs at defense plants radicalized many blacks. Across the country, African Americans were organizing to fight discrimination, and union head A. Philip Randolph was the spiritual and practical leader of this movement. In January 1941, Randolph called for thousands of blacks to march on Washington, DC, to demand fair treatment in the military and defense industries: "I think we ought to get 10,000 Negroes and march down Pennsylvania Avenue asking for jobs in defense plants and integration of the armed forces." At the time, few people took his statement seriously. The idea of African Americans taking such a confrontational stance in not only the nation's capital but a southern city was hard for many whites, and African Americans, to fathom. The *Chicago Defender* argued that getting 10,000 blacks together for such an effort "would be the miracle of the century." But during the months that followed black activists worked to make the march a reality.[23]

In March, Randolph announced that the protest would occur on 1 July. Across the country, blacks established March on Washington Movement chapters that sold buttons stating "Democracy Not Hypocrisy—Jobs Not Alms." Randolph issued an 8 Point Program for the movement stating, "for the Negro . . . the fight for democracy has meaning only when it grants to them the full measure of every right as well as of every obligation for which democracy stands." Randolph demanded abolition of segregation in the military, an end to job discrimination, and representation of blacks in all aspects of the defense program. In late spring, there were offices in Harlem, Brooklyn, Washington, Pittsburgh, Detroit, Chicago, St. Louis, and San Francisco, and thousands attended rallies to promote the cause. By May, Randolph, emboldened by the activity, announced that he expected 100,000 blacks to converge on the nation's capital.[24]

As the date drew nearer, and they received reports that the protest was going to be a reality, the president and his aides became increasingly concerned. They worried there would be a race riot that would be an international embarrassment to the president and would weaken his efforts to promote unity for the war effort. In response, FDR pressed Hillman and Knudsen to take action to improve the administration's profile on racial issues. In April, Hillman announced that Weaver was being transferred to the OPM to spearhead a new section devoted to "the integration of Negroes into the defense effort." Weaver's new title would be director of the Negro Employment and Training Branch.[25]

Hillman also released a letter that he had sent to holders of defense contracts arguing that discrimination against blacks was "extremely wasteful of our human resources" and urging them "to examine their employment and training policies at once." His cochair, Knudsen, who continued to oppose any government intervention in the area of hiring, refused to sign the letter. Hillman also made several speeches to black groups promoting these actions. In one, he noted that, through Weaver's efforts, black workers, including more than 2,500 carpenters, were being employed in the construction of military training facilities in the South. The editors of the *New York Amsterdam News* stated that Hillman had "spoken boldly" but argued that, "unless he follows through with something more punitive than a mere plea, his words are going to fall on deaf ears." The *Chicago Defender* called Hillman's remarks "a theatrical stunt intended only for the gallery."[26]

Throughout the spring, Weaver issued a flurry of press releases marking the achievements of his office in securing training and employment for blacks. In late April, he announced that several manufacturing companies had told him that they planned to train and hire black workers, including one unnamed aircraft plant that promised to take 1,200 blacks when their operation was fully functional. As the date of the march neared, and complaints about discrimination continued, Weaver began to get more specific commitments from employers. "Negro workers . . . are scheduled to play an important role in making America an 'arsenal for the democracies,'" a June release began. Among the deals brokered by Weaver's office were the promise by the Curtiss-Wright aircraft plant in Buffalo to train 1,200 black workers, an agreement from the Atlas Powder Company to recruit at least 1,000 black workers in Ohio, and a notice that E. I. Dupont de Nemours Company would hire at least 670 blacks at their Indiana ordinance plant.[27]

The fight over war discrimination placed Weaver in the awkward position he would occupy throughout his long career. Some civil rights leaders responded that Weaver's statements were premature: that the companies had not actually hired black workers; they only stated that they would open training classes to them and/or would hire in the future. Furthermore, few of the employers stated what kind of jobs would be available to blacks. Roy Wilkins accused Weaver's office of issuing a report on the Curtiss-Wright plant in Paterson, New Jersey, that "painted a rosy picture of employment for Negroes" that was "greatly at variance" with the feelings of blacks in the community, and Weaver agreed that the employment of 16 blacks at a plant of 16,000 workers was not a victory.[28]

As the date for the march approached, both civil rights leaders and FDR enlisted Eleanor Roosevelt to mediate the dispute. In late May, the First Lady convened a group for lunch at the White House to discuss discrimination in defense industries. She summoned Hillman and Weaver (who remembered it as his first White House visit) and grilled Hillman about what he was doing to end discrimination. Hillman stumbled about for an answer, and she pushed him to do more. Weaver later remembered that Hillman was "more responsive" thereafter, but the change produced only marginal improvements. Hillman, of course, was not the main problem—intransigent employers were.[29]

After the war ended, Weaver stated that he did not receive much help from the top officials in promoting fair treatment for blacks. "The OPM responded feebly to the demands of Negroes" before the march on Washington, Weaver asserted in 1946. Despite his constant requests for more people to investigate complaints and negotiate employment agreements, agency leaders concluded that the market would create new opportunities for blacks as white unemployment decreased. Federal intervention, they argued, was not necessary. Although this might be true in the long run, Weaver argued, discrimination prevented blacks from exploiting opportunities now. Dealing with this exclusion "could not be handled effectively by a staff of about ten field representatives," he concluded. Only a national commitment could solve the problem.[30]

In the months leading up to the war, Weaver did not deny that discrimination continued to plague most workplaces, but he focused on the improvements that his office observed. While the majority of the releases from his office promoted commitments to hire, Weaver also celebrated actual increases in black employment. In Michigan, he announced that 2,360 blacks were placed by the local office of the U.S. Employment Service during the first quarter of the year, and he trumpeted achievements in getting training classes in the aircraft industries open to blacks. However, the number of blacks actually enrolled in these classes remained low throughout the year.[31]

Weaver's press releases did little to assuage the complaints about continued discrimination. In May, Randolph declared that the march would go on, ending in a rally at the Lincoln Monument. In response, the White House did everything it could to prevent the protest from happening. In a last-ditch effort, on 18 June, the president invited Randolph and Walter White to meet with him and the production officials. Randolph told FDR that the march would go on unless the president issued an executive order banning segregation in the military and discrimination in all defense production programs. After Randolph and White convinced the president that they really planned to hold the march, FDR agreed to issue an order.[32]

For the next week, the parties negotiated over the content of the directive, which was finally issued on 25 June 1941. Executive Order 8802 declared that "it is the policy of the United States to encourage full participation in the national defense program by all citizens . . . regardless of race, creed, color, or national origin." The order directed all government agencies to take steps to prevent discrimination in their training programs and instructed them to place in each defense contract a provision prohibiting discrimination. Finally, the directive established a Committee on Fair Employment Practices (which would later be called the Fair Employment Practices Committee [FEPC]) within the OPM to "receive and investigate complaints of discrimination." The order made no mention of discrimination or segregation in the military.[33]

Weaver did not take part in the organization of the march, nor was he involved in the negotiations over the order, but he later claimed that he "knew exactly what was happening." Weaver stated that he supported the march and believed that it helped him in his efforts to move intransigent government officials toward recognizing the problem of discrimination. Although the releases that Weaver issued were interpreted by some to support the argument that the march was not necessary, Weaver claimed that he took other actions that supported Randolph's efforts, such as providing evidence of discrimination that march organizers could use to make their case.[34]

The president's declaration was far from everything that organizers had demanded, but Randolph agreed to call off the march. He and White called the order a "second Emancipation Proclamation." Though some people criticized the compromise, most black leaders praised the outcome. The *Chicago Defender* argued that the order was "one of the most significant pronouncements that has been made in the interest of the Negro for more than a century," and Lester Granger wrote that the president's "act was truly a momentous one." Some, however, questioned how the order would be enforced. Marjorie McKenzie, writing in the *Philadelphia Tribune*, argued that the FEPC, which would be run by volunteers and did not have the authority to compel employers to comply, would have little impact. Weaver's efforts at the OPM, she contended, were likely to produce more reform. McKenzie's comments presaged the future conflict that Weaver would have with the group.[35]

DURING THE SUMMER of 1941, Weaver organized his office within the OPM, hiring more than twenty professionals to receive and investigate claims of discrimination and to gather data on employment and training trends. The staff toured the country, meeting with employers and civil rights groups to negotiate agreements to hire black workers. In July, he issued a release stating that Brewster Aeronautical had agreed to train blacks for their facility at Long Island City. The announcement created a controversy that illuminates the difficult position he held as an activist operating within a system that changed only slowly and grudgingly. NAACP officials in New York had been watching the plant since it was organized. In early 1941, investigators accused the company of rejecting black applicants without consideration, a claim the company denied. In April, activists planned to picket the company's Manhattan headquarters but canceled the protest at the last moment when company officials promised to train and hire black workers.[36]

While African Americans did enter the training program affiliated with the company, Brewster Aeronautical was slow to employ black graduates. At the end of July, Weaver announced that Brewster had hired "a crew" of black sheet-metal workers for the plant, but NAACP officials felt the company had accepted only a few tokens to relieve the pressure. The organization had just received several complaints from blacks whom the company had rejected. Roy Wilkins reported that NAACP staff were "literally raging at Bob Weaver for the kind of stuff OPM has been sending out." He and White agreed to "call OPM to task" and to single out Weaver for criticism.[37]

On 1 August, the association issued a press release that began: "Contrary to the optimistic stories sent out from the Office of Production Management by Robert C. Weaver," the NAACP had learned that Brewster Aeronautical "had made no steps to drop its color bars." Acknowledging that Brewster Aeronautical had recently hired five black workers, the release stated that three qualified blacks had been turned down while white applicants were hired. "Most flagrant is the case of Edmond Van Osten, 31 of Brooklyn, who has nine years of experience as a sheet metal worker," they asserted. According to the NAACP, when Van Osten applied, the personnel officer told him that he "would not hire any more colored workers." Van Osten alleged that he saw thirty-five to forty whites hired for the same position while he was at the office. His allegations were supported by an official of the New York State Employment Service, who argued that, after hiring a small number of blacks, Brewster Aeronautical had continued to reject black applicants "without exception and regardless of their qualifications."[38]

Weaver responded immediately to the allegations. He pointed out: "If the company has hired any Negroes it certainly must have made at least an initial step toward dropping its color bar" and argued that the purpose of the releases was to alert blacks to new opportunities and to get them to enroll in the training programs. "Obviously, we have no illusions about the effect of the placement of a few colored workers," he wrote White. "Nor do we believe that a factual statement of such placement will lull Negroes into inactivity in this regard. On the other hand, we all have a responsibility to encourage colored workers to avail themselves of all training." In another press release, Weaver stated that the company had hired seven black workers since the end of June. He further argued that his office had investigated the claims of the three workers and found them unwarranted. The workers, Weaver argued, either did not have the requisite skills or had applied for jobs where there were more trainees than openings.[39]

Weaver complained that NAACP officials had "made an uninvestigated rumor the basis for an open attack on the reliability of my office," and White responded that the office had issued the releases to show that "extreme care should be used in preventing too optimistic reports being circulated regarding employment practices of defense industries which have hitherto discriminated." White was not alone in his criticism. Columnist Charley Cherokee, while acknowledging Weaver's "history-making gains for Negro skilled labor," argued that Weaver lessened his stature by "making grand optimistic announcements" whenever a few workers were hired.[40]

The exchanges between Weaver and the NAACP became so heated that other civil rights leaders worried about the creation of an insurmountable rift. White, however, stated that he and Weaver were good friends and that he expected that friendship to "continue always." He said that there was "nothing personal" in his criticism, but he contended that "Dr. Weaver's office is not checking as carefully as should be done" the true facts of the employment policies of defense companies. The workers Brewster Aeronautical hired were "tokens," and the NAACP thought that Weaver was making an "overstatement which would do harm to the efforts to break down discrimination." Wilkins wrote a colleague that "there is no great breach between Weaver and the N.A.A.C.P." and that he did not expect any "coolness" between their offices to linger.[41]

But the conflict among civil rights leaders paled in comparison with the violence committed against black job pioneers. Much of Weaver's attention, along with that of civil rights activists, focused on the expanding defense effort in Detroit. By 1941, people were streaming into the city to take jobs in the dozens of facilities that were gearing up to produce planes, tanks, and other war necessities. With the support of the union leadership, Weaver was able to negotiate agreements protecting the rights of black workers, but frequently the white union members ignored the directives of their own leaders. For example, in September 1941, when the Packard Motor Company promoted two blacks to the metal-polishing department, 250 white workers staged a sit-down strike. To assuage the protestors, management backed down and demoted the black workers. While Weaver fought this decision, the black workers, fearing for their safety, declined to return to work. Similar events occurred at several other area defense plants, revealing the numerous obstacles that black workers faced in their efforts to secure wartime jobs.[42]

IN ADDITION TO managing his office in the OPM, Weaver participated in shaping the president's Committee on Fair Employment Practices. Historians have judged the creation of the committee a formative moment in the civil rights movement. As the first government institution created specifically to promote racial equality, the FEPC deserves the status that it has received. However, most students of the agency have concluded that it had little practical effect on the job prospects of minority workers. Throughout the committee's short life, Weaver had a complicated relationship with the group. Because he was charged with the same responsibilities but working in a different agency, Weaver frequently found himself in competition with his civil rights peers. At the same time, the more aggressive tactics of the FEPC frequently put it at odds with Weaver, who generally pursued a path of quiet negotiation.

The president's executive order placed the FEPC under the oversight of the OPM, making Weaver an influential person in the group's organization. While most African Americans cheered the president's executive order, the institution he created was very limited in its authority. The FEPC's initial budget was only $80,000, so it could hire only a few staff members. Furthermore, the organization did not have the ability to subpoena or fine companies that violated the order. Rather, it had to rely on advocacy and persuasion. What the FEPC did have going for it were several members who took the issue of discrimination seriously. After much lobbying, the president appointed two African Americans, Chicago alderman Ernest Dickerson and porters union vice president Milton Webster, to the group. They were joined by David Sarnoff, chairman of RCA, and union leaders William Green of the American Federation of Labor and Philip Murray of the Congress of Industrial Organizations. The president asked Louisville newspaperman and southern liberal Mark Ethridge to chair the FEPC. Soon thereafter, the FEPC hired Lawrence Cramer, former governor of the Virgin Islands, as executive director.[43]

Lacking the resources to hire a full staff, Cramer decided to rely on Weaver and his office, giving them responsibility for investigating complaints and negotiating with employers. The FEPC would serve as a board of appeal when no solution could be reached. This approach, which was opposed by Dickerson and Webster, frustrated some civil rights leaders, including NAACP head Walter White. When White wrote to the FEPC to complain about discrimination at Brewster Aeronautical, Cramer replied that Weaver had briefed them on the matter and they had found no violations. White requested that the FEPC conduct an "independent investigation," which they declined to do.[44]

While Weaver and his staff continued to mediate disputes and create job opportunities at individual companies, the FEPC decided to focus on public relations to promote the cause of equal opportunity. After much discussion, and reluctance from some of the white members, they agreed to conduct investigative hearings in Los Angeles, Chicago, and New York. During the fall of 1941 and into early 1942, the hearings, which exposed the depth of discrimination in three major areas of defense production, drew great attention from black newspapers and not very much from anyone else.[45]

Weaver tried to use the embarrassment that the exposure created for companies and unions to negotiate agreements to hire black workers. In California, he succeeded in getting the boilermakers union, which prevented blacks from getting jobs at sites with labor agreements by denying them membership, to permit blacks to take jobs at Oakland shipyards. That the union required blacks to join "auxiliary unions" which required them to pay dues but gave them no influence over union policies disturbed Weaver and his staff, but their immediate concern was increasing the number of jobs, not promoting full equality within the labor movement. In other cases where the hearings exposed discrimination, such as in Chicago's General Motors plant, Weaver was unable to use the information to reform company policies.[46]

By mid-1941, FDR and most other people in the administration realized that it was only a matter of time before the United States would be forced to enter World War II. The Japanese attack on Pearl Harbor on 7 December 1941 made that decision easy. Immediately after declaring war on the Axis powers, Roosevelt moved to organize the wartime production system. Almost everyone agreed that the OPM had not been successful in managing the country's defense production, and in early January the president announced that he was creating the War Production Board (WPB) to oversee the use of materials and labor in the production of the ships, tanks, and other matériel necessary to win the war. Roosevelt chose former Sears, Roebuck executive Donald Nelson to run the organization. OPM head Knudsen found out from news reports that his job had been eliminated. Hillman was demoted to head of the Labor Division under Nelson. For the third time in three years, Weaver found himself transferred.[47]

In his new position as chief of the Negro Manpower Division, with the war mobilization heating up, Weaver saw progress in job opportunities for blacks. By February 1942, his office had contacted more than 600 firms involved in the defense effort, negotiated 248 agreements to employ blacks, and was in the process of negotiating another 204. The work of his office, Weaver argued, was producing results. In a survey of 158 plants, his staff found 33,335 African American workers. Blacks had succeeded in opening up several fields. In the aircraft industry, 5,286 blacks were at work in 49 plants, a dramatic increase for an industry that had employed only a handful two years earlier. In shipbuilding, where blacks had always been employed in large numbers, 13,000 African Americans toiled. That was in addition to the 14,000 blacks working in U.S. Navy yards, up from 6,000 two years earlier.[48]

But Weaver acknowledged that these victories were "not satisfactory numerically." At the time of Weaver's report, blacks, who constituted more than 10 percent of the population, represented just 3 percent of all war workers, and one federal survey found that firms still refused to consider hiring African Americans in half of the positions that were available. As a result, the unemployment rate for blacks remained three times higher than that for whites. In the face of continuing discrimination, black resentment in many cities increased dramatically. According to a report by the Office of War Information, a majority of blacks stated that they were worse off than they had been before the war, and most did not think that conditions would improve after the conflict ended.[49]

The work of Weaver's office, along with that of the FEPC and civil rights leaders across the country, certainly played a role in the improving, but still limited, job prospects for black workers. But the war economy, which caused the unemployment rate to plummet, was the main reason for the opening of job opportunities. By early 1942, with the military draft drawing more and more young men into the armed services at the same time that the federal government began spending the billions of dollars authorized for military production, employers were increasingly desperate for workers. They stole skilled and unskilled employees from each other, bidding up wage rates to ensure that they did not have to slow production for lack of bodies.

Witnessing the increasing competition for bodies, Roosevelt's advisors told him that the federal government needed to be more directly involved in the allocation of workers to ensure that vital production was not sacrificed to lesser needs. After a typically long and tortuous process, FDR created the War Manpower Commission (WMC), which he charged with determining how the workforce would be allocated between the factories and the military. Over its first year, Roosevelt dramatically expanded the commission's authority, and it would control the lives of Americans workers for the rest of the conflict.[50]

Sidney Hillman hoped that the president would appoint him to head the WMC, which was to replace his office, but Hillman's support among labor leaders and New Deal liberals had evaporated during his two years in government. Instead, Roosevelt chose former Indiana governor Paul McNutt, a rising star in the Democratic Party during the 1930s. In 1940, McNutt was widely rumored to be one of the top choices for the vice presidential nomination, and many talked about him as a successor to the president. During his two years directing the labor of more than fifty million Americans, however, McNutt's star would lose much of its luster.[51]

McNutt took the job cognizant of the need to include black workers in the expanding defense effort. When McNutt met with civil rights leaders soon after his appointment, he immediately announced that he was creating a Negro Division in the WMC to make sure that blacks were included in the manpower program. To run this division, McNutt had already hired Weaver, who left his job at the soon-to-be-dismantled Labor Division of the OPM.[52]

Weaver moved from his old position to the new one with relative ease, but the abolition of the OPM placed the FEPC in limbo. Committee members worried that the president was trying to dismantle the group, and FDR was feeling increasing pressure to control the FEPC, which had angered southerners by holding a series of hearings on discrimination in Birmingham, Alabama. Just weeks after the hearings, FDR surprised committee members by announcing that the FEPC would be placed under the oversight of McNutt and the WMC. Civil rights leaders objected that the transfer would undermine the independence of the committee and they protested to the president.[53]

FEPC leaders argued that they could not be successful with the WMC looking over their shoulders, and they criticized Weaver's efforts. Ernest Dickerson claimed that Weaver's methods had been tried for a year and a half before the issuance of the executive order with little positive impact. Board member Mark Ethridge claimed that, if McNutt's plan was adopted, Weaver would be the real director of the equal-opportunity program. Jonathan Daniels, a confidant of the president who took on an increasing role in the administration's racial policies during the war, preferred the approach of Weaver and Will Alexander (who was in charge of "other minorities")—quiet negotiation—over the FEPC's public declarations. This fact, of course, made Weaver even more suspect in the eyes of the more aggressive members of the FEPC board and staff, as well as civil rights activists outside the government.[54]

After several months of heated discussion and much pressure on the administration, McNutt announced that Weaver's division would be abolished and that his investigators would be transferred to the FEPC. The FEPC would have a budget to pay the regional staff as well as a staff in Washington, DC. Although the *Chicago Defender* announced the decision with the headline "And He's Out!" Weaver received yet another job title: assistant to the director of operations of the WMC. The FEPC succeeded in securing more autonomy than McNutt originally envisioned, but the commissioner still had the authority to approve all major actions. Most importantly, all decisions on future hearings were subject to McNutt's approval. The turmoil raised by the transfer of the FEPC caused Will Alexander to resign his post in disgust at the end of 1942, but Weaver stayed on, choosing to continue the fight from within. While Weaver's title changed frequently, his job remained the same—persuasion and negotiation with employers and training programs to open opportunities to African Americans.[55]

Many compromises had to be made in the pursuit of jobs for African Americans. The Sun Shipbuilding Company, located just south of Philadelphia in Chester, was a major provider of defense vessels and had employed blacks since its inception, generally in low-skilled occupations. In 1941 it informed Weaver that it planned to expand opportunities for blacks in several trades and double the number of black workers to 1,500. In 1942, Sun president John Pew, an advocate for black advancement in the paternalistic mode of Henry Ford, announced that the company would open a new yard and would hire more than 9,000 black workers to operate it. Although many cheered the possibility of higher-paying positions, the plan concerned civil rights leaders because Pew stated that the yard would employ only blacks, who would remain excluded from other shipyards.[56]

NAACP head Walter White immediately protested the creation of the segregated yard. While "not unappreciative of the importance to the 9,000 Negroes" who would be employed, he wrote Pew, White questioned the "wisdom and long-range value" of the segregated system and pointed out that blacks and whites had been working side by side in numerous defense industries and dying together in war. But the NAACP's opposition to Sun's plan brought it severe criticism from several black leaders, who questioned their "whole loaf or none policy." The editor of the *Philadelphia Record* told White that "under normal circumstances I'd go along with you in your objections" but claimed that "the advantages outweigh the Jim Crow implications." White argued that there was no reason to accept "second-class status." The demand for workers in the shipyards was so high, he claimed, that blacks could take jobs "on the same basis as anyone else."[57]

Unlike many other hiring announcements, Weaver's office did not trumpet Sun's plan. He later wrote that the decision to segregate workers was "unfortunate." White complained to the FEPC about the plan, but the committee declined to intervene, arguing that it could not make "hypothetical conjectures" when there was no complaint of discrimination by any aggrieved person. Yard Four opened in late 1942. By the end of the conflict, Sun employed over 15,000 black workers: 6,500 in the segregated yard, and the remainder in other yards.[58]

DESPITE THE GAINS in black employment and in the military, compromises like those at Sun Shipbuilding, combined with the continued intransigence within government and in the private sector, took their toll on many civil rights leaders. After January 1943, Weaver would have to continue the fight to reform the bureaucracy without his good friend William Hastie. For three years, Hastie, as aide to Secretary of War Henry Stimson, had struggled to improve the conditions for blacks in the military but had achieved only small victories. Segregation continued almost without exception, and the facilities and training programs for blacks, while separate, were far from equal. Hastie's arguments for the gradual integration of new services like the Air Corps were met with unyielding opposition in the armed services. Secretary of War Stimson, Undersecretary Patterson, Navy Secretary Knox, and their subordinates rejected any measures that they perceived would affect the "morale" of the forces. Seeing this constant opposition, Hastie decided that he could have a bigger impact by resigning and working "as a private citizen who can express himself upon such issues than as a member of the War Department under obligation to refrain from such public expressions."[59]

Civil rights leaders praised Hastie's decision. Journalist Louis Lautier wrote that "Bill Hastie has done an heroic thing." W. E. B. DuBois wrote in *Crisis* that there were two types of racial advisors in government. "One sort is the kind of upper clerk who transmits to the public with such apologetic airs as he can assume, the refusal of the department to follow his advice." The other kind "seeks to give advice and to get the facts and if he receives a reasonable amount of cooperation he works on hopefully. If he does not, he withdraws." To DuBois, it was "this second type of official alone who is useful and valuable. The other is nothing." Later that year, the NAACP awarded Hastie the Spingarn Medal, the highest honor the association bestowed, for his service to African Americans.[60]

Hastie resigned at the point that was in many ways the nadir of the effort to secure fair treatment for blacks. Just weeks later, McNutt would create another furor when he canceled hearings that the FEPC had scheduled to examine discrimination on southern railroads. The decision was a victory for southern segregationists, and civil rights leaders took it extremely hard. The editors of the *Pittsburgh Courier* called it "the final triumph of a long and consistent campaign to make the FEPC completely ineffective." Charles Hamilton Houston, who was serving as counsel to the FEPC, resigned, writing the president that it was time "government officials begin to realize that Negroes are citizens not wards," but FDR stood by the decision. Several committee members, Ethridge, McClean, Sarnoff, and Cramer resigned after the hearings were canceled, primarily for reasons unrelated to the decision, but many civil rights activists felt that the FEPC was being eliminated. In response to their vocal protests, Roosevelt told them that he still supported the organization and had created a committee to study the reorganization of the FEPC.[61]

After several months of more discussion about what to do with the committee, the president announced that he was creating a new office in the White House. To chair the reconstituted board, Roosevelt appointed Monsignor Francis Haas, who had led the National Labor Relations Board. He appointed several other liberals, including Justice Department lawyer Malcolm Ross, who were loyal to the administration. Though controlled by White House loyalists, the FEPC was rejuvenated by the decision. By the fall of 1943, the FEPC's twelve regional offices were actively investigating complaints of discrimination.[62]

After the war ended, Weaver argued that several institutional flaws prevented the FEPC from being more successful. The agency, he asserted, faced enormous pressure to produce immediate results. As a result, he felt, it neglected "long-run planning and programming." Weaver criticized the FEPC for failing to get government contracting agencies to enforce the nondiscrimination provisions that the executive order required. He also faulted the FEPC for failing to carefully investigate claims of discrimination before sending letters to employers accusing them of violating the order. The rush to judgment, he claimed, resulted in a loss of prestige for the organization.[63]

The biggest weakness of the FEPC, in Weaver's mind, was its decision to pursue individual complaints of discrimination instead of working, as his agency did, to negotiate changes in employment policies with companies prospectively. The FEPC's "legalistic," as opposed to Weaver's "economic," approach resulted in skewing its efforts toward the wrong employers, Weaver argued. In the aircraft industries, for example, many companies categorically refused to employ blacks. Blacks knew which companies had this policy, and they did not apply for jobs. Therefore, there were few complaints against the worst offenders. On the other hand, blacks flocked to the companies that were not totally exclusionary. When some of these applicants were rejected, they complained to the FEPC. As a result, the committee found itself investigating discrimination, which was real, at the most progressive companies and ignoring those with the worst records. This, Weaver claimed, "occasioned intense employer resentment against the FEPC." His views were seconded by his former associate, white southern liberal Will Alexander, who chided the FEPC for "always telling what they are going to do and not what they have done." Weaver, like Alexander, argued that more progress could be made by careful analysis and private negotiation than by public pressure. Both, of course, were necessary, but in terms of practical achievements, Weaver's efforts secured more jobs for blacks.[64]

THE RESOLUTION OF the FEPC controversy came just as a summer of racial tensions was beginning. The year 1943 marked a significant moment in race relations, signifying the growth of black assertiveness. Though they were not the first race riots, the conflicts of the summer, particularly the largest, in Detroit, gave notice to the country that African Americans would not accept second-class status without struggle, violent if necessary. The Motor City's racial situation since a February 1942 conflagration at the Sojourner Truth homes, a black public housing project in a white area, had only deteriorated, as blacks increasingly demanded equal treatment at workplaces, in unions, in housing, and particularly in the city's social life, and whites adamantly resisted all gains. No one was surprised when violence erupted in June, but many people were shocked by its severity. The conflict began with several small incidents at Belle Isle, a city park on the Detroit River. On 20 June, more than 100,000 people, the majority of them black, had traveled to the park to seek relief from the early summer heat. Late that night, several fights, some between military men on leave, broke out in the park and the adjacent area.[65]

The violence quickly spread to other sections of the city, where white mobs attacked blacks on the streets. At the same time, when a rumor spread that whites had attacked and killed blacks at Belle Isle, black youths in a nearby area began to attack whites. The violence lasted well into the next afternoon and was quelled only by the intervention of federal troops, requested by the governor several hours after it was clear they were needed. When it was all over, thirty-four people were dead, twenty-five of them black and nine of them white. Seventeen of the twenty-five blacks were killed by police bullets. Throughout the conflict, the police focused their attention on blacks, shooting people in the back and firing indiscriminately into black crowds, while allowing white rioters to continue their rampage.[66]

The Detroit riots were only the worst of the conflicts occurring during a summer which included race riots in Mobile, a mob of 10,000 whites in Beaumont, Texas, who killed two blacks and set fire to dozens of homes, and the "Zoot-Suit Riots" of Los Angeles, where groups of sailors attacked Mexican American and black youth. Then, in August, Harlem exploded for the second time in less than a decade. There, the immediate cause was a false rumor that a New York police officer had killed a black soldier. This brought thousands of blacks into the streets. The rioters concentrated on local businesses, smashing store windows and looting their stocks. While the New York Police Department did not unleash the wholesale attack that occurred in Detroit, when the conflict was over, six blacks were dead and 189 injured.[67]

Civil rights leaders blamed the violence on the continued efforts of whites to prevent blacks from becoming full-fledged citizens, while southern segregationists argued that the riots were the result of administration policies that made blacks "impudent." Congressman John Rankin (D-MS) blamed the FEPC, which was, he argued, "attempting to mix the races." Attorney General Francis Biddle was so concerned about race relations in urban areas that he recommended that FDR bar further migration of blacks to cities.[68]

During the summer, FDR confidant Jonathan Daniels played an increasingly important role in shaping the administration's racial policies. Born into a wealthy North Carolina family, Daniels's father served as secretary of the navy under Wilson. After graduating from college and failing out of Columbia Law School, Jonathan Daniels joined the family newspaper business. In the early 1930s, he became editor of the *Raleigh News and Observer,* a paper that he made a strong supporter of the New Deal. When the war started, Daniels came to Washington to work in the Office of Civilian Defense, and in 1943, he became administrative assistant to the president.

Viewed as a progressive (by southern standards) on race relations—Weaver described him as a "frightened liberal"—Daniels's most important responsibility was to advise FDR on the nation's racial situation.[69]

Much of Daniels's understanding of the problems facing African Americans evolved through his increasing contacts with Weaver. Weaver's soft-spoken manner and reputation as a "team player" made him attractive to the southerner, and Daniels sought out Weaver's advice. Weaver urged Daniels to get the president to commit to a more energetic effort to prohibit discrimination and to put the weight of the administration behind stopping racial violence. He argued that the roots of the violence lay in the continued discrimination blacks faced in jobs and housing and that morale among blacks was extremely low across the country. Sounding somewhat like the critics of civil rights activism, Weaver worried about the "reports of extreme racial chauvinism on the part of Negroes, of super-sensitiveness which complicates their problem of industrial employment and of a discrimination mindedness which influences their participation in the armed forces." He claimed that the treatment of blacks in the armed services was the largest cause of the problems, and he told Daniels that these obstacles could not be overcome by racial advisors in government agencies. Only the president, Weaver argued, could solve the racial tensions besetting the nation. Daniels took this advice to the president, who declined to act.[70]

During the fall of 1943, Weaver continued lobbying firms to hire blacks and government officials to remove obstacles in their programs. This job was made easier by the fact that ten million Americans were out of the job market and fighting the war. By the end of the year, however, Weaver decided that it was time to end his service in the federal government. The hot summer of 1943 clearly took its toll on Weaver. His memos to Daniels were much more emotional than the usual dry prose that he used in his government dealings. Still, Weaver did not make an event out of his decision to leave the government. There were no public letters or interviews as there had been with his friend Hastie. There were many reasons for Weaver's decision to leave the government after eleven years of service. He told one interviewer several decades later that "virtually no one within the administration shared his commitment to black participation."[71]

The creation of the new FEPC also hastened Weaver's departure. The president's reinvigoration of the committee had heartened activists and lessened the pressure on Weaver. But, although Weaver had good relations with many of the staff members, several of whom had previously worked for him, Weaver continued to disagree with the committee's approach to the problems of racial discrimination. The FEPC now had its own budget and a much-expanded staff, and it no longer needed the support of Weaver and his staff. Weaver saw his responsibilities in the employment sector decreased by the rise of the FEPC and, more importantly, the decline of opposition among large business to expanding black opportunities. At the same time, while the fighting in Europe and the South Pacific was just beginning in earnest, the defense production program was beginning to wind down.[72]

During the summer, Weaver began to tell friends that he was ready to leave, and several black papers reported his dissatisfaction with the White House. The editors of the *Chicago Defender,* who had been critical of Weaver, complained that his powers were being "usurped." Calling Weaver "one of the few real scholars of the race," the editors complained that "it is indeed regrettable" that the administration could not "employ the vision and clarity of the mind of Dr. Weaver to the full extent of his potentialities." Weaver told one interviewer that he was "being enmeshed in a maze of irrelevant and unimportant functions" in the WMC bureaucracy and that he wanted to get out.[73]

Announcing his resignation in early January 1944, Weaver told friends and reporters that he was leaving because congressional conservatives had taken control of the issues he cared about: jobs and housing. He advised blacks to organize to put Congress back in liberal hands in 1944, fearing that the gains made by the New Deal would be lost if the Right continued to hold power. Black journalists called the decision "the end of the black cabinet." Horace Cayton argued that Weaver was "the alpha and omega of bright young people to parade through Washington" and called it "an extraordinary thing" that the White House, given racial tensions across the nation, "would let the best trained Negro specialist" leave the government. "Because of what this indicates to the mentality of an administration, we have, all of us, black and white alike, lost plenty," Cayton concluded.[74]

Weaver celebrated the achievements that his office had made, but he believed that his agency had been far too timid in promoting equal treatment for blacks. In a few cities like New York, blacks had become fairly well integrated into the labor market. But in general, his superiors, Weaver argued, "ignored, delayed, or evaded" calls to push employers to hire more black workers. While McNutt and other officials said the right thing, "adopting fine statements of policy," their actions were softer than their words.[75]

By the time of Weaver's departure, the job situation for blacks was consistently improving but far from good. Blacks were only 3 percent of war workers in 1940, but by 1944 they constituted 8 percent of the workforce. The percentage of black skilled and semiskilled workers also increased significantly during the war years. Among the most significant gains were those in aircraft production and shipbuilding, the fields to which Weaver had devoted much of his attention. In the West Coast shipyards, particularly in Los Angeles (where they were 6.5 percent of workers) and San Francisco (where they represented 8.5 percent), blacks achieved major increases in their numbers. Despite the efforts of white workers to exclude them, the employment of blacks in southern yards also increased. The aircraft industry, which had employed fewer than 250 blacks in 1940, employed more than 100,000 by 1944, 6 percent of the total workforce. A significant percentage of these workers were black women.[76]

But blacks remained concentrated in the dirtiest, most dangerous jobs, particularly in the iron and steel industries. Despite significant gains, the percentage of black workers in the newly developing industries like scientific instruments, electrical production, and metalworking remained extremely small. In addition, blacks were concentrated in the largest companies. The overwhelming majority of smaller companies still excluded blacks without exception. When the war ended, and the massive factories inevitably scaled back production, this concentration of blacks would have significant implications.[77]

The war brought other gains to black workers. As a result of FEPC pressure, blacks increased their participation in the federal government. Government bureaucracies employed 60,000 African Americans at the beginning of the conflict (mostly in menial, low-paid positions), but by the end of the war there were 200,000 blacks in government service. In addition, while the Air Corps placed severe limitations on the number of blacks who were allowed to become pilots, it did train thousands of African Americans in aircraft maintenance and other ground operations. And while the navy had an almost-complete bar on blacks on its ships, it trained almost six thousand people in technical jobs to provide maintenance and other duties necessary to the naval program. The increase of black participation in training programs, one of Weaver's most determined pursuits, increased postwar opportunities for tens of thousands of workers.[78]

In 1944 black journalist Roi Ottley published a book on black America. Put together from articles first appearing in his newspaper column, Ottley titled the book *New World A-Coming: Inside Black America*. The purpose of the book was to chronicle the significant changes in the nation's race relations in the previous decade. It profiled many black leaders, including a long description of Weaver. "Top man today is handsome Doctor Robert C. Weaver," the entry began. Ottley described him as a man "who wears his clothes with a stylish flare, is of very light complexion—Negroes call him 'high yaller.' He is possessed of a refined intelligence, but is coolly aloof to acquaintances, and critics have pointed to this as a defect. Nicknamed 'Bob,' he is not one of the boys in a hail-fellow-well-met sense. Essentially, he is a student, discerning, deliberate, and removed." The book described the efforts of Weaver, Hastie, and others in the federal government to promote the interests of African Americans and retold the story of their role in President Roosevelt's decision to promote General Benjamin Davis. Widely reviewed in the media and read by black and white Americans, the book greatly increased Weaver's profile. By 1944, he was an established member of the black leadership class.[79]

Weaver was pleased with his status and with the significant gains made by African Americans during the war, but he left DC disheartened. He told reporters that he had planned on making a career of federal service, devoting himself to "the betterment of race relations." But he grew skeptical that significant progress could be made at the federal level in the postwar years. The future of race relations lay, he believed, in America's largest cities.

* 6 *

# Chicago and the Science of Race Relations

When he resigned from the War Manpower Commission (WMC), Weaver told reporters that his goal had been to make a career out of federal government service. However, the trials of the war years, and the constant pressure of being caught between intransigent bosses and, in Weaver's view, unrealistic activists, took their toll. No longer feeling that his impact was worth the aggravation, Weaver left federal service. He would return to Washington, DC, but not for almost twenty years.

His departure marked a major turning point in Weaver's career, beginning a decade in which he moved almost constantly from job to job in search of a place where he could best use his talents. Though these years were often frustrating for Weaver, they were also very productive. Between 1945 and 1948 alone, Weaver would publish two widely read books, be among the first Americans to visit the postwar Soviet Union, play a central role in the rise of a new approach to American race relations, and aid the NAACP's Supreme Court victory against racial discrimination in housing. By the end of this period, Weaver had established himself as one of the leading authorities on race relations in America. Although he would not be able to parlay his scholarly and activist experience into the academic position he desired, Weaver's postwar years were crucial ones in his path to power.

Weaver's first foray into this new world came in Chicago, a city that was physically and metaphorically at the center of the new regime of American race relations. From World War I through the end of World War II, the city saw its black population skyrocket, as hundreds of thousands of southern blacks boarded trains for what they called the "Promised Land." Chicago's racial history was as complex as the nation's. The site of the largest race riot in the country in 1919 and a place where job and housing discrimination ruled the lives of the city's black citizens and segregated them into a dense area called the South Side, Chicago was also the location of a vibrant black economic and social life and a place with a significant number of whites who looked favorably upon blacks' claims for equal treatment. During World War II, Chicago made significant progress in the fight against discrimination in war industries.[1]

During the postwar years, Chicago would become a focal point for the rise of a new framework that would come to be known as racial liberalism. By coincidence, Weaver left the government in the same month that Swedish economist Gunnar Myrdal published what quickly became the bible of this movement, *An American Dilemma: The Negro Problem and Modern Democracy*. The fruit of more than five years of work by Myrdal in collaboration with a large collection of American social scientists, the book served as the primary source for liberal intellectuals and policymakers and spurred the development of a new field that would have profound influence over American race relations. Weaver's years in Chicago marked the emergence of a new "science" of race relations: the development and implementation of theories positing that racial antagonism was primarily the result of ignorance. Though the theories took years to fully develop and were attacked as soon as they were formulated, their foundational principle was that, with careful direction from professionally trained experts, racial groups could learn to live in harmony.[2]

This new approach was paralleled by a growing focus by civil rights activists on legal reform. The emergence of a liberal Supreme Court aided the struggle against legal discrimination, providing civil rights lawyers with significant victories. They relied on social science theory and data to inform their legal arguments, increasing the importance of social scientists like Weaver in the assault on Jim Crow. Decisions such as *Shelley v. Kraemer*, in which the Court declared race-restrictive covenants unenforceable, were important steps on the road to *Brown* and the broader attack on segregation during the postwar years. Though grassroots organization and the struggle for political power continued to draw large numbers of African American activists, the framework of racial liberalism relied on professionals in the law and other fields to serve as mediators among the races. Weaver, one of the leading formulators of this approach to black progress, was a central actor in the creation of this new regime.

In the years after the war, Weaver and his peers toiled to influence American racial policies, winning some victories but making only slow progress in their efforts to end racial segregation. Through court cases and political activism, they succeeded in breaking down the legal barriers that supported discrimination and segregation. At the same time, they were unable to influence the deeper structures—political, social, and economic—that created a racially divided society. The successes and failures of their efforts illuminate the potential and limitations of the scientific approach to race relations, as well as the broader philosophy of liberalism out of which these theories grew.

WEAVER CAME TO Chicago at the behest of two men: his friend and patron Edwin Embree and Chicago mayor Edward Kelly. A product of the city's powerful machine, the Cook County Democratic Party, Kelly was appointed mayor in 1933 to replace Anton Cermak, who was killed in a botched assassination attempt on Franklin Roosevelt weeks before he was to enter the White House. Kelly, who served for fourteen years, became nationally known as a symbol of ethnic political power as he and Chicago party chair Pat Nash strengthened the big-city machine that would endure well into the 1980s. Although during his time Kelly wielded significant power in the national Democratic Party, he is primarily remembered as the leader of the nation's most corrupt big-city government and as the person who presided over a period of exceptional lawlessness in Chicago. At the same time, Kelly was successful in securing federal relief funds and employing thousands of Chicagoans in Works Progress Administration and other government projects, including the construction of the elevated-train line and the creation of Lakeshore Drive.[3]

Kelly also worked to incorporate African Americans into the political system, showing a sensitivity to their concerns that was significant compared with that of most political machines. He also appointed blacks to government positions, including developer Robert Taylor, whom he selected for the Chicago Housing Authority. As a result of his careful cultivation of black Chicagoans, Kelly won over a majority of formerly Republican black voters.[4]

Like other cities experiencing wartime growth, racial tensions in Chicago increased significantly as blacks demanded jobs and better housing. Many observers in Chicago and in Washington viewed the city as one of the more likely spots for racial conflict during the hot summer of 1943. Soon after the Detroit riots, Kelly announced that he was forming the Mayor's Committee on Race Relations "to advise the city government in developing steps to eliminate racial tensions." He appointed four black members (Robert Taylor, union leader Willard Townsend, YWCA head Ruth Smith, and Dr. Julian Lewis) and five white members (banker Morton Bodfish, businessmen J. S. Knowlson and Stuyvesant Peabody, union leader Anton Johanson, and Edwin Embree, whom Kelly asked to chair the group).[5]

The Mayor's Committee on Race Relations was a Progressive Era response to social problems: the appointment of wise men (and one wise woman) to investigate, mediate, and develop solutions to racial conflict. It was based on the idea that all Chicago residents had common interests and that elites could convince their "less educated" brethren to realize this fact. Though the committee had no legal powers, one analyst called it "an immediate success, both as a palliative and as a public relations coup." That Chicago did not witness a race riot during the summer was proof to many of the committee's effectiveness. Embree believed, however, that to prevent further racial violence the Mayor's Committee had to be professionalized, and he asked the mayor to triple the group's budget so that it could hire a staff. Kelly agreed to fund an office of six "experts" in race relations along with clerical staff.[6]

To run the committee, Embree turned to Weaver. The two men had kept in close contact throughout Weaver's government service and had met frequently to discuss the progress of race relations. Embree knew that Weaver was dissatisfied with the federal government, and he offered to bring Weaver to Chicago. Weaver had traveled frequently to the city during his years in Washington. He knew many of its African American leaders, and he had a good relationship with housing manager Robert Taylor. For Weaver, the job offered the opportunity to get out of the fishbowl of Washington, a place where every action was magnified in importance. Though it meant a significant change for Ella, who would have to resign her position at Howard University, she and her husband agreed that a change of scenery would be good for the family.

On 6 January 1944, Mayor Kelly announced Weaver's appointment. The press release quoted Embree, who said, "I regard Mr. Weaver as the very top man in the younger Negro group of the entire country," and "Chicago is honored in getting a man of his high ability and national standing to direct its city planning in race relations." Kelly stated, "I have wanted this important committee to get the very ablest man in America as its director, and I believe we have that man in Mr. Weaver." Weaver's friends and colleagues praised Weaver's decision. "Your appointment to this very unique and important position in Chicago, in my mind, is a very definite and signal step forward," Mary McLeod Bethune told him.[7]

Civil rights leaders were pleased because, although the committee approach was not new, the appointment of a black person to run the agency was a radical step in the context of the times. Weaver was an obvious choice for many reasons. He had Embree's confidence as well as that of White house race advisor Jonathan Daniels and other government officials. Although he had been criticized by some black leaders, almost all of them respected Weaver, and they could not condemn the decision to appoint a black man. Weaver left Ella and Robert Jr., who would join him after the semester ended, in Washington and set himself up in Chicago. Unable to quickly secure decent housing in this segregated city, Weaver took a room at Hull House, the settlement house founded by progressive leader Jane Adams.

Later in the year, Weaver was the subject of a flattering profile in the *Chicago Sun*, which declared his job "the toughest in Chicago." The writer described Weaver as "a husky, handsome, well-groomed man with mobile features, a trim mustache and keen, luminous eyes. Neither stuffy nor unctuous, he talks frankly and earthily, punctuates his speech with an occasional explosive epithet aimed at economists and their ilk. In his spare time he reads voluminously, writes for learned journals, and tinkers with mechanical gadgets—a throwback to his high school days as an apprentice electrician." At work, the writer wrote, Weaver was "a sober, down-to-earth economist who knows the difficulties of his job" and was "neither cynical nor bitter." Weaver took the job because "the federal government has gone about as far as possible" in dealing with race relations. According to Weaver, "It's up to communities to carry the ball the rest of the way." His goal was to educate white Chicago about "life in the Negro community" while at the same time "assisting Negro immigrants to practice good citizenship and adjust themselves to the community."[8]

His first task was to organize a series of public hearings to gather information on the state of black Chicago. Weaver and Embree focused the discussion on four issues: employment, housing, education, and police relations. On each issue, they concluded, the city had made progress, but it still had far to go to achieve full equality for all citizens. Weaver, Embree, and the other commissioners attempted to chart a middle course: recognizing problems in the city's race relations but noting the progress that had been made. During their first year, Weaver and his staff investigated complaints about discrimination in the police department's handling of racial conflicts and worked with police supervisors to train patrolmen in techniques to reduce racial tensions. They also mediated disputes arising from the entrance of blacks into formerly white neighborhoods and organized meetings between police and black leaders to increase cooperation. The group focused on increasing employment opportunities for blacks, particularly in white-collar occupations, lobbying downtown commercial stores and offices, most of which relegated blacks to janitorial positions, to hire blacks as salespeople and secretaries. They also pushed city administrators to increase the hiring of blacks in civil service positions.[9]

After nine months of operation, Embree told the mayor that "interracial relations continue to be much better in Chicago than in most of the large cities of the country," and he reported "excellent cooperation" from government departments. Embree proudly reported that the War Department considered their efforts "excellent work" that resulted in a decrease in "the causes of racial conflict." Weaver too believed that the efforts were "moving in the right direction," but he argued that much work remained. The committee, Weaver asserted, must undertake "social planning" to deal with the "underlying social and economic conditions which furnish the stuff out of which racial misunderstandings and antagonisms are born."[10]

Weaver spent much of his time focusing on the housing problems that vexed many Chicago African Americans. The city's severe shortage of decent shelter affected many residents, but it was particularly oppressive to blacks, who were excluded from almost all neighborhoods but those in the city's oldest, most dilapidated areas. The shortage was so severe in 1944 that the War Department proposed to take over the largest hotel on the South Side and turn it into a "reconversion center" for returning black troops, only deciding against such a plan after Weaver protested.[11]

A major obstacle limiting the housing options of blacks were "restrictive covenants," agreements between homeowners that bound them to refrain from selling or leasing their property to people of color. Proponents of covenants argued that they were necessary to protect property values, which declined, they claimed, when blacks or other minorities moved into a neighborhood. Although the strategy had been used for several decades, the number of properties subject to restrictive covenants rose substantially during the 1920s, particularly in large cities, and a significant portion of Chicago housing, primarily in middle-income neighborhoods, was subject to them. These agreements, which gave parties the power to sue a violating party for an injunction or damages, prevented whites, even those who may have wanted to sell or rent to blacks, from transferring their property, and they were responsible for keeping blacks in the already-overcrowded South Side ghetto.[12]

Restrictive covenants were of particular concern to the small but increasing number of professional blacks, who found themselves financially able to buy decent housing but prevented from doing so. Myrdal critiqued such agreements in *An American Dilemma,* arguing that "there exists a Negro upper and middle class who are searching for decent homes and who, if they were not shunned by the whites, would contribute to property values in a neighborhood rather than cause them to deteriorate." Weaver chose to focus on the problem early in his tenure, joining activists in the Chicago NAACP who were already fighting the covenants in court.[13]

In the summer of 1944, Weaver published an article on the topic in the *Journal of Land and Public Utility Economics,* in which he laid out most of the arguments against housing discrimination that he would use over the next decade. Restrictive covenants were not only wrong but ineffective, he argued. In addition, there was no evidence to support the allegation that the entrance of blacks into a neighborhood caused property values to decrease. To the contrary, the experience with public housing had shown that "the Negro is proving to be a good tenant and a good neighbor," Weaver asserted. If anything, recent studies revealed that the entrance of blacks increased values, because blacks paid higher prices for sale and rental housing. While it was true that neighborhoods experiencing the arrival of large numbers of blacks in cities like Chicago also saw the deterioration of these neighborhoods, the causes of such decline were not racial, Weaver argued, but economic. Blacks were moving into areas that were already "blighted." Because of discrimination and low incomes, blacks were forced to "double-up," increasing the number of people in an area. In certain areas, this decreased the incentive for owners and managers to maintain their properties, beginning a cycle of decline. This process was inevitable as long as blacks were limited in their housing options, Weaver argued.[14]

Furthermore, Weaver claimed, restrictive covenants gave "a false sense of security" because they had not and could not prevent the expansion of blacks into new areas. The housing needs of blacks were severe, and the housing market could profit from exploiting these needs. At the same time, new developments in other areas of the city would provide new opportunities for white families, who would depart, leaving vacancies that would be filled by blacks. Despite the efforts of whites to keep blacks out, Weaver argued, restrictive covenants would fail. Using Chicago as an example, Weaver stated that blacks were moving into several areas on the South Side and west of the central business district that were formerly restricted to whites.[15]

Though he believed that covenants were irrational, to overcome white homeowners' fears that blacks would lessen property values, Weaver proposed an alternative: residential restrictions based not on race but on occupancy and maintenance requirements. Property owners would agree that their homes would be used only for single-family residence, and they would meet community standards of care similar to those applied by homeowners' associations. Such agreements "would afford an opportunity for the Negro who has the means and the urge to live in a desirable neighborhood" and would "prevent, or at least lessen the exodus of all whites upon the entrance of a few Negroes," Weaver claimed. Weaver's work on restrictive covenants sought to open up opportunities to the growing black middle class, enabling them to find decent housing in new areas of the city. If this movement could be achieved without "panic selling" by whites, Chicago neighborhoods would prove that racial integration could work, Weaver believed. In the long run, he argued, such experiments in integration would pave the way for more comprehensive efforts.[16]

The fight against covenants sought to remove barriers to individual mobility, but Weaver, relying on his experience with public housing, also hoped to create new, large-scale experiments in racial integration. In the fall of 1944, after six months of work, the Mayor's Committee issued a report recommending the construction of a "planned community" on a site outside the black ghetto which included public and private housing. The project would meet the housing shortage facing blacks but would also "be open to all racial groups." The report, which received the support of black and white committee members, was never publicly released, because the mayor tabled it. Residents in white areas were already expressing opposition to new public housing projects that they thought would house blacks, and the idea of an avowedly integrated development was too radical for Kelly.[17]

Soon after the completion of this report, Weaver resigned from his position as the executive director. Weaver later argued that the mayor's refusal to support an integrated development was one reason for his resignation, but he also blamed larger, more structural constraints. However, Weaver never criticized the mayor publicly for failing to act. Instead, he found another job, again with Embree's help, and resigned with little fanfare.

Although Weaver was frustrated by the failure of political leadership in Chicago, he also felt that there were inherent limitations to the race relations committee approach. Most groups, created in periods of crisis, failed to deal with the structural problems that caused racial tensions, Weaver felt. "When the summer of 1944 passed without a serious racial clash, most intergroup committees were content to sit and wait for another crisis," he commented in 1946. Mayor Kelly had made the right statements about the need for racial cooperation, but when presented with ideas that were likely to raise the opposition of real estate interests as well as the white communities that represented the core of the Democratic Party, he chose to delay. A few years later, as Chicago's housing crisis grew and tensions over black movement increased, Kelly would be forced to take a stand. His limited support for racial integration would cost him his job.[18]

From Weaver's viewpoint, these hard choices had to be made, and he did not want to work for an administration unable or unwilling to act. Still recovering from his experience in wartime Washington, Weaver decided to get out of government completely. With the exception of his temporary job with the United Nations, he would not return to paid public service for more than a decade.

FRUSTRATED WITH THE inability of the political system to directly confront the roots of racial segregation, Weaver left the public sector to enter the emerging field of scientific racial management at the newly created American Council on Race Relations. Much of the framework for this new effort was established by a decade of work done by Gunnar Myrdal and his staff (particularly Weaver's friend Ralph Bunche). Few social science studies in American history have had more impact than *An American Dilemma*. The book, which exceeded fifteen hundred pages, provided the most comprehensive examination of black America ever produced. Although the product of immense scholarly study, its purpose was not as an intellectual exercise but rather to promote what Myrdal referred to as "social engineering." One historian called the book a "modern jeremiad to white Americans concerning the race issue."[19]

Myrdal claimed that the "American Dilemma" was the contradiction between the universally accepted "American Creed" (vaguely defined as the belief that all people were entitled to liberty, freedom, and opportunity) and the country's treatment of African Americans. "At bottom our problem is the moral dilemma of the American—the conflict between his moral valuations on various levels of consciousness and generality," Myrdal argued. The most poignant example of this dilemma was "the Negro," who, Myrdal claimed, "has not yet been given the elemental civil and political rights of formal democracy." But this contradiction could be resolved. Rejecting the arguments of American intellectuals, who reasoned that the state could have little impact on race relations, Myrdal argued that, in the postwar era, issues that were considered "predominantly a matter of individual adjustment will become more and more determined by political decision and public regulation." In this new era, he claimed, "fact-finding and scientific theories . . . will be seen as instrumental in planning controlled social change." In essence, Myrdal's argument was that social scientists, working with government, could promote societal reform: their efforts to amass and publicize the facts about the state of black Americans had the potential to convince white society to support needed changes.[20]

As he had so often in the past, Embree played the role of broker in the process of translating theory into practice. In March 1944 Embree and Weaver organized a meeting of civil rights leaders, scholars, and government officials from across the nation. At the conference, attended by, among others, Charles Hamilton Houston, Ralph Bunche, and Mary McLeod Bethune, the group discussed ways to prevent racial violence and to continue the momentum of civil rights activists in the postwar era. Embree already had in mind the creation of a new organization that would serve as a "clearinghouse and service center" with the responsibility for "bringing together and making available the knowledge and experience of those persons, public officials and private citizens, who have been most successful in dealing with minority group relations." Before the meeting he convinced the board of the Rosenwald Fund to appropriate $75,000 over three years to fund the new group.[21]

Two months later, Weaver and his former New Deal colleague Will Alexander called the first meeting of the Board of Directors of the American Council on Race Relations (ACRR), in Chicago. Among the board members were Edwin Embree, businessman Marshall Field, NAACP head Walter White, Mary McLeod Bethune, Rev. Francis Haas (former head of the Fair Employment Practices Committee [FEPC]), attorney Lloyd Garrison, writer Pearl Buck, and National Urban League head Lester Granger. The goal of the group was "to bring about full democracy in race relations" through the "discovery of fundamental knowledge" about racial problems. The organization sought to promote scholarly study of racial issues, to develop materials for use by government and private organizations, and to assist local communities in organizing programs of racial cooperation. Embree secured the support of several other foundations and liberal business leaders to fund the group.[22]

To run the new organization, Embree chose Alexander Liveright. Liveright had served as chief field representative of the WMC and had worked as regional director of the WMC in Philadelphia. Neither Embree's papers nor those of other participants in the ACRR's founding record the reasons for Liveright's selection, nor do they discuss why Embree declined to choose a man equally suited and obviously interested—Weaver. Given Embree's aspirations for the national impact of the group, Weaver's race was certainly a limiting factor. Chicago might have been willing to accept a black official as the public face of the city's race program, but southern segregationists, Embree believed, would not.

Embree selected Weaver as director of community services, the person who would serve as second-in-command and be in charge of developing programs that aided local race relations groups. At the time, Weaver did not record his feelings about taking a junior role, though he would later complain about this position. Dissatisfied with Chicago politics, Weaver quickly accepted the new position. In October, Weaver announced his resignation from the Mayor's Committee. He stated that "working in the City of Chicago has been one of the most pleasant experiences I have ever had," but he believed that the new job presented the opportunity "for doing similar work on a larger scale."[23]

By early 1945, the ACRR had a staff of nine professionals, including former government officials Philleo Nash (who would become Truman's main race relations advisor), Laurence Hewes, and Davis McEntire, all of whom had worked on racial issues during the war. During the ACRR's first year of operations, the group provided information and consultation to the more than four hundred local race relations committees that had been established since 1943. The staff aided local antidiscrimination efforts, created a manual (written by Weaver) for local race relations committees, and published a newsletter to report on activities across the country. In the summer of 1945, they organized the first Institute for Race Relations and Community Organization, a retreat for representatives of race relations committees and civil rights organizations, and they created a training program for police to help them deal with racial tension. They also focused on discrimination against Japanese Americans on the West Coast.[24]

Weaver's most important function at the ACRR was to continue his work on restrictive covenants, and he joined an increasing number of lawyers and activists in this effort. Over the next five years, Weaver played an important role in this legal struggle, which resulted in a major victory at the Supreme Court in 1948 that became the template for other civil rights struggles. By the time Weaver arrived in Chicago to take up his post on the Mayor's Committee, several Chicago attorneys were representing families that were denied the right to purchase or occupy homes in different parts of the city.

Working with attorney Loring Moore, Weaver served as an expert witness in several disputes and aided in the preparation of briefs in which he argued that restrictive covenants had serious negative effects on the Chicago housing market.[25]

Moore and Weaver received the support of the Chicago branch of the NAACP, which published a pamphlet entitled "Restrictive Covenants: In a Democracy They Cost Too Much." The brief argued that "race restrictive covenants undermine the foundation of our democracy" and told "the one and one-fourth billion people of color throughout the world that they are considered unworthy of an equal chance to live in the world." Because these agreements limited the availability of housing and increased its cost, blacks had paid $50 million more for housing in the past ten years than they should have, NAACP leaders claimed.[26]

Although lawyers hoped that courts would acknowledge the illegality of racially restrictive covenants, they understood that existing law was against them. Local and state courts across the country had approved such agreements during the 1920s, and not a single state had denied the power of residents to use race-restrictive covenants. In the 1926 case *Buckley v. Corrigan*, the U.S. Supreme Court also stated its approval of restrictive covenants. Justice Edward Sanford called the African American's petition against the covenant "so insubstantial as to be plainly without color of merit and frivolous." Such was the court's inability to conceive of the impact that such agreements had on American race relations.[27]

In the 1940s, restrictive covenants were an accepted aspect of housing policy. From the Federal Housing Administration (FHA) down to the local realtor, the real estate industry held as one of its central tenets that people of different races should not live together. The ethical code of the National Association of Real Estate Boards (NAREB) specifically stated that realtors should not introduce into a neighborhood "members of any race . . . whose presence would clearly be detrimental to property values." From its inception in 1934 until 1949, FHA regulations strongly suggested restrictive covenants in all federally financed housing.[28]

However, the widespread prevalence of such agreements did not deter civil rights lawyers. The lawsuits in Chicago, like those in several other states, were primarily directed at the high court in Washington, DC. Given the right case, a strong record, and a careful argument, lawyers believed they might be able to convince the U.S. Supreme Court to declare restrictive covenants unconstitutional. From 1945 to 1948, the attorneys representing individual clients, at the insistence of Thurgood Marshall and his colleagues at the NAACP national legal office, joined together to push for constitutional change in this area. Weaver, by 1945 recognized as the nation's foremost authority on the economic and social impact of restrictive covenants, played a central role in this coalition.[29]

In July 1945, NAACP head attorney Thurgood Marshall called together thirty-three of the nation's leading civil rights lawyers and activists to meet at Weaver's office to discuss the pending cases in the area of restrictive covenants. There they received reports from several attorneys handling cases, heard a presentation from Weaver on the use and impact of restrictive covenants, and debated the appropriate steps to get the issue in front of the court. After the meeting, Marshall announced that the NAACP was undertaking a new legal assault on restrictive covenants.[30]

In a memo to the participants shortly after the meeting, Weaver argued that the economic and social aspects of restrictive covenants should be emphasized both in the legal attack and in the public relations effort that would complement the court battles. "The most immediate effect of restrictive covenants is psychological in that they give legal sanction, and consequently, respectability to all other instruments for effecting residential segregation," he claimed. "In the whole network of devices and practices for exclusion, the race restrictive housing covenants have gained currency as a respectable and legitimate device. This is a fiction that must be dissipated by sociological and legal attacks." Weaver advised the lawyers to emphasize the economic impact of covenants as well as their effect on the exacerbation of social problems in black neighborhoods.[31]

Weaver and his colleagues also undertook a national campaign to raise public awareness about the problems caused by restrictive covenants. In September 1945, the ACRR published a pamphlet, written by Weaver, entitled "Hemmed In: ABC's of Race Restrictive Housing Covenants." "Of all the instruments which effect residential segregation, race restrictive covenants are the most dangerous" because they give the appearance of respectability to segregation, the pamphlet argued. "As long as the 'better people' in a community sign restrictions against certain groups and the courts enforce such agreements, other elements will 'protect' their neighborhoods against minorities too." The pamphlet also explained in simple terms the effect of covenants on residential overcrowding and neighborhood decline and again made the case for restrictions not based on race. Over the next year, the group distributed thousands of copies of the pamphlet around the country.[32]

Though it was praised by some people, Weaver's proposal for "occupancy agreements" (ensuring single-family residence) brought withering criticism from others. The *Chicago Defender*, in an editorial "The American Council Blunders," argued that Weaver had produced an "ill-advised brain child." By focusing on such standards, the editors claimed, Weaver was playing into the hands of racist white residents and landlords. "In effect what the American council proposes is that the great majority of Negroes, who are in the lower brackets and who have not the means, would continue to be hemmed in by covenants—but on the basis of class rather than race." Such distinctions, they argued, "have no more place in America than racial distinctions." The dispute highlighted the class-based tensions within the civil rights struggle over the appropriate mechanisms for racial progress, tensions that would become more difficult to resolve during the postwar years.[33]

BY 1945, ELLA and Robert Jr. had joined Weaver in the Windy City, and they set up a household in an apartment just outside the downtown "Loop." In 1946, with Robert Jr. in school, Ella began pursuing a doctorate in speech at Northwestern University—in 1947 she would become the first African American woman to obtain a doctorate in the field. Weaver continued to travel around the nation to work with race relations groups, and when he was at home he spent much of his time writing. His goal was to finish his first book, *Negro Labor: A National Problem*. When published in 1946, the book, an analysis of the work he had done in the early 1940s, placed Weaver in the middle of the national debate over the role of African Americans in the postwar economy. A scholarly study that Weaver hoped would establish him as a leading social scientist, one who would be sought after by the nation's elite schools, *Negro Labor* was a book that attempted to merge the most recent scholarship in labor economics with Weaver's personal experiences during the war manpower mobilization.

Much of the book was a republication of the numerous articles that Weaver had written during his years in the government's war employment agencies. It was divided into three sections: an analysis of the changes in black employment during the war, an interpretation of the problems of black workers, and an assessment of the future of the struggle for equal opportunity in the workplace. The first section began with a short review of the state of black workers before the war and then followed with an analysis of the problems facing blacks in the years of the defense buildup. Relying on data and analyses he prepared while in government, Weaver described the exclusion of black workers in several areas, focusing on aircraft production and shipbuilding, and he discussed the racial conflicts that arose in many industries when employers attempted to hire black workers. He then traced the beginnings of reform in employment policies, focusing on government construction initiatives and the effort to reform government training programs. The last chapters in the section examined the path of blacks into wartime jobs and described the areas where African Americans had succeeded and where they had failed to secure fair treatment. Despite many problems, Weaver concluded that the "changes in a period of four years represented more industrial and occupational diversification for Negroes than had occurred in the seventy-five preceding years."[34]

In the second part of the book, Weaver examined several aspects of the wartime employment struggle, discussing in greater detail the battles in the aircraft industry and in local transportation. During the war, the aircraft industry had made significant strides in employing black workers, whereas transportation agencies, because of violent opposition from white workers, did not make much progress. The section also included previously published studies of the role of management in successful employment strategies and the complicated relationship between black workers and labor unions. In the chapter "Governmental Approaches," Weaver presented a critical assessment of the government agencies regulating the labor market. He argued that neither the Office of Production Management nor the U.S. Employment Service had taken the issue of discrimination seriously. He also gave a negative assessment to the FEPC, which he argued had failed to bring about structural changes in employment policies because it focused on dramatic cases instead of long-range research and planning.

The first two sections of the book were a careful explication of the existing literature (much of which Weaver had written) on wartime employment. Most of the material was known to people in the field, but Weaver attempted to explain the issues in a manner accessible to the general, educated public. Weaver's critical assessments of government agencies would have surprised people who did not know him, given Weaver's public silence on these issues while in government service, but they would not have shocked those with whom he worked.

Whereas the purpose of the first two sections was to provide a comprehensive overview of the obstacles facing black workers and the efforts to overcome them, the third section was directed at postwar policymakers.

Weaver strongly supported liberal efforts to keep the federal government involved in economic planning. Like many others, the lesson he took from the war was that government intervention was necessary to maintain a robust economy. Arguing that "no element in the community will suffer more from our failure to secure full employment than our color minorities," Weaver endorsed federal legislation committing the government to a policy of full employment and called for a revitalization of government planning agencies. The section also examined the impact of postwar conversion, concluding that black workers, particularly women, would be hard hit by the inevitable unemployment that would occur. He argued that union officials, management, and government leaders would have to pay careful attention to the implementation of seniority rules in order to prevent racial tensions from increasing as veterans returned home. To smooth the dislocation, Weaver joined other liberal economists such as Harvard's Alvin Hansen in advocating a major public works program.[35]

Weaver used these arguments to support his primary conclusion that federal, state, and local governments needed to establish and support organizations to promote fair employment practices. Unemployment was going to occur. What was important was for the government to create "a feeling on the part of all groups that America is prepared to meet its post-war problems and that reconversion dislocations are to be of a temporary nature." This required, he claimed, the maintenance of government agencies to prevent job discrimination. Acknowledging that these agencies could not create jobs, Weaver asserted that they could "divide more equitably such work as is available at any such given time" and "sustain the morale of black America and its belief in American democracy." Such organizations were needed at the state and local levels too, because a federal agency would regulate only a limited number of companies. Although he praised the efforts of New York State, which had recently passed a fair employment practices law, Weaver was not optimistic about the chances for a comprehensive program, given the recent failure of Congress to adopt the bill making the FEPC permanent.[36]

Weaver worked hard during 1945 to finish the book, which he wanted to have released while Congress was debating whether to make the FEPC permanent. He pressured the publisher to release the book as quickly as possible, but they were reluctant to do so during the fall, which they thought was a bad time to market a serious work like Weaver's. Instead, Harcourt Brace released the book in January 1946, after the efforts to secure passage of the FEPC law had failed.[37]

The book was widely and very positively reviewed in both academic and popular media. The assessment of the *American Economic Review* was that "Dr. Weaver's volume deserves a wide reading." Because of its "careful marshalling of facts, its competent analysis of complicated problems, and its objective treatment of an issue so highly charged," it was "an excellent piece of work." Dale Yoder of the University of Minnesota, reviewing the book for the *American Sociological Review*, stated that the book was "well-written, clear-cut, incisive and informative," and Don Lesochier of the University of Wisconsin, writing in the magazine *Survey Graphic*, called it "a powerful critique of the color occupational system." Horace Cayton, writing in the *Chicago Tribune*, argued that "some organization should see that it is placed on the desk of every Senator," and John Davis, in a review published by *Crisis*, stated that the book was "full of really brilliant discussions which only a trained economist and government official of long experience could make."[38]

Weaver published *Negro Labor* at a time when the future of civil rights in America was being widely debated. After more than twelve years of FDR, the country was still acclimating itself to a new president, Harry Truman. A racial moderate during his years in the Senate, Truman supported some civil rights measures, but as the representative of the "border state" of Missouri, Truman did not have a strong record on the issue. One of his earliest battles as president involved the FEPC, which had been a lightning rod for segregationists since its creation. In 1944, southern politicians, led by Representative Howard Smith (D-VA), succeeded in cutting the committee's budget to $500,000. In 1945, they almost succeeded in eliminating all appropriations for the agency, and eventually settled for an agreement to fund it for one more year at $250,000, a sum that would allow the organization to wrap up its current activities. Truman opposed the cuts to the FEPC, but he did not use much of his political capital before acceding to the demands of southern Democrats. While accepting the appropriation bill, Truman stated that he favored a permanent fair employment committee.[39]

However, early in 1946, while stating his support for a permanent FEPC, Truman did little to prevent a weeklong Senate filibuster against the proposal. The president's inaction left the FEPC a dead issue that would not be revitalized for two decades and African Americans with little to celebrate, except for the appointment of William Hastie as the first black governor of the Virgin Islands. In his relations with Congress, Truman could avoid conflict by saying the right things but allowing southern Democrats to have their way. However, when racial violence increased after the war, the president was forced to do something. One of the first widely reported episodes occurred in Columbia, Tennessee, where the wounding of four police officers in the black section of town led to a systematic denial of civil rights to all blacks, as police rampaged through the homes of blacks looking for weapons, injured dozens of blacks, and killed two in custody. In another incident, a white policeman in Aiken, South Carolina, blinded a black serviceman who had recently returned home. The July lynching of four blacks, two of them women, in Macon, Georgia, also received national attention.[40]

After the Georgia incident, Weaver and ACRR staff, working with the NAACP, formed the National Emergency Committee against Mob Violence and asked Truman "to throw the full force of the federal government" behind "bringing before the bar of justice and convicting the lynchers." The group sponsored a rally in New York City, which was attended by 15,000 people, and a march to the Lincoln Memorial, in which another 15,000 participated. By September the committee had forty-seven organizations as members. Several of the group's leaders, including Walter White and Congress of Industrial Organizations secretary James Carey, met with Truman in his office and asked him to use the federal government to stop mob violence.[41]

In response to protest from civil rights leaders, Truman decided to appoint a Committee on Civil Rights. The idea of a committee to study American race relations had first been raised during the summer of 1943 in response to the riots, but Roosevelt had dismissed it without much consideration. On 5 December 1946 Truman issued an executive order creating the committee. He appointed fifteen members, including Charles Wilson, president of General Electric, as chair, two black members, Philadelphia attorney Sadie T. M. Alexander and Channing Tobias, union leader James Carey, and university presidents Frank Graham of North Carolina and John Dickey of Dartmouth. Truman asked the committee to study the whole spectrum of racial issues and to propose legislation to protect the civil rights of Americans. Though they lost the battle for a permanent FEPC, civil rights leaders made clear to the president that their demands for equal rights would not cease. Although reform was slow to come, the report the group produced would end up having a significant impact on American politics and the path of the civil rights movement.[42]

There is a profound irony to the fact that the publication of *Negro Labor* coincided with the demise of the FEPC bill. Over the course of the next decade, employment discrimination receded in importance to civil rights lawyers, and the battle for equality became focused on issues of educational and housing discrimination. Civil rights lawyers increasingly concentrated on issues of legal "status," attacking laws requiring racial segregation, and they gave less attention to economic issues. As the philosophy of racial liberalism moved from theory to action, advocates convinced themselves that abolishing these legal distinctions would lead to racial integration and a decline in discrimination. The strategic decision to adopt this approach coincided with liberal thinking about individual rights and was influenced by the growing struggle between the United States and the Soviet Union. Claims against Jim Crow gained power in the context of the U.S. critiques of communism, and as Myrdal had predicted, civil rights lawyers sought to exploit these contradictions. However, their neglect of economic concerns denied attention to a crucial aspect of black life.

As one of the leading thinkers in the area of racial liberalism, Weaver moved in the same direction and increasingly focused on housing matters. He left behind more than a decade of efforts to improve employment prospects for black Americans. In the 1960s, in response to War on Poverty efforts to revitalize declining cities, policymakers like Daniel Patrick Moynihan argued that the root of urban racial problems was monetary. There was no housing crisis among African Americans, he asserted—the problem facing poor blacks was that they could not afford decent housing. The government, he claimed, should focus on increasing African Americans' income. In the late 1940s, seeking to break the hold of Jim Crow, Weaver and most of the civil rights movement shifted their attention away from the economic issues that Moynihan and others would come to view as central to the progress of black Americans. Their decision would have a profound impact on the course of the civil rights movement.[43]

* 7 *

# Searching for a Place to Call Home

Weaver missed much of the 1946 debate over the Fair Employment Practices Committee because he was in the Soviet Union on a six-month contract with the United Nations Relief and Rehabilitation Administration (UNRRA), the agency charged with resuscitating war-ravaged communities with emergency food and industrial and agricultural assistance. His sojourn in the Ukraine marked the first detour from a career focused on the promotion of racial equality. Though leaving his family for six months to travel to a dangerous part of the world with few of the comforts of home seems a somewhat odd choice for Weaver, it was consistent with his upbringing. The son of a family of barrier breakers, Weaver hoped that his success in the position would provide further evidence that his race was no limit to his abilities. Raised to believe he had an obligation to disprove theories of racial inequality, Weaver jumped at the chance to show that he could handle the immense task facing the relief operation. His trip would begin a two-year period of almost-constant movement in search of an appropriate professional home. In 1948, the family would leave Chicago. However frustrated Weaver might have been during this time, it was one of great individual productivity as well as progress in the effort to promote racial equality.

Chartered in 1943 by agreement of the United States, Great Britain, the USSR, and China, UNRRA had yet to begin operations when Weaver signed up in early 1946. After the war ended, even though the devastated countries of Eastern Europe were desperate for assistance, the Soviets' concern about American infiltration—the Soviets wanted the goods but not their western bearers—slowed the negotiation process and prevented aid from reaching the region.[1]

William Hastie recommended Weaver to UNRRA Ukraine Mission chief Marshall McDuffie, who, desperate to find professionals trained in government financial operations, quickly hired him. After obtaining a leave of absence from his job at the American Council on Race Relations (ACRR), Weaver left for the Ukraine, where he worked as a supply officer in the relief effort. He was one of the first Americans to see firsthand the devastation experienced by the region, which had been known as "Russia's Breadbasket." After the Germans' retreat, the Ukraine's agricultural and industrial economy, which had been one of the Soviets' most successful efforts during the 1920s and 1930s, lay in ruins. Over its three-year run, UNRRA, led by New York governor Herbert Lehman, distributed almost $200 million in food, raw materials, and industrial equipment to aid in the reconstruction of the region. Originally, Weaver was responsible for tracking the delivery and distribution of construction supplies for rebuilding efforts. He also served as deputy of the mission and acting chief for several months, which meant he was in charge of the total reconstruction effort. During this time the mission spent $35 million. There, he made contacts with white professionals such as Lehman (then a senator from New York) and Averill Harriman (Weaver's future boss).[2]

While in the Ukraine, Weaver told a reporter that "the damage and suffering from the German invasion of Russia is so vast it has to be seen to be appreciated. Statistics alone cannot give the whole story." The housing situation was particularly dismal. However, Weaver did not say much about his time there after he returned to America. In October 1946, he wrote a short article for the ACRR newsletter on his impressions of race relations in the Soviet Union entitled "No Race Problem in Russia." In the article, Weaver claimed that "the Soviet Union has solved its minority problems by legislative, economic and educative action." Where before the revolution the country was "rife with anti-Semitism and national hatreds," at the present it was "relatively free from intergroup-tensions." According to Weaver, the Communist Party had excised prejudice from its operations, and schools and labor organizations were active in promoting cooperation among ethnic and racial groups. "Russia has shown the world that group prejudices can be modified," Weaver concluded.[3]

Unlike many of his friends, particularly John P. Davis, who had been drawn to American communism during the 1930s out of frustration with American politics and a belief that the ideology was more amenable to racial equality, Weaver never dallied with the party. His FBI file noted his 1940 membership in a Washington, DC, book cooperative, which agents said was "controlled" by Communists, but he was not an active participant and was a member for only a short time. Weaver's only contact with the House Un-American Affairs Committee came in 1944 when he was listed as a contributor to the National Citizens Political Action Committee (NCPAC). The organization, founded by Weaver's boss Sidney Hillman, aided politicians sympathetic to unions and received support from a multitude of liberals, including Arthur Schlesinger, Orson Welles, and Reinhold Niebuhr. Investigators termed it a "communist front," but the fact that Eleanor Roosevelt supported the enterprise weakened their case. The scion of an established, middle-class family, the owner of a summerhouse in an exclusive resort on the Chesapeake, and an avid, if small, stock investor, Weaver was as far from being a Communist as most Americans. However, opponents would later use his time in the Soviet Union to attack him.[4]

Later in the fall of 1946, Weaver wrote two short articles for the *Journal of Housing* on the state of the region's housing. He concluded that the Ukraine was making slow progress in rebuilding its housing stock, but he worried that the need to produce shelter quickly would result in poor planning and shoddy construction. However, these short pieces were the only writings Weaver published on his experiences. Weaver later told an interviewer that he had planned a speaking tour on his time in Russia but that he had canceled it after a friend told him that his observations about race relations and the success of the Soviet experiment were wrong. Also, in light of the increasing tensions between the United States and the USSR, Weaver concluded that it was best to stay clear of the topic, lest it interfere with his professional aspirations and his desire to promote racial progress. The few statements he did make would come back to haunt him two decades later at the hearings on his nomination to head the federal housing effort.[5]

IN NOVEMBER, WEAVER returned to an organization that, after two years of existence, faced an identity crisis. While the ACRR had provided important services to many local race committees, several board members believed that it had failed to achieve its goal of developing comprehensive approaches to race relations. The large number of attacks on blacks and other minorities, along with the retrenchment of the federal government in the area of civil rights, left activists frustrated with the ineffectiveness of the organization. ACRR staff had taken on many diverse tasks and initiated several efforts. Edwin Embree and other board members at the Rosenwald Fund, which continued to provide most of the ACRR's funding, expressed concern about the administration of Executive Director Alexander A. Liveright.[6]

To revitalize the agency, the board turned to University of Chicago sociologist Louis Wirth. One of the leaders in the field of "intergroup relations," Wirth, who was already a board member, was an obvious choice to run the ACRR. Born in Germany, Wirth immigrated to the United States as a child. A student of pioneering University of Chicago sociologists Robert Park and Ernest Burgess, Wirth received his doctorate in 1926, beginning what was to be an illustrious but abbreviated career. As a professor at Tulane University during the early 1930s, Wirth's outspoken advocacy of civil rights cost him his job. He was rewarded with a position at the University of Chicago, where he remained until his death in 1952. During the 1930s and 1940s, Wirth was a pioneer in the study of urban race relations, a consultant to several government efforts to relieve racial tensions, and an activist for civil rights groups, including the National Urban League and the American Jewish Congress.[7]

Embree stated at the group's founding that it would be concerned with research more than activism, but during its first two years the ACRR was involved in several projects that focused on grassroots organizing. Groups promoting racial cooperation were a new idea, and ACRR staff, including Weaver, were directly involved in the operations of many agencies. This approach stretched the group's resources and inhibited the research and planning that Embree envisioned. Wirth's selection clarified that the ACRR was going to be primarily an "institute," not an advocacy group.[8]

At the same time he accepted the job Wirth convinced the University of Chicago to create the Center for Training and Research on Race. The institute, which would also be run by Wirth and staffed by other university professors studying race relations, would develop and implement a scholarly research agenda to study racial issues in America and train students in the field of race relations. The ACRR would disseminate this research to professionals active in race relations and the general public. The professor agreed to serve as president of the organization, in charge of establishing the program, but the day-to-day operations would be managed by an administrative assistant.[9]

It does not appear that the board gave serious consideration to promoting Weaver for the job, which is not completely surprising considering he had spent most of the prior year working on his book and in Russia. Although Weaver maintained warm relations with Embree until Embree's death in the early 1950s, and Embree continued to support Weaver, as well as serve as his chief headhunter, by 1946 Weaver had decided that the ACRR was a flawed organization. If he and Embree ever disagreed about the organization's direction, they never put those feelings in writing. However, Weaver's actions revealed his dissatisfaction with the group. Weaver continued to do his job, providing guidance to local race relations groups and writing about trends in civil rights, but he did not play a leadership role in the organization. Instead, Weaver focused on his own projects—his books and other writing and his work against restrictive covenants. He refrained from public comments about the ACRR, following an approach that would mark the rest of his career. Embarrassed several times during his years in the federal government by speaking too freely, Weaver chose not to document his feelings about the group's limitations.

WHILE HE PULLED himself away from the daily administration of the ACRR, Weaver increased his efforts against discrimination in housing. In 1948, he played a major role in a signal victory for civil rights, the *Shelley* decision against restrictive covenants. Today the Supreme Court's 1948 landmark opinion attacking restrictive covenants is popularly known by the name of an African American from St. Louis, J. D. Shelley, but in fact the Court issued two opinions: *Shelley v. Kraemer,* which involved the constitutionality of the enforcement of covenants by state courts, and *Hurd v. Hodge,* which concerned such agreements in the District of Columbia. Both of these cases had two sets of plaintiffs. *Shelley* encompassed both Shelley's case, which arose from the Missouri Supreme Court, and *Sipes v. McGee,* which involved a Michigan dispute. The Missouri case was brought in 1945 by members of the Marcus Avenue Improvement Association, who had agreed to a racially restrictive covenant that they argued covered the house at 4600 Labadie Avenue in St. Louis, bought by the Shelleys, a black couple. The Shelleys attacked both the validity of the agreement and the policy behind restrictive covenants and succeeded in convincing a local judge that the restriction was invalid. The Missouri Supreme Court, however, reversed the decision and issued an injunction ordering the Shelleys to vacate the premises. In 1947, the Shelleys, represented by attorney George Vaughn, appealed to the U.S. Supreme Court.[10]

The Michigan case also commenced in 1945, brought by white Detroit property owners against Orsel and Minnie McGee to oust them from the house they had bought at 4626 Seebaldt Avenue. The plaintiffs argued that a restrictive covenant signed by property owners in the area limited occupancy to Caucasians, and they asked a district court to issue an injunction. Like parties in other suits, the McGees made a wide variety of allegations, contesting the fact that they were Negro, arguing that the covenant had not been properly created, and attacking the constitutionality of such agreements as well as the policy behind them. The trial court, however, rejected all of these arguments and awarded an injunction to the plaintiffs. The Michigan Supreme Court upheld the decision.[11]

At the same time that attorneys across the nation were attacking restrictive covenants, Charles Hamilton Houston was working on several cases in the District of Columbia. One of them involved James Hurd, who in 1944 purchased a house on Bryant Street in the North Capitol area. Houston later agreed to represent Raphael Uriculo, a white realtor who had purchased several homes in areas with restrictive covenants and sold them to African Americans. Uriculo had done quite well financially, despite the Washington Real Estate Board's termination of his membership for violating their code of ethics. At trial, the lead plaintiff in the Hurd case, Lena Hodge, testified that she would prefer an "untidy white person to a Negro, no matter how educated or cultured," and Houston attacked the validity of the covenant, argued that Hurd was in fact "American Indian," introduced testimony arguing that racial characteristics were impossible to prove, and presented studies, prepared by Weaver and Howard University sociologist E. Franklin Frazier, showing the negative impact of restrictive covenants on the housing opportunities of black DC residents.[12]

The evidence was not enough to convince the district judge, who upheld the covenants in both cases and declared the transfers void. Houston appealed, and the U.S. District Court of Appeals affirmed the decisions in *Hurd v. Hodge* and *Uriculo v. Hodge* by a vote of 2–1, arguing that the court had consistently approved such agreements for over twenty-five years. In a dissenting opinion, Judge Harry Edgerton relied heavily on the sociological and economic literature, citing Myrdal's *An American Dilemma* and Weaver's articles in the footnotes. "Negroes have a constitutional right to buy and use" property. Judicial enforcement of restrictive covenants, he argued, violated the Civil Rights Act of 1866 because the government was taking action that infringed upon the rights of a racial minority. He further claimed that restrictive covenants were bad policy because they increased racial animosities. The judge was alone in his view at the time, but he would soon be joined by other jurists.[13]

Many legal scholars believed that the campaign against restrictive covenants was a lost cause, but the postwar years were ones of significant change for the American legal system. In June 1947, the Supreme Court agreed to hear arguments in the *Shelley* and *Sipes* cases, and they did the same for the *Hurd* and *Uricolo* cases in October. Throughout the summer and fall of 1947, civil rights attorneys worked to craft their arguments for the Court. Because most of the existing law was against them, Marshall, Houston, and the other attorneys agreed that they would have to base their arguments on policy—restrictive covenants had a negative impact on society and therefore should not be favored. The attack, argued Justice Department attorney Phineas Indritz, who aided Houston in preparing his briefs, "must be supported by a full sociological presentation. Legal arguments, standing alone, may find a less fertile field for acceptance in this controversy which has so frequently been dominated by unspoken emotional preconceptions and misconceptions."[14]

To aid the attorneys, Weaver and Wirth agreed to coordinate the production of a memorandum on the "economic and social aspects of race restrictive covenants." Although the participation of the social scientists in a Supreme Court case was not novel, the extent of their involvement was significant and provided an early experiment in the sociolegal argument that would prove crucial to civil rights cases over the next two decades, most famously in *Brown v. Board of Education*. The economic and social analysis written by Weaver and Wirth took up fully one-third of Houston's 150-page submission. The introduction to their section stated that covenants had "drastically curtailed the ability of Negroes to secure adequate housing," were "a major contributor to the enormous overcrowding" that blacks endured, and were a direct cause of increases in "disease, death, crime, immorality, juvenile delinquency, racial tensions and economic exploitation."[15]

With the policy analysis as the foundation of their arguments, civil rights lawyers attacked judicial enforcement of restrictive covenants. In their briefs and at oral argument, the petitioners on the state cases claimed that enforcement of restrictive covenants violated the Fifth and Fourteenth Amendments and federal law. The *Sipes* brief ended by calling the case "a test as to whether we will have a united nation or a country divided into areas and ghettoes solely on racial or religious lines." In his brief, Houston claimed that the case had significant international ramifications, because restrictive covenants were an example of the failure of the United States to live up to the promises of equality under the law. These obstacles to racial mobility created "a divisive, caste society" that was "a direct danger to our national unity."[16]

The attorneys defending the covenants (who had the precedents behind them) presented briefs that were much shorter than those of the petitioners. They argued that the restrictions were allowed under existing law and that private agreements were necessary to protect the property rights of the owners. They were joined by several homeowners associations and the National Association of Real Estate Boards, which filed briefs in support of the lower-court decisions.[17]

The increase in national attention to civil rights issues brought the attorneys unprecedented support in their attack on restrictive covenants. More than twenty organizations, including the American Civil Liberties Union, the American Jewish Committee, the Congress of Industrial Organizations, and the National Bar Association, filed amicus briefs during the fall of 1947 asking the Court to repudiate the enforcement of restrictive covenants. The Justice Department also agreed to file a brief supporting the petitioners. In it, Solicitor General Philip Perlman argued that restrictive covenants "cannot be reconciled with the spirit of mutual tolerance and respect for the dignity and rights of the individual which give vitality to our democratic way of life."[18]

Although the weight of submissions opposing restrictive covenants greatly surpassed those in favor, the outcome of the case was far from certain. The prevalence of such agreements was starkly revealed when three Supreme Court justices (Stanley Reed, Wiley Rutledge, and Robert Jackson) all had to recuse themselves because they owned property that was subject to restrictive covenants. The remaining six judges, however, voted unanimously in favor of the petitioners, marking a major victory for civil rights. Acknowledging that restrictive covenants themselves could not "be regarded as a violation of any rights guaranteed to petitioners by the Fourteenth Amendment," the court declared, in *Shelley v. Kraemer,* that judicial enforcement of such agreements constituted "state action" in violation of the U.S. Constitution. Since the cases involved willing buyers and sellers, the Court declared it "clear that but for the active intervention of the state courts . . . petitioners would have been free to occupy the properties in question without restraint." The Court concluded that "freedom from discrimination by the States in the enjoyment of property rights was among the basic objectives sought to be effectuated by the framers of the Fourteenth Amendment."[19]

In a brief opinion, the Court also held, unanimously, in *Hurd v. Hodge,* that the Civil Rights Act of 1866 prohibited the enforcement of restrictive covenants in the District of Columbia. In neither of the cases did the Court cite the voluminous social science literature produced by Weaver and his colleagues and used in many of the briefs. The opinions relied solely on the argument that judicial enforcement of restrictive covenants constituted government action in violation of the law. But there was little question from the participants and analysts of the cases that the sociological arguments played a crucial role in the outcome.[20]

Civil rights groups responded to the decision with jubilation. "Live Anywhere," proclaimed the headline of the *Pittsburgh Courier*. "The ruling by the court gives thousands of prospective homebuyers throughout the United States new courage and hope in the American form of government," an NAACP release proclaimed. The *Chicago Defender*, in an editorial entitled "Let Democracy Flourish," declared that the decision had "ushered in a new era of racial relationships in Chicago and the nation." The *New Republic* claimed the decision was "a reaffirmation of the basic principle that the law can't be used as a weapon to deprive Americans, regardless of their color, creed or social condition, of equality of opportunity." At the same time, many civil rights leaders argued that the opinion was not going to have an immediate effect on the lives of most people. Attorney Loren Miller stated that it would be "folly to expect an overnight reversal of attitudes," and Walter White reminded blacks that real estate boards, neighborhood associations and other private groups remained strong enemies to black home seekers.[21]

WEAVER RECEIVED GLOWING praise for his role in the victory against covenants. His stature was further heightened by the June 1948 release of his second book, *The Negro Ghetto*. The product of more than a year of intense work, the book was a study of racial change in northern cities that quickly became required reading for students of urban policy. *The Negro Ghetto* was a history, sociology, and economic analysis of the black ghetto. It was also a vigorous critique of the system of restrictive covenants and of the government's role in supporting segregation. As a result of the effort, as well as his other activities, by the late 1940s Weaver was widely acknowledged to be the nation's foremost authority on urban policy and housing discrimination and a leading scholar of black America.

Weaver conceived the book in 1946 and spent much of 1947 working on it. He peppered his former colleagues Frank Horne, B. T. McGraw, and Corienne Robinson, all of whom had remained with the federal government's housing programs, for data on recent developments in public and private housing, and he merged their statistics with a review of the existing literature on African Americans in the city and added his own analysis of policy changes during the past decade. *The Negro Ghetto* was the first work to attempt a comprehensive survey of the relatively new phenomenon of large black populations in the urban North.

In the preface, Weaver, alluding to Myrdal, noted that recent discussions of "the race problem" focused on it as a moral issue and "tended to divert attention from the economic motivations and institutions that must be recognized and understood if we are to comprehend the nature of social problems and plan for their solution." While Weaver acknowledged the "psychological and moral" aspects of residential segregation, the goal of the book was to examine the economics of the ghetto. America's housing, Weaver claimed, was in "a bad situation . . . constantly getting worse." This fact was particularly true for black Americans. Although racial conflict was generally viewed as a southern issue, Weaver argued that segregation was also a northern problem. "If the north is to maintain face and traditions, it must start at once to do something to make real its pronouncements of civilized behavior in relations to Negroes and other colored people," he claimed.[22]

*The Negro Ghetto* was divided into four parts. The first section provided a detailed examination of the rise of the northern ghetto, beginning with a brief analysis of the black urban North in the nineteenth century and describing the rise of black ghettos from World War I through World War II. Racial segregation, Weaver argued, was not the common pattern before World War I, but in most large cities it had become the rule by the end of World War II. The intransigence of the black ghetto, Weaver claimed, separated it from prior iterations. Most immigrants groups lived in concentrated areas upon arrival in America. However, within a generation, they had moved into new neighborhoods. Both public and private institutions prevented African Americans from following this pattern. Weaver provided a detailed examination of the migration patterns of African Americans, the growth and limitations of black economic institutions, and the role of white organizations, particularly real estate boards, banks, and neighborhood groups, in restricting the access of blacks to better housing. While giving particular attention to the situation in Chicago, Weaver also described ghetto formation in Detroit, Philadelphia, Los Angeles, and other cities. He concluded the section with an analysis of economic gains by blacks during the war and pointed out that African American purchasing power was higher but still could not be used to secure decent shelter in the discriminatory housing market.[23]

The second part of the book traced the recent history of the government efforts to produce housing, focusing on the Federal Housing Administration. Although it had begun to support housing construction for African Americans, Weaver argued, the agency's underwriting policies continued to tacitly support restrictive covenants and did not promote integrated housing developments. Public housing's record with regard to segregation was mixed. Although it was responsible for several projects that had mixed-race tenant bodies, the majority of them were segregated.[24]

The legal and economic institutions responsible for entrenching the ghetto were the focus of the third part of the book, which relied largely on Weaver's earlier publications. While much of this section examined the rise, use, and impact of restrictive covenants, Weaver argued that these agreements were only the most popular of several methods to restrict the housing opportunities of African Americans. He described in detail the role of local real estate boards and financial institutions in obstructing the efforts of blacks to escape the ghetto. Banks, he argued, had been "a principal deterrent to mixed racial neighborhoods." The section also discussed the small but growing number of attempts by private builders to construct homes for middle-class blacks and the backlash these efforts faced from residents and politicians.[25]

As a result of this limited market, Weaver concluded, "the non-white family receives less housing value for the same price than does the white group." He showed this through detailed statistical analysis of housing costs in large northern cities. Weaver repeated his argument that restrictive covenants were incapable of preventing the expansion of black areas and concluded his assessment by arguing that "American cities have a choice to make. They can maintain strict residential segregation or they can initiate urban redevelopment and sound urban planning. They cannot do both."[26]

The final section addressed the future of urban housing and redevelopment, focusing on contemporary "slum clearance" efforts in many cities, which sought to demolish run-down buildings and replace them with housing for the middle class. Weaver declared that programs to revitalize American cities could be an "opportunity or threat" depending upon how they were implemented. He worried that they "carried a triple threat to minorities and good housing" because such plans might further increase racial segregation by displacing blacks from desirable areas and breaking up integrated neighborhoods. They could also result in a decrease in housing available to African Americans. Appropriately implemented, however, urban redevelopment could also be a chance to create "new patterns of living" for blacks. The new communities that would be created, he asserted, presented the best opportunity for experimentation in integration, because in such areas "opposition to minorities has not crystallized."[27]

*The Negro Ghetto* was widely reviewed and warmly received. Journalist Carey McWilliams called it "the finest study of its kind that has appeared to date: well-written, carefully documented, the summing-up of invaluable experience and insight." The *New York Times* review described the book as "a comprehensive, authentic survey of an acute social problem," and Professor William Bradbury, writing in the *American Journal of Sociology*, believed that the book was "likely to remain the standard work for a good many years." Weaver's friend Catherine Bauer wrote that the book was "a long-needed classic in the field," and planner Coleman Woodbury concluded it was "one of the most important books of our troubled times." Several reviewers favorably assessed Weaver's proposal for occupancy standards. City College professor H. A. Overstreet believed that the term would "find its way increasingly into the language of interracial housing." The book, combined with his participation in the *Shelley* victory, made Weaver a national authority on urban issues.[28]

*The Negro Ghetto* was released at a time of intense battles in cities across America, both on the streets and in the boardrooms and political clubs, over the future of American cities. Much of this activity centered on the issue of racial change. The restrictive covenant cases made such agreements less attractive, but white neighborhoods continued to use them to prevent the entrance of black Americans and other minorities. However, in changing areas like those on the South Side of Chicago, such efforts had little effect. One analyst concluded that they served as "little more than a fairly coarse sieve" in this area during the postwar years. Several judges refused to enforce them, and even when plaintiffs succeeded in court, they were frequently unable to prevent the swift racial turnover that began once blacks moved into a neighborhood. Witnessing the ineffectiveness of legal maneuvers to maintain racial barriers, some communities resorted to more violent responses to integration attempts. In the immediate postwar years, Chicago was the site of dozens of attacks by whites on black newcomers. Between May 1944 and July 1946 there were at least forty-six such incidents, twenty-nine involving arson attacks on black homes.[29]

Such attacks would only escalate. In 1947, they enveloped the Airport

Homes, a Chicago Housing Authority (CHA) development for returning war veterans on the city's southwest side. Under pressure from civil rights activists who complained of the severe housing shortage for black veterans, the CHA decided to place a small number of blacks in the 185-unit development. In November, when two African American families attempted to move into the project, they were met with a barrage of rocks and racial epithets. Thousands of people gathered outside the development, overturned vehicles, and attacked passing cars. In what turned out to be a career-ending decision, Mayor Kelly stood by the black veterans, stating that "all law-abiding citizens may be assured of their right to live peaceably anywhere in Chicago." The furor over Kelly's actions played an important part in the Democratic Party's decision to replace him as their candidate for mayor in the spring of 1947. The party's choice, Martin Kennelly, would not make the same mistake, and he would oversee the construction of the nation's most segregated city. Such actions, like those across the country, tempered the victory in *Shelley*. Changing the law was one thing. Changing society was another.[30]

Weaver would be a significant participant in the struggle for the postwar city, but he would not do this from Chicago. Instead, the Weavers returned to the East Coast, this time to New York City. After four years, Weaver and Ella had never settled into life in Chicago. Although there were other professional blacks in the city, they had few good friends there, and they were isolated from their friends and family in DC and New York. Weaver was on the road for much of these years, and the family spent most of their summers elsewhere, either at Highland Beach in Maryland or, when Weaver secured a part-time summer position at Columbia Teacher's College, in New York. Even when he was in Chicago, Weaver made few efforts to include himself in black or white society. During 1947, he spent much of his free time building an eleven-foot sailboat, which he then dismantled and shipped to their summer home.[31]

When she was not taking care of Robert Jr., Ella worked on her dissertation, a study of language development in youth. In 1947, she began teaching at the newly opened Roosevelt College. An experimental effort in community-based, integrated education, the college opened in 1945 at a "campus" in an office building in downtown Chicago. Ella taught classes in speech and drama. Although she enjoyed her job, Ella too longed to return to the East Coast.[32]

During this period, Weaver decided that his professional goal was to join his wife in academia. The publication of *The Negro Ghetto* in 1948 capped a decade of distinguished scholarly productivity for Weaver. Since the late 1930s, Weaver had produced two books and more than two dozen scholarly articles on issues of labor, housing, planning, and race relations. He did this while putting in long hours in government and private-sector jobs and serving on numerous boards of directors. This was certainly a record deserving of consideration by America's academic institutions, but the racial climate in American institutions was far from liberal.

In June 1945, Fred G. Wale of the Rosenwald Fund wrote to 509 college presidents to inquire about their plans to hire African American faculty. Noting that only fifteen blacks served on faculties at white institutions, Wale informed the presidents that over two hundred African Americans possessed doctorates and that many of them had achieved distinction in research and teaching. Currently, he argued, between two hundred and three hundred African Americans received master's degrees each year. The responses Wale received were telling. College presidents gave a wide variety of reasons for the failure to hire black faculty, ranging from arguments that white students would not accept them to claims that black scholars were needed at African American colleges. Even though a significant number of black PhD's had received their training at the nation's most elite institutions—twenty from the University of Chicago, fifteen from Harvard, and ten from Columbia—white administrators told Wale that they did not believe that there were any blacks qualified for the positions. This was at a time of major expansion at American universities, when the demand for professors was at its highest ever. Even in this climate, racial exclusion remained the norm, and African American scholars made only slow inroads into white academia during the postwar years.[33]

For most of them, black institutions remained the locations of academic opportunity. After he moved to Chicago, Weaver was constantly recruited by Howard University, which wanted him to join the economics department. In 1947, after Weaver had rejected an earlier offer of a nontenured position, Dean Charles Thompson offered him a job as professor of economics at a salary of about $5,000. Weaver would replace Abram Harris, who had left to take a position at the University of Chicago. Although Weaver's pay would be less than his $6,000 annual salary at the ACRR, he entered into serious negotiations with the administration and received approval to create an institute to promote research on housing and planning issues. In the end, however, he declined to take the position.[34]

By 1947, Weaver was aggressively pursuing an academic position, but he was much more interested in one at a white institution. In addition, he and

Ella had decided that they wanted to be in New York City. In 1946, Weaver received an offer from Columbia University Teacher's College to participate in their summer session. George Counts, director of the Foundations of Education Program, asked Weaver if he would be interested in teaching two courses, one on the "philosophical foundations of education" and one on political activism entitled "Civic and Political Education through Voluntary Organizations." Weaver quickly accepted the position and received permission from the ACRR to spend six weeks in New York City. His experience was very gratifying, and the college asked Weaver to return in the summer of 1948. Weaver accepted the offer, stating that he hoped it was "a step toward the affiliation with the College." Weaver later told an interviewer that he and Ella "had both fallen in love with New York City" and agreed that this was where they wanted to live.[35]

Weaver had never been pleased with the ACRR's administration, and this dissatisfaction did not change when Louis Wirth took over. After Wirth's hiring, the ACRR focused increasingly on scholarly research. The group was instrumental in the creation of the National Association of Intergroup Relations Officials (NAIRO), an organization of professionals and academics involved in race relations, and Wirth worked to shape the field into one with clear, standardized practices. With several notable exceptions such as his and Weaver's role in the restrictive covenants cases, Wirth decreased the role of the ACRR in specific civil rights causes and increased the academic focus of the agency.[36]

Many people considered Wirth temperamental and difficult to work with. In 1939, Gunnar Myrdal asked Wirth to serve as assistant director of his race study, but Wirth, who had problems with Myrdal's approach, declined, leading Myrdal to call him a "very queer person who did not keep the truth." The Swedish economist felt that Wirth held views about blacks that were less than progressive. Wirth told Myrdal that "the Negro does not fit into the modern machine age," and "there is a looseness in his life which explains many of the statistical differences [between whites and blacks]." Weaver had great respect for Wirth but remembered "he didn't suffer fools gladly. He was not a diplomat."[37]

Weaver later told his biographer Alma Rene Williams that he had resigned because he had trouble being "second in command." The most significant tension between the men revolved around the appropriate relationship between research and advocacy. Weaver favored research directed at specific social changes, but Wirth was more circumspect about the role of academics as activists. In 1948, Wirth criticized race relations committees for adopting "shot-gun approaches" to race relations rather than carefully studying the issues and developing a long-range plan. He criticized activists who were impatient and unwilling to wait until scientific studies of race relations had been completed. "They want practical results and they want the research workers to deliver them now," Wirth complained.[38]

The larger problem, for Weaver, however, was that it was clear that Chicago was not going to be a place where the civil rights movement would make its largest impact. The battles in white neighborhoods throughout the city laid bare the difficult road facing civil rights activists in achieving the goal of integration. Frustrated by growing obstacles to equality, Weaver was so intent on moving to New York that he resigned in June 1948 without a permanent job. At that point, the only paying occupation he was certain of was his summer position at Columbia. He did have several pending options that he believed were going to pan out, and so he and Ella decided to leave Chicago. Wirth's memorandum to Weaver acknowledging his resignation was reserved, expressing "sincere appreciation for the contributions you have made during your years of service," and Weaver's departure received only one line in Wirth's report to the board of directors.[39]

The Weaver family left Chicago in mid-1948 excited to be returning to the East Coast and looking forward to new opportunities in the nation's largest city. The metropolis they were moving to was not only the center of American finance and culture but also the home of the country's growing civil rights movement. Weaver, who was already a national civil rights leader, would take an increasingly important role in the most significant aspect of the fight for equality in the North: the struggle that would come to be known as the fair-housing movement. New York was a particularly appropriate place for the battles over access to housing, as it was the city that had the most ambitious plans for redevelopment. Throughout the 1950s, New York City would be a leader in the increasingly intertwined questions of race and urban policy. Weaver would play a central role in these battles.

* 8 *

# New York City and the Institutions of Liberal Reform

In 1952, Jackie Robinson, star of the Brooklyn Dodgers and the first African American to play in baseball's major leagues, decided to move his family to a new home in the suburbs. For over a year, Robinson's wife, Rachel, searched for a suitable place for their growing family. During this process, according to Robinson, the family "became even more acutely aware that racial prejudice and discrimination in housing is vicious. It doesn't matter whether you're a day laborer or a celebrity, as long as you're black." The Robinsons experienced many subtle attempts to prevent them from buying homes in white neighborhoods. In several circumstances, homes were taken off the market after they expressed interest. In other instances, the realtors dramatically increased the asking price.[1]

In the fall of 1953, a reporter for the *Bridgeport Herald* wrote about the Robinsons' failed efforts to buy a home in Stamford, Connecticut. Realtors in the area denied the article's claims and alleged that the controversy was the "politically inspired" work of "rabble rousers." In December, the community's leading ministers convened a meeting, and they decided to circulate among their congregations a statement affirming their opposition to discrimination. While they did not intend their actions as a "crusade," the statement proclaimed that the "exclusion of any person solely for reasons of race, creed or national origin could lessen the spiritual, economic and social development of the community." Later the same month, the Robinsons signed an agreement to purchase a house in the area.[2]

The Robinsons' struggle was part of an increasing focus on racial discrimination in the postwar years. Social, political, and economic change in the 1940s resulted in an invigorated civil rights movement that could no longer be ignored by the country's political elite. While progress was slow, legal and political victories, as well as personal successes like those of the

Robinsons, became increasingly common in the post–World War II years. The effort against housing discrimination is a crucial, yet neglected, aspect of the broader civil rights movement, and Robert Weaver was the leader.[3]

Weaver left Chicago excited to be moving back east and hoping to settle into academia. He told Frank Horne that he had decided to "slow down and enjoy life," and he believed that an academic job would enable him to live in financial security while providing him with the flexibility to continue civil rights activism. In the short term, Weaver's dreams would be fulfilled, as he would secure a position at New York University. Weaver's career in academia, however, was short-lived, lasting only a year. He would return to the ivory tower one day, but not until two decades had passed.[4]

Instead, as the civil rights movement gained momentum in the postwar years, Weaver was increasingly drawn into the struggle, where his experience, knowledge, and connections made him an invaluable member of the growing effort to fight racial discrimination in northern cities. Though the battle against segregation in education has received the most attention from historians, Weaver joined other activists in the equally important and hard-fought struggle against residential segregation. Through his work at the Whitney Foundation and his leadership of the National Committee against Discrimination in Housing, Weaver engaged the nation's political, business, and philanthropic elite in this effort. Although Weaver was already a well-known expert on housing issues, during this period he would develop a national reputation that would enable him to move into the high echelons of government, first in New York State and then in Washington.

In many ways, the city and state of New York were ahead of the nation regarding racial equality. In 1945, the state became the first in the nation to prohibit religious and racial discrimination in private employment, creating the State Commission against Discrimination (SCAD) to enforce the law. However, in the early years the law was more symbolic than real, as SCAD did little to respond to discrimination complaints and its leaders bragged that they had never used the agency's enforcement powers. Other aspects of city life also illuminated New York's complicated racial landscape. Many of the city's hotels and restaurants did not discriminate, but others did, leaving blacks confused and constantly aware of their fragile position in society. Similarly, while some New York educational institutions provided instruction on a nondiscriminatory basis, many private schools and colleges did not. If social relations were somewhat fluid, residential segregation was not. Many civil rights leaders blamed the 1943 Harlem eruption on the almost-total exclusion blacks experienced when they tried to access housing anywhere other than the northern Manhattan ghetto (or a similar one in central Brooklyn). The real estate industry systematically barred blacks from the overwhelming majority of city neighborhoods.[5]

The center of American liberalism, New York City was the best place to reform the nation's system of residential segregation. New York's racial landscape, like the city itself, was dynamic in the postwar years. Given the continued in-migration of blacks and Puerto Ricans and the movement of whites to the surrounding suburbs, no one could forecast what the future held. The region, therefore, presented great opportunities for positive, or negative, change. No aspect represented the dynamic state of the city more than its redevelopment program. After several decades of lobbying from urban planners and other activists, by the 1940s "slum clearance" initiatives (they would later be given the more positive-sounding name of "urban renewal") were under way. Advocates argued that their efforts would eliminate the chaos of the tenement neighborhoods and replace them with modern, efficient communities. During the postwar years, this initiative would rebuild large sections of the city while reshaping New York's racial geography.

In *The Negro Ghetto,* Weaver declared that redevelopment programs could be an "opportunity or threat" depending upon how they were implemented. They might displace blacks from desirable areas, be used to break up integrated neighborhoods, and result in a decrease in housing for African Americans. Appropriately implemented, however, urban redevelopment could also be a chance to create "new patterns of living" for blacks. As he had argued for a decade, new communities presented the best opportunity for experimentation in integration. Over the next decade and a half, Weaver would become a central participant in the struggle to implement the vision of an integrated city, both in New York and across the nation.[6]

Weaver's efforts were marked by the same characteristics that guided his work in DC and Chicago: a reliance on professional analysis of social problems and a focus on institutional reform through elite channels. Much of his work in this period concerned programs to aid middle-class blacks, in the belief that their success would open doors for their poorer brethren. Particularly after the passage of the 1949 Housing Act, Weaver and his colleagues lobbied incessantly to reform federal, state, and local housing policies and to push government bureaucrats to wield their power in support of racial integration. In the 1950s, activists succeeded in passing several laws in New York, and then in other states, that banned discrimination in the sale or rental of housing. Weaver's advocacy, writing, and organizational skills were crucial to these important victories. At the same time, he and Ella became important, if not particularly social, members of New York City's liberal community, serving as mediators between the white and black sectors of that elite.

The early 1950s, capped by the Supreme Court's renunciation, in *Brown v. Board of Education*, of "separate but equal," were a time of significant progress in the legal attack on racial discrimination. During these years, civil rights activists gained important allies in business and politics, and they began the long process of changing public attitudes regarding racial integration. One of the most important, and most frustrating, aspects of this struggle involved the effort to promote residential integration. Although they made important progress in removing legal barriers for blacks and other minorities during this period, the efforts of Weaver and his colleagues to bring about fundamental, lasting change in the nation's neighborhood racial rules would illuminate both the potential and the limitations of their approach.

SOON AFTER ARRIVING in New York, Weaver finalized negotiations to accept a position as visiting professor in Negro culture and education at New York University (NYU). An institution long in the shadow of its ivy-league neighbor Columbia, NYU was undergoing a major expansion in the postwar years. The administration hired Weaver under a grant given it by the Rockefeller Fund to create opportunities for African American scholars to teach at white schools. To secure Weaver, NYU administrators offered to pay him an additional $1,000 to supplement the $6,000 salary funded by the grant. In his first year, Weaver, who was located in the School of Education, taught three classes: two introductory classes in education and one on "voluntary organizations" in urban policy. Although he was still not particularly comfortable in the classroom, Weaver told Frank Horne that he was enjoying teaching and also appreciating having "free time." NYU officials were also pleased with their new addition. Ernest Melby, dean of the School of Education, told Rockefeller officials that Weaver was "an exceptional individual" who "as a representative of his racial group brings both distinction and inter-group understanding." Although the appointment was generally nonrenewable, NYU officials asked the fund to allow them to reappoint Weaver for a second year (the last year remaining on the grant).[7]

Weaver enjoyed interacting with students and faculty, but he most appreciated that his position enabled him to focus most of his time on research and activism. As he had in Chicago, Weaver continued to battle housing discrimination. He came to the city at a crucial moment in the battle for equal opportunity in housing. Although they celebrated the Supreme Court's *Shelley v. Kraemer* decision, few civil rights leaders believed that the federal agencies charged with implementing the housing program would apply the ruling wholeheartedly. By 1948, activists had spent more than a decade in a frustrated effort to reform federal housing programs, and they would spend another two decades before securing the full support of the federal government.[8]

The worst offender was the guarantor of America's suburban dreams, the Federal Housing Administration (FHA). Throughout its early history, the agency systematically rejected all efforts to include blacks in the housing market, but this practice drew increasing criticism. The *Shelley* decision in particular created intense concern for many builders, realtors, and their supporters in the government. In response, federal housing administrator Raymond Foley asked for a review of agency policies to see if they would have to be changed in light of the decision. The conclusion of his staff was that the agency could continue business as usual. They would no longer recommend restrictive covenants (a change Truman had ordered a year before), but they would do nothing to prevent them or other forms of discrimination. According to FHA commissioner Franklin Richards, it was not the place of government "to require private individuals to give up their right to dispose of their property as they see fit."[9]

Later that summer in 1948, Weaver met with other activists to craft a strategy to change federal policies, and they recommended that the president issue an executive order forbidding discrimination in all federal housing programs. However, officials were slow to respond. That fall, the government's position was put to the test at the development that would become the paradigmatic postwar community, Levittown, New York. Developer William Levitt planned a 17,500-house community on Long Island, New York, and he sought and received federal mortgage assistance and other support to build these homes for veterans. However, while several hundred thousand African Americans were eligible under the program, Levitt announced that he would sell and rent only to whites. Thurgood

Marshall asked the FHA to deny financial support to the Levitt Company, but Commissioner Richards, writing after the *Shelley* opinion, replied that he found nothing in the law "which would authorize this administration to refuse to insure mortgages" on the grounds that they were bound by racially restrictive covenants. Despite legal and political efforts of civil rights officials, Levittown opened in 1949 as a "whites only" community.[10]

In February 1949, Thurgood Marshall sent President Truman a long memo, written with Weaver's help, describing discrimination in federal housing programs and asking that he direct the FHA to "exclude all considerations predicated upon racial, religious or national distinctions." Over the next six months, Solicitor General Philip Perlman met with civil rights leaders and housing officials to negotiate over the proposal. FHA officials and their clients in the banking, building, and realty sectors adamantly opposed any presidential declaration, arguing that allowing blacks to purchase or rent anywhere would harm the housing market. Truman and his advisors, however, recognized the importance of the black vote to the Democratic Party and decided they had to act. In December 1949, Perlman announced that the FHA would not provide mortgage insurance for any properties that had recorded restrictive covenants subsequent to the promulgation of the Supreme Court ruling.[11]

Real estate executives blasted the announcement, but federal officials quickly calmed them by noting that the prohibition applied only to *recorded* restrictive covenants, not to "gentleman's agreements," and that it would be "an exceptional case where a property cannot receive Federal mortgage help." Civil rights activists were truly disappointed by the order and even more by the subsequent statements. They complained that the new rules would not affect existing restrictive covenants or reduce FHA hostility to mixed housing developments. The backtracking was typical of the Truman administration's approach to civil rights at midcentury. Stymied in most of its domestic initiatives and increasingly focused on the conflict in Korea, as well as the cold war in general, Truman was reluctant to use too much of his political capital on civil rights issues. He feared losing the support of southern Democrats on other matters, and therefore he did not want to take action in this sensitive area that would upset the patrons of Jim Crow.[12]

In New York City, activists were also frustrated in their efforts to breathe meaning into the exhortations of racial equality. There the battle focused on a new massive development named Stuyvesant Town. Spearheaded by master builder and "power broker" Robert Moses and sponsored by the Metropolitan Life Insurance Company, the middle-income apartment complex covered a seventy-two-acre tenement district on Manhattan's Lower East Side. While most of the city's progressive leadership supported "slum clearance" and affordable housing, civil rights activists were most concerned about the remarks of Metropolitan Life chairman Frederick Ecker regarding Stuyvesant Town's racial composition. "Negroes and whites don't mix," Ecker stated in 1944, declaring that the project would be for whites only.[13]

This statement started a flurry of activity at the city and state levels. Civil rights activists demanded that the city and state refuse to move forward on the project until Ecker agreed that Stuyvesant Town would admit tenants on a nondiscriminatory basis. Unable to secure governmental support, activists brought suit against Metropolitan Life and the city. The lead counsel on the case was Charles Abrams. Born in Russia, Abrams immigrated to New York as a child. Like many other working-class Brooklyn Jews, Abrams attended City College. He then became a successful real estate lawyer in Manhattan and an active supporter of housing reform. Abrams played a crucial role in the creation of the New York City Housing Authority and served as its counsel for the first four years of its existence. Paraphrasing Weaver's arguments in *The Negro Ghetto,* Abrams claimed that, instead of intensifying segregation, Stuyvesant Town could be a model for future integration efforts. Because it would be a new development, the residents would not have established views about what was acceptable for the neighborhood. Ecker's response to the complaints was to announce that his company would also build "model housing for colored folks," the Riverton Houses, in Harlem. Although NAACP officials condemned the project, many middle-class blacks, desperate for decent housing, welcomed the 1,200-unit development. Abrams lost the suit, but the battle energized black and white activists to organize against housing discrimination.[14]

Although their personalities could not have been more different—Abrams was an ebullient social butterfly who had opinions on everything—Weaver and Abrams would work closely together in civil rights and Democratic Party causes, developing a relationship that, while often contentious, lasted the remainder of their lives. Together, Abrams and Weaver would be founding members of what would come to be known as the fair-housing movement. Their efforts were crucial, because much more was at stake than discrimination in New York City. In 1949, after a decade of attempts, the federal government entered the urban redevelopment field, creating the potential for dramatic change in cities across the nation. Ushering in a new era of urban policy, the Housing Act of 1949 promised a decent home for everyone and sought to bring about this goal by providing funding to local governments to clear slums and redevelop them. Although other federal programs, particularly the highway initiative that began in the mid-1950s, also had a big impact on American cities, urban renewal and public housing came to be viewed, for better or worse, as the face of federal urban policy. The promise and limitations of that approach would be revealed over the next twenty years as cities demolished buildings and replaced them with expensive, middle-class, and publicly owned housing.[15]

The central premise behind the urban renewal program was that cities were succumbing to decline, called "blight" by urban planners. In order to revitalize these areas, cities needed to acquire run-down properties through the power of eminent domain. After the tenements and other buildings were demolished, the areas could be replanned and sold for redevelopment. As Weaver had said in his book, such efforts had the potential to dramatically help or hurt African Americans. The path of these programs, he and Abrams believed, depended on the intervention of professionals who would promote equal access to housing.[16]

To bring this about, they decided that permanent institutions were required. Along with Weaver and Abrams, two other people, both of whom would become Weaver's lifelong friends and colleagues, were crucial to this effort: Algernon Black and Hortense Gabel. Black, a graduate of Columbia College, was the director of the New York Ethical Culture Society. The society, founded in 1876 by wealthy, Reform Jews, described itself as "a humanistic religion based on the ideal that the supreme aim of life is working to create a more humane society." Active in many civil rights causes, Black's participation in the fair-housing movement emerged from his organization's commitment to equal treatment and its desire to protect its membership from discrimination.[17]

Born in the Bronx, Gabel would have a long history of opening doors for women in the legal field. Among the first women to graduate from Columbia Law School, she would later become a judge on the New York Supreme Court. Robert Moses's biographer Robert Caro described her as a "reformer with a healthy helping of the reformer's penchant for idealism." Gabel was drawn to the fair-housing effort through her friendship with Rabbi Stephen Wise, founder of the American Jewish Congress. Gabel was active in many civil rights causes throughout the 1940s and afterward, and throughout the 1950s she was the administrative mastermind behind the fair-housing movement.[18]

In 1949 and 1950, the foursome was responsible for the creation of two organizations that would be the leaders in the cause of fair housing: the New York State Committee on Discrimination in Housing (NYSCDH), founded in 1949, and the National Committee against Discrimination in Housing (NCDH), created a year later. Although they were incorporated separately, the organizations had the same staff (including Gabel) and the same participants. Black served as president of the NYSCDH, and Weaver was elected president of the NCDH. Both organizations drew their strength from the coalition of groups that supported fair housing. Most active among its constituent members were the NAACP and the American Jewish Congress. The boards of directors of the groups were filled with leaders of New York's liberal elite, including Judge Justine Wise Polier, Stephen Polier, Dr. Bryn Hovde (president of the New School for Social Research), Stanley Isaacs (New York City councilman), Judge Hubert Delany, and Mrs. Marshall Field. In the decade that followed, these organizations, with Weaver first as an active member and then as a supportive government insider, would be the leaders in the efforts of northern civil rights activists to combat the country's increasing residential racial segregation.[19]

Influenced by Gunnar Myrdal's arguments, fair-housing advocates believed that public awareness was the key to the successful implementation of the Housing Act. To that end, they organized a major campaign to convince the public that housing discrimination was wrong. The centerpiece of the campaign was the photo essay "Forbidden Neighbors," cowritten by Weaver. Released in November 1949, immediately after the passage of the Housing Act, the pamphlet argued: "These vast funds, which will be greatly enlarged by local expenditures, will have an enormous impact on interracial and group relations. Properly administered, the new law may serve as a major step in breaking down urban patterns of segregation."[20]

The pamphlet relied on the arguments that Weaver had made against restrictive covenants and claimed that "housing is the crux of the fight against group hatred," and that segregation was a moral and social problem requiring solution. Segregation was the cause of group hostilities, it resulted in social problems like crime and delinquency, and it was responsible for increased government expenditures. "More serious than the cash loss is the waste of human beings," the pamphlet continued. Furthermore, it pointed out that discrimination affected U.S. relations with other nations, where "our system of segregation has been more thoroughly publicized than our preachments on democracy and the equality of man."

Pointing to examples in public housing, the pamphlet argued that "racial integration works." To promote the benefits of open housing, the pamphlet was full of pictures of smiling groups of racially diverse children playing at these projects. If these efforts were continued, "Forbidden Neighbors" argued, integration could become the norm, not the exception. Toward that end, the pamphlet called upon citizens to take it upon themselves to make integration a reality. "Forbidden Neighbors" argued that equality "begins at home" but that organization was necessary to see that integration became a reality. By 1950, the group reported that it had distributed more than 10,000 copies.

Although the fair-housing movement was a coalition of many groups with strong ideas about civil rights, Weaver's perspective on these issues was very influential. Weaver had written frequently about the unfairness of the exclusion that blacks, particularly higher-income African Americans, experienced in the housing market. Throughout the 1950s, Weaver argued that a growing number of black families were able to pay for suburban housing but builders and policymakers were preventing them from participating in the market. "Under a free economy," he asserted, "the purchaser is supposed to have access to the total supply (within his price range) at the same time that the seller is supposed to have access to the total effective demand." In his analysis, the housing market failed to meet this standard. "Nowhere is the repudiation of the promise of a free, private enterprise economy better illustrated than in the development of postwar communities like Levittowns and Park Forest [a suburban Chicago development], where colored families, regardless of income and cultural attainments, are systematically excluded." The question for the policymakers, Weaver argued, was, "not so much whether we are going to continue with residential segregation, but a more immediate issue, and that is whether or not we are going to expand it with the stamp of government approval."[21]

Weaver's view was that antidiscrimination laws would enable a small number of middle-class blacks to move into new housing and provide a first step toward integration. He had no illusions that the process would be rapid: it would likely take several generations before the goal of full racial integration was achieved. Over the next decade, fair-housing activists would convince many Americans (though far from a majority) that integration was a good thing. However, the progress in changing abstract understandings about racial minorities was not paralleled by a corresponding reform in the responses to the actual arrival of racial minorities in most white neighborhoods. In principle, FHA-sponsored suburban housing, public housing, and urban renewal were racially neutral programs. In practice, combined with discrimination by builders and white residents, their role in entrenching the separation of races was crucial. Throughout his years in New York, and continuing in Washington when he was put in charge of these initiatives, Weaver and his peers would struggle to reform these programs, with limited success.

THE BATTLE AGAINST housing discrimination was Weaver's main concern, but this job did not pay the bills. To earn a living, Weaver would seek support from the white philanthropists whom he had cultivated throughout his career. In June 1948, the Julius Rosenwald Fund closed its doors. The foundation, which had done more to support civil rights causes, African American institutions, and minority individuals than any other philanthropy, was following the directives of its creator, who required that all funds be expended by the fund's twenty-fifth year. The closure put many organizations in crisis. Several that had relied on the Rosenwald Fund for the majority of their funding, including the American Council on Race Relations, would cease operations soon thereafter.[22]

That month, several hundred of the nation's civil rights leaders met in Chicago to celebrate the achievements of the Rosenwald Fund. The event, organized by Weaver, brought together business officials, academics, and politicians to praise the deceased founder and the fund's leader Edwin Embree. While acknowledging the crucial role of the fund in the advancement of civil rights, activists also worried about how their organizations (the fund had supported the NAACP, the National Urban League, as well as hundreds of secondary schools and dozens of black colleges) would replace the $22 million the philanthropy had spent during its life. The closure of the Rosenwald Fund left a gaping hole in the support structure of the Talented Tenth, a significant number of whose leaders had been supported by Rosenwald Fellowships.[23]

Into this void, partially, stepped John Hay Whitney. The forty-four-year-old Whitney was as close to American royalty as the nation had. Descendant of original settlers of the Massachusetts Bay Colony, relative of Eli Whitney, grandson of former secretary of state and Lincoln biographer John Hay, Whitney was from a family that was among the wealthiest and best known in the country. His forebears had been business partners of the Rockefellers and the Vanderbilts and had amassed fortunes surpassed only by those families. Whitney had added to his own fortune through investment banking and had become a Hollywood producer in the 1930s (his most significant investment was in *Gone with the Wind*).[24]

After World War II, Whitney, who had served in Europe and had been a prisoner of war, received access to a large portion of the immense estate that his father had left him, and he decided to form a foundation. In 1949 Whitney asked Edwin Embree, recently freed from his responsibilities with the Rosenwald Fund, to serve as a consultant to help shape the foundation's program. As he had in almost every initiative during the decade, Embree asked Weaver to help him on the project. Embree and Weaver recommended that Whitney use the foundation's resources to support the education of talented minority students, modeling their plan on the defunct Rosenwald Scholars program. They proposed the creation of the Opportunity Fellowship Program, which would "give impetus, encouragement and assistance to younger persons who have demonstrated exceptional promise and who, because of arbitrary barriers such as racial or cultural background or region or residence, have not had full opportunity to develop their talents." At a time when racial barriers at many of the nation's elite schools were just beginning to fall, the funds would ensure that the upwardly aspiring minority students had the resources they needed to finish their education so that they could go on to prestigious jobs. In the fall of 1949, Whitney agreed to the proposal and allocated $100,000 annually to be given to talented youth to pursue professional and graduate education.[25]

Soon after the Whitney Foundation board of trustees voted to approve the program, Whitney asked Weaver to run it. The decision was obviously Whitney's but it was also clearly supported by Weaver's friend Embree. Weaver did not hesitate to accept the job, which at $10,000 paid $2,000 more than he currently earned and was much more secure since much of his salary at NYU was supported by a grant about to end. While continuing to teach two classes, Weaver began working at the Whitney Foundation in December 1949.[26]

Over the five years that Weaver ran the program, the Opportunity Fellowships supported over two hundred young scholars. The majority were African American, but a significant number of fellowships went to Latinos, Asian Americans, and Native Americans. The program also funded students from Eastern Europe and several whites from Appalachia. They received grants from $1,000 to $3,000 annually to pursue studies in numerous fields, including law, medicine, social sciences, hard sciences, and the arts. In 1954, Weaver reported to the trustees that thirteen fellows had received PhD's, ten had received law degrees, and eleven had become medical doctors. The program also supported a large number of students in music, drama, and art, including opera singers Lenora Lafayette and Mattiwilda Dobbs and pianist Natalie Hinderas, many of whom became internationally known.[27]

In the twenty-one years the program operated, it supported almost one thousand individuals. During Weaver's term, he funded many students who would become leaders in their fields: the Whitney Foundation aided A. Leon Higginbotham, who would become a judge on the Third Circuit Court of Appeals, to pay for his studies at Yale Law School; it supported anthropologist Elliot Skinner, who would later become a professor at Columbia University; and it helped Andrew Brimmer, who would become the first African American member of the Federal Reserve Board, to pursue a doctorate in economics from Harvard. Several fellows went on to careers in the Foreign Service. He also aided one of the first Native Americans, Edward Dozier of the University of Oregon, to obtain a tenured position at an American university. As head of the program, Weaver oversaw the review of applications and personally interviewed most of the applicants. He also charted their progress through graduate school and thereafter.[28]

Weaver's position placed him in a position of power to influence the lives of the Talented Tenth of African Americans as well as other minorities. It also gave him access to the foundation world and a connection to one of the nation's richest men. Furthermore, the job provided the financial stability and time to pursue other goals. Weaver modeled his activities on those of his friend Embree, who had made himself a civil rights leader through the numerous volunteer activities he undertook while running the Rosenwald Fund. Since Whitney was familiar with the philanthropic world, he understood that much of Weaver's time would be devoted to public service. He supported Weaver in these efforts, believing that such activities were good public relations for the fund. The job was also attractive to Weaver because, unlike his position in Chicago, Weaver had no boss to oversee his daily activities. Weaver had a small staff to manage, but the position provided him great freedom and opportunities to involve himself in other causes. The issue of housing discrimination received the lion's share of Weaver's professional time.

Soon after Weaver took the job, the family moved to a new apartment on Riverside Drive, a lovely neighborhood on Manhattan's Upper West Side abutting Riverside Park and with beautiful views of the Hudson River and the New Jersey countryside. The move put Weaver closer to his office at Rockefeller Center. It also placed the Weavers in the center, at least physically, of the city's liberal community. If Manhattan's Upper East Side was the center of the city's blue-blood elite, the Upper West Side was where many of the nation's most important liberal thinkers, philanthropists, and activists lived. Robert and Ella were important, if not social, members of this influential club.

In his note to classmates marking the twenty-fifth anniversary of their graduation from Harvard College, Weaver wrote that "we live in Manhattan and love it," and they clearly did. Throughout the decade, Weaver became an increasingly important member of the city's liberal elite, active in numerous charitable, political, and advocacy organizations. But, as racial pioneers, as well as deeply private people, Weaver and Ella lived on the periphery of the Upper West Side social circle. Though they were friendly with many of the city's white and black leaders, they preferred to socialize in small groups and generally avoided the large parties that were the life of many activists. Shirley Siegel, Weaver's colleague in the fair-housing effort, remembered the period as a vibrant social world that mixed business and pleasure. Their mutual friend Charles Abrams was one of its most gregarious members, throwing parties frequently at his house. "I don't recall ever seeing Weaver at any of his parties," Siegel later observed. She described Weaver as a soft-spoken man who was "always the most gentlemanly of the group." Ella was a "lovely, gracious, southern, attractive woman. She was reserved also," Siegel recalled.[29]

Ella had her own busy schedule to maintain. In 1949 she took at job as assistant professor of speech at Brooklyn College. She would remain there for two decades. During this time, Ella trained thousands of students in the theory and practice of speech therapy. The chair of her department described Ella as an "altogether unusual person" and reported that "the entire staff are very happy to have her here." Over the years, Ella would be an important member of the Brooklyn College community, and she would also become a leader in her field.[30]

During the summer, the family retreated to what Weaver described as "a small cottage on the Housatonic River in Connecticut" that they bought in the early 1950s. The house, near the town of Oxford, Connecticut, had "bathing, swimming, and boating from our back yard, and the place always needs attention," he told his classmates. As he had since his youth, Weaver spent most of his free time working on the house and on other construction projects. He built several small boats and many pieces of furniture during the family's time there.

FREED FROM WORRIES about paying the bills by his job with the Whitney Foundation, Weaver continued to focus his efforts on the battle against housing discrimination. But, despite activists' constant pleading throughout the remainder of Truman's term, federal housing officials and their home-building clients rejected any changes to their standard practices. Symbolic of federal inaction was its acquiescence to another ambitious Levitt development, this one in the Bucks County suburb of Philadelphia. The new development of 17,300 homes in Morrisville, Pennsylvania, would provide housing to defense workers at U.S. Steel and their families. As before, Levitt stated that the homes would be for whites only, even though a substantial percentage of U.S. Steel's workforce was black. Civil rights leaders vehemently protested this decision. Weaver told federal housing leader Raymond Foley that "should this city be developed on a segregated basis . . . an ominous pattern will have been set for the entire country."[31]

But housing officials responded that the rules did not "forbid segregation" and they could not deny federal support to "persons who might be unwilling to disregard race, color or creed in the selection of their purchasers or tenants." Administrator Foley asked for patience and acknowledgment of the "many things he has done" for minorities. Weaver described Foley's efforts as "sending a child to do a man's work." Despite numerous protests, the FHA approved a massive loan to Levitt for the project.[32]

To placate his critics, Foley asked Weaver to join the Slum Clearance Advisory Committee, a group that would work with Nathaniel Keith, administrator of the new urban development program. Weaver joined several politicians, policymakers, and business leaders, including Pittsburgh mayor David Lawrence, banker Earl Schwulst, and planners Harland Bartholomew and Catherine Bauer, on the committee. The role of the group was to advise the program's leadership about regulations and guidelines. From the first meeting, Weaver raised concerns about the impact of renewal efforts on African Americans. He argued that relocation would put immense strains on black residents unless federal agencies required cities to provide housing on a nondiscriminatory basis. He further asserted, joining Bauer, that federal officials should require cities to build housing on vacant sites before allowing them to demolish buildings in slum areas.

Foley acknowledged his concerns but did little to address them. The position on the advisory panel gave him detailed information about the implementation of the program, but it provided no power to prevent the racial discrimination that clearance would promote.[33]

Weaver's experiences on the committee and in his other relations with federal officials disheartened him. In his 1952 address to the National Conference on Discrimination in Housing, Weaver gave an interim report on the impact of the urban renewal program, concluding that the effects were in some ways worse than expected. "What was not anticipated," Weaver asserted, was that urban renewal, "in combination with the continuation of FHA neglect of the Negro market, would engender a new and extremely costly racial discrimination in urban shelter." The initiative was still relatively new, but African American neighborhoods across the country were already being targeted for redevelopment. The demolition of working-class homes under the program, combined with a similar number of dislocations resulting from public housing development, exacerbated an already-tight housing market, and discrimination made it even more difficult for blacks to find adequate housing. At the same time clearance projects were reshaping urban racial geography, the public housing program was having its own impact. In some cities, the initiative had a positive effect on residential race relations, but in others it took on an ominous form, providing a mechanism for the entrenchment of segregation at an unprecedented scale.[34]

Because they had begun redevelopment efforts before the passage of the federal law, New York and Chicago were the furthest advanced in the implementation of the program. In New York, Robert Moses's "redevelopment machine" had several major public and private housing developments under construction or in the planning stages at midcentury, and federal funds enabled Moses to move these projects along more swiftly. Moses planned a major renewal effort in Manhattan and parts of Brooklyn. He envisioned the demolition of thousands of tenements and their replacement with modern high-rise apartments that would be attractive to middle-class professionals. Over the next two decades, federal, state, and local funds would enable the construction of several hundred thousand units of housing and bring about a dramatic change in the city's residential structure. Though he supported the efforts to clear dilapidated buildings and replace them with modern housing, Weaver would be constantly at odds with the "Power Broker" over the specific plans, which often disproportionately affected the city's black population.[35]

New Yorkers celebrated the commencement of renewal projects across

Manhattan and in selected parts of the other boroughs, but Weaver and his colleagues in the fair-housing movement quickly became concerned about the impact of demolition on working-class New Yorkers. They lobbied politicians and government officials to slow the redevelopment process while they developed a workable solution to the relocation problems faced by those who lived in the project areas (an estimated 325,000 people were dislocated in the decade following World War II). Properly planned, Weaver claimed, development projects could put "the stamp of government approval on open occupancy housing" and show that integration could work. But Robert Moses rejected this advice. New York's rebirth, he argued, could not wait for more planning. Any delays would imperil his efforts, and he threatened to resign if the mayor or other officials obstructed his plans.[36]

This policy had disastrous effects on the public housing program. In the early 1950s, fair-housing activists across the country succeeded in convincing public housing officials to accept racial integration, and several cities and states passed laws prohibiting racial segregation in public housing projects. In many cities, housing authorities discovered that the maintenance of segregated projects was just too inefficient and prevented them from achieving other goals. The New York City Housing Authority, long an opponent of "mixing housing and social problems," began to actively support integration efforts during the years. Open access in public housing was made necessary by the immense problems of relocation brought on by urban redevelopment. In order to quickly clear sites, public housing had to be more flexible in its tenant selection. As a result, public housing became the first true experiment in integrated living. According to Weaver, "untold numbers of racially-mixed neighborhoods in hundreds of urban centers in all parts of the nation prove that racially-democratic housing patterns are possible." The long-run implications of these victories, however, were problematic. Since blacks remained excluded from housing in many areas, "open occupancy" in public housing meant, in most large cities, that they were in the transitional phase from white to minority.[37]

In theory, blacks and Latinos uprooted by clearance projects could move to other parts of the city. In reality, housing discrimination severely limited their options. As a result, these refugees crowded into neighborhoods with deteriorating housing that whites no longer desired. Neighborhoods like the Brownsville section of Brooklyn, once a predominantly Jewish neighborhood, witnessed a rapid racial transformation during the decade as increasing numbers of the dislocated found shelter in the neighborhood's crumbling tenements and in the area's public housing inventory. An area where residents originally supported public housing and lobbied government officials to build there, by the early 1950s Brownsville had three large projects. The first, the Brownsville Houses, was racially integrated when it opened in 1948. However, as housing officials concluded that the neighborhood was destined to lose its white population, they increasingly directed blacks and Latinos to these dwellings. By 1960, their composition, like the rest of the neighborhood, would be overwhelmingly minority. It was a transformation that was repeated in districts across the city and country.[38]

Chicago's redevelopment program, which, like New York's, had begun before the passage of the federal act, had even more profound implications for that city's black population. In New York, redevelopment officials expressed support for the principle of equality even if they did not take such promises seriously in the implementation. In Chicago, public housing and slum clearance became the primary means by which the city's racial boundaries were forged in steel and concrete. Over the next twenty years, Chicago mayors used federal funds to separate the races, demolishing thousands of tenements and building a massive public housing complex for African Americans on the city's South Side. To ensure that whites and blacks remained separate, Mayor Richard Daley built a ten-lane interstate highway to cordon off the projects.[39]

Although New York and Chicago were the most extreme examples, these patterns were repeated across the nation. The implications for the future of cities, which most policymakers were oblivious to, were profound. Willing to pay high prices to secure decent housing, blacks were moving into new neighborhoods, creating what Weaver described as "pressure turnover, a process in which present occupants reluctantly leave their abodes under the impetus of high selling prices and of the fear of heralded neighborhood deterioration." As a result, Weaver argued, unlike prior policies which allowed private parties to create segregated living patterns, "today a local agency, operating with federal funds and blessed with approval of a federal agency, can and does affect the whole job of racial displacement."[40]

Policymakers in the Truman administration disappointed fair-housing advocates, but at least that regime had provided some moral support for the cause. When General Dwight Eisenhower took office in 1953, such affinity almost disappeared. Eisenhower's choice for Housing and Home Finance Agency (HHFA) administrator, Albert M. Cole, was a former congressman who was a vocal opponent of public housing, rent control, and many other federal housing policies. His nomination was vigorously opposed by most housing groups. "It is no exaggeration to say that his appointment would be disastrous to the national housing program," declared Hortense Gabel.[41]

Fair-housing advocates got little help from the head of the nation's housing program. After his confirmation, Cole argued that his job was to serve his clients—real estate developers and housing consumers—and that he was not concerned primarily with "social issues." He acknowledged that, "too often, the workings of our free economy do not provide solutions that benefit minorities," but he concluded that housing discrimination could be overcome by the education of home builders and neighborhood residents. His main proposal to solve housing discrimination was the creation of a special financing tool to promote voluntary home building for the "Negro market."[42]

Weaver complained that Eisenhower's housing program "utterly failed to come to grips with minority housing problems." The administration "would not prevent the overcrowding which is at the root of urban decay," because it did nothing to promote the production of decent housing for minorities. Relying on moral suasion to get developers to build housing for black homebuyers, Weaver argued, would not work. Racially restrictive practices could not "be overcome by exhortation and education" alone.[43]

Cole also attacked the one office in his agency, created by Weaver two decades earlier, working to promote the interests of blacks. In 1953, Cole replaced Frank Horne, the race relations head who had taken Weaver's job in 1940, with a political appointee, Louisville realtor Joseph Ray. NCDH leaders called the action "a mischievous step backward that would go far to destroy the non-political character of this technical office," and Weaver organized a group of national leaders to protest the decision. After a barrage of complaints, Cole decided not to fire Horne and instead gave him the new title of "advisor to the administrator," with no staff or clear functions.[44]

But during the years that followed, Cole systematically marginalized Horne, removing him from any positions of influence. He declined to replace Horne's staff members and directed that his office be left off distribution lists of important documents. Cole's dismissal of the office led even Ray, who was appointed with the understanding that he would keep a low profile, to complain. In 1955, Cole did fire Horne and his assistant Corienne Robinson Morrow (whom Weaver had brought to the federal government in 1934) on the pretense of budget restrictions. These actions severely limited the office that Weaver had established more than two decades before.[45]

By mid-decade, fair-housing advocates viewed federal lobbying efforts as hopeless and declared that "the period of negotiation with HHFA had been exhausted." "The record of the FHA with regard to the production of homes for minority groups has indeed been a sorry one," NCDH director Frances Levenson testified in front of the House Committee on Banking and Currency. Federal housing officials rejected calls for greater intervention into housing markets because they believed such activities exceeded their purview.[46]

The 1954 decision *Brown v. Board of Education*, which invalidated the separate but equal doctrine, was a momentous one in the history of race relations. Though it was not the first time the Supreme Court had supported African Americans in their efforts to break down the Jim Crow system, the decision was a ringing declaration of the judges' aspiration for a society where racial categories were irrelevant. Although the Court failed to support its professions of racial equality with the legal backing to fulfill this dream, the language of the opinion still had a profound impact on American society. After *Brown* the balance of legal power shifted against the protectors of legal segregation and toward those seeking racial justice.

However, in the everyday world of suburban development, urban renewal, and public housing, the racial trends moved in a direction antithetical to the goal of integration. The initiatives created in the postwar years changed the landscape of urban America, supporting a massive migration of the middle class to newly developed communities while rebuilding significant parts of city cores. Throughout these years, business leaders, policymakers, and journalists celebrated the progress the country was experiencing, remaining generally oblivious to the profoundly negative implications of these programs for African Americans and, in the long run, the cities to which they continued to migrate. Weaver and a small number of activists worked incessantly to raise awareness about the impact of housing discrimination on blacks and other minorities. Their complaints made only inconsistent headway in reforming these policies.

# * 9 *

# The First Cabinet Job

By the mid-1950s, the Weavers were established members of New York's liberal society. They lived in a nice apartment on Riverside Drive, summered in Connecticut, and socialized with the political and business leaders that shaped New York's daily life. Ella was a professor of speech at Brooklyn College, and their son, Robert Jr., was entering his teenage years and heading off to boarding school. Weaver earned a good salary in a position that provided him with the flexibility to involve himself in numerous housing and civil rights causes. He was a board member of the NAACP, the National Housing Conference, and the New York Health and Welfare Council. By all measures, Weaver had achieved a successful career, and he seemed satisfied with his life.

The election of W. Averell Harriman to the governor's seat of the nation's most populous state would dramatically change the Weavers' life and set Bob on a path that neither he nor his friends envisioned at the time. The changing politics of race in New York created an opportunity for the advancement of blacks in government, and as he had been during the Depression, Weaver would be a pioneer in this effort. The increasing power of the black vote, combined with Weaver's successful negotiation of the border between the worlds of African America and white America, placed him in a position to be one of the most influential African Americans in the country. During the late 1950s, through his work in one of the state's most controversial areas, rent control, Weaver would emerge as a national political leader.

At sixty-three when he decided to make his first official run for public office, Averell Harriman had already led a life that was the material of novels and movies. Born in 1891 to one of the wealthiest families in the country, Averell was the son of Edward H. Harriman, one of the nation's most powerful businessmen at the turn of the century, who left his heirs in excess of $75 million when he died. Averell Harriman was raised in the luxury of the nation's most exclusive elite: childhood in a Fifth Avenue mansion, schooling at Groton, and college at Yale. He then embarked upon his own illustrious business career, which included mining, movies, and airplane manufacturing.[1]

During the New Deal, Harriman was an influential advisor to President Roosevelt, working with the National Recovery Administration and other agencies. He was one of FDR's "dollar-a-year men" at the National Defense Advisory Committee (where he became aware of a young Harvard economist named Robert Weaver) and was one of Roosevelt's most important liaisons with Winston Churchill and with the Soviet government. He sat with the president when he met with Churchill and Stalin at Yalta and played a major role in shaping the postwar world order. Though he had never run for political office at any level, in 1952, with support from several party leaders, Harriman waged a spirited run for the Democratic presidential nomination, defeating Tennessee senator Estes Kefauver in the Washington, DC, primary by reaching out to black voters. But, in the end, Harriman endorsed the enigmatic, reluctant Illinois governor Adlai Stevenson (the person whom Truman and most liberals had wanted in the first place) for the nomination.[2]

Though Harriman was not a natural politician, the presidential campaign exhilarated him, and after Eisenhower defeated Stevenson, he nursed hopes that he could be the Democratic standard-bearer in 1956. In the meantime, many Democrats in New York pressed him to run for governor in 1954. After several months of vacillating, Harriman decided to challenge Congressman Franklin Delano Roosevelt Jr. for the job. The son of the former president was the darling of many New York City liberals, but many members of the Democratic establishment, including Democratic Party leader Carmine DeSapio, had both political and personal problems with the congressman, and at their convention they selected Harriman as the Democratic nominee, a decision that angered many progressives in the state.[3]

Harriman campaigned vigorously against state senator Irving Ives, who sought to replace the Republican governor Thomas Dewey, who had served for three terms. With the help of young political activists like Daniel Patrick Moynihan, Harriman attacked the Dewey administration for failing to respond to the numerous changes the state was experiencing. He campaigned actively in Harlem and other black communities, making civil rights an important issue. Harriman charged that Dewey failed to enforce antidiscrimination laws and vowed that they would be invigorated under his administration. He also promised to extend discrimination laws that regulated housing. In courting the black vote, Harriman faced a substantial challenge from Ives, who as a state senator had championed civil rights and sponsored the bill creating the state's antidiscrimination apparatus. Ives's moderate positions attracted many New York City liberals, winning him the endorsement of the *New York Times*, which called Harriman's proposals "pie in the sky" and complained that the candidate "luxuriates in the theory that there is an inexhaustible supply of money." The *New York Amsterdam News*, the largest paper serving the black community, also endorsed Ives.[4]

Despite the criticisms, most political observers felt that Harriman would cruise to a substantial victory, and he racked up an impressive margin in New York City. However, the pundits underestimated the upstate Republican vote, and in the end the election was so close that Governor Dewey had to impound the ballots and ask for a recount. After it was finished, Harriman was declared the victor by a margin of 11,000 votes out of 5 million cast. The candidate, who had never served as a public official in a full-time capacity before, entered office with a less-than-strong mandate. His biographer described Harriman as having "the onus of being Tammany Hall's handpicked candidate," facing "a reactionary Republican legislature," having "no sharply honed agenda," and knowing "little about his state."[5]

Aware that he had to secure the support of the party's liberal base, Harriman appointed several New York City progressives to his cabinet, including Charles Abrams to manage the rent control program. Aware of the important role the black vote played in his victory, soon after his election his staff promised that the governor would appoint blacks to positions of influence within the administration. Typifying the contradictory attitudes of the period, Harriman stated, "I intend to name many Negroes to my administration, but I will not take the question of race into consideration." The day before his inauguration, Harriman appointed Weaver deputy commissioner of housing.[6]

Harriman did not document the reason he chose Weaver, who was not active in the campaign and was likely to have favored Roosevelt. John Hay Whitney, who had known Harriman since he was a child, was one person who influenced Harriman's selection. Weaver later recalled that, when he was asked to join the administration (by Hortense Gabel, who herself had just accepted a job), he did not believe the offer was real. In the midst of entertaining guests, Weaver abruptly hung up on his friend and was forced to sheepishly call her back to ask if Harriman was serious. He was, and he quickly accepted the offer. Weaver's appointment met no opposition. Abrams, on the other hand, for years a vocal supporter of expanded government intervention in the areas of housing and civil rights, immediately became a target of conservative ire.[7]

Weaver's boss in his new position was Joseph McMurray. A native of New York City, McMurray had spent much of his career in Washington, DC, working with Senator Robert Wagner (D-NY) and directing the Senate Subcommittee on Housing. McMurray was a nationally known expert on housing policy, and he was also viewed as somewhat prickly. McMurray later remembered that when Harriman asked him to hire Weaver, he was reluctant. But after meeting with Weaver, he assented. Despite the state's fiscal constraints, McMurray and Weaver's Housing Division was one of the few to succeed in implementing new initiatives during Harriman's first year.

Soon after taking office, Harriman sponsored a bill to support the construction of "middle-income" housing similar to one proposed in Congress several times. The program would aid "the forgotten one-third"—those who made too much money to qualify for public housing but not enough to buy a home at the high prices asked by private developers. In DC, conservatives called the plan socialist and argued that the housing cooperatives envisioned by the act were un-American, and the bill failed to pass. In New York, however, activists were successful in getting legislative approval and an early victory for Harriman. The bill provided financing, through low-interest loans and tax exemptions. Over the next three decades, the "Mitchell-Lama" program, named for the bill's sponsors, would produce several hundred thousand units of decent housing. Weaver would be deeply involved in the new law's administration while continuing to spend most of his time promoting the cause of "fair housing," now from the inside.[8]

Weaver began his job in the Housing Division at a time of increasing attention to the problem of housing discrimination. During the early 1950s, while continuing to press for changes in federal rules, activists worked to increase the coverage of fair-housing laws in New York. Early in Harriman's term, they succeeded in securing passage of the Metcalf-Baker bill, which prohibited discrimination in federally insured apartments and single-family houses throughout the state. Buoyed by the *Brown v. Board of Education* decision, which, they claimed, "established the legal and constitutional ethic that a democratic government may not tolerate . . . segregation," activists argued that "affirmative action" was required "to give full meaning to these basic concepts." Harriman supported the bill, and it passed in the spring without much debate. One reason the proposal garnered little opposition is because it applied only to future construction.[9]

To show his commitment to eliminating discrimination, Harriman appointed a blue-ribbon committee to oversee the implementation of the law, chaired by developer James Scheuer. Scheuer, who in the 1960s would be elected to a seat in Congress that he would hold for almost thirty years, had been an active proponent of integrated housing and had opened his up-scale buildings to members of all races. Harriman directed the group to create "a climate of public opinion which would encourage harmonious acceptance of a pattern of non-discrimination." The governor appointed Weaver as the main administration liaison with the group. Soon thereafter, Weaver advised an aggressive campaign to show builders that the law would be enforced. In general, however, the committee focused on studying the problem by conducting investigations of the housing market for blacks and looking at the impact of racial discrimination. They took no action against the numerous violators of the law.[10]

During his first year in the Harriman administration, Weaver's main responsibility was similar to the tasks he held during the New Deal: serving as a watchdog against discrimination in state housing programs and promoting the administration's efforts in speeches and articles. The laws, he claimed, would aid developers because they would "disperse non-white demand over all developments," placing all developers on an equal footing. The number of minorities with the resources to purchase housing in suburban communities was small, Weaver argued; therefore, there would be "no general inundation" of the suburbs. Furthermore, he claimed, citing communities in Westchester County and Queens, there were many areas that "would be surprised to hear that Negro occupancy is supposed to depress property values." In these areas, he stated, "Negroes have been accepted without comment." These new neighbors "were improving and beautifying their properties to the benefit of the neighborhood." As he had argued in the past, Weaver claimed that the new laws would "accelerate the acceptance of colored families."[11]

Meant to regulate major subdivisions like Levittown on Long Island, the Metcalf-Baker law did increase the opportunities for black home seekers, but few families were interested in being pioneers in hostile communities. Not many blacks or other minorities had the financial means to pursue these opportunities, and those who did focused on New York City neighborhoods in Brooklyn and Queens that were already undergoing racial transition. Discrimination continued in suburban developments, and not many minorities were willing to invest the time it took to bring a claim of discrimination under the act. By 1957 fewer than a hundred complaints had been filed under the law. Nevertheless, these provisions were important symbolically in advancing the cause of fair housing, and they provided support for the argument that antidiscrimination laws were compatible with the housing market.[12]

WHILE HE CONTINUED his work against housing discrimination, Weaver also played an important role in the battle over educational segregation in the nation's largest city. Less than two months after the Supreme Court issued the first *Brown* decision, Dr. Kenneth Clark, the City College psychology professor whose work played such a prominent role in the case, gave a speech about the New York City public school system. Accusing the Board of Education of running a Jim Crow program, Clark cited statistics showing that most black and Latino children attended schools where more than 90 percent of their classmates were also people of color. The school board president, Arthur Levitt, first denied that there was any segregation in city schools and then responded by requesting a study of school integration by the Public Education Association, a private organization dedicated to improving New York schools.[13]

More than fifteen months later, the association released its report, which, according to the *New York Times*, "cleared" the city schools of the accusation that it "intentionally segregates Negro and Puerto Rican pupils." While the report did criticize the school board for "failing to promote integration," it focused most of its attention on the state of the schools attended by minority New Yorkers. These schools, the report concluded, were ten to twenty years older and had larger class sizes and higher rates of teacher turnover.[14]

In the interim, under increasing pressure from civil rights advocates, New York City mayor Robert Wagner Jr. asked the Board of Education to establish a commission to study the issue. New Board of Education chair Charles Silver asked outgoing chair Arthur Levitt (he resigned when he was elected state comptroller in 1955) to head the group. The Commission on Integration, which did not start its work in earnest until 1956, was composed of two dozen "civic leaders" and several Board of Education officials. Among the members of the group were Clark, NAACP official Ella

Baker, Joseph Monserrat, head of the Puerto Rican labor migration office, and Robert Weaver.[15]

Because of his experience in construction, Levitt asked Weaver to chair the Sub-commission on Physical Plant and Maintenance. With the aid of education officials, Weaver put together a report that showed marked differences in the facilities available to minority students, particularly in the Harlem and Bedford Stuyvesant areas. Recognizing that many of these schools were so outdated that they could not be rehabilitated, Weaver recommended a major program of new school construction. Appropriately located in areas that were racially diverse, Weaver argued, these new schools could contribute "to the stabilization of integrated population."[16]

Weaver's proposal for new construction was among the least controversial aspects of the commission's work, and it was roundly supported by all the members, who would have been ecstatic if throwing money at the problem would solve racial segregation. However, the most contested issue facing the Commission on Integration involved the crucial question of *where* the children would be sent to school. The zoning subcommittee was charged with the seemingly impossible task of figuring out a way to promote integration while maintaining what they called the "sanctity of the neighborhood school." When that group proposed new standards for the creation of school districts, unfounded rumors swiftly spread that the board was going to send white children from Queens and Staten Island to black areas and bus black children into white neighborhoods. Parents' organizations erupted, threatening violence if their children were required to change schools. Superintendent William Jansen quickly assuaged the fears of white parents, stating that, while he generally agreed with the subcommittee's recommendations, he would exercise "administrative discretion" in implementing them.[17]

The school board had no intention of radically changing the enrollment system, but even the small, experimental efforts that integration advocates recommended faced insurmountable obstacles. The focal point of much of the debate over school composition was a new facility in central Brooklyn, Junior High School 258. The school, built to replace several of the most decrepit facilities in the borough, was located in an area that was racially diverse. Civil rights leaders, particularly Rev. Milton A. Galamison, who headed the borough's NAACP chapter, argued that the school could serve as a model for integration not only in education but as a mechanism to promote racial integration in the surrounding neighborhood. At first, school officials agreed, and they crafted a zoning plan for the school that would create a racially balanced student body. But, under pressure from white parents, officials changed their minds. When the school opened in the fall of 1955, it was overwhelmingly African American.[18]

In response to complaints from civil rights activists, Superintendent Jansen stated that it would be "impossible" to integrate the school and forecast violence if the board tried to promote racial balance. He and board chair Silver promised greater resources for the school, falling back on the "separate but equal" doctrine the U.S. Supreme Court had just renounced. Upset about the failure of the board to promote integration, local activists became increasingly aggressive in their protests, organizing a picket of the school board headquarters and a campaign to get political leaders to intervene.[19]

These efforts put Galamison and his group increasingly at odds with the national leadership of the NAACP, which wanted to negotiate such matters behind closed doors. During the early 1950s, the NAACP had undertaken an effort to purge itself of "leftist influences," and it banned or marginalized hundreds of people who had been active participants in civil rights battles. While some members protested these exclusionary tactics, in the heightened atmosphere of the cold war most supported the national office's efforts. In 1956, Executive Director Roy Wilkins expressed concern at the activities of Galamison and his group, arguing that several of the activists had "communist affiliations." He also pressed Galamison to refrain from making public statements without clearing them with him.[20]

The debate within the civil rights coalition—grassroots action versus inside agitation—was as old as the struggle for equal rights. But Weaver and his friend Roy Wilkins had long ago chosen sides in this dispute. The consummate insider, Wilkins, who had taken the helm of the NAACP in 1955, was concerned about antagonizing government officials who publicly supported integration. He argued that it was important that activists work cooperatively with New York City officials, and he was particularly concerned that the efforts in New York not harm those under way in the South. If the zoning program spurred violent resistance among whites, "the consequences to the overall desegregation program, North as well as South, could be incalculably damaging." Weaver, an NAACP board member since 1953, stood by Wilkins and refused to join in the criticisms of Jansen. As Galamison became increasingly strident in his criticisms of the board—he publicly called for Jansen's resignation in late 1956—Wilkins worked to weaken the minister's influence. Activists and parents, however, continued to protest, telling the mayor that "we are tired of promises. We want action." The split within the civil rights community, however, weakened their position.[21]

The parents were not the only ones upset about the Board of Education's intransigence. During the summer of 1957, officials of the New York Urban League charged school officials with tearing "the heart out of the nation's most comprehensive school integration program," and Kenneth Clark charged Superintendent Jansen with "sabotage" in his refusal to implement the recommendations. Weaver made no public statements about the intragroup struggle, but he also became increasingly disenchanted with the Board of Education's lack of leadership on integration. Though the board approved all of the reports made by the Commission on Integration, education bureaucrats continued to interpret the recommendations so as to weaken their impact. Officials also sided with teachers in opposition to plans to transfer senior educators to lower-performing schools. The commission found that the schools with the largest minority populations also had the teachers with the least experience and training. But the teachers unions called the proposed transfers "sentencing them to Siberia" and opposed the proposals to balance the quality of teaching among all the schools.[22]

In the fall of 1957, at the exact time that Arkansas governor Orval Faubus was making a last stand for legal segregation in the South, New York City school officials were dragging their feet in implementing the recommendations to support integration in the city. Weaver told Harriman that he was "greatly disturbed by some recent developments," particularly the fact that the board was preventing a public release of the Commission on Integration's findings. In addition, Weaver and several other commission members complained to Mayor Wagner that the city budget drastically cut the funding to implement the integration plan, but neither the governor nor the mayor chose to intervene. Because he did not want to embarrass his boss or Mayor Wagner, Weaver never did make his objections public.[23]

The report, finally released in 1958, said all the right things about integration, recommending that school zoning plans "establish as a cardinal principle the objective of integration" and adopting almost all of the other recommendations made by its members. However, with the Commission on Integration's work done, the school officials who had opposed much of the program remained to implement the report. The few efforts they attempted to promote integration—for example, the busing of small numbers of black students to schools with vacancies—were met with violence by white residents, and school officials canceled the experiments. For the next decade, discussions about racial disparities in New York schools focused primarily on improving conditions in existing schools, not promoting integration by reorganizing their composition. As a result, racial segregation within the school districts, instead of declining, increased markedly. Frustrated with their inability to create a new system, many New York civil rights activists turned to another model, community-based schooling (in other words, separate but equal), in the mid-1960s.[24]

If *Brown* provided a window of opportunity to reshape the racial landscape of New York City schools, it was, indeed, sadly short-lived. Weaver never gave up on integration, but he did emerge from the school struggles with enhanced knowledge of the long battle ahead. He did not, however, change his view that the road to racial progress was through working to reform institutions from within.

ALTHOUGH WEAVER WAS powerless to create real integration in New York City schools, at the end of 1955 he took a position of great influence over the city's five million renters. In December, Harriman announced that he was transferring Weaver and Abrams to new jobs. Abrams left the rent control office to become the new chair of the State Commission against Discrimination (SCAD), the entity that enforced state discrimination laws, and Weaver took over Abrams's position as rent administrator. The appointment, which paid $20,000, made Weaver the first black cabinet official in the history of the state and brought him close to the state's political powers.[25]

The appointment was not without controversy within the administration. Abrams later commented that "Harriman had some initial doubts about whether Weaver could handle the job," reservations that Abrams shared, both men believing that "Weaver lacked political sense." Although he had been active in Democratic politics during the New Deal, Weaver had not devoted much attention to New York's political scene since his arrival. As an officer of the Whitney Foundation, he did not think it appropriate to be affiliated too closely with local officials, and he was dispositionally ill-suited to New York's bare-knuckles politics. The rent control position was among the state's most politically sensitive. Landlords hated the program and responded viciously to efforts to increase government regulation. At the same time, a wrong move by the administrator in favor of landlords would result in a swift and acrimonious response from tenant groups and the Democratic politicians who represented the city of renters. Abrams himself had struggled in the job and was the subject of much criticism from Republican legislators, and some of Harriman's advisors thought he should be eased out. The rent administrator job was different from any position Weaver had ever held before, and Harriman's advisors had many discussions before making the decision to appoint him.[26]

But, because Weaver's and Abrams's appointments served important political purposes, they went ahead with the change. Analysts interpreted the appointments as an effort to shore up Harriman's liberal support in the Democratic Party in advance of a 1956 presidential run. According to a *New York Times* reporter, the actions signaled "the abandonment of any effort to obtain support of southern delegates" and an effort to position Harriman as "the champion of minority rights in major Northern states with large urban Negro populations." Harriman's advisors, the reporter argued, believed that Weaver's appointment would increase support for the governor in Chicago, Philadelphia, Detroit, and other major cities.[27]

Whether or not this was true, Weaver, who had constant problems with McMurray, was happy about the change and jumped at the new opportunity. Weaver had never developed a decent working relationship with McMurray, who was a micromanager who worried about Weaver attracting too much of the spotlight. As he had in his relationship with Louis Wirth, Weaver chafed at being subordinate to a man who he thought was not his equal. During the year, Weaver had told friends that McMurray "made him miserable" and that he had discussed resigning with Harriman, who talked him out of it.[28]

In the release appointing Weaver, Harriman stated that Weaver had "made an effective contribution to the work of the Division of Housing." Harriman told Weaver that he was appointed because "the challenge of administering our Housing Rent Control laws demand that a person of your outstanding experience and ability should be at the helm." The appointment was front-page news in papers across the state. All of them noted that Weaver would be the first black cabinet official, but they did not dwell on the issue, choosing instead to focus on the continually contentious debate over the appropriateness of the program.[29]

A new rent administrator was necessary because Harriman was also concerned that SCAD had become a political liability. During the year, many liberals complained about the lack of effort by the agency to fight racial bias, and they lobbied Harriman to appoint an aggressive leader. Abrams's predecessor, Republican holdover Ward Arbury, had philosophically supported antidiscrimination laws but did not push his agency to enforce them. Activists cheered the selection of Abrams, a man whose fair-housing credentials were almost as strong and deep as Weaver's. According to Abrams, Harriman took the action in response to "a rash of unfavorable stories about Harriman sending Negroes back to the south in extradition cases." Whatever the reason, Harriman's decisions succeeded in gaining liberal acclaim.[30]

Weaver's housing and management credentials certainly qualified him for the rent administrator job, but it is interesting that Harriman does not appear to have considered putting Weaver in charge of the antidiscrimination program. Given his more than two decades of experience in housing and racial discrimination, Weaver was eminently qualified to become chair of SCAD, much more qualified than he was to run the rent control program. Despite the nation's progress on racial issues, the appointment of a black person to administer an antidiscrimination law was difficult for Harriman to conceive, even within the framework of racial liberalism. However, the rent appointment was a notable accomplishment, one that Weaver, who desired to prove that his abilities superseded his race, eagerly accepted.[31]

His selection moved Weaver higher in status among the state's liberal elite, and many people started talking about his running for political office. Soon after Weaver and Abrams were confirmed, Harriman attended a fundraising party for the National Committee against Discrimination in Housing. The event, at which Lena Horne sang, honored Weaver and Ella for their contributions to the cause of civil rights. The governor bragged that New York would "set a new standard" through the passage and enforcement of antidiscrimination laws.[32]

Weaver came to his new agency at a time when rent controls were struggling under a decade-long assault. Though the program had more life in New York than anywhere else in the country, even in that state rent control forces were on the defensive. Weaver's efforts to administer the program fairly and efficiently in the face of increasing criticism of the initiative were generally viewed as successful. At the same time, liberals criticized Weaver and the Harriman administration for overseeing a retrenchment of the state's protection of millions of tenants.

By 1955, rent control was almost fifteen years old and had been the subject of constant debate at the federal, state, and local levels. First tried during World War I, controls were reestablished in several cities during World War II. Immediately after hostilities ended in 1945, real estate groups lobbied to end the program, but federal officials argued that it would be even more important during the reconversion of the economy. Throughout the rest of the decade, supporters and opponents battled over the issue, each accusing the other of disregarding the public interest. Critics of rent control argued that it prevented the construction of desperately needed housing, while advocates claimed that the program protected tenants from exploitation at a time of severe housing shortages. Neither side prevailed in the argument, and for five years federal rent control swung wildly between deregulation and increased enforcement.[33]

The battles over rent control at the national level were nowhere more contested than those in the country's largest city, which had far more renters than any other area. Throughout the late 1940s, New York tenant leaders vigorously fought against any weakening of rent laws, and they succeeded in getting the New York City Council to pass laws to fill what proponents considered gaps in the federal system. Rent control was a central issue in the 1949 mayoral election, and candidates competed to top each other in showing their desire to protect tenants. Communist Party councilman Benjamin J. Davis called the city's controls "completely inadequate," while Republican-Liberal-Fusion candidate Newbold Morris argued that the rent laws promoted by Mayor O'Dwyer "gouged tenants instead of protecting them." Rent control was an issue favored by almost every New York politician, regardless of political affiliation. It received almost as strong support at the state level. When a court invalidated a city law as conflicting with the federal legislation, the state legislature stepped in to authorize the city to proceed with regulation.[34]

After an acrimonious debate in Congress during the 1950 session, it became clear that federal controls would soon be eliminated, which they were in 1952, and that states desiring to continue controls would have to secure their own legislation. New York was the first state to act on the issue. In March 1950, Governor Dewey signed legislation creating the Temporary State Rent Commission, which would be responsible for the regulation of rents in the state. Like much else related to rent control, the Temporary State Rent Commission was an odd organization. It consisted of nineteen members, some appointed by the legislature and some by the governor. The "administrator" of the rent control program served on the commission but was appointed by, and responsible to, the governor. In a period when Republicans controlled the legislature and the governor's seat, this arrangement did not seem problematic. However, when Harriman took office with the Republicans still in control of the legislature, the operations of the commission became more complicated.[35]

The legislature renewed the controls in 1951 and 1953, each time for two-year periods and each time subject to heated discussion. The new governor made extension of rent control one of his legislative priorities, and he recommended greater controls on evictions and rent increases. The power of tenants in New York was evidenced by the rapid agreement of Republicans that rent controls should continue. "There's no question that the housing shortage is still very acute in New York City," Assembly Speaker Oswald Heck stated before Harriman issued his message. After several days of hearings and vocal opposition from landlords, the renewal passed. Of the 2.2 million units covered by the law, more than 1.8 million were located in the five boroughs of New York City. It was these dwellings, housing almost half of the state's residents, that Harriman charged Weaver with protecting.[36]

With the security of a two-year extension passed before he took the job, Weaver focused his efforts during his first year on organizing the unwieldy agency. The "temporary" commission, now six years old, had almost eight hundred employees in fourteen offices across the state—though the overwhelming majority toiled in New York City. When he took office, Harriman directed his senior officials to relocate to Albany because he did not want to be accused by upstate Republicans of governing from New York City. But Harriman exempted the rent administration from this directive. It maintained its primary office on Broadway near Wall Street. From there, Weaver, his deputy and friend Hortense Gabel, and the rest of the senior staff managed the contentious program.[37]

Weaver's report on the first year of his administration revealed the immensity of the task. During the calendar year, the commission received 581,371 "applications," which involved disputes over rent increases, evictions, changes to the occupancy of units, or other disagreements between landlords and tenants. The New York City offices handled an average of 47,000 requests a month. During the year, staff processed 290,400 rent increases and ordered 16,654 rent decreases. The appeals section heard 8,749 protests. The accounting office audited 2,227 landlords, while the legal department handled 784 cases. Staff focused enforcement efforts on particularly egregious landlords, those who sought to evade rent controls through strategies such as collecting higher rents by promising services that they never provided, charging for furniture or appliances not provided, illegally converting single-family dwellings, and charging unwarranted broker's fees.[38]

At the same time that he was overseeing the commission operations, Weaver spearheaded the effort to increase public understanding of the program. He appeared on a weekly radio program to answer questions about rent control, and he was a regular participant on local television news programs. In the summer of 1956, the commission issued two pamphlets, "The Little Book on Rent Control" and "The Little Book on Evictions," that explained the rights and responsibilities of tenants and landlords in clear, nontechnical language. He also used his office to promote research on the housing problems of poor and middle-class New Yorkers and focused attention specifically on the needs of African Americans. In early 1957, Harriman publicly praised Weaver's administration of the program, stating that Weaver had made the commission more efficient and had followed the administration's mandate to concentrate "upon a factual, rather than emotional or political, approach." Less than a year after his appointment, Weaver described it as "a tough job and a large administrative one." But he liked the fact that he could "make up my own mind about decisions instead of trying to help some one else."[39]

Although Weaver's first year heading the rent control effort was relatively calm, 1957 would see him thrown into the middle of a heated debate. The battle over the program's renewal in early 1957 saw protests, parades, fights at public hearings, and the best (or worst) examples of political posturing. That Weaver was in the center of the storm placed him where no African American government official had gone before.

Though a person who entered in the middle of the 1957 rent control fight would never have believed it, all the contestants knew that the program was going to be renewed. During the first week of the year, Harriman stated that reauthorization would be one of his legislative priorities, and he declared that he would seek to enact the provisions the Republicans had rejected two years before. Republican leader Joseph Carlino, who was also chair of the Temporary State Rent Commission, announced that it would consider a variety of options, including elimination of state controls, decontrol of "luxury" apartments, and rent increases in consideration of increasing costs to landlords. But, as he had two years before, Assembly Speaker Oswald Heck calmed the worries of New York tenants by stating that he believed the controls would be renewed without substantial changes.[40]

At the end of January, Harriman released his rent plan. Arguing that the housing shortage had not improved, he called for a two-year renewal of the program and proposed greater regulation of rents in several areas.

Harriman stated that he would oppose any further efforts to eliminate controls in suburban communities or in upstate New York, arguing that such action would be "catastrophic." But he did make two concessions to opponents. Adopting a proposal Republicans had made two years before, the governor's legislation allowed for a recalculation of rents for certain types of properties. In addition, Harriman stated his support for decontrol of the most expensive apartments, though he argued that this could be done administratively. He stated that Weaver's staff was currently studying the issue and would make recommendations soon.[41]

Befitting the acrimonious issue, Harriman's proposals brought complaints from rent control supporters and opponents. The leader of the Liberal Party, an organization that had supported Harriman in the election, argued that the proposal would result in "significant increases for tenants in one and two-family houses," and many other liberal organizations attacked the legislation. Several Democratic legislators stated that they would oppose the bill if it was not amended, and they also criticized the governor for taking off the table issues that should have been used as bargaining chips in negotiations. Harriman argued that his administration wanted to be "fair with small property owners," and Weaver, who had stated that the change would affect about 250,000 units, released statistics claiming the number was only 10,000 to 15,000. Weaver argued that the bill had many benefits in that it would "plug all the loopholes" that landlords were exploiting to unfairly increase rents. Republican leaders argued that that the governor's acceptance of ideas that he had opposed, along with his vacillation after liberals complained, was proof of his lack of leadership.[42]

In the end, Harriman was able to assuage the concerns of Democrats, and his revised bill was introduced. Republicans responded with a proposal that would remove controls on all apartments renting for more than $150 a month when they became vacant. The change, they argued, would affect fewer than 10 percent of all units, and only those who could afford to pay market rents. Weaver argued that such action would be "the death knell of rent control" and claimed that 500,000 families would face an increase in rents. Such actions, he argued, would "drive away thousands of middle-income families and accelerate the trend toward making the heart of the city a two-class community, composed of the very rich and the very poor."[43]

At the end of February, the battle reached a fever pitch when the Temporary State Rent Commission held a public hearing to consider proposals for rent control. The day before the hearing, a group of landlords paraded through Times Square to protest the continuance of the program. They demanded an end to all controls within the year. The parade ended at the headquarters of the city Republican Party, where landlords chided staff members for their party's support of rent controls. That same day, a group of tenants who would be affected by the decontrol of expensive apartments also protested. One well-dressed elderly woman claimed that the administration proposal to decontrol their rents was "class discrimination."[44]

The next day Weaver described the hearing as a "circus." Although rent control supporters testified and were numerous in the audience, Republican chair Joseph Carlino packed the hearing with landlords and used the event to attack rent control and the Harriman administration in general. While Carlino grilled Weaver about the administration's plans, opponents in the audience jeered the administrator and prevented him from speaking. They held up placards that said "Help Control Creeping Communism" and "Commissar Weaver." One Democratic member commented that Carlino "handled Weaver more in the role of a prosecutor than as chairman of a joint legislative committee." In the audience, supporters and opponents shouted and jostled each other. After several hours of disorder, Carlino called a recess and brought in state troopers to restore calm.[45]

After the hearing, Weaver and Carlino got down to the hard business of negotiation, held both in private sessions and through the media. Whenever Carlino would make a proposal to decontrol some apartments, Weaver would release the information to the press and allow public criticism to weaken Republican resolve. Carlino proposed several plans to allow decontrol of more expensive apartments, but Weaver opposed them all. Weaver argued that allowing rent raises upon vacancy would give landlords an incentive to push out their tenants. "Fear would prevent the remaining occupants from demanding their rights," he claimed. In the end, the Republicans, realizing that the decontrol of expensive rents would hit their constituencies the hardest, agreed to allow Weaver to decontrol rents in expensive apartments without legislation.[46]

In the end, the Republicans on the commission approved a report proposing that rent controls be continued in New York City with only minor changes but that major changes be undertaken elsewhere. The report recommended removing controls in Buffalo and several other counties immediately and in all other areas of the state (including the suburbs of New York City) as apartments became vacant. These actions could be reversed if local governments voted to retain controls. In essence, the bill made rent control almost exclusively a New York City phenomenon. The Democrats on the commission opposed the changes and Weaver wrote a "minority report" that criticized the proposal, calling it "haphazard" and "phony." Decontrol, Weaver argued, would be "particularly disastrous in the New York City suburban areas." But Weaver had to acknowledge that the administration got most of what it wanted in the bill. After another week of political posturing, the legislature approved the Republican-sponsored proposal, and Harriman signed the bill, though he chided Republicans for their "callous disregard" of the needs of tenants outside the city.[47]

Considering the amount of energy and ink that went into the debates over rent control, the outcome seemed not worth the effort. The result was a victory for Harriman, but the fact that opponents were able to chip off yet more parts of the rent control apparatus was viewed by many as further evidence of the governor's weaknesses as a politician. One person who benefited greatly from the battle was Weaver. For two months, he was a constant presence on the news—on television and radio and in print. Weaver received unprecedented media attention for an African American, and his political profile dramatically increased. The fact that an African American official was deeply involved in an issue that had little to do with race was another remarkable fact, as was the lack of attention given to Weaver's race during the debates.

The remainder of Weaver's term as rent administrator was calm relative to the heated days of early 1957. He found himself in the middle of another, smaller battle when his office reached a decision on "luxury" apartments. After a year of studying the issue, in September 1957, Weaver announced that he was lifting controls on apartments that rented for $5,000 a year or more. The decision covered 600 apartments, mostly on the Upper East Side of Manhattan. Landlord representatives, who had expected over 5,000 expensive apartments to be decontrolled, quickly attacked the decision. Robert Fougner, head of the Metropolitan Fair Rent Committee, called the ruling "farcical" and argued that it could be "explained only on the grounds that this year and the next being critical election years." His organization filed a lawsuit alleging that the decision violated state law, but a New York Supreme Court judge later upheld Weaver's decision.[48]

Weaver and his staff also worked to protect the thousands of New Yorkers who lived in buildings that were called hotels. Under federal and state rent controls, hotels had not been regulated since the late 1940s, but many of these operations were in reality apartments. In 1958 Weaver, claiming that there were "hundreds of phony hotels" collecting "exorbitant rents," led an effort to reclassify many of these buildings as apartments and subject them to rent controls. Such decisions brought Weaver much criticism. One landlord wrote to Harriman complaining that the administrator was "a megalomaniac" and "totally unqualified." He asked for an investigation of Weaver's arbitrary decisions. At the same time, Weaver was criticized by others for being too lenient with landlords. Among one of the most controversial decisions in this regard was the approval of significant rent increases at Knickerbocker Village, a massive development on the Lower East Side built during the Depression. The rents, Weaver argued, had not been raised since this time, and the project was threatened with bankruptcy. Still, many of the tenants complained about the decision.[49]

Former colleagues remembered Weaver as a demanding boss who did not spend a lot of time socializing. A few years later, several of them had strong memories of being subjected to the "Weaver treatment," which they claimed was "marked by a politeness so unrelieved in its iciness that its victims felt they would be warmer if they curled up in a refrigerator." Morton Schussheim, whom Abrams brought to the rent administration and who stayed through Weaver's term and followed him to Washington, remembered Weaver as "an intellectual" who was "widely read in the field of housing." However, Weaver was pretty much a loner. "With Abrams, it was like he was my uncle," Schussheim remembered. "He had me come over to his house, stay over night. I never stayed over night at Weaver's house." Despite his cold personality, however, colleagues praised Weaver's management skills.[50]

Although rent control continued (and continues) to be controversial, Weaver's performance as rent administrator greatly increased his profile as an agile administrator and a political force to be reckoned with. His management of the large agency and his battles with New York Republicans earned him the respect of the general public in New York City and drew the interest of Democratic Party officials eager to find African Americans to promote within the power structure.

Weaver had a very successful term as rent administrator, but it would end in 1958 when his boss was voted out of office. A darling in 1952, Harriman's luster had worn off by 1958. Although promising "a bold and adventurous administration," Harriman offered few new programs. When he learned of the troubled position of state finances, Harriman directed his staff to look for programs to eliminate, and he did not support many new initiatives. "When it comes to spending money, I'm a conservative," he told reporters. An early review criticized his efforts, stating, "from the outside, the Harriman administration looks more confused than Dewey's." Staff struggled to get Harriman to focus on the details of administration. He preferred to talk about foreign policy rather than master the numerous issues facing the state.[51]

In 1956, Harriman's hopes to use his position as a stepping-stone to the White House were thwarted again by Adlai Stevenson, who won the Democratic nomination. Though Harriman received some support from Truman, his chances were deeply damaged by Eleanor Roosevelt's strong support of the former Illinois governor. Harriman reluctantly returned to Albany, having failed to achieve his primary purpose for becoming governor. While there, Harriman continued to struggle with an obstinate legislature. The Republicans were philosophically opposed to most of the initiatives the governor proposed, and the Democrats were too disorganized and demoralized to pose a challenge.[52]

Then, in 1957, Harriman made the fatal mistake of giving a public position to the scion of the nation's wealthiest family, Nelson Rockefeller. Harriman asked Rockefeller to chair a commission to revise the state's constitution, a task which the young man, who shared Harriman's attraction to public life, took on with great zeal. Though he failed to secure the passage of a referendum authorizing a Constitutional Convention, the effort brought Rockefeller much attention and public support. When the Republicans selected Rockefeller to run against Harriman in 1958, most political observers forecast trouble for the incumbent.[53]

The campaign pitted two of the nation's richest men, from two of its most famous families, against each other. In addition to having the same background and connections, the two men also shared a general view of government. If anything, Rockefeller's philosophy was more activist than Harriman's. But they were mirror opposites on the campaign trail. The reticent Harriman could not compete with the ebullient Rockefeller, who genuinely loved campaigning. Rockefeller's campaign took on the air of a crusade as people were drawn to the charismatic candidate. In addition to winning the endorsement of the *New York Times*, which called Harriman's record "barren of sufficient major accomplishments," Rockefeller also secured the support of the usually Democratic *New York Post*. He criticized Harriman for failing to stand up to the Democratic machine and for failing to respond to the loss of jobs in the state. Pundits pointed to several Harriman gaffes—including the parole of a major organized-crime figure and a fight within the Democratic Party over the nomination of a Senate candidate—and in the end voters chose the younger, better-looking moderate. On election day, Rockefeller amassed a margin of over 500,000 votes, sending Harriman home.[54]

The next day, Weaver wrote Harriman a note telling him that "it has been a great privilege to work with you" and expressing "admiration for the positions you have taken and for the dedication you have had for liberal issues." While the defeat was certainly a disappointment for Weaver, as it was for everyone in the administration, his four years working for Harriman dramatically increased his future prospects. Because he was involved in a sensitive, inherently political matter, Weaver got to know New York's Democratic leaders well. Weaver worked with all of the most influential people in New York government, including Senator Herbert Lehman, New York mayor Robert Wagner, and state comptroller Arthur Levitt. All of these people would be helpful to Weaver in his future activities. Because of his generally well regarded stewardship of the rent control program, New York City political leaders frequently referred to him as a potential candidate for office, and he was also courted for other government jobs. In 1958, Wagner publicly offered Weaver a position on the board of the reorganized New York City Housing Authority. Wagner wanted Weaver to take one of the two vacancies for the three-member board, which ran the city's massive, and increasingly troubled, public housing program. In the end, Weaver turned down the $30,000-a-year position, choosing to stay with Harriman. The Board of Trustees of Fisk University also wrote to inquire if he would be interested in serving as president, to follow his friend Charles Johnson, who died suddenly in 1956. Weaver declined this position too.[55]

Weaver was also called upon frequently to participate in discussions with national leaders on housing and other domestic issues. At the invitation of Harvard economist John Kenneth Galbraith, he served on the Economic Committee of the Advisory Council to the Democratic National Committee, a group that helped craft the party's domestic policy during the late 1950s. Through the council, Weaver interacted frequently with many of the party's national leaders. Weaver was sought after by business groups interested in urban redevelopment, such as ACTION, a national organization funded by the Ford Foundation to promote urban growth. All of these contacts would be crucial to Weaver when he moved to Washington two years later.[56]

In the meantime, like everyone else working for Harriman, Weaver needed a job. He did not have much to worry about, however. After more than a decade of demolition, relocation, and construction, New York City's "redevelopment machine" was breaking down. Change was something New

Yorkers were accustomed to, but the impact of continued migration (blacks and Latinos in, whites out), combined with the city's massive construction program, created a crisis in neighborhoods across the city. Weaver would play an important role in the effort to solve these problems. Even though the solutions Weaver and his colleagues adopted were flawed, his participation in these matters would further increase his political profile, opening up even more opportunities.

* 10 *

# The Path to Power

In 1958, University of Chicago political scientist Morton Grodzins published a short but prescient article that received little attention outside the small world of scholars of urban issues. In the first paragraph of the article, which was entitled "The Metropolitan Area as a Racial Problem," Grodzins stated the problem succinctly: "Almost nothing is being done today to meet the nation's most pressing social problem tomorrow. The problem can be simply stated in all its bleakness: many central cities of the great metropolitan areas are fast becoming lower class, largely Negro slums." Ten years later, the nation would be well aware of this fact, but in 1958 few of the country's leaders noticed the trend.[1]

The two years between Weaver's term with Harriman and his work in the Kennedy administration were ones of significant change for American cities as well as the nation. Through his leadership of the NAACP, his research on urban problems, and his involvement in New York City government, Weaver played a central role in the development of policies to deal with urban racial change. After Harriman's loss, Weaver remained deeply involved in New York City's housing and development efforts, and he would help nurture the beginnings of the War on Poverty at the nation's largest philanthropy, the Ford Foundation. In these efforts, Weaver continued using the same tools that he had mastered throughout his career, working to secure reform of existing programs through quiet negotiation with the nation's business and political leaders. However, by the end of the decade, many people would begin to question the viability of many aspects of this approach to civil rights. At the same time criticism of the initiatives Weaver was working to reform, particularly the public housing and urban renewal programs, increased. During the 1960s, many Americans, unaware of the festering troubles that had preceded the urban turmoil they were witnessing, would view the 1950s with nostalgia. But the failure to confront neighborhood change in the 1950s limited the influence of urban policies during the 1960s.

IN THE LATE 1950s, the nation's largest cities were witnessing two major trends: the rapid departure of middle-income whites to the suburbs and the equally rapid arrival of African Americans from the South. In 1958, blacks constituted 19 percent of Chicago's population, two and a half times the percentage in 1940. New York City's population experienced similar changes during the 1950s. Between 1940 and 1960, its black population more than doubled. More important than the fact of migration was where the people were going. Although segregation was not new, the intensity of racial separation was. The increasing division produced "communities in which people live their whole lives without, or with minimum, contact with the other race," Grodzins found. "With a Negro population numbering in the hundreds of thousands, and with this population densely concentrated, one can live, eat, shop, work, play, and die in a completely Negro community. The social isolation of the northern urban Negro is, for very large numbers, more complete than it ever was for the Negro rural resident in the South," he claimed.[2]

During the late 1950s, racial change occurred in neighborhoods across the nation, from the Roxbury section of Boston to Cleveland's eastside neighborhoods, Lawndale in Chicago, and the Watts section of Los Angeles. In each city, the combination of white suburbanization and black and Latino migration resulted in the rapid racial transformation of aging neighborhoods. These changes coincided with a significant increase in crime in most American cities. In New York, for example, the number of murders doubled between 1957 and 1964 (from 314 to 637), as did the total number of felonies and misdemeanors (from 173,830 to 375,155). These changes created an atmosphere of tension throughout America's large cities.[3]

Urban politicians, particularly those who represented areas "in transition," and professionals or those who worked with these populations such as the Board of Education and welfare departments were paralyzed by these changes. Few had experience with the new populations, and the small number of black political leaders did not have the capability to deal with the burgeoning population. City leaders also knew that racial change was occurring, but they chose to focus their efforts on urban redevelopment projects. These efforts, they believed, would be the most beneficial for cities, because they would ensure that middle-class, white, tax-paying residents remained. In addition, many of them thought, neighborhood change was an inevitability that they could do nothing about.

One of the few policymakers who was concerned about the long-term effects of urban racial change was Ford Foundation executive Paul Ylvisaker. A native of St. Paul, Minnesota, Ylvisaker had taken his Harvard doctorate in government to Philadelphia, where he worked for reform mayor Joseph Clark during the early 1950s. Clark was a prototypical urban progressive, favoring civil rights legislation while promoting urban renewal as the solution to the city's decline, and Ylvisaker played an important role in the City of Brotherly Love's efforts to respond to suburbanization. One historian described Ylvisaker as "a generalist with a philosophic bent" who "felt comfortable in academic circles but was himself more of an activist." In 1955 Ylvisaker joined the Ford Foundation to run their newly formed Public Affairs section. There, he focused on the problems of governments in rapidly suburbanizing areas. However, by the late 1950s, Ylvisaker realized that racial change was the crucial issue facing American cities.[4]

However, he struggled to convince his superiors at the Ford Foundation to focus on this issue. Founded in 1936 by Henry Ford to protect his family's control of the massive auto company, the organization held assets of $500 million in 1950, making it the largest private foundation in the country. Active internationally, at home the foundation adhered to Henry Ford's paternalistic support for African Americans, but even these efforts got it in trouble during the heightened racial atmosphere of the 1950s. During the early 1950s, the foundation supported efforts to improve African American educational and social institutions, but by 1952 southern segregationists were organizing boycotts of Ford dealerships in the South to protest the foundation's activities. Under increasing pressure from automobile executives, the foundation's leaders pulled back on their support for school integration.[5]

Although the foundation had a large staff based in New York, it also frequently hired academics and policymakers as "consultants" to work on specific projects. Usually the contracts ran for a year and were renewable at the discretion of the foundation. Consultancies were a lucrative way for academics to supplement their salaries, and they also provided support to colleagues "between jobs." In March 1959, Ylvisaker helped Weaver secure such a position. He later told an interviewer that he did this because Weaver's colleague in the fair-housing movement, developer James Scheuer, called him and said, "look, this Bob Weaver is great and he needs a job. He's got nothing right now." Ylvisaker called Weaver, and the two met several times to discuss possible projects for Weaver to undertake. After Weaver met with other Ford officials, the foundation agreed to hire him for a six-month position (extended to a year in October) at a pay of $20,000 annually.[6]

Ylvisaker played an important role in Weaver's hiring, and the two would work closely together for the year that Weaver held the position. But, under the original agreement, Weaver's assignment was not to work on issues of neighborhood racial change. Ford leaders remained reluctant to engage these issues, and they would have been even more opposed if they knew that one of the leaders of the effort was vice chair of the NAACP. Instead, Ford officials agreed to hire Weaver to investigate the status of black colleges, particularly those in the South, and to "survey the state of public-affairs research in selected Negro colleges and universities." This task, which required Weaver to engage with some of the country's more conservative black leaders—to be a black college president in the South required extreme moderation in order to survive—fit within the more moderate approach to racial issues that the foundation had adopted since its travails in the early 1950s.[7]

With no steady income other than Ella's Brooklyn College salary, Weaver happily accepted the position, and he spent much of the spring traveling the South to conduct interviews of the leaders of the nation's black colleges. Weaver saw two parts to his task. The first was to conduct research to help determine "what the future of Negro colleges and universities should be." Beginning with the assumption that integration was going to occur sooner or later, Weaver sought to provide an analysis of the role of existing black institutions in the process. He conceded that some of them "may wither away before this takes place," while others could succeed as integrated institutions, if they were strengthened.[8]

Over the next six months, Weaver gathered information, read up on current scholarship being produced by black academics, and met with the leadership of the nation's black colleges. He concluded, not surprisingly, that the institutions "vary greatly in quality and program." Weaver praised graduate programs at several schools, particularly Atlanta, Fisk, and Howard universities, but argued that others (such as Alabama State) provided "little more than a fifth year of an inadequate college course." In addition, he found that several colleges, particularly those in "border states," would have to become integrated or they would face closure. However, as integration remained only a future prospect for the South, Weaver concluded that black colleges there would continue to play a vital role. He criticized two of the oldest black institutions, Tuskegee and Hampton, for "failure to define clearly their function" but recommended that they, along with several other colleges, receive support from the foundation. At the same time, Weaver counseled against aid to many others. "It is doubtful if the academically poorer Negro colleges (as all poor colleges) serve any real good," Weaver argued.[9]

In his memoranda, which he later published as articles in the *Journal of Negro Education*, Weaver made several proposals to Ford staff, recommending pilot projects that the foundation could undertake to promote improvements in the quality of education at these institutions. His major focus was on improving the quality of faculty, which Weaver argued, rested on several changes, including increased pay, greater support for research, and improving the quality of students through more scholarships for talented high school graduates. He also recommended that the foundation organize a conference of the leaders of black colleges and the foundations that supported them to discuss their problems.[10]

At the end of 1959, Clarence Fauset, the Ford official in charge of the Education Program, who called Weaver "an intelligent and experienced Negro," told foundation head Henry Heald that Weaver "so far has not come up with anything that looks very promising." In the end, the foundation agreed to provide financial support to Atlanta University to improve its graduate programs, with the hope that it could become a racially integrated institution, but Weaver's efforts produced few other concrete results.[11]

The project Weaver aided with the most lasting impact was what would become known as the Gray Areas Program. Over time, the initiative has taken its place in the mythology of the 1960s as one of the most important precedents for the War on Poverty. At the time it was created, the project was an attempt by Ylvisaker to get the foundation to focus on issues of race relations without raising the fears of the more conservative trustees. Frustrated by his division's lack of success in developing creative responses to urban problems, in the late 1950s Ylvisaker began to shift his attention away from government reform and toward the people who lived in declining urban areas. For political purposes, Ylvisaker and Weaver and the staff of the Public Affairs Program framed the initiative as focusing on the "problems of migration." "We tend to forget that many of the social ills which we attribute to the new migrants had their counterparts in the pre–World War I era," Ylvisaker argued. This formulation placed the situation of newcomers to urban areas in the well-worn framework of ethnic immigrant studies, but the reality was that, during the 1950s, the overwhelming majority of new residents in most large cities were African American, and their problems were very different.[12]

While trying to avoid racial stereotypes, Ylvisaker and Weaver relied on Progressive Era "ecological" understandings of migrant neighborhoods. These residents, many of whom came from rural areas, needed help to adjust to their new settings. Ylvisaker claimed that the goal was to "citify" them. He and his staff proposed a program of research on the problems of migrants and financial support to local organizations for services to these new residents. The goals of the project were to offer information and analysis to policymakers about the shape and scope of the migration to cities and to promote successful programs to "accelerate the entrance of migrants into the mainstream of our life."[13]

The Public Affairs staff decided to name the project the Gray Areas Program, appropriating a racially neutral phrase that described the sections bordering the central business district. These areas were among the oldest sections in town, and they were burdened with declining housing, struggling businesses, and social problems. They were also the areas experiencing rapid racial change, but Ylvisaker chose the term to avoid association of the project with this trend.[14]

Weaver and Ylvisaker proposed giving experimental grants to create or grow organizations that would "reach the newcomer and let him know that the community is interested in him." These groups would focus on improving social conditions through the traditional means of "uplift." They would train new residents to find the services they needed, teach them "the basic individual and family behavior required by urban life," and provide them with "the minimum of skills and standards in housekeeping and environmental sanitation that are required in an urban environment." They also hoped that these groups could "assist in mobilizing the talents and indigenous leadership potential in migrant groups." These efforts, staff hoped, would provide models that could be replicated across the country.[15]

In early 1960 Ford trustees agreed to support the idea through the foundation's existing efforts in big-city schools. Under the auspices of the Great Cities School Improvement Program, the foundation gave grants to organizations that provided services to "culturally deprived" children and worked to improve contacts between schools and parents. A year later, Ylvisaker convinced the trustees to support a broader program of grants to local groups to provide comprehensive services to residents in the gray areas of ten cities. During the early 1960s, several of these organizations, in particular, Community Progress, Inc., in New Haven, Connecticut, and the Philadelphia Council for Community Advancement, evolved into the models for the Kennedy/Johnson administrations' War on Poverty.[16]

Since Weaver did not fit their image of a Ford consultant (i.e., he was not an academic from a prestigious institution of higher learning), some Ford officials had originally been reluctant to hire him. But, by the spring of 1960, Weaver had insinuated himself into the daily operations of the organization. A representative of the Rockefeller Foundation reported to his superiors that Weaver was Ylvisaker's main "formulator of programs and ideas." Writing to Senator Willis Robertson in 1961, Ylvisaker said, "Dr. Weaver carried out his assignment with distinction, imagination, tact—and with a rare measure of common sense," and he later told an interviewer that Weaver had been instrumental in the creation of the Gray Areas Program. However, Weaver's sojourn in the foundation world did not last long. In May 1960, he resigned his position, leaving to enter the world of power politics as a member of the newly created New York Housing and Redevelopment Board. Ford vice president Dyke Brown told staff it was "almost superfluous to comment on how capable and compatible a colleague we found him to be. He leaves a spot which no one will completely fill."[17]

WEAVER LEFT THE Ford Foundation for the opportunity to manage the country's largest, and (critics would argue) most troubled, urban renewal program. The Housing and Redevelopment Board (HRB) was the result of Mayor Wagner's very belated attempt to deal with the snowballing, and interrelated, problems of urban renewal, public housing, and neighborhood change. The complaints over the impact of urban renewal on poor black, white, and Latino New Yorkers were as old as slum clearance, but during the late 1950s evidence of stark corruption and inefficiency in the program made even the initiative's strongest supporters question its viability. These facts were compounded by the realization that the program was not succeeding in meeting the extremely optimistic promises made by promoters. Despite the expenditure of several billion dollars and the uprooting of hundreds of thousands of people (more accurately because of their uprooting), anyone living in New York could tell that the city was becoming more troubled. Crime and racial tensions were on the rise, as was the deterioration of neighborhoods thought stable just years before.

But the direct cause for the changes in New York's housing bureaucracy was the daily reports of the fraud, exploitation, and insider deals that marked the "Title I" program. The worst of the many troubled projects was the Manhattantown development, a major renewal effort on the Upper West Side. To build this middle- and upper-income development, Czar Robert Moses selected a group of politically connected businessmen with no development experience. In 1953, the city condemned six square blocks, including 338 buildings, at a cost of $15 million (paid for in federal dollars) and sold them to the project sponsors for $1 million (they did not even pay this amount—it was borrowed from the city). The contract required the sponsors to demolish all of the structures and begin construction on the new apartments within the year. However, by the end of 1955, most of the buildings were still standing. Instead of moving ahead with the project, the sponsors had "milked" the buildings—charging the remaining tenants rent while allowing the units to rapidly deteriorate. Investigators found tenants living in squalid conditions, with no heat or water, holes in ceilings, and rats everywhere.[18]

Despite the fact that this was a scandal worthy of front-page stories, the city's papers, in awe of Moses and his accomplishments and strongly supportive of urban renewal, were reluctant to act. However, the problems with the program became increasingly difficult to ignore as the decade progressed. In 1957, the project still had not commenced construction, the sponsors had spent the $2 million the city had loaned them as well as the millions they had received in rent, and all they had to show was a delinquent real estate tax bill of $600,000. To resuscitate the project, Moses found a real developer to buy them out. By 1959, the continued failure of the project, combined with increasing racial tensions across the city, awoke the press to the scandal of urban renewal. The *New York Post* published a series of articles on real estate owner Sidney Ungar, whose troubled management of a stable of slum buildings did not prevent him from securing designation as sponsor of a major development in Harlem. Like the Manhattantown promoters, Ungar failed to produce.[19]

In August, Wagner announced that he had hired a consultant to study the city's housing programs and propose a reorganization plan. Even though almost everyone knowledgeable about the subject recommended consolidating the city's many housing programs into one agency, the investigator, attorney J. Anthony Panuch, spent over six months and $150,000 on the study, primarily to allow Moses to ease himself out gracefully. In the interim, Panuch issued a report stating what Weaver and many others had said for a decade: that the relocation program was a scandal that had damaged thousands of families as well as many city neighborhoods.[20]

Panuch's report, finally released in early March 1960, recommended that the mayor create a new entity, the HRB, to be overseen by a chairman and two members. The agency would be responsible for the implementation of the urban renewal program as well as the city programs in middle-income housing and housing rehabilitation. The chair, who would share responsibility with two board members (to prevent the kind of consolidation of power that Moses had wielded), would be responsible for advising the city government on all housing issues and for representing the city in negotiations with state and federal governments and private parties.[21]

To chair the board, Wagner appointed J. Clarence Davies, a former realtor who was then running the city's relocation program. Soon thereafter, Wagner announced that he had selected Weaver and Walter Fried, who had been the regional head of federal urban programs, as the other board members. The selection of Fried and Weaver, two people who had been very critical of New York's program, was a major acknowledgment of the flaws in the city's urban renewal and housing initiatives.[22]

In his activities and writing on urban development, Weaver focused much of his attention on the impact of slum clearance on African Americans. In 1958 he and Frank Horne argued that the New York City program should conduct demolition only where the housing conditions were so bad that the units had to be torn down and should focus on building in areas where relocation problems would not be severe. If the city continued to uproot large numbers of people, they claimed, there was "a grave danger that urban renewal . . . will face such political opposition as to kill it." Relocation, Weaver argued, hurt not only blacks and Puerto Ricans but the city as a whole. As dislocated minorities moved to new neighborhoods, they pushed whites out of the city. In addition, as he had argued for a decade, Weaver continued to assert that urban renewal could never succeed in keeping the middle class in the city without the support of fair-housing laws to enable blacks and other minorities to deconcentrate.[23]

Although by 1960 increasing numbers of liberal intellectuals and academics, including Weaver's friend Hortense Gabel, were questioning the basic philosophy underlying the urban renewal program, Weaver continued to believe that it could work if implemented carefully. Weaver's position on urban renewal was that it was a crucial part of urban revitalization that, combined with improvements in public schools, could result in bringing middle-class families to the city. However, he viewed this as a long-term project. In the short run, Weaver openly stated (unlike most advocates, who avoided the question) that the percentage of racial minorities in the central city was likely to continue increasing. In addition, he argued, "while the size and squalor of slums may be decreased we shall not clear all of them." Carefully planned redevelopments could slow this change, Weaver agreed, but not stop it. Finally, Weaver claimed, urban renewal could succeed only if projects were built away from areas of minority concentration or, alternatively, where a middle-class community could emerge once a minority area was totally cleared, as in Washington's southwest section. Weaver supported "class integration," but he argued that there should be strict limits on the number of poor residents in any urban renewal plan; without such limits, the projects would fail. Weaver's prognosis for the city was one of slow reform, not the dramatic change promised by many redevelopment advocates.[24]

Weaver's colleagues adopted his moderate approach. In a report to the mayor a month after their appointment, the board outlined their plan for the new agency. In it, they promised to work closely with the City Planning Commission (which Moses had ignored, calling it full of "long hairs who never built anything"), and they committed to "consult" with the neighborhood groups that Moses disdained before finalizing any renewal plan. With regard to the most contentious aspects of the program, they promised to carefully supervise relocation efforts and to select only sponsors that had been carefully screened. However, while recognizing that many of the city's projects had been controversial, the board committed to continue almost all of them. They shelved only one project, a development on the Lower East Side, an area they found had already experienced "great upheaval," and they amended two others. But the overwhelming majority of the projects that Moses designed were continued.[25]

Although some activists expressed desire for more radical revisions, the media and housing advocates generally cheered the change in operations. Over the next six months, Davies, Fried, and Weaver met with government officials and neighborhood residents to discuss the promise and problems of the city. They received high marks for their commitment to negotiate with community groups in the project areas. The board also promoted new programs, focusing greater resources on the development of middle-income housing and creating a new loan program to support the rehabilitation of tenements. In its first annual report, the HRB claimed that "we have replaced the 'bulldozer approach' with a combination of new construction, rehabilitation and redevelopment," and Weaver reported that they had rejected one project specifically because of this concern. However, more than 10,000 New Yorkers were uprooted by projects during the year, and several times that number would be relocated for projects in the planning stages. In the end, during his short tenure, Weaver helped moderate the excesses of the program, but he and his fellow board members did not make any structural changes.[26]

Weaver's brief term as manager of New York's urban renewal program was an important credential that, added to his three years as rent administrator, certified his place as one of the nation's leading domestic policymakers. His ability to work with politicians and business leaders in a careful, diplomatic manner placed Weaver at the top of the list of candidates for these posts. His performance in these jobs, widely praised, increased his attractiveness to politicians looking to court the black vote while adhering to a framework of moderate, incremental change.

AT THE SAME time that he was immersing himself in the details of New York's massive redevelopment industry, Weaver found himself at the center of an increasingly heated debate over the course of the civil rights movement. His elevation to chairman of the board of the NAACP in January 1960 occurred just as the movement for equal rights was entering a new stage.

When Weaver took his position, the nation's oldest civil rights group had just celebrated its fiftieth anniversary. Although the NAACP continued to be far and away the largest organization of African Americans, the second half of the 1950s had been difficult years. After its signal victory in *Brown v. Board of Education,* the group was attacked from all sides, assaulted by the massive resistance of the South's political leaders while at the same time increasingly criticized by other black activists.

The focal point of these complaints was Roy Wilkins. When he replaced Walter White as executive secretary in 1955, Wilkins had already been running the organization for several years. A native of St. Paul, Minnesota, Wilkins had been active in the NAACP for more than three decades, and he had worked in the national office since the 1930s. Wilkins handled numerous organization activities, including conducting dangerous investigations in the South, editing the organization journal, *The Crisis,* and managing the group's crucial fundraising activities. He was an obvious choice to succeed White, though Thurgood Marshall and NAACP chief lobbyist Clarence Mitchell also wanted the job. The reserved executive could not match White's flamboyance, but he continued his former boss's cultivation of political leaders and white liberals. Though he increased outreach to the local chapters that provided the membership of the group, Wilkins focused primarily on securing legislative, judicial, and executive relief against racial discrimination.[27]

As was evident in the battle over school segregation in Brooklyn, Wilkins's desire to control the image of the organization resulted in frequent clashes between the executive director and the heads of local branches who wanted to take more aggressive approaches to civil rights causes. Wilkins's attention to the careful, generally quiet, work of cultivating and persuading the nation's elites to support civil rights conflicted with growing numbers of black activists who wanted to mobilize African Americans to fight in their communities.

This conflict was evident in Wilkins's relations with the Reverend Martin Luther King and the Southern Christian Leadership Conference (SCLC). When Rosa Parks ignited the Montgomery, Alabama, bus boycott in December 1955 by refusing to relinquish her seat, Wilkins had only been in charge a few months. Although he was skeptical about the efficacy of such efforts, Wilkins and the other NAACP officials worked closely with King and other local leaders (Parks herself had been chair of the local branch), providing financial and legal support throughout the battle. However, as the SCLC continued to grow and King received national attention for his nonviolent, grassroots tactics, tensions between the two groups intensified. Though King and Wilkins avoided criticizing each other, the SCLC increasingly became involved in areas that had been the NAACP's domain, particularly the struggle for voting rights in the South.[28]

Wilkins also had to deal with legal attacks on the organization from southern segregationists. After the *Brown* decision, several states attempted to eliminate the NAACP through legislation and persecution. The state of Louisiana, arguing that the organization was run by subversives, passed a law banning the group completely. In Virginia, legislators severely restricted the organization's ability to raise funds and ordered the group to release its membership list to state officials, a requirement that would have exposed blacks to harassment and worse. In Georgia, revenue officials tried to bankrupt the organization through legal action to collect income taxes they claimed its branches owed. And in Washington, DC, southern segregationists, after years of harassing the group through investigations, succeeded in getting the Internal Revenue Service to require the NAACP Legal Defense Fund to legally separate from the organization that had created it decades before.[29]

These efforts, however, did not stop the NAACP, and in November 1959 the group had over 310,000 members, more than it had had when the decade began (but still below the peak of the mid-1940s—it had 420,000 members in 1946). Weaver had served as a board member since 1953 and as vice chair since 1956, joining luminaries like Ralph Bunche, A. Philip Randolph, publisher Lewis Gannett, and musician Oscar Hammerstein II. In January 1960, board chair Channing Tobias, one of the "old lions" of the organization who was one of the longest-serving board members, announced that he was stepping down due to bad health. Weaver was an obvious choice to succeed him. In addition to the fact that he was the second-ranking board member, Weaver had known and worked with Wilkins for years. Since taking charge in 1955, Wilkins had worked to shape a board that would give him full support, and Weaver had been one of "the Caucus" that met before meetings to decide major issues. Weaver was, by temperament, a perfect head for the tradition-bound group. He had impeccable credentials and was well known and respected in liberal circles. In addition, he was certain to provide a steady presence, staying "on message" and always looking out for the interests of the organization. At the meeting where Tobias announced his resignation, the board elected Weaver unanimously.[30]

Less than a month later, on 1 February 1960, four black students from North Carolina Agricultural and Technical College—Ezell Blair, David Richmond, Joseph McNeil, and Franklin McCain—ushered in the new decade with a dramatic action that pushed the civil rights movement to the forefront of the nation's attention. They took the simple step of sitting down at the lunch counter of the Greensboro Woolworth's store and asking to be served. When they were denied on account of their color, they refused to leave. The next day, they were joined by more than two dozen fellow students, and over the week the protest spread to counters in other stores. By the next week, the protests had spread across the state, to Durham, Winston-Salem, Charlotte, Raleigh, among other cities. Soon, students were "sitting-in" at lunch counters in Virginia and Tennessee. Historian William Chafe called the event "a watershed in the history of America."[31]

In fact, students had undertaken similar action in Oklahoma City two years before and had succeeded in integrating lunch counters in that city. The 1960 action was special because it happened at the beginning of a new decade, at a time when television journalism had become an established form of news. The national broadcast of the events in North Carolina differentiated them from most previous civil rights efforts and was largely responsible for the swift and massive response to the students' actions.

The NAACP played no role in the spontaneous uprising, but local and national officials of the group were crucial supporters during the months that followed, providing financial and legal assistance to the hundreds of protestors who were arrested. Wilkins and others led protests at Woolworth and Kresge stores in New York City to highlight the discrimination that their executives refused to eliminate. Despite the NAACP's support for the students, during the spring many blacks criticized the group for being out-of-touch with the masses. At the April conference of young activists that resulted in the creation of the Student Non-violent Coordinating Committee (SNCC), Martin Luther King was quoted as saying that the sit-ins represented a move "away from the tactics which are suitable merely for gradual and long-term change." Many writers, as well as Wilkins himself, interpreted this statement as an attack on the NAACP's strategy. Black journalist Louis Lomax argued that the new movement had bypassed the NAACP and that it represented a dramatic change from the old methods of civil rights activism. The wave of protest, he argued in *Harper's* magazine, marked "the end of the great era of the Negro leadership class," specifically the NAACP, which had been the "undisputed commander."[32]

With Wilkins the unquestioned leader of the organization, the NAACP board chair had few responsibilities. Weaver ran the monthly board of directors meeting after choreographing it with Wilkins, and he infrequently acted as spokesperson for the organization. The public face of the group, however, was Wilkins. He was the leader of the lobbying effort to pass a new civil rights bill in Congress, he was the one who appeared to protest police abuse of blacks in the South, and he was the one who cajoled local activists to follow national NAACP policies.

One of the main functions of the board chair was to deliver the keynote address at the NAACP's annual convention, where delegates met to elect the board of directors and set policy. In June, NAACP leaders gathered in St. Paul, Minnesota, for the conference. Given the immense amount of attention that the civil rights movement received during the year, and the fact that the convention was the first national civil rights meeting since the sit-ins, Weaver's speech could have been a memorable event. He began by stating that he was "truly tempted . . . to be dramatic," given that it was his first keynote. But, instead, Weaver ended his first paragraph by saying, "I am sufficiently conditioned as a social scientist and sufficiently honest as an American and a Negro to avoid this temptation."[33]

Instead, Weaver chose the forum to engage in a thorough defense of the NAACP. "Recently much has been made over the fact that some young people feel the NAACP is too conservative." Reviewing the history of his participation in the organization over three decades, Weaver reminded the audience that such complaints were not new. "Dissatisfaction with the rate of progress on the color line and feelings that adults are too cautious are no new attributes of our youth," he claimed. "What is new is the courageous and effective direct action of Negro college youth for, and dedication to, real functioning democracy." However, although the students provided a crucial spur to action, Weaver concluded, the NAACP would remain the fulcrum of civil rights activity.[34]

The sit-ins, Weaver claimed, would not have been possible without the legal groundwork laid by NAACP lawyers over several decades to provide the constitutional foundations undermining Jim Crow. Because of these efforts, "the legal basis of racial segregation in public facilities has been destroyed, and slowly but surely we are translating a legal right into a reality." Weaver concluded by noting the irony that the association was critiqued from both sides. "To some we are moving too fast—as though Americans could be so described for demanding their basic rights. We can never press too hard for equality and human dignity! To others we have outlived ourselves because we are too conservative. Without laboring the dubious semantics of this latter point of view, let me say that there is one basic barometer by which any organization like ours can be measured. That is the size of its membership. Ours continues to grow." He closed by reading the Langston Hughes poem "Mother to Son," which ends "I'se still climbin'. And life for me ain't been no crystal stair."[35]

Although Weaver's service as board chair would last only a year, it was a tumultuous one for the civil rights movement. The year 1960 marked a turning point in the battle against discrimination and a rise in alternative, grassroots approaches to civil rights. As he had for two decades, Weaver walked a fine line between activists demanding rapid, structural change and the established power structure, which produced slower, more limited improvements. Having decided years ago that he would follow a path of "inside agitation," Weaver did not take the attacks on the NAACP personally, and he was generally magnanimous to critics. During the decade to come, however, the division between the two sides would widen, and Weaver would find it harder to continue his role as racial mediator.

THROUGHOUT HIS CAREER, Weaver had rejected suggestions that he run for political office. He was a government official, a scholar, and an activist, he argued, and was not suited to the world of politics. Always reserved, especially in public, Weaver did not fit the mold of a politician, and he certainly would not have enjoyed campaigning for public office. Even in the days when politicians were able to separate their private and public lives, Weaver would have resented the intrusions that a political life would have imposed on himself and his family. Yet, because he was an articulate, moderate African American who had been successful in government, Weaver could not avoid such suggestions. Soon after his national NAACP speech, the continuing exposures of corruption in the city's redevelopment program almost resulted in Weaver's elevation to the job of Manhattan Borough president.

One of the many outcomes of the newspaper reports criticizing the city's urban renewal program was the indictment of Manhattan Borough president Hulan Jack on charges of corruption. A native of British Guiana, Jack was a veritable Horatio Alger character. He moved to New York at the age of sixteen and worked as a janitor in a paper company. Over the next two decades, he worked himself up the ladder, eventually becoming vice president of the company. At the same time, Jack immersed himself in Democratic politics. Through hard work and constant loyalty to the party's leaders, Jack became one of the most powerful blacks in the organization. In 1940 the party's support enabled Jack to win a seat in the State Assembly, a position he held for thirteen years. In 1954 his allegiance to the machine was rewarded with the party's nomination for Manhattan Borough president. A position established when the five counties merged in 1898, each borough president was responsible for overseeing construction and development projects in his district, which brought them many opportunities to award supporters (or extort them). The borough presidents also sat with the mayor on the Board of Estimate, the institution that was responsible for approving the city's budget and charter changes and that held veto power over the City Council. The Democrats' selection of Jack was a recognition of the increasing political power of African Americans in the city, particularly through the voting bloc in Harlem.[36]

Although some African Americans wished that a different person had been chosen, all blacks cheered Jack's victory as a statement of progress for the race. Jack's election increased the power of the coalition he had formed with another Harlem institution, Congressman Adam Clayton Powell. The fiery minister of the Abyssinian Baptist Church, one of the nation's largest and most prosperous congregations, Powell cut a dashing figure in New York, Washington (when he decided to show up for his job), and the Caribbean (where he frequently vacationed). Although many liberals were suspicious of the flamboyant congressman, Powell earned the respect of many through his constant battles with southerners over civil rights issues. Powell was as exciting as he was unpredictable. In 1956, upset about his treatment by the Democratic Party both at home and in Washington, Powell announced that he was supporting Eisenhower in his bid for reelection, as well as black Republican Jacob Javits in his Senate race with Mayor Wagner. This decision caused a rift between Powell and party loyalist Jack, and over the next five years the two would engage in a bitter struggle for control.[37]

One thing that Powell and Jack shared was the constant attention of prosecutors at the local and federal levels. In 1960 both of them were indicted—Powell in a federal tax evasion case, and Jack by the Manhattan district attorney on conspiracy charges. The case against Jack rested on his relationship with real estate operator Sidney Ungar. In 1957 the *New York Post* reported that Ungar received approval for an urban renewal project in upper Manhattan, though he had no development experience. In a subsequent suit brought by Ungar against the paper for libel, it was revealed that Ungar had paid more than $4,000 for renovations to Jack's apartment, leading many to conclude that Jack had accepted a bribe to promote Ungar's interests. The revelations resulted in a yearlong political spectacle. In early 1960 the DA indicted Jack on corruption charges, but the charges were dismissed by a New York judge, whose decision was then reversed by the state Court of Appeals. The first trial against Jack resulted in a hung jury, but the second trial resulted in a swift conviction on several of the charges. Throughout the year, Jack was in and out of office, suspending and reinstating himself as borough president several times. Harlem leaders, even those who had feuded with Jack, claimed that the charges were racially motivated and argued that it was no coincidence that the city's two most powerful black politicians were under attack at the same time.[38]

Jack's conviction in December 1960 made him ineligible to serve as borough president, and political observers engaged in a heated debate over his successor. Several names were raised, but most agreed that the favorite was Weaver. Wagner, who was beginning an effort to distance himself from the Democratic machine, clearly wanted Weaver, who was close to reform Democrats such as Eleanor Roosevelt and City Council head Stanley Isaacs. The editors of the *New York Post* called him the "Man for the Job" in a glowing editorial that described Weaver as "an informed, able citizen with a notable record of public service" who looked "infinitely larger than most of the party hacks" who wanted the job. The editors complained that it was "sad" that most of Weaver's promoters focused on his race instead of his "distinctive intelligence, integrity and independence." Weaver also had the support of the *New York Times*, whose editors argued that Weaver would "handsomely" meet Wagner's stated desire to find "an outstanding independent Democrat."[39]

Had he taken the job of Manhattan borough president, Weaver would have immediately become the country's most powerful black elected official. But Weaver did not want the position. "Friends of Mr. Weaver . . . say he would rather stay in his present post," reported the *New York Times*, noting that Weaver and his wife led "a quiet and relaxed life" that they did not want to disrupt. The position eventually went to Edward Dudley, a judge on the Domestic Relations Court, but the pursuit of Weaver only continued to burnish his reputation as a leading African American official. However, the quiet life that Bob and Ella supposedly envisioned for themselves was not to last. Weaver did not become borough president, because he took a bigger, more important, and even more stressful job: running the nation's housing program.[40]

Through three decades of careful, diligent work, Weaver had made a name for himself as a talented public servant and racial advocate. His cultivation of the nation's liberal elite in the name of racial progress won him supporters in business, the media, and politics, as well as grudging acceptance by his opponents. Weaver's success in the political arena would open up opportunities heretofore unavailable to African Americans.

1. Robert Tanner Freeman, Weaver's maternal grandfather, the first professionally trained African American dentist.

2. Rachel Turner, Weaver's maternal grandmother, a significant force in his life.

3. Mortimer Weaver, Weaver's father, whom he called "puritan."

4. Florence Weaver, Weaver's mother, who read him Tennyson and Longfellow.

5. Robert Weaver as a child.

6. The Weaver home in the Brookland section of Washington, DC.

7. Weaver with the 1929 Harvard Debating Society: he was a team leader, but he was excluded from participating in several debates.

8. Weaver at his desk with an assistant. One of the few black professionals in the federal government during the New Deal and World War II, Weaver was a source of both pride among African Americans and discontent for segregationists.

9. Weaver at the opening of the University Homes in Atlanta, Georgia. Weaver played a major role in protecting the interests of blacks in the public housing program.

10. The Black Cabinet, 1938.

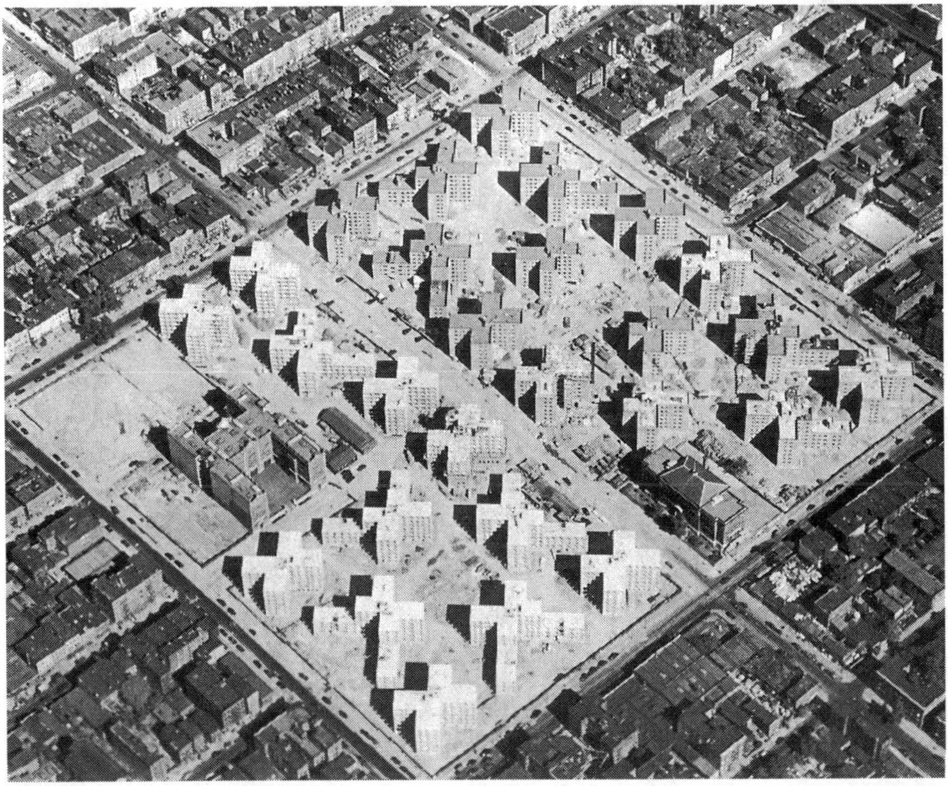

11. The Brownsville Houses, Brooklyn, a typical example of early public housing. At its opening in 1948, this housing development was racially integrated. By 1960, it was overwhelmingly Latino and African American.

12. Ella Weaver and Robert Weaver Jr. in the early 1940s. The Weavers were married for over fifty years. Robert Jr. was their only child.

13. Weaver and Lawrence Cramer, executive director of the Fair Employment Practices Committee. Weaver and Cramer were constantly embroiled in bureaucratic conflicts with each other.

14. Weaver at the Detroit NAACP Conference, 1944. During the war, Weaver traveled the country advising local groups battling racial discrimination.

15. Stateway Gardens, Chicago. Despite Weaver's efforts, by the 1960s, Chicago had the largest concentration of public housing in the nation, and it was among the nation's most segregated.

16. Weaver, with Charles Abrams and Governor Averell Harriman in 1957. Both men played important roles in Weaver's career.

17. Ella Weaver and Robert Weaver Jr., who had a troubled youth.

18. Weaver, President John F. Kennedy, and Ella Weaver at Robert's 1961 swearing in as HHFA director.

19. Weaver, Ralph Bunche, William Hastie, and Roy Wilkins at a celebration for Weaver's HHFA appointment.

20. Weaver and Ella in front of their DC apartment. The Weavers were popular subjects for Washington journalists.

21. Weaver receiving the NAACP Spingarn Medal, 1962.

22. Weaver and LBJ at the signing of 1965 Housing Act. Johnson called Weaver "a wise man" but hesitated before naming him HUD secretary.

23. Weaver, Robert Wood, and LBJ before announcement of Weaver's and Wood's 1966 HUD appointments.

24. Engelhardt cartoon of Weaver and LBJ. At Weaver's swearing in, Johnson acknowledged that the job might be "too much to put on the shoulders of one single man."

25. Weaver, Joe Califano, and LBJ in the Oval Office during the summer of riots, 1967.

26. LBJ signing the Civil Rights Act of 1968. Many of Weaver's friends called the act his greatest achievement.

27. Weaver at the 1968 opening of HUD headquarters.

* 11 *

# The Kennedy Years

## *A Reluctant New Frontier*

On 26 December 1960 Weaver received a call from New York mayor Robert Wagner, who asked Weaver to come to his office. Weaver thought that Wagner was going to offer him the job of Manhattan borough president, a position that did not interest him. But Wagner surprised him by saying that newly elected president John F. Kennedy wanted Weaver to join his administration. Wagner asked if Weaver was interested in running the Housing and Home Finance Agency (HHFA), and Weaver said he was. Two days later, Weaver flew to Palm Beach, Florida, to meet with the incoming president. After receiving two assurances—that Kennedy would pursue an executive order banning discrimination in federal housing programs and that, if a cabinet department on urban affairs was created, as Kennedy had promised during the campaign, Weaver would receive serious consideration—Weaver agreed to accept the nomination. Kennedy made the announcement at a press conference immediately after their meeting.[1]

In 1961 the HHFA was not exactly a high-profile institution. Unlike the Departments of State or Defense, it did not have legions of reporters investigating the intricacies of government policy. An opinion poll would have revealed that few Americans knew anything about the agency, and few members of Congress paid attention to its activities. Even in large cities with significant public housing and urban renewal programs, not many people were aware of the organization's influence. Most people thought of these initiatives as local government efforts.

During the 1950s, however, the HHFA had significantly increased the federal government's role in the lives of urban Americans. In the decade to follow, millions of Americans would look to Washington to solve the increasingly related problems of city decline and racial tension. The HHFA was an organization with over 11,000 staff members that managed a wide variety of programs, including mortgage insurance, public housing, urban redevelopment, local and regional planning, construction of public facilities (e.g., water and sewer systems), financing of college housing, and assistance to mass transit. It was an unwieldy agency with many fiefdoms—an institution that the president-elect chose Robert Weaver to direct.[2]

Throughout the 1950s, as chair of the National Committee against Discrimination in Housing (NCDH), Weaver had been a vocal critic of the urban renewal program's implementation. Weaver also locked horns with the Federal Housing Administration (FHA), which, he argued, had consistently prevented the creation of integrated neighborhoods. During the second half of the decade, when Weaver served as a local and state official, he tempered his language but continued to disparage many aspects of the HHFA program. Because of his vocal critiques of many aspects of federal policy in race and housing, and even more because of his color, many observers were surprised when President-Elect John F. Kennedy chose Weaver to head the HHFA. His three years working with Kennedy would provide an opportunity to expand the federal government's role in urban affairs and race relations. These opportunities would be limited by a timid president, a conservative Congress, and the politics of race.[3]

WHEN ELECTED, THE president was in many ways an unformed political entity. As a senator, Kennedy was not a vocal supporter of civil rights, and his aide Ted Sorensen later remarked that Kennedy "simply did not give much thought" to the issue during his Senate years. In the debates over the Civil Rights Act of 1957, Kennedy (who voted in favor of the final bill) sided with southern Democrats and worked to limit the scope of the act on several intermediate votes, raising the ire of Roy Wilkins and other civil rights activists.[4]

During the 1960 campaign, Kennedy did not make civil rights a major issue, but he made several statements to establish his support for the cause. One of the issues he chose to highlight his support for equal rights was housing. In August 1960, Kennedy held a news conference to criticize the Eisenhower administration and its approach to civil rights, focusing in particular on their intransigence in dealing with housing discrimination. Calling on the president to issue an executive order banning discrimination in federal housing programs, Kennedy stated, "If he does not do it, a new Democratic Administration will." Later, in October, Kennedy repeated this critique, stating, "one stroke of the pen would have worked wonders for millions of Negroes who want their children to grow up in decency." Campaign aides made sure that the remarks were widely reported in the black press.[5]

But many blacks were still skeptical about the young candidate and continued to support Republican nominee Richard Nixon, who had a decent, if undistinguished, civil rights record. In September, as the campaign was heating up, Kennedy asked to meet with Roy Wilkins and his board chair, Robert Weaver. They went to Kennedy's Georgetown home, where the candidate emphasized to them his support for civil rights. Wilkins left feeling "impressed with the candidate I had seen that evening." He later recalled, with the benefit of hindsight, that Kennedy had been "sizing up Weaver for future use."[6]

By October, it was clear to many observers that the election would be extremely close and that the black vote would be crucial to determining the winner. As a result, both candidates increased their activities in urban areas with large black populations. Several weeks before the election, the Kennedy campaign sponsored a meeting on civil rights in New York, bringing together more than four hundred political leaders and civil rights activists from across the country. The day after the conference, in response to questions about the Republicans' commitment to civil rights, vice presidential candidate Henry Cabot Lodge told a Harlem audience that, if elected, the Nixon administration would appoint an African American to a cabinet post. The next day, however, in a striking example of how both candidates were spun around by the politics of race, Nixon, concerned about his support in the South, repudiated the statement, and Lodge denied that he had made it. Kennedy stated that hiring on the basis of race was "racism in reverse, and it's worse," and Lyndon Johnson and other Democrats hammered the Republicans on the flip-flop for the rest of the campaign.[7]

During most of the campaign, Kennedy studiously avoided engaging in the debates over the battle for equality in the South. One of the few actions Kennedy did take, just weeks before the election, was to call Coretta Scott King when her husband was jailed in Atlanta to offer his assistance. Many observers felt that this symbolic act, more than any of his votes or other statements, swung African Americans to Kennedy. In the end, he won over three-quarters of the black vote. However, while most civil rights leaders were happy to see the end of Dwight Eisenhower's lackluster term, they remained uncertain about what the new president would do.[8]

After his election with strong support from African American voters, most political observers believed that Kennedy would appoint blacks to high positions in his administration. In December, Kennedy asked

Representative William Dawson (D-IL) to serve as postmaster general, but Dawson rejected the offer. Since that post was generally ceremonial and had little influence on government policy, several black newspapers questioned Kennedy's commitment to African Americans. Needing to find alternative appointees, Kennedy's advisors turned to Weaver.[9]

Several years later, Weaver stated that no fewer than twelve people claimed credit for his appointment to the HHFA, and he did have several supporters, including Kennedy confidants Arthur Schlesinger, John Kenneth Galbraith, and Adam Yarmolinsky, all, like Weaver, products of Harvard. They called him a "highly respected leader in the Negro community" and recommended him for jobs in the HHFA, Department of Labor, or the State Department. Frank Horne and James Scheuer also filed formal recommendations of Weaver. Scheuer noted that Weaver was a "nationally respected opinion leader in the areas of housing, urban renewal and inter-group relations," had an "excellent capacity to work with all kinds of people," and possessed "sophisticated political insight." Weaver believed that Averell Harriman and Philip Graham (editor of the *Washington Post*) also recommended him. Louis Martin, the highest-ranking African American in the Democratic Party, also pushed Kennedy to hire Weaver.[10]

Introducing Weaver to the press, Kennedy noted Weaver's "long experience in the field of housing" and claimed that "we have been most fortunate in securing his services." The journalists present asked Weaver only a couple of questions and then started to query the president about foreign affairs. When asked if he favored "a requirement that homes be available for sale to Negroes before they would be eligible for Federal insurance of mortgages," Weaver stated that it would be "premature to get into the technique that would be used," but that he favored the "idea of open occupancy and nondiscrimination in housing." Weaver also said that it was too early to judge the reaction of southern Democrats to the nomination of a black man for one of the highest posts in the government. Kennedy's response was more direct: "Well, I have selected a man who I think can do the job, and I am hopeful that that will be the judgment of all Americans."[11]

Weaver's nomination surprised many people in the field of housing and urban affairs. Many observers expected that Weaver's former boss Joseph McMurray, who had been staff director of the Senate Banking and Currency Committee for many years before taking the job in New York and was supported by the powerful Senator John Sparkman of Alabama, would be the nominee. Others thought that the selection would be an influential mayor such as Richard Lee, the mayor of New Haven, Connecticut.[12]

The appointment received only moderate interest in the mainstream media. The *New York Times* and *Washington Post* published stories, but most papers just copied from the wire services. Picking up Weaver's statement that he was "an electrician by trade," the *Star* described Weaver as "a housing expert who could probably rewire your home himself, and then sit down and talk economics with you on a Ph.D. level." The editors of the *Post* stated that Weaver was "well-prepared to direct the Nation's drive to improve its living quarters." The United Press International (UPI) stated that Weaver had "excelled in two fields—Government work and racial desegregation," by "fighting hard and working quietly," and it quoted Weaver as saying, "the key to victory for Negroes was to fight hard, legally, 'and don't blow your top.'"[13]

Not surprisingly, the black press trumpeted the announcement. The *Philadelphia Tribune, Pittsburgh Courier, Chicago Defender,* and *Baltimore Afro-American* all had front-page stories on Weaver's nomination. The *Courier* called the appointment "a telling blow" against housing discrimination "because the new administrator, not appointed to the job necessarily because of his race, but because of his ability, will serve as a symbol."[14]

While most editorials cheered the appointment, John Sengstacke, the editor of the *Chicago Daily Defender,* who had sparred with Weaver in the 1940s, was less optimistic about Weaver's impact on civil rights, reminding readers that in the late 1940s Weaver had favored replacing restrictive covenants with "occupancy covenants." The editorial also took issue with papers that billed Weaver as a "crusader for civil rights. "While Dr. Weaver doubtless is a capable administrator," the paper argued, "we're not quite sure his record justifies the word 'crusader.'"[15]

Kennedy's correspondence files show the public response to have been strongly in favor of the appointment. The White House received five times as many letters praising the decision as criticizing it. Most of the letters opposing Weaver claimed that their concern was not his race but his "communist associations," allegations propagated by southern segregationists in Congress. Where there is the "slightest suspicion of communist affiliation, regardless of whether the person be white or colored," Win Rhodes of Portuguese Bend, California, wrote, the nomination should be withdrawn. Several critics cited Weaver's work for the NAACP as evidence of his Communist affiliation. Others were explicit about their racial opposition. "You have served warning to the people of the South," stated Ann Tipton of Midland, Texas.[16]

Given Weaver's stated support for a policy of nondiscrimination in housing, opposition from southern politicians and organizations was to be expected. Southern members of the National Association of Home Builders and the National Association of Real Estate Boards organized efforts to prevent approval of his appointment by the Senate. "We do not oppose Dr. Weaver's appointment on his qualifications nor do we oppose his appointment on the basis of his race, but we do feel that anyone as biased and as prejudiced as Dr. Weaver would have a detrimental effect on the hom [*sic*] building industry of the United States," argued L. Clarke Jones, president of the Home Builders Association of Richmond. Although southern organizations opposed the nomination, the national real estate groups against which Weaver had struggled for much of his career remained silent.[17]

Both supporters and opponents played down the racial implications of Weaver's nomination, but in the context of the increasing demands for civil rights by blacks in the South and the North, Weaver's color played a crucial role in the debates. Weaver's nomination was to be considered by the Senate Committee on Banking and Currency, which was chaired by Virginia's junior senator Willis Robertson. While Robertson was usually outshone by his senior colleague, the ardent segregationist Harry S. Byrd, he understood the political implications of the appointment for his southern colleagues, and he quickly announced his opposition to Weaver. Robertson based his opposition on Weaver's support for nondiscrimination and his "communist affiliations."[18]

Given the composition of Robertson's committee, most observers felt that the nomination would be approved. In the Senate generally, seniority gave southerners great power, but the Committee on Banking and Currency had a strong majority of northern liberals, Democrat and Republican. Among the committee's members were Senators Paul Douglas (D-IL), Joseph Clark (D-PA), William Proxmire (D-WI), and Harrison Williams (D-NJ). Several of its Republican members, notably Prescott Bush (R-CT) and Jacob Javits (R-NY), were strong supporters of civil rights and an activist federal urban policy. Many of them announced their support for Weaver before the hearings. Only four of the committee's twelve members were from the South.[19]

After pressure from Senate Majority Leader Mike Mansfield (D-MT), Robertson agreed to expedite the Senate's consideration, and the committee began two days of public hearings on 7 February. Chairman Robertson began by stating that "this nomination is a controversial one." He claimed that he had asked the president to respond to a "number of complaints touching on the subject of his [Weaver's] loyalty" and stated that the president had failed to respond to the request. Because of confusion on this issue, the senator recessed the hearing for two hours until the letter from the president arrived. It stated: "As is customary in nominations of this importance, a report on Mr. Weaver was submitted to me by the Federal Bureau of Investigation, and this report was fully reviewed and evaluated." The FBI had, in fact, conducted a comprehensive evaluation, interviewing seemingly every white person Weaver had ever met, and it found no reason to oppose his nomination. Given that assurance, Robertson called the hearing to order.[20]

Weaver was introduced by his two home senators. Kenneth Keating (R-NY) called Weaver "an energetic and competent public servant," and Jacob Javits (R-NY) stated that Weaver had been examined "thoroughly in the marketplace of ideas and actions" and asserted that he had "no doubt whatever" regarding Weaver's "patriotism." Prescott Bush (R-CT) argued that "Dr. Weaver brings excellent qualifications and credentials to this very important post," and all of the northern Democrats praised him in their opening remarks. Weaver clearly had the support of the majority of committee members, but the southern Democrats, to varying degrees, criticized his statements and writings and questioned Weaver's actions and affiliations. Senator John Sparkman of Alabama, a leader in promoting public housing and other federal programs, questioned Weaver's administration of New York's rent control program and criticized Weaver's advocacy of open-housing laws. Sparkman argued that such policies would "stop this great housing program that we have going in this country, and I think this is a great program."[21]

Weaver parried the attacks with reserve and moderate language. "I do not think that you can legislate integration," he told Sparkman, but, he continued, the law "can give equal opportunity, and that is what I am concerned with." He argued that the goals of housing production and civil rights were compatible. Weaver later recollected that he believed that Sparkman, though he opposed open housing, actually supported Weaver's nomination. "I don't think," Weaver recalled, "Mr. Sparkman politically could afford to do anything but to oppose me. I would say looking back on the record that Mr. Sparkman's opposition was minimal."[22]

Both Sparkman and his colleague Wallace Bennett (R-UT) focused on Weaver's policy prescriptions and questioned him in a generally cordial manner. The personal attacks on Weaver were left to the junior senator from Texas, William Blakely. Appointed to replace Lyndon Johnson, Blakely would serve in the Senate only a short time (he would lose his seat in 1962 to Republican John Tower). At the hearings, he struggled through an attempt to discredit Weaver by unearthing his alleged Communist connections. Blakely began his questioning by noting that, as the junior senator on the committee, he had "great reluctance in this position to take a stand or to bring out information." He further told Weaver that he had been "genuinely impressed" by Weaver's "biography" as well as his "attitude" and "personality."[23]

Blakely then stated that Weaver "had a variety of associations with a number of organizations" that had been cited by the attorney general or by congressional committees for possible Communist connections. The first organization Blakely mentioned was the National Negro Congress, pointing out Weaver's participation in their 1937 annual meeting. Weaver responded by noting that he had cleared his attendance with the Interior Department and that he "was in fairly good company" because the president of the United States had sent greetings and "the then Republican Mayor of the city of Philadelphia greeted the conference in person." When questioned about his knowledge of "communist influence" in the organization, Weaver argued that he had not been involved in the organization of the Congress and had never been a member (he had, in fact, made at least two donations to the organization) and that, up until 1940, the group was not controlled by Communists.[24]

Blakely also asked Weaver if it concerned him that Weaver's book *Negro Ghetto* had been declared a "Book of Lasting Value" by the Workers Book Shop in New York City. "No," Weaver replied, "but anytime anybody would list my book as of lasting value, I do not think I would repudiate it." And, in an episode that left several committee members smiling, Blakely asked Weaver if he knew that a review of *The Negro Ghetto* had appeared in the journal *Masses and Mainstream*, written by "J. Crow, Realtor." Oblivious to the joke, Blakely pressed Weaver to respond. "I was unaware that he wrote book reviews," Weaver stated. Journalists covering the hearings reported that even Senator Robertson had to laugh at this colloquy.[25]

The last topics Blakely explored were Weaver's writings upon return from his 1947 trip to Russia and his long-term involvement with the NAACP. Reading from Weaver's article entitled "No Race Problem in Russia," Blakely asked whether this piece reflected his views. Weaver responded that "subsequent events have shown that I either did not see it as well as I might have seen it or things changed very rapidly about the way they have handled their minority problems." With regard to the Communist influence in the NAACP, Weaver responded that "the NAACP has a very brilliant history in opposing communism" and noted that J. Edgar Hoover had praised the group's efforts.[26]

The *Washington Post* called Blakely's questioning reminiscent of the McCarthy years. The editors of the *Baltimore Afro-American* agreed, arguing that Blakely "looked bad in his effort to prove Weaver guilty by association. . . . When Blakely finished his questioning, the impression was left that the late Senator Joseph McCarthy of Wisconsin, who was the Senate's champion of the smear by association, would have been embarrassed by the performance of the Texan." The following day, the committee concluded its consideration by taking public comments. The hearing lasted less than an hour. While several organizations sent letters of support or opposition, only one organization, the National Apartment Owners Association, sent a representative to testify at the hearings. Immediately after the hearings ended, the committee voted 11 to 4 to approve the nomination and send it to the full Senate.[27]

Senator Robertson, who controlled the presentation of the nomination to the full Senate, stated that the final vote would be delayed until after the Senate recess for the Washington's Birthday holiday. Worried that Robertson was trying to organize opposition, the White House insisted that the nomination be considered immediately, and a day later Senator Hubert Humphrey (D-MN) moved for unanimous consent to bring the nomination to the floor. Although Weaver's confirmation was certain by this point, several southern senators delayed the final vote with denunciations. Senator Robertson called Weaver a "man of demonstrated poor judgment and extreme views." Senator James Eastland (D-MS) revisited all of the allegations made by Senator Blakely in committee and then produced a long diatribe about the dangers of interracial housing. Eastland's primary evidence against interracial housing was a 1957 report by the *New York Daily News* on the decline of the Fort Greene Houses. Weaver and his policies, Eastland argued, were responsible for this situation. "Why it is desired to impose those conditions on the rest of the country, I cannot understand," Eastland argued.[28]

Senator John Stennis (D-MS) echoed Eastland's argument and claimed that, if Weaver was confirmed, "it would be a source of great regret on the part of the present administration, and would bring great trouble and harm to the administration of the housing program." Stennis argued that Weaver was committed to a policy of "forced housing" and that he would implement this policy in disregard of congressional direction. "I oppose Weaver because his record shows clearly and without question that he is more interested in promoting racial integration than he is in carrying out Federal housing policies enacted by Congress." Joe Clark (D-PA) called his colleague's statements "a sad commentary on the climate in this body, a climate which still protects an age which has decayed and passed away. That age is gone; it is dead; the country knows it; the world knows it. It is time, in my opinion, that this body learned it." After an hour of discussion, Weaver's appointment was approved by a voice vote on 9 February 1961.[29]

Weaver was sworn in at the White House on 11 February. In a very brief statement, President Kennedy said that he had "the highest confidence" in Weaver's "ability, his energy, his integrity, his loyalty." Weaver responded that he felt "deeply humble" in receiving this honor. The *New York Times* concluded that "Dr. Weaver got in on his personality, his intelligence, and his record." The editors stated that "we know that Weaver will fill it [the position] ably and loyally, and we wish him well," and the editors of the *Washington Post* stated their confidence that "he would prove himself up to the challenge."[30]

A few weeks later, Roy Wilkins organized a celebration for Weaver. Ralph Bunche, William Hastie, Frank Horne, and many of the country's black (male) elite attended. After a night of drinking, celebrating, and roasting, Weaver took the floor. He told his friends that his job was to produce decent housing for the people who needed it and that he expected at some point that many of the people in the audience would be unhappy with his priorities. However, he concluded, his job was to serve the entire nation.[31]

Reminiscing about the hearings in 1964, Weaver still felt anger about his treatment by Blakely, Robertson, and other senators: "The fact that from the point of view of a human being, because I was a Negro regardless of my qualifications, my capabilities or anything else, I was subjected to this long hearing—much of it irrelevant, much of it without any basis of fact–was demeaning. This was the sort of thing that naturally I resented, and I felt that this was again an evidence of the fact that Negroes in America are still not first class citizens." At the same time, he felt that the hearings gave him "a certain degree of exposure" that showed Congress and others that he "knew something about what I was doing, that I knew something about the job, and also that I had some degree of integrity and some degree of courage; that I wasn't going to equivocate, or I wasn't going to back up nor was I going to apologize for what I believed."[32]

AFTER QUICKLY PUTTING together his senior staff—for his deputy Weaver hired union leader Jack Conway (who would later become a leader of the War on Poverty), and for his counsel he drafted Milt Semer from the Senate Committee on Banking and Currency—Weaver set out to craft the administration's urban and housing programs. Kennedy had promised "bold new ideas" frequently during the campaign, and the HHFA leaders worked to form creative proposals. In general, however, they focused on improving existing programs.

The administration program was outlined in the president's first message to Congress. Entitled "Our Nation's Housing," Kennedy presented it on 9 March 1961. Finalized less than three weeks after Weaver's nomination was approved, the proposal was drafted by Weaver and his senior staff with very little participation from the White House. In general, the proposal was similar to those made by liberals in Congress during the late 1950s. It did not offer many new initiatives but rather called for the expansion of existing programs for urban renewal, public and elderly housing, and loans for improvement of infrastructure like water and sewer systems. In discussion with Senator Homer Capehart (R-IN), Weaver admitted that Kennedy's proposed increase in the housing budget for 1962 was $138 million and only $8 million of that was in grant authorizations (the rest were loans). "I could not resist the temptation of pointing out how narrow the New Frontier is with respect to housing," Capehart dryly noted.[33]

Hungry for an early victory, the White House lobbied hard to secure the bill's passage. Even though it was Weaver's bill, the White House took the lead in the lobbying effort, partly because of Weaver's race and partly because Kennedy's people did not trust Weaver's political instincts (which was not unusual: Kennedy's men trusted no outsider's political instincts). Though in the future he would be well known among members of Congress for his advocacy, Weaver did not express any concern about his marginalization. After two months of negotiation, the bill that emerged from Congress was substantially similar to the administration's proposal. While the *Wall Street Journal* argued that "irresponsibility" best described the bill, the *New York Times* called the bill "one of the new Administration's brighter legislative victories" and praised its shifting of attention "toward the cities and away from the new suburbs." Kennedy, with some overstatement, called the law the "most important and far-reaching Federal legislation in the field of housing since the enactment of the Housing Act of 1949."[34]

A week later, almost all of the parties involved in the bill's passage came to the White House for Kennedy's first bill signing. But there were two noticeable absences from the congressional delegation: Senator Sparkman and Congressman Albert Rains, who chaired the House Subcommittee on Housing. Both southerners had played crucial roles in pushing the bill through their respective houses, but they declined to attend because they feared that they would be photographed with Weaver, a picture that could be used against them by future political opponents in the increasingly segregationist climate (in fact, both men were targeted for defeat by segregationists in the early 1960s). Kennedy remarked that their absence was "like having Hamlet played without the prince," and he publicly thanked Weaver for his role in securing the bill's passage.[35]

Weaver's race prevented him from winning the public support of southerners in Congress, but his early performance made him popular in the rest of the country. The *Washington Star* reported in May of his first year that Weaver was the administration's most popular speaker. The housing director gave more than a dozen major speeches in the months immediately after his appointment. In April, Weaver appeared on the television program *Meet the Press* to discuss the administration's housing policy. His performance received rave reviews from journalists and administration officials.[36]

Later that spring, Weaver was the subject of a long and generally glowing profile in the *New York Times Magazine*. The introduction to the article pictured him looking out his apartment window at the redevelopment of Washington, DC. The writer described him as a "tall, heavy-set man with piercing eyes in a dreamer's face" who was "a salty blend of realism, organizational talent, mental agility and skill at unruffling feathers" and who kept his staff "on a seven-day work schedule." Though the writer described Weaver positively, he also noted that his personality was "not always that jovial. Underlying the amiability and reasonableness that are Weaver's trademark is an insistence on excellence that makes him intolerant of sloppy performance or faulty judgment." Weaver was known for working hard and having few close friends.[37]

During this period, Ella, for the first time in her career, received attention for her own accomplishments. The Washington media were fascinated by her because of her light skin and also because she had pursued a career of her own, an uncommon thing for a wife of a high government official. The *Washington Post* published a long article, entitled "There's No Conflict of Interest at House of Doctors Weaver," on Ella's background and current occupations. Noting that Ella had "always given priority to her husband's job," the article described her efforts to "set up house" in DC while maintaining an active schedule in New York. "People who don't know Ella Weaver or her background assume she is white," the reporter wrote, and Ella generally did not disabuse them of this belief. "I don't say, 'Hello, I'm Negro,' just as you wouldn't say, 'Good morning, I'm a catholic or whatever you are,'" she told the reporter. The article noted that Ella gave her full support to her husband and that "for two years they've had a reservation for a return trip to Europe but had to cancel at the last minute because of his work." The article also stated that she often served as her husband's primary editor.[38]

Returning to Washington for the first time in more than a decade, Weaver reestablished many old contacts but did not make many new friends. Ella reported that they both preferred "small intimate dinner parties—anywhere from six to 12 guests"—to going out. Even when Ella was in New York, Weaver chose to cook dinner for himself instead of going out. At lunch, Weaver also frequently dined alone. Even though his background was similar to many of Kennedy's advisors, he did not regularly interact with them. Kennedy and his people had little experience with African American professionals like Weaver, and Weaver did not think it productive to expend the energy necessary to gain access to their club, particularly since they were unlikely to allow him in. Publicly, Weaver joked about his role as racial ambassador. After attending the annual banquet of the Gridiron Club (a crucial institution of the political elite) with Carl Rowan, deputy assistant secretary of state for public affairs, one of the only other high-level African American officials, he told reporters, "I can tell you one thing about this integration, though. It's expensive. This tie-and-tails outfit cost me $118.[39]

Throughout his years in the Kennedy administration, Weaver would toil alone, working to prove that a black man could do the job as well as anyone else. Although he never became part of the inner circle, Weaver's first year in the administration was a success that included a significant legislative victory, a great deal of media attention, and strenuous efforts to reorganize his agency. As with all honeymoons, however, this period of glory would be short-lived.[40]

LIBERALS PRIDED THEMSELVES on Weaver's success, but positive feelings resulting from his acceptance by Washington's elite did little to stem the racial conflict erupting across the South. The Kennedy administration counseled caution, but young black and white activists were unwilling to wait to secure equal rights. In May 1961, thirteen of these pioneers left DC on an ill-fated bus tour destined for New Orleans to test the government's commitment to the right of integrated travel. When the "Freedom Riders" arrived in Birmingham, they were attacked by a mob while the police watched. The violence was broadcast nationwide, creating embarrassment for the White House and forcing the president to intervene. Kennedy and his brother Attorney General Robert Kennedy pleaded with Martin Luther King to get the riders to give up the crusade, but he refused, and they pledged to continue. The president, his brother, and other White House staff were disturbed by the violence, but they blamed civil rights activists for provoking it. The White House did not understand that activists were willing to risk their lives and would not accept promises of future action. They wanted results now.[41]

The administration was equally slow to act on the few civil rights commitments it had already made. Throughout his term, Kennedy would vacillate on the matter of housing discrimination, an issue he had proclaimed was so easy to solve during the campaign. That such a seemingly small action, the barring of discrimination based on race in the use of federal funds for housing, would take two years to secure in a liberal Democratic administration is stark evidence of the obstacles facing the achievement of true integration in 1960s America.

Soon after his confirmation, Weaver moved into a one-bedroom apartment in the southwest section of the city. The area had been cleared during the 1950s for the city's largest urban renewal project. Weaver said he wanted to "put his money where his mouth was" by supporting the development. Weaver's apartment selection was also an effort to make a statement about open occupancy—a response to critics who called the development an effort to replace a black ghetto with white professionals. The decision was evidence of Weaver's liberal bona fides, but less than six months later he decided to move to a larger apartment on Connecticut Avenue in the Woodley Park section. The luxury building he and Ella chose was known for housing many of the city's elite, and they were among the first black families in the area. Although many residents in the building welcomed them, the manager received a flood of abusive letters from those opposed to integration when the papers reported the Weavers' move. One note, from a segregationist who thought the Weavers were a mixed-race couple, "berated the fair-skinned Ella for marrying a Negro."[42]

The complaints reinforced the point that housing discrimination remained a serious obstacle that blacks who lacked the Weavers' clout and money struggled to overcome. Kennedy's promise to ban discrimination in federal housing programs was one of the few specific statements he made during the campaign, and civil rights leaders expected him to act soon after his election. Kennedy's advisors recommended that the first priority in the area of housing should be the passage of the Housing Act of 1961. Weaver agreed, and he asked his fair-housing friends to support the bill without pushing for antidiscrimination provisions. White House officials told fair-housing activists that an executive order would soon follow, but by the summer of 1961 many activists were getting restless. In August, NCDH leaders Charles Abrams, Algernon Black, Eleanor Roosevelt, and Roy Wilkins wrote Kennedy to press him to issue the order. Now that the Housing Act had passed, they argued, it was "imperative that effective Executive action insure equal opportunity in all federally-assisted housing activities."[43]

In September, the NCDH released a thirty-eight-page report describing discrimination in federal housing programs and calling on the president to issue an order banning such activities. "There is massive evidence that the Federal Government is actually promoting and strengthening nationwide patterns of residential segregation," they argued, citing the urban renewal and public housing programs as examples. The report called for a broad order that covered federal agencies, state and local agencies, and private organizations that administered federal housing funds.[44]

In conjunction with the issuance of the report, the NCDH launched a public relations effort it called the Stroke of the Pen Campaign. Calling on the president to sign the order presented to him, the NCDH organized a campaign of letter writing, editorials in newspapers and periodicals, and pressure on other governmental officials to call on Kennedy to ban housing discrimination. During the months that followed, the White House received thousands of pens along with letters asking him to sign the order.[45]

By the fall, administration officials—in the White House and at the Justice Department and the HHFA—were all busy considering options for a ban on discrimination. Several members of Kennedy's staff argued that the issuance of the order would interfere with the president's efforts to create a new Urban Affairs Department, and they counseled delay. Weaver urged the president to push ahead with regulations, and he was supported by many Democratic politicians. By November, most political observers assumed that an executive order would be issued soon. While the building industry and the real estate lobby clearly opposed the decision, they did little to fight it and seemed resigned to the decision. White House staff submitted a proposed order to Kennedy in mid-November, but he delayed in signing it because of opposition from southern congressmen. Given the increasing racial conflict in the South and the rising protest from liberals regarding White House inaction, issuing of a ban on government discrimination seemed to many to be a relatively painless way for the president to show his civil rights commitment. But Kennedy's political calculus was more complicated. He continued to feel that a decision would imperil his domestic agenda, so he delayed action.[46]

As he had many times during his career, Weaver found himself in a difficult position, caught between his longtime friends in the fair-housing movement and his loyalty to his boss. Weaver said very little publicly about the executive order during this period, but in a speech to the New York Chapter of the American Jewish Committee, he both urged legal reform to help minorities and claimed that such laws would not have a great impact. Assessing New York's urban redevelopment program, Weaver argued that the success of the urban renewal program depended upon the creation of "greater freedom of choice for Negroes in housing." But he noted that "segregation and integration are not the result of laws and executive orders but "in large measure [of] the way people behave." He further argued that it was "nonsense" to think that "Negroes have a burning desire to live next door" to whites.[47]

Civil rights activists continued throughout the fall to lobby the administration to issue the order, arguing that the "continued delay is becoming extremely disturbing." NCDH leaders told White House staff that the order should be issued before Congress reconvened, because southern senators could use it in their battle against the new cabinet department that the president wanted to create. "Once the order is promulgated," NCDH director Frances Levenson argued, "it is out of the way and can no longer be used for 'blackmail.'" Advising NCDH leaders before their meeting with White House officials, Levenson argued that the delay was weakening Weaver in his ability to maintain credibility. "There is a definite limit to the length of time Housing Administrator Robert Weaver can maintain the stance that, while he personally is committed to open occupancy, the policy must be established by the White House. There comes a point when such a position becomes untenable, and Administrator Weaver leaves himself open to considerable attack. (Roy Wilkins might make this point more strongly.) Restlessness with Mr. Weaver is already being seen in some segments of the Negro press."[48]

As the end of December approached with no executive order, several newspapers again urged the president. "There is nothing radical about this order," the editors of the *New York Times* stated on Christmas Day: "Every day of delay encourages the opposition. The President should now take a pen in hand and redeem his pledge." But days later the UPI reported that the president had decided not to issue the regulation because of concerns about the impact it would have on his 1962 legislative program. White House officials stated that the order would not be issued for several months, and maybe not until after the fall 1962 elections. The report quoted one Capitol Hill observer who said that issuing the directive would enrage southern Democrats and would be "just like waving a red flag in front of them. The White House just isn't in a position to alienate anybody." NCDH officials were told that the administration delayed so that it could push through the new cabinet department and make Weaver secretary. Within the administration, Weaver argued that the executive order was more important, but he did not make his views public.[49]

Two weeks later, the president made his first statement on the issue. At a 15 January news conference, in response to a question about his campaign pledge to sign the executive order, Kennedy said, "I stated that I would issue that order when I considered it to be in the public interest, and when I considered it to make an important contribution to advancing the rights of our citizens." Kennedy argued that his administration "in the last twelve months made more progress in the field of civil rights on a whole variety of fronts than were made in the last eight years," and he pointed to administration lawsuits to protect voting rights and the end of segregation in interstate travel. "So we are proceeding ahead in a way which will maintain a consensus, and which will advance this cause," Kennedy stated. He concluded that he was "fully conscious of" his prior statements and planned to "meet my responsibilities in regard to this matter." These remarks followed statements by administration officials that Kennedy did not plan to introduce any civil rights legislation during the 1962 congressional term.[50]

Kennedy's statement brought immediate criticism from civil rights activists and political leaders. Columnist Jackie Robinson stated that he "wondered if Mr. Kennedy has forgotten so soon that if it hadn't been for the votes of the Negro segment of the American public, he might not be entrenched at his Pennsylvania Avenue address." Robinson called it "a poor boast to say he has done more than a President who did little more than to take himself South to play golf with the most prominent segregationists," and he concluded, "If the President thinks he can satisfy the Negro because he has made some nice appointments of Negroes who already 'had it made'—or because he maintains a praiseworthy personal attitude on civil rights, he is sadly mistaken." Other civil rights leaders echoed Robinson's comments, but the president refused to budge.[51]

ADMINISTRATION OFFICIALS HOPED that the removal of the executive order from the political debate would ease the passage of their legislative program, but they were sorely mistaken. There remained many other obstacles to Kennedy's domestic agenda. Throughout 1962, Kennedy struggled with an intransigent Congress that opposed most of his domestic initiatives. The battle for a cabinet department for urban affairs, which JFK had proposed in his 1961 housing message, a debate in which race played a major role, was the first of several such defeats.

For years, advocates had been urging a cabinet department for urban affairs, claiming that it would focus national attention on the problems of cities and the urban areas that surrounded them. According to Senator Joseph Clark, a new department would give "the city dweller the same status and recognition that the farmer has enjoyed for more than a century." It would also, Clark asserted, "sharpen our thinking about the national responsibility for metropolitan affairs," help "harassed local officials," and give urban communities "an equal voice." Kennedy agreed and announced his support for the proposal.[52]

But the administration struggled to articulate what, exactly, the new department would do, relying instead on bureaucratic jargon. The purpose of the new department, according White House official David Bell, was to "provide for full recognition and consideration of the problems resulting from the rapid growth in the United States of our metropolitan areas and needs." The department, Bell argued, would "help in achieving consistent and flexible administration of the Government's community development and housing programs, give more effective leadership within the executive branch to the coordination of federal activities affecting urban and metropolitan areas, and foster consultation among Federal, State and local officials to contribute to the solution of urban and metropolitan development problems." Such vague generalities provided little confidence that the agency could succeed.[53]

Because he might become the secretary of the new department, the White House limited Weaver's role in the congressional debates. But Weaver did comment frequently in public on the need for a more coordinated federal urban policy. In a speech to the U.S. Conference of Mayors,

Weaver called the HHFA a "bureaucratic monstrosity" and said that within his agency there were "both overlapping areas of responsibility and areas where nobody seems to have any responsibility." In another speech Weaver focused on the administrative aspects of the proposal. "We need an efficient, consolidated structure that will place these vital, expanding programs in a Department under the direct surveillance of the President if we are to make yesterday's program effectively serve today's needs."[54]

However, hostility to the idea was high in Congress and elsewhere. Real estate and business groups opposed the proposal. O. G. Powell, president of the National Association of Real Estate Boards, stated that the administration's approach would "soon create a situation in which the mayors of our cities will have little to do other than perform the ministerial task of distributing federal money." The journal *Nation's Business* stated that "control of city governments could move to Washington. . . . It's likely your city would then be less responsive to your individual needs." Senate opponents dramatically claimed that the bill would "violate the principles of the Federal system, usurp the authority vested in State governments, crumble the walls of self-determination, demolish local leadership, and build ever higher the stronghold of Central Government." They further argued that the new department would allow corrupt city mayors to gain a direct link to the federal government for funds that would further entrench their power.[55]

Kennedy's political strategists worked to secure the bill's passage in the winter of 1961, but they fought an uphill battle. Most Republicans opposed the measure because they thought it would expand the federal government. In the Senate particularly, opposition also came from several southern Democrats who believed that Weaver would become the first black cabinet secretary. Senator John Sparkman of Alabama asked Kennedy for a private pledge that he would not appoint Weaver. When Kennedy refused, Sparkman announced that he would oppose the bill. Under the weight of strong opposition, the bill died on 24 January 1962, when the House Rules Committee, composed primarily of Republicans and southern Democrats, voted to prevent it from reaching the floor.[56]

Four Democrats voted against the bill, but President Kennedy blamed Republicans for the defeat. In a press conference the same day, Kennedy stated that he would again propose the department under the powers granted him by the 1949 Government Reorganization Act. The law allowed Kennedy to get around the Rules Committee by organizing the department subject to subsequent congressional approval. Kennedy further stated that he planned to appoint Weaver as the secretary of the new department. He argued that this was known on Capitol Hill and that "the American people might as well know it."[57]

Pundits called Kennedy's announcement a brilliant political move that put northern Republicans on the defensive, because they now would be perceived as voting against civil rights. Republicans criticized the president for making the policy debate a "racial issue." Congressman John Lindsay (R-NY), who supported the cabinet proposal, stated that, while he was a great admirer of Weaver, the "President's injection of the civil rights thing into it is a terrible shame, and I think it might hurt his bill too." Several newspaper editorials also criticized the president's move. "It is deplorable that the fact of Mr. Weaver's race is alienating southern Democrats' votes, for he seems fully qualified for the post," the *Washington Star* commented. "It is even more deplorable, however, that the fact of his race is being used in an attempt to coerce Members of Congress into voting for a Government reorganization plan in which, on its merits, they do not believe."[58]

To increase pressure on wavering representatives, Weaver appeared on the Sunday morning television program *Meet the Press*. In the interview, he stated that "a large segment of the population" would interpret a vote against the department as a vote against putting a black in the cabinet. In response, many opponents hastened to make clear that their opposition to the new department had nothing to do with their feelings about Weaver or his race. Senator Winston Prouty (R-VT) argued that he regarded Weaver as "one of the most capable public servants presently heading any Government agency in Washington." Congressman Gordon McDonough (R-CA) recognized Weaver as a "competent Administrator" and stated he would not oppose his appointment to the cabinet. "I personally would have been delighted to see Mr. Weaver or any other well-qualified Negro appointed to Mr. Kennedy's original Cabinet, and I wonder why this was not done," stated another representative.[59]

In the end, however, the proposal was soundly defeated in the House and Senate. At the time, political pundits viewed the rejection of the department for urban affairs as a major defeat for Kennedy. *Time* magazine called the Senate vote "a stunning rebuke to the administration." Kennedy himself admitted that he may have overreached in his attempt to create the department through the reorganization route. Although the cabinet bill was again introduced in 1963, Kennedy did not fight for its passage.[60]

Even though the effort to create the department failed, the conflict greatly increased Weaver's profile. He appeared several times on national television and was the subject of newspaper articles across the country. In a press conference following the rejection of his plan, President Kennedy joked that the people who opposed the department were ready to support Weaver "for any Cabinet position he wishes—Defense, State, Treasury or anything else." Kennedy told reporters that he was sure that Weaver was "grateful for those good wishes for a Cabinet position where there is no vacancy." In fact, during the debates, several senators had argued that Weaver should be appointed secretary of the Department of Health, Education, and Welfare (HEW), a position that everyone assumed was soon to be vacated by Abraham Ribicoff so that he could run for the Senate in Connecticut.[61]

As the nation's top African American official, Weaver became a major focus of the political battles between Democrats and Republicans for the black vote. He was frequently named as a potential Democratic candidate for the New York Senate seat of Republican Jacob Javits. Even Rev. Martin Luther King entered the debate, urging blacks to "use their political power at the polls this fall to defeat Congressmen who allowed the race question to sabotage their most cherished dream—a Negro in the cabinet of the federal government." To prove his party's civil rights credentials, Republican National Committee Chair Bob Wilson publicly urged the president to appoint Weaver to replace Ribicoff. Wilson made this statement in April, even though Ribicoff had told reporters he would not make a decision about resigning until the summer.[62]

Kennedy responded that the Republicans were using Weaver to court the black vote and that Weaver was better suited to his current position. But several insiders reported that the administration was seriously considering him for the job, and Weaver believed he could have had it had he told the president he wanted it. However, after a little research, Weaver decided HEW was "a hornet's nest." He told White House staff that he was not particularly interested in the HEW job but that he would do as the president desired. Later in the year he publicly stated that, while he would not turn it down, he did not want the job. After Ribicoff resigned, Kennedy appointed Cleveland mayor Anthony Celebrezze to the post.[63]

Weaver's profile was further increased when, in July 1962, the NAACP awarded Weaver its forty-seventh Spingarn Medal. According to the program, the medal was awarded for the "highest achievement of an American Negro"; Roy Wilkins stated that Weaver was being given the award for his "public service on the municipal, state and federal levels; for his pioneer role in the development of the open occupancy doctrine, and for his responsible and militant leadership in the struggle for civil rights." Previous winners of the award included W. E. B. DuBois, James Weldon Johnson,

Mary McLeod Bethune, and Weaver's good friends William Hastie and Ralph Bunche.[64]

In his speech, Weaver thanked his parents, who "never accepted for themselves or their children the psychological limitations of a color-caste system," and Ella, who had "blended—and at times subordinated—her own successful career to mine," while providing "a constant atmosphere of intellectual stimulation and affectionate criticism." He told the audience that he hoped that some day the award would not be necessary because blacks were no longer excluded from American life. However, while there had been improvements in opportunities for blacks, the accomplishments of many blacks remained unrecognized. More importantly, Weaver argued, an objective of the award was to "stimulate the ambitions of the colored youth." In this area, Weaver asserted, much more work remained to be done. "A much larger number of colored Americans are not only outside of the mainstream of our society but see no hope of entering it," he claimed. Weaver noted that, because some African Americans were succeeding while others were being left behind, conflict among blacks was increasing. "In a minority group it is safer to resent the class lines within the segregated society than to battle against color barriers which involve the dominant group as well." Much of this resentment, he believed, was the result of "middle-class chauvinism," the belief held by many Americans that their success was solely the result of their own hard work. "But success is a fickle mistress," Weaver told the audience. The larger problem with American society was that discrimination both prevented the ambitious from achieving and provided "an excuse for failure." Weaver worried that a "protective culture with values and behavior patterns all its own" was emerging within the black community. "Those who are conditioned by these protective devices resist the values and motivations of the dominant culture."[65]

The purpose of the NAACP, Weaver argued, was to break down racial barriers and create a culture of success within the black community. Alluding to the rise in popularity of separatist movements such as the Nation of Islam, Weaver stated that the NAACP and its approach were best suited to achieving these goals. "This is not the time to flirt with the romantic 'new approaches' which would repudiate the efforts which" had proven successful, he claimed. As in his 1960 keynote speech at the NAACP annual convention, Weaver continued to insist that the traditional approach to civil rights was the most appropriate method. Time and events, however, were making this assertion more difficult to maintain.[66]

## * 12 *

# Fighting for Civil Rights from the Inside

Cabinet or not, Weaver had a department with many programs and fiefdoms of power to run. His first years at the Housing and Home Finance Agency (HHFA) were devoted to bringing together its disparate parts, reaching out to his opponents in the real estate sector, and trying to reform federal urban policies that discriminated against minorities. In each of these areas, Weaver made progress, but the federal bureaucracy was a slow-moving ship at a time when urban deterioration and racial conflict were rapidly increasing.

Weaver struggled particularly with the Federal Housing Administration (FHA). The FHA, whose commissioner was appointed not by Weaver but by the president, had a long history of independence. Because its operations were funded through insurance premiums paid by home mortgages, FHA staff came to view themselves as employees of a quasi-private institution, not as part of the federal government. The FHA's clients—the home builders, financial institutions, and realtors that made up the housing industry—were happy with this arrangement and did not respond well to Weaver's efforts to control them.[1]

Another difficult area was the urban renewal program. Weaver later remarked that "of all the programs in the HHFA there was none that was more volatile, more fraught with problems, more dangerous for a democratic, people-oriented administration." Reminiscing two decades later about his early years at the HHFA, Weaver remembered that he had done "quite a bit of writing pointing out the deficiencies of urban renewal. Then I finally found myself in the unique position of administering a program of which I had been critical." Across the nation, as more and more cities began implementing their redevelopment plans, complaints about the program were increasing. In San Francisco, NAACP officials demanded that all renewal programs be halted until the city conducted a detailed study of their impact and produce a plan for integrated housing. In Syracuse, the Congress of Racial Equality (CORE) organized a protest against the city's urban renewal program. Eighty activists were arrested at the event, where several climbed on machinery at four renewal sites and refused to leave until the mayor met their demands to stop the clearance of blacks and to desegregate the city.[2]

Though he shared the protestors' concerns, Weaver spent a lot of time in his public appearances defending the urban renewal approach, particularly to African Americans. In Pittsburgh, he lauded the redevelopment efforts of city leaders and argued that in his administration there would be a shift away from demolition of housing toward rehabilitation. This, he claimed, would benefit blacks. "I hope it will become increasingly clear that urban renewal is an opportunity rather than a burden for those most directly affected by it," he stated. But he also defended renewal efforts in areas where African Americans were significantly dislocated. "There is no city in the country that has a brighter history of achievement than the City of New Haven," Weaver told New Haven residents. Activists in that city, however, took a different view, complaining about the disruption caused by the program. Just a few years later, these protests would turn violent.[3]

Weaver also defended the public housing program. In 1962, the Public Housing Administration marked the completion of the 500,000th unit of public housing. While this was still far from the goal of 810,000 units, the agency celebrated the fact that more than 2 million people, more than half of them children, lived in public housing. Despite its success in providing shelter, public housing was under increasing attack, not only from its longstanding antagonists in the real estate business and Congress but from its former supporters. In many small cities, public housing provided decent, affordable shelter to needy families. In these cases the program achieved its goals and did so in an efficient, effective manner. However, these successes were obscured by the scandal that public housing had become in many large cities. By the early 1960s, public housing in the nation's largest cities was overwhelmingly housing for minorities. In St. Louis, the tenant body was more than 80 percent black. The racial transformation of many projects was largely responsible for the decline in support for the program.[4]

Chicago became the poster-child of problem programs. There, fewer than 10 percent of the 30,000 public housing residents were white. That city, which twenty years earlier had, over Weaver's protests, undertaken a massive construction program, had succeeded in creating the largest black ghetto in the nation. As Weaver and others had forecast, the results were disastrous for the city and for the public housing residents, who lived in rapidly deteriorating communities besieged by crime, social problems, and failed management. Although Chicago was an extreme case, most large cities also reported a significant increase in crime at public housing projects. These changes mirrored similar transformations in other parts of most cities, but the deterioration in public projects, many only a decade old, was obvious, and supporters increasingly viewed the program as a failure.[5]

Despite the growing concerns, Weaver continued to support the initiative, responding that of course public housing sheltered families with economic and social problems. "This, in fact, is the job that public housing was set up to do." To blame public housing for these problems, Weaver argued, was "like blaming the doctor for the disease." Contradicting the assertions of the program's founders, he commented, "Good housing, however, is not itself a remedy for a family's ills, any more than a good hospital building can make you well. It does, however, offer the environment in which many of these family problems can be successfully treated." His agency, Weaver argued, was working with other parts of the federal government to bring social services to needy families.[6]

While Weaver publicly defended public housing, within his administration officials were increasingly frustrated with the decline of the buildings they had funded, and public housing administrator Marie McGuire told Weaver that the program needed substantial reform if it was to survive. The history of opposition to public housing and the current perceptions of the program, she argued, had "proven to be a drawback in accomplishing the substantive goal of providing suitable housing for those who cannot afford it." Instead of continuing to rely on the traditional structure of public housing, she proposed that the federal government seek to provide shelter by alternative methods such as subsidizing tenants to rent in the private market. Over the next decade, as public projects in large cities continued to deteriorate, these alternatives would become more attractive.[7]

In general, throughout his HHFA years, Weaver struggled to ensure that federal housing policies were implemented in a nondiscriminatory manner. The gap between aspirations and reality was, however, large at Weaver's agency. The story of a federally subsidized apartment building in Milwaukee, Wisconsin, illuminates the complicated problems Weaver faced in eliminating discrimination. In 1960, a 328-unit building opened on the north side of the city. The project was developed by the American Federation for State, County, and Municipal Employees (AFSCME) to house people uprooted by urban renewal projects in the city. In the late 1950s and early 1960s, AFSCME had undertaken several such projects across the nation, and in May 1962, Weaver visited the city to give a speech at the union's national convention. In the talk, Weaver praised the activities of AFSCME leader Arnold Zander and of other unions that had sponsored similar projects.[8]

A year later, however, local NAACP officials revealed that the project was exclusively white and had never accepted a black tenant. Blacks, NAACP leaders argued, were allowed to apply, but they met constant delays in processing that caused them to give up on the apartments. This was a particularly troublesome example of discrimination, given that the union had a significant number of black members. AFSCME leader Arnold Zander, who was also a national director of the liberal advocacy group Americans for Democratic Action, quickly announced that two black families would move into the apartments the next month, July, but eighteen months later federal officials found that there were no blacks in the development. Weaver's staff found this situation typical. "Although the union is racially integrated," they told Weaver, the union's eleven projects across the nation were "either segregated or have minimal Negro tenancy."[9]

When he was not dealing with crises, Weaver spent a great deal of time cultivating his constituents in the housing industry. Although he generally avoided the realtors lobby, which was philosophically opposed to much of the administration's program, Weaver felt he made significant progress with the home builders. "I went to their convention and made a very short speech and spent a couple of evenings with them. I think I probably won the support of a large number because I indulged in one of their favorite activities which was the consuming of whiskey." Through quiet persuasion, he believed he was making progress in changing attitudes, but time was against Weaver in his effort to reform the building industry from within.[10]

Weaver did succeed in placating some congressional opponents. Congressman Albert Thomas (D-TX), an influential member of the Appropriations Committee and a southern Democrat from Houston whom Lyndon Johnson later referred to as having "the prejudices typical of East Texas," wrote President Kennedy a glowing letter praising Weaver and his staff. "The agency, under the able leadership of Dr. Weaver, is doing an outstanding job," Thomas wrote. "Without a doubt, he is one of the most knowledgeable men in the United State in all phases of urban affairs." Thomas concluded that "the Subcommittee is exceptionally proud of the fine service he has rendered and we would like you to know that your choice of Dr. Weaver was an excellent one."[11]

However, by 1963 many housing activists had grown weary of the Kennedy administration's limited attention to urban problems. While they did not blame Weaver for this neglect, they began to complain loudly about the lack of new initiatives to deal with housing deterioration and neighborhood decline. At the annual convention of the National Housing Conference, a group in which Weaver had been an active member before his HHFA appointment, the membership passed a resolution stating that "the administration has failed to make any comprehensive analysis of needs or the adequacy of present programs." The "administration's attitude and its proposals are not good enough to meet our needs and aspirations," they concluded, and they demanded that the president convene a national conference on housing and community development. Kennedy's staff began to explore the idea but ultimately decided against it. Kennedy, who was never very interested in domestic matters, focused his attention on the Soviet Union and other international issues. Other than their efforts to spur economic growth in the country, his administration produced few domestic initiatives, leaving many liberals frustrated and critical and putting Weaver in the uncomfortable position of defending the administration against his former colleagues.[12]

STYMIED AT THE White House, Weaver spent most of his time trying to get his agency to work more efficiently. Although Weaver achieved success in this area, if there was any progress on the matter of housing discrimination, it was hard to see. The lack of improvement in this area and a maturing and increasingly aggressive civil rights movement increased pressure on Kennedy to fulfill his campaign promise. The defeat of the bill to create a cabinet-level urban affairs department gave fair-housing activists the opportunity to say "I told you so" to the president, but this was an empty victory since their real goal was the government's prohibition of discrimination. Soon after the defeat of the bill, National Committee against Discrimination in Housing (NCDH) leaders again called on the president to issue an order banning discrimination. By the end of 1962, they would achieve victory, but it was a slow, painful process that produced only limited returns.[13]

Throughout the spring and summer of 1962, fair-housing activists peppered the administration with demands for the issuance of the executive order. Newspapers across the country called for the president to sign the order. In Los Angeles, CORE activists picketed a speech by Kennedy to protest the delay. NAACP officials put out constant press releases calling on members to lobby the president. "The patience of Negroes and other enlightened Americans . . . is not inexhaustible," they warned the president. Under increasing pressure, the administration started to consider the issue again, and in July Kennedy counsel Ted Sorensen publicly predicted that the president would sign the order, though he did not say when this would happen.[14]

As reports increased that Kennedy would sign the executive order, many Democrats in Congress pressed him to reject it, or at least to wait until after the November elections. Southern Democrats were primarily concerned about the political impact of the order, but they focused their arguments on the economic effects. "An order of this nature is likely to result in a disastrous curtailment of activity in existing housing programs," Senator Sam Ervin (D-NC) wrote. John Sparkman (D-AL) claimed that it would "cripple badly the home-building industry, with a very serious impact on the economy of the country." He also used the turmoil created by civil rights agitation to argue against the order. "The already very confused and troubled situation which we have witnessed in Alabama and other parts of the South would simply be agitated all the more," he concluded.[15]

The majority of congressional opponents were southern, but others also asked the administration to reconsider. Congresswoman Martha Griffiths (D-MI) argued that "there is not time enough left before election for the white areas to understand the full implications of this order. . . . Most white people have resigned themselves to the fact of integration, but the suburbs of Detroit believe it will be years before it applies to their exact area." She presciently argued that the issuance of the order would have serious implications for Democrats representing suburban districts. She also warned, "If such an order is to be issued, it should not be issued immediately preceding an election because it will be interpreted as political and as an attempt to buy votes." Many observers expected the president to announce the order to mark the hundredth anniversary of the Emancipation Proclamation on 21 September, but congressional protests convinced the president to wait until after the elections.[16]

Instead, the White House tried to placate blacks with a lavish formal dinner to celebrate the event. Kennedy invited eight hundred African Americans and placed Weaver and Thurgood Marshall (whom Kennedy had appointed as a federal judge) "on prominent display." To white reporters, the White House dismissed the gala as a social event, but to black newspapers it trumpeted the fact that more African Americans attended the dinner than had visited the White House in the prior century and a half. Kennedy spokesmen argued it was evidence of a new day in Washington, but the event did little to calm the growing storm of criticism among civil rights leaders.[17]

The Democrats' moderate success in the midterm elections—they gained three Senate seats and lost two in the House—gave Kennedy enough comfort to finally take action on the housing matter. On 20 November 1962, more than two years after he first raised the issue, Kennedy signed an executive order banning discrimination in federal housing programs. He made the announcement in the most low-key manner possible, after proclaiming that the Soviets had agreed to remove all their bombers from Cuba and confirming that the Soviet missile silos had been dismantled. Kennedy stated that he was "directing Federal departments to take every proper and legal action to prevent discrimination" in housing owned, operated, funded, or insured by the federal government. Under the order, each agency would be responsible for securing its programs' compliance. It also established the President's Committee on Equal Opportunity in Housing, composed of government officials and public members, to oversee federal activities and recommend policy changes to the president.[18]

The order was similar to the one that had been considered in 1961 but more limited than that proposed by fair-housing advocates. While it covered all HHFA programs, it did not regulate the financial institutions that funded housing development, and it did not apply retroactively. The order directed agencies to use their "good offices" (i.e., persuasion) to get existing projects to comply. Exempting the sale of homes by individuals, the order applied solely to commercial builders. According to historian Carl Brauer, "so narrow had the order finally become that the president dispatched his brother Robert and [Justice Department official] Burke Marshall to break the news to Robert Weaver who he feared might resign in protest." Weaver remembered being greatly disappointed with the president's decision. But "I recognized the fact, as I said to Bobby, I had two choices. I either went along with that, or else I resigned. And I wasn't ready to resign, so I went along with it."[19]

Though they were frustrated by the narrow order, civil rights leaders praised the president's action. "The order strikes at the very heart of the segregated system," Dr. Martin Luther King announced. "Integrated housing is the primary means by which we will have a truly integrated society." Roy Wilkins claimed that the order placed "the national policy of no discrimination squarely on the housing field, and there can be no contention henceforth that the national policy is fuzzy." Weaver's former NCDH colleague Shad Polier declared the order "less than half a loaf" but continued that "even such crumbs are better than no bread at all." Jackie Robinson called Kennedy's decision "indicative of the fact that intelligent political leaders realize that appeasement of the South will not work."[20]

Not surprisingly, southern politicians vilified the decision. Senator John Stennis (D-MS) called it "an audacious usurpation of power by the Executive Branch," and Willis Robertson (D-VA) declared it "absolutely unconstitutional." Senator Herman Talmadge claimed that the order was "a grave disservice to the economic welfare of the United States." The homebuilding industry was relatively silent about the decision.[21]

Fair-housing activists were disappointed that the order was not as expansive as they desired. However, NCDH director Frances Levenson stated that it was "an important gain in practice as well as principle." To assuage civil rights leaders, Weaver publicly noted that broadening the order in the near future was a "possibility." The order did have an immediate impact on the realtors' industry, which changed its code of ethics to state for the first time that realtors who sold home to blacks in previously all-white neighborhoods did not violate association rules.[22]

For Weaver, the pleasure of securing the executive action for which he had lobbied for more than a decade was muted by events in his personal life. Just two weeks before, on 6 November, his son, Robert Jr., died as the result of a self-inflicted gunshot. According to the *Washington Star,* the twenty-two-year-old Weaver, who had a wife and two children, shot himself. New York police detectives speculated that Weaver was playing "Russian roulette," but Weaver's wife, Aida, said he was trying to prove that his revolver would not shoot ammunition made for an automatic weapon. He shot the gun at the floor several times, but it failed to discharge. Weaver then put the gun to his head, expecting it to jam, his wife said, but it fired.[23]

Weaver said very little, before or after, about his son, and Weaver's relatively voluminous files hold almost no record of Robert Jr., so it is very difficult to piece together the story of his life. However, the small bits of evidence there are point to an increasingly troubled existence up to his death. In April 1956, Robert Jr. and a friend were arrested near the Weavers' summer home in Connecticut. The two boys had been suspended from boarding school for smoking and had run away to the Weavers' cottage. They took the Weavers' boat down the Housatonic River, intending to go all the way to Florida. They were picked up by the Coast Guard somewhere near Greenwich. They were far from the first boys to do such a thing, and several people chalked it up to "adolescent adjustment."[24]

Most of the small pieces of evidence about Robert Jr.'s life come from the reports that Federal Bureau of Investigation (FBI) agents filed during Weaver's 1961 confirmation hearings. These documents are notoriously unreliable, particularly regarding African Americans. In general, the agents interviewed anyone who said they knew the subject and recorded whatever they said. Opinion was presented as fact, and the agents frequently included their own interpretations without evidence. In Weaver's case, for example, several informants stated that Weaver had acted inappropriately in trying to have his uncle Harry Burleigh declared incompetent in 1940. After a little investigation, FBI agents found that Weaver had not participated at all in the litigation over Burleigh's assets.[25]

When the FBI agents in New York City were directed to investigate Weaver after his nomination to run the HHFA, they fairly rapidly ascertained that he had no skeletons in his closet, so they spent a great deal of time investigating his son. The picture they put together was of a young man struggling to find his way in life, and doing it, according to some informants, without the help of his family. In 1958, Robert Jr. enlisted in the Air Force, but he left after less than a year. He moved back to New York City and soon thereafter married Aida Pacheco, a woman of Puerto Rican descent. The FBI's informants were in dispute on the matter, but according to several, his parents were not happy about the decision. One informant stated that Robert Jr. had "been dropped like a hot potato," and another argued that he "appears to be a child that has been left out of the family circle and can best be described now as somewhat down at the heels." However, another person told agents that he was "apparently doing well," while a different informant stated that he was a "well-mannered, lively and neat young man who has managed to stay out of any kind of trouble." He appeared, the informant stated, "to be on good terms with his family and speaks very highly of his father." Robert and Aida had two small children and were living in the Amsterdam Heights section when he died. According to the FBI reports, he had worked in several jobs since returning to New York City.[26]

Though Weaver never acknowledged it, or discussed the matter, most of his friends and colleagues thought the young man had committed suicide. Weaver was devastated by the loss, but he was typically reticent in expressing his emotions. He destroyed all of the hundreds of messages that he told

Charles Abrams he had received. Abrams was one of the few people he did share his feelings with, expressing thanks for Abrams's letter of condolence. Ella also wrote to thank Abrams, noting that Weaver was "not given to verbalizing" his feelings. Abrams's "beautiful letter of November 7th broke through that reserve and he permitted himself the relief of tears unashamedly. Having shared many years with a man who does not give in to this luxury, it had special meaning for me," Ella told Abrams.[27]

The Weavers buried their son in a private ceremony, and his father went back to work. He had a lot to do to mollify the critics, who worried that Weaver was just a "token" with little power. Kennedy's approach to the executive order on housing was typical of his approach to civil rights during his presidency: although sympathetic toward the activists' demands for equality, he was reluctant to push too hard against the southern political system. "If we drive [John] Sparkman, [Lister] Hill and other moderate Southerners to the wall with a lot of civil rights demands that can't pass anyway, then what happens to the Negro on minimum wages, housing and the rest," he told staff. Because of Kennedy's charm, the majority of African Americans continued to hold favorable opinions of him, but civil rights leaders were constantly frustrated by the administration's timidity. "We've gotten the best snow job in history. We've lost two years because we admired him for what should have been done years ago," one activist stated in 1962.[28]

By 1963, civil rights activists were tired of the administration's timidity. The increasingly vocal protests against racial violence, the denial of the right to vote, and general racial discrimination in the South became daily news on the nation's television networks and in the morning papers. After two years of prodding, in the spring, Kennedy acquiesced to demands that he introduce civil rights legislation, but his proposal was a very limited one that he did little to promote. At the same time, southern politicians became even more intransigent in their opposition to any change. The violent response to the demonstrations in Birmingham led by Martin Luther King galvanized public support for federal legislation, and Kennedy agreed to significantly expand his civil rights program to ban discrimination in public facilities and protect black activists from violence.[29]

To support the bill, in June civil rights leaders announced that, twenty-two years after A. Philip Randolph proposed the idea, they were organizing a "March on Washington for Jobs and Justice." King stated that it would be "one of the greatest demonstrations for freedom that has ever been held in America" and would serve as a "creative channel through which thousands of Negroes can nonviolently articulate their longing for freedom and human dignity." As President Roosevelt had two decades before, Kennedy opposed the march and told organizers that they could imperil his proposal if they went through with it. Throughout July, administration officials and other liberals lobbied King and the organizers to cancel the event, but they refused.[30]

On 28 August 1963, 250,000 people met in the nation's capital for a day of song and protest capped by Rev. King's "I have a dream" speech. It was a day unlike any before, as Americans of all races joined to demand the government make real the promises made by Lincoln a century before in his Emancipation Proclamation. Before they went home, the participants knew they had taken part in a historic moment. However, despite the warm feelings generated among liberals by the event, neither the march nor the more traditional lobbying effort were able to secure passage of the civil rights bill during the remainder of the 1963 term.[31]

As the highest ranking black in the federal government, Weaver was a symbol of civil rights progress, but other than his crucial role in the issuance of the executive order, he played little part in the administration's debates or discussions with civil rights leaders. "They didn't regard him as the spokesman or the expert on civil rights," his colleague Mort Schussheim remembered. Weaver accepted this position without complaint. "Almost by tacit understanding," he later recalled, "the President felt that since I was going to be involved in running a rather important area of government activity my concentration should be there and I should be used only casually in the race relations problems outside of my agency." A year later, Weaver summed up for a reporter his attitude about the role of his race in his work. "He has chosen stimulation of the broader metropolitan revolution as his lever to upgrade minorities along with the rest of urban America," the reporter claimed. "His immersion in civil rights, he says, is as a liberal, rather than a Negro. Black chauvinism, he feels, is no better than white chauvinism." Weaver preferred to be seen as a professional who was black rather than a racial advocate. His choice brought him respect for the work he was doing in housing, but it limited his ability to participate in decisions that shaped the course of racial progress.[32]

"It was a matter of personality," one colleague later argued. "If he had been bolder, if he had stuck his neck out, they would have had to include him." But all of Kennedy's civil rights advisors—Robert Kennedy, Burke Marshall, Harris Wofford, and Lee White—were white, and no blacks had an important part to play in these decisions. It is unlikely that they would have allowed Weaver a prominent role in these debates, and fearful of being rebuffed, he never attempted to intervene. Typical of Kennedy's attitude toward civil rights was his response to the March on Washington. Worried about embarrassment to the administration should the protest end in violence, Kennedy directed his staff to stay away from the Mall that day. Although it is possible Weaver rejected these orders, according to several associates he did not attend what many consider the most important event in American civil rights history. Weaver did not participate in the famous meeting Kennedy held with civil rights leaders after the March on Washington, nor was he present in any of the discussions between activists and other top government officials.[33]

Playing the good soldier, Weaver frequently praised the efforts of the Kennedy administration in civil rights. In speeches he pointed to the administration's attack on segregated transportation facilities, its suits against infringements on voting rights, and its intervention in civil rights conflicts in Alabama, Mississippi, and Georgia. "The record of President Kennedy in the field of civil rights speaks loud and clear to every American. This is a man who believes in equal opportunities for men of all races. And it is a man both willing and able to use the full force of the Presidency to achieve those opportunities," he claimed.[34]

In an interview six months after Kennedy's assassination, Weaver gave a favorable opinion of the administration's civil rights record. "Well, I think there were three ways you could look at it. And, I think this was the way the President looked at it. First, I think there was the question of basic commitment. Second there was the question of techniques. And, third the question of time. As far as the basic commitment is concerned, I think that there was never any faltering." Weaver pointed to the appointments of black officials and the revitalization of the President's Committee on Equal Opportunity in Housing as examples. Weaver nevertheless noted that, "at times, I, as many people who worked in this administration, probably felt that there was an overcautiousness on the part of the President." Weaver credited this timidity to the close election and to the fact that Kennedy was "much more a man of ideas and a man of concepts than a man of personal relations in the sense of being able to work with people and adjust himself and adapt himself to what one has to do to, apparently, get legislation through in this country."[35]

In the end, however, Weaver was heartened by his experiences as HHFA administrator. Although they had opposed his nomination, Weaver found it increasingly easy to work with the southerners who ran the Congress.

"There was an unwritten thing. I never discussed race with them, and they never discussed race with me. We discussed housing." Weaver believed that "a great deal of the southern position is for local consumption." While he did not "relish it," he accepted it.[36]

Weaver's management of the agency was emblematic of his personality—quiet, careful, and focused on incremental change. In general he avoided the spotlight, and did not attempt to gain influence within the White House. In the thousand days that Kennedy occupied the office, Weaver met with him on a significant matter—a dispute over the administration's mass-transit bill—only once. Weaver chose to work through White House aide Lee White. According to his HHFA legal counsel Milt Semer, Weaver was "basically a loner" who worked with only a few people. His colleague and friend Mort Schussheim had similar recollections. In a town where the term "power lunch" was coined, Weaver "would go off by himself to lunch an awful lot. He went to a deli in a hotel, I think the Ambassador Hotel on 16th and K, and he'd sit at the counter and order a sandwich." At the same time, his ability to get things done without bothering the president increased his esteem in the eyes of the White House. The nation's top black official, however, was clearly not a "player."[37]

Most observers considered Weaver's first three years at the HHFA a success, but the number of interested parties was few. The nation was still unaware of the problems that were festering in American cities, and the country's political leadership was not focused on these issues. The framework that had characterized Weaver's political agenda for thirty years—the methodical pursuit of racial reform through research, analysis, and persuasion—would achieve major successes in the years that followed, but it would also look increasingly anachronistic as these problems became more evident.

* 13 *

# The Great Society and the City

Possibly no single incident in the twentieth century affected American society more than the murder of the thirty-fifth president. The events of 22 November 1963 influenced American politics and culture for decades to come, creating suspicions of conspiracy that continue into this century. Kennedy's assassination not only shocked the nation but cast a pall over the federal government. Weaver remembered, "I was in Cleveland. I was going to do a TV show, a quiz show, when I heard the word and I couldn't continue." A week later, Weaver told a Boston audience that "this is a somber and serious moment in our history. . . . The events of recent days have brought home in a frightening way the price a Nation pays for its social neglects and shortcomings. For whether it is a warped mind, a distorted spirit, or a frustrated life that brings such disaster upon us, it is a disease nurtured in the soil of our own society and it springs from an infection that we must eliminate."[1]

While the nation grieved for the fallen president, in Washington attention turned to his successor. Because of his background and his voting record in the Senate, liberals were not enamored of Lyndon Johnson. Although he was not an active segregationist, for most of his career Johnson had sided with his southern brethren in opposing federal civil rights proposals. As majority leader, however, Johnson had pushed through the Civil Rights Act of 1957, the first civil rights law in eighty years. To Johnson and his backers, this was evidence of Johnson's support for equality. Civil rights leaders responded that Johnson had seen that most of the important provisions were removed before the bill was put to a final vote.[2]

Most liberals were upset when Kennedy selected Johnson for vice president, but as vice president, Johnson worked assiduously to develop his civil rights credentials. Directed by Kennedy to chair the President's Commission on Equal Opportunity (PCEO) (a thankless task given Kennedy's lassitude on the matter), Johnson organized a program called Plans for Progress that negotiated with business to increase their hiring of minorities. While not everyone agreed that these efforts were successful, Roy Wilkins later remembered that he began to see a change in Johnson's understanding of civil rights during the vice presidency. "He no longer held back," Wilkins claimed.[3]

Weaver knew Johnson by reputation when both were New Deal officials. As head of the Texas office of the National Youth Administration, Johnson had made a name for himself as a "young Turk" of the New Deal, and he used this office to bring public facilities to the poorest parts of the state. He also directed resources to his African American and Mexican American constituents, though always for segregated projects. In his oral history for the Johnson Library, Weaver remembered hearing "about this guy down in Texas who was running the National Youth Administration and he was shocking some people up on the Hill because he thought that the National Youth Administration benefits ought to go to poor folks." One of the first public housing projects built by the U.S. Housing Authority was located in Johnson's district. In the early 1960s, Weaver and Johnson had gotten to know each other as members of the PCEO.[4]

Although he recognized that the nation was still in shock over the fallen president, Johnson wasted little time in charting a course for the federal government. In the spring of 1964, he unveiled his vision for the future of America in a series of speeches. In May, Johnson told the University of Michigan graduating class that "we have the opportunity to move not only toward the rich society and the powerful society, but upward to the Great Society." This society, he argued, would be "a place where every child can find knowledge to enrich his mind and to enlarge his talents." Johnson cataloged the many aspects—health, housing, education—where the country still needed improvement, and he called on Americans to support his efforts to bring the weight of the federal government to bear on these problems. "We have the power to shape the civilization that we want. But we need your will, your labor, your hearts, if we are to build that kind of society," Johnson told the audience.[5]

During the next five years, Johnson would lead the country into a new era of domestic policy. The legislation passed during his term and a half would dwarf that of the subsequent forty years. When Johnson left office in 1969, the federal government was dramatically different than when he gave his speech in Ann Arbor. At the same time that he was revolutionizing domestic policy, Johnson would enmesh the country in its most damaging international conflict to date. The battle over Vietnam, which would spread throughout Southeast Asia, would have a profound impact on the country and would strongly influence and inhibit the president's domestic agenda.

The two years following Kennedy's assassination were ones of rapid change for urban America, for the federal government, and also for Weaver. During this period, social forces dramatically altered relations among America's racial groups while they reshaped the geography of urban society. As the administration's highest-ranking black official, Weaver played an important role in some of these changes but was noticeably absent in discussions of other important questions. At the end of his first two years with Johnson, Weaver would achieve a significant milestone in his career and in African American history, but not without a fight that would illuminate the potential and limitations of liberal approaches to racial equality and urban policy.

IN HIS FIRST year, no issue would occupy more of Johnson's time than civil rights. To the surprise of many, only five days after Kennedy's death, Johnson announced that his first major task would be the passage of civil rights legislation, arguing, "No memorial oration or eulogy could more eloquently honor President Kennedy's memory than the earliest possible passage of the civil rights bills for which he fought so long." Throughout the winter and spring of 1964, Johnson worked to secure the passage of the civil rights bill Kennedy had introduced. After the longest filibuster on record in the Senate, the bill passed and Johnson signed it in June. It was the most far-reaching civil rights law since Reconstruction, prohibiting discrimination in public accommodations, employment, and government programs. Its provisions created a framework for the expansion of equality to millions of Americans.[6]

Although civil rights advocates were ecstatic about the bill's passage, California voters reminded them that the roots of racial discrimination and segregation were deep and would take years to remove. There, opponents of fair-housing laws secured a major victory against the cause of civil rights. Their actions were particularly troubling to Weaver, who had spent his career fighting against housing discrimination and was hoping to use his influence over federal housing programs to expand opportunities for blacks and other minorities. Instead, Weaver spent the fall of 1964 in a losing battle to maintain the status quo.

The dispute involved a new California law called the Rumford Fair Housing Act. Passed in 1963, it prohibited discrimination in the sale or rental of housing in the majority of the state's new developments. Although activists cheered the victory, only weeks after Governor Edmund Brown signed the bill, the California Real Estate Association instituted a campaign to repeal it. By amending the state constitution to prohibit governmental interference with an individual's right to sell his or her property, opponents sought to invalidate the fair-housing law. Edward Mendenhall, an official of a national realtors organization, argued that the right to sell property was an "essential liberty" and claimed that the Rumford act created a situation of "forced housing." During the spring of 1964, 600,000 signatures were secured to put the proposition on the ballot. Their efforts were facilitated by the wording of the referendum, which phrased the initiative as a simple statement of the rights of individuals to control their property and de-emphasized its true intent.[7]

Fair-housing advocates argued that Proposition 14 was unconstitutional and immoral and that it would set a dangerous precedent. They claimed that it would repeal all state and local fair-housing laws and poison race relations in California. Opponents further argued that the proposition would hurt the state by putting it at odds with the federal government. They were supported by the housing administrator: Weaver wrote that the proposal "would raise serious questions as to the future of the urban renewal program in California." Because the federal executive order required recipients of federal funds to certify that they did not discriminate, Weaver had "considerable doubt" whether California's urban renewal projects would be authorized by his agency. California public officials also criticized the proposal. Governor Edmund Brown argued that the proposition was illegal and worried that it would incite organized hate groups; all of the state Democratic leadership and most Republican politicians opposed the proposition.[8]

During the fall of 1964, Proposition 14 became the most heated issue of the California election. Rev. Martin Luther King traveled to the state to declare, "All over the United States, Proposition 14 has become a symbol for segregation in schools and housing." Weaver visited California during the last days of the presidential campaign to repeat his opposition and warn that federal funding could be lost if the proposition passed. Proponents of the proposition criticized Weaver for insinuating himself into the matter. "I don't think California voters are going to be disturbed by Dr. Robert C. Weaver, who came out here from Washington as the big gun to start banging away at the people of California on how they will vote," Howard Byrum, head of the campaign, told reporters. In the end, the claims about the sanctity of property rights prevailed over the arguments of Weaver and civil rights activists, and Proposition 14 passed by a margin of nearly 2 to 1.[9]

In response, Weaver declared that the amendment had "created legal uncertainties" regarding the compliance of California agencies with federal law, and he directed urban renewal administrator William Slayton to halt the issuance of any new contracts within the state. NAACP officials initiated a lawsuit declaring the law unconstitutional. Two years later, the U.S. Supreme Court invalidated the proposition, but the passage of Proposition 14 highlighted the limits of the civil rights movement to promote equality through law, spurred movements in several other states to pass similar legislation, and presaged the future, more contentious debates over fair-housing law at the federal level.[10]

IN THE CALIFORNIA conflict, Weaver used urban renewal funds to enforce antidiscrimination laws. However, by 1964, urban renewal was under attack in cities across the nation for its negative impact on blacks and other minorities. It was also facing increasing criticism from academics and policymakers. The critiques were part of a larger reassessment, from the Left and the Right, of existing approaches to urban problems. As the nation's top housing official, Weaver, who had critiqued the program as an activist, now found himself urban renewal's most prominent advocate. Holding true to his New Deal roots, Weaver continued to believe that the most productive way to revive the city was through professional planning.

He would become increasingly isolated in these beliefs. By the early 1960s, many intellectuals were questioning the basic philosophy of urban renewal. They argued that, despite the investment of billions of dollars, cities had not been revitalized, and they complained that the dislocation caused by the program had resulted in the creation of more slums. Among the most vociferous critics of the program was Jane Jacobs, whose best-selling book *The Death and Life of Great American Cities* argued that urban renewal was destroying the fabric of the city. Published in 1961, the book examined the impact of the urban renewal program on neighborhoods in several cities. Describing the plight of areas like Boston's North End, Jacobs argued that the program had destroyed vibrant communities and replaced them with sterile developments. Jacobs criticized not only the impact of urban renewal on the residents of these neighborhoods but the philosophy behind the program. Newly developed areas were not the boon to the city that renewal promoters claimed, Jacobs stated. Rather, they replaced architecturally diverse, economically viable communities that provided social and economic support to the working class with upper-middle-class high-rises that could be sustained only with public funds. Urban redevelopment programs, she argued, did "not rest soundly on reasoned investment of public tax subsidies, as urban renewal theory proclaims, but on vast involuntary subsidies wrought out of helpless site victims."[11]

Urban renewal advocates were quick to respond to Jacobs's accusations. "Mrs. Jacobs has presented the world with a document that will be grabbed by screwballs and reactionaries and used to fight civic improvement and urban renewal projects for years to come," claimed the executive director of the American Society of Planning Officials. Redevelopment official Ed Logue argued that Jacobs had romanticized neighborhoods that were not viable and had ignored the facts of their decline. Despite their efforts, however, Jacobs's book became required reading for progressives by the mid-1960s.[12]

Faced with growing criticism, Weaver devoted increasing attention to defending the urban renewal program. In the spring of 1964, he published an article in the *Washington Post* in which he argued that "urban renewal is an instrument that hundreds of communities are successfully using to bring about change for the better." He pointed to projects in southwestern DC, Boston, St. Louis, San Francisco, and Philadelphia as evidence of the positive outcomes of the program. While Weaver acknowledged that the urban renewal program had problems, he argued that it had dramatically improved and that the critics were people who were "against it in the first place" and were "even more vehement in their attacks now that it is well on its way to accomplishing its mission."[13]

Throughout 1964 and 1965, Weaver gave numerous speeches in which he claimed that urban renewal was the right approach to restoring the city and that it could be implemented to protect minority and poor city residents. "The major achievement of urban renewal is that it has restored hope for older cities and worn out neighborhoods," he argued. Weaver agreed that the program had dislocated many people and that many of them were minorities, but he claimed that most of them had improved their situation. Urban renewal afforded minority residents the "opportunity to move into areas not previously open to them," and he argued that 30 percent of the units completed by the urban renewal program were occupied by nonwhites. He further noted that, as the program shifted from demolition to rehabilitation, more minority citizens would be served. Weaver also criticized Jacobs, calling her views "romanticized." In an interview on NBC's *Today* show, he said, "these urban neighborhoods were not quite as warm as she suggested," and he claimed that the North End of Boston was "atypical." Most renewal areas were beset with "social pathology" and "physical decline." They were districts of decay that could not be saved.[14]

Despite the growing critiques, when the administration released its 1964 housing proposals, the urban renewal program remained the most important facet of urban policy. But, because of budget constraints, the effort was funded at an even lower ($300 million less) level than Kennedy's previous proposals. As a result, critics of many political stripes blasted the administration. Many in Congress condemned the proposals. Senator Willis Robertson (D-VA), chair of the Senate Committee to which the bill was referred, called it the "biggest and vaguest and most dangerous housing bill that has ever been presented to Congress." On the other side, liberals complained that the proposals were not enough to deal with the significant problems facing American cities. Senator Joseph Clark (D-PA) stated that he intended to introduce an amendment dramatically increasing the funding in the bill. New York mayor Robert Wagner testified that, though he supported the bill, the amount of money proposed for urban programs in the bill was "wholly inadequate."[15]

In the end, Congress approved a housing bill that was even smaller than the administration's proposal, but liberals blamed the administration for lacking creativity. The editors of the *New York Times* argued that the bill failed "to strike at the heart of the nation's housing difficulties" and concluded that, "if the big city is to remain a place for ordinary people to live as well as work and if the suburb is to become more than an ugly sprawl and a commuters' nightmare, the president is going to have to lift his next housing bill out of the ruts of compromise and put it on a new intellectual level." Weaver agreed that the act "did not go as far as one might wish," and he sympathized with the "justifiable impatience" expressed by the *Times*, but he argued that the bill was only one of many initiatives the administration was undertaking to improve urban society. Among the efforts he cited was the Economic Opportunity Act.[16]

Although the War on Poverty has come to symbolize Johnson's effort to ameliorate America's racial crisis, that was not how the administration advertised the program at the outset. From the beginning, the War on Poverty was a program to provide opportunity to poor persons—whatever their race and whether they were in rural areas or in cities—to improve their situation through education, job training, and institution building. One of the program's architects, Adam Yarmolinsky, would later write that "the whole problem of the northern ghetto was still not seen in anything like its full depth and complexity" when they began the program. The initiative would later become symbolic of the failures of the Johnson administration to solve the crisis of the ghetto, but like most of the nation, Johnson and his staff had very little understanding of the problems.[17]

In his State of the Union message, Johnson made the antipoverty effort one of his focuses. "The administration today, here and now, declares unconditional war on poverty in America," he announced, and in January 1964 he asked for $1.5 billion to fund the effort. Later that month, Johnson asked Sargent Shriver, the head of the Peace Corps (and a Kennedy brother-in-law), to organize a task force to turn the broad ideas into legislation. Like all other senior administration officials, Weaver sent his ideas to Shriver. However, despite the fact that he had been a significant contributor to the Ford Foundation poverty project, Weaver was not asked, or did not choose, to take a significant role in shaping the poverty initiative. Weaver later argued that he was fully apprised of, and agreed with, the plans but was too busy with his housing responsibilities to participate in the discussions.[18]

Introduced in the spring of 1964, the Economic Opportunity Act of 1964 had five major facets: job-training programs for youth, including the Job Corps; the Community Action Program (CAP), which sought to "provide stimulation and incentive for urban and rural communities to mobilize their resources . . . to combat poverty"; the Volunteers in Service to America (VISTA) program, which recruited volunteers to aid in combating rural poverty; small-business loans and loans to small farms; the creation of the Office of Economic Opportunity in the White House to coordinate these and other antipoverty initiatives.[19]

After introducing the bill, Johnson and his staff devoted a great deal of time and effort to convincing the public of its importance. His administration worked assiduously to downplay the racial aspects of the bill and emphasize that poverty afflicted white people. In an address to the NAACP, Shriver said that "eighty percent of the poor people in America are white," and other government officials emphasized the rural nature of American poverty. In late April and early May, Johnson took two trips to promote the antipoverty initiative and to, in the president's words, "listen and learn" from the poor. On both the trips (the first a whirlwind tour to Indiana, Ohio, Pennsylvania, Kentucky, and Tennessee and the second to Appalachia), he gave almost exclusive attention to rural and small-town poverty.

Weaver went with him, along with the secretaries of the Departments of Agriculture, Labor, and Health, Education, and Welfare.[20]

The most controversial aspect of the War on Poverty would turn out to be the CAP, but when the task force was developing its proposal, the idea received widespread support. This was in part due to the fact that "community action" meant different things to different people. Several different strands of thought merged in the CAP, but the most influential were those developed by Weaver's former colleagues at the Ford Foundation. Paul Ylvisaker and David Hackett, who had been hired by Robert Kennedy while he was attorney general to develop a juvenile-delinquency program, argued that poor communities lacked the institutional infrastructure to function effectively and that the federal government could help by supporting the creation of new community-based organizations. These groups, they asserted, would provide a medium for poor residents to help themselves.[21]

As Shriver and his staff began to implement the act, the CAP soon consumed most of their time. Big-city mayors welcomed the additional resources, but many chafed at the more aggressive aspects of the effort to empower the poor. Mayor Richard J. Daley of Chicago called it "folly" to think that the poor could design and manage their own poverty programs, and many mayors complained about the CAP leaders who helped poor residents seeking to advance political goals.[22]

One local program that would receive particularly tough opposition from community action agencies was urban renewal. From the beginning, community action was directly at odds with the existing approaches, such as urban renewal, that gave power to professional planners and business leaders. But if Weaver saw these contradictions, he did not state them publicly. Rather, he claimed that community organization was compatible with urban renewal and that "stabilizing local organizations broadly representative of the community" played a crucial role in the operation of the urban renewal and public housing programs.[23]

JOHNSON'S EFFORTS TO reform the federal government won him the widespread support of Americans outside the South, and praise for some aspects of his program even within that region. With the nation still in shock from Kennedy's assassination, most observers forecast that Johnson would win election to the White House in 1964. Their predictions were made easier when the Republican Party tore itself apart selecting a candidate. Out of the battle emerged Arizona senator Barry Goldwater, an outspoken conservative who deeply opposed much of the New Deal and all of Johnson's initiatives. During the campaign, Johnson and his operatives exploited Goldwater's penchant for speaking his mind, letting Goldwater's words defeat him.[24]

Goldwater was a strong opponent of civil rights laws, and Johnson's campaign used this to court black voters who had voted for Nixon in 1960. Democratic officials gave no role to Weaver at the party's convention in Atlantic City, a decision they later regretted, as racial issues took center stage at the event. When the members of the Freedom Democratic Party tried to unseat their state delegation, arguing that it was chosen in an unconstitutional manner, it marked a new level of civil rights activism. Party leaders called Weaver's exclusion an "oversight" and a mistake. During the fall, however, Weaver was active in the campaign, making dozens of speeches. In late October, Weaver made a whirlwind tour of California, during which he headlined ten events in Los Angeles, San Francisco, and Sacramento. Weaver was the main speaker at several fundraisers and stumped for congressional candidates, including his former colleague and Kennedy press aide Pierre Salinger, who was running for the Senate. The state's Democratic Party head told Weaver that his efforts were a "tremendous help" and a big factor in the election returns. The president cruised to a landslide victory which brought thirty-seven new Democrats to the House of Representatives and two to the Senate. Like the rest of the administration, Weaver entered 1965 with high hopes for a vigorous and creative domestic policy.[25]

The president's landslide victory set the stage for the most active legislative session since the New Deal. During 1965, Johnson dramatically expanded the scope of the federal government's role in domestic affairs, passing landmark laws in the areas of health care, civil rights, education, environmental protection, and other fields. In the area of urban affairs, however, the Johnson team struggled to formulate a program. In 1964 the urban crisis had yet to become a national issue, but just a year later the country's attention focused increasingly on the problems festering in American cities. Johnson and his staff were forced to become quick studies on the problems facing American cities, and for help, they turned to many experts, including Weaver. They were not always satisfied with the results, and they frequently chided Weaver for his lack of creativity. The debates over urban policy, however, reveal how few new ideas anyone had about the significant problems of race and the inner city.

Soon after taking office, Johnson announced a plan to pull together "the best brains in the country" into a series of task forces to critically analyze government programs and propose alternative approaches. One of the fourteen was the Task Force on Metropolitan and Urban Problems, charged to study new ways of dealing with the needs of urban areas. Chaired by MIT professor Robert Wood, the task force included Jerome Cavanagh, mayor of Detroit, Paul Ylvisaker of the Ford Foundation, and University of California professors Nathan Glazer, Martin Meyerson, and Catherine Bauer Wurster (who died in an accident the week before the final report was presented). Johnson gave the task force a broad mandate, asking it to look at the "urban complex from downtown to the last outpost of the spread of great cities" and to develop "solutions based on contemporary tools to deal with present and emerging problems."[26]

According to Robert Wood, task force members were divided about the nature and extent of urban problems. "It was at the stage where a number of intellectuals still doubted that there was an urban crisis," he remembered in 1968. One task force member, businessman Karl Meninger, "didn't believe in cities," according to Wood. "He kept coming in saying we ought to all go back and live on the farm." As a result, the task force was unable to agree on many new approaches and proposed few new ideas to the president.[27]

In November, the group sent Johnson a forty-page report with a wide variety of proposals to improve federal urban policy. A few experimental initiatives to test alternative ideas for urban development were presented, but in general the report argued that existing programs needed to be planned more comprehensively and implemented more aggressively. The report did not radically differ from those produced by similar groups two decades earlier or from the proposals Weaver himself made to the White House during the year.[28]

When President Johnson gave his "Message on Housing" to Congress the following March, it included most of the task force's recommendations. Many American cities, Johnson argued, were "in need of major surgery to overcome decay," and the deterioration of these cities cast "a pall of ugliness and despair on the spirits of the people." At the same time, "new suburban sprawl reaches out into the countryside." The federal government could play only a small part in aiding urban areas. "The vast bulk of resources and energy, of talent and toil, will still have to come from state and local governments, private interests and individual citizens." But Washington did have a responsibility to provide resources and "serve as a catalyst and as a lever to help guide state and local governments toward meeting their problems." Regarding an overall urban policy, Johnson acknowledged that his administration was "still only groping toward a solution," but he argued that "the next decade should be a time of experimentation." The city, he concluded, should be a place where "every man feels safe on his streets," where "each of us can find the satisfaction and warmth which comes only from being a member of the community of man."[29]

Despite Johnson's flowery language, the response to the message was not particularly positive, and Johnson's proposals were critiqued from all parts of the political spectrum. Mayors across the nation slammed the small size of the program. Officials in New York City, who were becoming increasingly aware of the crisis facing them, were particularly critical. Weaver's old friend Hortense Gabel, now director of the city's redevelopment program, expressed "disappointment" in the program. Government officials there claimed that the program would mean only 3,000 units of additional public housing a year when 100,000 families had applied. Roger Starr, director of New York's Citizen's Housing and Planning Council, called the proposal "ridiculous" and directed his ire at Weaver. "I strongly suspect that this message was dictated not by his [Weaver's] view of what people need, but by his concept of what the Congress will support. And I think that's a crying shame for a Housing Administrator." Starr argued that Weaver should have resigned if he did not get Johnson's support for a full program. "Courage is a very rare commodity these days," Starr concluded. Even Johnson's limited (to liberals) program, however, faced strong opposition in Congress, where many members argued it went too far.[30]

The bill's major new proposal, which quickly became the most controversial, was for an experimental program to give "rent supplements" to those uprooted by urban renewal projects. The idea, first raised two decades earlier, would provide an alternative to public housing, enabling families to secure housing in the private market, with the government paying a share of the rent. The experiment represented a minuscule amount of the total funds authorized by the bill, but it almost dragged down the rest of the proposal. In essence, it provided assistance to families with incomes too high for public housing but too low to afford decent housing. For those families participating, the federal government would pay the difference between the rental value of the dwelling and 25 percent of the family's income. Rental subsidies provided an answer to several problems facing federal policymakers. First of all, they were, advocates argued, an efficient means to spur additional housing production with lower government expenditures, since the government would only pay a small amount per family, as opposed to the large amounts the government paid to build public housing.[31]

Rental subsidies could also ameliorate the problems facing many urban renewal efforts. Many families dislocated from clearance areas had incomes too high to qualify for public housing, which was already full in most cities anyway. Because they were forced to find housing in housing markets that were often tight, these families had to pay increasing portions of their income for rent. The assistance would lessen this burden and, as a result, housing administrators hoped, lessen opposition to urban renewal in general.[32]

Never explicitly acknowledged by officials but directly related to both the public housing and urban renewal questions was the issue of racial integration. In most cities, public housing had become minority housing—the vicious circle of local opposition, racially discriminatory siting decisions, and the general exclusion of racial minorities from most parts of urban areas created this situation. Racial segregation was further entrenched by the urban renewal program, which often cleared racially mixed low-income areas and replaced them with racially homogenized high-income developments. At the same time, dislocated minority residents found housing only in increasingly segregated areas. Rental subsidies could compensate for this process by providing dislocated families with greater resources to find decent housing and, hopefully, wider housing options.[33]

Because of its many implications, the rent subsidy initiative was the dominant issue in the congressional debates over the bill. At both the House and Senate hearings, liberal and conservative committee members criticized the program. Republicans contended that the program was "socialistic" and would have a deleterious effect on society. "To own one's home, no matter how modest, is the goal of the typical American family. The rent supplement kills the incentive of a family to achieve that goal," Republicans argued. Republicans further claimed that the program would, over its life, cost the federal government greatly in excess of its budget. From the other side, Senators Paul Douglas (D-IL) and William Proxmire (D-WI) claimed that there were millions of poor families who could benefit from rent subsidies and that they should be included in the program.[34]

Originally, Weaver opposed the rent subsidy idea. He argued that public housing and other existing programs could provide housing more efficiently and that they would be cheaper over the long run. However, the White House's desire to propose something new overwhelmed his objections.

Even though he had his own reservations, Weaver took the lead in lobbying for the bill. He testified at a congressional hearing that the program was limited to certain groups—specifically, the dislocated and those living in substandard housing—and that his agency would have clear guidelines to limit the program to those who could not afford decent housing in the city where they lived. In the end the bill passed but not before a massive lobbying effort by the administration barely kept the rent subsidy program in the legislation.[35]

The passage of the Housing and Urban Development Act was only one of many legislative achievements by the Johnson administration during 1965. In one year, Johnson secured passage of some of the most important federal legislation in more than a decade, creating the Medicare and Medicaid programs and dramatically increasing the federal government's support for education through the Elementary and Secondary Education Act and the Higher Education Act. Throughout the year, Johnson worked tirelessly to see his Great Society become a reality. At the same time, he secured passage of the Voting Rights Act, a feat that even the law's most ardent supporters did not think possible in the climate of massive white southern resistance.[36]

In his voting-rights speech, Johnson declared that "the real hero of this struggle is the American Negro. His actions and protests, his courage to risk safety and even to risk his life, have awakened the conscience of this Nation." His remarks and the subsequent passage of the bill marked for many the highpoint of the civil rights movement. But Johnson's many legislative victories during the first half of 1965 did little to assuage the growing unrest in many American cities. The summer of 1965 was a turning point in the history of American race relations, and the Watts riots in Los Angeles were its most significant event. The uprising there, which began just five days after the president signed the Voting Rights Act, shaped Americans' understanding of the problems facing Americans cities and their views on the possibility of interracial cooperation. The violence, which surprised Weaver and most black leaders by its ferocity, had a profound influence on Weaver's role as the highest-ranking African American in the federal government.[37]

The conflict began on Wednesday, 11 August, with a minor traffic accident, but when rumors spread through the Watts area that the police had abused a pregnant woman, a crowd of over a thousand people gathered at the scene and started throwing rocks at passing automobiles. The next day the area was relatively calm, but that night Watts erupted again. Thousands of people took to the streets, overturning cars and setting them on fire. By Friday an area of more than fifty blocks, including Watts and several other neighborhoods, was beset with violence. The conflagration continued through the weekend, and by the time it was over the total damage from the insurrection was devastating: 34 people killed, 1,032 injured, more than 600 buildings damaged, and 200 destroyed.[38]

The riots were televised across the nation, and dozens of newspaper reporters fanned out across the area. Helicopters captured the events live for millions of viewers. The conflict changed many Americans' views of cities and of their black inhabitants, and they deeply influenced Lyndon Johnson, who was stunned and paralyzed by the violence. After Watts, Johnson toned down his rhetoric on the issue of civil rights. The riots changed Johnson's understanding of the civil rights movement and influenced his thoughts on the role of black leaders in dealing with the problems of African Americans.[39]

Immediately after the riots calmed, Johnson directed his staff to find as many resources as possible to direct to the Watts area, and on 26 August he issued his first major public statement about the events. "We have all felt a deep sense of shock and dismay at the riots last week in Los Angeles. I have expressed my conviction that there is no greater wrong in our democracy than violent or willful disregard of the law." At the same time, he argued, "we must eliminate the deep-seated causes of riots such as those we witnessed." Johnson directed over $29 million in aid to Los Angeles in September.[40]

Disheartened by the events in Los Angeles, Johnson pushed his administration to craft an agenda to improve life in the city. One of the main vehicles for the administration program would be the newly created Department of Housing and Urban Development, which Congress authorized the same month as the riots. After Johnson's landslide election in 1964 brought along with it significant Democratic majorities in the House and Senate, most observers assumed that a department of urban affairs would be approved. When Johnson issued his housing message in March 1965, he made clear that the creation of the new department would be a priority for his administration.[41]

The only major difference between Johnson's proposal for the new department and Kennedy's was the name. It would now be called the Department of Housing and Urban Development (HUD). The response to the legislation was similar to the reaction two years earlier. Republicans continued to complain that the new department represented overreaching and centralization of government on issues that were local responsibilities. A House group led by Congressmen Bradford Morse (R-MA) and Donald Rumsfeld (R-IL) argued that hiring an "Urban Czar" in the White House would produce better results. But in the end Johnson had the votes for his proposal, which the House and Senate approved during the summer.[42]

Many of the nation's newspapers commented on the bill's passage—and illustrated the confusion over the department's purpose. The editors of the *Louisville Courier Journal* acknowledged that "the specifics of what it can accomplish we can only dimly perceive at this point" but they thought that the department's "potential" was "intriguing." The *Los Angeles Times* told its readers that places like their city "may become better places" to live but cautioned that "change, if any, will be gradual." The *Milwaukee Journal* concluded that "the great connotation of the act is symbolic." Over the rest of Johnson's term as president, the nation's opinion leaders would complain about HUD's failure, though they never agreed on its purpose. The man they would blame for the agency's inability to solve urban problems was Robert Weaver, the department's first secretary.[43]

* 14 *

# HUD, Robert Weaver, and the Ambiguities of Race

On 9 September 1965, President Johnson held one of his famous parties in the Rose Garden of the White House to sign the law establishing the Department of Housing and Urban Development (HUD). In his remarks, Johnson noted the many problems facing urban areas, and he acknowledged the crisis facing America. "Unless we seize the opportunities available now, the fears some have of a nightmare society could materialize," he claimed. The new department, Johnson argued, was "the first step toward organizing our system for a more rational response to the pressing challenge of urban life." In his remarks, Johnson thanked several senators and congressmen who had aided the bill's passage. Johnson had Weaver stand close by when he signed the bill, but in his remarks he made no mention of his Housing and Home Finance Agency (HHFA) head.[1]

Since for five years he had run the agency that would become HUD, since President Kennedy had stated his intention to appoint him secretary four years before, and since Johnson had given such attention to civil rights, most observers assumed that Johnson would quickly name Weaver the secretary. But Johnson made no comments on the matter, and his staff deferred questions on the new department's leadership. Weaver would eventually become the nation's first African American cabinet secretary, but not before four months of delay from Johnson and turmoil and embarrassment for Weaver. Johnson's tortuous path to Weaver illuminated many of the contradictions of Weaver's career and the complexities of racial liberalism and urban policy in the mid-1960s.[2]

Although in the end he secured the job, the very qualities that enabled Weaver to achieve success—his unassuming personality, his commitment to moderate change, and his agreement with the central premise of liberal government (reliance on professional expertise)—were all perceived as liabilities in this new era of urban turmoil. In addition, despite the significant progress made in the fight against racial discrimination, Weaver's color continued to pose a significant obstacle to his advancement. The irony that a man who had worked assiduously to earn the proper academic and career credentials would find these achievements held against him, and that a president committed to racial equality would hesitate to promote him, reveals the complicated nature of race in this period of turmoil.

JUST A MONTH before the HUD bill passage, at the August signing of the Housing and Urban Development Act of 1965, Johnson had made a point of singling out Weaver for praise. After thanking the many people who aided the bill's passage, Johnson said, "And last, but certainly not least–he has been for months the leader of us all in this field–the modest, retiring, and able Administrator–Bob Weaver, who finds not much satisfaction in the compliments paid him, not even in the recognition accorded him by his superiors, but who finds ample satisfaction in the achievements that come his way. And this Bill is a monument to him." The president's public statement was a high point in Weaver's career.[3]

Weaver was not one of Johnson's closest confidants, but the president did call on him for advice about many issues. Earlier in 1965, after heeding Weaver's advice about relations with black politicians, Johnson sent Weaver a signed photograph. "To Bob Weaver, A Wise Man," the inscription read. Johnson also discussed Weaver's status with Martin Luther King. King had called the president to report that civil rights leaders were very interested in getting him to appoint a black person to the cabinet. That action, he argued, "would be a great step forward for the nation" that would "do so much to give many people a lift who need a lift now." Johnson told King that he was "pretty half way committed" to Weaver, who was viewed as "a very able administrator and has done a good job." Johnson said that he felt a "moral obligation" to Weaver and compared him to an assistant pastor of a church who deserved promotion when the pastor retired.[4]

During the summer of 1965, however, Johnson expressed his doubts about Weaver to associates. In July, during one of his frequent telephone conversations with NAACP head Roy Wilkins, Johnson stated, "You know, I love Bob Weaver and I admire him, but Bob Weaver's not a dynamic fellow that we're going to need and I don't know whether we really want to insist on putting a Negro at the head of urban affairs when we get it." Johnson told Wilkins that "we ought to put someone that will do more for the Negro than a Negro can do for himself in these cities." He stated he wanted a "Goldberg type," referring to Supreme Court Justice Arthur Goldberg, and suggested Laurence Rockefeller as a potential candidate.[5]

After the bill creating the new department passed, and two weeks before the president signed it, John Macy, the head of the civil service and Johnson's main headhunter, recommended that Johnson appoint Weaver to the position. "Mr. Weaver has had a long and distinguished career in housing and urban matters, and he has served well in his capacity as Administrator of HHFA," Macy argued, and he noted that Weaver had been vetted by the FBI and that Macy had cleared the appointment with the Democratic National Committee and congressional leaders. However, Johnson decided to delay the appointment and search for other candidates. According to Johnson aide Joseph Califano, Johnson was afraid that he would not be able to get the Senate to confirm Weaver. In the aftermath of the Watts riots, Johnson worried that the Senate would not approve of a black person for the job. The HUD secretary would be the federal government's point person on urban issues, which had become increasingly complicated as urban rioting increased. In addition, Califano noted, "Weaver was not personally popular on the hill."[6]

Weaver did not receive much praise from those with the ear of the president. Throughout the fall, Johnson solicited advice from congressional leaders, administration officials, and other confidants. Weaver was not warmly regarded by his future colleagues in the cabinet. Secretary of Defense Robert McNamara argued that Detroit mayor Jerome Cavanagh, Budget Director David Bell, and Boston urban renewal head Ed Logue were all "superior to Weaver." Stewart Udall, Johnson's interior secretary, told the president that Weaver was "competent. He is not dynamic. He lacks the spark that might inspire the American people. Can he provide the challenging leadership you want and deserve? I seriously doubt it," Udall concluded. Udall recommended that Johnson select "one of the Rockefellers," though he did not specify which one.[7]

Members of Congress also were less than enamored with Weaver. Senator Abraham Ribicoff told Johnson, "I don't gather that there's anything inspirational about Weaver, and you're gonna have to have an inspirational man because your programs keep funneling into the cities." Robert Kennedy stated that he had "never been very impressed with Mr. Weaver" and repeatedly told Johnson that President Kennedy had made "no commitment" to him. Kennedy argued that "having a Negro heading up housing would create problems in the North as well as the South," and he agreed with Johnson that there would be "some advantage to having a white man in there." Attorney General Nicholas Katzenbach was also critical of Weaver. "I'm afraid he's not really up to the kind of job that you want done," he told Johnson.[8]

These comments laid bare the casual racism held by men who had never worked on a professional level with an African American. Though they all called themselves liberals, few of them believed blacks were equal to them in intelligence or performance. These men expected little from blacks and looked for evidence that supported their prejudices. But these criticisms also reflected the reality that Weaver was not a dynamic leader in the Johnson administration. Rather, he was a scholarly technocrat and a loner who did not frequently socialize with other high-level officials. This was partly because it was not in Weaver's personality to do so and partly because the "old boys club" was not fully open to him. Whatever the reasons for their negative opinions, the views of Johnson's advisors did not help his cause.[9]

During September, Johnson asked Califano and Macy to solicit suggestions from national leaders for the post. They received at least sixty serious recommendations. None of the other prospects were African American. Reviewing Macy's list, the president responded that "none of these appeal to me." Although Johnson and many others in the administration were less than effusive about him, Weaver received support from leaders across the nation. The White House mail on the topic was overwhelmingly in favor of Weaver's appointment. Boston urban renewal head Ed Logue told the president that Weaver would make "a first-rate Secretary" and argued, "Under Weaver's leadership the Housing Agency became, for the first time, an agency with a unified approach instead of a collection of scattered programs that were accidentally located in one place." Logue acknowledged that because Weaver was "a proud man" he was "perhaps not inclined to go out and attempt to cultivate the clientele of his agency assiduously," but Logue concluded, "Looking back over the last four, almost five years, I think he has stood the test very well, and I would hope has earned this promotion." Kansas City mayor Joseph McDowell called Weaver "the most refreshing HHFA Administrator we have had."[10]

Legislative politics during the fall hurt Weaver's standing with Johnson. The administration had barely protected the rent subsidy program during the consideration of the 1965 housing bill, and in the middle of October the House voted to eliminate funding for the program from its annual appropriations bill. Several senators attempted to have the money included in the final bill, but in the closing moments of the session the senators, eager to go home, gave up the fight.[11]

Part of the reason for the administration's defeat was the release of the program's proposed operating regulations before the vote. The regulations stated that in selecting projects consideration would be given to the proposal's contribution to furthering "equal opportunity in housing." Since, unlike public housing, the developments could be built without local approval, this preference for integration raised the ire of southern Democrats and northern suburban representatives. In addition, the vague wording of the rules allowed opponents to argue that the program could be used to help wealthy people, in violation of the law's spirit. Opponents interpreted the regulations to allow families with incomes well above the national median to secure federal subsidies. Some argued that under the rules families with assets of $25,000 were still eligible. Weaver responded that these claims were exaggerations and his staff quickly pulled the document, but the damage had been done. Columnist Arthur Krock argued that Weaver had "made several grave tactical errors which, superimposed on the burden the project already carried as clearly socialistic in concept, proved too heavy for it."[12]

The failure of Congress to fund the program was a major defeat for Johnson, and he blamed it on Weaver. Joe Califano later remembered that Johnson "privately blasted Weaver's 'political stupidity' in having anything on paper until Congress provided the funding." Califano also noted that Johnson "ignored the fact that he would have roasted Weaver unmercifully had the housing administrator not been ready, upon getting the appropriation, to award the first rent supplements." Johnson referred to the defeat frequently in his deliberations over Weaver. He lambasted Weaver for being "off in New Jersey making a Chamber of Commerce speech" when "he should have been in D.C. making sure the program was safe." He told Roy Wilkins that Weaver "pulled the biggest bonehead any man ever pulled" and informed him that Weaver could not be nominated because Senate Majority Leader Mike Mansfield was so upset about Weaver's performance that Mansfield told the president he could not support Weaver for HUD secretary.[13]

In later recollections, Weaver argued that "the faux pas was not mine, the faux pas was the FHA's. But when you are in a job like this, you know, when something happens, you don't go around saying, 'He done it,' or 'They done it,' you just take it." Weaver understood that the conflict might have had some impact on the president, but he believed that "the President and those around him knew what was happening, and I think they knew this was a matter of a political attack really on him and on this program. But it didn't help." With regard to complaints from Mansfield, Weaver said, "He certainly had never indicated anything to me of displeasure."[14]

OVER SEVERAL DAYS in late October and early November, legal issues surrounding the new department brought the question of Weaver's appointment to a head and almost resulted in Weaver's resignation. The law creating the department stated that it would come into being sixty days after the president signed the bill. As the 9 November deadline approached, Weaver and other members of his staff, along with others in the Johnson administration, began to worry about the legality of the new department. If Johnson did not appoint at least an acting secretary, Weaver argued, there would be no one to approve contracts and other decisions necessary for the federal government's housing programs to function. On 27 October Weaver went to Califano asking him to have the president sign several documents that were necessary to create the new department and designate an acting secretary.[15]

Johnson, who was recuperating in Texas from gall bladder surgery, did not want to appoint Weaver secretary or acting secretary. Congress had adjourned for the session, and Johnson argued that, even if he was ready to appoint Weaver, he did not want to do it during the recess, which would anger members of the Senate. Johnson did not want to designate Weaver as acting secretary because he worried that Weaver might make a mistake during this period that would require Johnson to expend additional political capital when he made the permanent nomination.[16]

He also was far from certain that Weaver was his man. In a long, rambling telephone conversation with Roy Wilkins on 30 October, Johnson tried to gauge the ramifications of choosing someone other than Weaver. He told Wilkins that "first of all, I like Weaver. He is a good man, he is a fair man, he likes me, we get along good together. We don't have any abrasiveness or any irritations or problems. I can't find any faults there. He knows more about the housing job than anybody in the Government." But, Johnson argued, citing the rent supplement loss, "he doesn't do his homework on the hill, he is not an imaginative person. His program for next year . . . just had to be sent back. It is just plain vanilla–about a C minus." He also argued that Congress would criticize the selection. "When I name him I am going to start catching hell that I have not picked an imaginative person, I have not picked the biggest man in this country for the job–that I just picked him because of his race. Now that is what is going to hit me and it is going to hit me pretty heavy in Congress where I am getting pretty weak." Furthermore, Johnson claimed, "a white man can do a hell of a lot more for the Negro than the Negroes can do for themselves in these cities. I don't think he will carry the handicap in these Congressional Committees that are packed and loaded."[17]

At the same time, Johnson worried that, if he did not appoint Weaver, it would disappoint the "little Negro boys in Podunk, Mississippi," and he felt that many blacks would say that, even though Johnson had done a lot for civil rights, "when you get down to the nut-cutting . . . this Southerner just couldn't quite cut the mustard—he just couldn't name a Negro to the Cabinet." Three days later he told Wilkins, "If I had my way I would certainly lean towards Weaver. But a good deal of that is just because of my feeling for the Negroes." Johnson speculated about making Weaver an ambassador or comptroller general, but he decided that "the only thing that is interesting at all to him is to be the first Negro in the Cabinet in a field where he has worked hard and where he has prepared himself." Johnson told Wilkins that his top choice for the job would be Laurence Rockefeller. Any of the Rockefellers—David, Nelson, and Laurence—were possibilities, but Dean Rusk and others had told him that "Laurence was the best of all of them."[18]

Wilkins, who had known Weaver for more than thirty years, did not press the president on the decision but mostly parroted Johnson's observations. "Laurence would be a ten strike and would help in alleviating this other situation," Wilkins replied. In a conversation the next day, Wilkins, in a very obtuse manner, explained to Johnson his view of the problems Johnson would have if he did not select Weaver. "Because the minority is sympathetic and emotional they would probably feel for the man as a symbol of the goal, even though they may or may not have any warm feelings for the man–only great admiration." There would be, Wilkins argued, "some slipping in affection on the part of the group itself." Never mentioning Weaver's name, Wilkins also stated that, since he had known "the man" for so long, he would "have to say something" if the president chose not to nominate him. But, if the president nominated Weaver, "I think looking a year ahead, you will be in trouble, the Department will be in trouble and he will be in trouble . . . when the situation becomes impossible, then he may have to withdraw." Wilkins told Johnson, "You have to get the best man and if we don't happen to have the best man then we will just have to keep on trying until we get the best one."[19]

Because of the complicated politics of the matter, Johnson decided to wait. "I am going to ask Weaver to stay on and do nothing until January.

Than I am going to ask the best five people in the world for this job for which he would be one," he told Wilkins. To enable him to delay the decision, Johnson directed Califano and Attorney General Katzenbach to write a memo declaring that the decision did not have to be made by the deadline. Katzenbach first determined that the president *did* have to act, but then he and Califano reinterpreted the statute to conform to the president's desires.[20]

Weaver's personal correspondence reveals varying emotions during this period. In early October, he wrote Frank Horne that "all I can do is wait. . . . As to how real the reported reservations are–anybody's guess is as good as another." Throughout October, he told people that he expected a decision very soon. Weaver received several inquiries into his availability, including job offers from Harvard University, the University of California, and City College of New York. Newly elected New York mayor John Lindsay also publicly stated that he would like Weaver to return to the city to chair the Housing and Redevelopment Board if he did not get the secretary's job. Weaver told suitors that his plans were "iffy," but he did not reject any of these entreaties.[21]

In later interviews, Weaver was emotional about this difficult period. He told an interviewer that he felt he should resign because "I did not want to be in the unfortunate position of being a sort of hanger-on on the one hand. And secondly, I did not think that anybody who would be the Acting Secretary would be able to get the sort of cooperation that one needed, and the department would not really get going." He remembered that the son of one of his associates told someone in his office, "Robert Weaver thinks he is going to be Secretary, but he ain't going to be Secretary," and that the boy's father resigned his position in anticipation of Weaver's departure. So, Weaver recalled, "I indicated strongly my attitude" to Califano and Lee White. He told several associates that he was resigning, he wrote a letter, and he "set up an appointment to see the President and tell him that." After being urged not to resign by Califano, White, and several others, Weaver said he decided to wait. "This waiting had become a very, very difficult thing," he remembered. "It was one of the times I must say my feelings toward President Johnson were less than warm."[22]

Califano's recollections of the period, which he recorded in a 1991 memoir, are more robust than Weaver's. When Califano told Weaver about Johnson's decision to delay, Weaver threatened to resign. "It would be embarrassing, downright humiliating," Weaver told Califano. "He was still angry when he left my office," Califano recalled, "but he did commit himself to sit tight." Hearing about Weaver's threats from Califano, Johnson became upset and told Califano to ask for Weaver's resignation. "Let him resign. If he's that arrogant, the hell with him. You just tell him to resign. Call him tonight and tell him," the president told Califano.[23]

The next day, when Weaver returned, Califano "suggested he consider resigning," because the president did not want to make a recess appointment. He was not going to make a decision until January, and he was going to consider other people. Weaver returned to his office and wrote a letter of resignation directed to Califano. "As you appreciate, I have been beset with conflicting emotions during the last few days," it began. Weaver acknowledged he would be "less than honest if I didn't say that I should like to be Secretary of the Department of Housing and Urban Development," but "I still have to live with myself and my values." Weaver was "not convinced that a recess appointment is fraught with the dangers you [Califano] delineated," and he was concerned that further delay would "bring an impossible administrative situation." Because he believed that HUD would face difficult problems if it was not organized immediately, he concluded that, "reluctantly, I must decline the offer to perform a holding operation which I cannot justify."[24]

When Califano called Johnson again to inform him that Weaver was drafting a resignation letter, Johnson told Califano, "what the hell is he doing that for? I don't want him to resign. You tell him not to resign." Johnson told Califano to say that he had no authority to accept Weaver's resignation; only the president could. "Weaver entered my office, letter in hand," Califano recollected. "He looked so broken–his dreams of a lifetime shattered over the past twenty-four hours–that I thought he might welcome the news. When he offered his handwritten letter of resignation, I said, 'The President doesn't want your resignation.' Weaver was utterly confused, so disconcerted and agitated that he spit his words out. 'No,' he said, 'I'm through. I don't want any more of this. I'm through.'" But Califano refused to accept Weaver's letter, and Weaver left to think about his decision. "That night," Califano continued, "Weaver called me. He sounded exhausted and tipsy. He wasn't happy with me or the President. But when the President called me late that evening to check on the situation, I was able to report, 'He's not going to resign. He'll sit it out.'"[25]

While Johnson complained about Weaver, the only person he fixed on as an alternative was Laurence Rockefeller. However, Johnson did not think that Rockefeller would accept the job, and it is unclear whether he ever discussed it with him. In the end much of Johnson's reason for delay appears to be his concern that Weaver would have difficulty gaining Senate approval. Johnson believed he could convince the senators, but not in his current health. "Nothing has to be done in November, Weaver is there running it," he told Wilkins. "What I want to do is come back to Washington and in my own way sit in my bedroom and talk to people and try to work this thing out to do what I am willing to stand on and defend." The knowledge that previous confirmation battles had weakened his and other administrations clearly weighed on Johnson. "I cannot have another Cabinet fight." Johnson asked Wilkins and Democratic Party leader Louis Martin to talk to Weaver and calm him down.[26]

According to Louis Martin, during this period Weaver was "in horrible shape psychologically." When Weaver read newspaper stories about Johnson interviewing other candidates, "Bob felt terribly humiliated," Martin remembered. "Bob was distraught," his colleague Morton Schussheim recalled. "The White House wasn't talking to him much." Many of Weaver's friends were telling him that he should resign, because the president had embarrassed him, but Ella, who knew he desperately wanted the job, told him to hang on and discouraged others from talking negatively. Martin told Weaver to stick it out. "I think I know this man. He puts whites through the wringer; he puts everybody through the ringer. Don't let it disturb you," he said. According to Martin, Johnson had him, Califano, and Lee White all telling Weaver different stories about the job. "This was the greatest game I've ever seen." Other friends told Weaver to persevere. Frank Horne wrote that "the administration is hunting high and low for a centerfielder when it has Willie Mays already on the roster."[27]

Although the confidential conversations between LBJ and his advisors did not become public for almost four decades, the White House and Weaver were both forced to make public comments on the matter. Press Secretary Bill Moyers told the media that Johnson was delaying his choice of a secretary until he received the report of the task force of urban experts he had organized. "There has been a meeting for sometime," Moyers stated, "of distinguished persons on the varied and complicated problems that the federal government must deal with in terms of meeting the overall city, or urban, problems of the next five decades." These "highly qualified Americans," Moyers stated, were going to "study very carefully, and very thoroughly, the question of how this department should be organized in order to get the best possible start." Moyers announced that all of the functions of the HHFA would be automatically transferred to HUD on 9 November and that there would be no problems with continuing the government's programs. Asked whether Weaver would be temporary head of the agency, Moyers responded that everyone would remain in their existing jobs. Moyers did not expect the task force to report before Christmas, and he stated that the president did not want to make a recess appointment. In addition, the president felt, "because of his illness and convalescence," that he had not had the opportunity "to talk personally to the people with whom he would like to discuss this in great detail." Moyers told the press that Weaver was one of half a dozen people being considered.[28]

On 8 November Weaver and counsel Milt Semer held a very awkward press conference to discuss the operations of the new department. Weaver began by stating that he realized there were many questions that the press might have about the new department, but he and Semer struggled mightily not to give any real answers. They repeated Moyers's statement that the staff would continue to operate as it had previously, and there would be no immediate changes to the organization. "Well, I think tomorrow what I will do will be what I am doing today," Weaver told reporters. Weaver said that they would continue to implement the 1965 housing act and that he did not foresee any immediate administration or morale problems, though he did acknowledge that problems might arise "after a while." After several minutes of avoiding questions about his feelings on Johnson's failure to select him, Weaver finally gave in. When asked, "would you still like this job?" Weaver replied, "yes." When asked why, Weaver stated, "because this is a field in which I spent most of my adult career. And these last four and a half years have been extremely exciting."[29]

Another reporter asked, "somebody said one of the reasons why you might not be chosen is because your experience is primarily in housing, and the urban part has to have a broader jurisdiction. Do you think that's a valid weakness, you might say, in your qualifications?" Weaver responded by referring to his last two books. "I think you'll find that my interests and my concern is more than for housing." As for his qualifications, Weaver finished, "that's for somebody else to decide."

Because he committed the faux pas of publicly stating that he wanted the job, Weaver was the subject of much discussion among political insiders. Commenting on the press conference, White House aide Harry McPherson wrote Joe Califano that "some of this boggles the mind." The editors of the *St. Louis Post-Dispatch* concluded that Weaver's statement "may have excluded him for consideration. That sort of arm twisting simply isn't cricket." Weaver later recollected that "you aren't supposed to do that, apparently. But hell, I wasn't going to stand up there and say, 'No.' Nobody would have ever believed me anyway, because if I didn't want to be, I would have quit before that." The whole incident led many reporters to conclude that Weaver was out of the running for the job, and several newspapers speculated that the mayor of a big city such as Chicago's Richard Daley or Detroit's Jerome Cavanagh would be named.[30]

Before early November, the question of Johnson's decision received only sporadic attention in the mainstream media. Not surprisingly, many black newspapers covered the issue with great interest. The editors of the *Chicago Defender*, responding to reports that Weaver would not be appointed, argued that Weaver was "perhaps the greatest authority to date on housing" and that none of the "other possible appointees" had the "experience and requisite background that Weaver could bring to the complex functions of the new federal government." The *Pittsburgh Courier* argued that Weaver's selection "would mean that a Negro was a full-fledged member of the top power structure and would counteract much of the urban Negro revolt to the Republicans reflected in many large and small urban community votes in the Nov. 2 election." The *Baltimore Afro-American* argued that many big-city politicians and real estate interests were opposed to Weaver because he "would move boldly to wipe out big-city racial ghettoes," and stated that "millions of Americans will be sorely disappointed if President Johnson bows to these pressures."[31]

Ignoring decades of civil rights work, several journalists argued that Weaver was not popular with African American leaders. Weaver, the *Baltimore Afro-American* reported, "has avoided direct involvement with the civil rights movement. He also has been criticized for not packing his agency with 'colored professionals.'" Louis Martin argued that Weaver "wasn't regarded as a very strong civil rights guy" and had to work to convince civil rights leaders to support him. "It wasn't antagonism, but they felt that Bob was, in the vernacular, a white folk's nigger." Other black journalists cataloged Weaver's weaknesses. Frank Stanley, president of the National Newspapers Association, noted that two criticisms of Weaver were that "he does not relate to the Negro masses" and that "he does not relate to the Negro members of Congress." Stanley rejected these criticisms and argued that they were irrelevant to the question of Weaver's qualifications.[32]

The increased attention given to Weaver forced civil rights leaders to take public stands on the matter. On 19 November Roy Wilkins and Whitney Young publicly expressed their support for Weaver. In his travels across the country, Wilkins stated, many blacks had asked him about Weaver's situation. He believed that blacks would be "disappointed" if Johnson chose someone else. "It could be that this might galvanize the Negro community into thinking that in rejecting Mr. Weaver he was rejecting them," Wilkins stated. While Wilkins asserted that "an appointment to the President's cabinet is not subject for lobbying in the ordinary sense of the word," he argued that "there's no question that he is regarded in the Negro community as having experience comparable to that needed for this department. So Negroes would be mightily pleased if he gets the job." Young claimed that "there has been quite a bit of discussion about this among Negro leaders who strongly support Mr. Weaver. The Negro leadership strongly feels that in the year 1965 there ought to be a Negro in the Cabinet."[33]

A day later, in response to arguments that the civil rights leaders' statements had hurt Weaver's chances, Wilkins insisted that he had been "making no threats" in his statements and had "the greatest respect for the President's sincerity on civil rights matters" and for Johnson's "political knowledge and acumen." *Business Week* reported "some surprise in Washington" regarding Wilkins's and Young's remarks, noting that Weaver's "lack of identification with the civil rights movement—even in these past five years—has made Negro civil rights leaders very cool to him." Just days later, Weaver, in one of his few press interviews, stated that "I feel the decision should be made—either way—on the basis of my record and not of my color."[34]

At the end of November, Johnson continued to express reservations about Weaver. He told Attorney General Katzenbach that if he appointed Weaver "you're liable to get yourself in the same shape you did after Reconstruction and take you another 100 years to get back. I doubt this fellow will make the grade and he'll be a flop and exhibit number one and if you get a white man he'll do a hell of a lot more and then you can be preparing your other people to do these things." But in the same conversation, it was apparent that Johnson had decided to select Weaver: "We've got to get a super man for number two place, and then send this fellow all around policy touring and let this second fella do the work with the Congress and with the President and with all the other people."[35]

In early January, Johnson told Thurgood Marshall that "there is a good feeling that Bob Weaver ought to be given a chance. I rather like Weaver if it were just up to me and my personal association. I rather think that I would give him a chance." When Johnson asked Marshall whether he would choose Weaver, Marshall said, "Yes I would. Honestly–and he is 100% reliable. That I know. I certainly would." Johnson told Wilkins that "I have watched him carefully and given him every chance in the world to stump his toe. He has not done that so far. He just functions as perfectly as you would have."[36]

Two recommendations completed Johnson's decision. The first came from MIT professor Robert Wood, who chaired Johnson's HUD task force. Wood, whom Johnson described as "an exceptionally able man" who had "done an outstanding job," told Johnson that Weaver's "experience in the administration of urban programs, especially housing programs, is unparalleled in this country." While acknowledging that Weaver "has a manner that does not excite sensationalism," Wood argued that this trait was a good one. It would "enable the potentially controversial programs to move forward with the caution that should permit them to flourish with a minimum of controversy." In managing an inherently flawed organization, Weaver had, Wood claimed, "succeeded in doing the impossible and in bringing new policy approaches and programs that have literally changed the entire direction and the entire tenor of America's housing and urban aid programs." Wood stated that Weaver was "as intellectually competent and as analytical of the urban scene as any major public figure in the United States today." Johnson called Wood "an objective fellow that does not allow the Negro question to enter into this."[37]

The other recommendation came from an unlikely source, Texas congressman Albert Thomas, chair of the Appropriations Committee. Weaver later described Thomas as a man who "knew more about HHFA than I did," because he had overseen the agency's budget for years. In a phone call, Thomas told Johnson, "you just stand with ole Doc Weaver because he's about as good a Negro I ever heard of in my life, he's honest and he's good and I back him." Johnson called Thomas "a typical East Texas boy" who "has all the prejudice of Nagadoches, Marshall and Shreveport," and he was impressed that Weaver had Thomas's confidence.[38]

ON 13 JANUARY Weaver received a message to report to the White House. He was told to arrive at the residence and not to tell anyone where he was going. There Weaver met the president, who told him that he planned to nominate him for secretary of HUD. Weaver left the White House and found a pay telephone to call Ella so that she could be there for the official announcement. Later that afternoon, the White House announced an unscheduled press conference in the Fish Room. There, accompanied by the whole cabinet, the president introduced Weaver and Robert Wood, whom the president had chosen as undersecretary of the new department.

Johnson stated, "After looking at over 300 outstanding potential candidates and talking to literally dozens of people about him, I have come to the conclusion that the man for the job is Robert Weaver." The nominee, Johnson continued, was "a deep thinker and a quiet but articulate man of action. He is as well versed in the urban needs of America as any man I know." His performance at the HHFA, Johnson added, "has been marked by the highest level of integrity and ability." Johnson called Wood "one of the most imaginative students of urban centers." After asserting that he was "presenting to the American people the best man I can to fulfill the pledge of this Administration," Johnson concluded his remarks by turning to Weaver and saying, "may the good Lord have mercy upon you."[39]

Three years later, Weaver remained perplexed by the process of his selection. When asked why Johnson waited so long, Weaver said, "Well, I don't know. That's the inscrutable–I frankly don't know." Califano later remarked that "Johnson delayed until virtually every major black and liberal leader had asked him to name Weaver so that he could remind them that he'd done something for them." Califano remembered that "the President left the new Secretary numb. He made it clear he could break or make Weaver–by doing both. He gave me a glimpse of a trait that sometimes drove him to crush and reshape a man before placing him in a job of enormous importance, much the way a ranch hand tames a wild horse before mounting it. To Johnson, this technique helped assure that an appointee was his alone."[40]

Reaction to the appointment was generally positive. A *Washington Post* editorial noted that Johnson chose the "best available man" and that Weaver had "served with distinction" in many positions. The editors of the *Milwaukee Journal* claimed that the choice was "a milestone in the history of his race and a splendid personal achievement by himself." The paper also praised Weaver's HHFA administration. "He has been just as 'color blind' as any white official would have been expected to be," the editors argued. The editorial in the *Pittsburgh Post-Gazette* argued that "Dr. Weaver will be able to give both knowledge and understanding to the achievement of the new goals of his department." The editors of the *Chicago Sun-Times* said that Weaver "will need not only the mercy of the Lord, but also the accumulated knowledge of his years. We wish him luck."[41]

Others were less effusive. The *St. Louis Post-Dispatch* argued that "perhaps a more aggressive table-pounder might fare better," while the *New York Times* noted that the appointment was made "despite some criticism of his abilities and his imagination" but wished Weaver "the best of luck in this monumental job." The editors of the *Washington Star* said that Weaver's "personal competency as demonstrated in a number of public posts" seemed to support Johnson's view that he was the most qualified.[42]

The announcement was met with joy in the black press and by civil rights leaders. The editors of the *New York Amsterdam News* said, "Weaver's appointment is the boldest strike toward the recognition of the Negro ever taken by an occupant of the White House." The *Baltimore Afro-American*, emphasizing Johnson's statement that Weaver was the "best qualified of some 300 persons," argued that this was "an encouraging sign that the nation at last is approaching the mature day when ability rates above color as a qualifying factor."[43]

The appointment illuminated the complicated role of race in Weaver's career. Many expressed contradictory attitudes about the meaning of the appointment, vacillating between praising its "historic nature" and noting it as a "victory for color-blindness." In his syndicated column, Whitney Young called the appointment "an indication of how far we've come" and a challenge "to all other institutions in our society–corporations, churches, educational institutions, etc.–to make equally significant appointments or promotions in their areas of responsibility." At the same time, he noted that Weaver's qualifications earned him the job without the factor of race. Though Johnson had obsessed about the reaction of blacks to his decision, he wrote to Young: "It matters not the color of a man's skin. What does matter is the commitment to the cause of his country and his capacity to rise to the challenge. These are assets that Bob Weaver brings to the job."[44]

Frank Horne told Weaver to remember the "thousands of hearts that were lifted as you were elevated to the seat you had surely won." He prodded Weaver to "shake free" from any restraints that may have hounded him and reminded him that, "in the long run, the vital questions will not be so much how long you will stay there but rather what you can do with it to help Joe and Sam in the street." Weaver promised Horne that he would "start to do the things that I have the power to do. I won't be reckless but I won't be hesitant either."[45]

Because Johnson and his staff worried that the delay had weakened Weaver's relations with Congress and his ability to manage the new department, Johnson vigorously worked to publicize that Weaver was his first choice. He called several senators to tell them that the reports that Johnson had offered the job to others were false. "My inclination was to appoint him right at the beginning but when I had my little confirmation problem I decided it would be wiser to let you all talk it over and let it cool. . . . I talked to our Senate friends when I got back and they said well they were irritated but that they would support him and confirm him. . . . I would like very much for it to be unanimous but he is and does represent my first choice and anything to the contrary is just discrediting Weaver," he told Senator William Proxmire.[46]

The Senate's consideration of Weaver in 1966 provided a stark contrast to his HHFA appointment in 1961 and signified both the president's political brilliance and major changes in the politics of race during the interim. Receiving word of Weaver's nomination, Senator Willis Robertson, who had voted against Weaver in 1961, quickly announced that he would support Weaver. "At one time I thought he was going to be prejudiced," Robertson stated, "but I've watched him very closely and I haven't found that he was prejudiced." The Senate Committee on Banking and Currency met on 17 January to consider Weaver's and Wood's nominations jointly. Senator Robert Kennedy, who had criticized Weaver only months before, introduced him to the committee, stating that he was "glad and happy and proud" that President Johnson had confirmed his brother's choice for the post. The hearing lasted less than an hour. Committee members made short statements generally praising Weaver and asked very few questions. After the committee voted unanimously to confirm the appointments, Senator Paul Douglas told the press that Weaver was "the first and only man" offered the job by Johnson. The appointments were sent directly to the Senate floor, which immediately confirmed Weaver and Wood.[47]

The next day, Weaver and Wood were sworn in by Federal Judge E. Barrett Prettyman at the White House. Roy Wilkins, Louis Martin, Whitney Young, Howard Dean, James Nabrit, several members of the cabinet and Congress, and union leader Walter Reuther were all in attendance. Johnson called it "a very proud moment for all of us and for all of America." Noting that others said that "the city has become unmanageable, unworkable, and unbelievable," Johnson stated that he did "not believe for a moment the cause of the American city is yet lost." The organization of the new department, Johnson argued, was "the beginning of a very exciting adventure. We are setting out to make our cities places where the good life is possible." Weaver, the president stated, "has his charge. It is to build our cities anew." Before issuing the oath, Johnson turned to Weaver and said, "Maybe that is too much to put on the shoulders of one single man. But we shall never know, Bob, until we try."[48]

* 15 *

# Power and Its Limitations

On 4 March 1966 *Time* magazine put Robert Weaver on its cover. "First Negro in the Cabinet: Trying to Save the Cities" was the headline, which conveyed a not-so-confident tone about whether the effort would succeed. The profile inside was generally positive toward Weaver, describing him as "a canny, cautious veteran of 22 years of Government manpower and housing bureaucracies," one of whose "most welcome qualities is that he himself is a lover of cities and a connoisseur of urban living." After describing Weaver's life in detail, the article listed the numerous problems facing American cities and the obstacles Weaver would face in reshaping his organization to respond to them.[1]

Given the national and international events of that turbulent period, Weaver's appointment competed with many other stories, but he certainly achieved celebrity status as the first black cabinet secretary, and he was the subject of much media attention. As he had consistently in the past, Weaver downplayed the issue of his race, arguing to the *Time* reporter that it should be "irrelevant." "I don't delude myself into thinking that I've ceased being a Negro because I've received recognition in the mainstream," he granted. However, he continued, "I would like to feel that I was appointed not because I was a Negro, but maybe in spite of that fact." Weaver presented himself to the nation as a sophisticated professional, not a black radical. According to the article, he was "a sybaritic, wholly citified man who loves Broadway plays, savors his stereophonic collection of Liszt and Chopin piano concertos . . . sips twelve-year-old bourbon. . . . dresses in banker-conservative clothing, favors dark suits and dark Homburgs at the office, a plum-colored smoking jacket and black leather slippers at home." The image he hoped to create was of a Park Avenue businessman, not a militant racial spokesman.[2]

Though Weaver would have preferred to ignore the racial aspects of his appointment, not surprisingly the African American media were most interested in him. He was the subject of long profiles in the two most popular black magazines, *Ebony* and *Jet*. Both articles emphasized his elite upbringing and his desire to transcend racial categories. "Race never has been a factor in Weaver's methodology and he would be the last to follow the tactics of several other Negro appointees," concluded journalist Simeon Booker. "First, he is no razzle-dazzle operator. Second, he is not afraid to take unpopular positions, and third, he is no social bug top heavy with prestige. . . . Weaver never worries about popularity–among Negroes or whites. He is determined to do a job and let the record speak for itself."[3]

Interviews with Weaver's colleagues and friends presented him as a hardworking but aloof person. "As complex as the cities he excels in, Weaver is a perfectionist in the Harvard tradition–determined as a Negro on his first integrated job, hardworking as if his salary depended on each day's output," and "a man with few continuing friends," Booker concluded. Frank Horne, his friend of thirty years, described him as "fundamentally reticent and definitely not an extrovert. . . . He grew up in a strong home, went to the best schools, and had little link with the ordinary 'Joe' in the street." Thurgood Marshall, then solicitor general, commented that "Harvard never contaminated Weaver" and argued that he was comfortable "whether in a group of Ph.D.s or a group of fellows at a cocktail party. Bob's not a stuffed shirt."[4]

Weaver's time to enjoy the accolades he earned through three decades of accomplishment was extremely short-lived. If 1966 marked the high point of Weaver's career, it marked even more significant changes for the Johnson administration. As the U.S. involvement in Vietnam increased, the president faced a growing wave of opposition to his foreign and domestic agendas. That Congress in an election year would be more critical of a president who could only lose luster after a record-breaking landslide victory and a legislative session that rivaled FDR's first is not particularly surprising. Johnson himself told his staff that they had to get their program through in 1965, because they would lose support thereafter. But the war in Asia heightened the natural tensions between the executive and Congress and weakened Johnson's public support.[5]

Since Congress passed the Gulf of Tonkin Resolution in August 1964, the United States had been drawn deeper and deeper into the Southeast Asia conflict. By 1966, a force that had been fewer than 20,000 "advisors" had grown to 325,000 young American women and men. As the fighting between American troops and the Vietcong increased, so did the casualties and, along with them, pressure on Johnson to end the conflict. However, each decision the president made in the hopes of ending the conflict had the opposite effect of entangling the United States to an even greater extent.[6]

The problems of Vietnam and domestic turmoil combined to produce a growing malaise in the country. The year 1966 marked a significant change in the attitudes of many Americans toward their government, including their representatives in Washington. Fading was the short-lived optimism that the federal government could solve all (or even most) societal problems. Nowhere was this change in attitude more profound than in the two areas to which Weaver had devoted his career. By the end of the year, the problems of race relations and the "crisis of the city" were merged. At the same time, the traditional liberal approaches to both these issues—the belief that professionally managed urban redevelopment programs could solve city decline and that legislation combined with professional mediation could overcome racial prejudice—were under attack. HUD's first year witnessed dramatic changes in the nation's understanding of these issues. As the nation's "urban czar" and its highest black official, Weaver was at the center of these conflicts.

WEAVER'S FIRST TASK was to reorganize the department to make it responsive to its mandate. But what was that mandate? Was HUD merely an elevation of the HHFA to cabinet status and a continuation of that agency's focus on construction projects? Was Weaver's job to represent "cities" or "urban areas"? Did HUD's purview include *all* urban problems, social and economic, in addition to housing? As several journalists noted in late 1965 and early 1966, neither Congress nor the administration had addressed these questions when the bill creating HUD was considered. Columnists Rowland Evans and Robert Novak called the department "novel in approach but fuzzy in detail" and claimed that the administration had muted questions about the agency's mandate during the debate over the bill out of fear that it would not pass. The editors of the *New Republic* argued that "Dr. Weaver and his HUD cohort will have to spend their first energies straightening out *their* new house before they can save the cities." Throughout 1966, Weaver and other policymakers within and outside HUD struggled with these questions. They never truly resolved them.[7]

Weaver received a great deal of advice in organizing his new department from the President's Task Force on Urban Affairs and Housing. Originally the task force was created in response to liberal complaints about Johnson's urban program. In the fall of 1965, Johnson, seeking to delay appointment of the HUD secretary, gave the group the additional responsibility of advising him on how to organize the new department. Chaired by Robert Wood, the task force included Senator Abraham Ribicoff, law professor Charles Haar, businessmen Edgar Kaiser and Ben Heineman, union leader Walter Reuther, civil rights leader Whitney Young, Budget Director Kermit Gordon, and planners Oscar Stonorov and William Rafsky.[8]

Although it proposed several new programs, much of the task force's final report advised the president on the organization of HUD, recommending, for example, that the existing fiefdoms of the Federal Housing Authority, Urban Renewal, and Public Housing be eliminated and that HUD be operated by regional directors who reported directly to Weaver and Wood. But the task force also focused on what exactly the new agency should do. They told Johnson that HUD should be responsible for more than just construction. HUD, they argued, must "recognize the integral relationship of the physical and social environments," while helping the president coordinate "federal activities which materially affect urban, suburban and metropolitan development." They advised the president to put the secretary in charge of a council of cabinet secretaries to make sure that their urban programs complemented each other.[9]

The most controversial task force recommendation was that the Community Action Program (CAP) be taken from the Office of Economic Opportunity and put under the responsibility of HUD. By late 1965, the CAP had become extremely controversial in cities across the country. Mayors like Chicago's Richard Daley were constantly complaining about the activities of community action agencies, which were working to organize the poor to demand better government services. The U.S. Conference of Mayors formally condemned the program for fomenting "class struggle" in cities. War on Poverty head Sargent Shriver stood by the embattled program, but Johnson became increasingly concerned about the CAP's political impact, and he told Califano to look into breaking up the War on Poverty initiatives and dividing them among existing agencies.[10]

The urban task force members (with two dissenters) agreed, arguing that the switch would "give HUD an active social agency that would challenge the rest of the department" while at the same time guaranteeing the CAP "a strong base of organizational support." In the end Johnson decided against the reorganization, telling staff that he thought the program was too new to be removed from the direct control of the White House and that he believed that the CAP's political problems were over.[11]

Because of the continuing debates over what the new agency would do, Washington insiders concluded that HUD had been weakened even before it began operating. Rowland Evans and Robert Novak asserted that HUD was "just a housing agency led by just a housing chief. That doesn't set pulses throbbing." Robert Semple, urban analyst for the *New York Times*, concluded that the result of these debates was that Weaver came "to his new post under rather unfavorable auspices." Weaver, he argued, could be "an excellent administrator, and a salesman with Congress" who could "transform a housing agency into a creative and powerful force in American life." However, Semple concluded, without the president's active support, Weaver "may end up just being another housing administrator."[12]

Johnson made the decision to have HUD focus on housing before his final selection of Weaver, and it is unclear whether this decision and the choice of Weaver were related. However, it is certain that Weaver did not think his agency should be in charge of "social programs" like community action. At Weaver's swearing in, Johnson declared that the new agency would have to deal with the American city's "human needs, as well as its bricks and mortar." Although Weaver agreed that HUD should play a major role in dealing with all urban problems, he did not—as others did—envision his agency taking over all programs that dealt with the cities. "I had little hope that all, or even most, federal activities related to urban affairs could be consolidated into a single department," Weaver later recalled. "In turf conscious Washington," he argued, such an approach would have created a great deal of controversy. His reluctance to take on more power and responsibility was consistent with Weaver's approach to government, but it would result in withering criticism over the next three years.[13]

Weaver's reorganization did not carefully follow the task force's recommendations (he later described them as "not worth a damn") but he did accept their general philosophy. Weaver shuffled the departments to weaken the established divisions of his agency and he placed a great deal of power in the regional directors. To assist him in this effort, Weaver hired as assistant secretaries four people well known in urban policy circles: Harvard law professor Charles Haar (Metropolitan Development), Philip Brownstein (Mortgage Credit), former Tucson mayor Don Hummell (Renewal and Housing), and Ralph Taylor (Demonstration Programs).[14]

Only months after their appointment, Weaver and his staff were already being criticized by members of Congress. Washington insider Marianne Means reported complaints that the new administration was ignoring congressional inquiries about its grants. "Weaver is a bright and talented man,"

Means wrote, but he was "blissfully staffing his new department with officials learned about city planning but ignorant of Congressional ways." Means directed her criticism particularly at Haar, who "arrogantly decided that his administration is to have nothing to do with Capitol Hill. He announced during a staff lecture that all grants would be made strictly on a merit basis and he conveyed the impression he felt this could not be done if anybody so much as spoke to a congressman." This inauspicious beginning would be compounded by the changing political climate in Congress.[15]

Weaver and his staff had very little time to get settled before the administration thrust them into a new legislative controversy by proposing a major new urban program that would eventually be called Model Cities. Though many people, including Weaver, later claimed credit for the idea, the Model Cities program resulted in large part from the prodding of union leader Walter Reuther. In the spring of 1965, Reuther told Johnson he should create a "Marshall Plan for the Cities" that would show the country's commitment to their residents. Reuther proposed that the federal government provide funding for the building of "total communities," which he described as "visible examples of new environments," with "new technologies of construction and prefabrication, new types of schools, new types of old age centers, recreational facilities and social services." The goal was to "set standards for the solution of the total job" of creating "physically beautiful and socially sound America." If successful, Reuther argued, the projects could be replicated across the nation.[16]

Directed by Johnson to develop the idea, the task force proposed a major new initiative they believed would, over the long term, solve urban decline. Calling their proposal Demonstration Cities, the group argued that "the size and scale of urban aids have been too small and too diffused" and that "present aid programs have often had the effect of entrenching archaic and wasteful practices." They proposed an initiative to fund comprehensive efforts to revitalize designated areas within selected cities. In order to receive funding, the cities would have to submit a detailed plan for how the funds would be used. Each city would receive, in addition to funds allocated under urban renewal, public housing, and other programs, extra grant funds for housing, employment, or social services.[17]

In his message transmitting the plan to Congress, Johnson stated that the "dream is of cities of promise, cities of hope, where it could truly be said, to every man his chance, to every man, regardless of his birth, his shining golden opportunity, to every man the right to live and work and to be himself and to become whatever thing his manhood and his vision can combine to make him." He proposed to spend more than $2 billion on the effort, which he renamed Model Cities, arguing that "the country is tired of demonstrations."[18]

The primary goal of the program, its creators asserted, was to empower local governments to solve the complex problems of the ghetto. The newly created Model Cities Administration, which would be overseen by HUD, would be responsible not only for aiding cities in dealing with the HUD bureaucracy but for helping them navigate the complicated array of government programs in all federal agencies. The initiative, administration officials argued, would work to overcome the obstacles cities faced in putting together comprehensive plans for housing and social services. It was also a way to placate mayors unhappy with the CAP.[19]

By the mid-1960s, increasing numbers of policymakers were expressing concern at the state of local government. The dynamic, progressive mayors of the 1950s, such as Philadelphia's Richardson Dilworth, who had received such glowing press even when their efforts failed, were now gone. They were replaced in many cities with career politicians who shared the same philosophy but faced growing budgets (the result of increasing demands by government workers and greater demands for social programs), decreasing tax revenues (resulting from the departure of middle-class whites), and escalating racial tensions in changing neighborhoods. In most cities, government was grossly unprepared to deal with these immense changes. The basis of the Johnson program was to aid these overwhelmingly Democratic officials in dealing with the problems in the cities' worst districts and regain control of these areas before decline spread.

Years later, his HUD colleague Charles Haar would argue that Weaver was never really supportive of the initiative. Weaver adamantly disagreed, arguing that he had proposed a similar idea just months before the task force met. As an administrator, however, Weaver must have been concerned about the implications of the program, particularly the requirement that HUD oversee and coordinate the activities of other federal departments, since he had earlier told White House officials, "It would be difficult for any agency to direct the activities of coordinate agencies of government." However, as the administration geared up for one of its renowned legislative campaigns, Weaver did not raise these concerns. In his congressional testimony on the legislation, Weaver stated that the program was designed "to help cities willing to face up to their responsibilities." The winning cities would have to examine their laws, codes, and tax systems and revise those that might impede the program and work to "encourage good community relations and counteract the segregation of housing by race or income." The legislation, he claimed, was the "cities' best hope."[20]

Reaction to the proposal was mixed. Many expressed support for the model-city idea but criticized the lack of funding. To carry out the program in any one large city would "easily gobble up all the money," the editors of the *New York Times* concluded. "Clearly, the figure proposed can only be regarded as provisional and preliminary." Several liberal members of Congress were skeptical. Congressman Henry Reuss (D-WI) asked why the administration proposed a new initiative before reforming urban renewal and other existing programs, and Senator John Sparkman (D-AL), while supportive of the idea, opposed giving Weaver the authority to determine which cities would be chosen. While they did not publicly state it, some members of Congress also worried about the requirement that applicants include a program for racial desegregation.[21]

The nation's mayors also responded to the initiative with trepidation, concerned about its impact on existing programs, and they worried about having to deal with yet another bureaucracy. Many also complained about the funding that the president proposed. The $2.3 billion Johnson recommended would be allocated over five years to more than 150 cities, meaning that an individual city's take would be relatively small. Mayor Lindsay called the program inadequate for the current needs. Democratic mayors Richard Daley of Chicago, James Tate of Philadelphia, and Jerome Cavanagh of Detroit supported the proposal but also complained that the funding was insufficient.[22]

House Republicans were very critical of the idea. The minority members of the Subcommittee on Housing argued that the proposal would create an open-ended liability on the part of the federal government to fund corrupt city governments. They also claimed that HUD was not capable of managing the efforts of other federal agencies, since it had trouble coordinating its own programs. Republicans were also concerned about the impact of the metropolitan planning grants. These provisions, they argued, would "place the shadow of HUD over every metropolitan area in our country" and drastically "reshape our Federal form of government." Given the lukewarm support of many liberals and the opposition of conservatives, many pundits argued that the bill would face great difficulties in Congress.[23]

AT THE SAME time it was fighting for model cities and several other urban programs, the administration took on another major battle in Congress:

housing discrimination. Weaver was once again placed in the middle of a complicated fight with major political implications. By the end of 1966, after two years of struggle, housing discrimination continued to be a major, unaddressed problem that threatened to further widen the growing gulf between black and white Americans.

Two years after President Kennedy made history by prohibiting discrimination in some federal programs, administration and fair-housing activists admitted that the order had had little impact in improving the access of racial minorities to housing. While the federal government continued to fund segregated housing, the fair-housing movement expanded dramatically. National Committee against Discrimination in Housing (NCDH) officials reported that there were at least a thousand fair-housing groups in the country. Through their efforts, seventeen states and twenty-eight cities had passed fair-housing laws.[24]

Activists continued to demand greater federal involvement, but they were frustrated by Johnson's weak response. In the spring of 1965, the President's Committee on Equal Opportunity in Housing, on which Weaver sat, issued a report recommending that federal antidiscrimination regulations be expanded to all housing financed by federally regulated banks, but it did not propose making the rule apply to housing already financed, as fair-housing activists had requested. NCDH chair Algernon Black called the recommendations "totally inadequate." But many in the administration had reservations about even this limited proposal. Like those on Kennedy's staff, many of Johnson's advisors believed that the president did not have the legal authority to expand the executive order. Attorney General Nicholas Katzenbach recommended that the president pursue legislation against housing discrimination instead of issuing an executive order, but he noted that this path was not without its disadvantages. "The housing issue, as indicated by the vote on Proposition 14 in California last year, may well be the most controversial and explosive of all civil rights issues," he told his boss.[25]

After several weeks of discussion in October and November, all of the president's White House aides agreed to pursue legislation instead of expanding the executive order. Vice President Humphrey and Katzenbach met with the President's Committee on Equal Opportunity in Housing and convinced them to change their recommendation. In the minutes of the meeting, David Lawrence noted that, while the decision was unanimous, several members had "serious reservations . . . as to the practicality" of convincing Congress to pass a fair-housing law.[26]

One might have expected Weaver to be a central participant in the administration discussions over the housing discrimination policy. Although several participants noted his support for administrative action instead of legislation, and although he was a member of the president's fair-housing committee and generally attended meetings, during the fall he was noticeably absent from the discussions. Weaver was not present when the committee decided to support the White House's recommendation, and presidential advisors Lee White and Joe Califano did not include Weaver's views in any of their reports to the president during the debates over administration strategy. It is hard to conceive that he was too busy to participate in meetings on a topic of such great importance to him, one to which he had devoted much effort over three decades. The only logical inference is that he did not support the decision. But, like a good soldier (and a canny bureaucrat who did not want to be on the losing side of the debate), he kept his opinion to himself.[27]

In his 1966 State of the Union address, Johnson gave his civil rights legislation prominent placement. "Justice means a man's hope should not be limited by the color of his skin," Johnson declared. But Johnson did not actually present a bill until late in April. The delay was partly the result of the drafting process, but it also had political motivations. Johnson hoped that by delaying introduction of the legislation until later in the term, he could appease civil rights groups without actually forcing a decision before the 1966 congressional elections. The bill included provisions protecting civil rights workers and increasing federal power over discrimination in the judicial system and education.[28]

The last section of the bill, which immediately became the focus of debate on a bill that otherwise received strong, bipartisan support, prohibited discrimination by "property owners, real estate brokers, and others engaged in the sale, rental or financing of housing." Noting that 1966 was the hundredth anniversary of the 1866 Civil Rights Act (which declared, "All citizens of the United States shall have the same right, in every State and territory, as is enjoyed by white citizens thereof, to inherit, purchase, lease, sell, hold and convey real and personal property"), Johnson argued that not enough had been done to "guarantee that *all* Americans shall benefit from the expanding housing market Congress has made possible." The time had come, he asserted, "for the Congress to declare resoundingly that discrimination in housing and all the evils it breeds are a denial of justice and a threat to the development of our growing urban areas."[29]

As the administration expected, liberals and conservatives both criticized the plan. Fair-housing advocates continued to argue that the president could eliminate discrimination immediately through the issuance of an executive order. Joseph Rauh, lawyer for the Leadership Conference on Civil Rights, described the bill as "a means of getting off the hook on an issue they don't want to face." He and other activists predicted that the housing discrimination section was the "negotiable part of the package" and extremely unlikely to pass especially in an election year. Senator Jacob Javits (R-NY) argued that an executive order would have accomplished the same thing and avoided "a bitter fight."[30]

Republicans and southern Democrats assailed the bill for exceeding federal authority. Senate leader Everett Dirksen (R-IL) called it "absolutely unconstitutional." He argued that housing purchases were an inherently local issue. "If you can tell me what interstate commerce is involved in selling or renting a house fixed to the soil, or where there is federal jurisdiction, I'll go out and eat the chimney off the house," Dirksen told reporters. Senator John Sparkman (D-AL) argued that the bill "clearly violates the right to free use and disposal of property."[31]

Not surprisingly, realtors were vigorously opposed to the bill, arguing that it would "destroy the American tradition of freedom of contract." Realtor James Lynch said that, "if this act is passed, we may as well repeal the Bill of Rights." As a result of lack of excitement on the part of liberals, strong opposition by conservatives, as well as election-year concerns for moderates, few pundits gave the bill much chance for passage.[32]

Conservative opposition to such legislation was long-standing, but the battle for fair housing was complicated by a growing conflict within the civil rights movement. By 1966 the latent tensions among activists over philosophy and strategy had grown into a rift that would not be repaired. Many blacks, frustrated by the continuing attacks on civil rights workers in the South and the hypocrisy of northern leaders who professed support for civil rights but watched as discrimination continued, gravitated away from a focus on racial integration toward nationalist ideologies.[33]

The Student Non-violent Coordinating Committee (SNCC) exemplified this transformation. Always wary of the mainstream civil rights groups, SNCC activists signaled a break with the others when they selected Stokeley Carmichael to head the organization. Carmichael stated that the existing philosophies of integration were inherently flawed and argued that blacks should focus on the development of their own institutions. Integration, he claimed, addressed racial issues "in a despicable way" by reinforcing, "among both black and white, the idea that 'white' is automatically superior and 'black' is by definition inferior." For this reason, he claimed, "'integration' is a subterfuge for the maintenance of white supremacy." Although other civil rights leaders strongly supported the fair-housing proposal, throughout 1966 Carmichael was a vocal critic of the bill.[34]

In an interview at the end of his term, Weaver was vague about his role in the administration's civil rights discussions, claiming that he was "primarily a person in the field of housing and urban development. I did not function as a person in race relations." Weaver stated that he had decided early on that he "could not do both things effectively, and I stuck to the knitting which I had been called in to do rather than try to cover the waterfront." In April 1966, however, Johnson told Califano that he wanted Weaver and Louis Martin to attend all meetings Johnson had on civil rights, particularly those with the White House Civil Rights Committee. Weaver told Johnson Library historians that he was present at many meetings with civil rights leaders, "primarily because of my own civil rights background, because I knew many of them personally." But, he concluded, "this was, I think, largely personal rather than racial, although the racial aspect obviously was there because the personal was related to the racial." Believing all African Americans "biased" on the questions, President Kennedy had excluded Weaver from civil rights discussions, but Johnson frequently reached out to black leaders. However, despite a career spent fighting discrimination, Weaver was reluctant at this time to take a prominent position in these debates.

With the benefit of hindsight, at least one close friend was critical of Weaver's approach during this period. "I think that Johnson did not regard Weaver as a strong man for his own causes and his people. If he had, he would have included him more in his inner circle. See what Bob didn't do was to claim the role of spokesman for the black community within the administration. He tended to hold back. He was a good manager but I don't think he was prepared to thrust himself into the battle," Mort Schussheim recollected. On Weaver's argument that he could not be a race leader, Schussheim commented, "that's a rationalization. I think if he had been a different personality, frankly, they could not have ignored him, because he was there and they couldn't fire him. He was there and he was doing a good job. I don't think that was his nature to thrust himself that way. He was an academic, basically. He was not a man who could be Richard the Lion Hearted in a crusade. He would be a policy adviser to Richard the Lion

Hearted, 'Let's take on those infidels,' and he might have picked up a sword, but he wouldn't be leading."[35]

Weaver did not frequently talk in public about the turmoil within the civil rights movement. But in his keynote address to the annual conference of the National Urban League in early August, Weaver made his feelings clear. Speaking to what was obviously a receptive audience, Weaver stated that the media was giving too much attention to militant leaders. "Until recently, a spokesman for Negro Americans was one who had a significant following," he told the group. "Today a publicized spokesman may be the individual who can devise the most militant cry and a leader one who articulates the most far-out position." This fact "disturbed" Weaver, who argued that "such images undermine those who speak with authority and have earned a significant and continuing following." The growing frustration among blacks, Weaver claimed, was real, and it was the reason that more people were attracted to radical statements: "Many nonwhites who have been repeatedly denied meaningful participation in the dominant society now look to substitute a social order which will afford them a significant role." But Weaver remained convinced that "most Negroes want to be able to believe in the promises of our democratic institutions." He continued to believe that racial integration provided the only hope for African Americans.[36]

The president's task of managing the violently diverging opinions on the nation's race relations was made more difficult by the continued racial conflict in many American cities. No city exemplified the increasing tension between blacks and whites more than Chicago, where the battle over housing discrimination hit the streets in a long summer of confrontation. At the center of the conflict were Martin Luther King and the Chicago Freedom Movement. In 1965 King decided to bring the Southern Christian Leadership Conference (SCLC) campaign to Chicago. Together with local activists, they decided to focus their attention on the housing discrimination that made the Windy City among the nation's most segregated. Arguing that housing discrimination was "a moral transgression, an offense against dignity of human beings and the American creed of equal opportunity," activists organized marches through all-white communities to dramatize the injustice of residential segregation.[37]

The reaction by white residents of working-class neighborhoods such as Gage Park and Marquette Park was swift and violent. In Marquette Park, whites threw rocks, bottles, and cherry bombs at the marchers and yelled "go home, niggers." When the protesters returned to their cars, they found that many had been set on fire and dozens had their tires slashed. When King himself led a march through Marquette Park, he was almost immediately hit in the head by a rock "as large as a fist," and a knife thrown at the civil rights leader barely missed him. King remarked that he had "never seen anything like it. . . . I've been in many demonstrations all across the south, but I can say that I have never seen—even in Mississippi and Alabama—mobs as hostile and hate-filled as I've seen in Chicago." After a summer of violence, the activists reached a weak agreement with Mayor Richard Daley and real estate leaders to promote open housing in the city.[38]

Historian James Ralph argues that the open-housing battles in Chicago "dramatically exposed the limits of the civil rights consensus," and they clearly influenced the debate over the Civil Rights Act. But unlike earlier protests in Selma and Birmingham and other southern cities in 1964 that galvanized support for federal legislation, the violence in Chicago had, if anything, the opposite effect: hardening opponents of fair housing without bringing together supporters. During earlier civil rights battles, Johnson used the conflict to rally support for his proposals, but he had little comment on the events in Chicago. He told his staff that protests were becoming counterproductive, and fearing reprisals from Daley and feeling increasingly distant from King, he did not use the conflict in Chicago in his efforts to secure passage of the antidiscrimination bill.[39]

In his congressional testimony on behalf of the bill, Weaver repeated a statement he had made a decade earlier, arguing that housing was "the one commodity in the American market that is not freely available on equal terms to everyone who can afford to pay." He claimed that the legislation would, by eliminating the scourge of discrimination, aid builders, because everyone would have to play by the same rules, and prevent block-busting and white flight by regulating unscrupulous brokers. But, realizing the extent of the opposition, the administration quickly began to take conciliatory positions. Just days after the bill was introduced, Attorney General Katzenbach agreed to exempt houses occupied by the owners from the law. Called the "Mrs. Murphy exemption," the proposal was advanced by several representatives who argued it would be unfair to regulate "little old ladies" who rented parts of their homes for "companionship." In a rare example of public disagreement, Weaver responded that he did not concur with Katzenbach's decision and stated that "any exemptions would weaken the bill."[40]

However, because of strong opposition to the housing section, it became clear that the bill would not be approved by the House without significant changes. In the end, Johnson decided to support the amendment, which passed in the House by one vote. Johnson acknowledged that it was not everything he wanted but argued that, nevertheless, the bill's significance was "large in both practical and symbolic terms." Civil rights leaders were disheartened. "I don't think the bill is worth passing like it is," King told reporters. Approving the amended bill would only "add to the tensions and violence in our Northern cities," he claimed. Lincoln Lynch, associate director of the Congress of Racial Equality (CORE), stated that "in essence the black man is being told by Congress that he only has constitutional rights in 40% of the nation's housing; in the other 60% he is not equal."[41]

Most observers thought that even the watered-down version would not pass the Senate. The reason was not that there were not enough votes—a majority appeared to support the bill. The reason was the Senate's voting rules. Southern Democrats would certainly oppose the legislation, and supporters would need a two-thirds vote to break a filibuster. After working for over a month to overcome the delaying tactic, administration officials gave up and declared the bill dead.[42]

Weaver was silent during much of the debate over the bill, but a few months later, in a speech to the National Association of Real Estate Boards annual convention, he argued that the passage of fair-housing laws was inevitable. There were some, he said, who denied free access to housing, "often on the ground that the seller has a right to choose the purchaser." Weaver told his audience that he had difficulty with that point of view. Residential mobility, he argued, was "required if we are to revitalize our cities." He invited realtors to "join the trend which is inevitable." Just two years later, Weaver would succeed in getting Congress to approve a bill banning housing discrimination that would be much stronger than the 1966 version. He would look at this victory as the capstone of his career. But by 1968 the nation's racial dynamics had changed so much that many others would dismiss the law's importance.[43]

THE BATTLES OVER housing discrimination, in the streets and the halls of Congress, were just one example of many revealing that, by 1966, the "crisis of the cities" was a major national issue. In August, the topic received a national platform from Senator Abraham Ribicoff. The former governor of Connecticut and secretary of health, education, and welfare used his chairmanship of the obscure Subcommittee on Executive Reorganization to organize a series of hearings, inviting administration officials, mayors from around the country, and other interested parties to testify. The hearings, which lasted several months and were widely covered by the media, illuminated the multiple obstacles facing American cities. While they produced substantive insights into urban problems, the hearings revealed the complete lack of agreement on the causes of these travails or the solutions to them.

Ribicoff was joined in the hearings by Robert Kennedy, whose presence dramatically increased media attention to the event. By 1966 Kennedy's feud with Lyndon Johnson was well known not only to Washington insiders but to the general public. Elected to the Senate from New York in 1964, Kennedy was generally supportive of the philosophy behind the Great Society, but he worked assiduously to distinguish himself from the president, proposing alternatives to administration programs. Kennedy was convinced that the administration's approach to urban problems was deeply flawed, and he remained skeptical about Weaver's ability to deal with these issues as HUD secretary. In the spring of 1966, he criticized Johnson's urban program. "It's too little, it's nothing, we have to do twenty times as much," he told friends. While he had yet to decide to run for president in 1968, Kennedy and his staff viewed the urban crisis as a crucial part of their campaign for a change in the White House. The Senate hearings provided an early platform for Kennedy's developing critique of Johnson's approach.[44]

Before the hearings started, Weaver and the other cabinet officials called to testify met with the president and his staff. Weaver, directed by Johnson, rewrote his testimony to pare down his discussion of the problems facing cities and to emphasize all the administration had done. Weaver would later rue this decision. Ribicoff told the president that he hoped to use the hearings to help the administration think of new ways to deal with urban problems, but when they began it quickly became clear that Johnson's people would be under fire. Weaver had prepared a forty-three-page statement to present to the senators, but he was not even able to begin before the senators peppered him with questions. Introducing Weaver, Ribicoff stated that HUD was too "brick and mortar oriented. You have to start thinking of people," he chided the secretary. Then Ribicoff and Kennedy, along with Senators Jacob Javits (R-NY), Ernest Gruening (D-AK), and Carl Curtis (R-NB), all began to grill the secretary. Was it not true, Ribicoff asked, that the government's welfare funds were going to pay landlords for substandard apartments? Weaver acknowledged that, yes, that was the case. How many substandard units are there in this country? Weaver did not know the figure off the top of his head. Are there any cities, Senator Curtis asked, that are not in crisis? Some, but every city has problems, Weaver answered. Javits asked whether the problem was not one of the proliferation of governments at the local level. Yes, this is a major concern, Weaver responded. More than an hour into the hearing, Weaver asked Ribicoff, "Mr. Chairman, might it be helpful if I present my statement before I answer questions about it?" A few minutes later, Ribicoff gave Weaver the floor.[45]

Weaver began his presentation by stating, "I am deeply disturbed by the present condition of the American city," but, he continued, "this administration has moved further, faster, with more understanding and a stronger sense of purpose to respond to the needs of our cities than any before it." The problems of cities would not be solved overnight or even in a decade, Weaver warned, but the Johnson administration was focused on "developing sound approaches which do treat the root causes" of urban problems. Weaver pointed to the Model Cities program, the rent supplement program, and his reforms in urban renewal as examples of the administration's approach.[46]

Soon after Weaver began to present his testimony, Senator Kennedy interrupted to criticize the administration's program. "I don't know whether we delude ourselves, Mr. Secretary, just by spending so much time going over what we have done, without really—we wouldn't be holding these hearings and you wouldn't be concerned as you are if it was not a fact that we are not doing enough. . . . I hope that we are not just going to go on and keep talking about every unit that we built in every part of the country," he stated. Kennedy told Weaver he had "the greatest respect for you and I believe that you know more about this problem than anybody in the United States," but it was clear that new approaches were needed. "The fact is the job is not being done," Kennedy stated. "We are still not solving the problem, and I don't think it is satisfactory." Weaver argued that he was describing new approaches that the administration was taking but Ribicoff responded, "No, I would say you are talking about the past." Both Ribicoff and Kennedy claimed that much more money needed to be spent on urban programs than the administration had proposed, and they argued that the administration had no overall plan of how to deal with the crisis.[47]

Weaver never did finish reading his statement before Ribicoff called the meeting to a close. He later remembered the hearings as "not one of my better presentations." The problem, Weaver argued, was that his remarks had "too many damn cooks," and he blamed the White House for pressuring him to include certain things. In the end, Weaver faulted himself for being "naïve" to the politics of the hearings, and he also criticized Ribicoff, who, he claimed, had cut off the discussion before Weaver got a chance to make his case.[48]

Although Weaver received the worst treatment from the committee, he was far from the only administration member who was aggressively questioned. Attorney General Katzenbach, who had served as Robert Kennedy's deputy when he was the nation's top lawyer, was next to testify. Katzenbach listed the administration's programs and described the Model Cities program as a means to provide a coordinated response to urban problems, but Kennedy called it "just a drop in the bucket for what we really need." After a very contentious conversation with his former assistant, Kennedy remarked, "I am just not satisfied." "You have made that clear, Senator," Katzenbach replied.[49]

Because of the tone of the attack against Weaver and the administration, the hearings received widespread attention. Even though they occurred in the middle of August, the hearing room was crowded with reporters and spectators. Articles describing the attacks of Ribicoff and Kennedy on Weaver and Katzenbach were on the front pages of newspapers across the nation. Many analyses focused on the difficulties the administration faced: under attack from liberals for not doing enough and from conservatives for doing too much. Journalists also noted that Congress had not been eager to pass most of the administration's proposals and had cut funding for several existing programs. Several mentioned that members of Congress were not happy with Weaver's performance. "Although critics regard Weaver as a competent technical expert. . . . they feel that he has not shown enough force in shaping new solutions to the broader problems of the megalopolis," the *St. Louis Post-Dispatch* reported.[50]

After the remaining administration officials testified, Ribicoff invited several of the nation's mayors to give their thoughts on the urban crisis. Mayor John Lindsay, touted as a presidential candidate after his defeat of the Big Apple's Democratic Party, argued that his city would need $50 billion in federal aid over the next decade to solve its problems. When Ribicoff stated that he did not think the government had that kind of money, Lindsay responded, "My job is to say what I think is needed." Mayor Jerome Cavanagh (Detroit) argued that a minimum of $250 billion (the annual federal budget for that year was a little more than $100 billion) would be needed in the next decade to revitalize all cities, while Mayor John Reading (Oakland) blamed the federal government for being at "the root of our cities' ills."[51]

The next set of hearings featured several people who were called to talk about ghetto life. Prominent among the witnesses were two African Americans, novelist Claude Brown, who was famous for his recently published book *Manchild in the Promised Land*, and Arthur Dunmeyer, a friend of Brown's who described himself as a "thirty-year-old grandfather." To the rapt attention of the senators, Brown and Dunmeyer described their life experiences in great detail. "You're in jail, whether you're in the streets or behind bars," Dunmeyer argued. "All the white community has tried to do so far is placate the Negro, keep the Negro cool," Brown claimed. Asked for recommendations to solve the problems, Dunmeyer proposed that the government find "all the numbers runners and dope peddlers and use them, see what they had to offer society."[52]

As the first series of what Ribicoff expected to be a year of hearings came to a close, the senator declared that they had already been productive in prodding the government to do more. He called on Johnson to introduce a tax increase of $10 billion to direct to city programs. Ribicoff also criticized the administration for failing to coordinate its initiatives, a job that had been "ignored in our headlong rush to adopt bigger and newer programs." He singled out HUD for criticism, saying that it was "not organized properly to take care of the problems."[53]

The media response to the hearings was less than positive. Television journalist David Brinkley said the hearings revealed the "illusion of bureaucratic omnipotence. That is, the assumption that all our domestic troubles can be blamed on fumbling and incompetent government agencies." Brinkley disputed this view. "If every bureaucrat in Washington had done everything right for the last fifty years we would still have slums. Hardly a big city in the world does not have them. So there must be more to it than that." The editors of the *Washington Star* focused their ire on Kennedy, calling his participation in the hearings the "kind of senatorial entertainment which adds nothing to his stature." Kennedy had "very little to teach anyone on the subject in hand except the extent of his animosity. . . . Free wheeling assaults upon public officials trying to deal with the problem contribute nothing to understanding or action in a field of need," they concluded.[54]

Johnson was, not surprisingly, given his sensitivity to any criticism and his extreme sensitivity to Kennedy, furious about the hearings. He claimed that Kennedy and Ribicoff were unfairly criticizing the administration when that administration had gotten all that it could from a reluctant Congress. To draw attention away from the Senate hearings, Johnson went on a three-day trip through New York and New England to highlight the administration's domestic initiatives.[55]

Highest among Johnson's priorities was the passage of the Model Cities bill, which he called "the most sweeping response ever made to our cities' needs." But winning support for the initiative was extremely difficult. Because of lukewarm support from liberals and active opposition from conservatives, many commentators declared the bill dead in the spring of 1966. Johnson's own advisors stated that the bill "excites no enthusiasm, either among Members or among any lobbying groups." During the summer, however, the Johnson administration undertook a full-scale effort to secure the bill's passage, including speaking tours by Weaver and Vice President Humphrey to elicit public support.[56]

The Senate approved the bill with relative ease, but the debates in the House were more contentious. Congressman Paul Fino (R-NY), who was a vocal opponent of the proposal from the beginning, argued that the legislation would result in Weaver's taking control of local educational systems and implementing a system of busing to achieve racial integration. Because cities were so desperate for money, Fino declared, they would accept the program without understanding its impact. "These metro governments are going to be L.B.J.s field headquarters. He and Dr. Weaver will run the country through these metro governments." With this bill, Fino claimed that Weaver would put "rent supplement" and "scattered-site public housing" in every suburb, draw up "civil rights and open housing legislation" in every city, redesign suburban taxes "to pay for slum schools," and put himself "at the head of the table in every city hall and board of education in this Nation." The result of this reallocation of power would be "forced school busing, pairing and redistricting" of schools.[57]

Supporters responded that Fino was using racial prejudice to stir opposition to a bill that had little to do with school busing or other issues of integration. "The Demonstration Cities and Metropolitan Development Act of 1966 is the real antiriot bill of the 89th Congress," argued Congressman Henry Gonzalez (D-TX). "It is the only well-considered, well-planned, and well-thought-out bill to prevent further riots and to help solve the numerous problems of cities that has been produced by Congress this year." To pressure House leaders to vote for the bill, the White House organized a group of twenty-two business executives, including David Rockefeller and Henry Ford II, to lobby for the bill. "America needs the demonstration cities act," they argued in a public statement. After passing an amendment clarifying that the program was not to be used to promote racial balance within schools, and rejecting several amendments that would have cut funding for the program, the House passed the bill by a narrow vote, and Johnson signed it into law. Over the next two years, the program would occupy much of Weaver's attention. It was an innovative idea, but HUD's efforts would be overwhelmed by urban decline and racial violence.[58]

The administration's celebration over a second successful legislative term was short-lived. In the November congressional elections, Democrats lost forty-seven seats in the House and three in the Senate. One of the Senate victims was liberal stalwart Paul Douglas (D-IL). The seventy-four-year-old had been a senator since 1948 and had played a major role in the passage of many important laws during his three terms. Despite health problems, Douglas waged a spirited campaign against liberal Republican Charles Percy, a businessman who had narrowly lost the governor's race two years before. A civil rights supporter, Percy did not generally exploit Chicago's racial tensions in the campaign, but the city's racial problems clearly played a significant role in the upset by Percy.[59]

Pundits dubbed the election the "white backlash." In several states racial tensions aided Republican candidates, particularly in California, where Ronald Reagan took the governor's seat, and in Florida, which elected a Republican governor for the first time since Reconstruction. *U.S News & World Report* called it a "protest vote of unexpected proportions" and claimed that it meant a tougher road for many Great Society programs. "Demands for bigger spending are almost certain to get more critical attention in the future than in the past," the editors wrote. Other journalists concluded that urban programs such as rent supplements and Model Cities were particularly vulnerable in the new Congress.[60]

On 10 November President Johnson made a telephone call to the 12,000 employees of HUD to congratulate them on their organization's first anniversary. "I want to thank all of you for the wonderful job you have done to bring greater opportunity, hope and beauty to our urban people. You must never lose sight of that goal." Later that month, Weaver reported to Johnson on HUD's progress during its first year. Weaver described the efforts to bring together the disparate parts of the HHFA and to shift the focus of the organization to "social and human values." "We are determined not to reflect the image of a federal agency that is slow-moving, unresponsive and bound in its own red tape." "We believe we have created an organization which will encourage action and innovation and which can respond to the human as well as the physical needs of the city." In response, Johnson commended Weaver and his staff for a "thoroughgoing and far-reaching reorganization." Others also praised HUD's efforts: "There are signs that a start is definitely being made in a new assault on the urban crisis," a reporter for the *Washington Post* wrote in November.[61]

But HUD did not receive positive reviews from everyone. Richard Lee, the mayor of New Haven, wrote to Joe Califano to inform him that, although he and other mayors were heartened by the creation of the new department, "a sense of frustration has set in because all it seems we have done is to create a new layer of bureaucracy and this, in turn, slows down the processing of our programs." A reporter for *House and Home*, the journal of the building industry, wrote that "Robert Clifton Weaver is fast becoming the Johnson administration's scapegoat of the year." Critics, the reporter stated, felt that Weaver had "proposed no new and imaginative programs to cure the festering ills of American cities." Weaver's first year as secretary was a trying one. As the administration's urban czar, he was under extreme pressure to quickly solve problems that had festered for decades but that had only recently drawn the nation's attention. The difficulties of the year would, however, pale in comparison to those that he and the nation would face in the next two years.[62]

* 16 *

# The Great Society, High and Low

By early 1967 it was clear to most observers, and to the president himself, that the Great Society was running out of steam, and facing so many obstacles, Johnson began to wonder "why he had ever wanted to be President." As the war in Vietnam took more of Johnson's time, his attention to domestic programs declined. But events in the summer prevented Johnson from focusing exclusively on winning the war. During 1967, urban violence swept the nation, making earlier conflicts seem minor. Riots in Detroit and Newark in particular dwarfed any seen before. The administration would face a flurry of proposals and criticism for its neglect of cities, and Weaver would endure withering criticism both within the administration and from outside as he struggled to manage the HUD bureaucracy and come up with ways to respond to urban decline.[1]

Out of this conflict emerged significant new legislative programs. In 1968 Weaver achieved his two major goals—the passage of a federal fair-housing law and a dramatic expansion of federal housing programs. Both laws marked significant progress and would spur the construction of thousands of units of housing while at the same time opening opportunities to African Americans and other minorities. But these victories would be clouded by the continued trouble within American cities and the escalating conflict in, and over, Vietnam, both of which would lead to Johnson's decision to withdraw his name from the presidential ballot. Like his boss, Weaver would depart Washington at the end of 1968. Worn out after seven years of leading a federal agency, he would leave the administration of these new programs to other people.

COMPARED TO PRIOR years, the administration's legislative program for 1967 was small, and this reluctance to promote new initiatives was particularly evident in the urban agenda. Johnson and Weaver both agreed that they would focus on implementing existing programs, but for different reasons. Johnson's concern about the federal budget deficit and his reluctance to use his limited political capital influenced his opposition to new ideas. Weaver was worried that HUD was already overextended and having difficulties managing its existing portfolio. The paucity of new initiatives brought criticism from liberal circles. Weaver argued that "this year there are more vitamins than calories in the serving bowl. And frankly, I don't believe that is bad at all," but advocates for cities were not impressed. Liberals in Congress also denounced the president's limited program. Senator Ribicoff declared that the president had not shown leadership in securing additional funding for cities and released his own program, which recommended spending an additional $7 billion annually on urban affairs. Weaver responded that Johnson had "given more leadership to this field than any other president we have ever had" and argued that Congress had failed to approve many of the initiatives the president had already proposed.[2]

The actions of Congress throughout the spring supported Weaver's claims. In May, that body, by a margin of 61 votes, cut all funds for the rent subsidy program. Congressman Paul Fino led the assault against the program, arguing that it would be used for "block-busting" by introducing racial minorities into suburban areas. Weaver accused House Republicans of "victimizing the poor" by their actions. "It is shocking that in this period of tension in our cities, the leadership of a major political party could be so insensitive to the nation's needs as to abandon those who are in the greatest need," he stated. Republicans also tried to drastically cut funding for the Model Cities program. It took a major effort by the administration and congressional supporters to save the appropriation for that program. The next month, responding to continual complaints by Fino and other representatives, the House voted to eliminate funding for the "Metropolitan Expediters" originally included in the program, removing one of the most innovative aspects of the program.[3]

The House also gave a stinging rebuke to one of the administration's few new initiatives. As part of the poverty program, Johnson recommended that the federal government fund local efforts to rid slums of rats, a problem highlighted during the Ribicoff hearings the year before. Weaver and his staff proposed that the federal government provide $40 million to local governments for extermination programs, but House Republicans and some Democrats ridiculed the bill. Representative H. R. Gross (R-IA) joked that the administration wanted to create a "rat corps" presided over by "a high commissioner of rats," and James Haley (D-FL) said it was "a monstrosity of a bill. Let's buy a lot of cats and turn them loose." The body rejected the proposal by a vote of 207 to 176. The president called the vote "a cruel blow to the poor children of America," and several editorials criticized the opponents for their callousness. Such was the tone of political debate in Washington during this period of crisis.[4]

Observers forecast continued opposition to the administration's urban program, but the events of the summer of 1967 would dramatically change the debate over what to do about America's cities. By this time, Americans were used to reports of summer violence in the nation's ghettos. The conflicts of 1967, however, were several magnitudes greater than the nation had witnessed in previous years. A federal study of urban riots that year reported 8 major disorders, 33 serious riots, and 123 minor uprisings across the nation in cities as diverse as Omaha, Tampa, Kansas City, Hartford, and Nashville.[5]

The worst violence occurred during July, and it began in the city of Newark, New Jersey. Like many others, the conflict began with a seemingly minor incident: the 12 July traffic stop of John Smith, a black cabdriver, near a public housing project. When Smith protested, several police brutally beat him in full view of many African Americans. A large crowd soon gathered in front of the precinct station. After a small skirmish between residents and the police officers, community leaders were able to defuse the situation, but the next evening a larger crowd gathered outside the police station. People began throwing rocks at the building, and the police responded with tear gas and nightsticks.[6]

Just blocks away fires and looting consumed the local business district. The police cordoned off the area but did not enter it; instead, they fired their guns into the air to warn looters to stop. The arrival of untrained National Guard troops made the situation worse, as many fired indiscriminately into the crowds. Several residents, including a three-year-old girl and a seventy-three-year-old man, were shot by police officers, and others were killed by stray bullets which appeared to come from the National Guard. By the end of the weekend, when the riot subsided, twenty-three people—twenty-one blacks, one white fireman, and one white police detective—had been killed.[7]

The terrible stories out of Newark shocked the nation, but the riots that began a week later in Detroit dwarfed those in New Jersey. Troubled police relations were also responsible for this conflict, which began when the Detroit police raided some after-hours clubs in the heart of the black community. In response to this harassment, hundreds of people took to the streets and began setting fire to stores. Looting continued throughout the next day; the police cordoned off the area but did not intervene. As in Newark, the arrival of the National Guard did little to slow the riots, and Guardsmen were responsible for several deaths. According to federal investigators, the Guardsmen "placed buildings under siege on the sketchiest reports of sniping." By Monday, much of Detroit was in chaos. Police reported hundreds of incidents of sniper fire, most of which were later deemed false. On Monday, the mayor and the governor called on President Johnson to send in the army to quell the disorder, and by late Tuesday the troops had brought the city under control. When the riots were over, forty-three people were dead—thirty-three black and ten white.[8]

In many ways the riots marked a turning point in American society. "How the march on Washington turned into Newark is something that will be explained with lies for years to come," columnist Jimmy Breslin observed. "Right now, one thing is certain. Nobody is marching anymore." Editorialists across the nation blamed the civil rights leadership, which they argued was powerless to deal with ghetto residents. "The civil rights movement is now in the process of collapsing, while its established and traditional leaders sit silent and shaken," the editors of the *Washington Post* argued. "As for the Negro slum, it has demonstrated that it has no leaders and follows none of the organizations that have claimed to lead it." Breslin quoted a black radical who said, "In Washington, they show you Robert Weaver. They tell you, look, we got a Negro in the cabinet. You know what everybody says about Weaver? They say, 'He's light and bright and damn near white.' Who knows him?"[9]

The editors of the *New York Times* blamed President Johnson's parsimony for failing to respond to urban needs. "They may not realize it themselves, but slum dwellers are in revolt at least in part because the cities in which they are condemned to live have become unlivable," they argued. "If peace and order are to be permanently restored to America's cities, the broader problems of urban and human rehabilitation must be tackled with far more vigor and imagination than have yet been displayed." Hugh Sidey, writing in *Life* magazine, noted the irony that Johnson, "a man of the open plains," would be judged on his response to urban problems. In reality, no one could explain the causes of the riots or develop solutions to the numerous problems facing the areas in which they occurred. That did not stop them, however, from blaming Robert Weaver.[10]

The country's political leadership, unable to think of concrete solutions to the complicated problem, fell back on partisan debate over who was responsible for the violence. The Republican leadership issued a statement accusing the president of fomenting rioting by vetoing a crime bill for the District of Columbia that many considered unconstitutional, and demanding "law and order" measures. They called for an investigation of the role of Communist agitators in the violence, for which, Senator Dirksen stated, they had strong evidence. Southern Democrats blamed the passage of civil rights bills for the violence and condemned the Supreme Court for its role in allowing increased lawlessness. Johnson was bewildered about how to respond to the conflict. As the riots in Detroit subsided, he made a prime-time television appearance deploring violence and announcing the creation of a commission, chaired by Otto Kerner, governor of Illinois, to study the causes of the riots.[11]

Weaver himself said very little about the riots, but he was truly unnerved by the level of violence, because it represented a direct attack on the approaches that he had taken throughout his career. Between the conflicts in Newark and Detroit, in testimony on Capitol Hill supporting the administration's urban program, Weaver used the violence to support more funding for existing programs. "The troubled and tragic events in Newark," he stated, "underscore the immediacy of the problems of our cities. While we condemn disorder and violence in urban America, we must also understand why they occur. They are the inevitable consequences of scores of decades of neglect, discrimination and deprivation. They reflect community despair and hopelessness, frequently evidenced by a disenchantment with dominant values. Only basic gigantic, and well directed positive action will prevent their recurrence." Weaver himself was increasingly aggravated by the lack of administration support for urban programs. At lunch with his friends Louis Martin and Roger Wilkins, he complained, "we can't fix cities on the cheap," and according to Wilkins, "he was very frustrated about the impact of the Vietnam war." But Weaver backed administration arguments against wholesale adoption of new programs. This was necessary, he claimed, "lest we again make promises that cannot be fulfilled, thereby augmenting the hopelessness that is already too prevalent." In the weeks after the riots, Johnson went on the offensive against his critics, and he lobbied Congress aggressively to fund the programs they had cut.[12]

Before the violence of July, the "crisis of the city" was a major topic, but after the eruptions in Newark and Detroit, the discussion became even more urgent. Everyone who fashioned himself a leader had an opinion about what should be done. The riots also focused what had been a vague, amorphous discussion about the nation's urban areas on a specific question: how to tame the black ghetto. Five years before, dealing with the increasing racial tensions within cities was only one of many issues facing policymakers. By 1967, it had become the only one.

To address the problem, many business and civic leaders turned to Weaver's agency. Throughout the rest of the summer and the fall, business, civic, and political leaders offered a dizzying array of proposals to bring peace to American cities. However, most of the ideas were undeveloped and focused primarily on the need to spend a great deal more money. The Urban Coalition, a group of businessmen and politicians created after the riots, called for the creation of one million public and private jobs and "bold and immediate steps to provide a decent home for every American." Whitney Young recommended an immediate appropriation of $10 billion to HUD for the construction of new housing in ghetto areas. The jobs created by this construction funding, Young argued, should go to ghetto residents. Senator Jacob Javits proposed the creation of an Urban Development Bank modeled on the World Bank. While acknowledging the reluctance of Congress to approve much smaller programs, all of the advocates argued that with public pressure the funds would be provided. Speaking for the Urban Coalition, John Lindsay argued that, "if our defense commitment, our commitment to space, or any other commitment made before our urban areas were beset by agony is blocking a vigorous effort to end these agonies, those commitments should be reassessed."[13]

Two of the most detailed proposals for dealing with the urban crisis came from moderate Republican senator Charles Percy and Johnson's nemesis Robert Kennedy. Both focused on improving housing conditions in the ghetto, which they claimed was the problem most responsible for the violence. A few years earlier, Weaver might have happily debated the merits of these proposals. But because their proponents were political enemies of the president with an election just a year away, and because their approaches would weaken HUD programs that were just getting established, Weaver became an implacable opponent. While neither bill was ultimately approved, the debates over these proposals illuminate the politicization of the ghetto and the difficulties facing Weaver in trying to craft a response to long-festering problems.

The centerpiece of Percy's urban policy was a program for homeownership. "A man who owns his home acquires with it a new dignity," Percy argued. "He doesn't burn it down, but instead begins to take pride in what is his own, and pride in conserving and improving it for his children." Percy proposed a federal corporation to provide low-interest loans for the construction and purchase of homes in ghetto areas. Contrasting his approach with that of the Democrats, who, he claimed, promoted "new ways of making the poor man not merely dependent, but doubly dependent–once on the landlord and once on the dole," Percy argued that his program would be "a New Dawn of opportunity for the poor but honest man."[14]

The positive response to Percy's proposal put the administration on the defensive. Weaver aggressively attacked the bill, taking the unusual step of issuing a press release when it was introduced. "While well-intentioned," Weaver argued, the proposal "indicates little real understanding of the problems of producing housing within the economic means of the poor." Weaver listed numerous objections to the bill, noting that it would affect only a small number of people, ignored local government, failed to provide for relocation of people uprooted by development, and would create a new, unnecessary federal bureaucracy. Furthermore, many of the people who purchased their homes would lose them. Weaver presciently claimed that for many people homeownership was "a snare and a delusion and it can be a cruel hoax because in many instances with these low down payments, with these long periods of loans after three years they will have negative equity. And if they lose their jobs, or if they are sick, they will lose their home. And if you think you have disillusionment and you think you have despair and potential violence in the ghetto now, what's going to happen if this occurs in large numbers?" he asked.[15]

Critics stated that Weaver's response "merely reinforced the charge [made by Democratic members of Congress] that HUD is too 'negative' and too defensive about what the administration has done without maintaining an open attitude to new ideas and concepts." Percy was far from the first person to propose low-income homeownership. Liberals, including Weaver's friend Charles Abrams, had made similar recommendations. Because of the strong support for Percy's idea, congressional Democrats started to pressure the White House to offer an alternative, and over Weaver's objections the administration started to study the idea of low-income homeownership more carefully.[16]

Weaver also attacked Robert Kennedy's proposal to revitalize the ghetto. Like Percy, Kennedy argued that greater private investment was necessary to solve the urban crisis. Kennedy's legislation provided a complex system of tax credits and low-interest mortgages to private investors that would, he argued, enable private corporations to produce housing for low-income persons at a profit. Under Kennedy's plan, these tenants in the apartments would be trained to take ownership of the buildings, and the developers would receive incentives to sell the units to the residents. Kennedy estimated that his proposal would support the production of hundreds of thousands of housing units at a lower cost. He argued that his program was better than the administration's because it was not "a welfare approach; it avoids requiring low- and moderate-income people to rely on receiving Government help every month," like the rent subsidy initiative.[17]

Earlier in the year, the administration had considered a similar idea, but as he did with Percy's proposal, Weaver attacked Kennedy's program, calling it "a significantly backward step." In a reversal of the Senate hearings the year before, when Kennedy attacked the administration's program, Weaver made a point-by-point criticism of the proposal, arguing that it would not help the poor, who could not afford the rents in the housing that would be developed, and claiming that the program would cost the government far in excess of existing initiatives to produce affordable rental housing. Weaver also criticized Kennedy's focus on building within the ghetto, arguing that it "would tend to strengthen the barriers that already confront the poor and the minority groups and prevent them from breaking out of these areas and becoming assimilated into the general stream of our society." He and Kennedy engaged in a heated debate in which Kennedy accused Weaver of misrepresenting the bill and dismissed Weaver's claims that HUD was increasing production in existing programs.[18]

As the Percy and Kennedy proposals reveal, during 1967 the debate over the ghetto shifted from a discussion over racial integration to a focus on the need to improve conditions in these areas. While continuing to discuss the broader issues of poverty and racial segregation, the immediacy of the crisis, combined with the growing frustration with efforts to reform local government, led the Johnson administration to focus on something it could, it felt, do: build housing. Existing programs, Johnson argued, could make significant improvements in ghetto life if they were fully funded and efficiently implemented. While he continued to demand that Congress allocate sufficient funds, Johnson and his staff constantly peppered Weaver with memos inquiring about the status of the administration's housing programs.[19]

Weaver and his staff responded by proposing several initiatives to make existing federal programs work more efficiently. They announced they would give priority to urban renewal and public housing proposals that could be completed quickly, and they proposed an experimental effort to fund low-income housing projects built and managed by private developers. Weaver and his staff hoped that guaranteeing private developers a profit would give them an incentive to participate, speeding the production of new housing. To placate critics and explore new ways to produce housing, Johnson formed yet another task force, the Committee to Rebuild America's Slums, chaired by shipbuilding magnate Edgar Kaiser. Johnson also created a program in which the nation's leading insurance companies would provide $1 billion in financing for housing in low-income, urban neighborhoods. Later in the year, he announced the formation of a new organization, called the Urban Institute, to study urban problems.[20]

Despite these numerous, and, over time productive, initiatives, the administration continued to receive withering criticism about its neglect of urban issues, and opponents slammed HUD for its inefficiency. They blasted the Federal Housing Administration (FHA) in particular for its inability to manage the affordable housing programs under its supervision. Senator Edward Brooke (R-MA), the first African American elected to that body since Reconstruction, citing a project in Malden, Massachusetts that was delayed for several years because of the FHA's obstructionism, questioned whether the agency was "committed to progress." He complained that only 40,000 units in the moderate-income program were produced in six years, when the administration had promised it would produce 60,000 each year. "Weaver responded that the FHA had made significant improvements in its process, but Brooke remained "unconvinced." He recommended that HUD be reorganized and that affordable housing programs be removed from the FHA's oversight.[21]

Although politics played a role in the Republicans' attack on the FHA, White House officials agreed with the criticism, and staff reported that the FHA's operation was "virtually a scandal. Despite the desperate need for low and low-moderate income housing, FHA has not come near building the housing actually authorized by Congress." White House aide Joseph Califano reported to the president that there was "little evidence available" to suggest that Weaver's actions were making any impact on the FHA. Weaver blamed much of the problem with the FHA on the fact that it was administered locally and that local FHA officials, who were often patronage hires recommended by members of Congress, were frequently unqualified for their jobs (among Weaver's examples of unqualified local managers were a former schoolteacher, a sales manager for an oil company, and a former sports-radio editor). Weaver proposed changing the hiring process, but administration officials were reluctant, fearing congressional backlash.[22]

During the summer of 1967, former senator Paul Douglas enabled HUD's critics to attack the agency without traveling to Washington. He did this through the auspices of the Commission on Urban Problems, a group created by Congress. The president hoped that Douglas, whom he had selected to head the committee, would support the administration's efforts. But Weaver found his fears that the group would be used to attack HUD operations justified. Frustrated with the continuing trouble in American cities, Douglas decided to conduct a full-scale study of the urban crisis. After hiring a large staff, Douglas took the commission on the road, conducting thirty-two days of hearings in sixteen cities between May and October 1967.[23]

HUD came under constant criticism during these hearings, which drew both urban experts and ordinary citizens. In New Haven, a city that many viewed as emblematic of the successes of urban renewal, residents damned the program. Neighborhood activist Stephen Papa told the commission that 12,000 to 15,000 people had been uprooted. These people, he argued, were "the backbone of the community." Defending the hearings, Douglas told Weaver, "sometimes you need critics from the outside to help you overcome internal obstacles," but Weaver argued that the criticisms interfered with his programs and provided grist for congressional conservatives. However, the commission was congressionally authorized, and the White House's hands were tied. As a result, Douglas's group became yet another sounding board for complaints about the administration in general and Weaver in particular.[24]

At the end of its second year, Weaver's department had more critics than supporters. The *Wall Street Journal* praised Weaver's "new boldness" in creating a common set of goals for HUD's agencies and pushing HUD offices to be more responsive to the needs of the poor. But others argued that the department had made little progress. The leaders of the National League of Cities acknowledged that no agency could "reverse the tide which has been rising for years" in such a short time, but they concluded that HUD had failed to define its mission and argued that the "flow of press releases" from the agency was "not representative of its limited achievements." A writer in the *Washington Post* directly criticized Weaver for failing to make the public case for more aid to cities. "For the past two years his speeches have sounded as though they were written by the mimeograph machine," he wrote. "He is, in fact, trying desperately to stay out of public controversy."[25]

AMONG WEAVER'S HARSHEST critics were his friends in the fair-housing movement. Amid much fanfare, the National Committee on Discrimination in Housing announced the publication of a thirty-one-page pamphlet, "How the Federal Government Builds Ghettos," which laid the blame for urban ills directly at the door of the Johnson administration. "Every day Federal money and power are used to build racial ghettoes," the pamphlet began. It made seventeen "charges" against the administration, most of which focused on HUD (though they never named Weaver as directly responsible), claiming, among other things, that the agency's efforts were "ineffectual and understaffed" and enforced by officials who were "out of sympathy" with nondiscrimination policies.[26]

The administration, the pamphlet argued, was not racist; it was bumbling. "The road to segregation is paved with weak intentions—which is a reasonably accurate description of the Federal establishment today. Its sin is not bigotry (though there are still cases of bald discrimination by Federal officials) but blandness; not a lack of goodwill, but a lack of will." As one of many examples, the pamphlet cited the fact that HUD had recently granted its "Award of Merit" to a suburban subdivision which had been cited by state officials for discrimination. While never naming him directly, the National Committee against Discrimination in Housing (NCDH) made many veiled charges against Weaver, arguing that "today's federal housing official commonly inveighs against the evils of ghetto life even as he pushes buttons that ratify their triumph—even as he OK's public housing sites in the Heart of Negro slums, releases planning and urban renewal funds to cities dead-set against integration, and approves the financing of suburban subdivisions from which Negroes will be barred." The group recommended that HUD establish a new housing discrimination division and fire people not sensitive to the issues.[27]

Weaver's public response revealed the extent to which he took the accusations personally. A day after the NCDH released the pamphlet, Weaver distributed to the press an eight-page response, calling the report "both inaccurate and unfair." He argued that the administration had taken "unprecedented steps" to produce housing for all people and open access to minorities. Under his leadership, Weaver continued, HUD had undertaken investigations of discrimination and worked to process complaints quickly.

It had also conducted sample reviews of real estate brokers to ensure that they were not discriminating, and it had worked with local housing and urban renewal agencies to promote racial integration. But none of these actions, Weaver argued, would "bring into being the open city or achieve the goals which both the Committee and I have long set for urban America," because the HUD secretary's powers were limited: "Regardless of my personal commitment to open occupancy in housing, I am sworn as a Federal official to carry out the laws of the land." To ensure fair housing for all would require "new legislation, revision of existing laws and greater receptivity for change in racial housing patterns than now exists," he claimed.[28]

Weaver undertook several actions to respond to criticisms of his efforts, issuing orders to his administrators to increase their oversight of housing programs and leaking a "confidential memorandum" that he had distributed to his administrators telling them that they had to improve minority access to housing. NCDH officials responded, "We have the greatest respect for our long-time friend and colleague, Secretary Weaver, but we do not find his statement responsive to the problem of discrimination." Even though the president had proposed legislation, fair-housing leaders argued, this did "not in any way negate his constitutional power to direct that Federal programs be administered affirmatively to eliminate racial discrimination and segregation in housing." Assessing the conflict, the editors of the *Baltimore Afro-American* argued that Weaver "projected as negative an attitude as . . . federal agencies generally exhibit in dealing with fair housing problems."[29]

Weaver's files reveal ample evidence of the major problems facing HUD offices in preventing discrimination and promoting integration. According to his staff, during the four years since the issuance of the antidiscrimination order, the FHA had investigated fewer than two hundred complaints. Of those complaints, only thirty-five resulted in the complainant's acquisition of the desired housing. More than 40 percent of the cases were dismissed because HUD had no authority under the law. Although publicly Weaver supported the administration line that legislation was required, he continued to argue to the White House that expanding the executive order against discrimination was legal and would improve the situation. Johnson's staff, however, were reluctant to take action.[30]

HUD's own study of the FHA concluded that the agency had failed to prevent discrimination. An internal review revealed that only 3 percent of new homes (13,832 out of 410,574) that were covered by the executive order had been sold to African Americans since 1962. HUD officials were "distressed" and "appalled" at this finding. To spur a change, Phillip Brownstein, director of the FHA, told district directors that they had "been measured and found wanting" and warned them that, if they did not ensure that more housing was made available to African Americans, they should "step aside for men who can provide leadership in these areas."[31]

Segregation in public housing was one of the most intransigent problems. Weaver's staff collected thirty-three complaints about new public housing projects that resulted in increased racial segregation in the first four years after the executive order took effect. In only eight of these did the housing authorities agree to changes in their plans after being questioned by HUD staff. Chicago continued to be one of the most egregious violators. Despite constant protest in the city and from the federal government, Mayor Richard Daley continued to focus that city's construction program in the same area that the city had chosen two decades before. By the mid-1960s, this area included over 20,000 units of public housing, the largest concentration in the country. They rapidly deteriorated while violence and social problems increased. By the 1970s, these projects would be considered the worst in the nation.[32]

The urban renewal program faced similar problems. Despite the efforts of Weaver and his staff to make the program more sensitive to racial minorities, civil rights leaders reported that many cities were still using redevelopment funds to entrench segregation. Fair-housing activists claimed that in Louisville, Kentucky, the relocation program directed blacks to apartments in the city's West End while sending whites to other parts of town: "Urban renewal in Louisville is designed to accomplish, and in fact does accomplish, wholesale Negro removal from the downtown area to areas of racial isolation," they stated. Activists complained to HUD officials, but they did not respond. NCDH leaders asked Weaver to deny all HUD funds until the city adopted an open-occupancy plan, but Weaver argued there was "no legal basis" for such action.[33]

Activists also complained about the Model Cities program, which they felt was really "gilding the ghetto," not promoting racial integration. They told Johnson that the program could be "a thrust toward creation of the Great Society, or it can be used to repeat the cycle of ghettoization for generations to come." Weaver's good friend (and NCDH board member) Frank Horne, echoing Weaver's statement about the urban renewal program two decades earlier, argued that model cities constituted a "promise and a threat, depending upon what our model is for the racial residential patterns of American cities."[34]

Horne was confident that Weaver would implement the program effectively, commenting that Weaver and Johnson were "people with unique understanding of the need for firm action . . . to remove racial restrictions." But Weaver felt that his hands were tied. When Congress passed the Model Cities law, it specifically forbade Weaver from using it to promote integration. NCDH officials, Weaver told the president, wanted "to force me to come out with a pledge for a positive racial integration in the model cities program." This, Weaver argued, "was contrary to the legislative history and the action of the Congress" and would "result in problems for us on the Hill." Weaver contended that the NCDH was wrong in its analysis of the administration's policy. "The alternative of 'perpetuating the ghetto' vs. dissolving it is without substance: we must do both," he stated.[35]

The president continued to pursue fair-housing legislation during 1967, but this time his strategy was even more measured than the year before. After much internal discussion over the administration's civil rights agenda, Johnson decided to introduce another bill that banned discrimination in housing. The major difference in the proposal was that it would require compliance gradually over two years, applying first to larger projects and then to individual homes. Administration officials hoped that this process would show the public that the law would not cause drastic changes in neighborhoods. Activists blasted the proposal, arguing that it was "token fair housing legislation. The chair of the American Jewish Congress, Howard Squadron, argued that the ghetto "cannot be dealt with bit by bit." Other civil rights leaders, however, supported the administration.[36]

The president called his proposal the "next and more profound stage of the battle for civil rights," but he was slow to engage in this struggle, and his staff did not actively pursue it. Most administration officials remained pessimistic about the proposal's chances in 1968, but Weaver lobbied hard within the administration to get them to act. With his prodding, joined by pressure from civil rights activists and liberals in Congress, the president's civil rights legislation became the dominant issue for the congressional term that began in January. In January 1968 the president announced his intention to make its passage a priority.[37]

Two weeks, later, Senator Walter Mondale (D-MN) introduced the administration's fair-housing bill, beginning a debate that would last almost five weeks. Senator Edward Brooke (R-MA), a cosponsor of the bill, argued that fair housing was crucial to ending urban violence. "No other solution will work," he asserted. As Weaver and other activists had done for years, the bill's promoters focused on the desires of middle-class blacks in making their case. Senator Mondale argued that "it is impossible to gauge the degradation and humiliation suffered by a man in the presence of his wife and children when he is told that despite his university degrees, despite his income level, despite his profession, he is just not good enough to live in a white neighborhood." The bill, he declared, would enable the private market to work as it should. The only people who would move would be upstanding middle-class families that would contribute positively to their new neighborhoods. These people deserved to live the American dream just like their white counterparts. As Weaver had argued two decades before, these pioneers would be role models who would show that integration was a good thing.[38]

Throughout the month of February, the opponents of the bill engaged in a filibuster, presenting long speeches listing its defects. But, by the end of February, civil rights advocates had become confident that they would be able to pass a fair-housing measure. The 1966 congressional elections, ironically, gave them greater support in the Senate. Many of the Republicans who had defeated Democrats—including Charles Percy of Illinois, Mark Hatfield of Oregon, Howard Baker of Tennessee (who was also Minority Leader Everett Dirksen's son-in-law), and Edward Brooke of Massachusetts—supported the legislation and believed that black votes were crucial to the future of the party. They pressured Everett Dirksen to change his mind and worked to get other Republicans to end the southern Democrats' filibuster.[39]

The passage of the bill was aided by the 1 March release of the report of the president's riot commission. Chaired by Otto Kerner, governor of Illinois, the commission had conducted hearings around the country throughout the fall and spring and spent over a million dollars on more than a dozen studies of conditions within black urban areas and the causes of racial tensions. The final document, which was over four hundred pages long, blamed white racism for the riots and argued that the nation was "moving toward two societies, one black, one white—separate and unequal." It called for a massive program of housing, education, and employment costing several billion dollars. The commission also recommended the passage of a "national, comprehensive and enforceable open occupancy law." That recommendation was echoed days later by a group of national business leaders, including Edgar Kaiser and James Roche, chair of General Motors, who argued that the legislation was "urgently needed."[40]

Although the report's content and recommendations were disputed by many—including the president himself, who was upset that the report did not note the many accomplishments of his administration—it gave further support to fair-housing advocates. On 5 March the Senate finally broke the filibuster, and on 11 March an exhausted Senate approved the civil rights bill, the only legislation it had considered for two months. Attention then shifted to the House, where Minority Leader Gerald Ford (R-MI) objected to many of the Senate bill's provisions. Given the opposition of southern Democrats, a large number of Republican votes were necessary if the bill was going to succeed. Throughout March, Weaver, other administration officials, and their supporters in the House lobbied Ford and other members to agree to the Senate version. Many observers believed that the bill faced a long delay, if not defeat.[41]

Then, on the afternoon of 4 April James Earl Ray shot Martin Luther King in Memphis, Tennessee. The assassination sent the nation into chaos—riots erupted in 125 cities and at least 39 people were killed. The assassination and the violence that followed plunged the president into despair. "Everything we've gained in the last few years we're going to lose tonight," he told his staff. The events brought out strong emotions in the usually reserved Weaver. His colleague Ed Lashman remembered that, "after the assassination, I had a long conversation with Weaver. The FBI wanted him out of sight, so we went back to his apartment and drank a lot of whiskey. Weaver talked about his reservations about King and about his hatred of J. Edgar Hoover. He had an awareness of the crosscurrents in his own development and was aware of the reasons people might not see him as successful as some more flamboyant leaders."[42]

The next day, Johnson organized a meeting of civil rights leaders that Weaver attended. The gathering was mostly an opportunity for the activists to vent their frustrations, but when it was over they agreed to work for the passage of the civil rights bill as a testimonial to King. Less than a week later, the House passed the bill. At the bill signing, the president stated, "In the Civil Rights Act of 1968 America moves forward and the bell of freedom rings out a little louder."[43]

The passage of the fair-housing law was the culmination of two decades of effort by civil rights activists, but few vocally celebrated the achievement. NAACP leaders forecast that the law would be extremely valuable, but by this time many blacks were beginning to join more radical activists in questioning the philosophical framework that had driven the movement for several decades. Interviewed in the *Chicago Defender*, self-described militant Russell Meek called the law "nothing more than a miserable gesture. . . . If we have to wait for the assassination of one of our black leaders before Congress will even serve up a bill such as the one in question, then the graveyards will be full of black leaders and we'll still be in slavery."[44]

Columnist William Raspberry, writing in the *Washington Post*, celebrated the bill's passage as a symbolic victory but concluded that the law "doesn't begin to get down to where the problem is." Like most civil rights laws, Raspberry argued, this one would benefit primarily the middle class. "Don't expect much dancing in the ghetto streets," Raspberry advised. Weaver later described the bill as "just about as good an act as we could have gotten. . . . If it had been any better and had more teeth in it as some wanted to see, we wouldn't have had a chance of getting it through." The fact was, he had concluded, that most American still did not support open occupancy.[45]

By 1968 many activists were tiring of the traditional legal approach to equality. Increasingly, they were focusing on economic issues and disregarding the goal of racial integration. Soon after Johnson signed the bill, Rev. Ralph Abernathy, King's successor in the Southern Christian Leadership Conference (SCLC), arrived in Washington to lead the "Poor People's Campaign." The group, which King had organized before his death, planned a series of protests to demand greater federal assistance to the poor in housing, education, and job training. For weeks, hundreds of protestors from around the country lived in a "tent city" near the Capitol to bring attention to the needs of the poor. Abernathy told congressional leaders that their requests were more important than laws providing theoretical access to neighborhoods that the poor could not afford.[46]

The White House sent Weaver as its representative, and he received a tongue-lashing. The protestors demanded more money for housing, greater involvement of the poor in urban planning, and requirements that poor people be hired to work on federally funded construction projects. They claimed that Weaver had failed to promote the interests of the poor during his term as HUD secretary. One member of the group, Colleen Buckley of Columbus, Ohio, told Weaver, "if you can't do the job, quit and give it to someone who can." SCLC leader Jesse Jackson was somewhat more reserved in his statement. He told Weaver that "this is the only time I ever wished it was a white man that had the job." Jackson wanted to "pitch a bitch, but you're black too, and you're in a bind," he told Weaver. Weaver told the group that he agreed with their requests but that it was Congress that would determine how much he could do. In the end, the Poor People's Campaign received much press but produced few results. It did, however, highlight once again the increasing dissatisfaction with old methods and their administrators.[47]

During any other year, the passage of the Fair Housing Act would have been seen as a dramatic step forward in the nation's race relations. After all, it was only seven years since President Kennedy concluded that issuing a limited directive prohibiting discrimination in a small part of federal housing programs—a regulation pertaining to a fraction of the housing covered by the 1968 law—was not possible. The act provided powers of a magnitude many times what was considered feasible at the beginning of the decade and signified that the federal government was behind African Americans in their efforts to live wherever they chose. However, 1968 was not any year. By the time the bill was passed, few people felt it provided much of an answer to the racial problems that beset the nation.

A MONTH AFTER Lyndon Johnson signed the Fair Housing Act, Weaver achieved what he viewed as an equally important victory: the passage of the largest federal housing bill in a generation. At any other time, the passage of the Housing and Urban Development Act, which represented the most sophisticated attempt of the federal government to deal with both city and suburban problems, would have been hailed by liberals as a landmark in urban policy. But Weaver's success was muted by the nation's changing social climate. By the end of the year, he would depart Washington with mixed feelings about the future of American cities.

Technically, the law emerged from the efforts of several groups the president organized to think of new housing programs, but Weaver was responsible for putting it together. Much of the bill was similar to the proposals made by Senators Percy and Kennedy that Weaver had previously criticized. After meeting with several policymakers and constituent groups, Weaver and his staff proposed a major expansion of existing urban development programs and several new ones. Recognizing the continuing opposition to integrated housing, Weaver's proposals focused on housing production. "The basic economic, political and social forces at work to produce and intensify economic/racial segregation are powerful," he argued, and asserted that "early reversal of the trend is too much to expect with realism." Instead, while recognizing that progress toward racial integration remained "the principal goal," he recommended focusing on the "critical immediate need for reduction in the housing and social problems in inner-city areas." This was a major change in approach, but Weaver felt the times necessitated it. Large-scale racial integration, if it was going to occur, had to be done in the context of increased production of affordable housing and the revitalization of the inner city. To accomplish this, Weaver proposed to immediately double the funding for affordable housing and to set a goal of producing 500,000 units a year during the 1970s. According to the plan, the federal government would support the construction of 600,000 units of public housing and 400,000 units of rent-subsidized housing in the next four years, almost three times the amount produced in the preceding four years.[48]

In addition to these new housing programs, Weaver asked for substantial increases in funding for the urban renewal and Model Cities programs. Finally, accepting the political pressures for homeownership, he proposed a program to subsidize the purchase of homes by low-income persons. Weaver stated that the approach "cannot, and should not, be a universal goal" and that many people would need counseling and preparation before they would be ready to buy a house. He further claimed that the homeownership program would be risky and recommended that the federal government set aside funds to protect the government from inevitable losses. Nevertheless, he favored giving the idea a try.[49]

Since 1966, Johnson had been increasingly concerned about the expanding federal deficit, pushing his staff to cut programs where possible. With the continuing military expansion in Vietnam, the budget situation had not improved by 1968, but Johnson, like others, was greatly disturbed by the riots the previous summer, and he decided to support Weaver's proposals. In early 1968, Johnson stated that he was going to call for major increases in funding for federal housing programs, announcing a goal of producing six million units of low- and moderate-income housing over the next decade. Johnson's decision to recommend a major new program was made easier by the fact that, since his proposals were to authorize increased funding in the future, they would not have major budgetary impacts for at least a couple of years. Johnson could therefore make sweeping proposals without having to deal with the financial consequences immediately.[50]

In late February, Johnson presented his program, stating that "today, America's cities are in crisis," a crisis that was decades in the making but had to be dealt with immediately. "There is no time to lose," Johnson claimed. He recommended an increase in funding for his antipoverty programs and proposed the Housing and Urban Development Act of 1968, a $4.6 billion bill that included all of Weaver's proposals. The response to Johnson's message was overwhelmingly positive.

Liberals who had previously claimed that Johnson scrimped on urban programs celebrated the program, and conservatives, somewhat chastened by the riots, were more muted in their opposition than they had been in the past. The mayor of Philadelphia, James Tate, representing the U.S. Conference of Mayors, argued that the bill would "open a new era" and "permit us to reach the goal which we have so long sought." One member of Congress argued that "the question is no longer should we. It is simply how can we. And today the President has proposed an answer." Even lobby groups that generally opposed Johnson's initiatives, such as the National Association of Real Estate Boards, supported the plan. One of the few in Congress to aggressively attack the bill was Senator Robert Kennedy, who argued that the initiative would not produce as much housing as his own proposals.[51]

Few people in the administration or outside believed that the nation's housing industry could produce this amount of housing without radical changes in its structure. But the announcement fit Johnson's political approach: to make bold pronouncements that established a framework for action even if the proposed goals could not be fully achieved. The large expenditures envisioned by the bill seemed relatively reasonable when compared to those recommended by the Kerner commission, which released its report a short time after Johnson's special message. While the members of the riot commission did not put a price tag on their recommendations, their proposals, which mirrored the administration's in the housing area but called for even greater funding, would have cost many times what the president recommended. In contrast to Johnson's proposals in previous years, the bill, with Weaver as the lead lobbyist, sailed through both houses.[52]

On 1 August President Johnson signed the Housing and Urban Development Act at a ceremony in front of HUD's new headquarters. Johnson called the act a "Magna Carta to liberate our cities" that was "vast in scope and in promise." Singling out Weaver for his role in the bill's passage, Johnson stated: "I believe that history will mark this first day of August 1968, as the day and the time and the moment when farsighted people turned the clock ahead, setting the hands of progress to the tempo of man's racing needs." Weaver said the act would provide "a new sense of excitement and optimism that we can solve the massive urban problems that have plagued us for so long."[53]

The achievement, however, was tempered for both Johnson and Weaver because both knew that they would not be around to see the law implemented. In March, Johnson, under assault from all sides because of the Vietnam War and domestic turmoil and reeling from the strong showing by Eugene McCarthy in the New Hampshire Democratic primary, had decided not to run for reelection. At the end of a national television address that was advertised as a report on the conflict in Vietnam, Johnson shocked the nation by stating, "I shall not seek, and I will not accept, the nomination of my party for another term as your President." Johnson said that he did not want "the presidency to become involved in the partisan divisions" that were developing, and that he thought he could serve the country better in this period of turmoil by withdrawing from the race.[54]

Like the rest of the cabinet, Weaver was not informed of the decision until the president began his speech. That night, he sent Johnson a note telling him the speech was "inspired by deep patriotism and selflessness," but hoping "that events of the next four months will modify your decision." Weaver concluded the note by stating that he and his staff pledged their "loyalty and devotion to you." But Weaver had informed Johnson of a similar decision just two weeks before. In early March, Weaver told the president that he planned to resign after the fall elections, no matter who was in office. Weaver said that he was interested in taking a job as president of a newly formed division of the City University of New York named Bernard M. Baruch College.[55]

Weaver later recollected that he resigned because he had "run out of gas. . . . I got that one indication that is almost foolproof, and that was I found myself becoming very defensive. I found myself becoming very sensitive to criticism, and as soon as anyone criticized anything I was doing, immediately trying to hit back in my own mind. And I think when that happens, you are beginning to lose some degree of your objectivity." He wanted to relieve the president of the decision whether to reappoint him and to relieve himself of worry about that decision. In addition, he said he had promised Ella, who had retired the year before because of health problems, that he would leave the job at the end of Johnson's term.[56]

Weaver's friend Frank Horne tried to talk him out of the decision. "The more I think of the idea, the less I like it," he wrote Weaver in April. Granting that Weaver had "been through the meat grinder" and deserved to move into academia or become a high-priced consultant, Horne argued that "the next four years will certainly be fast-moving in the field of race relations" and would be "crucial to the direction and temper of the next several decades." Horne reminded Weaver that "for the first time in your professional life you have the backing of law to attempt and actually to do some of the things we had the audacity to dream about thirty years ago."[57]

But Weaver was anxious to pursue new opportunities New York. In May, after he was formally offered the job and word began to leak out, he asked the president if it would be acceptable for university officials to announce his hiring. On 14 May Weaver told reporters that he planned to resign after the November elections, saying that "new blood is needed in this post." A day later, CUNY officials announced his appointment, which would not begin until January 1969.[58]

Before leaving, Weaver experienced a few more victories and several defeats. In September, HUD staff celebrated the opening of their new office building. Constructed in the southwest DC redevelopment area, the ten-story, $26 million building was described by *New York Times* architecture critic Ada Louise Huxtable as a "handsome, functional structure that adds quality design and genuine 20th century style to a city badly in need of both." Weaver called the building, which was designed in double-Y form, "not only urban but urbane . . . useful but graceful . . . practical but also experimental and innovative." The president stated that it was "bold and beautiful."[59]

But Weaver also saw his two major legislative achievements decimated by fiscal conservatives in the House, who drastically cut the appropriations for Model Cities, urban renewal, and other housing programs. Working out of the spotlight, Republicans and southern Democrats on the House Appropriations Committee used their power to curtail funding for the initiatives that were the center of Johnson's urban agenda. Weaver also had to fight to save the fair-housing program from irrelevance after the House eliminated all funding to administer the law. Weaver requested $11 million to hire the 850 people he said were needed to staff fair-housing offices across the country, but the House Appropriations Committee refused the request. "Without manpower, the fair housing legislation is a meaningless gesture," Weaver told reporters. In the end, he had to settle for a $2 million allocation. The cuts meant that the agency could not adequately investigate or mediate claims of discrimination, which would have significant implications for the success of the program.[60]

When asked to discuss the accomplishments of his administration, Weaver said that one of the things he was most proud of was his organization of the new department. He also mentioned his efforts to end discrimination within federal housing programs and the creation of the Model Cities program. Weaver asserted that his administration had "laid a substantial foundation on which to build for the future" but acknowledged that "obviously we haven't solved the urban problem nor have we solved the housing problem." Among the most pressing problems were the need to have an effective land policy and the problems that arose from the localized nature of American government. Many of the problems facing urban areas, he argued, could not be solved by the federal government even if it wanted to intervene.[61]

On 21 December eight hundred people gathered at the Washington Hilton to celebrate the accomplishments of Robert Clifton Weaver. Chaired by former HEW secretary John Gardner, the Weaver Testimonial Committee included almost fifty members of the nation's political, civil rights, and business elite, including Roy Wilkins, Whitney Young, Walter Reuther, General Motors head Arjay Miller, Senator John Sparkman, Congressman Wright Patman, and Edgar Kaiser. Johnson sent a note to be read at the ceremony stating, "Our esteem and affection for you is second to none. And our gratitude for your loyalty and devotion to duty can never be fully repaid." At the dinner, Joe Califano praised Weaver as "a scholar of the American city," and argued that "we are approaching the turn of the tide in our cities because Bob Weaver has led us to this point with a touch of greatness." Gardner stated that Weaver had served with "great distinction." Weaver responded that "it has been a rewarding experience, one that I will always cherish."[62]

Accepting Weaver's formal resignation in December, Johnson wrote him that "because they change old relationships and ways of doing things, people who break new ground are often unpopular with many of their fellow men. It is a tremendous tribute to you Bob that you have made great strides and changed a lot of those old relationships while maintaining the respect and affection of those with whom you dealt and worked." Johnson told Weaver that he appreciated "your humanity, your integrity, your extremely hard work, and your unflappability."[63]

Weaver presided over HUD during one of the nation's most tumultuous periods. Although the era is remembered as one of urban decline and violence, in terms of legislation Weaver's tenure oversaw the passage of more laws regarding the issues under his purview—housing production and antidiscrimination—than any period before or since. More affordable housing was built under the Housing and Urban Development Act of 1968 than under any other federal law. The fair-housing law, although it still has many critics who say it exceeds federal authority and others who call it toothless, was a major step forward in the battle against discrimination and has a daily impact on this nation. Weaver's longtime friend Mary Washington argues that the bill is Weaver's "greatest legacy. To see every day in the newspapers, wherever you are across the country 'Equal Housing,' it gives me chills to know how momentous that legislation was and how few people even know about it or who was responsible for it. That was the capstone of his career, to get that bill passed."[64]

Although Weaver was never one of Johnson's main confidants, he played an important role in major administration discussions. The crisis of the cities was one of the country's most crucial domestic issues, and Weaver was the point man. "We put an awful lot on his back on the model cities legislation. I'm constantly calling him saying go see this Congressman," Johnson aide Joseph Califano recollected. "He was under a lot of pressure." With regard to Weaver's marginal role in other civil rights issues, Califano concluded, "I don't think he was excluding Weaver—most of these cabinet officers spent most of their time running their offices, and he had one of our gems, once we passed model cities we wanted something delivered, so he had a lot of pressure on him. . . . it's not like he's running some department that's some routine backwater." Roger Wilkins, who spent a lot of time in the White House as one of Johnson's main advisors on race relations, was direct about the criticisms of Weaver: "Word on the street was that he was weak, but this was created by white people. Many administration people lived lily-white lives and did not personally believe in black achievement."[65]

His former colleagues praised Weaver's efforts. "I think, all things considered, he did a good job. I don't think anyone could have done a better job," Califano concluded. Edward Lashman, who as head of liaison with Congress for Weaver spent a great deal of time with the secretary, was also complimentary. "Weaver was a very sophisticated guy. He was not surprised and not overwhelmed by the job. How can we get these things going was the focus, not the complaints of some protestors." According to Lashman, "Weaver didn't pick fights he didn't need to or if he didn't think he could win. His talent was his ability to work with people and see them change without losing face. He was able to help people to see that change was not only advantageous to the organization but to the individuals." Weaver's personality was charming and unthreatening, and as a result, he got along with Congress well. "He was comfortable working with the Dixies and understood their limitations," Lashman concluded. "He was also a really decent guy, just straight, there was nothing devious about him, we were always on the same page, you got what you saw . . . that's important because I can compare him to a lot of other people in the administration," Califano added.[66]

* 17 *

# An Elder Statesman in a Period of Turmoil

Like the administration in general, Weaver limped out of Washington. He was pleased with the progress they had made, frustrated that Congress had continued to curtail his initiatives through funding cuts, and, most of all, happy to be finished with the overwhelming pressures of running an agency in that difficult period. He was also delighted to return to New York City, if not to the job that awaited him. It was clear to his friends that the presidency of Baruch College would not have been his first choice had he other options. But the job offers that at least some cabinet secretaries had come to expect upon leaving federal service were not there for Weaver.

In January 1969, Weaver returned to New York to stay. He would live in the city for the next twenty-eight years, until his death, and would continue to contribute his time and knowledge to solving urban and racial problems. During the 1970s, Weaver would lead a major public institution through a formative period in the history of American universities, and he would serve on the boards of numerous public and private organizations, most importantly the Municipal Assistance Corporation, the entity created to bring the city back from the brink of financial collapse. Throughout the decade, one that was an economic and social disaster for American cities in general (and New York in particular), Weaver would witness the scaling back or elimination of many of the initiatives he had promoted. Despite these travails, Weaver would remain optimistic about the future of cities and of African Americans. Others, however, would not agree, and Weaver would find himself, as well as his approaches to these issues, increasingly marginalized in American politics.

ALTHOUGH THE INSTITUTION he was chosen to lead had been established decades earlier, Weaver was the first president of Bernard M. Baruch College. Since its creation in 1919, the school, originally known as the City College School of Business, had been the neglected stepchild of its prestigious affiliate, the City College of New York. Weaver arrived at a crucial moment for the school, its initial period of independence in the newly created City University of New York (CUNY) system. The short period Weaver served was a time when Baruch was just establishing itself as a separate school. Among his many tasks were to figure out how the school would balance the demands of business school training with the desire to prepare students in the liberal arts; to establish a separate identity from City College and to compete with the other CUNY schools for the best students; to create an administrative infrastructure for the new school; and to deal with the increasing agitation by students for greater influence over the institution. Although he was promised full support from the officials who hired him, Weaver faced these challenges in a period of economic instability and budgetary restrictions. After eighteen eventful months on the job, a period in which he would endure several student-sits, city-wide school protests, and complaints from faculty, Weaver would resign his position.

Until 1968, Baruch College was a subsidiary of the City College of New York. Founded as the Free Academy in 1847 for the education of the sons of clerks and foremen, City College has a rightfully earned illustrious place in the history of New York City. Known by many New Yorkers as the "proletarian Harvard," over the years, City College produced a substantial portion of the city's business, political, and cultural leaders. The list of famous graduates includes Supreme Court Justice Felix Frankfurter, composer Ira Gershwin, and Secretary of State Colin Powell in addition to seven Nobel Prize laureates. Particularly during the first decades of the twentieth century, when few elite colleges admitted the children of immigrants, City College served as an institution of upward mobility for tens of thousands of New Yorkers.[1]

During the 1800s, students studied a classical curriculum of Latin, history, mathematics, and philosophy. However, at the turn of the century, as New York cemented its place as the nation's financial and business center, City College administrators began to offer training to the swelling number of managers, clerks, and other professionals who were becoming the backbone of the city's middle class. In 1919, after decades of discussion, the Board of Trustees announced the creation of the School of Business and Civic Administration. Immediately popular among the thousands of

New Yorkers working in the city's financial sector, the school, which occupied a building at Twenty-third and Lexington, quickly overflowed with students taking courses in accounting, economics, management, and the liberal arts. From the beginning, the school's status was inferior to the rest of City College, whose main campus was located on St. Nicholas Terrace in northern Manhattan. It struggled to secure resources for construction, to hire new teachers, and to serve the tens of thousands of students who entered its doors.[2]

After ten years in a building where many floors lacked heat or water, in 1929 faculty and students celebrated the opening of a new, eight-story building on Twenty-third Street, but it was almost immediately inadequate to serve the growing school population. Throughout the 1930s, 1940s, and 1950s, faculty and students pressed City College administrators to expand the school's facilities, but several plans never got off the drawing board. In 1953, hoping to increase the school's prestige, administrators decided to name the school the Bernard M. Baruch School of Business, honoring a City College graduate and financier who led the World War I mobilization. They hoped the decision might bring financial support from Baruch, who was then in his eighties, but the efforts to secure money for new facilities proved futile. However, in 1961, when the state approved the merger of several New York City schools, including Hunter and John Jay Colleges, into the City University of New York system, many people believed that a new campus would soon be a reality for Baruch.[3]

Throughout the decade, administrators discussed plans for a new campus, none of which came to fruition. At the same time, Baruch officials did achieve greater independence. After several years of study and discussion, in 1967 the CUNY trustees agreed to separate Baruch from City College. Instead of being run by administrators 150 blocks to the north, the college would have its own president, its schools (Business, Liberal Arts, and Public Administration) would have their own deans, and the departments, many of which had previously been appendages of their counterparts at City College, their own heads. The plan also called for the construction of a new campus in Brooklyn, selected at the behest of local politicians hoping to use the new campus to jump-start the revitalization of the area.[4]

Having agreed to separate Baruch from City College, the next task facing CUNY administrators was to find a president for the new school. Most faculty and students expected them to choose Dean Emmanuel Saxe, who had been the school's leader for a decade and had played a major role in the school's growth. But city officials wanted the appointment to make a dramatic statement about the CUNY system. The crucial person behind Weaver's appointment was Julius Edelstein, a man who spent his career as a behind-the-scenes power broker in New York City and national Democratic politics. After serving as a journalist in World War II, Edelstein became advisor to Presidents Roosevelt and Truman. In the 1950s, he took on a series of jobs in New York City, eventually becoming Mayor Robert Wagner's primary policy and political advisor. Weaver had known Edelstein for more than two decades, and Edelstein had frequently recruited him for government jobs, including the urban renewal position Weaver held in 1960. Aware that he was interested in resettling in New York, Edelstein pressed CUNY officials to offer Weaver the job of Baruch College president.[5]

When he announced Weaver's appointment on 15 May 1968, Porter Chandler, chair of the Board of Higher Education (which oversaw the CUNY system), stated that "Secretary Weaver's acceptance symbolizes the emerging role of the university as a vital resource in the solution of our nation's urban problems." Weaver stated that he envisioned "an institution which will become the prototype of the urban university as an idea-generation and action-implementation center for meeting the paramount domestic challenge of our time." He said that the opportunity to create a new college campus was what drew him to the job, because it gave him the chance to use "novel concepts" and to "mold, with others, an institution of higher education."[6]

The release announcing Weaver's appointment emphasized that the school would focus on solving urban problems through its business, public administration, and city-planning programs. According to CUNY leaders, there would be "an emphasis on community relations and economic development," and the school would, "from its inception, place special emphasis upon expanding educational and professional opportunities for the city's minority population." The statement, which tacitly acknowledged the widespread criticism that CUNY schools had not well served the city's black and Latino students, also put Weaver at a disadvantage with his constituents. Although he was more than qualified for the position, many faculty and students believed that he had been appointed primarily because of his race.[7]

Although Weaver accepted the job in May 1968, he would not take office until the Johnson administration ended in January 1969. According to Baruch historian and former faculty member Selma Berrol, Weaver "was not a popular choice" among the faculty and students, and he did not endear himself to them during the months that followed. Between his appointment and the time he actually took office six months later, Weaver appeared on campus only a couple of times. He briefly attended the first faculty meeting of the new college in September, but he did not actively participate in the discussions, leading many to question his interest in the job. Many faculty members believed that Weaver would not assume the presidency if Vice President Hubert Humphrey was elected president, and several felt that he "might not have accepted the appointment in good faith." Whether or not he intended to stay in DC, which appears unlikely, Weaver's continued work at HUD left the school without a leader during its formative stages. When Weaver arrived in January, problems were already emerging regarding the school's share of the CUNY budget, the reorganization of the schools and faculty, and the role of the students in the administration. Weaver, exhausted from several years of nonstop work and stress, began his term in a difficult position and would struggle to gain the confidence of the faculty and students.[8]

Although Weaver, as always, downplayed his race in his dealings with Baruch constituents, one of his first tasks as president was dealing with complaints about the marginalization of black students on campus. Across the country, student demands for a "relevant" college experience increasingly focused on the inclusion of African American, Latino, and feminist studies in the classroom. The number of black students at Baruch was extremely small (only 120 out of 2,600 day students), but this did not prevent them from making their voices heard. Less than two months after he took office, Weaver experienced his first sit-in, as more than a dozen African American students took over his office. Calling themselves the Society of Koromantee, they demanded the development of an African studies program at the school and the hiring of specialists in this area. Weaver called their requests "fairly reasonable" but said that he was limited in what he could do by a budget situation that was "horrible." Although the students left mollified for the short term, it was not an auspicious start for the new administrator.[9]

Among Weaver's first administrative tasks was organizing the schools and hiring deans to manage them. In the spring of 1969, he hired several new staff, including a dean of students, and appointed a dean of the School of Liberal Arts. At the same time, he oversaw the appointment of dozens of new faculty members—122 new scholars joined the faculty between 1968 and 1972—particularly in the liberal arts. In addition to overseeing the reorganization of the schools, Weaver and his staff worked to increase student satisfaction. Historically, a substantial portion of Baruch students held full-time jobs and fit classes in between other obligations, but the number of students whose primary occupation was academia increased during the 1960s. This led to demands for greater focus on "student life," and Weaver increased support for student organizations and programs.[10]

During his years at HUD, Weaver was a frequent commencement speaker, and he always discussed the issue of campus unrest. While arguing that students should not run universities, Weaver agreed that it was appropriate for students to participate in major decisions at their schools. In the spring of 1969, Weaver canceled all scheduled activities for a program named Rights and Responsibilities Day. The purpose of the event was to initiate a conversation among faculty, staff, and students about the appropriate mechanisms for student participation. Weaver posed the following questions, among others, for discussion: What is the function of a college? Should it be predominantly a center for teaching and learning, a center for research, an instrument for social change, or a center for some other purpose? Another goal of the day was to discuss the "soundest machinery for decision-making in the College" and to explore the question of who should participate in the process. Finally, Weaver asked students to consider "what are the acceptable methods and tactics for bringing about changes in the policies and practices of the College," and "what should be the policy on breaches of College rules?" Through these discussions, Weaver sought to channel student protest in productive ways and to establish procedures to "assure fair and healthy controversy where differences exist." Throughout the year, he met with student leaders and groups and held "fireside chats" for students.[11]

At the June 1969 commencement, Weaver claimed several achievements, including the reorganization of the business curriculum and the establishment of several faculty/student committees. He stated that the college had "laid the foundations of a strong tradition of student participation in decision-making . . . without confrontation but through understanding and cooperation." Although Weaver might have believed that his approach was successful in preventing the protest that plagued other campuses, he would soon be proven wrong. Conflict at Baruch would not approach the ferocity of that at many other campuses across the nation in this turbulent period, but during the spring of 1970 the campus would be closed for more than a week as the result of student strikes. Weaver would manage these protests with more tact and success than many other university presidents, but the conflict would contribute to his decision to resign his post.[12]

Although the protests at other schools focused frequently on opposition to the war in Vietnam and philosophical concerns about the state of higher education, at Baruch the issues were more prosaic. Students were certainly worried about international and domestic affairs, but what caused them to walk out was the decision by Chancellor Albert Bowker to raise the fees they paid to the school. Since 1847, what most distinguished City College from other institutions was that it was free, and this was, to many New Yorkers, sacrosanct. Throughout the 1960s, as education budgets at the city and state level grew, increasing numbers of politicians and administrators called for requiring students at CUNY institutions to pay tuition at a level similar to that charged by the state system, but all such proposals met with stiff resistance. As an alternative, administrators began to charge student "fees" for athletics and recreation. In the spring of 1970, Bowker proposed to increase student fees from $60 to $110 a semester.[13]

In response, on 16 April 1970, at the same time students at Columbia University were attempting to shut down the school to protest the university's involvement in military research and the oppression of black Harlem, and students at New York University were protesting to support union efforts among the staff, students at several CUNY schools, including Queens College, Hunter College, and Baruch, went on strike. The grievances varied across CUNY schools, but at Baruch the two big issues were the lack of maintenance in the building and the student fees. That afternoon, more than a hundred students sat down in the lobby, blocking the elevators that led to classrooms and beginning a generally peaceful protest that would last for several days. Adopting and amending a favorite slogan of the period, protestors chanted "Hey, Hey, BHE [Bureau of Higher Education], how many times you're gonna raise our fee?" After several hours of negotiation, Weaver ordered classes canceled for the day. Although he was angry that the students forced him to cancel classes, Weaver agreed with the protestors' complaints. He immediately issued a statement saying that he was "in complete sympathy with student opposition to proposed increases in student fees" and that fee increases should be a last resort and vowing to "fight to see the increases are kept as small as possible." Student leaders called Weaver's response tepid and claimed that he "hemmed and hawed" when asked to support their efforts with CUNY leadership. "Once again Bobby boy has used his office as something to hide behind," the editors of the student newspaper charged.[14]

The protests, which were generally calm and well behaved, forced the cancellation of class for the rest of the week. Although Weaver met with student leaders frequently, he was not able to convince them to call off the action. Early the next week the strike subsided, eased by the Passover holiday that canceled classes for Tuesday and Wednesday. By Thursday, classes were back in session but sparsely attended. A week later, after a CUNY-wide protest that failed to convince the chancellor to rescind the fee increase, the student protestors were back in class, and they and their classmates were most concerned with how they would be graded for the semester. Weaver convened a faculty/student committee that agreed that students would not be punished. A week later, faculty, staff, and students joined Weaver in a memorial service for the four students murdered at Kent State University in Ohio. After that incident, the upheaval at Baruch seemed mild in comparison. Weaver later argued that "a lot of wasted motion and energy, not to mention patience and goodwill, could have been saved if the protestors had known . . . what the President could act upon" and what he could not. Though weary from two weeks of constant pressure, Weaver reported with pride that "we have not had any violence or serious vandalism."[15]

But the conflict took its toll on Weaver, who decided to resign his position. On 9 June Weaver gave the commencement address at his own school. In his short remarks, he took the opportunity to reflect on how the conflict at Baruch fit into the larger turmoil facing American society. "This era of college life is replete with uncertainties, and we at Baruch experienced ours this spring," he began. What had occurred at Baruch, he asserted, was "but a phase of what is happening in society." Although he did not agree with all of the tactics of student protesters, the "grave social issues"—among them the immorality of the conflict in Vietnam, racial discrimination, environmental degradation, and continuing poverty—the protestors were raising were real. "It would be folly to try to justify inaction and inarticulateness because the champions of change seem often to go about it in unacceptable ways." But it was not enough for protestors to complain. "They must also propose alternative values and institutions. It is not enough to criticize what exists: to warrant support one must also propose viable substitute patterns." And, he continued, while he believed that students had an important role to play in the management of the university, they were not qualified to run the institution. "If college students have the capacity to determine what should be taught and who should teach it, they are miscast as students."[16]

In the end, Weaver challenged the graduates to "question values and institutions" and "resist the temptation to believe that you can avoid the difficult, unfamiliar, and, at times unpleasant." The day was called commencement, he argued, because it was the beginning of their work. However, for Weaver, the day represented the end of his toil at Baruch. Less than two weeks later, he announced he was stepping down, effective 1 September. In his resignation letter, Weaver wrote that he had taken the job of building a new college. However, he felt that, "largely because of uncertainty and inadequacy of financing," he was unable to "make substantial progress toward this goal." Weaver called the funding for the college "inadequate" and concluded that the results of his work at Baruch were "not commensurate with the effort."[17]

To the Baruch community, Weaver wrote that "the past two years have had their frustrations and conflicts, but they have also had their stimulations and rewards." Although he felt that some progress had been made in creating a modern university, he stated, "I have come to the conclusion that for me to continue in office is to mislead all of you about the immediate prospects for dramatic improvement and growth in the college." Weaver's major concern was the failure of administrators to provide funding for the development of the Brooklyn campus. After more than a year of promises, Baruch still had no budget for the new buildings, and state and local officials cut the university's budget for the 1970 fiscal year. Weaver also feared that his budget was insufficient to prepare for the increase in the number of students that the college expected to follow the "Open Enrollment" initiative—the city's commitment to provide a postsecondary education to all New York City public school graduates. Although his announcement surprised many in the Baruch community, it did not shock the officials at the Bureau of Higher Education. The board's press release blandly stated, "We regret Dr. Weaver's resignation and understand the reasons that prompted it." Chancellor Bowker, however, called his departure "a profound loss."[18]

Weaver's friends were not surprised by his decision. "He was not interested in going to Baruch," remembered HUD colleague Mary Washington. "He knew he wouldn't be there long." According to former HUD official Edward Lashman, Weaver was "initially pleased and flattered with the Baruch offer," but he was frustrated with the administration. "He wasn't cut out for wiping professors' noses and students' asses," Lashman concluded. Although Weaver was frustrated by the slow pace of progress at Baruch, he did leave a legacy of new faculty hires, expansion of programs for minorities, and an invigorated administration. In addition, although the hope for a new campus did not come to fruition (thirty years later, the college would open a new "vertical campus" two blocks from the original building), the college did expand its facilities. One faculty member called these efforts major achievements "unappreciated by a man whose academic life had been spent at Harvard."[19]

STRUGGLING TO MANAGE a campus in turmoil, Weaver did not have the time to actively participate in the debates over federal urban policy, but he worried greatly about the changes that the new Republican administration was adopting. After squeaking to victory over Vice President Hubert Humphrey, Richard Nixon spent much of his early term struggling to craft a policy toward cities, which continued to be troubled by violence, deterioration, and economic turmoil. An expert in foreign affairs, Nixon had never shown much interest in questions of housing, race relations, or the other major aspects of domestic policy. The continued decline and increasing racial animosity within American cities, however, prevented him from ignoring these questions. By the end of Nixon's presidency in 1974, the federal government's approach to race relations and urban troubles would dramatically differ from the approach being pursued when Weaver left Washington, and many of the programs Weaver created would be eliminated. That even few Democrats opposed these changes was a stunning rebuke to Weaver and the other veterans of the Great Society.[20]

To replace Weaver at HUD, Nixon chose his former presidential rival George Romney. A wealthy businessman, Romney was a moderate "Rockefeller Republican" who had served as Michigan's governor during the 1960s. While frequently arguing for local solutions to urban problems, Romney also believed that the federal government should play an active role in rebuilding urban areas and in opening up the suburbs to minorities. Nixon, however, had different ideas about the federal government's role in these issues. In his 1968 campaign, Nixon promised to return power to the states and cities, a philosophy he referred to as "New Federalism." In the first year of his term, Nixon spoke frequently about the "bureaucratic monstrosity, cumbersome, unresponsive, ineffective," that Washington had become, and HUD was a primary target. In a television address on 8 August 1969, Nixon assailed the main tenets of liberalism that had infused government policy from the New Deal through the Great Society. "A third of a century of social experimentation has left us a legacy of entrenched programs that have outlived their time or outgrown their purposes," he claimed. The time had come, Nixon argued, for "a New Federalism in which power, funds, and responsibility will flow from Washington to the States and to the people."[21]

While the administration pushed its proposals to eliminate initiatives such as Model Cities, Democrats, who still held a majority in Congress, worked to preserve Lyndon Johnson's agenda. In 1970, Congress reauthorized all of the existing programs and directed the president to develop an "urban growth policy." Observers believed that the president would veto the bill, but he signed it into law in January 1971. Romney tried to add additional programs to HUD's portfolio, particularly in the area of housing discrimination, and this led to increasing animosity between the secretary and the president. Spurred by a report of the U.S. Commission on Civil Rights that called for an end to "exclusionary zoning," Romney and his staff argued that the administration should punish suburban communities that blocked low-income housing. Nixon, seeing a direct conflict with his "suburban strategy," an effort to entrench the Republican Party in these areas, rejected the idea.[22]

Romney's efforts to expand HUD's influence were also hampered by problems within existing federal housing programs. In January 1971, Representative Wright Patman of Texas released a staff study exposing fraud and abuse in the home ownership program established by the Housing and Urban Development Act of 1968. Over the next few years, the scandals would become well-known and oft-repeated examples of the major flaws in the federal housing bureaucracy. In general, they involved collaborations of real estate speculators and corrupt home inspectors and appraisers who took advantage of unsophisticated homebuyers and lax housing officials. Often, these scandals occurred in neighborhoods that were in transition from white to black and/or Latino. A realtor would locate a dilapidated building and purchase it from owners wishing to vacate the neighborhood. The realtor would bring in a rehabilitation crew to do superficial repairs. Then, an appraiser would value the home at substantially more than it was worth and sell it to an unsuspecting buyer. All of these abuses were ignored by FHA officials, who felt pressure to implement the program. The result was that the homebuyer would quickly face a large expense for repairs that he or she could not afford. Often, the house would be abandoned, leaving it to the FHA in foreclosure. The federal government suffered the financial losses, along with the homeowners, and the neighborhoods faced the problems that came with increasing vacancies.[23]

Faced with increasing reports of abuse and corruption, even supporters like Representative Thomas Ashley (D-WI) remarked, "It looks like we passed some bad legislation." The complaints coincided with the continued decline of many cities. In New York, for example, public officials called the situation evidence that American civilization was in decline. Across the country, neighborhoods continued to deteriorate, crime continued to increase, and families departed for the suburbs. Even though these problems were years in the making, many people blamed Lyndon Johnson's programs for the crisis. In response to the mounting evidence of problems in federal housing programs, Romney and Nixon decided to freeze funding for housing construction, drawing withering criticism from Democrats. However, in the midst of the scandal and continued and dramatic urban decline, HUD found few supporters. Although the problems involved the laws that he had worked so hard to promote, Weaver refrained from making any public statements during the controversy.[24]

In January 1973, Nixon's State of the Union address reemphasized his commitment to returning power to the states and building "self-reliance" in local governments. "Abroad and at home, the time has come to turn away from the condescending policies of paternalism," Nixon declared. Later in the month, Nixon stated that his officials would cease accepting applications for urban development grants and instead use these funds for a "revenue-sharing" program that would allow states and local governments to spend the money without federal oversight. Under his proposal, HUD would be drastically reduced in authority. "The time has come to reject the patronizing notion that Federal planners, peering over the point of a pencil in Washington, can guide your lives better than you can," Nixon argued.[25]

After more than two years of attacks on the programs that he had created, in February 1974, Weaver ended his self-imposed public silence and criticized Nixon's proposals. In a speech to the Mortgage Bankers of America, Weaver argued that Nixon had "distorted" the programs' performance "to justify their suspension." Weaver went on to say, "Black Americans were seriously—and adversely—affected by the January 1973 moratorium and tens of thousands of blacks that might now have housing were denied it." He acknowledged that the initiatives were not "free from defects," and he asserted that such "new and complicated" programs were "sure to need constant evaluation and revision." The problems, Weaver claimed, were caused by an "unusually rapid build-up," "inept administration," and the constant reorganization of HUD, which led to "administrative chaos" and prevented officials from doing their jobs. Citing a report from the Brookings Institute, a Washington think tank, that concluded that the programs had "provided high quality housing for more than two million families," Weaver argued that they had done far more good than harm, and that the corruption could be avoided by better management. Furthermore, he claimed, the programs had achieved one of their main goals, enabling more African Americans to move to the suburbs.[26]

Weaver's defense fell on deaf ears on Capitol Hill. Later that month, the Senate approved a bill that eliminated almost all federal housing initiatives and merged them into one grant program. The Senate debate revealed how little support remained for active federal direction of urban development. Senator Hubert Humphrey, as vice president one of the strongest supporters of Model Cities and other Great Society initiatives, argued that the new program would "give cities a new flexibility and responsibility in community development matters, one long overdue." While several senators criticized the Nixon's moratorium, none supported the continuation of the Model Cities program or other Johnson initiatives.[27]

In the House, a few representatives expressed reservations over this major change in federal policy. Congressman Ralph Metcalf (D-IL) argued that the Model Cities program had been of "tremendous benefit to Chicago and to other major cities in the country." Congressman Parren Mitchell (D-MD) argued that the legislation was "exclusionary" and "punitive toward those cities that have made progress in the past." Other representatives worried about the removal of federal controls. "While local autonomy is very important," Congressman Donald Fraser (D-MN) argued, "without some guidelines we run the risk of wasting part of the community development funds and failing to meet the most pressing needs in our urban areas." In the end, Congress passed the bill, eliminating almost all of the programs Weaver had struggled to create.[28]

Weaver did not testify on the bill, nor did he issue any public statements during the congressional debates over the proposal. Later that year, he criticized the act, claiming that "despite the rhetoric" it would be a failure. Weaver argued that turning over power to local governments would ensure that little affordable housing was built in the suburbs and would result in further economic and racial segregation. The act, he claimed, would be "less successful than its predecessors in promoting greater choice of housing opportunities and avoiding undue concentration of lower-income persons." A few years later, he argued that his predictions had come true: "Under the guise of returning the problem back to the people . . . which, we were told, knows best how to handle it, the Federal government was virtually relieved of its monitoring responsibilities for civil rights laws." The result was that many local governments had used the federal funds to prevent the construction of affordable housing instead of promoting it.[29]

The "Section 8" program and the Community Development Block Grant (CDBG) program enacted by the 1974 legislation were both ideas percolating during Weaver's years at HUD. Section 8, which provided funds to individuals to help them pay the rent for apartments that they had found for themselves, was presaged by the rent supplement program that Weaver had created in the mid-1960s, and the CDBG program was similar to programs promoted by Senator Robert Kennedy and others during the 1960s. Over the thirty years following their enactment, both would be responsible for the rehabilitation of vacant housing and the construction of new units of affordable housing. They would serve millions of poor Americans and greatly assist the revitalization of many struggling neighborhoods. At the same time, the 1974 act was responsible for substantially weakening HUD as an agency. During the 1960s, Weaver and other policymakers debated how much of a role the federal government should play in helping cities rebuild and urban areas manage the problems of growth. They never resolved the question, and in 1974 Congress gave up trying. Though HUD would continue to exist, it would never recover the influence that it had during the decade after it was created.

SINCE HE WAS one of the creators of much of the legislation that Congress eliminated, it is not surprising that Weaver was a marginal participant in the debates over national urban policy during the early 1970s. His views, which were obviously biased in favor of the existing programs, were not very influential to politicians or the journalists that followed the issues. The fact that he had been a high-ranking official in an administration that, particularly in the early 1970s, was widely disparaged by members of both parties further increased his marginalization. However, Weaver had a seat at the table during the decade's most intense urban crisis: the near bankruptcy of New York City. As a member of the board of the Municipal Assistance Corporation (MAC), the state-chartered agency which helped the city finance its operations, Weaver was present when crucial decisions over the future of the nation's largest city were made. However, his actual influence was negligible, and he watched as the board, along with conservative ideologues at the local and federal level, attempted to dismantle the programs New York liberals had championed for decades, many of which were only starting to reach the African Americans Weaver was appointed to represent.[30]

By the early 1970s, the city's financial difficulties were decades old, but they escalated in the late 1960s. A number of factors—a dramatic decline in manufacturing jobs (600,000 lost between 1950 and 1980), a loss of 800,000 residents, and increased costs due to wage demands from city workers—all played a significant role. But the city was also caught in national and international trends over which it had no control. The federal budget deficits created by the twin obligations of financing the Vietnam War and expanding domestic programs caused inflation to skyrocket during these years, and the city's costs of borrowing increased dramatically. All of these factors created turmoil within the financial markets and put pressure on the nation's banks. These institutions were themselves under financial stress after a decade of uncontrolled and often irresponsible lending, much of it in real estate speculation and third-world development.[31]

During the 1960s, the city relied on short-term borrowing through municipal bonds to finance operations. By mid-1974, many banks and other investors, as a result of the city's financial insecurity, as well as their own financial problems, were reluctant to purchase these bonds. This placed the city in a crisis, as it had $3.4 billion in short-term debt and would need to borrow $5 billion in the next year to pay the bills. Throughout the rest of the year, local and state officials worked with leaders of major banks to stabilize the city's financial affairs. But lenders had little faith in the city's new mayor, Abraham Beame, an accountant who had been a stalwart of the Brooklyn Democratic machine for decades. Taking office in 1974, Beame spent most of the year denying that there was a problem and then promising to make budget cuts that never materialized.[32]

In the spring of 1975, with insolvency looming, the city's major financial leaders, including David Rockefeller of Chase Manhattan Bank, William Spencer of Citibank, and Ellmore Patterson of Morgan Guaranty, demanded measures to ensure the city's financial soundness. They met with Mayor Beame and told him that the city would need state and federal assistance to meet its obligations. While Beame and his administration struggled to respond to the crisis (his advances to President Gerald Ford for assistance from the federal treasury were abruptly rejected), the business leaders came up with their own plan, put together by Felix Rohatyn, an ebullient partner in the investment firm of Lazard Freres, who had come to be known as "Felix the Fixer" for his ability to broker deals among the country's business and political leaders. During Memorial Day weekend, Rohatyn met with several financial leaders at the Greenwich, Connecticut, home of Richard Shinn, president of Metropolitan Life Insurance Company (a major bond purchaser), and worked out a deal to create the MAC. Appointed head of that organization soon thereafter, for the next twenty years Rohatyn would be the public face of New York City's financial rehabilitation and would receive international praise and criticism for his efforts.[33]

The basic premise of the MAC was that the city could no longer secure loans from the private market on its own and needed the support of a more financially stable entity. The MAC was a state-chartered agency that issued long-term bonds and transferred the funds to the city to pay expenses. The bonds were "backed" with a guaranty from the state and repaid from city sales taxes. To ensure that the city was restored to financial integrity, the MAC could refuse to disburse the funds to the city until it believed that the city had a plan to balance the budget. The MAC board also had to approve all of the city's borrowing and had access to all city finances. In essence, in return for money, the city turned over much of its power to an unelected body.[34]

Under the law creating the MAC, the governor picked five members of the MAC board, and the mayor selected four. Although the MAC would be responsible for making decisions that affected all New Yorkers, very few aspects of that diverse melting pot were represented. The governor and mayor filled the board with representatives of the business elite, including Rohatyn, Thomas Flynn, a partner at Arthur Young and Company, William Ellinghaus, president of New York Telephone, and securities executives John Coleman and George Gould. Governor Hugh Carey selected the only African American on the board, Robert Weaver. Through his work as HUD secretary and as a board member of both New York Life Insurance and Bowery Savings Bank, Weaver was well known to New York's financial community. Between its creation and 1 September, the MAC board met, officially, nineteen times to plan for the sale of $1.5 billion in bonds and to press Mayor Beame for layoffs and budget cuts. Joined by Chase chairman David Rockefeller and other financial leaders who attended several MAC meetings, Rohatyn, Ellinghaus, and Flynn did most of the negotiating for the group. The other board members were mostly passive participants.[35]

Though necessary to right New York's financial ship, the MAC provided the framework for an assault on the governmental health, housing, and educational services that had distinguished New York from the rest of the country. Led by conservative ideologues like Nixon Treasury Secretary William Simon, those opposed to the "New York approach" to governance saw an opportunity to roll back the liberal state. Before coming to Washington, Simon headed the municipal bond division at Salomon Brothers and was a vocal critic of the city's governmental structure. He called the salaries of municipal workers "absurd" and their pensions "appalling," and he blamed New York liberals for imposing their "socialist" views on the rest of the country. The expanded federal government, he claimed, was based on the New York model, and it had negatively affected the nation's culture and economy.[36]

He was joined in this view by many members of Congress, who, according to *New York Times* writer Fred Ferreti, thought "the city was a haven for 'welfare cheats' (read that 'lazy niggers'), for people with an overabundance of chutzpah (read that 'Jew'), for 'minorities who want a free ride' (read that 'Puerto Ricans and other Hispanics'), for arrogant smart asses who don't give a damn about the rest of the country." Simon and others wanted to make an example of New York because of its excesses of liberalism. They took it on themselves to extract punishment for the city's deviant policies, and they pushed their agenda with the MAC leadership.[37]

The first institutions facing assault were CUNY and the mass transit system. The transit system was run by a regional authority (the Metropolitan Transportation Authority, or MTA), and an increase in fares, which federal officials demanded, would have no impact on the city's bottom line. The establishment of tuition at CUNY, as Mayor Beame told officials, would produce $34 million dollars a year when the city budget was in excess of $12 billion. These were symbolic efforts, Rohatyn acknowledged, but, he argued to the board, "an overkill was required, if for no other reason than the shock impact," because "it was apparent from what the banking community had said that the city's way of life is disliked nation-wide." During the summer, MAC officials pressured city leaders to increase the subway fare by 40 percent (from thirty-five to fifty cents) and to charge tuition equal to that charged by the state university system. They also got Beame to issue an across-the-board wage freeze on all municipal workers.[38]

If Weaver said anything about these cuts, which hit the poorest New Yorkers the hardest, it is not evident in the minutes of the MAC board or elsewhere. Several months later, he told African American state assemblyman Arthur O. Eve that "you may be sure" that "when and if specific issues affecting minorities come before MAC, I shall not hesitate to express my feelings and present what I believe to be the interests of those so long disadvantaged." But during the first year of MAC proceedings, no comments or complaints by Weaver are reflected in the minutes. According to journalists Jack Newfield and Paul DuBrul, who produced the first comprehensive assessment of the financial crisis, Weaver "proved to be a passive, acquiescing member of the new governing agency."[39]

Few people disputed that the city's books were unbalanced, but there were many ways to bring the budget back in line, including renegotiating some of the loans, which paid extremely high interest, with bankers. The city could have also focused the layoffs on the more than 5,000 political appointees, many of whom had highly-paid, no-show jobs. But the MAC board ignored other, less painful ways to restore the financial stability of the city. According to board member and future secretary of health and human services Donna Shalala, "there was tremendous pressure to get the Mayor to do something. . . . The process wasn't rational. There was possibly a half hour of discussion about raising the fare; that's all. There was never a set of staff papers prepared, so we could study it. We did no background work. We had no hard facts. That's the horror of it. We were just throwing together a list of things that might be cut."[40]

Despite the significant cuts and increased charges that the city implemented during the summer of 1975, the MAC still had difficulties selling its bonds on the private market. In the end, it had to rely on local banks and government pensions to purchase a majority of the notes. Private investors, according to brokers, were still skeptical about the mayor's ability to make the necessary reductions in the size of local government. With another round of financing necessary to stave off the city's default, Governor Carey again intervened, securing the passage of legislation that directed $2.3 billion in grants and loans to the city and created a new entity, the Emergency Financial Control Board (EFCB), to run the city's finances. The EFCB, which included the governor, the mayor, the state and city comptrollers, and three private-sector members (Rohatyn, Ellinghaus, and Colt Industries president David Margolis), had even broader powers over the local government than the MAC, which was afterward relegated to selling bonds. Over the next few years, the EFCB oversaw the dramatic contraction of New York City government—among the casualties: twenty-eight day-care centers closed; eleven eye clinics (serving 10,000 children) shut down; a decrease in the number of CUNY students by 62,000 and the loss of 1,000 faculty jobs; the loss of 8,000 public school teachers (a disproportionate number of them black and Hispanic, since they were the last hired); and a total loss of 25,000 city jobs in the years thereafter. The austerity it imposed was sufficient to enable the city to secure the support of President Ford, who agreed to provide short-term loans from the federal treasury.[41]

The crisis, and specifically the creation of the MAC and EFCB, had a more profound impact on the democratic nature of New York City and other cities that experienced similar crises in the decades to come. As journalists Jack Newfield and Paul DuBrul argued, "the coup that looked like salvation transformed New York City's representative form of government. The theoretical repositories of the people's will—the mayor . . . the elected legislators—lost much of their authority, which shifted decisively . . . to the bankers and businessmen who dominated MAC and EFCB. Decision making shifted from the semi-public forum of the Board of Estimate to an endless round of private meetings in boardrooms, summer homes, and law offices." No labor leaders served on the MAC in its early years, nor did a representative of the middle- and working-class residents that made up the city. There were no Latinos on the board. Though they did not name Weaver explicitly, Newfield and DuBrul obliquely criticized him for his failure to represent the interests of his race, stating, "the blacks who are present do not speak for, and are not in contact with, the propertyless black masses of New York City."[42]

Weaver served on the MAC board for almost two decades, but after the first year, the organization itself did not play an active role in the city's administration. The New York City fiscal crisis was a critical moment in American history because it spread "the belief that the market could better serve the public than government, that government was an obstacle to social welfare rather than an aid to it. . . . Because New York served as a standard-bearer for urban liberalism and the idea of a welfare state, the attacks on its municipal services and their decline helped pave the way for the national conservative hegemony of the 1980s and 1990s." It is sadly ironic that Weaver, who was an important member of the team that brought about the New Deal and Great Society, was seated at the table when their ideological and practical underpinnings were demolished.[43]

After leaving Baruch, Weaver spent the rest of his professional career ensconced at the Upper East Side campus of Hunter College. Formerly a preparatory school for women, Hunter was incorporated into the CUNY system in the 1960s. With a long background in training teachers, Hunter had already made an impact on New York City, but during the 1970s its leaders, including Weaver, steered the school increasingly toward a focus on urban problems. Hunter was one of the first schools in the nation to offer a doctorate in urban studies. Although he did not spend much time in the classroom, Weaver was a mentor to dozens of graduate students during his years there.

When he was not dealing with administrative duties, Weaver continued to focus his energy on housing issues, particularly the discrimination that had concerned him for decades. In 1974 he returned, twenty years after leaving the office, to the presidency of the National Committee against Discrimination in Housing (NCDH). For the next decade, Weaver devoted a significant amount of time to lecturing on housing discrimination, raising money for the NCDH, and assisting local efforts to promote the enforcement of the fair-housing law. In 1979 he led the effort to amend the law to provide it with greater enforcement powers. Noting that it was crucial in putting the federal government behind victims of housing discrimination, Weaver and others complained that the law did not have the teeth to make violators abide by the regulations. In large part, this was because HUD was, Weaver argued, "limited to the velvet glove of conciliation." It could not impose monetary penalties significant enough to ensure compliance. The amendments, which failed to pass (despite constant pleas throughout the 1970s and thereafter, the Fair Housing Act was not amended until 1988), would have enabled HUD to impose sanctions that Weaver believed were "required if we are to deter significantly the continuation of housing discrimination."[44]

As he had for decades, Weaver continued to argue that the only way to secure true racial integration was to open up the suburbs to middle-class blacks. He attacked the efforts of many suburban communities to protect themselves through "exclusionary zoning," ordinances that prevented the development of affordable housing through limits on construction such as forbidding more than a small number of houses per acre or prohibiting the construction of apartments. Although such laws were almost always racially neutral, their true impact was to limit the options of African Americans and other minorities who did not have the money to afford the expensive housing that suburban zoning required. To combat such efforts, Weaver argued that state governments and the federal government had to take greater control over land use regulation.[45]

Writing to his Harvard classmates in 1979 to mark the celebration of their fiftieth college reunion, Weaver described his career as "an exciting life full of varied experiences and enlivened by associations with interesting people." He was pleased that he had been able to "continue to learn and become involved in social and intellectual (and often ideological) issues." At age seventy-two, he planned to continue writing on housing and urban issues and advocating for equal treatment for all. Despite the problems that continued to trouble the nation, he remained optimistic about the possibilities for positive change. His life, he argued, was evidence of the progress the nation had made. "The satisfactions of such opportunity have blunted the disappointments and sorrows that are a part of living," he concluded.[46]

During the early 1980s, Weaver was a vocal critic of President Ronald Reagan's domestic policies, particularly his efforts to restrict the enforcement of fair-housing laws. In 1983, he told fair-housing advocates that, "over the past few years, there are clear signs that we are losing ground. We are faced with an administration that is, at best, indifferent to fair housing concerns and, at worst, making efforts to undermine the very foundations on which the structure of equal housing opportunity rests." Through both its interpretations of fair-housing law and its lack of support for enforcement activities, the Reagan administration significantly decreased the enforcement of the law Weaver called the crowning achievement of his career. HUD officials relied almost exclusively on voluntary compliance with the law and adopted a toothless agreement with the National Association of Realtors, a longtime opponent of fair-housing laws, that enabled real estate agents to flout their spirit. Like other civil rights activists, Weaver damned the administration for its retrograde approach. At the same time, he remained optimistic that principles animating fair housing would prevail. "This administration does not represent the wave of the future. It is a temporary aberration. The nation has made a firm commitment to decent housing and fair housing for all Americans. . . . I am convinced that neither the Federal Government nor the American people are prepared to renege on that commitment," he concluded.[47]

Weaver and Ella frequently entertained friends at their Park Avenue apartment, and they traveled widely. During his last decade, Weaver spent a great deal of time with Ella, who suffered from many illnesses in her final years. When she passed in 1991, Mary Washington remembered, "it took a lot out of Bob. They were very close." On 17 July 1997, Weaver himself died peacefully at his home. The *New York Times* published an obituary that chronicled Weaver's long career and described him as a "portly, pedagogical man." The editors of the *Washington Post* called his life one of "many firsts" and concluded, "his greatest legacy may be the work he did, largely out of public view, to dismantle a deeply entrenched system of racial segregation in America." In August, several hundred people gathered at the Schomburg Center for Research in Black Culture in Harlem for a memorial service for Weaver. In a letter read at the service, Lady Bird Johnson remembered Weaver as "a good dependable friend, and always the consummate gentleman." "Bob," she wrote, "deserves a place of high honor in our nation's history." President William Clinton called Weaver "a wise and effective advocate for civil rights and a visionary leader for housing opportunity" who provided "a strong and steady voice for desegregation in housing, education and government employment." Clinton called on the attendees to use Weaver's memory to "renew our commitment to make our cities all that they should be for all our people."[48]

Two years later, Weaver's friends, in particular his former HUD colleagues Mary Washington and Morton Schussheim, succeeded in lobbying

Congress to name the HUD building after the agency's first secretary. The sponsor of the bill, Senator Daniel Patrick Moynihan (D-NY), commented that Weaver "will be missed but properly memorialized" by the legislation. Congressman James Oberstar (D-MN) concluded that "Dr. Weaver led a rich, full life marked by professional accomplishments and excellence" and called the designation "fitting and proper." President Clinton signed the bill at the end of 1999.[49]

# Conclusion

Robert Weaver passed away as American cities were entering a new era. The end of the twentieth century witnessed a construction boom in cities across the nation, and economic and demographic trends resulted in many positive changes. After decades of decline, Weaver's adopted home of New York actually grew in population during the 1990s, and in his birthplace of Washington, DC, many neighborhoods long abandoned were being reclaimed. As more young adults and retirees chose to settle within cities, older neighborhoods witnessed revitalization, gaining new housing, businesses, and other facilities. These trends, however, were balanced by the poverty, violence, and social problems that continue to burden many areas. The "comeback" touted in many newspaper articles was an uneven one in most cities—it remains easy to find neighborhoods where abandoned housing and social neglect are widespread. Many cities, particularly those in the section of the Midwest that has been renamed the "rust belt" have struggled to participate in these trends at all.

American cities still have a long way to go to dig out of the economic and human crisis that exploded during Weaver's years as HUD secretary. Lyndon Johnson, Robert Weaver, and their colleagues had the misfortune of being in power when a "perfect storm" of social upheaval, racial change, and economic restructuring all combined to hit the country at the same moment. During the 1970s, neighborhood deterioration, social problems, and deindustrialization intensified in most cities, and millions of residents left for the suburbs. These long-developing trends, not any particular government program, are primarily responsible for the turmoil that cities faced during these years. By the 1980s, the crisis began to ebb in some cities, but even in those places the years of neglect left large swaths of territory decimated. It will take many more decades of progress to bring these places out of the poverty and decay that they continue to struggle against.

As residents return to some cities, many local governments have turned their attention to the public housing projects that Weaver championed. In Chicago, Philadelphia, St. Louis, and other cities, the large developments built during the 1940s and thereafter have fallen to the wrecking ball and have been replaced by smaller (sometimes mixed-income and racially integrated) neighborhoods. In 1993, Congress created the HOPE VI initiative, which was an explicit rejection of traditional public housing. The goal of the program was to bring new investment and optimism to neighborhoods suffering from concentrated poverty. Over the past decade, HUD has funded, through this program, the destruction of more than 80,000 public housing units and their replacement with new models of affordable (and not so affordable) housing. Although public housing continues to provide desperately needed shelter to several million low-income Americans, the program was never able to break free from the negative images attached to it from its inception, and most people have cheered the projects' demise.

Public housing and urban renewal remain among the most contested aspects of the New Deal–Great Society enterprise in which Weaver played such a crucial role. Though many of the initiatives created during these periods (Social Security and Medicare are the most obvious examples) maintain wide popularity, critics continue to blame Franklin Roosevelt and Lyndon Johnson and their activist agendas for the economic and social problems the country has faced. In 1992, almost thirty years after the Watts riots, when Los Angeles again burned, President George H. W. Bush's press secretary Marlin Fitzwater pointed to "misguided Great Society programs" as the cause of the uprising. Critics argue that these initiatives took away local control, created dependency among their clients, and obstructed progress within American cities. They ignore the fact that the federal government's assistance has been crucial to most of the country's progress since the Great Depression. Without federal aid, millions of elderly Americans would be hungry, millions of families would be without health care, and our highways would have long ago crumbled (that is, if they had ever been built in the first place). The question today is not whether the federal government should play an important part in domestic policy—that debate was settled long ago—but what its priorities should be.

Although the arguments over the appropriate role of the federal government in American life continue today, in the field of urban affairs the influence of Washington, DC, has consistently declined since the early days of

HUD. At the beginning of the twenty-first century, the federal government plays only a small part in the effort to redevelop aging neighborhoods or to assist cities and suburbs in managing the problems of infrastructure, housing, and social services. Weaver's years at HUD, an era of growing federal involvement in urban problems, were an exception to the long-standing rule of decentralized government and local responsibility.

Throughout the last decades of the twentieth century, American suburbs continued to grow, drawing wealthy and middle-class families, and their money, from cities. In many cities, a majority of the urban poor are people of color. Many argue that cities cannot bear the burden of caring for the country's underprivileged alone: they have neither the economic resources nor the political power to solve the social and economic troubles which burden them. In the face of constantly increasing need, city politicians demand more assistance from the federal government and their state governments, but these pleas have fallen on deaf ears. Many advocates argue for regional approaches that would exploit the tax base of wealthier suburbs to provide a fairer distribution of responsibility for these problems. The competition, they argue, is not between city and suburb but between regions, and therefore suburban residents, having a significant stake in the viability of their cities, should help them get out of their predicament. This approach has won a few converts, but not many. Robert Weaver, along with his peers, envisioned a significant federal role in the project of rebuilding cities and creating opportunities for their residents. Throughout the postwar era, Weaver was also one of the strongest advocates of regional approaches to these problems. During his years in Washington, Weaver moved the government in these directions. Many of these experimental efforts were flawed, but they provided models for reform in cities that may have succeeded given more time. However, those trends reversed soon after Weaver departed. With a few exceptions, Washington, DC, today remains aloof from involvement in urban revitalization. Although he was unable to fully implement it, Weaver's legacy of an active federal urban effort is one that many today are hoping to resuscitate.

Unlike the story of American urban policy, which is one of fairly steady retrenchment, the legacy of the civil rights struggles in which Weaver participated is much more complicated, providing evidence of both significant progress and unmet aspirations. Although people continue to critique, from the Right and the Left, the civil rights laws Weaver championed, the legal framework established in the postwar years—of nondiscrimination and equal opportunity—remains dominant. Since the 1970s, policymakers have battled over the implementation of these laws, particularly over the meaning of the term "affirmative action," but the basic philosophy, that a person's race should have no impact on his or her legal rights as an American citizen, is widely accepted. Weaver and his peers achieved significant victories in their battle against racial discrimination. The court decisions and legislation they secured opened up opportunities for millions of African Americans and other people of color.

One of the most profound changes in American society that these laws brought about is the dramatic growth in African American suburbanites over the past two decades. As blacks gained economic security, they, like white Americans before them, flocked to suburbs across the nation. This trend (which has generally been unexamined, at least relative to the constant attention focused on the black ghetto) is one of Weaver's greatest legacies. The increase in housing opportunities for blacks has turned the post–World War II hopes of fair-housing activists into reality.

This demographic change is evidence of the complexity of modern race relations. Although discrimination continues to influence the lives of people of color, the role of racial prejudice is much more difficult to disentangle from issues of class than it was during the postwar years. In the suburbs and the cities, African Americans have more opportunities today than ever before. The barriers have fallen in almost every aspect of society—in business, politics, academia, and elsewhere. Although Weaver's attainment of several high-level positions was exceptional at the time, it is no longer novel to see blacks take on important roles in all professions.

At the same time, the entrenchment of poverty in the black ghetto remains one of the nation's most intractable problems. Decades of social disorder and government neglect have combined to create a level of poverty that has become increasingly hard to break. The economic deprivation which many blacks continue to endure is the reason for the persistence of nationalist ideologies that argue that African Americans should take care of themselves by establishing and maintaining their own institutions. Weaver rejected these approaches, and he continued to fight them as they gained power during his later years.

At the same time, across the country, racial segregation remains a reality. Even middle-class African Americans in suburban areas live, generally, in areas where blacks constitute a disproportionate share of the population. This reality has caused some people to declare the framework of racial liberalism—the assertion that race relations would be improved by education and contact between blacks and whites—a failure and to claim that residential integration is an unachievable dream.

Weaver would reject this claim. He argued frequently that significant improvements in the country's race relations would come only after several generations. Although he is a marginal figure in our public discussion today, Weaver's framework for progress, one of slow, incremental change and the assimilation of blacks into American society, remains a powerful one. African Americans have neither the resources nor the political power (nor, for most blacks, the desire) to establish an alternative society. As Weaver recognized, the only way to secure fully equal status is through the creation of one community, a place where a person's color is irrelevant. This was and remains the organizing principle of the nation's largest activist groups, including the NAACP and the National Urban League, even though many African American leaders today are reluctant to give this principle the forum it deserves.

Weaver never wavered from this philosophy, nor did he ever shy from forcefully advocating it. His legacy is a large one that includes a lifelong struggle for racial integration, a pursuit of African American political power, and several successful government interventions into American economic and social life. His efforts resulted in many positive changes in race relations and urban affairs. At the same time, his approach had many limitations. Like other New Deal liberals, Weaver's unyielding faith in professional expertise ignored the reality that all policy decisions have winners and losers and that the distribution of political power determines these outcomes. Weaver's framework did not include a significant role for grassroots organization and therefore left African Americans and others unable to fully protect their interests. Lacking political influence, blacks and other minorities bore the burden of even liberal programs such as urban renewal. In addition, the shift of power to professionals that Weaver and others advocated concentrated influence in a small number of people. Although some of these leaders were genuinely concerned with the needs of African Americans, they did not have all the solutions to the complicated problems of race and urban policy. The result was that alternative perspectives and approaches were ignored. For example, Weaver and other policymakers held steadfast to the public housing model as the best way to provide shelter to the poor long after most local politicians and many activists had given up on the initiative. Similarly, Weaver and his cohort placed too much faith in urban planning to solve the problems of urban development and supported programs that placed an unfair burden on the poor and people of color. A comprehensive response to the intertwined problems of race and urban policy requires a multifaceted approach, one that includes both professionals and community-based leaders, to achieve true structural reform.

More than anything, however, Weaver's legacy is as a model of leadership. Well aware of the personal consequences, Weaver chose a role that he knew would leave him isolated throughout his life. His position as mediator between white and black Americans made him suspect to both groups and created lifelong tensions that he accepted, generally, with magnanimity. Weaver understood that, as a racial pioneer, he would often be alone in his efforts to bring about meaningful change. Although his success came with many benefits, his choices also weighed on him personally. Weaver considered this sacrifice a worthy and necessary one to achieve the goal of true racial equality. Although the conflicts raised by his life, particularly over the role of government and the meaning of race in our society, have not been, nor ever will be, fully resolved, Robert Weaver played an important part in thrusting these issues to the forefront of the American debate.

# Abbreviations Used in Notes

| | |
|---|---|
| Abrams Papers | Charles Abrams Papers, Microfilm, John M. Olin Library, Cornell University, Ithaca, NY |
| Baruch | Special Collections, Baruch College Archives, Baruch College Library, New York, NY |
| Bethune Papers | Mary McLeod Bethune Papers, Microfilm |
| Black Papers | Algernon Black Papers, Rare Book and Manuscript Library, Columbia University, New York, NY |
| BND | New Deal Agencies and Black America, Microfilm |
| Bunche Papers | Ralph Bunche Papers, Schomburg |
| Califano Papers | Joseph Califano Papers, LBJL |
| CETR | Committee on Education and Training Research, Special Collections, University of Chicago Library, Chicago, IL |
| Davies Papers | Dorothy Davies Papers, JFKL |
| Davis Papers | John P. Davis Papers, Schomburg |
| Douglas Papers | Paul H. Douglas Papers, Chicago Historical Society, Chicago, IL |
| DuBois Papers | W. E. B. DuBois Papers, Microfilm |
| Education | Office of Education (RG 12), NARA |
| Ella Weaver Papers | Ella Haith Weaver Papers, Schomburg |
| FDRL | Office Files, Franklin Delano Roosevelt Presidential Library, Hyde Park, NY |
| Ford | Ford Foundation Archives, New York, NY |
| Frazier Papers | E. Franklin Frazier Papers, Howard University, Moorland Spingarn Library, Washington, DC |
| Gaither Papers | Henry Gaither Papers, LBJL |
| Harriman Papers | W. Averell Harriman Papers, Special Collections, Syracuse University Library, Syracuse, NY |
| Hastie Papers | William H. Hastie Papers, Microfilm |
| HHFA Papers | Housing and Home Finance Agency Papers, JFKL |
| Hillman Papers | Sidney Hillman Papers, Catherwood Library, Cornell University, Ithaca, NY |

| | |
|---|---|
| Horne Papers | Frank S. Horne Papers, Amistad Library, Tulane University, New Orleans, LA |
| Houston Papers | Charles Hamilton Houston Papers, Howard University, Moorland Spingarn Library, Washington, DC |
| HUA | Harvard University Archives, Cambridge, MA |
| HUD | Department of Housing and Urban Development (RG 207), NARA |
| HUR | Harvard University, Records of the Registrar's Office, Cambridge, MA |
| Ickes Papers | Harold Ickes Papers, Franklin D. Roosevelt Presidential Library, Hyde Park, NY |
| Interior | Department of the Interior (RG 48), NARA |
| JFKL | John Fitzgerald Kennedy Library, University of Massachusetts, Boston, MA |
| Johnson Papers | Charles S. Johnson Papers, Amistad Library, Tulane University, New Orleans, LA |
| LBJ Civil Rights | Civil Rights in the Johnson Era, Microfilm Collection University Press |
| LBJL | Lyndon Baines Johnson Library, University of Texas, Austin, TX |
| LOC | Library of Congress, Washington, DC |
| Logan Papers | Rayford Logan Papers, Howard University, Moorland Spingarn Library, Washington, DC |
| Macy Papers | John Macy Papers, LBJL |
| McPherson Papers | Harry McPherson Papers, LBJL |
| NAACP | National Association for the Advancement of Colored People, Microfilm |
| NAACP, part 1 | Meetings of the Board of Directors, Annual Conferences, 1909–1960 |
| NAACP, part 2 | Personal Correspondence of Selected NAACP Officials, 1913–1950 |
| NAACP, part 3 | The Campaign for Educational Equality, NAACP, 1914–1955 |
| NAACP, part 5 | The Campaign against Residential Segregation, NAACP, 1913–1939 |
| NAACP, part 10 | Peonage, Labor, and the New Deal, NAACP, 1940–1955 |
| NAACP, part 13 | The NAACP and Labor, NAACP |
| NAACP Papers | National Association for the Advancement of Colored People Papers, LOC |
| NARA | National Archives and Records Administration, Silver Spring, MD |
| NCA&TCA | North Carolina Agricultural and Technical College Archives, Greensboro, NC |
| NCDH Papers | National Committee against Discrimination in Housing Paper, Amistad Library, Tulane University, New Orleans, LA |
| NHA | National Housing Authority (RG 196), NARA |

| | |
|---|---|
| Nixon Papers | Papers of President Richard M. Nixon, NARA |
| NNC | National Negro Congress, Microfilm |
| OCD | Office of Civil Defense (RG 171), NARA |
| OEM | Office of Emergency Management (RG 214), NARA |
| Panzer Papers | Fred Panzer Papers, LBJL |
| RAC | Rockefeller Archive Center, Sleepy Hollow, NY |
| RCW Papers | Robert Clifton Weaver Papers, Schomburg |
| Romney Papers | George Romney Papers, Bentley Historical Library, Ann Arbor, MI |
| Rosenwald Papers | Julius Rosenwald Fund Papers, Amistad Library, Tulane University, New Orleans, LA |
| Schomburg | Schomburg Center for Research in Black Culture, New York, NY |
| Sorenson Papers | Theodore Sorenson Papers, JFKL |
| Terrell Papers | Mary Church Terrell Papers, LOC |
| UNH Papers | United Neighborhood Houses Papers, Social Welfare History Archives, University of Minnesota Library, Minneapolis, MN |
| USEP Papers | U.S. Employment Service Papers (RG 183), NARA |
| Wagner Papers | Mayor Robert F. Wagner Papers, New York Municipal Archives, New York, NY |
| Washingtonia | Washingtonia Collection, Martin Luther King Library, Washington, DC |
| WHCF, JFKL | White House Central File, JFKL |
| WHCF, LBJL | White House Central File, LBJL |
| White Papers | Lee White Papers, LBJL |
| Wilkins Papers | Roy Wilkins Papers, LOC |
| Wirth Papers | Louis Wirth Papers, Special Collections, University of Chicago Library, Chicago, IL |
| WMC | War Manpower Commission (RG 110), NARA |
| WOP | War on Poverty, Microfilm |
| WPB | War Production Board (RG 179), NARA |
| Wright Papers | James C. Wright Papers, Howard University, Moorland Spingarn Library, Washington, DC |
| Young Papers | Whitney Young Papers, Special Collections, Columbia University, New York, NY |

# Notes

## CHAPTER 1

1. Letter to Cicero Edwards from Robert Clifton Weaver, 24 March 1939, RCW Papers, reel 1; letter to M. A. Harris from Robert Clifton Weaver, 11 September 1970, RCW Papers, Supplement, box 4; letter to H. C. Edwards from James M. Dunning, dean, Harvard School of Dental Medicine, 2 May 1950, RCW Papers, reel 1; Alma Rene Williams, "Robert C. Weaver: From the Black Cabinet to the President's Cabinet" (PhD diss., Washington University, St. Louis, 1972), 1; Werner Solors, Thomas A. Underwood, and Caldwell Titcomb, eds., *Varieties of Black Experience at Harvard* (Cambridge, MA: Harvard African-American Studies, 1986), 14.

2. Williams, 1; "Address by Robert Clifton Weaver to Ladies Auxiliary of the National Dental Association," 7 August 1961, HHFA Papers, box 2; Letitia Woods Brown, *Free Negroes in the District of Columbia, 1790–1846* (New York: Oxford University Press, 1972), 100; letter to M. A. Harris from Robert Clifton Weaver, 11 September 1970, RCW Papers, Supplement, box 4.

3. Constance Green, *The Secret City: A History of Race Relations in the Nation's Capital* (Princeton, NJ: Princeton University Press, 1967), 75–90.

4. Williams, 2–3.

5. Williams, 2–3, 6; Albert J. Farley, "Veteran D. C. Court Clerk, Is Buried," *Washington Afro-American*, no date, RCW Papers, reel 3.

6. House of Representatives, "Memorial of Colored Citizens," 22 January 1873, Misc. Doc. 58.

7. Willard Gatewood, *Aristocrats of Color: The Black Elite, 1880–1920* (Fayetteville: University of Arkansas Press, 2000), 38–43; Jacqueline M. Moore, *Leading the Race: The Transformation of the Black Elite in the Nation's Capital, 1880–1920* (Charlottesville: University of Virginia Press, 1999), 11–13.

8. Gatewood, 44; letter to Robert Clifton Weaver from Clara Bruce, 11 February 1938, RCW Papers, reel 1.

9. Green, 139; Gatewood, 53, 355; Moore, 79, 162–165.

10. Moore, 16, 21; Gatewood, 283; Williams, 9; Anacostia Museum and Center for African American History and Culture, *The Black Washingtonians* (Hoboken, NJ: Wiley, 2005); "Berean Served Area for 66 Years, Seeks Higher Goals," Washingtonia.

11. Green, 125–127; Moore, 5.

12. Green, 129.

13. Gilbert Ware, *William Hastie: Grace under Pressure* (New York: Oxford University Press, 1984), 9.

14. Green, 159–160; Ware, 9. Mortimer's salary taken from Weaver Application for Freshman Aid, 20 March 1925, HUA.

15. "Brookland: An Old, Solid Suburb in Northeast," *DC North*, August 2003.

16. Robert Clifton Weaver, 19 November 1968, LBJ Oral History, LBJL; Williams, 5; Ware, 9; A. H. Raskin, "Washington Gets 'the Weaver Treatment,'" *New York Times Magazine*, 14 May 1961.

17. Williams, 8; Raskin.

18. Green, 190–193.

19. Williams, 5.

20. Moore, 86–111; Thomas Sowell, "Black Excellence: The Case of Dunbar High School," *Public Interest* (Spring 1974): 3–21; "A Very Special Monument," *New Yorker*, 20 March 1978.

21. Howard H. Long, "The Support and Control of Public Education in the District of Columbia," *Journal of Negro Education* 7 (July 1938): 390–399; Mary A. Morton, "The Education of Negroes in the District of Columbia," *Journal of Negro Education* 16 (Summer 1947): 325–339; Jonathan Scott Holloway, *Confronting the Veil: Abram Harris, Jr., E. Franklin Frazier, and Ralph Bunche, 1919–1941* (Chapel Hill: University of North Carolina Press, 2002), 40–41; letter to Robert Mattingly from William Hastie, 14 November 1974, Hastie Papers, reel 39.

22. Moore, 88–89, 108–111; Sowell, 6; Green, 137; Hundley, *The Dunbar Story* (New York: Vantage Press, 1965).

23. "Saturae: A Review of the Class of 1922," Wright Papers, box 4.

24. "A Very Special Monument," 104–107.

25. Moore, 95; Ware, 8; "Preparing a Black Elite," *Washington Afro-American*, 15 March 1975.

26. "A Very Special Monument," 105–106; Robert Clifton Weaver, "Commencement Speech," Coppin State Teachers College, 10 June 1955, RCW Papers, reel 2; Robert Clifton Weaver, "Personal Record and Certificate of Honorable Dismissal," 1925, HUR.

27. "Dunbar Captures Second and Third Honors," *Washington Post*, 25 May 1925; "Oratory Contest Candidate Named," *Washington Star*, Robert Clifton Weaver file, HUR; Williams, 7–8.

28. Williams, 9.

29. Robert Clifton Weaver Personal Record, HUR; letter to Walter L. Smith, 27 July 1925, Weaver Personal Record, HUR.

30. Solors, 8–20; W. E. B. DuBois, *A Negro Student at Harvard, at the End of the Nineteenth Century*, oral history printed in Sollors, 39–42; Marcia Graham Synott, *The Half-Opened Door: Discrimination and Admissions at Harvard, Yale, and Princeton, 1900–1970* (Westport, CT: Greenwood Press, 1979), 83.

31. Sollors, 83–97; Synott, 49–51; Nell Painter, "Jim Crow at Harvard: 1923," *New England Quarterly* 44 (December 1971): 628.

32. Painter, 629; Sollors, 84–85; Synott, 49.

33. Synott, 51, 81, 84.

34. Letter to William Bentnick-Smith from Robert Clifton Weaver, 15 March 1966, HUD, box 184.

35. Williams, 9–10; letter to Robert Clifton Weaver from Dean H. J. Hughes, 6 March 1826, Weaver Personal Record, HUR; letter to Robert Clifton Weaver from Robert E. Bacon, 22 March 1926, Weaver Personal Record, HUR.

36. Robert Clifton Weaver interview with Joe B. Frantz, 19 November 1968, RCW Papers, Supplement, box 8; Robert Clifton Weaver, "Address to Harvard University Graduate School of Design," 5 May 1961, Harvard University School of Design Vertical Files, Cambridge, MA; Robert Clifton Weaver, "Charter Day Speech," Howard University, 1 March 1963, HHFA, box 3.

37. Ware, 34; Brian Urquart, *Ralph Bunche: An American Life* (Boston: Norton, 1993), 43.

38. Letter to Robert Clifton Weaver from Dean A. C. Hanford, 28 March 1928, Weaver Personal Record, HUR; "R. C. Weaver Awarded Medal for Oratory," *Washington Post*, 11 March 1928; "Maeterlink's Blue Bird Is Dunbar's Spring Play," *Washington Post*, 22 April 1928.

39. "Debating," *Harvard Nineteen Twenty-nine Class Album*, 166; Weaver interview with Frantz, 19 November 1968, RCW Papers, Supplement, box 8.

40. *Afrocentric Voices: Harry T. Burleigh*, http://www.afrovoices.com; letter to M. A. Harris from Robert Clifton Weaver, 11 August 1970, RCW Papers, Supplement, box 4.

41. David Levering Lewis, *W. E. B. DuBois: The Fight for Equality and the American Century, 1919–1963* (New York: Henry Holt, 2000), 222.

42. "Funeral of Weaver at Howard Tomorrow," *Washington Post*, 13 May 1929; "High School Notes," *Washington Post*, 4 October 1925; "Howard to Debate with Harvard Team," *Washington Post*, 23 February 1928.

43. Letter to Richard Martin from Robert Clifton Weaver, 16 February 1962, HHFA, box 2; "Cities: Hope for the Heart," *Time*, 4 March 1966.

44. Edward S. Mason, "The Harvard Department of Economics from the Beginning to World War II," *Quarterly Journal of Economics* 97 (August 1982): 410; Richard Parker, *John Kenneth Galbraith: His Life, His Politics, His Economics* (New York: Farrar, Straus, and Giroux, 2005).

45. Parker, 12.

46. Mason, 400–403; Parker, 45.

47. Parker, 47–51; Mason, 419.

48. Letter to Edward Mason from Robert Clifton Weaver, 27 March 1956, RCW Papers, reel 2. "Letters to File from Arthur Cole," 9 February 1931; W. L. Crum, February 1931; F. W. Taussig, 11 February 1931; F. C. Packard, 7 February 1931; all in Weaver Personal Record, HUR. On Taussig, see Robert Clifton Weaver interview with Phoebe Roosevelt, 18 February 1992, RCW Papers, Supplement, box 8.

49. Parker, 46–47; Williams, 12.

50. "1934 Bulletin," *North Carolina Agricultural and Technical College*, NCA&TCA; Williams, 13.

51. Letter to Chairman, Harvard Committee on Graduate Scholarships, from Warmoth Gibbs, 3 February 1932, NCA&TCA.

52. "Harvard University, Division of Economics, History and Government, Examinations for the Degree of Ph.D., 1930–1931," RCW Papers, reel 1; letter to W. E. B. DuBois from Robert Clifton Weaver, 29 January 1931, RCW Papers, Supplement, box 5; Robert Clifton Weaver, "The High Wage Theory of Prosperity" (PhD diss., Harvard University, 1934); letter to Glenn McLaughlin from Robert Clifton Weaver, 25 June 1934, RCW Papers, reel 1.

## CHAPTER 2

1. "Statement of the Negro Industrial League concerning the Code of Fair Competition in the Textile Industry," no date, NNC, reel 1.

2. "Statement of the Negro Industrial League"; Hilmar Ludvig Jensen, "The Rise of an African American Left: John P. Davis and the National Negro Congress" (PhD diss., Cornell University, 1997), 315–317.

3. Jensen, 317–318; Robert Clifton Weaver interview with Phoebe Roosevelt, 18 February 1992, RCW Papers, Supplement, box 8; Raymond Wolters, *Negroes and the Great Depression: The Problem of Economic Recovery* (Westport, CT: Greenwood Publishers, 1970), 110–111; Patricia Sullivan, *Days of Hope: Race and Democracy in the New Deal Era* (Chapel Hill: University of North Carolina Press, 1996), 46; "Cotton Mills Seek Accord with Labor," *New York Times*, 30 June 1933.

4. Roger Biles, *New Deal for the American People* (Dekalb: Northern Illinois University Press, 1991), 10–11; David Kennedy, *Freedom from Fear: The American People in Depression and War, 1929–1945* (New York: Oxford University Press, 1999), 87; Harvard Sitkoff, *A New Deal for Blacks: The Emergence of Civil Rights as a National Issue; The Depression Decade* (New York: Oxford University Press, 1978), 35.

5. Sitkoff, 36; Joe William Trotter, "From a Raw Deal to a New Deal? 1929–1945," in *To Make Our World Anew: A History of African Americans*, ed. Robin D. G. Kelley and Earl Lewis (New York: Oxford University Press, 2000), 411; Nancy Weiss, *Farewell to the Party of Lincoln: Black Politics in the Age of FDR* (Princeton, NJ: Princeton University Press, 1983), 47–48.

6. Kennedy, 98–101; Biles, 29.

7. Jonathan Scott Holloway, *Confronting the Veil: Abram Harris, Jr., E. Franklin Frazier, and Ralph Bunche, 1919–1941* (Chapel Hill: University of North Carolina Press, 2002), 5–8; David Levering Lewis, *W. E. B. DuBois and the Fight for Equality in the American Century, 1919–1963* (New York: Henry Holt, 2001), 320–325; Kenneth Janken, *White: The Biography of Walter White, Mr. NAACP* (New York: Free Press, 2003), 180–182.

8. Holloway, 7–10.

9. Kennedy, 177–183; Biles, 79.

10. Sitkoff, 54, 48–49; Biles, 176.

11. Jensen, 311–312; James Hodges, *New Deal Labor Policy and the Southern Textile Industry* (Knoxville: University of Tennessee Press, 1986); Louis Galambos, *Competition and Cooperation: The Emergence of a National Trade Association* (Baltimore, MD: Johns Hopkins University Press, 1966).

12. "Statement of the Negro Industrial League concerning the Code of Fair Competition in the Textile Industry," no date, NNC, reel 1.

13. Jensen, 305–307.

14. Jensen, 312–313; Weaver interview with Roosevelt, 18 February 1992, RCW Papers, Supplement, box 8; Richard Parker, *John Kenneth Galbraith: His Life, His Politics, His Economics* (New York: Farrar, Straus, and Giroux, 2005).

15. Jensen, 317–318; Weaver interview with Roosevelt, 18 February 1992, RCW Papers, Supplement, box 8; Sullivan, 46; "Cotton Mills Seek Accord with Labor," *New York Times*, 30 June 1933.

16. "Resolution Adopted by the 24th Annual Conference of the National Association for the Advancement of Colored People," 29 June 1933, NNC, reel 1; letter to Friend from Walter White, 20 July 1933, NAACP, part 10, reel 15; "National Urban League, Survey of the Month," *Opportunity*, September 1933.

17. Jensen, 320–323.

18. Janken; Walter White, *A Man Called White: The Autobiography of Walter White* (Athens: University of Georgia Press, 1995).

19. Jensen, 321–322, 325; Janken, 236–237; "The Negro Industrial League," July 1933, NNC, reel 1; *Pittsburgh Courier*, 15 July 1933.

20. "Low Wages in Lumber Industry Spurs Fight for 'New Deal' in South," *Pittsburgh Courier*, 29 July 1933; "Statement of the Negro Industrial League concerning the Code of Fair Competition for the Lumber and Timber Products Industry," 21 July 1933, NNC, reel 1; "Negro Industrial League, Report," September 1933, NNC, reel 1; "Summary of Work Already Accomplished and Suggested Next Steps in Program for the Joint Committee on National Recovery," 15 September 1933, NAACP, part 10, reel 9; Jensen, 331–332.

21. Jensen, 330–334.

22. "Summary of Work Already Accomplished and Suggested Next Steps in Program for the Joint Committee on National Recovery," 15 September 1933, NAACP, part 10, reel 9; Jensen, 330; "Negro Industrial League, Report," September 1933, NNC, reel 1.

23. *Washington Tribune*, 27 July 1933; "Survey of the Month," *Opportunity*, September 1933; Jensen, 332.

24. "Youth and Age at Amenia," *Crisis*, October 1933; Holloway, 10–13; Sitkoff, 250–251; Wolters, 221–227.

25. "Suggested Plan for Coordination of Negro Organizations for the Purpose of Integrating Interests of the Negro in All Federal Recovery Projects," 10 July 1933, NNC, reel 1; Wolters, 158–159; Jensen, 342–347.

26. Jensen, 339–347; letter to Walter White from Roy Wilkins, 14 August 1933, NAACP Papers; letter to William Hastie from Roy Wilkins, 22 August 1933, Hastie Papers, reel 36; "Release, Joint Committee in Capital before NRA Includes NAACP," 25 August 1933, NAACP, part 10, reel 15.

27. Letter to John P. Davis from Frances Williams, 8 September 1933, NAACP, part 10, reel 9; letter to Frances Williams from John P. Davis, 11 September 1933, NAACP, part 10, reel 9; letter to George Hayes from Walter White, 14 August 1933, NAACP, part 10, reel 9; letter to Robert Clifton Weaver from John P. Davis, 30 October 1933, RCW Papers, reel 1; Jensen, 352.

28. Edwin Embree and Julia Waxman, *Investment in People: The Story of the Julius Rosenwald Fund* (New York: Harper Brothers, 1949); John B. Kirby, *Black Americans in the Roosevelt Era: Liberalism and Race* (Knoxville: University of Tennessee Press, 1980), 14.

29. Letter to Robert Clifton Weaver from John P. Davis, 30 October 1933, RCW Papers, reel 1; letter to Robert Clifton Weaver from Edwin Embree, 30 October 1933, RCW Papers, reel 1.

30. Kirby, 13–16.

31. Kirby, 13–16; Sitkoff, 77.

32. Kirby, 14–17.

33. Sullivan, 48.

34. Weaver quoted in Sullivan, 48.

35. Kirby, 14–17; Sitkoff, 77.

36. Sullivan, 25–34.

37. Sullivan, 34–38.

38. "NAACP Release, Protest Lodged against White Adviser for Negroes," 25 August 1933, NAACP, part 10, reel 15; "W. E. B. DuBois, Postscript," *Crisis*, October 1933; Jensen, 344–345.

39. Kirby, 19–20; "Meeting of Special Industrial Recovery Board," 18 September 1933, NNC, reel 1.

40. Jensen, 333, 352; letter to John Henry Williams from Robert Clifton Weaver, 11 September 1933, RCW Papers, reel 2; letter to Robert Clifton Weaver from John P. Davis, 3 October 1933, RCW Papers, reel 1.

41. Letter to Robert Clifton Weaver from Clark Foreman, 30 October 1933, RCW Papers, reel 1; Weaver interview with Roosevelt, 18 February 1992, RCW Papers, Supplement, box 8; letter to John P. Davis from Robert Clifton Weaver, 6 November 1933, RCW Papers, reel 1.

42. Letter to Clark Foreman from John P. Davis, 7 November 1933; letter to Harold Ickes from John P. Davis, 7 November 1933; letter to Robert Clifton Weaver from John P. Davis, 8 November 1933; all in RCW Papers, reel 1.

43. Letter to Robert Clifton Weaver from John P. Davis, 8 November 1933, RCW Papers, reel 1.

44. "Release for Afternoon Papers of Thursday," 9 November 1933, Ickes Papers; "Foreman Names Two Aides in Interior Department," *Baltimore Afro-American*, 11 November 1933; letter to Clark Foreman from Roscoe Conkling Bruce, Blacks in the New Deal, BND, reel 7; letter to John P. Davis from Clark Foreman, 8 November 1933, RCW Papers, reel 1; "Bruce Letter in the Dunbar News," 29 November 1933, RCW Papers, reel 3; "Negro Appointments," *Pittsburgh Courier*, 18 November 1933. For reports, see "Appointments," *Opportunity*, December 1933; "Foreman Names Two Additions to Staff," *Chicago Defender*, 18 November 1933; Kirby, 38.

45. Letter to Robert Clifton Weaver from George Streator, 10 November 1933, RCW Papers, reel 2; letter to Robert Clifton Weaver from George Streator, 25 November 1933, RCW Papers, reel 2.

46. John A. Davis, "We Win the Right to Fight for Jobs," *Opportunity*, August 1938, 230–237; Holloway, 51.

47. Holloway, 52–63; Brian Urquhart, *Ralph Bunche: An American Life* (New York: W. W. Norton, 1993), 44–45.

48. Gilbert Ware, *William Hastie: Grace under Pressure* (New York: Oxford University Press, 1984), 81; Harold Ickes, *The Secret Diary of Harold Ickes: The First Thousand Days* (New York: Simon and Schuster, 1955), 416; "Appointments," *Opportunity*, December 1933.

49. Memo to Secretary of Labor from Lawrence Oxley, 18 January 1935, Oxley Files, USEP Papers, box 3; Ware, 82; Sitkoff, 66.

50. Memo to Clark Foreman from Robert Clifton Weaver, 22 November 1933, RCW Papers, reel 2.

51. Letter to Clark Foreman from Robert Clifton Weaver, 28 February 1934, RCW Papers, reel 1.

52. Sitkoff, 78; "Department of Commerce, Committee Discusses Negro Problems," 6 March 1934, NNC, reel 2; "Minutes of the First Meeting of the Interdepartmental Group Concerned with the Special Problems of the Negro Population," 7 February 1934, Racial Discrimination, part 1, Interior; Weiss, 76–77.

53. Wolters, 128–129, 140.

54. John P. Davis, "The Maid-Well Garment Case," *Crisis*, December 1934; Wolters, 123.

55. Robert Clifton Weaver, "A Wage Differential Based on Race," *Crisis*, January 1934; Wolters, 103.

56. Wolters, 120–122; Jensen, 428.

57. Weaver, "A Wage Differential Based on Race"; Ira D. Reid, "Black Wages for Black Men," *Opportunity*, March 1934; Sullivan, 52; Wolters, 104–105.

58. Wolters, 105–106.

59. Letter to Frances Williams from John P. Davis, 2 June 1934, NAACP, part 10, reel 9; letter to George Hayes from George Arthur, 3 April 1934, Blacks in the New Deal, BND, reel 14; memo to Frances Williams from Walter White, 10 October 1934, NAACP, part 10, reel 9; Jensen, 404; Kirby, 159; Janken, 237–239.

60. Sullivan, 53; Kirby, 37; "Weaver Named to Economic Advisor's Post," *Chicago Defender*, 25 October 1934; "Employees—Dr. Weaver Succeeds," *Baltimore Afro-American*, 27 October 1934.

## CHAPTER 3

1. Mark Gelfand, *A Nation of Cities: The Federal Government and Urban America, 1933–1965* (New York: Oxford University Press, 1975), 24–25; David Kennedy, *Freedom from Fear: The American People in Depression and War* (New York: Oxford University Press, 1999), 134.

2. Gail Radford, *Modern Housing for America: Policy Struggles in the New Deal Era* (Chicago: University of Chicago Press, 1996), 90; Gelfand, 54–59.

3. John Mollenkopf, *The Contested City* (Princeton, NJ: Princeton University Press, 1983), 65; Kennedy, 178; Gelfand, 47.

4. Radford, 96–101; Michael W. Straus and Talbot Wegg, *Housing Comes of Age* (New York: Oxford University Press, 1938), 45–51.

5. Robert Clifton Weaver, *Negro Labor: A National Problem* (New York: Harcourt, Brace,

1946), 10–11; memo to Clark Foreman from Robert Clifton Weaver, 22 November 1933, RCW Papers, reel 2; Gilbert Ware, *William Hastie: Grace under Pressure* (New York: Oxford University Press, 1984), 82; Robert Clifton Weaver interview with Phoebe Roosevelt, 18 February 1992, RCW Papers, Supplement, box 8.

6. Marc W. Kruman, "Quotas for Blacks: The Public Works Administration and the Black Construction Worker," *Labor History* 16, no. 1 (1975): 37–51, especially 38–39.

7. Robert Clifton Weaver, "An Experiment in Negro Labor," *Crisis*, October 1936; Weaver interview with Roosevelt, 18 February 1992, RCW Papers, Supplement, box 8.

8. Weaver interview with Roosevelt, 18 February 1992, RCW Papers, Supplement, box 8; Weaver, "An Experiment in Negro Labor"; "Minutes of the Interdepartmental Group concerned with the Special Problems of Negroes," June 1934, Racial Discrimination, part 1, Interior; Kruman, 40–42; Patricia Sullivan, *Days of Hope: Race and Democracy in the New Deal Era* (Chapel Hill: University of North Carolina Press, 1996), 55; John B. Kirby, *Black Americans in the Roosevelt Era: Liberalism and Race* (Knoxville: University of Tennessee Press, 1980), 22.

9. Ware, 82.

10. Weaver interview with Roosevelt, 18 February 1992, RCW Papers, Supplement, box 8; "Learning for Langston Terrace," http://www.wam.umd.edu/~kaq/langston.html; letter to Mr. Slattery from Clark Foreman, 29 January 1934, BND, reel 7.

11. Weaver, "An Experiment in Negro Labor," 297–298; letter to Lawrence Oxley from Robert Clifton Weaver, 13 September 1935, BND, reel 13; memo to Robert Clifton Weaver from J. R. McGuiness, no date, BND, reel 13; letter to Robert Clifton Weaver from A. F. Hinrichs, 13 August 1936, BND, reel 13; Kruman, 42–44.

12. Harvard Sitkoff, A *New Deal for Blacks: The Emergence of Civil Rights as a National Issue; The Depression Decade* (New York: Oxford University Press, 1978), 67; Sullivan, 55; John P. Davis, "A Black Inventory of the New Deal," *Crisis*, May 1935; Raymond Wolters, *Negroes and the Great Depression: The Problem of Economic Recovery* (Westport, CT: Greenwood Publishers, 1970); Kruman, 44.

13. Carol A. Flores, "U.S. Public Housing in the 1930s: The First Projects in Atlanta, Georgia," *Planning Perspectives* 9 (1994): 405–430, especially 410–411; Frank Ruechel, "New Deal Public Housing, Urban Poverty, and Jim Crow: The Techwood and University Homes in Atlanta, Georgia," *Historical Quarterly* 81, no. 4 (1997): 915–937; Florence Fleming Corley, "Atlanta's Techwood and University Homes Projects: The Nation's Laboratory for Public Housing," *Atlanta History* 31, no. 4 (1987): 17–36.

14. Flores, 411; Corley, 20; "The Atlanta Housing Project," *Crisis*, June 1934.

15. Flores, 412–419; Corley, 26; "Atlanta Housing Project."

16. Memo to Horatio Hackett from Harold Ickes, 30 November 1934, BND, reel 7; "Message from the Administrator of Public Works to the Annual NAACP Conference," 30 June 1935, Racial Discrimination, part 1, Interior; Addendum No. 5 to Specifications for the Techwood Housing Project, NNC, reel 2.

17. Weaver, "An Experiment in Negro Labor," 296–297; "Message from the Administrator of Public Works to the Annual NAACP Conference."

18. Letter to Robert Clifton Weaver from Alonzo Moron, 5 March 1937, RCW, reel 1; letter to Robert Clifton Weaver from Alonzo Moron, 7 June 1937, RCW Papers, reel 1.

19. Weaver, "An Experiment in Negro Labor," 297; "Message from the Administrator of Public Works to the Annual NAACP Conference," 30 June 1935, Racial Discrimination, part 1, Interior; "The Negro in a Program of Public Housing," *Opportunity*, July 1938; Kruman, 48–49.

20. Corley, 30; Flores, 421–422; letter to Robert Clifton Weaver from Alonso Moron, 1 April 1938, RCW Papers, reel 1.

21. Kirby, 34–35.

22. Memo to Clark Foreman from Robert Clifton Weaver, 22 November 1933, RCW Papers, reel 2.

23. Memo to Clark Foreman from Robert Clifton Weaver, 22 November 1933, RCW Papers, reel 2; Kirby, 23; Radford, 100–102. There were also two projects in Puerto Rico and one in the Virgin Islands.

24. Radford, 100–101; "First 45 Tenants in New PWA Homes," *New York Times*, 1 November 1937; letter to Langdon Post from Walter White, 1 November 1937, NAACP, part 5, reel 1.

25. Memo to Clark Foreman from Robert Clifton Weaver, 24 December 1933, RCW Papers, reel 1; Ruechel, "New Deal Public Housing, Urban Poverty, and Jim Crow," 930; Robert Clifton Weaver, *The Negro Ghetto* (New York: Harcourt, Brace, 1948), 75, 179.

26. Roger Biles, *New Deal for the American People* (Dekalb: Northern Illinois University Press, 1991), 177–178.

27. Letter to Robert Clifton Weaver from Walter White, 24 November 1933, RCW Papers, reel 2.

28. W. E. B. DuBois, "Postscript," *Crisis*, January 1934; Sitkoff, 251–252; David Levering Lewis, *W. E. B. DuBois and the Fight for Equality in the American Century, 1919–1963* (New York: Henry Holt, 2001), 336–341.

29. W. E. B. DuBois, "Postscript," *Crisis*, March 1934; "Segregation—a Symposium," *Crisis*, March 1934; Ware, 70–71; Lewis, 336–341.

30. Weaver interview with Roosevelt, 18 February 1992, RCW Papers, Supplement, box 8; memo to Clark Foreman from Robert Clifton Weaver, 24 December 1933, RCW Papers, reel 1; Hilmar Ludvig Jensen, "The Rise of an African American Left: John P. Davis and the National Negro Congress" (PhD diss., Cornell University, 1997), 369, 421; Kirby, 44.

31. Memo to Harold Ickes from Clark Foreman, 19 March 1935, RCW Papers, reel 1; memo to Clark Foreman from Robert Clifton Weaver, 18 March 1935, RCW Papers, reel 1; letter to Rayford Logan from Arthur Logan, 12 January 1935, Logan Papers, box 17.

32. "Charge of 'Un-American' Talk in TVA Brings Official Defense," *Washington Post*, 31 August 1938; Charles H. Houston and John P. Davis, "TVA: Lily-White Reconstruction," *Crisis*, October 1934; "Charter Day Dinner Held at Howard U.," *Washington Post*, 5 March 1935; "Dr. Weaver Tells Coppin Grades to Stress Thinking," *Baltimore Afro-American*, 29 June 1935.

33. Kirby, 25.

34. Arthur Logan, "General Findings with Respect to the New Deal and the Negro," August 1936, Logan Papers, box 17.

35. "Our Leadership (?) in Washington," *Chicago Defender*, 9 February 1935; Kenneth

Robert Janken, *Rayford Logan and the Dilemma of the African-American Intellectual* (Amherst: University of Massachusetts Press, 1993), 101–102.

36. On the demise of the NRA, see Alan Brinkley, *The End of Reform: New Deal Liberalism in Recession and War* (New York: Vintage Press, 1995), 46–47.

## CHAPTER 4

1. Cheryl Greenberg, *Or Does It Explode? Black Harlem in the Great Depression* (New York: Oxford University Press, 1991); Cheryl Greenberg, "The Politics of Disorder: Reexamining Harlem's Riots of 1935 and 1943," *Journal of Urban History* 18, no. 4 (August 1992): 395–441, especially 407–408.

2. Robert Clifton Weaver, "The New Deal and the Negro: A Look at the Facts," *Opportunity*, July 1935, 200–202.

3. "Open Letter from Ralph Bunche and John Davis," March 1935, NNC, reel 1; Jonathan Scott Holloway, *Confronting the Veil: Abram Harris, Jr., E. Franklin Frazier, and Ralph Bunche, 1919–1941* (Chapel Hill: University of North Carolina Press, 2002), 70–74; Hilmar Ludvig Jensen, "The Rise of an African American Left: John P. Davis and the National Negro Congress" (PhD diss., Cornell University, 1997), 508–509; "Program for National Conference," NNC, reel 1; Ralph Bunche, "A Critique of New Deal Social Planning as It Affects Negroes," *Journal of Negro Education* 1 (January 1936): 59–65.

4. Holloway, 75; Raymond Wolters, *Negroes and the Great Depression: The Problem of Economic Recovery* (Westport, CT: Greenwood Publishers, 1970), 357–358; Jensen, 510–511; Lawrence S. Winner, "The National Negro Congress: A Reassessment," *American Quarterly* 22, no. 4 (Winter 1970): 883–901, especially 884; Beth Tompkins Bates, "A New Crowd Challenges the Agenda of the Old Guard in the NAACP, 1933–1941," *American Historical Review* 102, no. 2 (April 1997): 340–377, especially 360; Senate Committee on Banking and Currency, *Hearings on the Nomination of Robert C. Weaver, 7 and 8 February 1961* (Washington, DC: Government Printing Office, 1961), 87. Weaver did, however, give the NNC a $10 donation; see letter to Robert Clifton Weaver from John P. Davis, 2 April 1936, NNC, reel 8.

5. John P. Davis, *Let Us Build a National Negro Congress* (Washington, DC: National Negro Congress, 1936), 30; *The Official Proceedings of the National Negro Congress* (Washington, DC: National Negro Congress, 1936); Winner, 885.

6. Nancy Weiss, *Farewell to the Party of Lincoln: Black Politics in the Age of FDR* (Princeton, NJ: Princeton University Press, 1983), 205–207.

7. Weiss, 210; Harvard Sitkoff, *A New Deal for Blacks: The Emergence of Civil Rights as a National Issue; The Depression Decade* (New York: Oxford University Press, 1978), 95–96; Weaver, "The New Deal and the Negro."

8. Weiss, 218–219.

9. Sitkoff, 94; Patricia Sullivan, *Days of Hope: Race and Democracy in the New Deal Era* (Chapel Hill: University of North Carolina Press, 1996), 93.

10. Letter to James Farley from Robert Clifton Weaver, 22 August 1936, RCW Papers, reel 1; letter to Robert Clifton Weaver from Paul Williams, 16 November 1936, RCW Papers, reel 2.

11. Weiss, 136–156; John Kirby, *Black Americans in the Roosevelt Era: Liberalism and Race*

(Knoxville: University of Tennessee Press, 1980), 107–122; Sitkoff, 78–82; Jane Motz, "The Black Cabinet: Negroes in the Administration of Franklin D. Roosevelt" (MA thesis, University of Delaware, 1964).

12. Weiss, 141, 152; Richard Bardolph, *The Negro Vanguard* (New York: Vintage, 1959), 364; letter to Robert Clifton Weaver from Frank Horne, 19 July 1936, RCW Papers, reel 1; cable to Frank Horne from Robert Clifton Weaver, 21 July 1936, RCW Papers, reel 1.

13. Weiss, 143; Sitkoff, 80; Richard Robbins, *Sidelines Activist: Charles S. Johnson and the Struggle for Civil Rights* (Jackson: University Press of Mississippi, 1996), 80.

14. Sitkoff, 80; Kirby, 111–119; Robert Clifton Weaver, "Speech to Americans for Democratic Action," 31 January 1963, HHFA Papers, box 3.

15. "Minutes of Meeting," 7 August 1936, Bethune Papers, part 2, reel 7; "Dr. Weaver on Federal Council on Negro Affairs," 29 November 1939, Bunche Papers, box 30; letter to Miss Edmunds from Mary McLeod Bethune, 29 September 1939, Bethune Papers, part 2, reel 7; Weiss, 137–138; Motz, 27.

16. Motz, 22–24; Weiss, 148.

17. T. Arnold Hill, "The Government as Employer and Philanthropist," *Opportunity*, May 1933; Charles Johnson, "The Army, the Negro and the Civilian Conservation Corps, 1933–1942," *Military Affairs* 36, no. 3 (October 1972): 82–88, especially 82; John A. Salmond, "The Civilian Conservation Corps and the Negro," *Journal of American History* 52, no. 1 (June 1965): 75–88, especially 83; Sitkoff, 51; Roger Biles, *New Deal for the American People* (Dekalb: Northern Illinois University Press, 1991), 177.

18. Salmond, 82; memo to Harold Ickes from Robert Clifton Weaver, 9 September 1935; letter to John Studebaker from Robert Fechner, 24 July 1935; memo to Harold Ickes from John Studebaker, 2 February 1937; all in Negro Education File, Education, box 12.

19. Robert Clifton Weaver, untitled memo, RCW Papers, Supplement, box 7; Ira D. Reid, Robert C. Weaver, Preston Valien, and Charles S. Johnson, *The Urban Negro Worker in the United States, 1925–1936* (Washington, DC: Government Printing Office, 1938–1939); letter to Harry Hopkins from Harold Ickes, 3 February 1934, BND, reel 7; letter to Sara Southall from Robert Clifton Weaver, 17 May 1948, RCW Papers, reel 2.

20. Johnson, 3–5; Bernard Braxton, "Security for the Negro Wage Earner," *Crisis*, July 1940, 210–212.

21. Robert Clifton Weaver, "Training Negroes for Occupational Opportunities," *Journal of Negro Education* 7 (1938): 486–497; Robert Clifton Weaver, "The Public Works Administration School Building Aid Program and Separate Negro Schools," *Journal of Negro Education* 7 (1938): 366–374; Robert Clifton Weaver, "Economic Factors in Negro Migration Past and Future," *Social Forces* 18 (October 1939): 90–101.

22. Letter to Commissioner of Motor Vehicles from Robert Clifton Weaver, 29 July 1935, RCW Papers, reel 1.

23. Letter to Bill Dean from Robert Clifton Weaver, 3 March 1936, RCW Papers, reel 1.

24. Letter to Robert Clifton Weaver from Glenn McLaughlin, 12 August 1935, RCW Papers, reel 1; "Dr. Weaver to Marry Teacher," *Baltimore Afro-American*, 25 July 1935; "She's a Busy Cabinet Wife," *Washington Daily News*, 24 January 1966; "There's No Conflict of Interest at House of Doctors Weaver," *Washington Post*, 30 July 1961; "Mrs. Weaver Believes in the Attainable," *Washington Post*, 23 January 1966.

25. "There's No Conflict of Interest at House of Doctors Weaver," *Washington Post*, 30 July 1961; letter to Robert Clifton Weaver from Ella D. Haith, 11 July 1935, Ella Weaver Papers, box 1.

26. Morton Schussheim interview with author, 3 November 2005; Mary Washington interview with author, 7 December 2005.

27. Letter to Paul Williams from Robert Clifton Weaver, 23 November 1936, RCW Papers, reel 2; letter to William Hastie from Robert Clifton Weaver, 1 September 1937, RCW Papers, reel 1.

28. Mary Washington interview with author, 7 November 2005.

29. Gail Radford, *Modern Housing for America: Policy Struggles in the New Deal Era* (Chicago: University of Chicago Press, 1996); Nathaniel S. Keith, *Politics and the Housing Crisis since 1930* (New York: Universe Books, 1973); H. Peter Oberlander and Eva Newbrun, *Houser: The Life and Work of Catherine Bauer* (Vancouver, BC: UBC Press, 1999); A. Scott Henderson, *Housing and the Democratic Ideal: The Life and Thought of Charles Abrams* (New York: Columbia University Press, 2000).

30. Radford, 105–106; Harold Ickes, *The Secret Diary of Harold Ickes*, vol. 2, *The Struggle Inside, 1936–1939* (New York: Simon and Schuster, 1954), 237.

31. J. Joseph Huthmacher, *Senator Robert F. Wagner and the Rise of Urban Liberalism* (New York: Atheneum, 1971), 207–216; Radford, 185–190; Keith, 33–36; Mark Gelfand, *A Nation of Cities: The Federal Government and Urban America, 1933-1965* (New York: Oxford University Press, 1975), 62–63.

32. "Straus to Direct Federal Housing," *New York Times*, 19 October 1937; Roger Biles, "Nathan Straus and the Failure of U.S. Public Housing, 1937–1942," *Historian* 53, no. 1 (Autumn 1990): 33–46, especially 34–35; Eugenie Ladner Birch, "Woman-Made America: The Case of Early Public Housing," *AIP Journal*, April 1978, 130–143.

33. Letter to Robert Clifton Weaver from Robert Taylor, 27 September 1937, RCW Papers, reel 1; letter to Walter White from Paul Williams, 21 October 1937, NAACP, part 5, reel 1; letter to Robert Clifton Weaver from Robert Taylor, 9 November 1937, RCW Papers, reel 2.

34. Letter to A. L. Foster from Walter White, 15 November 1937, NAACP, part 5, reel 1; "Memo for Files from the Secretary," 22 December 1937, NAACP, part 5, reel 1; letter to Robert Clifton Weaver from Walter White, 22 December 1937, RCW Papers, reel 2; Robert Clifton Weaver interview with Frances Hardin, 30 November 1973, RCW Papers, Supplement, box 8; letter to Walter White from Corienne Robinson, 28 November 1937, RCW Papers, reel 2; "Robert C. Weaver Named Aid to Nathan Straus," *Washington Post*, 10 February 1938.

35. Letter to Robert Clifton Weaver from Campbell Johnson, 14 February 1938, RCW Papers, reel 1; letter to Robert Clifton Weaver from Forrester Washington, 3 March 1938, RCW Papers, reel 2; letter to Robert Clifton Weaver from C. L. Alexander, 10 February 1938, RCW Papers, reel 1; letter to Robert Clifton Weaver from T. Arnold Hill, 19 January 1938, RCW Papers, reel 1.

36. Robert Clifton Weaver, "The Negro in a Program of Public Housing," *Opportunity*, July 1938, 1–6; Public Housing Authority, "Order No. 96," 14 April 1938, Historical File, NHA, box 33; letter to Robert Clifton Weaver from J. R. Henderson, 19 March 1938, RCW

Papers, reel 1; letter to Robert Clifton Weaver from Alonzo Moron, 27 December 1937, RCW Papers, reel 1.

37. Weaver, "The Negro in a Program of Public Housing," 198–203, especially 203; letter to Alonzo Moron from Robert Clifton Weaver, 8 April 1940, RCW Papers, reel 1; Robert Clifton Weaver interview with Phoebe Roosevelt, 18 February 1992, RCW Papers, Supplement, box 8.

38. Letter to Robert Clifton Weaver from Dewey Jones, 21 December 1938, RCW Papers, reel 1; letter to Robert Clifton Weaver from Walter White, 4 October 1938, RCW Papers, reel 2; letter to Robert Clifton Weaver from Walter White, 26 March 1940, RCW Papers, reel 2; letter to Alonzo Moron from Robert Clifton Weaver, 10 May 1940, RCW Papers, reel 1; letter to Robert Clifton Weaver from Alonzo Moron, 8 April 1940, RCW Papers, reel 1; Marc Kruman, "Quotas for Blacks: The Public Works Administration and the Black Construction Worker," *Labor History* 16, no. 1 (Winter 1975): 37–51, especially 48; Robert Clifton Weaver, "Federal Aid, Local Control, and Negro Participation," *Journal of Negro Education* 11 (January 1942): 47–59, especially 57.

39. Letter to Josephine Gomon from Walter White, 23 December 1937, NAACP, part 5, reel 1; letter to Robert Clifton Weaver from Paul Williams, 16 August 1939, RCW Papers, reel 2; stenographic transcript of telephone conversation between Robert Clifton Weaver and Alonzo Moron, 31 May 1939, RCW Papers, reel 1; letter to Harold Ickes from Dr. Leroy Morris, 3 January 1939, Racial Discrimination, part 1, Interior.

40. Stenographic transcript of telephone conversation between Robert Clifton Weaver and Alonzo Moron, 31 May 1939, RCW Papers, reel 1.

41. Joel Schwartz, *The New York Approach: Robert Moses, Urban Liberals and the Redevelopment of the Inner City* (Columbus: Ohio State University Press, 1993), 56–57; Wendell Pritchett, *Brownsville, Brooklyn: Blacks, Jews, and the Changing Face of the Ghetto* (Chicago: University of Chicago Press, 2002), 98.

42. Weiss, 149; U.S. Housing Authority, "Bulletin No. 18 on Policy and Procedure: Site Selection," DuBois Papers, reel 50.

43. Robert Clifton Weaver, "Racial Minorities and Public Housing," Proceedings of the National Conference of Social Work, 1930, RCW Papers, Supplement, box 6.

44. Press release, "Win Fight against Jim Crow in New Jersey Housing Project," 18 November 1939, NAACP, part 5, reel 4; letter to W. Clifford Harvey from Walter White, 4 June 1940, RCW Papers, reel 2.

45. Weaver, "Federal Aid, Local Control, and Negro Participation," 46–59, especially 55–57; Robert Clifton Weaver, "Racial Policy in Public Housing," *Phylon* 1 (1940): 149–161, especially 151.

46. Radford, 192.

47. On the conservative response to the New Deal, see David Kennedy, *Freedom from Fear: The American People in Depression and War* (New York: Oxford University Press, 1999), 323–362.

48. Biles, "Nathan Straus and the Failure of U.S. Public Housing, 1937–1942," *Historian* 53, no. 1 (Autumn 1990): 33–46; Keith, 37–38; Radford, 191–192.

49. Robert Clifton Weaver, "The Negro as Tenant and Neighbor," speech given at the Third National Negro Congress, 28 April 1940, NAACP, part 10, reel 11; "Opposition Tac-

tics Imperil Housing Bill," *Washington Post*, 30 May 1940; Alvin White, press release, Associated Negro Press, undated, RCW Papers, reel 3.

50. "Opposition Tactics Imperil Housing Bill," *Washington Post*, 30 May 1940; letter to Walter White from Congressman F. L. Crawford, 4 June 1940, RCW Papers, reel 2; letter to Walter White from Congressman Robert W. Kean, 4 June 1940, RCW Papers, reel 2; letter to Walter White from Congressman Jessie Sumner, 4 June 1940, RCW Papers, reel 2.

51. Alvin White, press release, Associated Negro Press, undated, RCW Papers, reel 3; Weaver, "Federal Aid, Local Control, and Negro Participation," 47–59.

52. Jensen, 510–512; Wolters, 358–359; Winner, 887–900; Bates, 369–370.

## CHAPTER 5

1. Richard Bardolph, *The Negro Vanguard* (New York: Vintage, 1963), 353–354; Harvard Sitkoff, *A New Deal for Blacks: The Emergence of Civil Rights as a National Issue; The Depression Decade* (New York: Oxford University Press, 1978), 307–308; Gilbert Ware, *William Hastie, Grace under Pressure* (New York: Oxford University Press, 1984), 97–98; Thomas Lee Grant, "Black Cabinet Members in the Franklin Delano Roosevelt Administration" (PhD diss., University of Colorado, 1981), 192–197.

2. Bardolph, 353–354; Sitkoff, 307–308; Ware, 97–98; Roi Ottley, *New World A-Coming: Inside Black America* (Boston: Houghton Mifflin, 1944), 259–260. The story of the president's call was reported by Ted Poston and Roi Ottley, but eighteen years later, Weaver said that, while it was possible, he could not testify to its truth." Letter to Richard Bardolph from Robert Clifton Weaver, 30 September 1958, RCW Papers, reel 1.

3. David Kennedy, *Freedom from Fear: The American People in Depression and War* (New York: Oxford University Press, 1999), 427–428.

4. Paula Pfeffer, *A. Philip Randolph, Pioneer of the Civil Rights Movement* (Baton Rouge: Louisiana State University Press, 1990), 47; letter to Walter White from Robert Clifton Weaver, 23 August 1940, RCW Papers, reel 2.

5. Cited in Sitkoff, 300–302; Andrew Edmund Kersten, *Race, Jobs and the War: The FEPC in the Midwest, 1941–1946* (Urbana: University of Illinois Press, 2000), 12.

6. Alan Brinkley, *The End of Reform: New Deal Liberalism in Recession and War* (New York: Vintage, 1996), 180–181; George Q. Flynn, *The Mess in Washington: Manpower Mobilization in World War II* (Westport, CT: Greenwood Press, 1979), 4–5.

7. Steve Fraser, *Labor Will Rule: Sidney Hillman and the Rise of American Labor* (New York: Free Press, 1991); Brinkley, 217–220.

8. Fraser, 452–461; Brinkley, 217–220.

9. Letter to Walter White from Louis Lautier, 1 July 1940, NAACP, part 13, series A, reel 18; Lee Finkle, "Quotas or Integration: The NAACP versus the *Pittsburgh Courier* and the Committee on Participation of Negroes," *Journalism Quarterly* 52, no. 1 (1975): 76–84, especially 79.

10. Kersten, 13; "A.T.&T. Engineer Named to Staff of Defense Board," *Washington Post*, 10 July 1940; "Office Memorandum from Leon Keyserling," 29 July 1940, RCW Papers, reel 1; letter to Robert Clifton Weaver from Thurgood Marshall, NAACP, part 13, series C, reel 7.

11. NDAC press release, 31 August 1940, NAACP, part 13(A), reel 18; "No Jim Crow in Defense Trades," *Pittsburgh Courier*, no date, RCW Papers, reel 3.

12. Robert Clifton Weaver interview with Phoebe Roosevelt, 18 February 1992, RCW Papers, Supplement, box 8; Fraser, 478–479; Kersten, 13–14; Merl Reed, *Seedtime for the Modern Civil Rights Movement* (Baton Rouge: Louisiana State University Press, 1991), 13.

13. Robert C. Weaver, *Negro Labor: A National Problem* (New York: Harcourt, Brace, 1946), 44–46.

14. Weaver, *Negro Labor*, 47–48, 59; NDAC press release, 15 October 1940, NAACP, part 13(A), reel 18; "Informal Memorandum for Mr. Dooley from Robert Clifton Weaver," 20 December 1940, Bureau of Training, Training within Industry Service, General, 1940–1945, WMC, box 10.

15. Robert Clifton Weaver, "The Defense Program and the Negro," *Opportunity*, November 1940.

16. Sitkoff, 304–305; "The White House Jim Crow Plan," *Crisis*, November 1940, 350; Herbert Garfinkel, *When Negroes March* (New York: Atheneum, 1969), 33.

17. "Notes on Conference at the White House," 27 August 1940, RCW Papers, reel 2; "Memorandum as Suggested Basis on Alleged Discrimination against Negroes in the Armed Forces," 27 September 1940, RCW Papers, reel 2; Sitkoff, 306–307; Brinkley, 187.

18. "White House Blesses Jim Crow," *Crisis*, November 1940; Sitkoff, 306–307, Garfinkel, 34–35.

19. Flynn, 5–6; Brinkley, 180–181; Fraser, 456.

20. Kersten, 16–17; letter to Walter White from Arthur St. Cyr, 16 October 1940, NAACP, part 13(A), reel 3; letter to Walter White from Robert Clifton Weaver, 22 January 1941, NAACP, part 13(A), reel 3; letter to William Knudsen from Walter White, 8 January 1941, NAACP, part 13(A), reel 3; letter to Walter White from H. G. Wilde, 25 January 1941, NAACP, part 13(A), reel 3; Louis Ruchames, *Race, Jobs and Politics: The Story of FEPC* (1953; repr., Westport, CT: Negro Universities Press, 1971), 14.

21. Weaver, *Negro Labor*, 109–118; "Limit Negro Air Jobs," *Kansas City Star*, 17 March 1941; NAACP press release, 13 June 1941, NAACP, part 13(A), reel 3.

22. NAACP press release, 10 June 1941; NAACP press release, 28 March 1941; letter to Roy Wilkins from Robert Clifton Weaver, 30 April 1941; all in NAACP, part 13(A), reel 3.

23. Joe William Trotter, "From a Raw Deal to a New Deal? 1929–1945," in *To Make Our World Anew: A History of African-Americans*, ed. Robin D. G. Kelley and Earl Lewis (New York: Oxford University Press, 2000), 442–443; Garfinkel, 38–39; Pfeffer, 47; Reed, 13; Sitkoff, 314–315.

24. "8 Point Program, March on Washington Movement; Group Issues Call for Job March in Nation's Capital for July 1," *Pittsburgh Courier*, 17 May 1941; Pfeffer, 48–49; Sitkoff, 316–318; Trotter, 443.

25. OPM press release, 11 April 1941, NAACP, part 13(A), reel 18.

26. OPM press release, 11 April 1941, NAACP, part 13(A), reel 18; OPM press release, 12 April 1941, NAACP, part 13(A), reel 18; Fraser, 479; "Address by Sidney Hillman to Annual Conference on the Negro in Business," 18 April 1941, NAACP, part 13(A), reel 18; *New York Amsterdam News*, 19 April 1941; Kersten, 15.

27. OPM press release, 29 April 1941; OPM press release, 10 May 1941; OPM press release, 21 June 1941; OPM press release, 26 June 1941; all in NAACP, part 13(A), reel 18.

28. Letter to Robert Clifton Weaver from Roy Wilkins, 5 June 1941, General Office Files, NAACP, part 2, box 343; letter to Roy Wilkins from Theodore Poston, 6 June 1941, NAACP, part 2, box 343; "Memorandum to Sidney Hillman from March on Washington Committee," 2 May 1941, RCW Papers, reel 2; letter to E. C. Davison from C. R. Dooley, 24 January 1941, Bureau of Training, Training within Industry Service, General Files, 1940–1945, WMC, box 10; letter to Robert Clifton Weaver from Louis Lautier, 12 May 1941, Bureau of Training, Training within Industry Service, General Files, 1940–1945, WMC, box 10; "Defense Job Bars 4 Women," *Philadelphia Tribune*, 2 January 1941.

29. Joseph Lash, *Eleanor and Franklin: The Story of Their Relationship Based on Eleanor's Private Letters* (New York: W. W. Norton, 1971), 533; Robert Clifton Weaver, "Eleanor, LBJ and Black America," *Crisis*, June–July 1972, 186–193.

30. Weaver, *Negro Labor*, 134–135.

31. OPM press release, 10 May 1941, NAACP, part 13(A), reel 18.

32. Letter to Fiorello LaGuardia from A. Philip Randolph, 5 June 1941, OCD, box 90; memo from Wayne Coy to Franklin Delano Roosevelt, 16 June 1941, OEM, box 11; Reed, 14–15; Kersten, 16–17; Sitkoff, 317–320.

33. Kersten, 17–18; Reed, 14–16.

34. Robert Clifton Weaver interview with Frances Hardin, 30 November 1973, RCW Papers, Supplement, box 8.

35. "Negro March on Washington Committee," no date, OCD, box 90; Lester Granger, "The President, the Negro and Defense," *Opportunity*, July 1941, 204–207; "End Job Bias—Roosevelt," *Pittsburgh Courier*, 21 June 1941; Kersten, 18; Sitkoff, 322–323; Reed, 15–16.

36. OPM press release, 1 July 1941, NAACP, part 13(A), reel 18; OPM press release, 26 June 1941, NAACP, part 13(A), reel 18; "Survey Says Aircraft Firms Bar Negroes," 2 February 1941, NAACP, part 13(A), reel 18; NAACP press release, 26 April 1941, NAACP, part 13(A), reel 2.

37. OPM press release, 26 July 1941, NAACP, part 13(A), reel 2; memo to Miss Crump from Roy Wilkins, 1 August 1941, NAACP, part 13(A), reel 2.

38. NAACP press release, 1 August 1941; letter to Robert Clifton Weaver from Thurgood Marshall, 4 August 1941; memorandum to Mr. White from Mr. Reeves, 8 August 1941; all in NAACP, part 13(A), reel 2.

39. Letter to Walter White from Robert Clifton Weaver, 4 August 1941; OPM press release, 9 August 1941; both in NAACP, part 13(A), reel 2.

40. "Confidential to Mr. White from Mr. Reeves," 9 August 1941; letter to Robert Clifton Weaver from Thurgood Marshall, 11 August 1941; NAACP press release, 15 August 1941; letter to Thurgood Marshall from Robert Clifton Weaver, 18 August 1941; letter to Robert Clifton Weaver from Walter White, 28 August 1941; all in NAACP, part 13(A), reel 2. Cherokee quoted in Reed, 32.

41. Letter to Walter White from Anson Phelps Stokes, 27 August 1941; letter to Anson Phelps Stokes from Walter White, 28 August 1941; letter to Anson Phelps Stokes from Walter White, 6 September 1941; letter to Gloster Current from Roy Wilkins, 9 October 1941; all in NAACP, part 13(A), reel 2.

42. Kersten, 98–99; Weaver, *Negro Labor,* 65–70.

43. Kersten, 19; Reed, 22–24.

44. "Minorities in Defense," October 1941, RCW Papers, reel 3; Reed, 23; letter to Thurgood Marshall from Larry Cramer, 13 August 1941, NAACP, part 13(A), reel 2; letter to Mark Ethridge from Walter White, 14 August 1941, NAACP, part 13(A), reel 2.

45. Reed, 33–45; Kersten, 19–32.

46. Reed, 269–270; WPB press release, 24 January 1942, Hillman Papers, box 20; Kersten, 27–28.

47. Brinkley, 182–186; Fraser, 483.

48. Memo to Sidney Hillman from Robert Clifton Weaver, 11 May 1941, Hillman Papers, box 108; Robert Clifton Weaver, "Racial Employment Trends in National Defense," *Phylon* 3 (1942): 22–30; Lester Granger, "Vocational Opportunity and the Victory Goal," *Opportunity,* March 1942, 74–77.

49. Memo to Sidney Hillman from Robert Clifton Weaver, 11 May 1941, Hillman Papers, box 108; Lee Finkle, "The Conservative Aims of Militant Rhetoric: Black Protest during World War II," *Journal of American History* 60 (December 1973): 692–713, especially 700–701; Flynn, 150.

50. Richard Polenberg, *War and Society: The United States, 1941–1945* (Westport, CT: Greenwood Press, 1980), 20–21; Flynn, 15–17.

51. Flynn, 9–11.

52. Kersten, 38; Flynn, 152–155; "Negro Manpower Unit to Be Formed," *Washington Post,* 21 June 1942.

53. Reed, 75–88; Kersten, 39; "FEPC Is Captured by the South," *Crisis,* September 1942, 279; "We Want Work Dammit Department," *Chicago Defender,* 29 August 1942; "FEPC Stronger, Says FDR," *Chicago Defender,* 22 August 1942.

54. Reed, 81–82; August Meier and Elliot Rudwick, *Black Detroit and the Rise of the UAW* (New York: Oxford University Press, 1979), 148.

55. Reed, 87–88; "And He's Out," *Chicago Defender,* 31 October 1942; "McNutt, Maclean Talk: FEPC Gets More Power," *Pittsburgh Courier,* 31 October 1942; Flynn, 155.

56. Weaver, *Negro Labor,* 35; OPM press release, 1 July 1941, NAACP, part 13(A), reel 18; "War Jobs for Negroes Doubled in Year Here: 17,000 Employed Now," *Philadelphia Record,* 28 May 1942; Herbert Northrup, "Negroes in a War Industry: The Case of Shipbuilding," *Journal of Business of the University of Chicago* 15, no. 3 (July 1943): 160–172, especially 167.

57. Letter to John Pew from Walter White, 1 June 1941; "Three Pressure Groups Seek to Control the Destinies of the Negro in America," *Washington Afro-American,* 30 July 1942; letter to Orrin Evans from Walter White, 9 June 1942; letter to Walter White from Orrin Evans, 12 June 1942; letter to Herman Laws from Walter White, 6 July 1942; letter to Walter White from Herman Laws, 16 June 1942; all in NAACP, part 13(A), reel 18.

58. Weaver, *Negro Labor,* 35; letter to Larry Cramer from Walter White, 2 June 1942, NAACP, part 13(A), reel 18; letter to Walter White from Larry Cramer, 29 June 1942, NAACP, part 13(A), reel 18; Northrup, "Negroes in a War Industry," 167; "Training the Negro for the Production Frontline," *Machinery,* December 1943; "Negroes Present Awards," *New York Times,* 9 April 1944.

59. Ware, 99–130; "Hastie Resigns," *Pittsburgh Courier*, 25 January 1943; "Judge Hastie Awarded Spingarn Medal for '43," *Chicago Defender*, 20 March 1943.

60. Ware, 131; Philip McGuire, "Judge Hastie, World War II, and Army Racism," *Journal of Negro History* 62 (October 1977): 351–362, especially 357–358.

61. Reed, 91–93; Genna Rae McNeill, *Groundwork: Charles Hamilton Houston and the Struggle for Civil Rights* (Philadelphia: University of Pennsylvania Press, 1983), 164; Kersten, 40–41.

62. Reed, 104–112; Kersten, 42; "FEP Reaches Agreement with WMC on Procedure," *Chicago Defender*, 17 July 1943.

63. Weaver, *Negro Labor*, 138–139.

64. Weaver, *Negro Labor*, 143–144; Reed, 97.

65. Kersten, 105; Dominic Capeci and Martha Wilkerson, *Layered Violence: The Detroit Rioters of 1943* (Jackson: University Press of Mississippi, 1991), 2–30; John Morton Blum, *V Was for Victory: Politics and American Culture during World War II* (New York: Harcourt Brace, 1976), 200–203; Kennedy, 773.

66. Thurgood Marshall, "The Gestapo in Detroit," *Crisis*, August 1943, 232–233, 246; "The Police in Riots," *Crisis*, August 1943; Capeci and Wilkerson, 90; Blum, 203.

67. Julius Thomas, "Race Conflict and Social Action," *Opportunity*, October 1943, 165–167; Blum, 205–206; Polenberg, 129–130; "Police Riots Sweep Nation," *Pittsburgh Courier*, 26 June 1943; Cheryl Greenberg, "Politics of Disorder: Reexamining Harlem's Riots of 1935 and 1943," *Journal of Urban History* 18 (August 1992): 395–441, especially 427; Martha Biondi, *To Stand and Fight: The Struggle for Civil Rights in New York City* (Cambridge, MA: Harvard University Press, 2003), 11.

68. "The Riots," *Crisis*, July 1943; Blum, 204; "Biddle Asks Bar on Dixie Trek to North," *Chicago Defender*, 14 August 1943; "Text of Biddle Letter Proposing Ban on Dixie Negro Migration into North," *Chicago Defender*, 21 August 1943.

69. Weaver interview with Hardin, 30 November 1973, RCW Papers, Supplement, box 8; Charles Eagles, *Jonathan Daniels and Race Relations: The Evolution of a Southern Liberal* (Knoxville: University of Tennessee Press, 1982); Reed, 94.

70. Memo to Jonathan Daniels from Robert Clifton Weaver, 4 September 1943, OF 4245g, FDRL, box 10; memo to Jonathan Daniels from Robert Clifton Weaver, no date, OF 4245g, FDRL, box 8.

71. Jane Motz, "The Black Cabinet: Negroes in the Administration of Franklin D. Roosevelt" (MA thesis, University of Delaware, 1964), 55; Grant, 256.

72. Kersten, 45; Motz, 32, 55; "Weaver, Alexander Due for Ouster from WMC," *Chicago Defender*, 12 June 1943; Horace Cayton, "Black Cabinet," *Pittsburgh Courier*, 8 January 1944.

73. "Dr. Weaver and the Black Cabinet," *Chicago Defender*, 16 July 1943.

74. "Report Weaver to Resign from WMC Position," *Chicago Defender*, 8 January 1944; "Weaver Resigns, Sees Race Gains in Danger," *Chicago Defender*, 15 January 1944; Horace Cayton, "Black Cabinet Has Disappeared from the National Scene," *Pittsburgh Courier*, 5 February 1944; Charley Cherokee, "National Grapevine," *Chicago Defender*, 12 February 1944; "Weaver Quits WMC Position," *Pittsburgh Courier*, 15 January 1944.

75. Weaver, *Negro Labor*, 139–140.

76. Weaver, *Negro Labor*, 70–84, 121–128, 88–91.

77. Weaver, *Negro Labor*, 91–92.

78. Weaver, *Negro Labor*, 137, 90–91; Flynn, 157.

79. Ottley, 262.

## CHAPTER 6

1. On Chicago see Arnold Hirsch, *Making the Second Ghetto: Race and Housing in Chicago, 1940–1960* (New York: Cambridge University Press, 1983); James Grossman, *Land of Hope: Chicago, Black Southerners, and the Great Migration* (Chicago: University of Chicago Press, 1991); Lizabeth Cohen, *Making a New Deal: Industrial Workers in Chicago, 1919–1939* (New York: Cambridge University Press, 1990); Andrew Kersten, *Race, Jobs and the War: The FEPC in the Midwest, 1941–1946* (Urbana: University of Illinois Press, 2000), 48–54.

2. Gunnar Myrdal, *An American Dilemma: The Negro Problem and Modern Democracy* (New York: Harper and Row, 1944); David Southern, *Gunnar Myrdal and Black-White Relations: The Use and Abuse of "An American Dilemma," 1944–1969* (Baton Rouge: Louisiana State University Press, 1987); Walter Jackson, *Gunnar Myrdal and America's Conscience: Social Engineering and Racial Liberalism, 1938–1987* (Chapel Hill: University of North Carolina Press, 1990).

3. Roger Biles, *Big City Boss in Depression and War: Mayor Edward J. Kelly of Chicago* (DeKalb: Northern Illinois University Press, 1984).

4. Biles, 90–102.

5. Memo to Jonathon Daniel [*sic*] from Will Alexander, 16 July 1943, OF 4245g, FDRL; "Mayor Kelly Names Ten to City Anti-riot Board," *Chicago Defender*, 17 July 1943; Kersten, 49–50; Biles, 125–127; Hirsch, 43–44.

6. "Mayor Kelly's Race Commission," *Chicago Defender*, 7 August 1943; Hirsch, 50–51; Biles, 127.

7. Press release, 6 January 1944, Rosenwald Papers, box 179; letter to Robert Clifton Weaver from Mary McLeod Bethune, 7 February 1944, RCW Papers, Supplement, box 5.

8. Sydney J. Harris, "Here Is Chicago," no date, RCW Papers, reel 3; "Summary of Mayor's Conference on Race Relations," February 1944, Houston Papers, box 19; "Embree Sums Up Mayor's Racial Group Findings," *Chicago Defender*, 28 February 1944.

9. "Mayor's Committee on Race Relations," *Race Relations in Chicago*, December 1944, 5, 9–10; memo to Edwin Embree from Robert Clifton Weaver, 26 April 1944, Rosenwald Papers, box 179; Robert C. Weaver, "Racial Tensions in Chicago," *Social Service Yearbook*, 1945, 6.

10. Letter to Edward Kelly from Edwin Embree, 7 September 1944, Rosenwald Papers, box 179; letter to Edward Kelly from Edwin Embree, 8 September 1944, Rosenwald Papers, box 179; Weaver, "Racial Tensions in Chicago," 8.

11. *Race Relations in Chicago*, December 1944, 12–14.

12. Clement Vose, *Caucasians Only: The Supreme Court, the NAACP and the Restrictive Covenant Cases* (Berkeley and Los Angeles: University of California Press, 1959), 5–13; Herman Long and Charles S. Johnson, *People vs. Property: Race Restrictive Covenants in Housing* (Nashville, TN: Fisk University Press, 1947), 11.

13. Myrdal, 625.

14. Robert Clifton Weaver, "Race Restrictive Housing Covenants," *Journal of Land and Public Utility Economics* 20 (August 1944): 183–193.

15. Weaver, "Race Restrictive Housing Covenants," 185–188.

16. Weaver, "Race Restrictive Housing Covenants," 191–192. For an analysis of this approach, see Preston H. Smith, "The Quest for Racial Democracy: Black Civic Ideology and Housing Interests in Postwar Chicago," *Journal of Urban History* 26, no. 2 (January 2000): 131–157.

17. "Living Space for Chicago's People, Report of the Subcommittee on Housing," October 1944, RCW Papers, reel 3.

18. Robert C. Weaver, *Negro Labor: A National Problem* (New York: Harcourt, Brace, 1946), 315; "Weaver Resigns Post on Mayor's Committee," *Chicago Defender*, 21 October 1944.

19. Jackson, 186–187; Myrdal, 4, lxxi.

20. Myrdal, 19–20, 1022–1023, 80; Southern, 58–59; Jackson, 192–193, 198.

21. Memo to the Sponsors of the Chicago Conference, March 1944, Houston Papers, box 19; minutes of the Julius Rosenwald Fund, 20 March 1944, Houston Papers, box 19.

22. Memo to Board of Directors from Robert Clifton Weaver, Johnson Papers, box 68; memo to Board of Directors from Louis Wirth, 7 March 1947, Wirth Papers, box 14; "American Council on Race Relations, Report," August 1950, Wirth Papers, box 5.

23. "American Council on Race Relations Newsletter," January 1945, CETR, box 35; letter to Edward Kelly from Robert Clifton Weaver, 16 October 1944, Rosenwald Papers, box 179; letter to Morton Bodfish from Edwin Embree, 17 October 1944, Rosenwald Papers, box 179.

24. "Director's Newsletter," February 1945, CETR, box 35; "Director's Newsletter," July 1945, CETR, box 35; letter to Edwin Embree from Robert Clifton Weaver, 1 October 1945, Rosenwald Papers, box 159.

25. "Restrictive Covenants: In a Democracy They Cost Too Much," NAACP, part 5, reel 21; Vose, 70–72; memorandum to Mr. Marshall from Marian Wynn Perry, 16 December 1946, NAACP, part 5, reel 21.

26. "Restrictive Covenants: In a Democracy They Cost Too Much," NAACP, part 5, reel 21; "Cases in All Parts of City Being Fought in Chicago's Courts," *NAACP Chicago Branch Bulletin*, 19 May 1945; "Covenant Suit Would Evict 1000 Families," *Chicago Defender*, 5 February 1944.

27. Vose, 10–19; *Buckley v. Corrigan*, 271 U.S. 323, 330 (1926).

28. "National Association of Real Estate Boards, Code of Ethics" (NAREB, 1924), 3.

29. Vose, 62.

30. Letter to National Legal Committee from Thurgood Marshall, 13 June 1945, NAACP, part 5, reel 20; "Tentative Agenda for Conference on Restrictive Covenants," NAACP, part 5, reel 20; "NAACP Legal Meeting Maps Drive at Two-Day Conference," 12 July 1945, NAACP, part 5, reel 20; Vose, 58–64; "Race Pacts Don't Pay, Group Told," *Chicago Daily News*, 10 July 1945.

31. "Preliminary Notes on Coordination of Legal and Social Attacks on Race Restrictive Covenants," no date, NAACP, part 5, reel 20.

32. ACRR, "Hemmed In: ABC's of Race Restrictive Housing Covenants" (Chicago: ACRR, 1945).

33. "The American Council Blunders," *Chicago Defender*, 8 January 1945.

34. Weaver, *Negro Labor*, 78.

35. Weaver, *Negro Labor*, 251, 263–264, 270, 280.

36. Weaver, *Negro Labor*, 308–314.

37. Letter to Robert Clifton Weaver from John Woodburn, 10 August 1945, RCW Papers, reel 2.

38. Joel Seidman, "Negro Labor: A National Problem," *American Economic Review* 36, no. 3 (June 1946): 452–454; Dale Yoder, "Negro Labor: A National Problem," *American Sociological Review* 11, no. 6 (December 1946): 771; Giles Hubert, "Negro Labor: A National Problem," *National Bar Journal* 4, no. 2 (June 1946): 167–168; Julius Thomas, "The Right to Work," *Opportunity*, April–June 1946, 98; "Comments on Negro Labor: A National Problem," RCW Papers, reel 3.

39. Donald R. McCoy and Richard T. Ruetten, *Quest and Response: Minority Rights and the Truman Administration* (Lawrence: University Press of Kansas, 1973), 13–16; Barton Bernstein, *Politics and Policies of the Truman Administration* (Chicago: Quadrangle Books, 1970), 271–273; William C. Berman, *The Politics of Civil Rights in the Truman Administration* (Columbus: Ohio State University Press, 1970); Kersten, 128–134.

40. McCoy and Ruetten, 27–28, 32–33, 43–47; Bernstein, 274–277.

41. McCoy and Ruetten, 46–48.

42. McCoy and Ruetten, 49–53; Bernstein, 277–278.

43. Risa Lauren Goluboff, "Let Economic Equality Take Care of Itself: The NAACP, Labor Litigation, and the Makings of Civil Rights in the 1940s," *U.C.L.A. Law Review* 52 (June 2005): 1393–1486; Daniel Patrick Moynihan, *Maximum Feasible Misunderstanding: Community Action in the War on Poverty* (New York: Free Press, 1969).

## CHAPTER 7

1. George Woodbridge, *UNRRA: The History of the United Nations Relief and Rehabilitation Administration* (New York: Columbia University Press, 1950), 231–256; "UNRRA," *International Organization* 3, no. 3 (August 1949); Grace Fox, "The Origins of UNRRA," *Political Science Quarterly* 65, no. 4 (December 1950): 561–584.

2. Woodbridge, 238–240; Alma Rene Williams, "Robert Weaver: From the Black Cabinet to the President's Cabinet" (PhD diss., Washington University, St. Louis, 1972), 84; "Robert Clifton Weaver Employment Record," 13 February 1947, CETR, box 35.

3. "Weaver to Russia as UNRRA Official," ACRR Report, April 1946; "Associated Negro Press Article," Rosenwald Papers, box 160; "No Race Problem in Russia—Weaver," ACRR Report, November 1946.

4. "PAC Termed Communists' Active Front," *Washington Post*, 4 October 1944.

5. Robert Clifton Weaver, "Russia's War-Ravaged Ukraine Faces Enormous Housing Needs, Part I, The Present," *Journal of Housing*, February 1947, 41–42; Robert Clifton Weaver, "Russia's War-Ravaged Ukraine Faces Enormous Housing Needs, Part II, The Future," *Journal of Housing*, March 1947, 71–72; Senate Committee on Banking and Cur-

rency, *Hearings on the Nomination of Robert C. Weaver, 7 and 8 February 1961* (Washington, DC: Government Printing Office, 1961), 96–99.

6. Minutes of the Julius Rosenwald Fund, 3 October 1946, Houston Papers, box 19.

7. On Wirth, see Roger A. Salerno, *Louis Wirth: A Bio-Bibliography* (New York: Greenwood Press, 1987).

8. Confidential memo to ACRR Board, 20 December 1946, CETR, box 28.

9. Memo from Clarence Pickett to Board of Directors, 20 December 1946, CETR, box 28; memo to Board of Directors from Louis Wirth, 7 March 1947, Wirth Papers, box 14.

10. Clement Vose, *Caucasians Only: The Supreme Court, the NAACP and the Restrictive Covenant Cases* (Berkeley and Los Angeles: University of California Press, 1959), 83, 109–121.

11. Vose, 125–136.

12. *Hurd v. Hodge*, 334 U.S. 24, 27 (1948); Vose, 74–95; Genna Rae McNeil, *Groundwork: Charles Hamilton Houston and the Struggle for Civil Rights* (Philadelphia: University of Pennsylvania Press, 1983), 178–179.

13. *Hurd v. Hodge*, 162 F.2d 233, 238, 243 (DC Circuit 1947); Vose, 95–99; David Southern, *Gunnar Myrdal and Black-White Relations: The Use and Abuse of "An American Dilemma," 1944–1969* (Baton Rouge: Louisiana State University Press, 1987), 132–133; McNeil, 178–179.

14. "Minutes of Meeting N.A.A.C.P. Lawyers and Consultants on Methods of Attacking Restrictive Covenants," 6 September 1945, NAACP, part 5, reel 22; letter to Charles Abrams from Phineas Indritz, 14 August 1947, NAACP, part 5, reel 22; Vose, 159.

15. Letter to Walter White from Louis Wirth, 15 April 1947, NAACP, part 5, reel 20; "Memorandum of Conference with Charles Houston from Marian Wynn Perry," 11 September 1947, NAACP, part 5, reel 22; "Background Materials on Restrictive Covenants," 8 March 1948, NAACP, part 5, reel 20; *Hurd v. Hodge*, "Consolidated Brief for Plaintiffs," 17 November 1947, U.S. Supreme Court Archives, 40, 73. On the use of sociological analysis in the NAACP legal assault on Jim Crow, see Mark Tushnet, *The NAACP Legal Strategy against Segregated Education* (Chapel Hill: University of North Carolina Press, 1987); Vose, 159–163.

16. McNeil, 181; Vose, 184–190; "Consolidated Brief for Plaintiffs," 90.

17. Vose, 197–199.

18. Vose, 163–164, 191–197; Southern, 134–135; McNeil, 181–182.

19. *Shelley v. Kraemer*, 334 U.S. 1, 13, 19 (1948).

20. *Hurd v. Hodge*, 334 U.S. 24, 34 (1948); "Fights Realty Covenants," *New York Times*, 15 December 1947; "Clark Condemns Race Property Ban," *New York Times*, 5 December 1947.

21. NAACP press release, 3 May 1948, NAACP, part 5, reel 22; "Live Anywhere," *Pittsburgh Courier*, 8 May 1948; "Let Democracy Flourish," *Chicago Defender*, 8 May 1948; Vose, 212–214.

22. Robert C. Weaver, *The Negro Ghetto* (New York: Harcourt, Brace, 1948), vii–x.

23. Weaver, *Negro Ghetto*, 7, 41–42, 70–72.

24. Weaver, *Negro Ghetto*, 166–167, 178, 198.

25. Weaver, *Negro Ghetto*, 226-227.

26. Weaver, *Negro Ghetto*, 261, 275.

27. Weaver, *Negro Ghetto*, 324, 328.

28. "Comments on the Negro Ghetto," RCW Papers, reel 3; Catherine Bauer, "Comment on the Negro Ghetto," RCW Papers, reel 3; letter to Lambert Davis from Coleman Woodbury, 30 June 1948, RCW Papers, reel 2; H. A. Overstreet, "Northern Complacency Punctured," *N.Y. Saturday Review of Literature*, 17 July 1948.

29. Arnold Hirsch, *Making the Second Ghetto: Race and Housing in Chicago, 1940–1960* (Chicago: University of Chicago Press, 1998), 30–31, 53.

30. Hirsch, 50, 76; Roger Biles, *Big City Boss in Depression and War: Mayor Edward J. Kelly of Chicago* (DeKalb: Northern Illinois University Press, 1984), 147–148.

31. Simeon Booker, "Robert C. Weaver: Quiet Man Wins Spot in Cabinet," *Ebony*, 21 April 1966.

32. "History of Roosevelt University," http://www.roosevelt.edu/aboutru/history.htm.

33. A. Gilbert Belles, "The College Faculty, the Negro Scholar and the Julius Rosenwald Fund," *Journal of Negro History* 54 (October 1969): 383–392, especially 384–385; James D. Anderson, "Race, Meritocracy and the American Academy during the Immediate Post–World War II Era," *History of Education Quarterly* 33 (Summer 1993): 151–171; "Negro Faculty Members of Northern Universities and Colleges," Frazier Papers, box 21.

34. Letter to Robert Clifton Weaver from Ed Lewis, 7 May 1947, RCW Papers, reel 1; letter to Robert Clifton Weaver from Ed Lewis, 26 May 1947, RCW Papers, reel 1; letter to Charles Thomas from Robert Clifton Weaver, 9 June 1947, RCW Papers, reel 2.

35. Cable to Robert Clifton Weaver from George Counts, 31 October 1946; cable to George Counts from Robert Clifton Weaver, 31 October 1946; letter to Robert Clifton Weaver from George Counts, 1 November 1946; letter to Robert Clifton Weaver from George Counts, 7 November 1946; letter to George Counts from Robert Clifton Weaver, 13 October 1947; all in RCW Papers, reel 1. Williams, 85.

36. "Progress Report on ACRR Activities," June–September 1947; ACRR, minutes of Regular Meeting of Board of Directors, 2 April 1948; both in CETR, box 28.

37. Southern, 16; Salerno.

38. Walter Jackson, *Gunnar Myrdal and America's Conscience: Social Engineering and Racial Liberalism, 1938–1987* (Chapel Hill: University of North Carolina Press, 1990), 284.

39. Memo to Robert Clifton Weaver from Louis Wirth, 4 June 1948, CETR, box 24; "Progress Report," April–June 1948, CETR, box 28.

## CHAPTER 8

1. Jackie Robinson and Alfred Duckett, *I Never Had It Made* (New York: Putnam, 1972), 117.

2. "Robinson Rouses Home Sale Dispute," *New York Times*, 12 December 1953; "Robinsons to Buy Home," *New York Times*, 18 December 1953.

3. For exceptions to the neglect of the fair-housing struggle, see Martha Biondi, *To Stand and Fight: The Struggle for Civil Rights in Postwar New York City* (Cambridge, MA: Harvard University Press, 2003); Stephen Grant Meyer, *As Long as They Don't Move Next*

*Door: Segregation and Racial Conflict in American Neighborhoods* (Lanham, MD: Rowman and Littlefield, 2000).

4. Letter to Frank Horne from Robert Clifton Weaver, 7 November 1948, Horne Papers, box 3.

5. Biondi, 19, 80–82, 98–99, 107; Joshua B. Freeman, *Working-Class New York: Life and Labor since World War II* (New York: New Press, 2000), 179–200; Craig Steven Wilder, *A Covenant with Color: Race and Social Power in Brooklyn* (New York: Columbia University Press, 2000), 204–205.

6. Robert Clifton Weaver, *The Negro Ghetto* (New York: Harcourt, Brace, 1948), 328.

7. Letter to Robert Clifton Weaver from Ernest Melby, 5 October 1948, General Education Board Papers, RAC, series 1.2, box 259; letter to Robert Clifton Weaver from Vice Chancellor, 5 November 1948, RCW Papers, reel 2; letter to Frank Horne from Robert Clifton Weaver, 7 November 1948, Horne Papers, box 3; letter to Robert Calkins from Ernest Melby, 18 May 1949, General Education Board Papers, RAC.

8. This section relies in part on the work of Arnold Hirsch, "Choosing Segregation: Federal Housing Policy between *Shelley* and *Brown*," in *From Tenements to the Taylor Homes*, ed. John Bauman, Roger Biles, and Kristin Szylvian (University Park: Pennsylvania State University Press, 2000), 206–225; Arnold Hirsch, "Containment on the Home Front: Race and Federal Housing Policy from the New Deal to the Cold War," *Journal of Urban History* 26 (January 2000): 158–189, especially 161; Arnold Hirsch, "Searching for a 'Sound Negro Policy': A Racial Agenda for the Housing Acts of 1949 and 1954," *Housing Policy Debate* 11 (2000): 393–441.

9. Memorandum from Franklin Richards, Commissioner, Federal Housing Administration, to Raymond Foley, Administrator, Housing Home Finance Administration, 21 May 1948, NAACP, part 5, reel 5; Hirsch, "Choosing Segregation," 211.

10. "Minutes of Conference in Connection with the Federal Housing Administration," 5 August 1948, NAACP, part 5, reel 5; Barbara Kelly, *Expanding the American Dream: Building and Rebuilding Levittown* (Albany: State University of New York Press, 1998), 17; "Release, NAACP Anti-bias Plea Rejected by FHA Head," 4 November 1948, NAACP, part 5, reel 5.

11. Hirsch, "Containment," 164; "Truman Puts Ban on All Housing Aid Where Bias Exists," *New York Times*, 3 December 1949. On Truman and civil rights, see Donald R. McCoy and Richard T. Ruetten, *Quest and Response: Minority Rights and the Truman Administration* (Lawrence: University Press of Kansas, 1973), 96–147; Barton Bernstein, "The Ambiguous Legacy: The Truman Administration and Civil Rights," in *The Politics and Policies of the Truman Administration*, ed. Barton Bernstein (Chicago: Quadrangle Books, 1970), 269–314, especially 283–287.

12. "Realty Men Fear Havoc in Building over Curb on Bias," *New York Times*, 4 December 1949; "No Change Viewed in Work of F.H.A.," *New York Times*, 4 December 1949; Bernstein, 296.

13. A. Scott Henderson, *Housing and the Democratic Ideal: The Life and Thought of Charles Abrams* (New York: Columbia University Press, 2000), 122, 127–129; Biondi, 122–123.

14. Henderson, 132–134; Biondi, 123–124.

15. Wendell E. Pritchett, "Where Shall We Live? Class and the Limitations of Fair Housing Law," *Urban Lawyer* 35 (Summer 2003): 399–470.

16. Wendell E. Pritchett, "The 'Public Menace' of Blight: Urban Renewal and the Private Uses of Eminent Domain," *Yale Law and Policy Review* 21 (2003): 1–52.

17. Columbia University has in its Rare Book and Manuscript Library a number of Black's papers, which reveal his involvement with numerous endeavors.

18. Robert Caro, *The Power Broker: Robert Moses and the Fall of New York* (New York: Vintage, 1974), 961.

19. "Toward Democracy in Housing, May 1949," Black Papers, box 9; "The Work of the National Committee against Discrimination in Housing and the New York State Committee on Discrimination in Housing," no date, Black Papers.

20. "Memorandum from Hortense Gabel, Report on Meeting of Advisory Committee on Urban Redevelopment Conference," 12 September 1949, UNH Papers, box 42; "Press Release of the New York State Committee on Discrimination in Housing," 1 November 1949, UNH Papers, box 42; New York State Committee on Discrimination in Housing, "Forbidden Neighbors" (1949).

21. Robert Clifton Weaver, "Habitation with Segregation," 1949, RCW Papers, Supplement, box 8; Robert Clifton Weaver, "Address at the Luncheon Meeting of the Sixth Annual Conference on Discrimination in Housing," 21 May 1954, RCW Papers, Supplement, box 7.

22. Edwin R. Embree, *Investment in People: The Story of the Julius Rosenwald Fund* (Chicago: Julius Rosenwald Fund, 1949).

23. Julius Rosenwald Fund, "Program," RCW Papers, reel 3; letter to Charles Johnson from Robert Clifton Weaver, Rosenwald Papers, box 60; press release, Rosenwald Papers, box 88.

24. E. J. Kahn, *Jock: The Life and Times of John Hay Whitney* (New York: Doubleday, 1981).

25. Kahn, 176–178; Esther Raushenbush, *John Hay Whitney Foundation: A Report of the First Twenty-five Years* (New York: John Hay Whitney Foundation, 1972), vol. 1, ix–xi; memo to Tex McCrary from Robert Clifton Weaver, 23 May 1950, Johnson Papers, box 7; Robert Clifton Weaver taped interview, no date, RCW Papers, Supplement, box 8.

26. Letter to Robert Clifton Weaver from John Hay Whitney, 22 November 1949, RCW Papers, reel 2.

27. "1952–1953 Fellowship Program," 9 April 1952, Johnson Papers, box 7; "Opportunity Fellows, 1950–1954: An Interim Report," 19 October 1954, Johnson Papers, box 52; "Opportunity Fellowships," December 1952, Johnson Papers, box 57.

28. Kahn, 179; Raushenbush, 64–65, 70–71.

29. "Robert C. Weaver, Harvard Class of 1929," *25th Anniversary Report*, HUA; Shirley Siegel interview with author, 14 October 2005.

30. Letter to Harry Gideonese from J. M. O'Neill, 24 May 1950, Ella Weaver Papers, box 1.

31. William Piggot, "The Geography of Exclusion: Race and Suburbanization in Postwar Philadelphia" (MA thesis, Ohio State University, 2002), 15; David Popencoe, *The Suburban Environment* (Chicago: University of Chicago Press, 1977), 113; letter

to Raymond Foley from Robert Clifton Weaver, 20 November 1951, Horne Papers, box 3; NCDH, "Executive Director's Action Report," 24 December 1952, Abrams Papers, reel 14.

32. "Remarks by Weaver, December 1950," NCDH Papers, box 1; letter to Raymond Foley from Robert Clifton Weaver, 20 November 1951, Horne Papers, box 3; "Executive Director's Action Report," NYSCDH, UNH Papers, box 42.

33. Letter to Robert Clifton Weaver from Raymond Foley, 9 December 1949, RCW Papers, reel 1; letter to Robert Clifton Weaver from Nathaniel Keith, 6 January 1950, RCW Papers, reel 1; Slum Clearance Advisory Committee, "Survey of the Second Meeting," 7 March 1950, RCW Papers, reel 3.

34. Robert Clifton Weaver, "Address at the National Conference on Discrimination in Housing," 20 May 1952, RCW Papers, Supplement, box 6.

35. Joel Schwartz, *The New York Approach: Robert Moses, Urban Liberals and the Redevelopment of the Inner City* (Columbus: Ohio State University Press, 1993); Freeman, 124.

36. Caro, 965–968; Schwartz, 124; Wendell E. Pritchett, *Brownsville, Brooklyn: Blacks, Jews, and the Changing Face of the Ghetto* (Chicago: University of Chicago Press, 2002), 120–121; Robert Clifton Weaver, "Recent Developments in Urban Housing and Their Implications for Minorities," *Phylon* 15 (1955): 290.

37. Robert Clifton Weaver, "Cooper Union Forum Address," 16 December 1951, RCW Papers, reel 2; Charles Abrams, *Forbidden Neighbors: A Study of Prejudice in Housing* (New York: Harper and Brothers, 1955), 309–310; Meyer, 142; Pritchett, *Brownsville, Brooklyn,* 98–99; Hirsch, "Searching for a 'Sound Negro Policy,'" 415.

38. Pritchett, *Brownsville, Brooklyn,* 99–100; Schwartz, 115–120.

39. Arnold Hirsch, *Making the Second Ghetto: Race and Housing in Chicago, 1940–1960* (Chicago: University of Chicago Press, 1999).

40. Robert C. Weaver, "Address at the National Conference on Discrimination in Housing," 20 May 1952, RCW Papers, Supplement, box 6; letter to Raymond Foley from Robert Clifton Weaver, 20 November 1951, Horne Papers, box 3.

41. "Memorandum from Hortense Gabel to Members and Friends of the Committee on Discrimination in Housing," 20 February 1953, UNH Papers, box 42; Meyer, 154–155.

42. Albert Cole, "What Is the Federal Government's Role in Housing?" 8 February 1954, UNH Papers, box 58; letter to Albert Cole from Robert Weaver and Hortense Gabel, 13 January 1954, RCW Papers, reel 1.

43. Letter to Albert Cole from Robert Clifton Weaver and Hortense Gabel, 13 January 1954, RCW Papers, reel 1.

44. NCDH press release, "Groups Protest Threat to Dismiss Frank Horne," 10 September 1953, UNH Papers, box 58; "Race Counselor," *Washington Post,* 17 September 1953; "The Horne Case: A Report and a Call for Vigilance," 23 October 1953, UNH Papers, box 52; Hirsch, "Searching for a 'Sound Negro Policy,'" 420–421.

45. "Affidavit of Robert C. Weaver," 28 June 1954, RCW Papers, reel 2; Hirsch, "Searching for a 'Sound Negro Policy,'" 420–422; "U.S. Housing Aide Quits," *New York Times,* 9 July 1956; Charles Abrams, "Segregation, Housing and the Horne Case," *Reporter,* 6 October 1955.

46. Frances Levenson, "Testimony before the House Committee on Banking and Currency," 21 May 1956, Black Papers, box 9.

## CHAPTER 9

1. Rudy Abramson, *Spanning the Century: The Life of W. Averell Harriman, 1891–1986* (New York: William Morrow, 1992), 21–62.

2. Abramson, passim.

3. "Harriman Enters Democratic Race for Governorship," *New York Times*, 26 July 1954; "Roosevelt Amateurs Pitted against Harriman Old Pros," *New York Times*, 28 August 1954; Abramson, 504–509.

4. "Civil Rights Goal Set by Harriman," *New York Times*, 26 September 1954; "Harriman Invites Harlem's Support," *New York Times*, 4 October 1954; "Our Next Governor," *New York Times*, 25 October 1954; "Our Choice for Governor," *New York Amsterdam News*, 23 October 1954.

5. "State Edge, 11,629," *New York Times*, 3 November 1954; Abramson, 514–515.

6. Martha Biondi, *To Stand and Fight: The Struggle for Civil Rights in New York City* (Cambridge, MA: Harvard University Press, 2004), 219–220; *Amsterdam News*, 4 September 1954, 11 December 1954, and 11 January 1955; "Harriman Defers Decision on Asking Rise in Income Tax," *New York Times*, 31 December 1954; A. Scott Henderson, *Housing and the Democratic Ideal: The Life and Thought of Charles Abrams* (New York: Columbia University Press, 2000), 158–159.

7. Alma Rene Williams, "Robert C. Weaver: From the Black Cabinet to the President's Cabinet" (PhD diss., Washington University, St. Louis, 1972), 91.

8. Richard O. Davies, *Housing Reform during the Truman Era* (Columbia: University of Missouri Press, 1966), 118–120; Joseph McMurray interview with Frank Munger, 4 April 1963, Syracuse University Archives, Syracuse, NY; Williams, 95; Executive Chamber, press release, 28 March 1955, Harriman Papers, box 1309; Housing, no date, Harriman Papers, box 1671; Robert Clifton Weaver, "Recent Developments in Urban Housing and Their Implications for Minorities," *Phylon* 16 (1955): 275–282, especially 281.

9. New York State Committee on Discrimination in Housing, "New York Needs a Fair Housing Practices Law," December 1956, UNH Papers, box 58; "Harriman Widens Housing Bias Ban," *New York Times*, 16 April 1955.

10. Governor's Office, press release, 8 July 1955, Harriman Papers, box 26; "First Annual Report of Housing Advisory Council," 24 October 1956, NAACP, part 5, reel 11; memo to James Scheuer from Robert Clifton Weaver, 22 July 1955, RCW Papers, reel 2.

11. Robert Clifton Weaver, "The Effect of Anti-discrimination Legislation upon the FHA and VA Insured Housing Market in New York State," *Land Economics* 31 (1955): 301–313, especially 305, 308, 309–310; Robert Clifton Weaver, "Can Democratic Racial Patterns Be Extended to Government Insured Housing?" 14 July 1955, Harriman Papers, box 26.

12. Wendell E. Pritchett, "Where Shall We Live? Class and the Limitations of Fair Housing Law," *Urban Lawyer* 35 (Summer 2003): 432–433.

13. "City Schools Invite Inquiry of 'Jim Crow' Allegations," *New York Times*, 14 July 1954; Clarence Taylor, *Knocking at Our Own Door: Milton A. Galamison and the Struggle to Integrate New York City Schools* (New York: Columbia University Press, 1997), 53–54; Gerald Markowitz and David Rosner, *Children, Race, and Power: Kenneth and Mamie Clark's Northside Center* (Charlottesville: University of Virginia Press, 1996), 95–96.

14. "City Schools Cleared in Segregation Study," *New York Times*, 7 November 1955; "School Segregation Here?" *New York Times*, 8 November 1955.

15. "Preliminary Statement of Board of Education Resolution for Action," 23 December 1954, NAACP, part 3, reel 6; "City Unit to Study School Equality," *New York Times*, 18 November 1955; Taylor, 54.

16. Sub-commission on Physical Plant and Maintenance, "Report," 16 June 1956, Commission on Integration Papers, series 261, New York City Municipal Archives, New York, NY, folder 40; "Schools Get Plan to Wipe Out Bias," *New York Times*, 17 May 1956; "City Schools Open a Major Campaign to Spur Integration," *New York Times*, 24 July 1956.

17. Markowitz and Rosner, 98–99; "Text of the Board of Education Statement on Integration Here," *New York Times*, 26 February 1957.

18. Taylor, 57, 65.

19. Taylor, 66.

20. Taylor, 50–55; Biondi, 167–169.

21. Memorandum to Mr. Wilkins from Mr. Morsell, 14 November 1956, NAACP, part 3, reel 6; Taylor, 67–69; "Integration Plea Charges City Lag," *New York Times*, 12 July 1957.

22. "School Board and Jansen Are Attacked by Urban League on Integration Reports," *New York Times*, 28 July 1957; "Critics of Jansen Ask to Query Him," *New York Times*, 5 August 1957; Taylor, 74; Markowitz and Rosner, 99.

23. Letter to Averell Harriman from Robert Clifton Weaver, 6 August 1957, NAACP, part 3, reel 6; letter to Board of Education from Executive Committee, 25 September 1957, Commission on Integration Papers, series 261, New York City Municipal Archives, folder 1; letter to Mayor Wagner from Executive Committee, 17 April 1957, Commission on Integration Papers, series 261, New York City Municipal Archives, folder 1.

24. New York Board of Education, "Toward the Integration of Our Schools: Final Report of the Commission on Integration," 1958; Taylor, 80–81; Markowitz and Rosner, 102, 106.

25. "Harriman Shifts Three State Aides," *New York Herald Tribune*, 15 December 1955; "Harriman Gives Weaver State's Top Rent Post," *Albany Times Union*, 15 December 1955; "Harriman Names Negro as Rent Administrator," *Syracuse Post-Standard*, 15 December 1955; "The Political Pot," *New York Age-Defender*, 31 December 1955.

26. Charles Abrams interview with Frank Munger, 27 February 1963, Syracuse University Library, Syracuse, NY.

27. "Harriman Spurs Housing Bias War," *New York Times*, 55 December 1955; Abramson, 538–539.

28. Williams, 95.

29. "Harriman Shifts Three State Aides," *New York Herald Tribune*, 15 December 1955; "Harriman Gives Weaver State's Top Rent Post," *Albany Times Union*, 15 December 1955; "Harriman Names Negro as Rent Administrator," *Syracuse Post-Standard*, 15 December 1955.

30. Abrams interview with Munger, 27 February 1963, Syracuse University Library; Governor's Office, press release, 14 December 1955, Abrams Papers, reel 17.

31. Abrams interview with Munger, 27 February 1963, Syracuse University Library.

32. "Harriman Urges Bias End," *New York Times*, 8 February 1957.

33. Neil Lebowitz, "Above Party, Class or Creed: Rent Control in the United States, 1940–1947," *Journal of Urban History* 7 (August 1981): 439–470.

34. "Dewey Acts to Freeze Rentals in State at Present OPA Levels," *New York Times*, 30 June 1946; Joel Schwartz, "Tenant Power in the Liberal City, 1943–1971," in *The Tenant Movement in New York City, 1904–1984*, ed. Ronald Lawson (New Brunswick, NJ: Rutgers University Press, 1986), 142, 146; "Morris Says City 'Gouges' Tenants," *New York Times*, 22 September 1949; "Council Approves Rent Control Bill Backed by O'Dwyer," *New York Times*, 11 January 1950; "State Validates Rent Law of City," *New York Times*, 11 January 1950.

35. "Senate Keeps Curb on Rents to Jan. 1: 6-Month Option Set," *New York Times*, 13 June 1950; Davies, 122–123; "State Takes Over Control of Rents: G.O.P. Bill Signed," *New York Times*, 30 March 1950; Schwartz, 152–153.

36. "Text of Governor's Special Message on Rent Control," *New York Times*, 20 January 1955; "Harriman Urges Tighter Rent Law, 2-Year Extension," *New York Times*, 21 January 1955; "State G.O.P. Committed to Keep Rent Control on Residences Here," *New York Times*, 13 January 1955; "Harriman Signs, Scores Rent Bill," *New York Times*, 28 April 1955; "Rent Curbs Lifted on 272,500 Units," *New York Times*, 1 July 1955; "2,229,100 Rentals under State Curb," *New York Times*, 1 August 1955; "Report to Averell Harriman from Charles Abrams," 1 July 1955, Harriman Papers, box 81.

37. Abramson, 521; Temporary State Rent Commission, "Report on Rent Controls in New York State," 1955, Syracuse University Archives, 13.

38. "Report on Rent Controls in New York State," 1955, 16–47.

39. "Report on Rent Controls in New York State," 1955, 30; Temporary State Rent Commission, "The Little Book on Rent Control," 1956; Temporary State Rent Commission, "The Little Book on Evictions," 1956; "State Issues Booklet on Rent Controls Designed to Reduce the Number of Disputes," *New York Times*, 7 May 1956; "Text of Harriman's Special Message on Rent Control," *New York Times*, 24 January 1957; "It's a Tough Job—He Likes It," *New York Post*, 4 March 1956.

40. "Harriman Plan to Keep Rent Law to Stir a Sharp Legislative Fight," *New York Times*, 5 January 1957; "2 State Leaders See Continued Rent Law," *New York Times*, 7 January 1957.

41. "Text of Harriman's Special Message on State Rent Control," *New York Times*, 24 January 1957; "Harriman Urges Two Moves to Ease Rent Controls," *New York Times*, 24 January 1957.

42. "A.D.A., Liberal Party Split on Rent Issue," *New York Times*, 12 February 1957; "Rent Plan Splits Harriman Forces," *New York Times*, 28 January 1957; "Memorandum by Robert C. Weaver, State Rent Administrator," 11 February 1957, Harriman Papers, box 312; "Rent Chief Lists Gains for Tenants," *New York Times*, 1 February 1957; "Harriman Calls Rent Plan 'Fair,'" *New York Times*, 25 January 1957; "G.O.P. Charges Harriman Tries to Cover Up Rent Increases," *New York Times*, 9 February 1957; "Rent Bill to Limit Rise to Small Properties," *New York Times*, 11 February 1957.

43. "Statement of Robert C. Weaver, State Rent Administrator," 27 February 1957, RCW Papers, reel 2; "Governor Heals Rift on Rent Bill," *New York Times*, 7 February 1957; "G.O.P. Urging Limit on Control of Rents," *New York Times*, 25 February 1957; "Weaver

Sees 'Death of Controls' if Legislature Enacts GOP's Plan," *New York Post*, 28 February 1957; "Study Plan of G.O.P. to Lift $150 Rent Lid," *New York Post*, 25 February 1957; "G.O.P. Rent Plan Scored at Albany," *New York Times*, 26 February 1957; "Rent Chief Warns on Lifting Control," *New York Journal American*, 27 February 1957; "500,000 Families Face Rent Rise under GOP Plan, Weaver Warns," *New York Post*, 27 February 1957; "Weaver, Landlords Clash on Controls," *NY World-Telegram*, 27 February 1957.

44. "Landlords Stage Rent Law March," *New York Times*, 27 February 1957.

45. "Heckling and Disorder Stall Albany Rent Curb Hearing," *New York Times*, 28 February 1957; "Patriots of Real Estate," *New York Post*, 28 February 1957; "Weaver Sees 'Death of Controls' if Legislature Enacts GOP's Plan," *New York Post*, 28 February 1957.

46. Robert Clifton Weaver interview with Frank Munger, 28 February 1962, Syracuse University Archives; "G.O.P. Won't Act on 'Luxury' Rents," *New York Times*, 15 March 1957; "GOP Offers New Rent Decontrol Plan—Weaver Denounces 'War of Nerves,'" *New York Post*, 8 March 1957; "Albany Reports Rent Law Gains," *New York Times*, 14 March 1957; letter to Averell Harriman from Robert Clifton Weaver, 14 March 1957, RCW Papers, reel 1; "G.O.P. Faces Split on City Rent Curb," *New York Times*, 16 March 1957.

47. "Report of Temporary State Rent Commission," 18 March 1957, RCW Papers, reel 2; "Minority Report on Rent Control," RCW Papers, reel 2; "State Unit Backs 2-Year Rent Curb," *New York Times*, 19 March 1957; "Weaver Calls GOP's Rent Plan 'Phony,'" *New York Post*, 19 March 1957; "Democrats Slam GOP on Rent Curb Plan," *Long Island Daily Press*, 25 March 1957; "Weaver Says Secret GOP Revision Opens Loophole for Rent Rise Here," *New York Post*, 25 March 1957; "Rent Control Kept in 12 Cities, 15 Towns," *New York Times*, 15 July 1957; "Control of Rents into '59 Is Voted," *New York Times*, 30 March 1957; "Terms New Law Victory for City but Detrimental to Upstate Dwellers," *New York Times*, 23 April 1957.

48. "Temporary State Housing Rent Commission, Administrative Improvement Report," 15 October 1957, Harriman Papers, box 1309; "Rent Chief Frees 600 Luxury Units," *New York Times*, 17 September 1957; "City Rent Ruling Is Called Proper," *New York Times*, 27 December 1957.

49. "Temporary State Housing Rent Commission, Administrative Improvement Report," 15 October 1958, Harriman Papers, box 1904; letter to Daniel P. Moynihan from Robert Clifton Weaver, 3 July 1958, Harriman Papers, box 313; "State Lists Hotel as Rooming House," *New York Times*, 1 July 1958; "Small Hotel Operators Charge Politics in State's Drive to Reclassify Buildings," *New York Times*, 14 October 1958; letter to Averell Harriman from E. G. Volence, 10 February 1958, Harriman Papers, box 313; Weaver interview with Munger, 28 December 1962, Syracuse University Archives.

50. A. H. Raskin, "Washington Gets the 'Weaver Treatment,'" *New York Times Magazine*, 14 May 1961; Morton Schussheim interview with author, 3 November 2005.

51. Abramson, 516–519, 526–531; "Harriman Becomes 'the Guv,'" *New York Times*, 3 July 1955.

52. Abramson, 532–542.

53. Abramson, 542–546; Joseph Persico, *The Imperial Rockefeller: A Biography of Nelson A. Rockefeller* (New York: Simon and Schuster, 1982).

54. Abramson, 564–569; "Harriman Routed," *New York Times*, 5 November 1958.

55. Letter to Averell Harriman from Robert Clifton Weaver, 5 November 1958, RCW Papers, reel 1; Weaver interview with Munger, 28 December 1962, Syracuse University Archives; "State Rent Chief Declines City Job," *New York Times*, no date, RCW Papers, reel 3; letter to Robert Clifton Weaver from Philip Widenhouse, 27 November 1956, RCW Papers, reel 2; letter to Philip Widenhouse from Robert Clifton Weaver, 28 November 1956, RCW Papers, reel 2.

56. Letter to Robert Clifton Weaver from John Kenneth Galbraith, 29 July 1957, RCW Papers, reel 1; letter to Robert Clifton Weaver from Fred Kramer, 28 February 1957, RCW Papers, reel 1.

## CHAPTER 10

1. Morton Grodzins, "The Metropolitan Area as a Racial Problem" (repr., Pittsburgh: University of Pittsburgh Press, 1969), 1.

2. Grodzins, 2–3, 11.

3. Gerald Gamm, *Urban Exodus: Why the Jews Left Boston and the Catholics Stayed* (Cambridge, MA: Harvard University Press, 1999), 225; Becky Nicolaides, *My Blue Heaven: Life and Politics in the Working-Class Suburbs of Los Angeles, 1920–1965* (Chicago: University of Chicago Press, 2002); Wendell E. Pritchett, *Brownsville, Brooklyn: Blacks, Jews, and the Changing Face of the Ghetto* (Chicago: University of Chicago Press, 2002), 153.

4. Alice O'Connor, "Community Action, Urban Reform, and the Fight against Poverty: The Ford Foundation's Gray Areas Program," *Journal of Urban History* 22, no. 5 (July 1996): 586–625, especially 601–603; Alice O'Connor, "The Ford Foundation and Philanthropic Activism in the 1960s," in *Philanthropic Foundations: New Scholarship, New Possibilities*, ed. Ellen Condliffe Lagemann (Bloomington: Indiana University Press, 1999), 169–194, especially 171; Gregory K. Raynor, "The Ford Foundation's War on Poverty: Private Philanthropy and Race Relations in New York City, 1948–1968," in *Philanthropic Foundations*, ed. Lagemann, 195–228, especially 215.

5. Raynor, 199–205.

6. Paul Ylvisaker Oral History, 27 September 1973, Ford, 22; letter to Robert Clifton Weaver from Joseph McDaniel, 24 March 1959, RCW Papers, reel 1; letter to Robert Clifton Weaver from Verne Atwater, 11 October 1959, RCW Papers, reel 1.

7. Letter to Robert Clifton Weaver from Joseph McDaniel, 24 March 1959, RCW Papers, reel 1.

8. Letter to Paul Ylvisaker from Robert Clifton Weaver, 15 February 1959, Grant no. L9–263, Ford.

9. Memo to Clarence Fauset from Robert Clifton Weaver, 15 September 1959, Project no. L9–263, Ford.

10. Memo to Clarence Fauset from Robert Clifton Weaver, 15 May 1959, Project no. L9–263, Ford; memo to Clarence Fauset from Robert Clifton Weaver, 15 September 1959, Project no. L9–263, Ford; Robert Clifton Weaver, "The Private Negro Colleges and Universities—an Appraisal," *Journal of Negro Education* 29, no. 2 (Spring 1960): 113–120; Robert Clifton Weaver, "The Negro Private and Church-Related College: A Critical Summary," *Journal of Negro Education* 29, no. 3 (Summer 1960): 394–400.

11. Memo to Henry Heald from Clarence Fauset, 25 November 1959, Project

no. L9–263, Ford; memo to Henry Heald from Clarence Fauset, 26 January 1960, Project no. L9–263, Ford; memo to Files from Clarence Fauset, 3 February 1960, Project no. L9–263, Ford.

12. Ylvisaker Oral History, 27 September 1973, Ford, 23; Edgar Hoover and Raymond Vernon, eds., *Anatomy of a Metropolis, the Changing Distribution of People and Jobs within the New York Metropolitan Region* (Cambridge, MA: Harvard University Press, 1959); O'Connor, "Community Action, Urban Reform, and the Fight against Poverty," 605–606.

13. Memo to Henry Heald from Dyke Brown, 23 December 1959, Project no. L9–517, Ford; O'Connor, "Community Action, Urban Reform, and the Fight against Poverty," 606.

14. Raymond Vernon, *The Changing Economic Function of the Central City* (New York: New York Area Development Committee, 1959).

15. Memo to Henry Heald from Dyke Brown, 23 December 1959, Project no. L9–517, Ford.

16. O'Connor, "Community Action, Urban Reform, and the Fight against Poverty," 610–611.

17. Interview with Paul Ylvisaker and Robert Weaver, 15 March 1960, Rockefeller Foundation Papers, RG2, General Correspondence, 1960, RAC, reel 18; letter to Verne Atwater from Robert Clifton Weaver, 4 May 1960, RCW Papers, reel 1; letter to Willis Robertson from Paul Ylvisaker, 3 February 1961, Henry Heald Papers, box 12, Ford; Ylvisaker Oral History, 27 September 1973, Ford, 23; memo to Joseph McDaniel from Dyke Brown, 6 May 1960, RCW Papers, reel 1.

18. Robert Caro, *The Power Broker: Robert Moses and the Fall of New York* (New York: Vintage, 1974), 979–980.

19. Caro, 1024.

20. Caro, 1062–1063; "Mayor Initiates Sweeping Study of All Housing," *New York Times*, 21 August 1959; "Reform of Relocation," *New York Times*, 17 December 1959; J. Anthony Panuch, *Relocation in New York City: A Report to Mayor Robert F. Wagner* (New York: Office of the Mayor, 1959).

21. J. Anthony Panuch, *Building a Better New York: Final Report to Mayor Robert F. Wagner* (New York: Office of the Mayor, 1960); "3-Man Authority to Guide Housing Urged on Mayor," *New York Times*, 10 March 1960. Weeks before, the Citizens Housing and Planning Council had proposed a similar reform; see Citizens Housing and Planning Council of New York, *Toward a Better New York* (New York: CHPC, 1960).

22. "Davies to Fill in as Housing Chief," *New York Times*, 13 April 1960; "Mayor Hints Weaver and Fried Will Get Housing Board Jobs," *New York Times*, 19 April 1960; letter to Robert F. Wagner from J. Clarence Davies, 11 April 1960, Wagner Papers, reel 2253; Mayor's Office, press release, 13 April 1960, Wagner Papers, reel 2253; Mayor's Office, press release, 3 May 1960, Wagner Papers, reel 2253; "Weaver Named to Housing Board," *New York Amsterdam News*, 1 May 1960.

23. "Housing in New York City," 30 September 1959, Program no. l9–931, Ford; Robert Clifton Weaver, "Address at the National Conference on Discrimination in Housing," 11 December 1958, Black Papers, box 12; Robert Clifton Weaver, "Class, Race and Urban Renewal," *Land Economics* 36, no. 3 (August 1960): 235–251, especially 242.

24. Weaver, "Class, Race and Urban Renewal," 244–246, 251.

25. J. Clarence Davies, Walter S. Fried, and Robert Weaver, "Report to Mayor Robert F. Wagner," 1 June 1960, Wagner Papers, reel 2253; "Housing in New Focus," *New York Times*, 6 June 1960.

26. "West Side Groups May Renew Area," *New York Times*, 14 August 1960; "Compromise Adds Co-ops in Cadman," *New York Times*, 1 September 1960; "City Plans Rise in Housing Loans," *New York Times*, 29 September 1960; "City Loans Ready on Old Buildings," *New York Times*, 19 November 1960; Housing and Redevelopment Board, *Annual Report, 1961* (New York: City of New York, 1961); letter to Paul Ylvisaker from Robert Clifton Weaver, 21 November 1960, General Files, 1960, Ford.

27. Gilbert Jonas, *Freedom's Sword: The NAACP and the Struggle against Racism in America, 1909–1969* (London: Routledge, 2005), 305–312.

28. David J. Garrow, *Bearing the Cross: Martin Luther King, Jr., and the Southern Christian Leadership Conference* (New York: Vintage, 1988), 91–92, 97–100.

29. Roy Wilkins, *Standing Fast: The Autobiography of Roy Wilkins* (New York: Da Capo, 1994), 241–242; "Along the N.A.A.C.P. Battlefront," *Crisis*, February 1957, 100–104; NAACP, "Report of the Secretary for the Month of November 1956," 10 December 1956, NAACP Papers, series 3, box A31.

30. NAACP, "Board of Directors Meeting," 4 January 1960, NAACP Papers, LOC, series 3, box A26; NAACP, press release, 7 January 1960, NAACP Papers, LOC, series 3, box A33; Jonas, 321; Martha Biondi, *To Stand and Fight: The Struggle for Civil Rights in New York City* (Cambridge, MA: Harvard University Press, 2004), 169.

31. William Chafe, *Civilities and Civil Rights* (New York: Oxford University Press, 1980), 99; Claybourne Carson, *In Struggle: SNCC and the Black Awakening of the 1960s* (Cambridge, MA: Harvard University Press, 1981), 9–12; Garrow, 129; Wilkins, 267.

32. "Along the N.A.A.C.P. Battlefront," *Crisis*, April 1960, 250–251; "Along the N.A.A.C.P. Battlefront," *Crisis*, May 1960, 313–314; Wilkins, 269; Garrow, 137; Nat Hentoff, "A Peaceful Army," *Commonweal*, 10 June 1960; Louis Lomax, "The Revolt against the 'Negro Leaders,'" *Harper's*, June 1960, 43.

33. "Keynote Address by Robert C. Weaver," NAACP, part 1, Supplement, reel 12; "Fifty-first Annual NAACP Convention—Accent on Youth," *Crisis*, August–September 1960, 405–409.

34. "Keynote Address by Robert Clifton Weaver," NAACP, part 1, Supplement, reel 12.

35. "Keynote Address by Robert Clifton Weaver," NAACP, part 1, Supplement, reel 12.

36. Edwin Levinson, *Black Politics in New York City* (New York: Twayne Publishers, 1974), 89; Kenneth Jackson, ed., *The Encyclopedia of New York City* (New Haven, CT: Yale University Press, 1995), 129 (borough presidents).

37. Charles V. Hamilton, *Adam Clayton Powell: The Political Biography of an American Dilemma* (New York: Atheneum, 1991); Levinson, 109–143.

38. Levinson, 92–93.

39. "Man for the Job," *New York Post*, 21 December 1960; "Hulan Jack's Successor," *New York Times*, 31 December 1959.

40. Levinson, 94; "Aftermath of a Suit," *New York Times*, 11 July 1960; "Hulan Jack Plans Stir Wide Debate," *New York Times*, 7 November 1960; "Back Negro for Jack's Old

Job," *New York Amsterdam News*, 17 December 1960; "Jack Is Convicted on 3 Counts at 2d Trial: Will Lose Borough Post," *New York Times*, 7 December 1960; "DeSapio-Wagner Deal," *New York Times*, 12 December 1960; "Mayor Ignores Tammany on Borough Presidency," *New York Times*, 29 December 1960; "Bob Weaver Appointment Certain to Be Confirmed," *Pittsburgh Courier*, 14 January 1961.

## CHAPTER 11

1. Robert Clifton Weaver Oral History, JFKL, 12–14.

2. "Urban Policy Task Force Report," JFKL, 22.

3. "Weaver Is Sworn in as Housing Chief," *New York Times*, 12 February 1961.

4. Theodore Sorenson, *Kennedy* (New York: Harper and Row, 1965), 471; Carl M. Brauer, *John F. Kennedy and the Second Reconstruction* (New York: Columbia University Press, 1977), 12, 20–21; Mark Stern, *Calculating Visions: Kennedy, Johnson, and Civil Rights* (New Brunswick, NJ: Rutgers University Press, 1992), 17; Nick Bryant, *The Bystander: John F. Kennedy and the Struggle for Black Equality* (New York: Basic Books, 2006), 75–77.

5. Stern, 32; "Needed—a Stroke of the Pen," October 1961, Black Papers, box 9; J. Anthony Lukas, "Integrated Housing: A Matter of Timing," *Reporter*, 15 February 1962; Taylor Branch, *Parting the Waters: America in the King Years, 1954–1963* (New York: Simon and Schuster, 1988), 341.

6. Roy Wilkins, *Standing Fast: The Autobiography of Roy Wilkins* (New York: Da Capo, 1982), 278.

7. "Lodge Denies Pledging Negro Cabinet Post," *Washington Post*, 19 October 1960; "Johnson Urges G.O.P. Debate," *Washington Post*, 20 October 1960; Brauer, 42; Bryant, 175–176; Stern, 36.

8. Brauer, 47–51; Alex Poinsett, *Walking with Presidents: Louis Martin and the Rise of Black Political Power* (Lanham, MD: Madison Books, 1997), 80–85; Hugh Davis Graham, *Civil Rights and the Presidency* (New York: Oxford University Press, 1992), 32; Branch, 339–360, 368–369.

9. "Dawson Postmaster?" *New York Amsterdam News*, 17 December 1960; "Why I Couldn't Accept a Cabinet Job: Bill Dawson," *New York Amsterdam News*, 24 December 1960; Poinsett, 88–90; Bryant, 216; "Robert Weaver Is Picked as Federal Housing Chief," *New York Times*, 30 January 1960.

10. Weaver Oral History, JFKL, 14–15; Staff Files, Davies Papers, JFKL; Poinsett, 101–102.

11. "Kennedy Nominates Robert C. Weaver for HHFA," *House and Home*, 261, 40; "Transcript of Kennedy-Weaver Press Conference," *New York Times*, 1 January 1961.

12. Weaver Oral History, JFKL, 62; Nathaniel Keith, *Politics and the Housing Crisis* (New York: Universe Books, 1973), 139.

13. UPI, "Weaver's Fight on Bias Firm but Well-Tempered," 1 January 1960; "D.C. Born Weaver Tagged 'Intellectual,'" *Washington Post*, 31 December 1960; "Weaver for Housing," *Washington Post*, 2 January 1961.

14. "Weaver Appointment Called Historic," *Pittsburgh Courier*, 7 January 1961; "Dr. Weaver to Get Top HHFA Job," *Baltimore Afro-American*, 7 January 1961; "Negro Ap-

pointee Will Direct Big Gov't Program," *Philadelphia Tribune*, 3 January 1961; "Weaver to Spur Anti-bias," *Chicago Defender*, 7 January 1961.

15. "The Weaver Appointment," *Daily Defender*, 5 January 1961.

16. "Win Rhodes to JFK," 8 February 1961; "Rosa Mcwane Whaley to JFK," 21 January 1961; "Ann Tipton to JFK," 8 February 1961; all in Davies Papers.

17. "They Can't Block It," *Baltimore Afro-American*, 4 February 1961.

18. "A Squire from Virginia," *New York Times*, 9 February 1961; "2 Senate Committee Heads Oppose Weaver for Housing Job," *Washington Post*, 6 January 1961.

19. "Kennedy to Fight for Weaver Choice," *Baltimore Afro-American*, 4 February 1961; "Weaver Approval Seems Certain Despite Opposition from South," *Pittsburgh Courier*, 4 February 1961.

20. Senate Committee on Banking and Currency, *Hearings on the Nomination of Robert C. Weaver, 7 and 8 February 1961* (Washington, DC: Government Printing Office, 1961), 3–4; Weaver Oral History, JFKL, 56; "Nomination of Weaver Hits Snag," *Washington Post*, 8 February 1961; "Runaround," *Washington Post*, 8 February 1961.

21. Committee on Banking and Currency, *Hearings on the Nomination of Weaver*, 5–6, 16–18, 76–79.

22. Weaver Oral History, JFKL, 73–74.

23. Committee on Banking and Currency, *Hearings on the Nomination of Weaver*, 84; Simeon Booker, "Top Negro in Kennedy Cabinet," *Jet*, 23 February 1961.

24. Committee on Banking and Currency, *Hearings on the Nomination of Weaver*, 88–90.

25. Committee on Banking and Currency, *Hearings on the Nomination of Weaver*, 92–93, 96; Sam Gaston, "A Negro Takes Over Federal Housing," *Look*, 11 August 1961.

26. Committee on Banking and Currency, *Hearings on the Nomination of Weaver*, 97–99; Booker.

27. "Dr. Weaver Sworn in at White House," *Baltimore Afro-American*, 18 February 1961; "Weaver Probe Shows Revival of McCarthyism," *Washington Post*, 12 February 1961; "Senators Back Weaver, 11 to 4, after Clashing Testimony," *New York Times*, 9 February 1961.

28. 87th Cong., 1st sess., *Congressional Record* 107 (9 February 1961): 1965, 1994.

29. 87th Cong., 1st sess., *Congressional Record* 107 (9 February 1961): 1996, 1983; "Senate Confirms Choice of Weaver," *New York Times*, 10 February 1961; "Weaver Is Confirmed as Director of Housing," *Washington Post*, 10 February 1961.

30. "Remarks of the President at the Swearing-in Ceremonies of Robert C. Weaver," HHFA Papers, box 2; "Weaver Sworn in as Housing Chief," *New York Times*, 12 February 1961; "Weaver and the Senate," *Washington Post*, 10 February 1961.

31. A. H. Raskin, "Washington Gets the 'Weaver Treatment,'" *New York Times Magazine*, 14 May 1961.

32. Weaver Oral History, JFKL, 58–60.

33. "Our Nation's Housing, Message to Congress," 87th Cong., 1st sess., 9 March 1961, House Doc. 102, 1–2; "The President Has a Plan," *Atlanta Journal*, 19 March 1961; "For Housing—the Same, but More," *Business Week*, 18 March 1961; "Mr. Kennedy Wants Speed on Housing," *New York Herald*, 11 March 1961; "New Ground," *Washington Star*,

11 March 1961; letter to Mark Gelfand from Robert Clifton Weaver, 17 November 1972, RCW Papers, Supplement, box 5; Keith, 142–143.

34. Weaver Oral History, JFKL, 93–94; "Senators Widen Housing Measure," *New York Times*, 19 May 1961; "Housing Bill Sent to the President," *New York Times*, 29 June 1961; Housing Act of 1961, Major Provisions, Henry Wilson Papers, JFKL, box 4; "The Housing Bill," *New York Times*, 5 July 1961; "Remarks of the President at the Signing of S. 1922," White Papers, box 6.

35. "The Fight in the Senate," *House and Home*, June 1961; "New Housing Law Hailed," *Washington Post*, 8 July 1961; letter to Robert Clifton Weaver from John F. Kennedy, 18 July 1961, WHCF, JFKL, box 481.

36. "Cities and People: Weaver Popular as Speechmaker," *Washington Star*, 7 May 1961; Alma Rene Williams, "Robert C. Weaver: From the Black Cabinet to the President's Cabinet" (PhD diss., Washington University, St. Louis, 1972), 129–130.

37. Raskin, "Washington Gets the 'Weaver Treatment.'"

38. "There's no Conflict of Interest at House of Doctors Weaver," *Washington Post*, 30 July 1961.

39. "Washington Gets the 'Weaver Treatment.'"

40. Morton Schussheim interview with author, 7 December 2005.

41. Stern, 58–59; Garrow, 154–157.

42. Don Oberdorfer, "Will Negroes Crack the Suburbs," *Saturday Evening Post*, 22 November 1962; A. H. Raskin, "D.C. Gets the Weaver Treatment," *New York Times*, 14 May 1961; Williams, 133.

43. Weaver Oral History, JFKL, 159–160; letter to the president, 22 August 1961, WHCF, JFKL, box 373; Brauer, 85.

44. "A Call on the President of the United States for the Issuance of an Executive Order in All Federal Housing Programs," September 1961, Abrams Papers, reel 14.

45. Memo from Black to NCDH Board re Launching of "Stroke of the Pen" Campaign, 4 October 1961, Abrams Papers, reel 14; Lee White Oral History, 25 May 1964, JFKL, 84; Stern, 51; Branch, 587.

46. "Kennedy Ponders Order to End Bias in Housing Aided by U.S.," *Washington Post*, 29 September 1961; "Ban on Color Line in Housing Is Due," *New York Times*, 28 September 1961; memo to Lee White from Harris Wofford, 29 September 1961, WHCF, JFKL, box 373; Reuther to John F. Kennedy, 21 November 1961, WHCF, JFKL, box 373; McDonald to JFK, 23 October 1961, WHCF, JFKL, box 373; Dilworth to JFK, 19 October 1961, WHCF, JFKL, box 373; Mosk to John F. Kennedy, 20 October 1961, WHCF, JFKL, box 373; "Order to Ban Bias in Housing Ready," *New York Times*, 27 November 1961; "Only Politicians Excited," *New York Times*, 17 December 1961; "Kennedy Decision on Housing Bias Order Expected by Mid-December Advisors Report," *Wall Street Journal*, 28 November 1961.

47. "Address by Robert Clifton Weaver to New York Chapter, American Jewish Committee," 17 October 1961, RCW Papers, Supplement, box 6; "Weaver Says Urban Renewal Depends on Mobility for Negroes," *New York Times*, 18 October 1961.

48. Memo from Frances Levenson re Background Memorandum regarding Appointment with Attorney General Robert Kennedy, 3 November 1961, Abrams Papers, R14; cable

from Abrams to John F. Kennedy, 14 December 1961, Abrams Papers, reel 14; "N.A.A.C.P. Presses for Housing Edict," *New York Times*, 18 December 1961; Lukas.

49. "Mr. Kennedy Should Sign," *New York Times*, 25 December 1961; "Kennedy to Delay Executive Order Barring Discrimination in Federally Aided Housing," *Wall Street Journal*, 26 December 1961; David Lawrence, "Are Principles Obsolete? Bias Story Is Deplored," *New York Herald Tribune*, 27 December 1961; "Discrimination Order on Housing Is Delayed," *New York Times*, 28 December 1961; memo from Frances Levenson to NCDH Board, 29 December 1961, Black Papers, box 9; Brauer, 85; Weaver Oral History, JFKL, 158; "President Pushed to Place a Negro in Cabinet Post," *Pittsburgh Courier*, 6 January 1962; Stern, 52; Sorenson, 481.

50. "Transcript of the President's News Conference on World and Domestic Affairs," *New York Times*, 15 January 1962; "Kennedy Asks New Rights Laws but Is Unlikely to Push Adoption," *New York Times*, 12 January 1962.

51. Jackie Robinson, "The President and Civil Rights," *Defender*, 3 February 1962; "Resolution on Civil Rights and the Kennedy Administration," 4 January 1962, WHCF, JFKL, box 372.

52. 87th Cong., 2d sess., *Congressional Record* 108 (11 January 1961): 542; "Congress Gets Kennedy's Plan for Urban Post in Cabinet," *New York Times*, 19 April 1961; 87th Cong., 2d sess., *Congressional Record* 108 (18 April 1961): 5676; Joseph Clark, "To Come to the Aid of Their Cities," *New York Times*, 30 April 1961, 90; 87th Cong., 2d sess., *Congressional Record* 108 (24 April 1961): 6203; Mark Gelfand, *A Nation of Cities: The Federal Government and Urban America, 1933–1965* (New York: Oxford University Press, 1975), 326.

53. 87th Cong., 2d sess., *Congressional Record* 108 (24 April 1961): 6202.

54. "Weaver in Plea for New Agency," *New York Times*, 15 June 1961, 21; "Address by Robert Weaver to the National Association of Mutual Savings Banks," 1 May 1961, Legislative History, HUD; Gelfand, 328.

55. "NAREB Hits Two Kennedy Proposals," *Realtor's Headlines*, 1 May 1961, Legislative History, HUD; "Washington Reaches for Your City Hall," *Nation's Business*, November 1961; "The Doomed Cities," *Wall Street Journal*, 4 May 1961, 12; House of Representatives, *House Minority Report*, 87th Cong., 2d sess., 1962, 32; Senate, *Senate Minority Report*, 87th Cong., 2d sess., 1962, 25.

56. "Urban Affairs Post Imperiled as G.O.P. Stiffens Opposition," *New York Times*, 17 January 1962; "President Faces Test This Week on Cabinet Post," *New York Times*, 22 January 1962; "House Rules Unit Kills Urban Bill; President to Act," *New York Times*, 25 January 1962; memo from Lee White to John F. Kennedy re Department of Urban Affairs and Housing, 21 August 1961, White Papers, box 18; Brauer, 331–332.

57. John B. Willmann, *The Department of Housing and Urban Development* (New York: Praeger, 1967), 24–25; "Reorganization Plan No. 1 of 1962, Message from the President of the United States," 87th Cong., 30 January 1962, Senate Doc. 320; Sorenson, 481; Brauer, 129; Gelfand, 333.

58. James Reston, "President Squares Off," *New York Times*, 25 January 1962; Arthur Krock, "Politics as Played on the New Frontier," *New York Times*, 26 January 1962; Bureau of National Affairs, "Report for the Business Executive," 1 February 1962; "Urban Affairs," *New Republic*, 5 February 1962; Willmann, 26–27; "Kennedy Accused on Urban Moves,"

*New York Times*, 27 January 1962; "Strictly Political," *Washington Star*, 20 February 1962; "GOP, Dixiecrats Peril Weaver's Cabinet Bid," *Pittsburgh Courier*, 27 January 1962; Bryant, 300.

59. "Weaver Raises Question of Bias in Urban Dispute," *New York Times*, 16 February 1962; 87th Cong., 2d sess., *Congressional Record* 108 (19 February 1962): 2222; 87th Cong., 2d sess., *Congressional Record* 108 (21 February 1962): 2418; "Democrats Will Press Urban Unit Showdown," *Washington Post*, 7 February 1962; "Mansfield Slates Urban Vote Today," *New York Times*, 20 February 1962; "Big Backfire," *Time*, 2 March 1962; Brauer, 130–131; Gelfand, 335; Sorenson, 482.

60. "The Weaver Case: Negro Views," *Newsweek*, 5 March 1962; "Big Backfire," *Time*, 2 March 1962; "Debacle," *Newsweek*, 5 March 1962; "Helping Our Cities," *Washington Post*, 20 February 1962.

61. "Remarks of Congressman Gordon McDonough," 87th Cong., 2d sess., *Congressional Record* 108 (21 February 1962): 2418; "Weaver Is Top Choice to Succeed Ribicoff," *Washington Star*, 21 January 1962; "Weaver as HEW Head Seen Urban Plan Risk," *Washington Post*, 22 January 1962.

62. Gould Lincoln, "Will Weaver Get the HEW Post?" *Washington Star*, 20 March 1962; "Weaver Is Top Choice to Succeed Ribicoff," *Washington Star*, 22 March 1962; letter to John F. Kennedy from Bob Wilson, 5 April 1962, Weaver File, WHCF, JFKL.

63. Memo to John F. Kennedy from Larry O'Brien, 27 April 1962, WHCF, JFKL, box 173; Lyndon Baines Johnson Oral History, LBJL, 21–22; "The Weaver Case," *Negro Views*, 5 March 1962; "Weaver Declines John F. Kennedy Bid to Cabinet," *Jet*, 26 July 1962; "Weaver Denies Any Desire to Become Chief of HEW," *Washington Star*, 9 July 1962; "Weaver Reluctant on Ribicoff's Post," *New York Times*, 9 July 1962. Kennedy aide Ted Sorenson later wrote that Kennedy decided against Weaver for fear of southern opposition and also because northern liberals told the president that Weaver was needed where he was (Sorenson, 274).

64. "Weaver Is Honored as Outstanding Negro," *Washington Post*, 9 July 1862.

65. Robert Clifton Weaver, "Speech to 1962 NAACP Annual Convention," RCW Papers, Supplement, box 8.

66. Weaver, "Speech to 1962 NAACP Annual Convention," RCW Papers, Supplement, box 8.

## CHAPTER 12

1. Robert Clifton Weaver Oral History, JFKL, 27–32, 232–234.

2. Robert Clifton Weaver Oral History, JFKL, 38; Robert Clifton Weaver interview with Morton Schussheim, 19 December 1985, RCW Papers, Supplement, box 7, 6; "Anti-bias Drive Stirs Strife over Renewal Planning," *House and Home*, October 1963.

3. Letter to Robert Clifton Weaver from Jack Wood, NAACP, part 5, Supplement, reel 4; Robert Clifton Weaver, "Address to P. L. Prattis Testimonial Dinner," 20 October 1961, HHFA Papers, box 2; Robert Clifton Weaver, "Address to Family Service Association of America," 13 November 1961, RCW Papers, Supplement, box 6; Robert Clifton Weaver, "Telephone Statement to Freedom Rally at New Haven, Connecticut," 2 October 1961, HHFA Papers, box 2.

4. Lawrence Friedman, *Government and Slum Housing* (Chicago: Rand McNally, 1968), 140–142.

5. Roger Biles, "Public Housing and the Postwar Urban Renaissance, 1949–1973," in *From Tenements to the Taylor Homes: In Search of an Urban Housing Policy in Twentieth Century America*, ed. John F. Bauman, Roger Biles, and Kristin M. Szylvian (University Park: Pennsylvania State University Press, 2000), 149.

6. "Milestone Will Be Marked Here on Wednesday," *New York Times*, 25 March 1962; Robert Clifton Weaver, "Address to Family Service Association of America," 13 November 1961, RCW Papers, Supplement, box 6.

7. Memo to Robert Clifton Weaver from Marie McGuire, 12 August 1963, HUD, box 116.

8. "Weaver Praises AFSCME Housing," *Convention Daily*, 3 May 1962, ASCME President's Papers, Jerry Wurf Collection, Labor and Urban Archives, Wayne State University, Detroit, MI, box 2. Thanks to Will Jones for this material.

9. "1st Negroes to Get Union's Apartments," *Milwaukee Journal Sentinel*, 21 June 1963; memo to Robert Clifton Weaver from Philip Brownstein re Monthly Report on Equal Opportunity in Housing, 4 February 1965, HUD, box 168.

10. Robert Clifton Weaver Oral History, JFKL, 53.

11. Letter to John F. Kennedy from Albert Thomas, WHCF, JFKL, box 174.

12. Nathaniel Keith, *Politics and the Housing Crisis* (New York: Universe Books, 1973), 148–149.

13. Letter to John F. Kennedy from Charles Abrams, 26 March 1962, WHCF, JFKL, box 98.

14. "Half Measures on Housing Bias," *Boston Herald*, 10 April 1962; "Stroke of the Pen," *New York Post*, 11 April 1962; "Discrimination in Housing; How It Hurts the Economy," *Newsweek*, 3 September 1962; "The Campaign for an Executive Order," NAACP, part 5, Supplement, reel 4; "Aide Predicts Kennedy Will Curb Housing Bias," *New York Times*, 21 July 1962.

15. Letter to John F. Kennedy from Sam Ervin, 6 October 1962, WHCF, JFKL, box 373; cable to John F. Kennedy from John Sparkman, 16 November 1962, WHCF, JFKL, box 98; letter to John F. Kennedy from J. W. Fulbright, 4 September 1962, WHCF, JFKL, box 373.

16. Letter to Larry O'Brien from Martha Griffiths, 18 September 1962, White Papers, box 21; "Rites Today Mark 100th Year of Emancipation Proclamation," *New York Times*, 22 September 1962; "Kennedy Decides on Housing Edict," *New York Times*, 22 October 1962; Lee White Oral History, 24 May 1964, JFKL, 90–91; Carl M. Brauer, *John F. Kennedy and the Second Reconstruction* (New York: Columbia University Press, 1977), 206.

17. Nick Bryant, *The Bystander: John F. Kennedy and the Struggle for Black Equality* (New York: Basic Books, 2006), 368–369.

18. Theodore Sorenson, *Kennedy* (New York: Harper and Row, 1965), 482; "Transcript of the President's News Conference on Foreign and Domestic Affairs," *New York Times*, 20 November 1962; "Executive Order 11063, Equal Opportunity in Housing," *Federal Register* 27 (24 November 1962): 11527–11530.

19. "President Bars Bias in Housing," *New York Times*, 21 November 1962; Burke

Marshall Oral History, 29 January 1964, JFKL, 58; Robert Clifton Weaver Oral History, JFKL, 27; Brauer, 208.

20. "Dr. King Hails Housing Order: Stennis Charges Power Move," *New York Times*, 21 November 1962; "Order Gets Applause of Leaders," *Baltimore Afro-American*, 1 December 1962; "Dear Colleague Letter from Shad Polier," 29 November 1962, Black Papers, box 13; "New Order Spotlights Kennedy's Courage," *Chicago Defender*, 1 December 1962; "The Housing Order and Its Limits," *Commentary*, January 1963.

21. "Dr. King Hails Housing Order: Stennis Charges Power Move," *New York Times*, 21 November 1962; "Officials Hopeful on Housing Order: South Is Critical," *New York Times*, 22 November 1962.

22. Memo to NCDH Board from Frances Levenson, 5 December 1962, Black Papers; "Edict on Housing May Be Widened," *New York Times*, 5 December 1962; "New Realty Code Will Help Negroes: Sales Curb Eased," *New York Times*, 16 March 1963.

23. "Gunshot Fells Weaver Son in N.Y.," *Washington Post*, 7 November 1962; "Son of Housing Chief Kills Self in Gun Game," *Washington Star*, 7 November 1962; "Son of Robert Weaver Accidentally Kills Self," *Jet*, 22 November 1963.

24. FBI File, Robert Clifton Weaver, New York, 161–171.

25. On the FBI investigations of African Americans, see Kenneth O'Reilly, *Racial Matters: The FBI's Secret File on Black America, 1960–1972* (New York: Free Press, 1989).

26. FBI File, Robert Clifton Weaver, New York, 161–171.

27. Edward Lashman interview with author, 9 November 2005; Morton Schussheim interview with author, 3 November 2005; Robert Clifton Weaver to Charles Abrams, 24 November 1962, Abrams Papers, reel 9; letter to Charles Abrams from Ella Weaver, 28 December 1962, Abrams Papers, reel 9.

28. Kennedy quoted in Brauer, 62; civil rights activist quoted in Brauer, 212.

29. Mark Stern, *Calculating Visions: Kennedy, Johnson, and Civil Rights* (New Brunswick, NJ: Rutgers University Press, 1992), 88–93.

30. King cited in Stern, 93–97.

31. Stern, 107–112.

32. "U.S. Housing's Man with a Mission," *Business Week*, 17 October 1964; Schussheim interview with author, 3 November 2005.

33. Robert Clifton Weaver Oral History, JFKL, 165; Brauer, 71.

34. Robert Clifton Weaver, "Address to Houston Negro Chamber of Commerce," 25 January 1963, HHFA Papers, box 3.

35. Robert Clifton Weaver Oral History, 153, 210–211.

36. Weaver interview with Schussheim, 19 December 1985, RCW Papers, Supplement, box 7, 16; Robert Clifton Weaver Oral History, JFKL, 74.

37. Milton Semer Oral History, 10 September 1968, JFKL, 42–44, 54; Schussheim interview with author, 3 November 2005. In his autobiography, Roy Wilkins remembered that Weaver was in the Oval Office when Kennedy confronted Mississippi governor Ross Barnett for disregarding the U.S. Supreme Court ruling on the admission of James Meredith to the state university. However, the White House diaries do not record Weaver's presence. See Roy Wilkins, *Standing Fast: The Autobiography of Roy Wilkins* (New York: Da Capo, 1982), 286.

## CHAPTER 13

1. Robert Clifton Weaver Oral History, JFKL, 27; Robert Clifton Weaver, "Address to the National Social Welfare Assembly," 3 December 1963, Harvard University Graduate School of Design Files.

2. The literature on the Johnson administration is immense. See Irving Bernstein, *Guns or Butter: The Presidency of Lyndon Johnson* (New York: Oxford University Press, 1996); John A. Andrew, *Lyndon Johnson and the Great Society* (Chicago: Ivan Dee, 1998); Mark Stern, *Calculating Visions: Kennedy, Johnson, and Civil Rights* (New Brunswick, NJ: Rutgers University Press, 1992). On the Civil Rights Act of 1957, see Stern, 120, 134–141.

3. Stern, 151–153.

4. Stern, 117–118; 120; Robert Clifton Weaver, LBJ Oral History, LBJL, 28–29.

5. "Remarks at the University of Michigan," 22 May 1964, *Public Papers of the Presidents, Lyndon B. Johnson, 1963–1964* (Washington, DC: Government Printing Office, 1964),704–707; "President Urges New Federalism to 'Enrich Life,'" *New York Times*, 23 May 1964.

6. "Address to Congress," 27 November 1963, *Public Papers of the Presidents, Lyndon B. Johnson, 1963–1964* (Washington, DC: Government Printing Office, 1964); Stern, 160–185; Bernstein, 43–81; Andrew, 23–55.

7. Lloyd Zimpel, "Showdown in California," *Commonweal*, 30 October 1964, 153–155; "California and Conn. Enact Fair Housing Statutes," *Trends in Housing*, May–June 1963, Black Papers, box 13; "President of Realtors Puts Property Rights First," *New York Times*, 11 November 1964; Stephen Grant Meyer, *As Long as They Don't Move Next Door: Segregation and Racial Conflict in American Neighborhoods* (Lanham, MD: Rowman and Littlefield, 2000), 179; Robert Self, *American Babylon: Race and the Struggle for Postwar Oakland* (Princeton, NJ: Princeton University Press, 2004), 167–168.

8. Memo to Bill Oliver from Max Mont, no date, and memo to Roy Wilkins from Tarea Hall Pittman, 30 July 1964, both in NAACP, part 5, Supplement, reel 2; "Facts about Proposition 14," Black Papers, box 16; "Speakers Handbook for Opposition to the Segregation Amendment," NAACP, part 5, Supplement, reel 2; "Brown Demands End to Initiative Abuses," *Los Angeles Times*, 21 October 1964; "Prop 14 Passage Seen by Brown and Cranston," *Los Angeles Times*, 28 October 1964; "Californians against Prop 14," *Los Angeles Times*, 26 October 1964.

9. "Proponents of Prop 14 Give Weaver Reply," *Los Angeles Times*, 21 October 1964; "Prop 14 Called Peril to Urban Renewal Fund," 20 October 1964; NCDH press release, 6 November 1964, Abrams Papers, reel 14; "Prop 14 Approved by a Big Margin," *Los Angeles Times*, 4 November 1964; Meyer, 181; Self, 168.

10. "U.S. Funds for State Renewal Jobs Cut Off," *Los Angeles Times*, 11 November 1964; letter to Roy Wilkins from Robert Clifton Weaver, 23 November 1964, NAACP, part 5, Supplement, reel 2; NAACP press release, 18 December 1964, NAACP, part 5, Supplement, reel 2; "NCDH Acts to Combat Referendum Movement," *Trends in Housing*, January–February 1965, Black Papers, box 13.

11. Jane Jacobs, *The Death and Life of Great American Cities* (New York: Random House, 1961), 5. Her first critique of the program was published in 1956: "Jane Jacobs, "The Missing Link in City Redevelopment," *Architectural Forum*, June 1956. For a careful examina-

tion of Jacobs's role in the developing critique of urban renewal, see Christopher Klemek, "Urbanism as Reform: Modernist Planning and the Crisis of Urban Liberalism in Europe and North America, 1945–1975" (PhD diss., University of Pennsylvania, 2004), chap. 3.

12. Cited in Klemek, 121.

13. Robert Weaver, "Urban Renewal Is Dispossessing Its Critics," *Washington Post*, 5 April 1964.

14. Robert Clifton Weaver, "Successes and Failures of Urban Redevelopment in the U.S.," speech to the New York Bar Association, 22 April 1965, NAACP, part 5, Supplement, reel 4; Robert Clifton Weaver, "Current Trends in Urban Renewal," *Land Economics* 30 (1963): 326; "Transcript of Interview," *Today Show*, 18 August 1964, HUD, box 146.

15. "Johnson's Economy Drive Trims Budget by Estimated $2 Billion," *New York Times*, 3 January 1963; Senate, *Hearings before a Subcommittee of the Committee on Banking and Currency, on S. 2468, 19 February 1964* (Washington, DC: Government Printing Office, 1964); "Johnson Housing Bills Assailed in 2 Parties as Hearings Open," *New York Times*, 18 February 1964; "Mayor Asks Rise in U.S. Housing Aid," *New York Times*, 21 February 1964; "Housing Bill Rated Too Much, Too Little," *New York Times*, 21 February 1964.

16. "President Signs Housing Aid Bill," *New York Times*, 3 September 1964; "Housing in the Great Society," *New York Times*, 18 September 1964; "Robert Weaver, Letters to the *Times*," *New York Times*, 21 September 1964.

17. On the War on Poverty's origins, see Alice O'Connor, *Poverty Knowledge: Social Science, Social Policy, and the Poor in Twentieth Century U.S. History* (Princeton, NJ: Princeton University Press, 2001); Gareth Davies, *From Opportunity to Entitlement: The Transformation and Decline of Great Society Liberalism* (Lawrence: University Press of Kansas, 1996); Adam Yarmolinsky, "The Beginnings of OEO," in *On Fighting Poverty*, ed. James Sundquist (New York: Basic Books, 1969).

18. "State of the Union Address," 9 January 1964, *Public Papers of the Presidents, Lyndon B. Johnson, 1963–1964* (Washington, DC: Government Printing Office, 1964); Scott Stossell, *Sarge: The Life and Times of Sargent Shriver* (Washington, DC: Smithsonian Institution Press, 2004), 346–347.

19. "Special Message to Congress Proposing a Nationwide War on the Sources of Poverty," 16 March 1964, *Public Papers of the Presidents, Lyndon B. Johnson, 1963–1964* (Washington, DC: Government Printing Office, 1964), 380; Robert Dallek, *Flawed Giant: Lyndon Johnson and His Times, 1961–1973* (New York: Oxford University Press, 1998), 79; Davies, 35.

20. Davies, 45–46.

21. James Patterson, *America's Struggle against Poverty, 1900–1985* (Cambridge, MA: Harvard University Press, 1986), 146–147; O'Connor, 124–132.

22. Allen Matusow, *The Unraveling of America: A History of Liberalism in the 1960s* (New York: Harper, 1986), 246.

23. Robert Clifton Weaver, *Testimony before the House Ad Hoc Subcommittee on the War on Poverty Program on the Economic Opportunity Act of 1964, 10 April 1964* (Washington, DC: Government Printing Office, 1964), 473.

24. Dallek, 166–184.

25. Letter to Robert Clifton Weaver from Elizabeth Gatov, 3 November 1964, HUD, box 146.

26. Vaughn Davis Bornet, *The Presidency of Lyndon B. Johnson* (Lawrence: University

Press of Kansas, 1983), 118–120; "Notes for Meeting with Task Force on Metropolitan and Urban Problems," 9 September 1964, WOP, reel 15.

27. Robert Wood, LBJ Oral History, LBJL, 8.

28. Task Force on Metropolitan and Urban Problems, "Summary of Recommendations," 30 November 1964, LBJL, ii–vii. For Weaver's proposals, see memo to Lee White from Robert Clifton Weaver, 21 July 1964, HUD, box 166.

29. "Special Message to Congress on the Nation's Cities," 2 March 1965, *Public Papers of the Presidents, Lyndon B. Johnson, 1963–1964* (Washington, DC: Government Printing Office, 1964), 231–240.

30. "Mayors Tell Humphrey of Problems, Criticize Plan for Housing, Cities," *Washington Post*, 9 March 1965; "Mrs. Gabel Disappointed in Johnson Housing Plan," *New York Times*, 15 March 1965; "The Cities: A Small Beginning," *New York Times*, 3 March 1965; "President's Housing Message Scorned by Many Here," *New York Times*, 4 March 1965.

31. Robert Clifton Weaver, *Testimony before the House Subcommittee on Housing Hearing on H.R. 5840, 25–31 March 1965* (Washington, DC: Government Printing Office, 1965), 179; "Task Force Report" (Washington, DC: Government Printing Office, 1965), 24–26; "Housing Program Emphasizes Rehabilitation, Provides Rent Aids," *Washington Post*, 28 February 1965; Nathaniel Keith, *Politics and the Housing Crisis* (New York: Universe Books, 1973), 160–161; Mark Gelfand, *A Nation of Cities: The Federal Government and Urban America* (New York: Oxford University Press, 1975), 372.

32. "Rent Assistance Plan Spelled Out by Weaver," *Washington Post*, 15 March 1965.

33. Tom Wicker, "Washington: Johnson's Housing Victory," *Washington Post*, 25 June 1965.

34. Weaver, *Testimony before the House Subcommittee on Housing Hearing on H.R. 5840, 25–31 March 1965*, 231; "Housing and Urban Development Act of 1965," 21 May 1965, House Report 365, 176, 180; "Housing and Urban Development Act of 1965," 28 June 1965, Senate Report 378, 100.

35. "Housing Program Gains in Senate," *New York Times*, 25 June 1965; "Memo to Lyndon Baines Johnson from Larry O'Brien," 25 June 1965, Henry Wilson Papers, LBJL, box 8; "6 Votes Save Rent Subsidy; House Passes Housing Bill," *New York Times*, 1 July 1965; 89th Cong., 1st sess., *Congressional Record* 111 (28 June 1965): 14,883; "Speaker Calls Rent Bill Hardest Task in Years," *Washington Post*, 4 July 1965.

36. Dallek, 185–238.

37. "Special Message to the Congress: The American Promise," 15 March 1967, *Public Papers of the Presidents, Lyndon B. Johnson, 1967* (Washington, DC: Government Printing Office, 1967), 285.

38. On the riots, see Gerald Horne, *The Fire This Times: The Watts Uprising and the 1960s* (Charlottesville: University Press of Virginia, 1995); Becky Nicolaides, *My Blue Heaven: Life and Politics in the Working-Class Suburbs of Los Angeles, 1920–1965* (Chicago: University of Chicago Press, 2002).

39. "Time to Sober Up," *St. Louis Globe-Democrat*, reprinted in *Los Angeles Times*, 22 August 1965; "A Summer Carnival of Riot," *Los Angeles Times*, 13 August 1965; Joseph Califano, *The Triumph and Tragedy of Lyndon Johnson* (College Station: Texas A&M Press, 2000), 62; Bernstein, 385–386; Dallek, 223–224.

40. "Statement by the President upon Announcing a Program of Assistance to Los An-

geles," 26 August 1965, *Public Papers of the Presidents, Lyndon B. Johnson, 1965* (Washington, DC: Government Printing Office, 1965), 453; memo to Lawrence Levinson from Ernest Friesen re Los Angeles, 29 October 1965, LBJ Civil Rights, reel 6; Dallek, 224.

41. "Weaver Sees Housing Office," *New York Times*, 24 February 1964; "Message from the President of the United States Relative to the Problems and Future of the Central City and Its Suburbs," 2 March 1965, House of Representatives Doc. 99, 3.

42. House of Representatives, Department of Housing and Urban Development, *Hearings before a Subcommittee of the Committee on Government Operations*, 89th Cong., 5 and 6 April 1965, 18; 89th Cong., 1st sess., *Congressional Record* 111 (11 March 1965): 4675; "G.O.P. Group Offers Urban Affairs Plan," *New York Times*, 12 March 1965; Gelfand, 378; "Establishing a Department of Housing and Urban Development, and for Other Purposes," 89th Cong., 11 May 1965, House Report 337, 5, 9, 13; "Establishment of a Department of Housing and Urban Development, Report of the Committee on Government Operations," 2 August 1965, Senate Report 536, 13, 39; "Vote Housing Post," *Chicago Tribune*, 12 August 1965; "Final Approval Given Urban Dept," *Washington Post*, 1 September 1965; "Office on Housing Set Up in Cabinet," *New York Times*, 10 September 1965.

43. "U.S. Urban Role to Expand Slowly," *Los Angeles Times*, 16 August 1965; "Cities Get Voice in Cabinet," *Milwaukee Journal*, 12 August 1965.

## CHAPTER 14

1. "Johnson Signs Urban Department Bill but Delays in Appointing Secretary," *Washington Post*, 10 September 1965; Lyndon B. Johnson, "Remarks at the Signing of Bill Establishing a Department of Housing and Urban Development," 9 September 1965, *Public Papers of the Presidents, Lyndon B. Johnson, 1965* (Washington, DC: Government Printing Office, 1965), 985; "LBJ Signs New Urban Dept. Bill," *Chicago Defender*, 11 September 1965; "Naming of Urban Cabinet Post May Be Delayed 60 Days," *Baltimore Afro-American*, 18 September 1965; Nathaniel Keith, *Politics and the Housing Crisis since 1930* (New York: Universe Books, 1973), 167.

2. "The Cabinet: Surrogate for the Cities," *Time*, 20 August 1965. Articles speculating on Weaver's appointment included "Senate Passes Bill to Create Cabinet Post on Urban Affairs," *St. Louis Post-Dispatch*, 11 August 1965; "Cabinet Urban Department Approved by Senate, 57-33," *Chicago Sun-Times*, 12 August 1965.

3. "Remarks of the President at the Signing Ceremony of the Housing and Urban Development Act of 1965," 10 August 1965, HUD, box 179.

4. Robert Clifton Weaver Oral History, LBJL, 5; Lyndon B. Johnson telephone conversation with Martin Luther King, 15 January 1965, LBJL.

5. Lyndon B. Johnson telephone conversation with Roy Wilkins, 15 July 1965, LBJL.

6. Joseph A. Califano, *The Triumph and Tragedy of Lyndon Johnson* (College Station: Texas A&M Press, 2000), 128; memo to Lyndon B. Johnson from John Macy, 24 August 1965, Macy Papers, box 626.

7. Memo to Lyndon B. Johnson from Robert McNamara, 25 November 1965, Macy Papers, HUD file; memo to Lyndon B. Johnson from Stewart Udall, 17 June 1965, Macy Papers, HUD file.

8. Lyndon B. Johnson telephone conversation with Abraham Ribicoff, 1 September

1965, LBJL; Lyndon B. Johnson telephone conversation with Robert Kennedy, 1 September 1965, LBJL; Lyndon B. Johnson telephone conversation with Nicholas Katzenbach, 29 November 1965, LBJL.

9. Roger Wilkins interview with author, 5 October 2005.

10. Memo to Lyndon B. Johnson from John Macy, 17 September 1965, Macy Papers, HUD file; memo to Lyndon B. Johnson from Joe Califano, 23 September 1965, WOP, reel 15; memo to Joe Califano from John Macy, 5 November 1965, Macy Papers, HUD file; Ed Logue to John Macy, 7 October 1965, WHCF, LBJL, Name File, W136; Joseph McDowell to Lyndon B. Johnson, 2 September 1965, WHCF, LBJL, Name File, W136.

11. "Johnson Set Back on Rent Subsidies," *New York Times*, 16 October 1965; "Subsidies on Rent Gain a Reprieve," *New York Times*, 20 October 1965.

12. "Congressman Ford Interviewed," *Radio TV Reports*, 26 October 1965, HUD, box 136; letter to Congressman Torbert MacDonald from Milton Semer, 20 October 1965, HUD, box 136; Arthur Krock, "In the Nation: Blocking the Rent Supplement," *New York Times*, 24 October 1965.

13. Califano, 127–128.

14. Robert Clifton Weaver Oral History, LBJL, 37. In November, Congressman James Harvey (R-MI), one of the people responsible for removing the rent supplement funding, wrote Johnson to say that he admired Weaver and that Johnson should not blame Weaver for the failure to fund the program. Lyndon B. Johnson telephone conversation with Roy Wilkins, 4 November 1965, LBJL.

15. Robert Clifton Weaver Oral History, LBJL, 34–37; Califano, 127–128.

16. Califano, 128.

17. Lyndon B. Johnson telephone conversation with Roy Wilkins, 30 October 1965. In July, however, Johnson praised Weaver for the "remarkably effective job" accomplished by his task force: memo to Robert Clifton Weaver from Lyndon B. Johnson, 29 July 1965, WHCF, LBJL, box 288.

18. Lyndon B. Johnson telephone conversation with Roy Wilkins, 30 October 1965, LBJL.

19. Lyndon B. Johnson telephone conversation with Roy Wilkins, 1 November 1965, LBJL.

20. Lyndon B. Johnson telephone conversations with Roy Wilkins, 1 November 1965 and 4 November 1965, LBJL; Califano, 127–128.

21. Letter to Frank Horne from Robert Clifton Weaver, 2 October 1965, Horne Papers, box 25; letter to Robert Clifton Weaver from William Wheaton, 14 October 1965, RCW Papers, Supplement, box 3; letter to Robert Clifton Weaver from William Nash, 5 December 1965, RCW Papers, Supplement, box 3; letter to Robert Clifton Weaver from Buell Gallagher, 6 January 1966, RCW Papers, Supplement, box 3; "N.Y. Makes Bid for Weaver if He Doesn't Receive LBJ Cabinet Post," *Pittsburgh Courier*, 25 December 1965.

22. Robert Clifton Weaver Oral History, LBJL, 34.

23. Califano, 127–128.

24. Draft letter to Joseph Califano from Robert Clifton Weaver, no date, RCW Papers, Supplement, box 3.

25. Califano, 129.

26. Lyndon B. Johnson telephone conversation with Roy Wilkins, 4 November 1965, LBJL; Robert Clifton Weaver Oral History, LBJL, 34–35.

27. Louis Martin Oral History, LBJL, 22–23; Morton Schussheim interview with author, 3 November 2005; Mary Washington interview with author, 7 December 2005. See also Alex Poinsett, *Walking with Presidents: Louis Martin and the Rise of Black Political Power* (New York: Madison Books, 1997), 130–133; letter from Frank Horne to Whitney Young, Young Papers, box 59.

28. Transcript of Moyers press conference, no date, WHCF, LBJL, box 252; "Johnson Delays Naming Urban Cabinet Officer," *Los Angeles Times*, 5 November 1965; "LBJ Delays Naming Chief of Urban Department till January," *Chicago Sun-Times*, 5 November 1965.

29. Transcript of Weaver press conference, 8 November 1965, WHCF, LBJL, box 288; "Weaver Would Like to Head New Cabinet Unit," *New York Times*, 9 November 1965; "Weaver Admits He Would Like Job as Head of New Housing Department," *Los Angeles Times*, 9 November 1965; "HUD Begins Its Existence with Bureaucratic Calm," *Washington Post*, 10 November 1965.

30. "Weaver Says He Wants New Cabinet Post," *St. Louis Post-Dispatch*, 9 November 1965; "Weaver Would Like to Head New Cabinet Unit," *New York Times*, 9 November 1965; memo to Joe Califano from Harry McPherson, 9 November 1965, WHCF, LBJL, box 288; "A Man for the Cities," *St. Louis Post-Dispatch*, 14 November 1965; Robert Clifton Weaver Oral History, LBJL, 35–36; "Dr. Weaver Seen out of Cabinet Race," *Baltimore Afro-American*, 30 October 1965; "Manhunt," *Newsweek*, 22 November 1965; "Johnson Decision on Housing Nears," *New York Times*, 2 January 1966.

31. "The New Cabinet Post," *Chicago Defender*, 11 September 1965; "Weaver Wants Cabinet Post," *Pittsburgh Courier*, 20 November 1965; "Dr. Weaver—the Logical Choice," *Baltimore Afro-American*, 25 November 1965.

32. Louis Martin Oral History, LBJL, 27; "Dr. Weaver Seen out of Cabinet Race," *Baltimore Afro-American*, 30 October 1965; "Weaver Is Logical Choice for Cabinet," *Pittsburgh Courier*, 2 October 1965.

33. "Cabinet Gets Negro, Little Else," *Chicago Defender*, 22 January 1966; "2 Negro Leaders Endorse Weaver," *New York Times*, 20 November 1965.

34. "Wilkins Softens Stand on Weaver," *New York Times*, 21 November 1965; "The Great Society's Advance Man," *Business Week*, 22 January 1966; Herbert Wechsler, "The Long Wait," *New York Post*, 15 December 1965.

35. Lyndon B. Johnson telephone conversation with Nicholas Katzenbach, 29 November 1965, LBJL. Bill Moyers and HEW Secretary John Gardner recommended that Johnson appoint Weaver along with deputies. Moyers called them "junior Goldbergs," and Gardner argued that Johnson should "buttress" Weaver "with strong and imaginative assistants" like Martin Meyerson, Philip Brownstein, and Whitney Young. Memo to Lyndon B. Johnson from Bill Moyers, 11 December 1965, Legislative Background, Dept. of HUD, LBJL, box 1; memo to Lyndon B. Johnson from John Gardner, 29 December 1965, Macy Papers, box 626.

36. Lyndon B. Johnson telephone conversation with Thurgood Marshall, 3 November 1966, LBJL; Lyndon B. Johnson telephone conversation with Roy Wilkins, 5 January 1966, LBJL.

37. "Summary of Robert Wood's Views on Robert Weaver for HUD," WHCF, LBJL, box 255; Lyndon B. Johnson telephone conversation with Roy Wilkins, 5 January 1966, LBJL; Robert Wood Oral History, LBJL, 24.

38. Lyndon B. Johnson telephone conversation with Roy Wilkins, 5 January 1966, LBJL; Lyndon B. Johnson telephone conversation with Roy Wilkins, 4 November 1965, LBJL; Weaver interview with Morton Schussheim, RCW Papers, Supplement, box 18.

39. "LBJ Names First Negro to Cabinet," *Chicago Sun-Times*, 14 January 1966; "Weaver Named to Cabinet as Head of New Urban Agency," *St. Louis Post-Dispatch*, 14 January 1966; "Robert C. Weaver: Quiet Man Wins Spot in Cabinet," *Ebony*, 21 April 1966; "Press Conference of the President of the United States," 13 January 1966, Macy Papers, box 626; "Transcript of the President's News Conference on Foreign and Domestic Matters," *New York Times*, 14 January 1966; "President Names Weaver to Head Housing Agency," *New York Times*, 14 January 1966; "Weaver Is Named to Urban Department," *Washington Post*, 14 January 1966.

40. Robert Clifton Weaver Oral History, LBJL, 36; Califano, 130.

41. "A Negro in the Cabinet," *Chicago Sun-Times*, 15 January 1966; "Secretary Weaver," *Washington Post*, 15 January 1966; "The Weaver Appointment," *Milwaukee Journal*, 14 January 1966; "A New Urban Era," *Pittsburgh Post-Gazette*, 17 January 1966.

42. "Weaver in Cabinet," *Washington Star*, 15 January 1966; "The Weaver Appointment," *New York Times*, 15 January 1966; "City Man in the Cabinet," *St. Louis Post-Dispatch*, 17 January 1966.

43. "The Weaver Appointment," *New York Amsterdam News*, 22 January 1966; "Secretary Robert Weaver," *Baltimore Afro-American*, 29 January 1966.

44. Whitney M. Young, "Weaver in Cabinet a Challenge to All U.S.," *Baltimore Afro-American*, 29 January 1966; letter to Whitney Young from Lyndon B. Johnson, 15 January 1966, WHCF, LBJL, box 255.

45. Letter to Robert Clifton Weaver from Frank Horne," 18 January 1966, Horne Papers, box 3; letter to Frank Horne from Robert Clifton Weaver, 20 January 1966, Horne Papers, box 3.

46. Lyndon B. Johnson telephone conversation with William Proxmire, 17 January 1966, LBJL.

47. Senate Committee on Banking and Currency, "Nominations of Robert C. Weaver and Robert C. Wood," 17 January 1966 (Washington, DC: Government Printing Office), 2, 5; "Senate Unanimously Confirms Weaver for Cabinet," *New York Times*, 18 January 1966; "Weaver's Long Wait," *Time*, 23 January 1966; "Senate Speedily Puts Approval on Weaver as 1st Urban Secretary," *Washington Post*, 18 January 1966.

48. "Remarks of the President at the Swearing in Ceremony of Robert Weaver as Secretary of the Department of Housing and Urban Development and Robert C. Wood as Undersecretary of Housing and Urban Development," 18 January 1966, Legislative Background, HUD, LBJL, box 2; "Historic Day as Weaver Takes Office," *Baltimore Afro-American*, 29 January 1966; "HUD Chiefs Take Oath at White House," *Washington Post*, 19 January 1966; "Weaver Asked to Make Cities in U.S. Livable," *Los Angeles Times*, 19 January 1966; "Weaver Sworn in as Head of New Cabinet Department," *St. Louis Post-Dispatch*, 18 January 1966.

## CHAPTER 15

1. "Cities: Hope for the Heart," *Time*, 4 March 1966.

2. "Cities: Hope for the Heart," *Time*, 4 March 1966.

3. Simeon Booker, "Robert C. Weaver: Quiet Man Wins Spot in Cabinet," *Ebony*, 21 April 1966.

4. Booker.

5. "The Changing Mood of Congress: How Outlook Is Shifting," *U.S. News & World Report*, 2 May 1966; Robert Dallek, *Flawed Giant: Lyndon Johnson and His Times, 1961–1973* (New York: Oxford University Press, 1998), 279, 299–300. See also Gareth Davies, *From Opportunity to Entitlement: The Transformation and Decline of Great Society Liberalism* (Lawrence: University Press of Kansas, 1996), 136.

6. Dallek, 358–371.

7. Rowland Evans and Robert Novak, "Inside Report: The HUD Headache," *Washington Post*, 14 January 1966; "Weaver's HUD," *New Republic*, 29 January 1966.

8. "Task Force Is Charting Program for Federal Urban Department," *Washington Post*, 18 November 1965.

9. Task Force on Urban Affairs and Housing, "Proposed Plan of Organization," 14 December 1965, WOP, reel 15; memo to Lyndon B. Johnson from Harry McPherson, 9 December 1965, WOP, reel 14.

10. Scott Stossel, *Sarge: The Life and Times of Sargent Shriver* (Washington, DC: Smithsonian Institution Press, 2004), 410–411; Dallek, 330–331; Davies, 90–93; Joseph Califano, *The Triumph and Tragedy of Lyndon Johnson* (College Station: Texas A&M Press, 1999), 78–80.

11. Task Force on Urban Affairs and Housing, "Proposed Plan of Organization," 14 December 1965, WOP, reel 15; letter to Robert Wood from Whitney Young, 24 December 1965, HUD Legislative Background, LBJL, box 2; Joseph A. Califano interview with author, 7 December 2004; "Study to Advise Shift of Community Action to Urban Department," *Washington Post*, 25 December 1965; Evans and Novak.

12. Evans and Novak; "Johnson Rejects Shift on Poverty," *New York Times*, 7 January 1966; "Weaver in Cabinet but Job Is Unclear," *New York Times*, 16 January 1966.

13. "At Last, the HUD Guessing Game Ends: Weaver Gets Job—and Some Helpers," *House and Home*, February 1966; Robert Clifton Weaver, "The First Twenty Years of HUD," *APA Journal*, Autumn 1985, 463.

14. Robert Clifton Weaver Oral History, LBJL, 41–42; memo to Lyndon B. Johnson from Robert Clifton Weaver re Organization of the Department of Housing and Urban Development, 25 February 1966, Weaver Subject Files, HUD, box 7; "Weaver to Decide Budget and Plans," *New York Times*, 26 February 1966; "3 Agencies Downgraded in HUD Reorganization," *Washington Post*, 26 February 1966; "Chief of Renewal Quits Urban Post," *New York Times*, 25 March 1966; Harold Wolman, *The Politics of Federal Housing* (New York: Dodd Mead, 1971), 168–169.

15. "HUD Irritating Source of Its $$," *Washington Star*, 6 April 1966.

16. Memorandum to Lyndon Baines Johnson from Walter Reuther, 13 May 1965, WOP, reel 15; Charles Haar, *Between the Dream and the Reality: A Study in the Origin, Fate, and Legacy of the Model Cities Program* (New York: Little, Brown, 1975), 36.

17. Memorandum to President Johnson from Joseph Califano, no date, Legislative Background Files, Model Cities, LBJL; Special Task Force on Cities, "Issues and Questions," no date, WOP, reel 15; "Sweeping Shifts Are Mapped for Cities by Presidential Panel," *New York Times*, 15 November 1965; Bernard J. Frieden and Marshall Kaplan, *The Politics of Neglect: Urban Aid from Model Cities to Revenue Sharing* (Cambridge, MA: MIT Press, 1975), 37; "Proposed Programs for the Department of Housing and Urban Development," WOP, reel 15.

18. "Program for American Cities," 26 January 1966, WOP, reel 14; "New Urban Plan Would Use Federal Funds to Eradicate Slums," *New York Times*, 26 January 1966; "Johnson Submits $2.3 Billion Plan to Rebuild Slums," *New York Times*, 27 January 1966; Frieden and Kaplan, 51.

19. Jeff Sheshol, *Mutual Contempt: Lyndon Johnson, Robert Kennedy and the Feud That Defined a Decade* (New York: Norton, 1997), 244–245.

20. Charles Haar Oral History, LBJL, 50; Robert Clifton Weaver Oral History, LBJL, 38; "Robert Clifton Weaver to Kermit Gordon," 10 January 1964, HUD, box 136; Wolman, 87, 102; House of Representatives Subcommittee on Housing, *Demonstration Cities, Housing and Urban Development, and Urban Mass Transit*, 89th Cong., 2d sess., 28 February 1966 (Washington, DC: Government Printing Office), 33–34, 46; Califano, 131.

21. "Program for the Cities," *New York Times*, 27 January 1966; "Attacking a Big Problem," *Christian Science Monitor*, 29 January 1966; Ada Louise Huxtable, "Toward Excellence in Urban Redesign," *New York Times*, 21 February 1966; "Slum Plan Stirs Concern in House," *New York Times*, 7 March 1966; "Democrats Voice Doubt about Model City Plan," *Washington Post*, 1 March 1966; "HUD Control of Slum Fight Is Opposed," *Washington Post*, 23 April 1966; Dallek, 319.

22. "Daley Says Johnson Will Need More Funds for His Urban Plan," *New York Times*, 5 March 1966; Frieden and Kaplan, 57; Haar, 63.

23. "Housing and Urban Development Act of 1966," 15 July 1966, House Report 1699, 63–65; "Move on to Save Bill to End Slums," *New York Times*, 23 May 1966; Califano, 131.

24. "How the Fair Housing Laws Are Working," *Trends in Housing*, November–December 1965, Black Papers, box 13.

25. Memo to Lyndon B. Johnson from David Lawrence, 2 April 1965, LBJ Civil Rights, reel 8; NCDH, press release, 7 May 1965, WOP, reel 14; memo to Lyndon B. Johnson from Katzenbach, 25 September 1965, LBJ Civil Rights, reel 8.

26. Memo to Lyndon B. Johnson from David Lawrence, 2 April 1965, LBJ Civil Rights, reel 8.

27. Memo to Lyndon B. Johnson from Hubert Humphrey, 9 June 1965, LBJ Civil Rights, reel 8. Weaver did not participate in the meeting with Katzenbach, Humphrey, and the President's Committee on Equal Opportunity in Housing at which the decision was made; memo to Lyndon B. Johnson from Fowler, 20 November 1965, LBJ Civil Rights, reel 8.

28. "Annual Message to the Congress on the State of the Union," 12 January 1966, *Public Papers of the Presidents, Lyndon B. Johnson, 1966* (Washington, DC: Government Printing Office, 1966); "Ban on Color Line in Housing Is Asked," *New York Times*, 13 January 1966; memo to Lyndon B. Johnson from Califano, 16 November 1965, LBJ Civil Rights,

reel 8; "Fair Housing Bill Nears Congress with Little Chance of Passage," *New York Times*, 16 March 1966.

29. "Text of President's Special Message to Congress Urging New Civil Rights Legislation," *New York Times*, 29 April 1966; "Civil Rights," *Time*, 6 March 1966; "President Urges Congress to Ban All Housing Bias," *New York Times*, 29 March 1966; "Johnson Calls for Stiff New Rights Laws," *Washington Post*, 28 March 1966.

30. NCDH, press release, 28 April 1966, Black Papers, box 13; "New Steps Asked by Wilkins," *New York Times*, 17 May 1966; "Rights Group Says 'Fair Housing' Reinforces Segregation Patterns," *Washington Post*, 30 April 1966; "Rights Units Cool to Legislation on Housing Sought by Johnson," *New York Times*, 23 January 1966; "Fair Housing Bill Nears Congress with Little Chance of Passage," *New York Times*, 16 March 1966; "Frontier for 66," *Newsweek*, 9 May 1966; "Javits Gives Up His Demand for a Rights Bill Time Limit," *New York Times*, 4 May 1966.

31. "Dirksen Assails Fair Housing Plan," *New York Times*, 3 May 1966; "Civil Rights," *Time*, 13 May 1966; "I'll Eat the Chimney," *Newsweek*, 13 May 1966; "U.S. Rights Unit Asks Senate to Strengthen Johnson Bill," *New York Times*, 11 June 1966; "LBJ Asks All-Out Bias Law: Congress," *House and Home*, May 1966.

32. "Rights Groups Cool," *House and Home*, June 1966; "Fair Housing Bill Nears Congress with Little Chance of Passage," *New York Times*, 16 March 1966; "Civil Rights? Yes: Fair Housing? Well," *New York Times*, 8 May 1966.

33. Claybourne Carson, *In Struggle: SNCC and the Black Awakening of the 1960s* (Cambridge, MA: Harvard University Press, 1981), 191–211.

34. Carson, 203–205; Kwame Ture and Charles V. Hamilton, *Black Power: The Politics of Liberation* (New York: Vintage, 1967), 54.

35. Mort Schussheim interview with author, 7 December 2005.

36. Robert Clifton Weaver, "Address before the National Urban League Annual Conference," 1 August 1966, HUD, box 219.

37. The story of the Chicago Freedom Movement is ably told in James Ralph Jr., *Northern Protest: Martin Luther King, Jr., Chicago, and the Civil Rights Movement* (Cambridge, MA: Harvard University Press, 1993); Brian Berry, *The Open Housing Question: Race and Housing in Chicago, 1966–1976* (Cambridge, MA: Ballinger, 1979); David Garrow, *Bearing the Cross, Martin Luther King and the Southern Christian Leadership Conference* (New York: Vintage Press, 1988), 430–525.

38. Ralph, 120–123; King quoted in Roger Biles and Richard J. Daley, *Race, Politics and the Governing of Chicago* (Dekalb: Northern Illinois Press, 1995), 128; Garrow, 498–500.

39. *Louisville Courier* cited in Ralph, 176; Ralph, 180–182.

40. *Civil Rights Act of 1966, Hearings before the House Judiciary Committee*, 89th Cong., 2d sess., 12 May 1966, 1355, 1357; "Katzenbach Bows to Mrs. Murphy," *New York Times*, 6 May 1966; "Fair Housing Loopholes Opposed by Weaver," *Washington Post*, 13 May 1966; "Weaver Disputes Katzenbach View," *New York Times*, 13 May 1966.

41. Tom Wicker, "The Holy and the Unholy," *New York Times*, 1 August 1966; "Exemption of 60% in Open Housing Voted by House," *New York Times*, 3 August 1966; "House Defeats Attempt to Maim Open Housing," *Washington Post*, 5 August 1966; "A Symptom of Anger," *Newsweek*, 22 August 1966; "Exemption of 60% in Open Housing Voted

by House," *New York Times*, 4 August 1966; "House Backs Curb on Housing Bias," *New York Times*, 6 August 1966; "Civil Rights Bill Passed by House in Vote of 259-157," *New York Times*, 10 August 1966; "Johnson Hails Rights Bill as 'Milestone' for Justice," *New York Times*, 11 August 1966; "The Policing Job Washington Is Now Trying to Get," *U.S. News & World Report*, 22 August 1966.

42. "Housing Bias Curb Backed in Senate," *New York Times*, 2 September 1966.

43. "Realtors Oppose Open Sales Laws," *New York Times*, 18 November 1966; Robert Clifton Weaver, "Speech at the Annual Convention of NAREB," 17 November 1966, HUD, box 217.

44. On the feud see Sheshol, 244–248; Stossel.

45. Memo to Lyndon B. Johnson from Marvin Watson, 28 July 1966, WOP, reel 15; Senate Subcommittee on Executive Reorganization, *Federal Role in Urban Affairs, Hearings*, 89th Cong., 2d sess., August–September 1966, 95, 151; "Katzenbach Blames Misery in Ghettoes, Not Reds, for Rioting in Cities," *St. Louis Post-Dispatch*, 17 August 1966; Adolph Slaughter, "Sacred Cow Bites the Dust," *Chicago Defender*, 27 August 1966.

46. *Federal Role in Urban Affairs*, 177.

47. *Federal Role in Urban Affairs*, 205–206; "Ribicoff, RFK, Scold Weaver on Ghettoes," *Washington Post*, 17 August 1966; "In the Cities NO Problem Is Easy," *New York Times*, 21 August 1966; "A Family Affair," *Newsweek*, 29 August 1966; Sheshol, 245; Davies, 143.

48. Robert Clifton Weaver Oral History, LBJL, 15.

49. *Federal Role in Urban Affairs*, 299; "Katzenbach, RFK Clash on City Needs," *Washington Post*, 18 August 1966; "Katzenbach Warns Senate 30 to 40 Cities Face Riots," *New York Times*, 18 August 1966.

50. "In the Cities No Problem Is Easy," *New York Times*, 21 August 1966; William S. White, "Second Assault: Kennedy Bloc Now Jabbing at Urban Program," *Washington Post*, 23 August 1966; "Kennedy Chides Johnson on Cities," *New York Times*, 16 August 1966; "Congress Gets Call to Act on City Problems," *St. Louis Post-Dispatch*, 16 August 1966; "Cities: The Bonfire of Discontent," *Time*, 26 August 1966.

51. "Senate Summons Mayors to Discuss Ghetto Problems," *Washington Post*, 22 August 1966; "$50 Billion Is Needed by N.Y., Lindsay Says," *Washington Post*, 23 August 1966; "What the Mayors Told the Senators," *Nation's Cities*, October 1966.

52. *Federal Role in Urban Affairs*, 29 August 1966, 1087; "Two Slum Menchildren Give Stories to Senators," *Washington Post*, 30 August 1966; "Senators Hear Sordid Stories of Ghetto Life," *St. Louis Post-Dispatch*, 30 August 1966; "Senators Hear of Life in the Ghetto: You're in Jail, Whether You're in the Streets or behind Bars," *New York Times*, 30 August 1966.

53. "Ribicoff Asks Taxes for Rebuilding Cities," *Washington Post*, 29 August 1966; "City Ills Probers Blame Administration as First Phase Ends," *Washington Post*, 2 September 1966.

54. Brinkley cited in memo to Lyndon B. Johnson from Harry McPherson, 2 September 1966, LBJ Civil Rights, reel 11; *Washington Star* cited in Sheshol, 246–247.

55. "Urban Hearings Vex White House," *New York Times*, 29 August 1966; Califano, 134; Sheshol, 246; "LBJ Vows to Take Profit Out of Poverty," *Chicago Sun-Times*, 20 August 1966.

56. "No Demonstration Cities," *New York Times*, 15 May 1966; "Move on to Save Bill to End Slums," *New York Times*, 24 May 1966; memorandum to President Johnson from Henry Wilson, 30 May 1966, Legislative Background, Model Cities, LBJL, box 2; memo to Joseph Califano from Robert Weaver re Next Steps, Demonstration Cities Bill, no date, Secretary Files, HUD, box 4; "Senate Approves Johnson Slum Aid," *New York Times*, 20 August 1966; "Weaver's Trade," *Time*, 24 October 1966.

57. 89th Cong., 2d sess., *Congressional Record* 112 (13 October 1966): 26,612–26,614, 26,624–26,625; Frieden and Kaplan, 59.

58. "Transcript of the President's News Conference on Foreign and Domestic Matters," *New York Times*, 7 October 1966; "Demonstration Cities Bill Urged by 22 Top Business Executives," *New York Times*, 11 October 1966; 89th Cong., 2d sess., *Congressional Record* 112 (13 October 1966): 26,617, 26,628; 89th Cong., 2d sess., *Congressional Record* 112 (14 October 1966): 26,991; "Demonstration Cities Bill Passed by House, 178-141," *New York Times*, 15 October 1966; Haar, 88.

59. Roger Biles, *Crusading Liberal: Paul H. Douglas of Illinois* (DeKalb: Northern Illinois University Press, 2002), 191–199.

60. "The New Congress," *Newsweek*, 21 November 1966; "Johnson Program Faces House Snag," *New York Times*, 13 November 1966; "Effects of Election," *U.S. News & World Report*, 21 November 1966.

61. "Telephone Statement by the President to HUD Employees from the Lyndon B. Johnson Ranch," 10 November 1966, Califano Papers, box 47; "Report to the President on Organization of the Department of Housing and Urban Development," WHCF, LBJL, box 253; letter to Robert Clifton Weaver from Lyndon B. Johnson, no date, WHCF, LBJL, box 253; "HUD Shows Promise on Birthday," *Washington Post*, 21 November 1966.

62. Letter to Joe Califano from Richard Lee, 16 November 1966, WOP, reel 15; "Weaver's Frustrating Year—Errors, Politics Mar HUD Start," *House and Home*, November 1966.

## CHAPTER 16

1. Robert Dallek, *Flawed Giant: Lyndon Johnson and His Times, 1961–1973* (New York: Oxford University Press, 1998), 391.

2. Dallek, 400; "The State of the Union," *New York Times*, 12 January 1967; Martin Nolan, "A Belated Effort to Save Our Cities," *Reporter*, 26 December 1967; "Ribicoff Proposes Urban Reshuffle," *New York Times*, 24 January 1967; "City Aid Still in Trouble," *Nation's Cities*, May 1967; Weaver testimony before the Senate Subcommittee on Executive Reorganization, *Hearings on the Federal Role in Urban Affairs*, 90th Cong., 1st sess., 18 April 1967, 3657.

3. "GOP Poses Major Threat to Key Housing Proposals," *Washington Post*, 10 April 1967; "Rough Sledding Seen for Rent Aid," *New York Times*, 7 January 1967; memo to Marvin Watson from unnamed aide, 20 May 1967, WOP, reel 14; "House, 232 to 171 Bars Expansion of Rent Subsidies," *New York Times*, 18 May 1967; "House Kills New Rent Subsidy Funds," *Washington Post*, 18 May 1967; "Race Overtone Seen in Defeat of Rent Subsidy," *Washington Post*, 22 May 1967; "House Ban on Rent for Poor Denounced," *Baltimore Afro-American*, 27 May 1967; "Envoys to Cities Barred by House," *New York Times*, 17 June 1967.

4. Joseph Califano, *The Triumph and Tragedy of Lyndon Johnson* (College Station: Texas A&M Press, 1990), 212–213; Robert Clifton Weaver Oral History, LBJL, 16; "Bill to Fight Rats Is Killed in House," *New York Times*, 21 July 1967.

5. *Report of the National Advisory Commission on Civil Disorders* (Kerner Report) (Washington, DC: Government Printing Office, 1968), 65; "Spreading Fire," *Time*, 28 July 1967.

6. *Report of the National Advisory Commission on Civil Disorders* (Kerner Report) (Washington, DC: Government Printing Office, 1968), 30–33; Komozi Woodard, *A Nation within a Nation: Amiri Baraka (LeRoi Jones), Black Power Politics* (Chapel Hill: University of North Carolina Press, 1999), 74–78; "Race Relations: The Ghetto Explodes in Another City," *New York Times*, 23 July 1967.

7. *Report of the National Advisory Commission on Civil Disorders* (Kerner Report) (Washington, DC: Government Printing Office, 1968), 35–38; memo to Lyndon B. Johnson from Ramsey Clark, 21 July 1967, LBJ Civil Rights, reel 7; Woodard, 82.

8. Sidney Fine, *Violence in the Model City: The Cavanagh Administration, Race Relations and the Detroit Riot of 1967* (Ann Arbor: University of Michigan Press, 1989), 32, 57, 99; *Report of the National Advisory Commission on Civil Disorders* (Kerner Report) (Washington, DC: Government Printing Office, 1968), 48–61.

9. Jimmy Breslin, "Marching Phase Is All Over," *Washington Post*, 30 July 1967; "Failure in the Movement," *Washington Post*, 26 July 1967.

10. "Sickness of the Cities," *New York Times*, 28 July 1967; Hugh Sidey, "The Big-Sky Man Hemmed in by the City," *Life*, August 1967.

11. "Bills Offered for Probe of Urban Riots," *Washington Post*, 26 July 1967; "President's Address to the Nation on Civil Disorders," 27 July 1967, *Public Papers of the Presidents, Lyndon B. Johnson, 1967* (Washington, DC: Government Printing Office, 1967), 722–723.

12. Roger Wilkins interview with author, 5 October 2005; Weaver testimony before the Senate Subcommittee on Housing and Urban Affairs, *Housing Legislation of 1967*, 90th Cong., 1st sess., 17 July 1967, 15; "Weaver Cites Riots in Plea," *Baltimore Sun*, 18 July 1967; "Riot Prevention Urged by Weaver," *New York Times*, 18 July 1967; "Johnson Appeals for Swift Action on 3 Urban Bills," *New York Times*, 20 August 1967; "Johnson Decries Urban Fund Cuts," *New York Times*, 4 November 1967.

13. "Coalition Urges U.S. to Act to Spur Jobs in the Cities," *New York Times*, 25 August 1967; Whitney Young, "Housing Can Rebuild Slums and Lives," *New York Times*, 9 November 1967; "Javits Proposes a Bank to Aid Slums," *New York Times*, 14 September 1967.

14. "Washington: Keep Your Eye on the Little Guy," *New York Times*, 23 April 1967; Charles Percy, "A New Dawn for Our Cities: A Home Ownership Achievement Plan, Speech to Kiwanis Club of Chicago," 15 September 1966, 90th Cong., 1st sess., *Congressional Record* 113 (11 January 1967): 166; "Percy Introduces Bill on Housing," *New York Times*, 21 April 1967; "Percy's Pulling Power," *Chicago Daily News*, 22 April 1967; Harold Wolman, *The Politics of Federal Housing* (New York: Dodd, Mead, 1971), 77; National Home Ownership Foundation, press release, 21 April 1967, WHCF, LBJL, box 1.

15. Robert Weaver, UPI interview, 10 June 1967, reprinted in *Congressional Record*, 29 June 1967, 18037; "What Got into Mr. Weaver," *Economic Opportunity Report*, 1 May

1967, reprinted in *Congressional Record*, 15 May 1967, 12,715–12,716; Martin Nolan, "The Belated Effort to Save Our Cities," *Reporter*, 28 December 1967.

16. "HUD's Anniversary: A Frustrating Two Years," *Nation's Cities*, November 1967; "Aid to Poor Asked for Owning Homes," *New York Times*, 16 May 1967; "Democrats Seeking Alternative to Percy Plan on Homeowners," *New York Times*, 23 July 1967; "White House Backs a Homeowner Plan to Counter Percy's," *New York Times*, 10 August 1967.

17. Robert F. Kennedy testimony before the Senate Finance Committee, *Hearings on Tax Incentives to Encourage Housing in Urban Poverty Areas*, 90th Cong., 1st sess., 14 September 1967, 58, 63, 71; "A Kennedy Plan Seeks Slum Jobs and Lower Rents," *New York Times*, 5 July 1967; Wolman, 79.

18. "White House Kills Urban Housing Plan," *New York Times*, 6 January 1967; *Hearings on S. 2100*, 90th Cong., 1st sess., 14 September 1967, 129, 138; "RFK Slum Housing Plan Scored," *Washington Post*, 15 September 1967.

19. Dallek, 417; memo to Lyndon B. Johnson from Joe Califano re Status of Major New Program Initiatives, 2 December 1967, WOP, reel 15; Wolman, 59.

20. Memo to Joe Califano from Robert Wood, 16 May 1967, WOP, reel 1; "HUD Spells Out Its New Policy: Homes for the Poor Will Come First," *Washington Post*, 17 June 1967; memo to Lyndon B. Johnson from Robert Clifton Weaver re Increasing the Supply of Housing for Low-Income Families, 7 September 1967, WOP, reel 15; "Weaver Names Three Cities for New HUD Plan," *Baltimore Afro-American*, 9 September 1967; "Statement by the President on the Formation of a Committee to Rebuild America's Slums," 2 June 1967, HUD, box 291; "Insurance Groups to Invest Billion in Slum Property," *New York Times*, 14 September 1967; "Breakthrough in the Slums," *New York Times*, 15 September 1967; "Johnson Chooses 'Think Tank' Panel on Urban Issues," *New York Times*, 7 December 1967.

21. *Congressional Record*, 29 August 1967, 24,390–24,391; "Housing Policies: FHA under Fire," *Washington Post*, 14 September 1967; "Two Top Negroes at Odds: The Issue: Federal Housing," *U.S. News & World Report*, 11 September 1967; "Coalition in Senate Planning to Reduce Role of the F.H.A.," *New York Times*, 20 September 1967; Martin Nolan, "A Belated Effort to Save Our Cities," *Reporter*, 28 December 1967, 16–21.

22. Memo to Joe Califano from Bruce Terris, 12 September 1967, WOP, reel 15; memo to Lyndon B. Johnson from Joe Califano, 23 September 1967, Califano Papers, box 13; "FHA Using Bigger Share to Aid Slums," *Washington Post*, 16 November 1967; "FHA Eases Lending Policy," *Cleveland Press*, 16 August 1967.

23. Howard Shuman, "Behind the Scenes and under the Rug," *Washington Monthly*, July 1979, 14–22; Roger Biles, *Crusading Liberal: Paul H. Douglas of Illinois* (Dekalb: Northern Illinois University Press, 2002), 204–205.

24. *Hearings before the National Commission on Urban Problems* (Washington, DC: Government Printing Office, May–June 1967), 179; letter to Robert Clifton Weaver from Paul Douglas, 15 January 1968, HUD, box 372; letter to Paul Douglas from Robert Clifton Weaver, 23 July 1968, HUD, box 372; memo to Joe Califano from Fred Bohen, 25 November 1967, WOP, reel 14; Shuman, 18; Biles, 205.

25. "New Task at HUD: Weaver Aims to Push Older Agencies Deeper into Attack on Slum Ills," *Wall Street Journal*, 21 December 1967; "HUD's Anniversary: A Frustrating Two

Years," *Nation's Cities*, November 1967; "Housing Politics: FHA under Fire," *Washington Post*, 14 September 1967.

26. NCDH, "How the Federal Government Builds Ghettos, Rights Group Says Government Helps Build Ghettos," *New York Times*, 9 February 1967; "Federal Government Gets Shelled for 'Building Ghettos,'" *Chicago Daily Defender*, 25 February 1967.

27. NCDH, "How the Federal Government Builds Ghettos, Rights Group Says Government Helps Build Ghettos," *New York Times*, 9 February 1967, 17; "Rights Group Raps Federal Housing Ghettoes," *Washington Post*, 9 February 1967.

28. Statement by Robert C. Weaver, 8 February 1967, McPherson Papers, box 23, 1–2; "Secretary Weaver Calls Bias Charges Unfair," *Baltimore Afro-American*, 13 February 1967.

29. "U.S. Urban Agency Acts to Curb Bias," *New York Times*, 16 February 1967; letter to Lyndon B. Johnson from Ed Rutledge and Jack Wood, 7 March 1967, McPherson Papers, box 23; "Dr. Weaver Should Crack Down on Housing Bigotry," *Baltimore Afro-American*, 25 February 1967.

30. Memo to Harry McPherson from Robert Clifton Weaver, 24 September 1966, HUD, box 206; memo to Harry McPherson from Robert Clifton Weaver, 27 May 1967, HUD, box 303.

31. "F.H.A. Asks Aides to Get Housing for Minorities," *New York Times*, 21 November 1967; "Remarks of Phillip N. Brownstein to FHA Officials," 13 October 1967, *HUD Administrative History*, vol. 2, LBJL.

32. Memo to Harry McPherson from Robert Clifton Weaver, 27 May 1967, HUD, box 303.

33. Letter to Robert Wood from Neal Gold, 19 June 1967, HUD, box 303; letter to Ed Rutledge from Robert Clifton Weaver, 10 May 1967, HUD, box 303.

34. Memo to Lyndon B. Johnson from Robert Clifton Weaver, 9 February 1967, LBJ Civil Rights, reel 8; Frank Horne, "Model Cities: Threat and Promise," speech to NCDH Executive Committee, 13 April 1967, HUD, box 303.

35. Horne; memo to Lyndon B. Johnson from Robert Clifton Weaver, 9 February 1967, McPherson Papers, box 23; memo to Harry McPherson from Robert Clifton Weaver, 22 March 1967, McPherson Papers, box 23.

36. "Nondiscrimination in Housing," Fair Housing, Legislative Background, LBJL, box 1; "Open Housing Idea in Stages Studied," *New York Times*, 13 January 1967; Hugh Davis Graham, *The Civil Rights Era: Origins and Development of National Policy* (New York: Oxford University Press, 1990), 267; "Liberals Assail Housing Concept," *New York Times*, 15 January 1967; "President Seeks to Abolish Housing Bias in 3 Stages," *New York Times*, 15 February 1967.

37. "Open Housing Bill Proposed in Senate," *New York Times*, 23 March 1967; "Weaver Blasts Fair Housing Inaction," *Chicago Daily Defender*, 26 August 1967; "2 in Cabinet Push Urban Fair Housing Law," *New York Times*, 22 August 1967; "President Urges Rights Measures to End Injustice," *New York Times*, 25 January 1968; Dallek, 517.

38. *Congressional Record*, 6 February 1968, 2278, 2279; *Congressional Record*, 14 February 1968, 2985; Graham, 270; "Liberals Eye Rider on Open Housing," *Washington Post*, 12 January 1968; *Congressional Record*, 20 February 1968, 3421.

39. *Congressional Record*, 19 February 1968, 3345; "Dirksen Holds the Key," *New York Times*, 20 February 1968; "Bid to Halt Rights Debate Fails in Senate by 7 Votes," *New York Times*, 21 February 1968; "LBJ Appeals for Passage of Rights Bill," *Washington Post*, 29 February 1968; "Dirksen Explains Rights Shift: 'Time and Reality' Make You Older and Wiser," *New York Times*, 28 February 1968; Graham, 271.

40. *Report of the National Advisory Commission on Civil Disorders* (Kerner Report) (Washington, DC: Government Printing Office, 1968), 263; "The Riot Report: Ghetto Discrimination Begins at Birth," *New York Times*, 3 March 1968; "Statement by Leading Businessmen on Fair Housing Legislation," 3 March 1968, LBJ Civil Rights, reel 8.

41. Dallek, 516; Califano, 262; "Senate Cuts Off Debate on Rights by Scant Margin," *New York Times*, 5 March 1968; "Senate Votes Cloture on Civil Rights Debate, Tables Amendment," *Washington Post*, 5 March 1968; letter to Speaker John McCormick from Lyndon B. Johnson, 11 March 1968, LBJ Civil Rights, reel 8; "Riot Panel's Report Criticized by Cohen," *Washington Post*, 26 March 1968; "Senate Approves Civil Rights Bill by 71 to 20 Vote," *New York Times*, 12 March 1968; "Explanation of H.R. 2516 as Passed by the Senate," 15 March 1968, LBJ Civil Rights, reel 8; "Rights Bill Vote Pushed in House," *New York Times*, 14 March 1968; "Rights and Votes: The House on Housing," *New York Times*, 17 March 1968; "Rights Bill in House," *Washington Post*, 15 March 1968.

42. Edward Lashman interview with author, 9 November 2005.

43. Dallek, 533, 534; "Aftermath of Riots—What Next?" *U.S. News & World Report*, 22 March 1968; "Washington Is Shaken: Leaders Call for Calm," *New York Times*, 5 April 1968; "Dr. King's Death Expected to Spur Rights Bill," *New York Times*, 6 April 1968; "Johnson Puts Off Congress Speech," *New York Times*, 7 April 1968; "Johnson, Negroes Confer," *Washington Post*, 6 April 1968; Lyndon B. Johnson, "Remarks of the President at the Ceremony for the Bill Signing of the Civil Rights Bill of 1968," 11 April 1968; "House Passes Civil Rights Bill," *Washington Post*, 11 April 1968.

44. "Black Leaders Differ on Value of Rights Measure," *Chicago Defender*, 13 April 1968.

45. William Raspberry, "Civil Rights Act Won't Help in the Ghetto," *Washington Post*, 14 April 1968; Robert Clifton Weaver interview for the Civil Rights Documentation Project, 12 March 1969, RCW Papers, Supplement, box 8.

46. "Leaders of Poor Call Senate to Help Create 2 Million Jobs," *New York Times*, 1 May 1968.

47. Alma Rene Williams, "Robert C. Weaver: From the Black Cabinet to the President's Cabinet" (PhD diss., Washington University, St. Louis, 1972), 218; "Officials Get a Scolding," *Washington Post*, 1 May 1968; letter to Robert Clifton Weaver from Poor People's Campaign, 2 May 1968, Gaither Papers, box 36; Weaver interview for Civil Rights Documentation Project, 12 March 1969, RCW Papers, Supplement, box 8.

48. "Summary of Report by Task Force on Housing and Urban Development," 12 October 1967, Task Force Files, LBJL.

49. "Summary of Report by Task Force on Housing and Urban Development," 12 October 1967, Task Force Files, LBJL, 3; "Follow the Leader as Played by Lyndon B. Johnson," *Wall Street Journal*, 7 March 1968; Paul George Lewis, "Housing and American Privatism: The Origins and Evolution of Subsidized Home-Ownership Policy," *Journal of Policy History* 5 (1993): 28–51, especially 32.

50. "Annual Budget Message to the Congress, Fiscal Year 1969," 29 January 1968, *Public Papers of the Presidents, Lyndon B. Johnson, 1968* (Washington, DC: Government Printing Office, 1968), 103. Johnson also proposed a tax increase at the same time. "Johnson Proposes Sharp Rise in Spending for Public Housing and Rent Subsidies," *New York Times,* 30 January 1968; memo to Henry Gaither from Human Resources Programs Division, 30 October 1967, Task Force Files, LBJL; Dallek, 404–405.

51. "Special Message to Congress on Urban Problems: The Crisis of the Cities," 22 February 1968, *Public Papers of the Presidents, Lyndon B. Johnson, 1968* (Washington, DC: Government Printing Office, 1968), 249; "Johnson Proposes Major U.S. Housing Program," *Christian Science Monitor,* 24 February 1968; "President Urges Private Capital to Help in Cities," *New York Times,* 23 February 1968; "Crisis of the Cities," *New York Times,* 23 February 1968; Tate testimony before House Subcommittee on Housing, *Hearings on Housing and Urban Development Legislation and Urban Insurance,* 90th Cong., 2d sess., 12 March 1968, 230, 391; *Congressional Record,* 29 February 1968, 4661; *Congressional Record,* 26 February 1966, 2986; Kennedy testimony before Senate Subcommittee on Housing and Urban Affairs, *Hearings on Housing and Urban Development Legislation of 1968,* 90th Cong., 2d sess., 5 March 1968, 623; Williamson testimony before Senate Subcommittee on Housing and Urban Affairs, *Hearings on Housing and Urban Development Legislation of 1968,* 90th Cong., 2d sess., 5 March 1968, 258.

52. Memo to Lyndon B. Johnson from Robert Clifton Weaver, 7 March 1968, WHCF, LBJL, box 255; *Congressional Record,* 27 May 1968; *Congressional Record,* 24 May 1968, 14,973; "$5 Billion Plan on Housing Voted by Senate, 67 to 4," *New York Times,* 29 May 1968; "Final House Vote Backs Housing Aid," *New York Times,* 11 July 1968; Lewis, 30–31.

53. "Remarks upon Signing the Housing and Urban Development Act of 1968," 1 August 1968, *Public Papers of the Presidents, Lyndon B. Johnson, 1968* (Washington, DC: Government Printing Office, 1968), 866–67; "Johnson Approves 'Massive' Program to House the Poor," *New York Times,* 2 August 1968; "Weaver Lauds New Housing Bill as Great Effort to Cure City Ills," *Chicago Defender,* 10 August 1968.

54. Dallek, 529.

55. Letter to Lyndon B. Johnson from Robert Clifton Weaver, 31 March 1968, WHCF, LBJL, Name File, W136; Robert Clifton Weaver Oral History, LBJL, 6; letter to Lyndon B. Johnson from Robert Clifton Weaver, 19 December 1968, WHCF, LBJL, box 255.

56. Robert Clifton Weaver Oral History, LBJL, 5–6.

57. Letter to Robert Clifton Weaver from Frank Horne, 26 April 1968, Horne Papers, box 3.

58. Cable to Lyndon B. Johnson from Califano, 13 March 1968, WHCF, LBJL, box 255; "Weaver Due to Resign after Nov. 5," *Washington Post,* 15 May 1968; "Weaver to Head Baruch College," *New York Times,* 15 May 1968.

59. "Architecture: The House that HUD Built," *New York Times,* 22 September 1968; "Remarks by Robert C. Weaver at Dedication of HUD Building," 9 September 1968, Panzer Papers, box 367; "Johnson Dedicates HUD Office," *Washington Post,* 10 September 1968.

60. "Conferees Approve $14.5 Billion Bill," *New York Times,* 19 September 1968; "Weaver Sees Housing Goal Setback," *Washington Post,* 30 October 1968; "Housing Mea-

sure Is Voted by House," *New York Times*, 20 September 1968; "Housing Bill Called Too Little," *Washington Post*, 20 September 1968; Graham, 275.

61. Robert Weaver, "Look Back and Ahead," press conference, 29 October 1968, RCW Papers, Supplement, box 7.

62. Letter to John Gardner from Charles Abrams, 17 December 1967, Abrams Papers, reel 12; letter to Robert Clifton Weaver from Lyndon B. Johnson, 5 December 1968, WCHF, LBJL, Name File, W136; "Robert C. Weaver Praised for 'Improving Urban Living,'" *Baltimore Afro-American*, 21 December 1968.

63. Letter to Robert Clifton Weaver from Lyndon B. Johnson, 2 January 1969, WHCF, LBJL, box 255.

64. Mary Washington interview with author, 7 December 2005.

65. Joseph A. Califano interview with author, 10 December 2004; Roger Wilkins interview with author, 5 October 2005.

66. Joseph A. Califano interview with author, 10 December 2004; Edward Lashman interview with author, 9 November 2005.

## CHAPTER 17

1. Selma Berrol, *Getting Down to Business: Baruch College in the City of New York, 1847–1987* (New York: Greenwood Press, 1989), xi.

2. Berrol, 12–14.

3. Berrol, 22, 76, 114–115.

4. Berrol, 124, 130–133.

5. Berrol, 5; "An Important Figure Who Never Made History," *LaGuardia Live Wire*, December 2002, http://www.lagcc.cuny.edu/livewire/21/article19.asp.

6. "Weaver to Head Baruch College," *New York Times*, 16 May 1968; "Robert C. Weaver to Head College Planned in Brooklyn," *New York Post*, 16 May 1968.

7. Baruch College press release, RCW Papers, Supplement, box 1; Berrol, 141–142.

8. Berrol, 141.

9. "Negroes Seek Gains at Baruch College," *New York Times*, 22 February 1969; Berrol, 142.

10. Berrol, 166.

11. "Late Bulletin: Rights and Responsibilities," *Baruch Today*, 28 April 1969, Baruch; "Community to Spend Today Discussing Rights and Responsibilities," *Ticker*, 6 May 1969; "News," Baruch College, 5 May 1969, Baruch; "Fireside Weaver," *Ticker*, 9 December 1969.

12. "Remarks of Dr. Robert C. Weaver, President of the Bernard M. Baruch College," 12 June 1969, RCW Papers, Supplement, box 1.

13. Berrol, 170.

14. "Unrest Simmers at 7 Colleges," *New York Times*, 17 April 1970; "College Turmoil Continues Here: Baruch Classes Off," *New York Times*, 18 April 1970; "Councilman Urges Inquiry into Student Protests," *New York Times*, 21 April 1970; "Statement by Robert C. Weaver," 17 April 1970, Baruch; "The Strike," *Ticker*, 17 April 1970; "Apathy at Baruch Is Dead," *Baruch Today*, 23 April 1970, Baruch; Berrol, 171.

15. "Minutes, General Faculty Meeting," 28 and 29 April 1970, Baruch; "Pres. Weaver

Appoints 13 Faculty Members to Committee of 26," *Ticker*, 29 April 1970; "Minutes, General Faculty Meeting," 12 May 1970; "Protest IV," *Baruch Today*, 11 May 1970, Baruch; "Address by Robert Clifton Weaver at Baruch College Commencement Exercises," 9 June 1970, RCW Papers, Supplement, box 6; letter to Don Hummel from Robert Clifton Weaver, 19 May 1970, RCW Papers, Supplement, box 1; Berrol, 171.

16. "Address by Robert Clifton Weaver at Baruch College Commencement Exercises," 9 June 1970, RCW Papers, Supplement, box 6; "Baruch Graduates Warned by Weaver on Violent Protest," *New York Times*, 10 June 1970.

17. Letter to Frederick Burkhardt from Robert Clifton Weaver, 22 June 1970, Baruch; "Weaver to Quit Baruch College; He Cites Financial Inadequacy," *New York Times*, 23 June 1970; Berrol, 172.

18. "Weaver's Statement to His Baruch Community," *Ticker*, 24 June 1970; "Weaver to Quit Baruch College; He Cites Financial Inadequacy," *New York Times*, 23 June 1970.

19. Berrol, 172–173.

20. On Nixon's domestic policy, see Timothy Conlan, *New Federalism: Intergovernmental Reform from Nixon to Reagan* (Washington, DC: Brookings Institution Press, 1988).

21. "Romney Meets the Voters," *New York Times*, 17 September 1967; memo from Richard Van Dusen to John Ehrlichman re HUD Programs, 18 March 1969, Romney Papers, box 7; "The President's Policy on Cities," *New York Times*, 30 January 1970. On Nixon's New Federalism, see Michael Reagan, *The New Federalism* (New York: Oxford University Press, 1972), 126–128; "Statement of Richard P. Nathan," in *A New Federalism, Hearing before the Senate Subcommittee on Intergovernmental Relations*, 93d Cong., 1st sess., 21 February 1973, 94–99; "President Urges Governors to Aid New Federalism," *New York Times*, 2 September 1969.

22. "House Passes Bill with Broad Provisions for New Communities," *New York Times*, 20 December 1970; "Urban Housing Bill Is Signed by Nixon, Now at Camp David," *New York Times*, 2 January 1971; "Rights Panel to Urge Fund Curb on White Suburbs," *New York Times*, 29 August 1970; memo to John Ehrlichman from Leonard Garment, 15 March 1971, Romney Papers, box 13; "Romney Seeks Clear Path for Housing for Poor," *New York Times*, 7 June 1970; "Government Promises Pressure for Integrated Suburbs," *U.S. News & World Report*, 28 June 1971; "Romney Bars Plan Proposed by Nixon Panel," *New York Times*, 17 August 1970.

23. "U.S. Report Finds Fraud in Housing," *New York Times*, 6 January 1971; Irving Welfeld, *HUD Scandals: Howling Headlines and Silent Fiascoes* (New Brunswick, NJ: Transaction, 1992); Brian D. Boyer, *Cities Destroyed for Cash: The FHA Scandal at HUD* (Chicago: Follett Publishing, 1973).

24. "Lag in Housing Spurs a Drive to Alter Law," *New York Times*, 22 March 1971; "Romney Hits Hard at Subsidy Scandals," *Business Week*, 19 February 1972; "Sparkman Assails Nixon for Refusing to Spend $8 Billion," *New York Times*, 4 March 1971.

25. "He Has Staked Out a Conservative Course," *New York Times*, 14 January 1973; "Annual Budget Message to the Congress, Fiscal Year 1974," 29 January 1973, *Public Papers of the Presidents, Richard Nixon, 1973* (Washington, DC: Government Printing Office, 1973), 46–47; "Nixon Attack on Grant Programs Aims to Simplify Structure, Give Greater Lo-

cal Control," *National Journal*, 20 January 1973, 76–89; "State of the Union Message to Congress on Community Development," 8 March 1973, *Public Papers of the Presidents, Richard Nixon, 1973* (Washington, DC: Government Printing Office, 1973), 171–180; "U.S. Commitment to Renew Cities Is in Doubt under New Program," *New York Times*, 30 January 1973.

26. "Increased Role in Housing Urged on U.S. by Weaver," *New York Times*, 8 February 1974.

27. Memo re Better Communities Housing Legislation, 29 April 1974, WHCF, Housing Files, Nixon Papers, box 3; "Nixon Aides Push Housing Measure," *New York Times*, 19 February 1974; "Compromise Bill to Spend $10 Billion," *Business Week*, 16 March 1974; "Senate Approves Housing Aid, 76-11," *New York Times*, 12 March 1974; "$10 Billion Proposal Facing Opposition in the House and from Nixon Administration," *New York Times*, 12 March 1974; 93d Cong., 2d sess., *Congressional Record* 118 (11 March 1974): 6169.

28. 93d Cong., 2d sess., *Congressional Record* 118 (20 June 1974): 20,256, 20,259, 20,260; "Ford Signs Bill to Aid Housing: $11.9 Billion Authorized for 3 Years Gives Localities Greater Control in Plans," *New York Times*, 23 August 1974.

29. Robert Clifton Weaver, "Housing the Disadvantaged in 1974," RCW Papers, Supplement, box 6; Robert Clifton Weaver, "Fair Housing Strategies: A Reassessment," 1979, NCDH Papers.

30. The New York City financial crisis has received a great amount of scholarly attention. See Joshua B. Freeman, *Working-Class New York: Life and Labor since World War II* (New York: New Press, 2000), 256–287; Jack Newfield and Paul DuBrul, *The Abuse of Power: The Permanent Government and the Fall of New York* (New York: Viking Press, 1977); Robert W. Bailey, *The Crisis Regime: The MAC, the EFCB, and the Political Impact of the New York City Financial Crisis* (Albany: State University of New York Press, 1984); Eric Lichten, *Class, Power and Austerity: The New York City Fiscal Crisis* (South Hadley, MA: Bergin, 1986); William K. Tabb, *The Long Default: New York City and the Urban Fiscal Crisis* (New York: Monthly Review Press, 1982).

31. Freeman, 256–257.

32. Freeman, 258–259; Lichten, 129; Newfield and DuBrul, 170–171.

33. Bailey, 24; Newfield and DuBrul, 178–180; Lichten, 128.

34. Bailey, 26–27; Freeman, 260–261.

35. Newfield and DuBrul, 180–181; Lichten, 130; Bailey, 30.

36. Freeman, 260–261.

37. Freeman, 259.

38. Newfield and DuBrul, 186, 194; Freeman, 262–264; Lichten, 136.

39. Newfield and DuBrul, 180.

40. Bailey, 35; letter to Representative Arthur Eve from Robert Clifton Weaver, 18 February 1976, RCW Supplement, box 2; Newfield and DuBrul, 186–187, 190.

41. Freeman, 265–267, 270–271; Bailey, 37–39; Lichten, 138–139; Newfield and DuBrul, 188, 195.

42. Newfield and DuBrul, 178, 182.

43. Freeman, 272.

44. Robert Clifton Weaver, "The Evolution and Significance of the Proposed Fair Hous-

ing Amendments Act of 1979," *Crisis*, December 1979, 422–424; "Strengthening of Housing Law Urged," *Milwaukee Journal*, 14 November 1979.

45. Robert Clifton Weaver, "Meeting Our Housing Needs," speech given at Florida Atlantic University, 9 January 1976, RCW Papers, Supplement, box 6; Robert Clifton Weaver, "Fair Housing Strategies: A Reassessment," 1979, NCDH Papers.

46. Robert Clifton Weaver, "Fiftieth Anniversary Report, 1929," HUA.

47. Robert Clifton Weaver, "Restating the Case for Fair Housing," speech given at NCDH annual conference, 11 April 1983, RCW Papers, Supplement, box 7.

48. "Robert C. Weaver, 89, First Black Cabinet Member, Dies," *New York Times*, 19 July 1997; "Robert C. Weaver," *Washington Post*, 21 July 1997; letter to the Family and Friends of Robert C. Weaver from President Bill Clinton, 15 August 1997, RCW Papers, Supplement, box 1; letter to Robert C. Weaver Memorial Service from Lady Bird Johnson, 29 August 1997, RCW Papers, Supplement, box 1.

49. S 67, 106th Cong., 1st sess.; HR 1236, 106th Cong., 1st sess.; 106th Cong., 1st sess., *Congressional Record* 145 (23 March 1999): 4153; 106th Cong., 1st sess., *Congressional Record* 145 (18 November 1999): 12,867.

# Figure Credits

**1, 2, 3, 4, 5, 6, 9, 12, 16, 17, 19, 20, 21, 25, 27** Robert C. Weaver Photograph Collection, Photographs and Prints Division, Schomburg Center for Research in Black Culture, The New York Public Library, Astor, Lenox, and Tilden Foundations.

**7** Harvard University Archives, call no. HUD 929.04, p. 166. Copyright 1929 by Richard G. West and John W. McPherson.

**8** Courtesy of the Library of Congress, LC-USW3-001658-C. Photo by Pat Terry.

**10** Courtesy of the Library of Congress, LC-USZ62-107174.

**11** Courtesy of the Brooklyn Public Library.

**13** Courtesy of the Library of Congress, LC-USE6-D-010813.

**14** Courtesy of the Library of Congress, LOT 13074, no. 545.

**18** Photo by Abbie Rowe, White House photographer, February 11, 1961.

**26** Courtesy of the Library of Congress, LC-USZ62-95480.

**22, 23** LBJ Library photos by Yoichi R. Okamoto.

**24** Reprinted with permission of the *St. Louis Post-Dispatch*, copyright 1966.

# Index

Made in the USA
San Bernardino, CA
30 August 2018